INDUSTRIAL RELATIONS IN
INTERNATIONAL PERSPECTIVE

Industrial Relations in International Perspective
Essays on Research and Policy

Edited by

Peter B. Doeringer

with
Peter Gourevitch
Peter Lange
Andrew Martin

HOLMES & MEIER PUBLISHERS, INC.
New York

First published in the United States of America 1981 by
HOLMES & MEIER PUBLISHERS, INC.
30 Irving Place, New York, N.Y. 10003
Copyright © 1981 by Peter B. Doeringer

Library of Congress Cataloging in Publication Data

Main entry under title:
Industrial relations in international perspective.
   1. Industrial relations – Research – Addresses,
essays, lectures. I. Doeringer, Peter B.
HD6961.I559 1979   331'.07'2   79–13690
ISBN 0–8419–0525–8

PRINTED IN HONG KONG

Contents

Notes on the Contributors

Peter B. Doeringer is Professor of Economics at Boston University. He has taught at Harvard University and the London School of Economics. His publications include *Internal Labor Markets and Manpower Analysis* and a number of monographs and articles on labour markets, manpower policy, and industrial relations.

B. C. Roberts is Professor of Industrial Relations at the London School of Economics where he chairs the Department of Industrial Relations. He has served as President of both the British Industrial Relations Association and the International Industrial Relations Association. He has published widely on industrial relations matters including *Trade Unions in a Free Society.*

George Strauss is Professor of Business Administration at the University of California, Berkeley, where he is also Associate Dean and Associate Director of the Institute of Industrial Relations. He is the editor of *Industrial Relations* and has published widely in the field of industrial relations.

Peter Feuille is Associate Professor of Labor and Industrial Relations at the University of Illinois, and has taught at SUNY, Buffalo, the University of Oregon and the University of California, Berkeley. He specializes in problems of public sector unionism and has written *The Impact of Police Unions.*

Shirley Goldenberg is Associate Professor of Industrial Relations at McGill University. She has published *Professional Workers and Collective Bargaining* and is on the Executive Board of the Industrial Relations Research Association.

H. D. Woods is Professor of Industrial Relations at McGill University. He has been an adviser to the Canadian Government on industrial relations matters and was chairman of the Commission of Enquiry into the Construction Industry. He has published *Labour Policy and Labour Economics in Canada.*

Derek Robinson is a senior research fellow at the Institute of Economics and Statistics at Oxford where he is also a Fellow of Magdalene College. He served as co-chairman of the British Government's Pay Board. His publications include *Wage Drift, Fringe Benefits, and Manpower Distribution.*

Walter Korpi teaches political science at the University of Stockholm. He has written widely on labour and politics in Sweden, including *Why do Workers Strike?*

Gino Guigni is Professor of Law at the University of Rome and has also taught at the University of Bari. He is an adviser to the Italian Government and to Italian trade unions. He has written *Labour Grievance Settlement in Western Europe.*

Mikio Sumiya is a Professor of Labour Economics at the University of Tokyo. His writings include *History of Labour Union Movement in Japan*, among many other articles and books on Japanese labour relations.

Heinz Hartmann is Professor of Sociology at the University of Münster, where he also works as a research fellow at the Institut Für Sozial- wissenschaft. His publications include *Codetermination in West Germany.*

Wolfgang Conrad teaches at the University of Münster, where he also works as a research fellow at the Institut Für Sozialwissenschaft.

Jean-Daniel Reynaud is director of the Conservatoire des Arts et Métiers at the University of Paris, where he teaches industrial relations. He is President of the International Industrial Relations Association and has written a two-volume work, *Les Syndicats en France.*

Peter Gourevitch is an Associate Professor of Political Science at McGill University, and has published articles concerning regional government in France and Italy, and European political development.

Peter Lange is an Associate Professor of Government at Harvard University. His writings have included investigations of the Italian Communist Party.

Andrew Martin is a Political Scientist at the Center for European Studies and has published essays on the comparative politics of Economic Policy, specializing in Sweden.

Acknowledgements

We wish to thank our numerous colleagues who participated at one stage or another in the development of this manuscript. We are also grateful to the Jacob Wertheim Committee on Industrial Relations and to the Center for International Affairs, both of Harvard University, for their financial support of the project.

A special debt is owed to the Contributors to this volume. Their studies of industrial relations research were completed in 1975 and were far more comprehensive than could be accommodated in a single volume. As a result, many important references had to be omitted. Throughout the project, the Contributors universally demonstrated a level of patience, understanding, and commitment that made a long collaboration worthwhile.

Peter B. Doeringer
Peter Gourevitch
Peter lange
Andrew Martin

1 Industrial Relations Research in International Perspective

Peter B. Doeringer

As economies grow, become more complex, and develop international interdependences, labour comes to play a larger role in political and economic affairs. Regardless of national economic objectives, or of the way in which labour and management relate to these objectives, the activities of industrial relations systems are inevitably of growing concern to national and international economic policy. Such developments are reflected in the content of industrial relations research.

This book grew out of a frustration with the thinness of English-language materials on the details of industrial relations in advanced market economies. While it has been relatively easy to obtain descriptions of the formal structure of industrial relations in such countries – their labour laws, union structure, bargaining arrangements, and so forth – it has been far more difficult to gain insights into the informal, more fundamental, workings of the various systems.[1] Moreover, there has been no systematic way for scholars to familiarize themselves with the native-language literature or to identify the significant research issues being pursued in various countries.

To help remedy this problem, this collection of bibliographic surveys was commissioned, resembling the 'Reviews' of industrial relations research occasionally prepared for the United States by the Industrial Relations Research Association.[2] Leading industrial relations scholars in eight countries – Canada, France, Germany, Italy, Japan, Sweden, Britain and the United States – were asked to identify the major research themes in their respective countries since 1960 and to assess the strengths and gaps in the research record. A similar task was undertaken in the multinational area.

What began as a bibliographic probe of modest dimensions has resulted in a substantial volume, valuable both as a research tool and a history of ideas and thinking in industrial relations. The essays portray a rich and vital picture of industrial relations practice as mirrored in each country's industrial relations research.

The different research patterns that emerge as countries face common industrial relations problems are not dominated by the idiosyncrasies of scholarship. Instead, researchers have responded to the concerns of public and private industrial relations policy by documenting, analysing, prescribing and often helping to implement new approaches. The body of industrial relations research in each country thus provides a unique window into industrial relations practice and industrial relations ideology.

Viewed internationally, industrial relations research is flourishing. In some countries – the United States and to some extent Canada – the maturity of the industrial relations system and the existence of a substantial body of research combine to make major research break-throughs more difficult. This may account for the sense of stagnation felt by many in the industrial relations field in the United States. In other countries – most notably Italy – where the redefinition of the industrial relations system is a matter of intense debate, and where the research base is weak, there is a strong sense of excitement and progress in both research and practice.

Changes in industrial relations and, therefore, advances in industrial relations research, are never smooth. Just as industrial relations systems emerge in the process of industrialization, so must they be adapted to changing market and political circumstances in advanced economies. This process of change may be fitful and erratic, but it is unceasing. The record of the sixties in Britain, for example, dramatizes how even a seemingly stable industrial relations system must confront the need for change.[3]

The challenge of industrial relations research, a challenge which seems to be well met in the countries examined, is to chronicle such change and to provide the facts and analysis to help policy-makers to understand change. This collection of essays encourages an optimistic view of the capacity of scholarship to keep pace with these ever-evolving relations among workers, employers and governments.

In the first part of this chapter, the pattern of industrial relations research in the countries surveyed is briefly reviewed. The second section examines the role of ideology and theory in industrial relations research. In the third section, the growing influence of the industrial relations factors in public policy is discussed. The chapter concludes with a comment on the future of industrial relations research.

Patterns of Industrial Relations Research

The range and diversity of the various essays defy summary in any complete way. It is possible only to provide the most general assessment of each country's industrial relations research and to make some selective observations about the emerging patterns.

The Industrial Relations System: Structure and Change

An overview of industrial relations research in the countries studied suggests that there is a close correspondence between the type of research undertaken and the structure of the industrial relations system. National systems of industrial relations develop rule-making arrangements which define the structure of the system. There may be formally organized institutional machinery or the procedures may be informal and highly idiosyncratic. The formal arrangements may be comprehensive, covering rules at the plant, industry, regional and national levels; or they may be fragmentary. Experience shows that formal, comprehensive arrangements usually come to dominate the more fragmentary and informal ones.

These structures must evolve to meet the requirements of the political, economic and technological environments of each country. But because such evolution occurs through trial and error, institutions develop slowly and environments also change, the structure of the system never fully stabilizes.

Systems just beginning to establish their rule-making arrangements face significant choices with respect to structure and tend to rely on *ad hoc* rule-making in the meantime. Systems at an intermediate stage in the developmental process will have formally organized rule-making arrangements at one or more levels in the structure and will be seeking to extend this formalization to other levels. Mature systems will be more concerned with *adjustments* to what is a basically complete formal structure.

These differences in comprehensiveness and formality of the rule-making arrangements, and in the degree of compatibility between the structure and the system's environments, influence the style and pattern of industrial relations research.

In mature systems, such as those in Canada and the United States, research tends to involve the study, *by discipline*, of marginal changes in the system or of issues at its periphery. Research tends to be organized by topic or problem and is often empirical rather than philosophical. Where the formal system is incomplete (i.e. where the full institutional structure of local, sectoral and national relationships has not been developed), as in Japan, research tends to focus on detailed examination of central industrial relations themes and on more speculative work on issues at the frontiers of the system.

Industrial relations systems in need of being realigned with their market and political environments present a more complicated research picture. Where the need for change can be anticipated, reform tends to focus on *procedures* and is often carefully supported by research on different procedural alternatives. Typically, the commissions or legislative bodies charged with making the formal system adhere more closely to industrial relations realities or to the country's economic and political goals, and seek the advice and assistance of the scholarly community. The Donovan Commission and the National Board for Prices and Incomes in Britain are examples of how a mature industrial relations system can plan for (if not always accomplish) the gradual changes needed to regularize its work-place industrial relations and achieve national economic goals.[4]

Where the pressures for the reform of the industrial relations system are more radical and immediate, research takes on a more ideological flavour. Italy best exemplifies this case.[5] The focus on work-place issues in Italy reflects the underdevelopment of employee representation at the work-place. Italy has neither the organized enterprise unionism of North America and Japan, the tradition of shop-steward representation of Britain nor the codetermination of Germany. Although industry-wide bargaining has occurred, backed by a high degree of political involvement, Italy has lacked the sectoral and regional industrial relations framework which give added depth to bargaining in France. Informal arrangements for determining work rules and for representing labour have been inadequate.

The predictable result has been an upsurge in localized conflict as a means of expressing the unmet needs of workers. The subsequent response of the system has been for unions to establish control over informal work-place organizations and over collective bargaining procedures at the local level.

While similar inadequacies in representation and neglect of local issues have plagued other Continental countries, the problems were less urgent and the adaptations more gradual. France faced a drive similar to Italy's to extend its formal industrial relations system to the local level.[6] And like Italy, its response has been to implement procedural reforms in plant-level industrial relations through a political accommodation involving regular union and employer channels. In the Federal Republic of Germany, reform has also been largely procedural, focusing on improvements in work-place representation, in new methods of dealing with conflict, and in revamping the arrangements for skill training.[7]

The debates in the European Economic Community over industrial relations structure provide an interesting complement to the experience of the individual member countries. As part of their efforts to harmonize economic and social policies, the EEC countries face the problem of finding a common industrial relations framework. Considering the lessons of work-place unrest in its member countries since the late sixties, it is obvious that national bargaining will need to be supplemented by some formal policy of work-place representation. In casting about for 'continental' solutions to this problem that will be acceptable to both employer and union representatives in the EEC countries, the German model of codetermination possesses the advantage of flexibility.[8] It allows for formal representation without defining too precisely the tie between work-place organizations and national unions.

Topics in Industrial Relations Research

A strict comparative analysis of industrial relations research by subject area among the countries is hampered by differences in the way that industrial relations is approached as a field of study. There are obvious variations arising from the disciplinary focus and in the definition of topics considered to fall under the term 'industrial relations'. More important, however, is the impact of ideology in shaping the framework within which research questions are formulated.[9] In the Anglo-Saxon countries, for example, research is generally categorized by subject area, whereas in those countries with Marxist influences (and for those authors working within a Marxist framework), industrial relations issues are only one component of a larger concern with the evolution of society and relationships between the classes. Thus, any overview of industrial relations research organized by topic must necessarily do some violence to Marxist research by arbitrarily dividing the whole into parts. With that caveat, some similarities and some differences in research pattern can be discussed.

Mainstream Issues

In all the countries discussed here, there has been research on the kinds of industrial relations issues usually considered as 'mainstream' in the Anglo-Saxon tradition.[10] Collective bargaining, trade union history and structure, conflict and its resolution, and legal regulation of the industrial relations system, are universal concerns. Within these broad areas, however, research emphasis has varied from country to country. For example, in Sweden and Italy, where there is no tradition of *formal* plant-level bargaining or a strong shop stewards' movement, research on work-place issues has tended to be more theoretical than empirical. Italian researchers approach bargaining principally from a legal perspective, whereas relatively little emphasis is placed on wage bargaining or on conflict. Research in the United States and Canada has been more concerned with public-sector bargaining than it has been in other countries.

Work-place industrial relations

Beyond these mainstream issues, however, there is considerable diversity in research patterns. Research on bargaining structure, particularly with respect to activities at the work-place level, flourished in all countries during the sixties and the seventies. In the countries experiencing considerable worker unrest – Italy (1968/69), France (1968) – the drive to create new industrial relations arrangements at the work-place understandably spurred research. However, even in countries showing greater stability in work-place relations, such as Britain, Sweden and Germany, concern with increases in wildcat strikes and with economic performance stimulated research attention. The Donovan Commission in Britain (1965) was the first systematic attempt to examine the role of work-place bargaining in an industrial relations system and to suggest reforms. Similarly, Swedish and German research addressed the issue of improving work-place representation following increases in wildcat strikes in 1969/70.

The treatment of work-place issues illustrates well the influence of ideology on industrial relations research. In Italy and France, the organizing principle for studies of work-place movements was one of class. Class interests have been consistently identified as the core of worker unrest, and analyses have traced these interests through the political process to their gradual assimilation by established union movements. In the 'procedural reform' countries, Britain and Germany, class identity has not emerged as sharply in the research on work-place bargaining, and class issues are confined largely to radical critiques of reform proposals. In Japan, the United States and Canada, where work-place unions are traditionally strong, class rarely features in the literature on work-place industrial relations.

Related to class identity at the work-place are questions of hierarchy and alienation. Research in Germany, France and Italy has examined hierarchy as an instrument of capitalist control. France, in particular, has explored the question of *autogestion*, or worker control, as an alternative style of work-place management. These same countries, along with Sweden, have examined worker alienation, often as it relates to the role of technology.

In the United States, Britain, Canada, Germany and Sweden, much research on work-place issues is from a technical and managerial perspective and is often directed at issues of interest to practitioners. Human relations approaches in industry have been a major subject in the United States and Canada, and personnel management is topical in Germany. In Italy, human relations has also been an important research theme, but from the viewpoint of class relations and capitalist control, rather than as a style of personnel management. Behavioural approaches, both human and organizational, have become important in the United States and Canada, and occupational health and safety at the work-place is a growing concern of industrial relations research in the United States and Sweden.

Labour Economics

Although labour economics has not been a dominant research discipline in most countries, labour markets are widely studied. The most advanced work has been in the United States, where there is also substantial companion literature on the economic analysis of manpower training programmes. In many of the countries (the United States, Sweden, Germany), labour-market analysis focusses on the changing occupational structure and its implications for skill development. Wages and wage structure are important themes in Britain, Sweden and

Japan. Japan naturally has focused on the internal labour markets of enterprises and also on the role of labour migration from rural to urban areas in the course of economic development.

Changes in the occupational structure have also been tied to issues of the 'new working class'. This term encompasses a range of meanings from *embourgeoisement* in Britain to problems of integrating tradition-ally non-union work groups into working-class movements in France and Italy.

Researchers in Italy, Sweden, the United States, Japan and Britain have examined the economic impact of unions. Wage effects have been most often analysed, although Japanese research is more concerned with the relation of unionization to lifetime employment and the *nenkō* system. In Sweden, the major emphasis has been on wage structure and the tension between the solidaristic wage policy of the LO (Con-federation of Swedish Trade Unions) and the wage ambitions of white-collar and professional groups. Researchers in both Sweden and Britain have been interested in the problem of wage drift at the work-place.

Dual labour markets and labour-market segmentation have been recent 'sources of research controversy in Italy, Japan and the United States. Italy and Japan have long understood their economies in dualist terms: the Italians emphasizing the north–south, rural–industrial split and the Japanese distinguishing between the sector of large enterprises and the rest of the economy. In both these countries, questions of class structure and of income distribution are often a part of the analysis. In the case of the United States, dual-market studies are divided between institutional and radical approaches. The former are concerned with the 'rules of play' governing labour markets and the implications of these rules for economic structure and economic behaviour; the latter are more directly concerned with income distribution in a class context.

Economic policy

The final broad area of industrial relations research is on economic policy. In the United States, and in Britain, there has been considerable research on incomes policy. The labour–management relations com-ponent of this research has been much higher in Britain, reflecting the stronger role of national bargaining in wage determination and the widespread conviction that wage restraint must rely on labour manage-ment institutions, and may require some industrial relations reform. United States research is more closely tied to traditions of labour economics and to the labour market foundations of the Phillips curve. In Italy, France and Sweden there is an emphasis on the role of unions and of labour politics in economic planning. In Italy, the discussion tends to be ideological and philosophical, whereas in France (with its tradition of indicative planning) and in Sweden (with its tradition of centralized bargaining and close ties between the government and labour and management organizations), there is substantial research on the actual development of joint economic programmes and the reliance on a tripartite approach to economic policy. Interestingly, research suggests that both Sweden and France appear to be relying more heavily on the collective bargaining process, and the extension of that process to the plant level, to achieve both local and national economic objectives.

Issues of productivity and inflation have been touched upon in some countries Italy, Japan and Sweden have shown a modest interest in the inflationary aspects of industrial relations, with the Swedes tying this interest into research on the Rehn model of labour-market policy. The British, and to some extent the Swedes, have undertaken research on productivity, the Swedes stressing its link with training and economic growth and the British examining productivity and productivity bargaining as an approach to incomes policy.

Issues of income distribution and inequality are implicit in all research with a Marxist orientation. The United States also has a substantial body of literature on discrimination and poverty and the distribution of earned income, but it emphasizes the legal and programmatic approaches to income distribution rather than its class connotations. Japan has been peripherally interested in these issues as part of studies on economic dualism, and both Sweden and Britain have examined the problem of low pay in connection with private or public wage policies.

Summary

Obviously these diverse patterns of research cannot be fully explained. Certain general influences can, however, be identified. The ideology of each researcher clearly plays a role in shaping his or her approach to industrial relations, but the more interesting question of the overall ideological balance of research in each country lies in its political and intellectual traditions. Despite marked ideological differences, the 'mainstream' topics reflect common problems to be resolved within the various industrial relations systems. The research reported in this book describes the specific dimensions of these issues as they have evolved in each country. It represents, more often than not, part of the quest for new solutions.

A second factor of common concern is 'crisis' in industrial relations structures. Particularly in countries where the structure of the industrial relations system is no longer compatible with the system's environments, serious discontent with existing arrangements runs high. In the sixties and early seventies this discontent was manifest in the area of work-place relations and was articulated both through spontaneous worker action and established political and bargaining channels.

Although the international economic prosperity of the late sixties eased the restraints on the expression of worker discontent in all countries, the research record shows that discontent was far less where formal bargaining structures were established at the local level. Even in countries with long-established traditions of formalized work-place bargaining, however, crises can arise wherever gaps exist in the system or where a part of the structure has become obsolete. In the United States, for example, the current interest in public-sector bargaining reflects an area of active experimentation to fill a gap in the system. Similarly, the Donovan Commission and Bullock Reports in Britain and the Sudreau Report in France can be seen as attempts to fill gaps in the formal industrial relations structure and to tackle problems of obsolescence.

Finally, this international survey of research on industrial relations underscores the universal interest of governments dealing with economic interdependences. Limiting industrial relations conflict is a prominent example of such concern. The growing tendency for governments in advanced market economies to consult with, and even defer to, labour and management on a far broader range of policies, however, indicates an increasing role for industrial relations analysis in the formation of public policy.

Industrial Relations Ideology and Industrial Relations Theory

This research survey provides a commentary on the ideological and theoretical perspectives governing industrial relations research in each country. Research seems to cluster around two ideological themes: the pluralist–institutionalist approach and the class approach. The former, characterized particularly by work in the Anglo-Saxon countries, tends to focus on procedural and institutional approaches to problem-solving in industrial relations.[11] The latter, of which Italy is the prototypical country, is as much concerned with workers and the working class as with unions and bargaining. Politics, political action and the tensions between employers and employees are prominent in class-oriented research. Less attention is devoted to the actual procedures and practice of industrial relations. A number of countries, especially Sweden, France and Japan, combine these two ideologies. In France, for example, Reynaud stresses that even class-oriented research by Marxist scholars has a strong vein of pragmatism allowing empirical research to coexist with ideological interpretation.[12] In Sweden, the high degree of union organization guarantees close correspondence between class and union issues, and the long tenure of Social Democratic government has blurred the distinctions between collective bargaining, national industrial relations policies and class issues. In Japan, two distinct ideological schools of research exist, one following the Anglo-Saxon pattern of pluralism and institutionalism, the other a mixture of 'German' social policy and Marxism.[13]

Parallels can be found in the use of 'theory' in industrial relations research. Three major divisions were visible in the research surveyed: (*a*) a systems approach to industrial relations (following Dunlop's *Industrial Relations Systems*[14]) stressing social pluralism, the development of representative institutions and the analysis of the industrial relations rules, (*b*) a Marxist approach stressing class relationships and the political and economic struggles between classes, and (*c*) a 'pragmatic' approach in which theory plays little or no role in the research. As with ideology, all three types of research are represented in the countries surveyed, but the balance varies. The Anglo-Saxon countries and Germany exhibit a strong penchant for the 'systems' model. Much of the research in France and Italy is organized around Marxist concepts. Japan has both Marxist and 'systems' schools of research, while Swedish research tends to be less theoretical.

Not surprisingly, where industrial relations research has a strong 'systems' bent, economics has been an important research discipline. This has been accompanied by a trend towards quantification. In the countries where class issues arise frequently in the research literature, sociology, history and law are more influential disciplines.

Because the various approaches to industrial relations theory are identified with contending political ideologies, the differences between these theories tend to be emphasized. The debate between these approaches goes back at least to the early twentieth century in the United States, when the Wisconsin school worked on alternative theories to Marx's as an explanation of 'business' unionism in America.

More recently, the debate has been renewed by critiques of the pluralist–institutionalist approach from the radical left. These critiques have formed an important part of the recent research literature in Britain, but are also emerging in countries such as the United States and Sweden. The main thrust of the criticism is that pluralist–institutionalist analysis is too conservative, too concerned with controlling conflict for the benefit of the *status quo*, and too involved with institutions instead of individual workers.[15]

Basically, these critics would argue that pluralist–institutionalists define labour unrest as symptomatic of a malfunctioning industrial relations system and as a sign of the need for reform. Reform is seen as a procedural matter in which labour and management organizations, sometimes in cooperation with government, are interested in reorganizing the structure of the industrial relations system, in order to eliminate the unrest. The pluralist–institutionalists tend to avoid normative assessments of the results of reform. By implication they endorse procedures which leave the balance of power between labour and management unchanged.

The competing view is that unrest is a manifestation of the stifled ambitions of individual workers or of small work groups – ambitions which are being frustrated by management and by the bureaucratic insensitivity of formal labour organizations. At stake in the issue of unrest is the distribution of power in society and the distribution of income that flows from power. Unrest is treated as a normal feature of the exercise of power and as such should be recognized as one more instrument in the economic and political bargaining over reorganization of the power structure.

This focus on workers and power leads naturally to class as an organizing device for analysis. At the work-place level, technology and management become the backdrop against which worker behaviour is studied. At the national level, worker protest and collective political action are seen as the instruments through which the working class responds to capitalist pressures as articulated by government.

The irony of this criticism is that it is levelled at research derived from a worker-oriented tradition – the Oxford school in Britain and the Wisconsin school in the United States. Admittedly, this tradition is non-Marxist, but it is a tradition concerned with understanding and articulating labour issues in societies where working-class consciousness is weak and where working-class political power is disorganized.[16] In place of political mobilization by class, the early pluralist–institutionalists advocated advancing the interests of workers by promoting unionization on the one hand and broad programmes of social welfare on the other. Such a broad-based strategy of social policy inevitably encourages a variety of political coalitions, many of which cut across class lines as conventionally defined.[17]

Bargaining over wages and working conditions may divide labour and management in a narrow sense, but both groups share in the common fortunes of their industry and of the national economy. Many labour organizations and managements have remarkably similar views when it comes to matters such as tariff policy, rate regulation, or minimum wages. Much of the theorizing about 'job control' unionism in the United States is more aptly perceived as a statement on the threat of unorganized workers to both labour and management in companies where collective bargaining is practised.

From this perspective, industrial relations cannot be approached solely from the study of class interests. It involves the analysis of the processes of accommodation among diverse clusters of interests. Public policy is seen as more than an instrument for the advancement of class interests. Its role is to promote collective social interests and to reconcile competing group interests where necessary.

Where class-oriented research is inclined to favour unfettered worker democracy, and procedures which articulate grass-roots worker sentiment, the pluralist-institutionalist school is not class-oriented and therefore judges procedures in terms of their consistency with political and economic interdependences among various groups in society. Indeed, a major characteristic of the pluralist–institutionalist school is that it tends to favour collective entities over individual workers as the vehicle for articulating labour interests. Collective organizations such as unions are seen not only as 'efficient' means for representing individual interests, but also as devices for weighing and aggregating these interests and for providing accountability for economic and political decisions once a consensus has been agreed on.

Having indicated the issues that divide the two schools of industrial relations theory, some areas where the two points of view are in substantial agreement should also be mentioned. Indeed, industrial relations research may well be moving in directions that are likely to promote reconciliations between the contending theoretical positions rather than drive them further apart.

Class-oriented scholars tend to judge industrial relations systems by their success in furthering working-class interests. While researchers in the pluralist–institutionalist tradition would not accept such a narrow measure of performance (and are often accused of avoiding any normative judgements about the distribution of power or economic benefits in an industrial relations system), they are nevertheless concerned with overall performance. For example, the Wisconsin school was clearly pro-labour in its research focus and its policy prescriptions. More recently, issues of inflation, growth and productivity have been major criteria used by pluralist–institutionalists in assessing the performance of national or sectoral industrial relations systems. Traditionally, research on work-place industrial relations in the United States has been concerned with equity and fairness as perceived by individual workers and there is increasing interest in matters of job satisfaction, work quality and alienation.[18] In the European context, there is a widespread belief among industrial relations specialists working along pluralist–institutionalist lines that incomes policies designed to stabilize national economies must also reduce earnings inequalities and raise low pay.[19]

A further prospect for reconciliation between these two schools is likely to be found in the future treatment of the relationship between industrial relations and markets, technology, and power. For both schools, markets and technology have been thought to be largely determined exogenously. That is to say that industrial relations, or class relations, are in part the result of reactions by the parties to market and technological circumstances. Concerning the issue of power, some of the pluralist–institutionalists have viewed it as part of the context in which the industrial relations system operates. Of course, for class-oriented researchers, power is inherent to the internal dynamics of the class system.

Various research studies, particularly those concerned with issues of economic policy, suggest that labour and management no longer take markets or technology as given. Instead, labour and management try to influence market structure and to control technology through the exercise of economic and political power. In the coming decades, research on industrial relations will have to confront the difficult task of treating market control and technology, as well as the development and use of power, as partly endogenous to industrial relations systems. As the viewpoints of the competing theories are broadened the theories are likely to become more similar in their focus and their conclusions.

Industrial Relations, Public Policy, and Research

The on-going changes in industrial relations systems will influence research in the coming years. In those countries engaged in restructuring their industrial relations systems, for example, the experiments and reforms of the seventies will need to be assessed. Learning the lessons for public policy from experience will require a broad foundation of empirical research. For industrial relations systems where reform is more gradual, however, research will be narrower and more closely tied to the needs of practitioners.

The most significant challenge to research will be to assist in the integration of industrial relations decisions into the larger fabric of economic policy-making.[20] Industrial relations decisions have an undeniable impact on economic performance, often to the dismay of national economic planners. The concern with the harmonization of industrial relations policy among the EEC countries and with the regulation of multinational enterprises are recent examples of the growing governmental awareness of the impact that labour and management have on market behaviour.

As market regulation and control becomes a more widespread part of industrial relations activities, it creates new pressures to place the substance of industrial relations more squarely in the public domain. Few countries, however, have the necessary mechanisms, or even the analytical knowledge, to promote compatibility between industrial relations decisions and national economic objectives.

France and Sweden have made the greatest progress in bringing the industrial relations system into the sphere of national economic planning and management. France, with its tradition of indicative planning, consults with labour and management on legislative proposals and has delegated to them some matters previously decided by legislation. In Sweden, legislation affecting industrial relations is often simply an extension of trade union policy and provides a framework within which further bargaining can take place.[21]

In the United States, Canada and Britain, the integration of the industrial relations system into economic policy-making has been limited to lobbying activities by labour and management and to their participation on commissions and advisory bodies. The major exceptions have been the brief periods of labour–management cooperation during wartime.[22]

Progress in this area for most countries will require new modes of policy-making. Moreover, long-standing antagonisms that have characterized many labour and management relationships will have to be overcome as well.[23] It is likely that the first steps towards forging such integrated policy-making procedures will involve narrow issues of common concern to labour, management and government. What will often appear as *ad hoc* solutions to industrial relations problems of national significance, however, will gradually build the institutional capability required for more effective labour and management participation in national economic policy-making. Where successful, these institutional arrangements will invariably acquire larger responsibilities in economic management. If industrial relations research is to contribute to the development of such policy approaches, the disciplinary divisions that have eroded industrial relations as a scholarly specialty will again need to be blurred and field research will need to be re-emphasized.

Concluding Observations

The wealth of facts, ideas and theories provided in the chapters that follow invites comment on the future direction of thinking on industrial relations issues.

Patterns of Research

Common to all the countries studied are a series of research areas that may be characterized as 'mainstream'. These topics – industrial conflict, union history, wages and labour markets, and so forth – are identifiable as the core of the area in each of the countries studied. The list of core topics has been relatively stable historically and changes slowly. Research in the eighties is not likely to depart in substantial ways from the present pattern.

Beyond the core search topics, however, are a variety of issues from which significant new research themes will emerge. Such themes tend to be connected with issues in the development and reform of industrial relations systems.

Judging from the research record of the sixties and seventies an inventory of gaps in industrial relations systems and of areas where economic or social change have rendered current industrial relations arrangements outdated should provide an indicator of key research areas for the future. One such example is the emphasis on work-place bargaining arrangements in Europe. Other likely issues for the future are labour's political role, industrial relations in unorganized employment and centralization versus decentralization in bargaining structure.

Public Policy

Much of public policy towards industrial relations has traditionally emphasized alternatives to industrial conflict, and the development of social welfare policies. For the future, these concerns are likely to receive less attention. The emerging focus will be on the relationship between industrial relations and economic performance.

Domestic policies in industrialized countries will be directed at easing the strains caused by inflation, unemployment and declining rates of economic growth. At the same time, domestic policy will strive to place greater weight on considerations of equity and equality. The growing international economy will also force greater attention to be paid to matters of trade and employment. There will be a search for new policy instruments to replace the current emphasis on various combinations of labour-market adjustment policies. To contribute to this policy development, researchers will need to understand the twin worlds of government and industrial relations.

Pluralism and Class

Pluralism and class conflict have been the competing assumptions underlying most industrial relations research. Both assumptions have their weaknesses in theory and practice. They will have to be more effective in integrating considerations of power, markets and technology into their analytical frameworks if they are to depict accurately new developments in industrial relations. They will have to rebalance their philosophical focus – pluralism developing more of a concern with the normative results of industrial relations systems, and class approaches recognizing the need for a more pragmatic understanding of industrial relations – if they are to provide a basis for analysing industrial relations experience.

Tripartism

Whether from a pluralist or a class perspective, industrial relations systems will continue to be governed by processes of economic and political bargaining. As gaps in the formal industrial relations systems are filled and as reforms in industrial relations and public policy are introduced, these bargaining processes will inevitably require more formal tripartism. As bipartism is replaced by tripartism in economic and social decision-making, research will have to provide the tools and understanding needed to merge public and private industrial relations policies.

Convergence

Finally, some observations should be made about the issue of convergence of industrial relations systems. In 1960, Kerr, Dunlop, Harbison and Myers foresaw a world-wide tendency for technological and market forces associated with industrialization to push industrial relations systems towards uniformity.[24] This view was the subject of considerable debate and was subsequently modified by the original proponents to reflect their judgement that convergence was only a *tendency* that is unlikely to result in anything resembling identical systems among industrialized countries.[25]

The studies presented in this volume do not tackle the problem of convergence directly. Each in its own way, however, presents findings which have a bearing on whether industrial relations systems are approaching some common set of arrangements. They support a restated convergence hypothesis – convergence not in form, but in the broader sense of developing alternative solutions to problems common to all industrial relations systems. The corollary to this hypothesis is that differences observed among industrial relations systems are not simply random, but are rooted in individual-country responses to the underlying compulsions of industrial evolution.

Convergence, in this sense, can be seen in historical patterns of response to the problems posed by industrialization. For example, all industrialized countries show a tendency to institutionalize, in formal ways, the structure of their arrangements for making the rules of industrial relations. This, in turn, makes industrial relations systems more amenable to control by labour, management and government.

Similarly, all systems respond to the need for balance – introducing reforms, or more radical changes, in areas where pressures from obsolescence are mounting. Where industry-wide bargaining machinery is relatively more adequate than plant-level bargaining, the latter will be the focus of reform. Where the means of resolving industrial conflict or wage inflation are missing, these will gradually be adopted. Where efficiency has been stressed over normative considerations this imbalance will eventually be redressed.

Convergence can also be understood as part of the dilemma of national goal-setting. Industrialized societies develop multiple goals, many of which are incompatible. Growth and equality, full employment and price stability, industrial peace and free collective bargaining are difficult to accomplish simultaneously. Both class and pluralist theories of industrial relations recognize that choices must be made among these conflicting goals, that one set of goals must be pursued at the expense of another. Eventually, the neglected goals must be recognized and new priorities pursued for a time.

Convergence must thus be seen within a three-part framework. Firstly, it is the result of responses to problems common to all industrial relations systems. Secondly, it is the process by which gaps in areas in the institutional arrangements of industrial relations systems are filled. Finally, it is the realization that, over a span of time all industrial relations systems must selectively respond to multiple and often incompatible goals. Much of what we observe as 'differences' among systems is the result of differences in the goals being pursued at a particular point of time.

The essays in this volume portray industrial relations systems through the eyes of researchers. They draw together much of what is known about the dynamics of industrial relations systems in industrialized economies. The point of such a codification of the 'state of the art' of industrial relations research, however, is not primarily to resolve debates over convergence and philosophy. It should help to guide both scholars and practitioners in the important task of shaping the future of national and international systems of industrial relations.

NOTES

1. The volume by C. Kerr *et al.*, *Industrialism and Industrial Man* (Cambridge, Mass.: Harvard University Press, 1960) and the body of research growing out of their 'Inter-University Study of Human Resources in National Development' is helpful in developing a comparative understanding of the formal aspects of industrial relations arrangements in a number of countries. For a recent example of a survey of formal industrial relations developments in European countries, see S. Barkin (ed.), *Worker Militance and Its Consequences* (New York, Washington, and London: Praeger, 1975).
2. See, for example, the most recent survey in W. L. Ginsburg *et al.*, and B. Aaron, *et al.* (eds.), *A Review of Industrial Relations Research*, Vols. I and II (Madison, Wisconsin: Industrial Relations Research Association, 1970, 1971).

3. See the *Report of the Royal Commission on Trade Unions and Employers' Associations* Summary and Study Papers, 1–11 (London: HMSO, various dates); *In Place of Strife* (London:HMSO, 1969) a White Paper prepared by the British Labour Party, and the subsequent experience under the National Industrial Relations Act.

4. See Royal Commission, *op. cit.*, and the reports of the National Board for Prices and Incomes (London: HMSO, various dates).

5. See chapter 9.

6. See chapter 7.

7. See chapter 6.

8. See chapter 10.

9. This point is nicely developed in chapter 5. These problems are further compounded by the perspectives of the individual authors in selecting key pieces of research and assessing national research patterns.

10. G Strauss and P. Feuille develop the 'mainstream' theme in chapter 3, as do H. D. Woods and S. Goldenberg in chapter 2.

11. For a discussion of pluralism in industrial relations research, see chapter 11.

12. See chapter 4.

13. Sumiya discusses this division in chapter 8.

14. J. T. Dunlop, *Industrial Relations Systems* (New York: Henry Holt & Co., 1958).

15. For excellent summaries of these critiques, see J. H. Goldthorpe, 'Industrial Relations in Great Britain: A Critique of Reformism', in *Politics and Society*, 1974, pp. 419–51 and A. Fox, 'Collective Bargaining, Flanders and the Webbs', *British Journal of Industrial Relations*, Vol. XIII, no. 2, July 1975.

16. See S. Perlman, *A Theory of the Labor Movement* (New York: Macmillan, 1928) and H. Clegg, *A New Approach to Industrial Democracy* (Oxford: Basil Blackwell, 1960).

17. For a slightly different approach to these issues, see R. Dahrendorf, *Class and Conflict in Industrial Society* (Stanford: Stanford University Press, 1959).

18. See S. H. Slichter, 'The American System of Industrial Relations: Some Contrasts with Foreign Systems' in J. T. Dunlop (ed.) *Potentials of the American Economy: Selected Essays by Sumner H. Slichter* (Cambridge: Harvard University Press, 1961), and *Work in America: Report of a Special Task Force to the Secretary of Health, Education and Welfare* (Cambridge: the MIT Press, n.d.).

19. See L. Ullman and R. Flanagan, *Wage Restraint: A Study of Income Policies in Western Europe* (Berkeley, Los Angeles and London: University of California Press, 1971), F. Blackeby (ed.), *An Incomes Policy for Britain* (London: Heinemann Educational Books, 1972), and OECD, *Wage Determination* (Paris: OECD, 1974).

20. See J. T. Dunlop, *Statement Before the Subcommittee on Production and Stabilization of the House Committee on Housing and Urban Affairs*, (Washington: GPO, 6 February 1974), J.–D. Reynaud, 'The Role of Trade Unions in National Political Economy' in S. Barkin *et al.* (eds.) *International Labor* (New York: Harper & Row, 1967), and J. T. Dunlop,

'Political Systems and Industrial Relations', *International Institute for Labor Studies Bulletin*, no. 9, 1972, pp. 99–116.
21. See, for example, the recent Swedish legislation on codetermination and work-place representation.
22. See D. Q. Mills, *Government, Labor and Inflation: Wage Stabilization in the United States* (Chicago and London: University of Chicago Press, 1975).
23. See J. -D. Reynaud, 'Industrial Relations and the Negotiation of Change', *International Institute for Labor Studies Bulletin*, no. 9, 1972, pp. 3–16, for a discussion of negotiation for political and economic change.
24. See Kerr *et al.*, *op. cit.*
25. J. T. Dunlop *et al.*, *Industrialism and Industrial Man Reconsidered* (Princeton: The Inter-University Study of Human Resources in National Development, 1975), pp. 35–9.

2 Industrial Relations Research in Canada

H. D. Woods and Shirley B. Goldenberg

A review of industrial relations research is complicated in Canada, as it is in the United States, by the lack of clear agreement on the parameters of industrial relations. While some scholars have an interdisciplinary approach to industrial relations as a field of study, others are involved in research impinging on various aspects of the subject from the perspective of a particular discipline, such as economics, law, history, political science, sociology, or psychology. Although this chapter will concentrate primarily on 'mainstream' industrial relations research, a major section will be devoted to labour and manpower economics. Research in the emerging fields of labour history and behavioural science will also be considered. Much of the relevant legal research will be covered in the section on public policy.

The Evolution of Industrial Relations Research

The first of many important public inquiry commissions into labour–management relations was appointed before the end of the nineteenth century (*Royal Commission on the Relations of Labour and Capital*, 1889). A book on the subject was published by a future prime minister of Canada early in the twentieth century (King, 1918). Serious academic research on industrial relations, however, has been very largely a post-Second World War phenomenon. Relatively few investigations carried out in the earlier period could meet the test of rigorous scientific method. This review will consider developments in research since the Second World War, with emphasis on the work of the past decade.

Recent bibliographical research (Isbester, Coates and Williams, 1965; Wood, Kelly and Kumar, 1970; Tremblay, 1969; Le Blanc and

Thwaites, 1973) shows that graduate theses and journal articles on a wide range of industrial relations topics began to appear in significant numbers in the mid-1940s. While this reflected a growing interest by Canadian scholars in industrial relations, as late as 1960 only a few major books had been published as a result of university research. However, some of these, such as Logan's (1948) history of trade unionism in Canada and Trudeau's (1956) volume on the asbestos strike, are still regarded as classics. This period also produced some of the earliest academic research on public policy in labour relations (Woods, 1948; Logan, 1956) and the first general overview of industrial relations in Canada (Jamieson, 1957, revised in 1973).

The adoption of new collective bargaining legislation at the federal level and in a number of provinces during and after the Second World War and the growing body of experience under this legislation gave a significant impetus to research by legal scholars, relying heavily on case material. Most of the early legal writing on industrial relations was restricted to an analysis of particular aspects of the law and its application, such as the use of the injunction (Carrothers, 1956), arbitration procedures and decisions (Curtis, 1957), and the functions and decisions of labour relations boards and boards of conciliation (Crysler, 1949). In a later work, Crysler (1957) covered a broad area of statutory and case law, mainly in Ontario and at the federal level, but Beaulieu (1955) provided the most interesting exception with his wide-ranging comparative study of labour legislation in France, Britain, the United States, Canada and Quebec, and his serious analysis of the problems that arise in the application of the law at each stage of the collective relationship. Gérard Picard's book (1957) on a proposed new labour code for the province of Quebec was also based on an analysis of labour legislation in other countries. However, his treatment of foreign experience is confined to an introductory chapter. The book provoked considerable comment at the time, and it is interesting to note that some of his major proposals, such as the extension of bargaining rights to previously excluded groups (civil servants, professionals) and a modification of his proposals for a labour court, have been adopted in Quebec (*Labour Code*, Revised Statutes of Quebec, 1964, c. 141, as amended 1969).

Scholarly research in industrial relations became more firmly established in the first half of the sixties. While the number of published volumes remained relatively limited, the areas of interest broadened. Legal scholars continued to write on a variety of topics: the status of trade unions (Cameron and Young, 1960), the role of regulatory bodies

(Bromke, 1961), labour arbitration (Carrothers, 1961), collective bargaining law (Carrothers, 1965), the enforcement of the collective agreement (Curtis, 1966), and restrictive practices with respect to unions and labour (Crysler, 1967). This period saw the publication of a comprehensive study of public policy and labour economics (Woods and Ostry, 1962), an interesting study of government intervention in the settlement of disputes (Anton, 1962) and a small but well-documented study of early labour history (French, 1962). The first book on staff relations in the Canadian Civil Service (Frankel, 1962) was a harbinger of things to come. Some public inquiries (H. C. Goldenberg, 1962; Norris, 1963; Freedman, 1965; Heaney, 1965; Montpetit, 1966) also formed landmarks. The second half of the decade brought a great increase in research activity which has continued to the present day. Thus, the period under primary consideration here represents the most prolific years of industrial relations research in Canada. In fact there is now sufficient published material on 'mainstream industrial relations' that selecting from it is difficult and must, at times, be arbitrary.

There is a similar problem of selection with respect to the material on labour economics, a field that had an earlier academic start than industrial relations and that is actually considered its parent discipline in Canada as in the United States. The unemployment problems of the Depression in the thirties gave impetus to serious academic research in this field (e.g. Marsh, 1935).

As work-related research in the behavioural sciences, such as organizational behaviour, is in a much earlier stage of development with more still in progress than actually published, this field has presented fewer problems of selection.

The Locus of Industrial Relations Research

An examination of the literature shows that most of the significant contributions to industrial relations research in Canada have originated in government departments or the universities. Unions and employers' organizations have confined their research efforts mainly to data collection designed to meet the needs of particular bargaining situations and the preparation of highly subjective briefs to government and to commissions of inquiry, or for public relations purposes. Even when central labour and management organizations use fairly sophisticated research methods the results are usually intended to serve specific goals and thus seldom meet the criteria of objective research.

The Canadian Construction Association has been an important exception on the employer side. It commissioned an objective study of the industry which resulted in the publication of a major volume by two editors and thirteen other independent contributors (H. C. Goldenberg and Crispo, (eds.), 1968). Published simultaneously in English and French, this volume represents the most ambitious and exhaustive examination of industrial relationships in a particular industry ever undertaken in Canada. Although it was not a public inquiry, some of its recommendations have had important policy implications.

Government

Regular government publications on industrial relations date back to 1900 when the *Labour Gazette* began as a monthly publication of the Federal Department of Labour. This publication has continued without interruption to the present. As jurisdiction over labour relations in Canada is divided between the federal government and the provinces, both levels of government have conducted research on a regular basis. Although these studies are largely for internal use, a number are fairly widely disseminated for public information (especially note those of the Economics and Research Branch of the Canada Department of Labour), as are studies sponsored by government agencies such as the Economic Council of Canada, Statistics Canada and the Pay Research Bureau.

A few public inquiries commissioned by government have covered the entire spectrum of labour relations, such as the McKinnon Report in Nova Scotia (1962), the Task Force on Labour Relations at the federal level (Woods *et al.*, 1968), and the Rand (1968) and Cohen (1972) Commissions in Ontario and Newfoundland respectively. The majority of public investigations, however, have been undertaken in response to specific problem situations such as a strike or violence in a particular industry, or with a view to introducing policy changes in an area, the public sector for example.

The public inquiries have been a stimulus to academic research. The federal Task Force on Labour Relations undertook in 1966–69 the most comprehensive investigation of labour–management relations in Canada. It commissioned nearly a hundred supporting studies by scholars in a number of disciplines recruited from universities across the country. The publication of many of the Task Force studies virtually doubled the serious Canadian literature (books) on industrial relations in less than a five-year period. Some scholars have continued research interests flowing from their original Task Force assignments, and this in turn has added to the literature (e.g. Malles, 1973). Thus a significant interdependent relationship has been established in Canada between government-sponsored research and university research. In addition, many academicians act as arbitrators and mediators in labour disputes and as members of administrative tribunals.

The universities

Labour law, labour economics, industrial sociology and psychology, as well as labour history, are taught for the most part in the departments of the basic discipline concerned. The core subject matter of industrial relations such as collective bargaining and public policy, and most recently organizational behaviour, are now given in the interdisciplinary setting of faculties of business or commerce. Some of the major universities also have separate industrial relations departments or centres. While most of these sponsor conferences and contribute to research, the Industrial Relations Department at Laval and the Industrial Relations Centre at Queen's deserve special mention for the particular contributions they have made, both through their own research activities and the publication facilities they have provided for others.

The Department of Industrial Relations at Laval publishes the bilingual *Relations Industrielles – Industrial Relations.* This journal began publication in 1946 and was adopted as the official organ of the Canadian Industrial Relations Research Institute (CIRRI) when that organization, the Canadian counterpart of the Industrial Relations Research Association (IRRA) in the United States, was established in 1963. The bilingual nature of the journal has helped to bridge a gap between French and English scholars in the field. The publication of a French–English glossary of industrial relations terms at Laval (Dion, 1975) has facilitated the accurate translation of contract terms and clauses in labour legislation. A comprehensive *Dictionary of Industrial Relations* (Dion, 1976) made a further contribution to the interpretation of these terms as well as providing other useful information on labour statistics, labour history and a chronology of labour legislation. While the author deserves full credit for conceiving the idea for this monumental work; and for carrying it to fruition, there is no doubt that the availability of graduate students and the collaboration of colleagues have resulted in an atmosphere at Laval that is particularly conducive to research.

The publications of the Industrial Relations Centre at Queen's University include research, reprint and bibliographical series as well as a comprehensive annual review by its director (Wood). Although most of the Centre's publications are the work of its own scholars, the research and reprint series include the writing of scholars from other universities as well as some practitioners in the field. The centre has also published a detailed and comprehensive labour law casebook (Labour Relations Law Casebook Group, 1970, 2nd edition, 1974).

The areas of research interest

Canadian research reflects particular interest in problem-prone industries, notably construction. There is also considerable interest in new groups bargaining collectively (white-collar workers, professionals and civil servants); in disadvantaged groups in the labour force (women, the handicapped, racial minorities); and in problems flowing from technological change, new methods of work and work relationships, and general problems like inflation and unemployment. There has also been some serious research on various aspects of labour history, including the ideological evolution and political involvement of the labour movement and the social implications of particular strikes. Concern with a wide variety of policy issues, from recognition procedures to dispute resolution, has generated some of the most significant academic research in the field as well as some major public investigations.

But in spite of the growing research activity in so many areas of industrial relations and some interesting studies of foreign systems intended to provide a better perspective on the Canadian experience (Isaac, 1970; Malles, 1969, 1973), there has been remarkably little theoretical writing, and certainly no serious attempt to develop an indigenous theory or philosophy of labour relations in Canada. This apparent lack may be explained in large measure by the strong influence of the United States both on the development of the Canadian industrial relations system and on the direction of industrial relations research. Even the few attempts at theoretical writing on industrial relations owe a considerable debt to earlier American thinking on the subject. For example, Hameed's (1970) effort to establish an integrated theory of collective bargaining is derived from widely accepted but hitherto unrelated theories of unionism, management and negotiation, all developed by American scholars. A model for the analysis of industrial relations systems on which the Federal Task Force based its research design (Craig, 1975) is a refinement and extension of Dunlop's (1958) theory. Hameed, like Craig, tried to establish a more dynamic relationship than Dunlop did between the industrial relations system and other subsystems of society, also by use of an input–output model. This has provided a valuable framework for the organization of his interesting book (Hameed, 1975).

The public sector is one area of industrial relations in which Canada has taken major policy initiatives over the United States and in which bargaining experience has been more extensive. Paul Phillips (1974) has made a serious attempt at theory in this area, using a series of diagrammatic bargaining models to compare the pressures on the parties in the private sector and in sectors representing varying degrees of public interest.

The American influence and its implications

The role of American business interests in the early industrialization of Canada and the initiative of American-based unions in organizing Canadian workers continues to be reflected in the figures on United States corporate domination of major sectors of the Canadian economy (Gray, 1972), and in the fact that nearly half of unionized workers in Canada are in local branches of international unions, whose membership, headquarters and executive personnel are overwhelmingly American (*Labour Organizations in Canada*, annual). Considering the union and corporate links between Canada and the United States and the similar technology and work environment in comparable trades and industries, it is not surprising that the structure of labour–management relations, the nature of the bargaining process–in fact the major issues dividing the parties and the resulting clauses in collective agreements– are remarkably similar. Much American research in industrial relations, as in other areas of social science, particularly in the newer field of organizational behaviour, has been found to be equally relevant in Canada.

In view of the American head start in research on industrial relations and related areas of study and the superior American resources for research and the dissemination of research results, there has been a tendency for Canadian scholars to avoid the ground already covered by researchers in the United States. They have accepted American thinking where it seems applicable to Canada and concentrated their efforts on areas in which the Canadian experience has differed from the American.

The American influence has become a subject of research in itself, particularly by economists, both in government and the universities. The interdependent relationship between the Canadian and American industrial relations systems has stimulated considerable interest in wage comparisons (Downie, 1970). Other research has been generated by interest in the extent of American influence and its implications for Canadian autonomy. The authors are generally agreed on the extent of American economic penetration, but differ in their interpretation of its implications (Brecher and Reisman, 1957; Levitt, 1972; Gray, 1972). Although some concern has occasionally been expressed over the imposition of inappropriate American precedents, remarkably little of the recent criticism of multinational corporations operating in Canada has been directed at their industrial relations practices (Crispo, 1974).

While much of the early criticism of international unionism reflected the concerns of the business community, there has also been significant resistance to the American influence by nationalist elements within the labour movement. This resulted in the organization of some important Canadian-based unions, but never succeeded in seriously undermining the dominant position of the international unions. Crispo (1967) concluded in his major study on international unions that their influence in Canada has been positive on the whole, confirming the view expressed a few years earlier by Kruger (1964). However, Crispo recommended that greater autonomy be given to Canadian sections of American-based unions to meet the growing nationalist aspirations of their members. Some branches of United States unions in Canada have already achieved considerable autonomy and a few have recently withdrawn from their American parent bodies.

Some of the more significant differences between the Canadian and American experience flow from distinctive characteristics of the Canadian environment, notably the constitutional division of jurisdiction under the federal system and the existence of the two separate linguistic and cultural communities.

Industrial Relations Research

Crispo (1978a) recently published the first and only general textbook on Canadian industrial relations. Apart from a few other books that defy classification because of the breadth of their coverage, such as

Jamieson's general overview of Canadian Industrial Relations (1957, revised 1973) and several collections of readings on a wide spectrum of labour relations (Miller and Isbester, 1971; Hem Jain, 1973, 1975; Harish Jain, 1971; Hameed, 1975), most of the Canadian research falls under well-defined subject headings.

Labour History

An early historical study devoted exclusively to labour was on the Winnipeg general strike of 1919 (Masters, 1950). This strike has continued to interest serious historians, both in the context of more general works (e.g. Morton, 1957; McNaught, 1959) and as a topic of interest in itself (McNaught and Bercuson, 1974). The most recent publication on the subject is probably the most complete (Bercuson, 1974). In addition to dealing with the events of the strike and its immediate antecedents, Bercuson examines the development of unionism and the social impact of the Depression and war in the two decades that preceded the strike. By focusing attention on earlier examples of labour unrest and on the history of poor relations that existed between labour and government, Bercuson, like Trudeau (1956) in the case of the asbestos strike, interprets the outburst in Winnipeg as the result of a natural progression of events rather than as an isolated phenomenon.

Although many of the institutional studies of the labour movement as well as some studies of particular strikes might well be classified as labour history, few of the authors of these studies have been concerned with the period prior to 1900 or with aspects of working-class life apart from the organized labour movement. Lately, however, there has been a growing interest in the earlier stages of labour and working-class history. This is reflected in a number of recent publications (e.g. P. Phillips, 1967; North and Griffin, 1974; Kealey, 1974; Langdon, 1975; Hamelin, Larocque and Rouillard, 1970; Bélanger and Bernier, 1973; Rouillard, 1974; De Bonville, 1975) and in reprints of previous studies which, though not written as historical works, may provide valuable source material on conditions existing in an earlier period (e.g. reprint, 1973 of first Royal Commission Report, 1889; also Bradwin, 1928, republished 1972). Forsey (1965) has provided some carefully documented insights into the early stages of labour organization, but many students of the earlier period have been hindered by the paucity of source material. The publication of the first specialized bibliography of primary sources in Canadian working-class history (Hann, Kealey, Kealey and Warrian, 1973) has provided a valuable reference guide for scholars in this field, as has the retrospective bibliography on the work world in Quebec, published in French (Le Blanc and Thwaites, 1973). The recently published memoirs of one of the founders of the Catholic labour movement (Charpentier, 1971), though not a historical study in itself, may also be noted as a useful reference for students of labour history.

The formation in 1970 of a committee on labour history within the Canadian Historical Association and the publication of an annual newsletter by this committee, dealing with published studies and on-going research including a considerable number of graduate theses, were important signs of the emerging interest in the application of the techniques of historical research to the study of various stages of Canadian working-class life. Publication of an annual bilingual journal of labour history, *Labour/Le Travailleur*, under the auspices of the Canadian Historical Association, began in spring 1976.

Management Structure

The employer side in Canada includes private, public and quasi-public enterprises ranging from sole proprietorships, through various kinds of partnerships and private and public limited liability corporations as well as all manner of government and private agencies. There is a vast range in the size, nature and location of operations, and a significant proportion of foreign investment, including a large number of wholly-owned American subsidiaries in some major sectors of the economy. The conglomerate corporation stretches over many disparate activities. Labour relations are highly fragmented on the management side. The Canadian Manufacturers' Association and regional and local Chambers of Commerce express views on labour relations, but they have no collective bargaining function. While employers in a particular industry sometimes join together for bargaining purposes at local or regional level (Bauer, 1974) there have been legal impediments to formalizing these *de facto* relationships, notably the requirement in most jurisdictions for certification on a single-employer basis. Arthurs and Crispo (1968) recommended formal accreditation of employers' associations in the construction industry and the law has since been amended to permit this in several jurisdictions.

A few studies have dealt with management attitudes with respect to labour relations (Mikalachki, Forsyth and Wettlaufer, 1970; Bélanger, 1970). Other studies of management, though they do not focus on the collective relationship, as such, are of more than peripheral interest for industrial relations, particularly in Quebec, because of their concern with matters such as corporate adaptability to bilingualism (Morrison, 1970) and differences between French and English management styles (Kanungo, in Jain and Kanungo, 1977).

Behavioural Science

Although the emphasis in industrial relations research has been on collective relationships, it is important to note other aspects of the world of work that have recently been receiving considerable attention. Personnel administration, organizational behaviour and related subjects are now prominent in university programmes. A considerable body of research is in progress on attitudes towards work and work relationships (see Canada Department of Labour, *Industrial Relations Research*), and some serious new journals have been established (e.g. *Canadian Journal of Behavioural Science; Studies in Personnel Psychology*). However, there is still virtually complete reliance on American texts for teaching purposes. The first Canadian volume on organizational behaviour with relevance to industrial relations was Jain and Kanungo (1977).

The limited attempts at theory in the behavioural science area draw heavily on earlier American thinking (e.g. Larouche and Delorme, 1972; Larouche, Levesque and Delorme, 1973; Larouche and Belzile, 1974; Belzile and Larouche, 1975; Evans, 1971, 1972, 1973) as does much of the empirical research on attitudes, motivation, job satisfaction and superior–subordinate relations. Some Canadian scholars are now using theories and methodology developed in the United States for research on distinctive Canadian problems such as French–English differences (Kanungo, in Jain and Kanungo and Kanungo, 1977) and the impact of conditions of work in the far North (Cram, 1972).

There is a growing concern in Canada, as in other industrialized countries, with the problem of worker alienation and its consequences for industrial relationships. But while this concern has resulted in a few experiments with a view to humanizing the work-place and has generated some new research initiatives as well as some important conferences, there has been little published research to date and the conferences still rely heavily on American source material and expertise.

The latter point is dramatically illustrated in the proceedings of a major symposium sponsored by the Canada Department of Labour on the quality of working life (Portigal (ed), 1974).

Loubser and Fullan (1970) did a serious study on worker attitudes to change arising from industrial conversion. Some sociologists (Meissner, 1971) have been interested in the relationship between the requirements of the job and off-the-job behaviour. Others have been more interested in changes in the broader social context in which industrial relations take place, such as the emerging values of the younger worker (Westley and Westley, 1971) and their ramifications in the world of work. This converges with the interests of the behavioural scientists who are concerned with motivation and job satisfaction. While some sociologists, like the Westleys, are proposing the adoption of European schemes for 'worker participation' in management as a solution to worker alienation in Canada, there has been little or no serious research on the feasibility of introducing these schemes in the North American context. After an extensive study of recent developments in the field of industrial democracy in Western Europe, and a thoughtful analysis of the relevance of the concept for North American industrial relations, Crispo (1978b) concluded that worker participation in the decisions that affect them in Canada, as in the United States, will continue to be accomplished primarily through collective bargaining supplemented by grievance procedure.

The Labour Movement

Although trade unions represent only one-third of non-agricultural paid workers in Canada, their importance lies in the fact that they have succeeded in organizing the key sectors of the economy. There is a very high rate of unionization in the automotive, aircraft and steel industries, in mining, logging, pulp and paper, printing, transport, longshoring and meat-packing. In other sectors, such as clothing, textiles and construction, the major firms are organized. The public sector, including hospitals, schools and government employment, is virtually 100 per cent unionized. The pattern-setting effect of negotiated settlements in these sectors gives the trade union movement an influence beyond its numerical strength and it is not surprising that this has been a major area of research interest.

Over 70 per cent of organized workers in Canada belong to unions affiliated with the Canadian Labour Congress (CLC) and nearly 10 per cent are in a Quebec-based movement, the Confederation of National Trade Unions (CNTU), some of whose affiliates have recently broken away to form a small independent federation, the *Centrale des Syndicats démocratiques* (CSD). The rest of the unionized workers are scattered between unaffiliated national and international unions and independent local organizations (*Labour Organizations in Canada*, annual).

The CLC came into being by merging two existing labour federations, the Trades and Labour Congress of Canada (TLC) and the Canadian Congress of Labour (CCL). *Relations Industrielles*, vol. 12, nos 1–2, 1957, is devoted entirely to a discussion of this merger.

In looking over the one hundred years or so of union development that culminated in the formation of the CLC, some Canadian scholars have dealt in considerable detail with the evolution of union structure (Logan, 1948; Hardy, 1958; Forsey, 1958; Crispo, 1967; Abella, 1973; Babcock, 1974). In the process, they have identified particular sources of tension, notably the issue of American domination and the conflict between craft and industrial unionism. Others have been interested in the philosophy of the labour movement as reflected in political action (French, 1962; Horowitz, 1968; Robin, 1968; Miller, 1971; Abella, 1973). The most recent publication on the subject (J. Williams, 1975) provides an overview of developments in union structure and ideology from the first attempts at labour organization in Canada until the early seventies.

The TLC and the CCL, like their American counterparts, the AFL and CIO, divided respectively along craft and industrial lines, with the CCL also representing the major all-Canadian unions. In spite of the fact that approximately half its members belong to international unions which are also affiliated with the AFL–CIO and that its predecessor federations, like some of its present affiliates, had to struggle against domination by their American counterparts (Crispo, 1967; Abella, 1973), the CLC since its inception has enjoyed virtually complete autonomy in relation to the American central federation. Nevertheless, the CLC is weak in relation to its own affiliates. With the bread-and-butter function of collective bargaining being handled by the unions themselves, the locus of power in the Canadian labour movement is in the affiliated unions and their national or international headquarters rather than in the CLC. The Congress has limited functions, two of which are to make representations to government and represent labour on various boards. Another is to oversee and police relationships among its affiliated unions. Kwavnick's research reveals an almost obsessive concern by the CLC leaders with protecting the position of the Congress as spokesman for labour at the national level. He notes that this is virtually an institutional imperative in view of its otherwise limited functions (Kwavnick, 1970, 1972).

While the main union gains in Canada like the United States have been achieved through collective bargaining, supplemented by non-partisan legislative pressures, organized labour in Canada from its earliest days has also placed considerable emphasis on direct political participation. This is in contrast to the philosophy of 'Gomperism' that has prevailed in the United States. In considering the evolution of union philosophy, Kovacs (1971) notes that in spite of the dominant American influence on the development of Canadian unionism, some American theories of the labour movement, such as Perlman's (1928) job-conscious union philosophy, may not be entirely applicable in Canada. Horowitz (1968) compares the Canadian and American political systems to explain why the leadership of organized labour in Canada would cast its lot with a socialist party rather than follow the American example of working within the major political parties. It should be noted that in spite of the historical relationship between union and socialist movements in Canada, with which Robin (1968) has dealt in such detail, no unions were directly associated with a political party until 1932 when the first viable 'labour party', the CCF, was formed. Most of the research on the political action of the labour movement, including the major studies by Horowitz (1968) and Abella (1973), concentrates on the period after 1930.

The political involvement of Canadian unions as well as their attitude at the bargaining table has reflected a philosophy of gradual reform rather than a rigid ideology of class confrontation. This is particularly evident in Abella's study (1973) which shows the struggle of the CCL to rid itself of communist-dominated affiliates. Recently, however, a coalition of unions in Quebec has been challenging the legitimacy of the political system. This is a particularly interesting phenomenon as the Quebec labour movement for many years was the most conservative in the country. The ideological evolution of the labour movement in Quebec has been the subject of considerable scholarly research.

Labour in Quebec: A Special Case

Tremblay's (1972) study represents the most up to date and thorough research on the development of union ideology in Quebec, while Trudeau's (1956, trans. 1974) introduction to *The Asbestos Strike*, though written considerably earlier, provides the most penetrating analysis of the social context in which this ideology has evolved. Trudeau's contribution remains valid in the present context because much of the militancy of the labour movement in recent years has its roots in the frustrations of an earlier period, a period in which social thought was dominated, with little exception, by the Roman Catholic Church, and in which public policy in labour relations was the most repressive in the country.

The defeat, in 1960, of a traditionally-oriented and long-entrenched political regime, the Union Nationale, by a reform-minded Liberal Party is recognized as a turning-point in the social history of Quebec. With this change in government, the province embarked on a period of extensive social reform that became known as *la révolution tranquille* (the quiet revolution) and telescoped into a brief time-period changes that were spread over many decades in the rest of North America. These changes included the upgrading and extension of health and educational services as well as the extension of collective bargaining rights, including the right to strike, to employees in a wide range of professional and public services where such rights had previously been denied. The watchword of this period was *rattrappage* (catching up). S. B. Goldenberg (1975) deals with the impact of these changes on the labour movement, citing the impatience to upgrade substandard wages and working conditions in a climate of rising expectations, rapid social change and widespread questioning of established institutions and practices as a partial explanation, at least, of the rising union militancy and rash of strikes that followed the liberalization of labour legislation – still very much a part of the industrial relations scene in Quebec. Dion (1973) has dealt with labour–management relations during the quiet revolution and with the subsequent politicization of the labour move-ment in the not-so-quiet times that followed. Roback (1975), among others, has considered various facets of the politicization of the labour movement in Quebec, a phenomenon that reached its peak in the public-sector negotiations of 1972 and formed the subject matter of a conference at Laval in 1973 (Dion (ed.), 1973).

Although slightly more than half the unionized workers in Quebec are in local branches of national or international unions affiliated with the CLC (Bernard, 1970), the story that distinguishes the development of trade unionism in Quebec from the rest of Canada and that has generated some of the most interesting research is the story of the Catholic labour movement, now the Confederation of National Trade Unions (CNTU), formerly the Canadian and Catholic Confederation of

Labour (CCCL). The change of name in 1960 from CCCL to CNTU was the culmination of a process of ideological change that began in the mid-1940s.

All historical accounts agree that 'confessional unionism' was not a spontaneous workers' movement. The first Catholic unions were organized at the turn of the century on the initiative of the clergy to 'protect' French Canadian workers (and their employers) from the 'radical' influence of the 'religiously neutral' international unions that were sending their organizers into Canada. The influence of the Catholic Church was dominant in these unions until the Second World War. It supported a no-strike policy, as the purpose of 'confessional unionism', by definition, was to maintain rather than upset the *status quo*.

Although increasing industrialization and urbanization had gradually transformed the social and economic climate in which confessional unionism first took root, the impact of the Second World War accelerated the process of change to the point that the very survival of the movement was threatened. The challenge for survival was met by a new type of leadership that took control at this time, an intellectual leadership produced by an innovative educational influence in Quebec, the faculty of social sciences at Laval University. The new leaders set the movement on a road to militancy from which it never turned back. The postwar years saw a number of prolonged and bitter strikes which escalated dramatically in the sixties, a period marked by bitter rivalry for membership with other unions (Dion, 1967; Roberge, 1969). By the beginning of the seventies, however, the CNTU decided to form a common front with other unions bargaining in the public sector and embarked on a collision course with the provincial government (Boivin, 1972, 1974). This, in turn, had serious repercussions within the CNTU as some of its affiliates disagreed with the politicization of negotiations in the public sector and broke away in protest.

In some cases (Logan, 1948; Dofny and Bernard, 1970; Desrosiers and Héroux, 1973), the early history of the Catholic unions is included in broader studies of the labour movement. Other authors (e.g. S. Barnes, 1959) have studied the evolution of this unusual movement as a subject in itself. Some have also studied its relationship to the rest of the Canadian labour movement, notably the question of affiliation with the CLC that was debated in the fifties (e.g. Dion, 1957). One study (Solasse, 1970) deals with its rather unique activities in the area of consumer protection. But much of the most significant research on the CNTU has focused on major strikes, some of which represent landmarks in the social history of Quebec as well as in the development of the labour movement.

Collective Bargaining

The collective bargaining literature includes a wide range of material on the structure, process and results of bargaining, much of which is discussed under specific topic headings.

Apart from Quinet's (1971) discussion of the role of research in centralized bargaining in the federal public service, as well as his thoughtful study of the costing of collective agreements (Quinet, 1974), the literature reflects more interest in the bargaining process and its results than in the preparation for negotiations. The negotiation process as such has been empirically understudied in Canada as in the United States, due to the difficulty of gaining access to on-going negotiations. However, some valuable studies have been produced *ex post facto* by government-commissioned inquiries.

Some scholars have looked at the bargaining process and its results in relation to macro-economic issues, but much of the collective bargaining research has taken the form of case studies of particular industries such as railways (Peitchinis, 1970), broadcasting (Samlalsingh, 1970), meat-packing (Craig, 1964) and construction, to mention just a few. The construction industry has generated more serious research, public and private, than any other single industry (e.g. H. C. Goldenberg, 1962; H. C. Goldenberg and Crispo (eds.), 1968; Woods, 1970; Hébert, 1971, 1977; Rose, 1972, 1973; Waisberg, 1974; Cliche *et al.*, 1975; Malles, 1975).

There have also been numerous public investigations of problem-prone industries or sectors such as the postal service (Montpetit, 1966), longshoring (*inter alia* L. A. Picard, 1967 and A. J. Smith, 1970) and fisheries (Green, 1970). Although these and other public inquiries have almost invariably been triggered by a particular crisis, the search for underlying causes of an overt conflict situation has usually involved a thorough study of the industrial relationships of the industry. Thus, industry studies resulting from public inquiries have made a significant contribution to the literature on the structure, process, and results of collective bargaining.

One approach to the study of bargaining issues has been through the comparative analysis of collective agreements. The analysis of contract clauses has shed interesting light on general trends in collective bargaining and on differences as well as similarities between negotiated issues in the private and public sectors (Quinet, 1974; also regular reports by the Pay Research Bureau).

New Groups, New Issues

The question of unionization and the adoption of bargaining relationships by new groups such as white-collar, professional and government employees has added a new dimension to the labour– management relationship, brought new issues to the bargaining table and created some policy problems. There are no legal bars to collective bargaining for white-collar employees in the private sector as there have been for the salaried members of some professions and, until recently, for civil servants. But there has been significant psychological resistance to collective bargaining, and to joining the mainstream labour movement (though less so in Quebec), as well as strong opposition by employers. W.D. Wood's doctoral dissertation (1959) was a pioneering study in the field of white-collar unionism in Canada, but there is paucity of research in this area, possibly because of the limited white-collar bargaining experience (Wood, 1975).

Professional workers have been traditionally resistant to collective bargaining, although S.B. Goldenberg (1970) showed that this resistance can vary considerably both between and within professional groups. Her study analysed the general problems at each stage of the bargaining relationship as well as some issues peculiar to the nature of professional occupations, such as the protection of professional standards and responsibilities and the recognition of individual merit in the context of a collective relationship. Muir (1968) dealt with similar problems, as well as some important policy issues, in his exhaustive research on teacher bargaining. Later, the Professional Institute of the Public Service of Canada commissioned a study of its own structure and activities, under the auspices of the McGill Industrial Relations Centre (Bairstow *et al.*, 1972), with a view to assessing its effectiveness in protecting professional interests through collective bargaining and making suggestions for change. The most recent development in the professional sector is the issue of collective bargaining for university faculty (Adell and Carter, 1972). The Canadian Industrial Relations Research Institute devoted its 1975 conference to this subject (see *Relations Industrielles*, vol. 30, no. 4, 1975).

Public Employees

The adoption of collective bargaining by government employees has raised important new issues and has stimulated a significant body of research. Boivin's (1974) study of public-sector bargaining in Quebec is one of the few to analyse bargaining experience. A study of the National Joint Council of the Public Service of Canada (L.W.C.S. Barnes, 1975) is particularly interesting in that it bridges pre-bargaining and post-bargaining periods. Barnes traces the evolution of this bipartite consultative body before the adoption of formal bargaining relationships in the federal public service and analyses its continuing role as an adjunct to collective bargaining. The same author is currently engaged in a study of the first ten years of collective bargaining experience in the federal public service.

Work Stoppages: Some Major Strikes and their Implications

Work stoppages have been a prominent research theme. Canadian researchers tend to focus on strikes that have become landmarks in the evolution of labour–management relations, although much policy-oriented research is directed primarily towards containing or avoiding conflict. Flood's case study of a wildcat strike (1968) identifies the sources of latent hostility leading to conflict. D.A. Smith (1972) and Kelly (1974) have investigated the determinants of strikes.

Francoeur (1963) has edited an interesting volume in which he and other contributors deal with five strikes, apart from asbestos, that marked the history of the Catholic labour movement in Quebec between 1937 and 1959. The last of these, the strike of French producers on the national television network, had particularly significant repercussions. It was a powerful stimulus to French Canadian nationalism and it contributed to the ascendancy of the CNTU. According to S.B. Goldenberg (1970), it should also be considered a major milestone in the struggle for professional bargaining rights. Other strikes in Quebec have had less public impact but form an important part of labour history.

Dumas (1971, trans. 1975) has made an interesting contribution by analysing a number of the strikes that took place in Quebec between 1934 and 1944, many of them by international unions. Some of her material is presented through the eyes of the actual participants and sheds new light on the struggles of the labour movement before legal recognition procedures became available.

Jamieson (1970) has done the broadest and most comprehensive research on industrial conflict ever undertaken in Canada. Presented in chronological order, by region and by industry, his study for the Federal Task Force provides a lengthy and detailed examination of labour unrest between 1900 and 1966, with emphasis on the socio-economic context in which the major strikes occurred. Other scholars have preferred to concentrate on a narrower range of labour struggles, chosen for their particular significance. Abella (1974), for example, edited a volume which starts with the 1919 Winnipeg general strike and ends with a chapter on asbestos. It also deals with two particularly significant disputes in the automobile industry, the General Motors strike at Oshawa in 1937 and the Ford strike at Windsor in 1945. The Oshawa strike is recognized as a landmark in the struggle of the CIO to spread industrial unionism in Canada; the Ford strike resulted in a famous arbitration award that established the principle of the agency shop in Canada.

Labour Relations Policy

Public policy in labour relations in Canada reflects an early concern with industrial peace as a goal (Selekman, 1927; Logan, 1956) as distinct from the structuring of institutional relationships which became the major preoccupation after the passage of the Wagner Act in the United States in 1935. A compulsory conciliation and strike delay system was the essence of Canadian federal policy for over three decades until the tensions of the Second World War and pressure from the unions led to a shift in policy towards the American system of compulsory collective bargaining. The Canadian policy that emerged from the Second World War borrowed heavily from Wagner and Taft–Hartley principles and procedures, but by retaining compulsory intervention and strike suspension and expanding the application to all industries it created a policy based on two principles and two sets of procedures whose interaction would have an important influence on the way collective bargaining would function, and on the results flowing therefrom (Woods, 1955). While the federal legislation continued without amendment until 1972 the provinces early tended to go their separate ways and some have introduced particularly innovative legislation (see Cutler, 1970 and Gagnon, Le Bel and Verge, 1971 on Quebec, and Arthurs, 1975 on British Columbia).

Although there have been a few interesting studies of the position of workers under individual contracts of employment and the implications for public policy (e.g. D'Aoust and Rousseau, 1970; Doucet, 1974), most of the research on labour relations policy has been predicated on the existence of a collective relationship. The first comprehensive examination of Canadian collective bargaining policy was by Logan (1956). It described the Canadian system of state interference since its general inception in the forties, against a background of lesser interference affecting a section of the economy over the period from 1900 to the Second World War. Nearly two decades later, Woods (Woods and Ostry, 1962) re-examined the experience, attempted to analyse emerging differences in policy by governmental jurisdiction, and evaluated policies and policy trends. A revision of this work (Woods, 1973) updated significant policy developments in the federal and provincial jurisdiction.

Intervention in Negotiation Disputes

Canadian research on intervention in interest disputes came after compulsory conciliation boards and the postponement of the strike right were more or less universal. The studies were, on the whole, critical of compulsory conciliation boards, and were influential in their gradual elimination in private-sector disputes (W. G. Phillips, 1956; Cunningham, 1958, 1970). Research on the Ontario experience (Kelly, 1974) shows that a significant proportion of recent settlements have involved conciliation procedures. Brown (1970) explored the intervention issue in a comparative study of arbitration of interest disputes in several countries, including Canada.

The Bargaining Unit

The establishment of an appropriate bargaining unit is a necessary preliminary to collective bargaining. But in Canada the bargaining unit problem is in some respects more difficult than in the United States. The fact that the constitutional distribution of powers between the central government and the provinces reflects a decentralized federalism in contrast to the highly centralized federalism of the United States, and that in Canada, statutory control of collective bargaining has linked the right to strike with the fulfilment of certain conciliation obligations, has to some extent placed obstacles in the way of multi-province bargaining units. This was noted by Downie (1971) who, however, also noted that some interprovincial and even international *de facto* bargaining units do emerge in spite of the constraints of compulsory conciliation under independent political jurisdictions. *De facto* bargaining units on a multi-employer basis have also emerged at the regional or provincial level, in spite of legal provisions for local certification. Jamieson (1971) and McKechnie (1971) discuss this phenomenon with respect to the West Coast lumber industry and Ontario haulage industry respectively.

A major examination of the bargaining unit problem in general terms was undertaken by Herman (1966). A comparative examination of the development of law and policy regarding craft bargaining units in Ontario and the United States by Willes (1970) revealed the difficulty of reconciling the principle of freedom of choice of bargaining instruments with the goal of industrial stability. While other groups such as professional employees have had particular problems in defining appropriate bargaining units, to be discussed in a later section, the bargaining unit issue has been most acute in construction, an industry that has provoked a disproportionate share of policy problems in Canada.

Construction

The construction industry has received considerable attention because severe instability in construction labour relations leads to turbulence, corruption and much illegal behaviour in general. Indeed there has been a marked tendency in this industry for collective bargaining and bargaining structure to break down.

Bertram (1968) examined the evolution of bargaining structure (units) down to 1967. The same issue had been studied in Ontario by H. C. Goldenberg (1962), who urged the adjustment of public policy to establish bargaining units in construction on a geographic basis, and by Woods (1970) in Nova Scotia, who also recommended the elimination of site certifications. Of particular interest is the move toward province-wide, multi-trade sectorial bargaining in the Quebec construction industry. This was imposed by law in the late sixties and was designed not only to establish one bargaining unit for the Province, but to transfer bargaining rights from the established national and international construction trade unions to the union federations or centrals in the Province. The new procedures also abandoned the principle of sole right to bargain so characteristic of North American policy and replaced it by a modified principle of representativeness of European origin. Cinq-Mars (1970) and Sauvé (1971) provide a general discussion of sector bargaining, Cardin (1969) discussed modifications to the law that would be required for sector bargaining and Hébert (1971) evaluated the Quebec experience in construction. A recent study for the Economic Council of Canada (Hébert, 1977) is a thorough analysis of the Quebec experience.

The problem of instability in construction labour relations is not limited to concern over the impermanence of site certification and the bargaining unit. Arthurs and Crispo (1968) analysed the power relations between unions and employer associations and concluded that the latter are vulnerable to destructive union tactics and need legal support. Their proposal for the accreditation of employer associations has been adopted in a number of Provinces (Rose, 1972, 1973).

Public concern over work stoppages, corruption, law-breaking and violence has led to a number of exhaustive investigations in recent years, the two most important being in Ontario (Waisberg, 1974) and Quebec (Cliche *et al.*, 1975; Cliche *et al., Recueil des annexes*, 1975). British Columbia has recently appointed a special inquiry commission (James Kinneard, Commissioner) to promote better industrial relations in construction and to report, *inter alia*, on the advisability of legislative reform. Malles (1975) has produced a thorough summary analysis of problems peculiar to the construction industry and their implications for public policy.

Automation

Automation or technological change has provoked a vigorous controversy in Canada. Economists have been concerned with the question of the employment impact of change both in micro and macro terms (Beach, 1967, 1971) or with the human adjustment problem (Kruger, 1971). Cardin (1967a) suggested the restructuring of union and employer organizations and the establishment of broader bargaining units to cope with some of the manpower problems arising from technological change. But policy-oriented research with respect to automation is best illustrated by the royal commission established to investigate the issue on the Canadian National Railways resulting from the introduction of diesel locomotives and the attendant redundancy problem (Freedman, 1965). The commissioner attempted to find a way around an issue that had been investigated in more limited terms some years earlier (Kellock *et al.*, 1958).

Rights Arbitration

In the field of enforcement of collective agreement obligations, Canadian law at the federal level (and in all but one of the provincial jurisdictions) in effect outlaws the strike and lock-out during the life of a collective agreement and requires final and binding resolution of disputes regarding the interpretation, application or administration of the agreement. There has been some interesting research on the historical development of this policy (Curtis, 1966) and an important study of the legal status of collective agreements in Canada compared with other countries (Adell, 1970).

The problem of enforcement of arbitration awards as well as decisions of administrative tribunals such as labour relations boards has generated some serious research, notably by legal scholars (see Weatherill, 1966; Cutler, 1968). For although the law declares arbitration awards to be final and binding, this has not precluded resort to the courts, albeit on limited grounds (deficiency in the jurisdiction of the arbitrator, error in the law on the face of the award, denial of natural justice). There have been some important journal articles on the judicial review of arbitration awards (e.g. Thompson, 1971; Adams, 1971; Verge, 1973; Weiler, 1971, 1974) and on legal aspects of rights arbitration such as the application of the rule of impartiality (Bergeron, 1975). Carrothers' work (1961) long stood out for its exhaustive treatment of the law of grievance arbitration as compared with other studies that focus on particular issues. However, a few recent publications have also been remarkably comprehensive. Brown and Beatty (1977) developed a coherent analytical framework in which the details of thousands of reported cases were examined. Palmer (1977) did likewise in his important legal text. Morin's (1975) study, though limited to Quebec, covers a wide range of experience in grievance arbitration.

The problems associated with contracting-out and the introduction of technological change have cropped up frequently in research and writing on grievance arbitration. Contracting-out was examined by Young (1964) in a comparative study of Canadian and American law, policy and experience. The issue of technological change and the legal obstacles presented by the prohibition of the strike and compulsory arbitration was raised by Fryer, a trade union writer (1967). Malles

(1968) undertook an examination of the industrial relations aspects of technological change in the Swedish context, although he was not specifically concerned with the problem of arbitration. The most complete examination of the policy problem regarding technological change was undertaken by Weiler (1969). He suggested the possibility that the duty to bargain should remain on issues not covered by the collective agreement (approximately the position in the United States) and that these would also be strikable issues. This would leave decisions regarding residual rights to the arbitrators, rather than settling the issue by statute as at present.

Civil liberties

A major problem issue for industrial relations in Canada, as in other countries, has been the preservation and protection of civil liberties in the context of the power of employers and unions. Notable among those studying this problem are Carrothers, whose major work (1965) deals with collective bargaining law in general; Adell (1966), who analyses the statutory, judicial and administrative jurisprudence with respect to the so-called 'employer free speech' problem in Canada and the United States; Palmer, whose study (1970) of decision-making and democracy in trade unions presents valuable insight into power relations within unions, including the vexatious issue of union security, the rights to membership, and procedural protection of the right; and Christie and Gorsky (1970) who examined unfair labour practices of both management and unions, as well as the protection or lack of protection in the law, and proposed legislative changes designed to protect civil rights within the power context of the employment nexus and union–management relations. More recently, the Cliche (1975) and Waisberg (1974) Commissions were concerned with the suppression of civil liberties of members within the construction unions, as was the Norris Commission that investigated labour problems in Great Lakes shipping some years earlier (1963).

New Groups and Public Policy

Important new policy issues have arisen over the question of extending bargaining rights to groups that were previously excluded from the coverage of labour legislation, notably members of the licensed professions and federal and provincial government employees.

Although some provinces still exclude salaried members of the licensed professions such as medicine, law, architecture and engineering from the coverage of labour legislation, the trend in recent years has been to reduce the number of professional exclusions from statutory bargaining rights. While Goldenberg dealt with a number of policy problems in her Task Force study on professional workers (S. B. Goldenberg, 1970) she identified the provision for managerial exclusions from the bargaining unit, a problem faced by white-collar workers in general (Reed, 1969), as the most serious impediment to the use of existing labour legislation by certain salaried professional workers, particularly engineers. She found this still to be the case in her later study with Fraser (Fraser and Goldenberg, 1974). In Quebec and Ontario, the only provinces in which they bargain collectively, professional engineers have refused to use the certification machinery originally envisaged for blue-collar workers for fear that this would result in an undue proportion of managerial exclusions from professional bargaining units (Cardin, 1967b).

There has also been considerable debate and some serious research on the anomalous position of other categories of workers whose dependent relationship gives them the economic characteristics of employees but who may not meet the technical definition of employee under labour legislation. This has been the position of milkmen and taxi-drivers hired on a contractual basis (Morin, 1970) and fishermen paid on a share-of-the-catch basis (Steinberg, 1975). Arthurs (1965) coined the term 'dependent contractor' to apply to workers in these and similar categories. The Task Force (Woods *et al.*, 1968) recommended amendments to the law to guarantee them collective bargaining rights.

Public-sector Bargaining

There is no question that the extension of collective bargaining rights, in some cases including the right to strike, to senior level government employees represents the most fundamental change in labour relations policy in Canada since the Second World War. This development makes the public sector one of the few areas of labour relations in which Canada has taken the initiative over the United States.

Public inquiries have been undertaken in some jurisdictions prior to granting bargaining rights in the public service (Heaney *et al.*, 1965;

Frankel, 1967; Revell, 1972; Higgins *et al.*, 1972) or with a view to reassessing bargaining relationships (Little, 1969; Finkelman, 1974). The Heaney Committee recommended a formal collective bargaining relationship between the federal government and its employees, with compulsory arbitration of unresolved interest disputes. The law that was subsequently enacted, the Public Service Staff Relations Act, 1967, went much further by introducing an innovative method of dispute-resolution involving a pre-bargaining choice by the bargaining agent between conciliation procedure, with the ultimate right to strike, and binding arbitration. Although the public service unions first showed a preference for the arbitration route, the trend recently has been against arbitration and almost two thirds of the employees in the federal public service are now in bargaining units that have opted for the con-ciliation/strike method of settling interest disputes. Barnes and Kelly (1975) see important policy implications in this trend, noting, *inter alia*, that the scope of arbitrable issues must be broadened if arbitration is to be considered a meaningful alternative to the strike.

Although the practice of unilateral decision-making by the government as employer has been largely abandoned in Canada, no consensus has yet emerged among the policy-makers on the most appropriate mechanism by which to reconcile the rights that are available to workers in the private sector with the particular characteristics and constraints of public service employment. This is recognized as a major challenge to governments as employers (Hodgetts and Dwivedi, 1974) and continues to generate serious research as well as important discussions between academicians and practitioners in the field (Gunderson, 1975).

Some of the researchers (e.g. S. B. Goldenberg, 1973a; Arthurs, 1971; Kruger, 1974) have analysed and compared the wide range of policy alternatives currently in effect in different jurisdictions for the definition of bargaining units, the recognition of bargaining agents, the process and scope of collective negotiations and the settlement of interest disputes. Others have focused on particular issues such as grievance handling and appeal procedures (Aggarwal, 1973, Garant, 1972) but the majority have concentrated on dispute settlement (e.g. S. B. Goldenberg, 1973b; Kruger, 1970), particularly on some of the bolder experiments with the right to strike, notably at the federal level, New Brunswick and Quebec where, in spite of provisions in the law for the protection of essential services in the event of a legal strike, there have been some serious problems of enforceability. Brian Williams (1973) has questioned the appropriateness of traditional bargaining procedures for resolving differences in the public sector, not because of the sovereignty argument, but because of the different power relationship, notably the lack of economic accountability, as compared with the private sector. He suggests, among other things, the adoption of forced-choice arbitration for the resolution of wage and salary issues as a substitute for economic pressures in reaching agreement in the private sector.

A particularly valuable analysis by Boivin (1974) examined the problem of bargaining and bargaining power in the public sector of the province of Quebec against a background of collective bargaining theory. In addition to an outline of the development of power relations and public policy in the public sector, the study deals with the conflicting roles of government and the problems associated with the attempt to introduce collective bargaining on a private-sector model in the context of a sociopolitical milieu involving a politicized labour movement.

Bargaining rights in the public service have usually been granted under separate legislation, with modifications to the private-sector model. Garant (1971) noted that the extension of collective bargaining rights to government employees in Quebec has involved an interesting fusion of administrative and labour law, with the former still regulating the structure and organization of the Civil Service and the latter, with certain modifications, regulating the new collective relationship. In a later article, Garant (1972) discussed the particular disciplinary requirements in the Civil Service as compared with the private sector, analysed the changes brought about by collective bargaining and grievance procedure, and compared the appeal procedures available to civil servants covered by the collective agreement and those who are excluded from bargaining rights.

Emergency Disputes

In Canada, as in other countries, the most vigorous controversy in the policy area is over emergency disputes. Significant research has been carried out under the authority of royal commissions, commissions of inquiry, and special task forces. Prominent among these is the very useful study of Verge (1970) in which the author examines conflicting views regarding the criteria advanced by other writers, especially in the United States, and reveals the difficulties facing those who would build public policy on a predetermined set of emergency criteria. A most valuable study by Arthurs (1970) examined Canadian legislative experience in essential industry disputes; compared it with that of the United States, a number of European countries and Australia; at-

tempted to define policy objectives in essential-industry labour relations; examined various techniques for settling essential-industry
disputes; and advanced certain proposals for an 'industrial peace act'.
The Task Force (1968) to whom Arthurs submitted his report, while
borrowing heavily from the study, advanced its own modified proposals
for a Public Interest Disputes Commission. In Ontario, Rand (1968)
recommended that authority be granted to the Lieutenant Governor in
Council to declare an industry 'essential' and refer a dispute to
compulsory arbitration. The Cohen Report (1972) in Newfoundland
advanced somewhat similar proposals covering 'essential' industries
under both private and public ownership.

One of the most recent studies to appear concerns labour relations in
the public sector in the province of Manitoba (1974). This product of
consultation and deliberation by a joint labour–management committee supported by the work of social scientists, while concerned with
all aspects of public-sector industrial relations, faced up to the
emergency dispute issue as it might occur in the Civil Service, in
municipalities, and in various crown agencies. In essence its recommendations have been influenced by a desire to preserve and strengthen
collective bargaining as far as possible, to impose on the parties of direct
interest the burden of protecting the public from emergencies, and
therefore to reduce the need for intervention of public authority to an
absolute minimum.

Picketing, Boycotting and Enforcement of the Law

Finally there is the question of permissible behaviour in the event of a
legal strike. Although workers engaged in a legal strike are protected
under Canadian law in their status as employees (Dunsmore, 1973), they
are subject to certain restrictions. For example, they are barred from
receiving unemployment insurance (Hickling, 1974) and may be liable to
damages and injunctions flowing from particular activities related to the
strike, notably picketing and boycotting. Christie (1967), in a comparative study of the liability of strikers in the law of tort in England and
Canada, examined, *inter alia*, the development of statutory restrictions
on picketing and the judicial interpretation thereof. Both the Rand
Report (1968) and the federal Task Force (Woods *et al.*, 1968) dealt with
the issue of picketing and the use of the labour injunction. This has also
been a subject of serious research by a number of legal scholars (e.g.
Carrothers and Palmer (eds.), 1966). Associated with the broad issue of

picketing is the particular question of secondary action. This has generated considerable research, also by legal scholars (e.g. Patterson, 1973; Batlett, 1974; Beatty, 1974).

Labour Economics

Labour economics, as distinct from industrial and employee re-lationships, has been the subject of research by Canadian scholars for a considerable period. This review of research reveals a preoccupation with labour supply (including population studies, the changing labour force, participation, and factors such as immigration and emigration, and the changing quality of the working population) with labour demand and the interaction of supply and demand in the labour market. The major question of the trade-off between unemployment and inflation and the issue of incomes policy has attracted the attention of many economic analysts.

Labour Supply

Throughout its history Canada has experienced a heavy flow of both immigration and emigration and public policy has shown a pre-occupation with immigrants, especially in relationship to industrializ-ation. Interest in the quality of the immigrant flow and its relation to manpower needs, as well as a decline in sociopolitical and ethnic considerations, is reflected in a change in public policy in the late sixties (Ostry and Zaidi, 1972) as well as in studies by Kalbach (1970), by Officer (1970), and in a major work by Hawkins (1972). Industrial-ization itself has tended to shift research interest towards the quality of the labour force, educational and training issues, and mobility.

Labour force research reflects these interests. As with most Canadian research in industrial relations, government agencies – the Dominion Bureau of Statistics (and its successor, Statistics Canada), the Economic Council, and the Departments of Labour and of Manpower and Immigration – have been especially important.

Somers (1971) outlined succinctly the evolution of manpower prob-lems and the development of manpower policies in Canada, and has drawn attention to the influence of The Economic Council on the establishment of the Department of Manpower and Immigration in 1966. Manpower research has been aided by a published bibliography on manpower management (C. B. Williams, 1968) which classifies research and writing under the general headings of employment, unemployment, manpower planning and utilization. A short but valuable paper by Meltz (1974) outlined the major efforts in manpower research and its application to industrial relations.

Population statistics have been collected decennially since 1871 and are now supplemented by a monthly sample Labour Force Survey. These data have been used to study demographic trends. Ostry (in Woods and Ostry, 1962) examined census statistics since 1871 to determine demographic trends, and this was later revised (Ostry and Zaidi, 1972).

Important contributions to statistical analysis of population and the labour force were made by others (Illing, *et al.*, 1967; Keyfitz, 1950; Ryder, 1954). Special attention was directed to immigration and emigration by a number of scholars (McDougall, 1961; Pickett, 1965; Pankhurst, 1966). The composition of the post war immigrant labour force was examined fully by Davis and Gupta (1968), and by Kalbach (1970).

Mobility

The phenomenon of the international movement of skilled and professional manpower was studied by Parai (1965) and Comay (1972). Internal demographic trends were examined by Anderson (1966), and Levitt (1960) produced the first regional study of population movements in the Atlantic Provinces. Sociological influences on labour mobility were examined in a section of New Brunswick by Melzer and Philbrooke (1974).

The question of internal mobility of the labour force was examined by Vanderkamp (1973) who showed that the charges of serious inflexibility in the labour market are fallacious. Similarly, Courchene (1970) concluded that internal migration is economically induced as workers respond to interprovincial earnings differentials. At the same time, Vanderkamp (1970), in a brief article, concluded that an economic effect of outmigration of unemployed is to create new unemployment in the supplying area.

The Economic Council of Canada (1964), in its first annual review, emphasized the importance of an adequate supply of properly trained and highly skilled manpower for the achievement of the economic goals of the country (Department of Manpower and Immigration, 1968;

Ostry and Zaidi, 1972). With this emphasis on training as a means of improving the quality of the labour supply, and of solving structural problems and improving the labour market, there was a shift in research interest towards training and education in relation to manpower and employment needs. Bertram (1966); Keys and Wright (1966); Illing and Zsigmond (1967); Zsigmond and Wennas (1970); Weiermair (1974) explored the usefulness of employer surveys for purposes of assessing and forecasting educational needs in occupations and occupational groups and concluded that vacancy data could be used to show general trends in educational requirements in broad occupational groups.

An especially interesting international conference (Somers and Wood, 1969) studied the application of cost–benefit techniques of analysis and evaluation to manpower policies. A valuable annotated bibliography on cost–benefit analysis and the economics of education was produced by the Queen's Industrial Relations Centre (Wood and Campbell, 1970).

In a broad-based study for the Economic Council covering twenty-four occupations in the professional and technical categories, Dodge (1972) concluded that, while there is a strong correlation between occupation and schooling, occupational income differentials are attributable more to artificial barriers to entry, such as licensing, than to schooling. The question of the appropriate role of the state in manpower training was examined by Ozay (1970) and by Gunderson (1974).

Labour Demand

The composition of the labour force in the long run reflects the demand for various classes of labour. Canadian policy has attempted in a number of ways to influence labour supply in the direction of greater conformity with demand. Immigration policy has been concerned with both the size and quality of the immigration flow. Similarly, internal manpower policies have involved programmes directed to upgrading unemployed workers and subsidizing movement from labour-redundant to labour-shortage areas. Research has been concerned with changes in the occupational and industrial composition of the labour force reflecting long-run changes in demand (Meltz, 1965; Ostry, 1967; Scoville, 1967), and with the question whether the high levels of unemployment in recent decades resulted from structural changes in demand or from aggregate labour demand deficiency (e.g. Winder, 1968).

Unemployment and Inflation

Canada, like many other countries after the Second World War, experienced a rapid increase in money wages and in prices, and engaged in the general discussion of the nature of inflation. Ostry (Woods and Ostry, 1962) raised the issue from the Canadian point of view and anticipated the later debate on the trade-off between inflation and unemployment. Kaliski (1964) was one of the first to study the trade-off relation in Canada, and Reuber (1964) discussed the policy implications of the same issue covering the fifties. Vanderkamp (1966) and Zaidi (1970) examined wage adjustment and trade-off relationships for Canada, employing quarterly data for the period from 1946 to 1962. Two important contributions by David Smith (1966 and 1967) explored the case for an incomes policy in an inflationary period and reviewed experiments along these lines in several other countries. Wood and Kumar (1976) compiled a book of readings on the Canadian wartime and foreign experience in this field following the adoption by the Canadian government of a programme of prices and incomes restraint.

A major effort (Bodkin *et al.*, 1967) explored the factors affecting price determination and the interrelation between movements in prices and costs, and productivity levels and incomes. Later Bodkin (1969) revisited the debate of the thirties as to whether real wages tend to rise or to fall with an increasing utilization of the labour force over the course of the business cycle. Using Canadian and United States data, he concluded that there is little support for the view that real wages are inversely related to cyclical utilization of the labour supply and that classical diminishing returns is probably confined to a range close to full utilization of labour and capital factors. A particularly useful conference held at Queen's University brought together Canadian and foreign economists of wide-ranging views regarding inflation and employment and resulted in the publication of a series of papers and commentaries on the issues (Swan and Wilton, 1971). Kaliski (1972) again addressed himself to the problem of the trade-off between inflation and unemployment, considered the later developments in theory, and evaluated various econometric models. Canadian scholars were giving increasing attention to the validity of the Phillips curve or indeed even to its existence as employed by some econometricians (Rowley and Wilton, 1974). Recently there has appeared a valuable symposium by a group of scholars in Quebec universities (Belzile *et al.*, 1975) which examines the inflation problem in both the economic and social context.

Other Contributions

A few economic studies of value that do not fit easily into any of the classifications used in this chapter are worthy of mention. Downie (1970), for example, examined wage behaviour in five industries operating in both the United States and Canada, with the object of developing theoretical underpinnings for an understanding of bi-national wage patterns and, concurrently, of similar domestic phenomena, and to provide empirical data on Canadian industrial relations. Kumar (1971) tested the stability of the labour share of national income in Canada for the period 1926–66. Cousineau and Lacroix (1977) studied the process of wage determination in the private and public sectors and the differences between them for the period 1967–75.

Conclusion

In spite of a late start, there has been a marked increase in industrial relations research in Canada in recent years, a significant proportion of which has been problem-oriented and sponsored or inspired by government. There has been less research of a purely academic nature; certainly very few contributions to theory. No distinctive schools of thought have emerged in Canada as they have in the United States and some other countries. These findings may be attributed in large measure to the slow development of graduate training in the social sciences in Canada and the consequent American head start in industrial relations teaching and research, much of which is equally applicable in the Canadian context. There was little reason for Canadian scholars to duplicate American work.

Most signs indicate that industrial relations research in Canada is alive and well that the prognosis for the immediate future is good. The industrial relations system as such is undergoing considerable strain. Carrothers (1975) has summarized the current strains under five major headings:

(1) An alarming increase in man-hours lost through work stoppages accompanied by a rise in the rate of rejection by union members of tentative settlements.

(2) An increase in wage settlements substantially in excess of the rate of inflation and any increase in national productivity.

(3) An increase in the number of illegal work stoppages and other forms of unlawful behaviour.

(4) An increasing politicization of disputes.

(5) An accumulation of public and private harm from disputes in essential services.

There will consequently be no shortage of problems to study in the foreseeable future. Industrial relations research, being problem-oriented, thrives in times of trouble. The challenge will be to select the research areas which will most contribute to problem-solving in times of stress. The following areas are suggested for further investigation:

The effect on industrial relations of the dispersion of authority and decision-making

The dispersion of authority and decision-making is caused on the one hand by the presence in Canada of international business and international unions and on the other by a decentralized federalism. Involved in the latter is the question of the appropriate bargaining unit, including the problem of sequential bargaining which has long been a factor in construction and other areas, but which has recently come to the fore on the national scene because of a series of work stoppages affecting the export of grain. Grain handling and transportation have to run the gauntlet of a series of bargaining situations involving different unions and different employers and even different statutory provisions (depending on whether the employees concerned fall under private- or public-sector labour legislation and whether they are in the federal or provincial jurisdiction). The potential for dislocation, and consequently for research, is self-evident.

The implications of public policy

Industrial relations research has probably been strongest in the policy area. Yet there has been little research on the practical implications of public policy, particularly on those aspects that are so much an accepted part of the Canadian–American system that they are seldom questioned, e.g. the effect of the requirement for majority support on union recognition (Bain, 1969; R. J. Adams, 1974), or the effect of exclusivity of bargaining rights on non-members of the union in the bargaining unit. Although there is room for research on the implications of certain policies that are common to Canada and the United States, a more useful contribution might be made by examining in depth the experience under unique Canadian policies such as the right to strike in public interest and public employment situations and the provision for compulsory arbitration of grievance disputes. The statutory requirement for centralized bargaining in construction and certain public services in Quebec also provides a unique Canadian laboratory situation that can be used to examine certain implications of centralized negotiations such as the difficulty of applying a centrally negotiated agreement at the local level and the effect of 'bargaining at the top' on the relationship between unions and their members. Other aspects of Canadian public policy such as social security legislation and unemployment insurance may have important implications for industrial relations, particularly regarding labour force participation (Steinberg, 1974). More research is needed in these areas.

The labour movement

While the organized labour movement has been studied fairly exhaustively from a historical and institutional perspective, more research should be encouraged on the general problem of labour in politics and on the politicization of particular bargaining situations. More work is also indicated on strains and tensions within the labour movement, as reflected in the phenomenon of break-away groups from international unions, and other rivalries and schisms.

Divergence in collective bargaining behaviour between Canada and the United States

It may require considerable research to explain the recent divergence in collective bargaining behaviour between Canada and the United States in relation to settlement levels and to the relative volume of overt conflict such as strikes, lock-outs and illegal activities. All these have been significantly higher in Canada, in marked contrast to previous experience.

Job attitudes, opportunities, and quality of working life

The halting beginnings of research in the sociology of work and the life-styles of the working class need to be expanded, especially with regard to traditionally disadvantaged groups in the labour market such as women, native peoples, and immigrants. Similarly, the special problems posed by the bilingual and multi-cultural character of Canada calls for intensive studies of group goals and attitudes and the difficulties of adjustment to and integration into industrial employment and industrial life. A recently published volume on the position of women in the world of work (Cook, 1975) is an example of the kind of research that is needed.

The Economics of industrial relations

The fact that courses on the economics of industrial relations still rely heavily on American material illustrates the relative weakness of Canadian research in this area and the need for improvement. One finds little or nothing in the Canadian research literature on the economics of collective bargaining, on how economic factors shape collective bargaining in particular industries. There is little regarding the economics of trade unions, including the effects of unions on wage differentials; little or nothing on such questions as how wage settlements are affected by the method of settlement or how wages relate to employee benefits; little or nothing about the relationship between macro-economic policies and collective bargaining results.

It is to be hoped that the recent (1975) introduction of an anti-inflation programme in Canada involving, *inter alia*, strict controls on wages, will open the door to an expansion of economic analysis and to research on the implications of a policy of wage control on collective bargaining and on industrial relations in general.

In David Smith's (1966) study of income policy, he makes a special plea for more social science research independent of government influence. While recognizing that good government research is obviously important, he suggests that its confidential nature on controversial matters emphasizes the need for complementary, unconstrained research under private auspices. The solution is to be found in the expansion of unrestricted financial support for private non-profit research institutes and university social science departments.

REFERENCES

Abella, Irving, *Nationalism, Communism, and Canadian Labour: The CIO, The Communist Party and the Canadian Congress of Labour, 1935–56* (Toronto: University of Toronto Press, 1973).

——, (ed.), *On Strike, Six Key Labour Struggles in Canada 1919–1949* (Toronto: James, Lewis and Samuel, 1974).

Adams, George W., 'Grievance arbitration and judicial review in North America', *Osgoode Hall Law Journal*, Vol. 9, no. 3 (1971), pp. 443–509.

Adams, Roy J., 'Solidarity, self-interest and the unionization differential between Europe and North America', *Relations Industrielles*, Vol. 29, no. 3 (1974), pp. 497–512.

Adell, B. L., *Employer 'Free Speech' in the United States and Canada* (Kingston, Ontario: Industrial Relations Centre, Queen's University, 1966), Reprint Series no. 8.

——, *The Legal Status of Collective Agreements in England, the United States and Canada* (Kingston, Ontario: Industrial Relations Centre, Queen's University, 1970), Research Series no. 10.

Adell, B. L. and Carter, D. D., *Collective Bargaining for University Faculty in Canada* (Kingston, Ontario: Industrial Relations Centre, Queen's University, 1972), English and French.

Aggarwal, Argun P., 'Adjudication of grievances in the Public Service of Canada', *Relations Industrielles*, Vol. 28, no. 3 (1973), pp. 497–547.

Anderson, Isabel B., *Internal Migration in Canada, 1921–1961* (Ottawa: Economic Council of Canada, Queen's Printer, 1966), Staff Study no. 13.

Anton, F. R., *The Role of Government in the Settlement of Industrial Disputes in Canada* (Toronto: CCH Canadian Limited, 1962).

Arrow, Kenneth J., 'The social discount rate', in *Cost-Benefit Analysis of Manpower Policies*, ed. by G. G. Somers and W. D. Wood (Kingston, Ontario: Industrial Relations Centre, Queen's University, 1969), pp. 56–75.

Arthurs, Harry W., 'The dependent contractor: A study of the legal problems of countervailing power', *The University of Toronto Law Journal*, Vol. 16, no. 1 (1965), pp. 89–117.

——, *Labour Disputes In Essential Industries*, Study no. 8, Task Force on Labour Relations (Ottawa: Queen's Printer, 1970).

——, *Collective Bargaining by Public Employees in Canada: Five Models*, Series on Comparative Studies in Public Employment Labour Relations (Ann Arbor: Institute of Labor and Industrial Relations, University of Michigan, Wayne State University, 1971).

——, 'The dullest Bill: reflections on the Labour Code of British Columbia', *U.B.C. Law Review*, Vol. 9, no. 2 (1975), pp. 280–340.

Arthurs, Harry W. and Crispo, John, 'Countervailing employer power: accreditation of contractor associations', in *Construction Labour Relations*, ed. by H. C. Goldenberg and John Crispo (Ottawa: Canadian Construction Association, 1968), Ch. 9, pp. 376–415.

Babcock, Robert H., *Gompers in Canada: A Study in American Continentalism Before the First World War* (Toronto: University of Toronto Press, 1974).

Bain, George Sayers, 'The growth of white-collar unionism and public policy in Canada', *Relations Industrielles*, Vol. 24, no. 2 (1969), pp. 243–78.

Bairstow, Frances; LeBel, Hélène; Downie, Bryan M., and Kleingartner, Archie, *The Professional Employee in the Public Service of Canada* (Montreal: Industrial Relations Centre, McGill University, 1972).

Barnes, L. W. C. S., *Consult and Advise: A History of the National Joint*

Council of the Public Service of Canada, 1944–1974 (Kingston, Ontario: Industrial Relations Centre, Queen's University, 1975), Research and Current Issues Series, no. 26.

Barnes, L. W. C. S. and Kelly, L. A., *Interest Arbitration in the Federal Public Service of Canada* (Kingston, Ontario: Industrial Relations Centre, Queen's University, 1975), Research and Current Issues Series, no. 31.

Barnes, Samuel H., 'The evolution of Christian trade unions in Quebec', *Industrial and Labor Relations Review*, Vol. 12, no. 4 (1959), pp. 568–81.

Batlett, R. H., 'The Hot Cargo Clause', *Alberta Law Review*, Vol. 12 (1974), pp. 378–402.

Bauer, Julien, 'Les employeurs et leurs associations face aux syndicats et aux pouvoirs publics au Québec' (unpublished thesis, Université de Paris, 1974).

Beach, Earl, 'La théorie économique de l'automation', *Relations Industrielles*, Vol. 22, no. 3 (1967), pp. 400–10.

——, 'Hicks on Ricardo on machinery', *Economic Journal*, Vol. 81, no. 324 (December 1971), pp. 916–22.

Beatty, David M., 'Secondary boycotts: a functional analysis', *Canadian Bar Review*, Vol. 52 (1974), pp. 388–425.

Beaulieu, Marie-Louis, *Les conflits de droit dans les rapports collectifs du travail* (Québec: Les Presses de l'Université Laval, 1955).

Bélanger, Laurent, *Evolution du patronat et ses répercussions sur les attitudes et pratiques patronales dans la province de Québec*, Study no. 14, Task Force on Labour Relations (Ottawa: Queen's Printer, 1970).

Bélanger, Noël and Bernier, Jacques, *Les travailleurs Québecois: 1851–1896* (Montreal: Les Presses de l'Université du Québec, 1973).

Belzile, Bertrand; Boivin, Jean; Laflamme, Gilles and Sexton, Jean, eds., *Inflation, indexation et conflits sociaux* (Quebec: Les Presses de l'Université Laval, 1975).

Belzile, Bertrand and Larouche, Viateur, 'Motivation au travail des familles à faible revenu: tentative de mesure', *Relations Industrielles*, Vol. 30, no. 1 (1975), pp. 60–82.

Bercuson, David J., *Confrontation at Winnipeg* (Montreal: McGill–Queen's Press, 1974).

Bergeron, Yves, 'De la règle d'impartialité en matière d'arbitrage de griefs', *La revue du Barreau* (une publication du Barreau du Québec), Vol. 35, no. 2 (1975), pp. 163–201.

Bernard, Paul, *Structures et pouvoirs de la fédération des travailleurs du Québec*, Study no. 13, Task Force on Labour Relations (Ottawa: Queen's Printer, 1970).

Bertram, Gordon W., *The Contribution of Education to Economic Growth* (Ottawa: Economic Council of Canada, Queen's Printer, 1966) Staff Study no. 12.

——, 'The Structure and Performance of Collective Bargaining Systems', in *Construction Labour Relations*, ed. by H. C. Goldenberg and John Crispo (Ottawa: Canadian Construction Association, 1968), pp. 416–519.

Bodkin, Ronald G., 'Real wages and cyclical variations in employment, a re-examination of the evidence', *Canadian Journal of Economics*, Vol. III, no. 3 (August 1969), pp. 353–74.

Bodkin, Ronald G.; Bond, Elizabeth P.; Reuber, Grant L., and Robinson,

T. Russell, *Price Stability and High Employment, The Options for Canadian Economic Policy* (Ottawa: Economic Council of Canada, Queen's Printer, 1967), Special Study no. 5.

Boivin, Jean, 'La négociation collective dans le secteur public québécois: une évaluation des trois premières rondes (1964–1972)', *Relations Industrielles*, Vol. 27, no. 4 (1972) pp. 679–708.

——, *The Evolution of Bargaining Power in the Province of Quebec Public Sector (1964–1972)* (Québec: Département des relations industrielles, Université Laval, Les Presses de l'Université Laval, 1974).

Bradwin, Edmund, *The Bunkhouse Man: A Study of Work and Pay in the Camps of Canada 1903–1914* (New York: By the Author, 1928. Republished Toronto: University of Toronto Press, 1972).

Brecher, Irving and Reisman, S. S., *Canada–United States Economic Relations* (Ottawa: Queen's Printer, 1957).

Bromke, Adam, *The Labour Relations Board in Ontario* (Montreal: Industrial Relations Centre, McGill University, 1961).

Brown, Donald J. M., *Interest Arbitration*, Study no. 18, Task Force on Labour Relations (Ottawa: Queen's Printer, 1970).

Brown, Donald J. M., and Beatty, David M., *Canadian Labour Arbitration* (Agincourt, Ontario: Canada Law Book Ltd., 1977).

Cameron, James C. and Young, F. J. L., *The Status of Trade Unions in Canada* (Kingston, Ontario: Industrial Relations Centre, Queen's University, 1960).

Canada Department of Labour, *Collective Bargaining Review* (Annual).

——, *Industrial Relations Research in Canada* (Annual).

——, *Labour Organizations in Canada* (Annual).

——, *Strikes and Lockouts in Canada* (Annual).

——, (Woman's Bureau) *Women in the Labour Force* (Annual).

Cardin, Jean-Réal, *Canadian Labour Relations in an Era of Technological Change*, (Ottawa: Economic Council of Canada, Queen's Printer, 1967a), Special Study no. 6.

——, 'Le code du travail: deux ans d'expérience', *Relations Industrielles*, vol. 22, no. 3 (1967b), pp. 327–43.

——, 'La négociation collective par secteurs et le droit québécois du travail', *Relations Industrielles*, Vol. 24, no. 3 (1969), pp. 467–88.

Carrothers, A. W. R., *The Labour Injunction in British Columbia* (Toronto: CCH Canadian Limited, 1956).

——, *Labour Arbitration in Canada* (Toronto: Butterworths, 1961).

——, *Collective Bargaining Law in Canada* (Toronto: Butterworths, 1965).

——, 'Who Wants Collective Bargaining Anyway', *Relations Industrielles*, Vol. 30, no. 3 (1975), pp. 319–30.

Carrothers, A. W. R., and Palmer, E. E. (eds.), *Report of a Study on the Labour Injunction in Ontario* (Toronto: Queen's Printer, 1966).

Charpentier, Alfred, *Cinquante ans d'action ouvrière: les mémoires d'Alfred Charpentier* (Quebec: Les Presses de l'Université Laval, 1971).

Chernick, Jack, *Adaptation and Innovations in Wage Payment Systems in Canada*, Study no. 5, Task Force on Labour Relations (Ottawa: Queen's Printer, 1968).

Christie, I. M., *Liability of Strikers in the Law of Tort* (Kingston, Ontario:

62   *Industrial Relations in International Perspective*

Industrial Relations Centre, Queen's University, 1967), Research and Current Issues Series no. 5.

Christie, I. M. and Gorsky, Morley, *Unfair Labour Practices: An Exploratory Study of the Efficacy of the Law of Unfair Labour Relations in Canada*, Study no. 10, Task Force on Labour Relations (Ottawa: Queen's Printer, 1970).

Cinq-Mars, Normand, 'Négociation locale et négociation sectorielle', *Relations Industrielles*, Vol. 25, no. 3 (1970), pp. 465–84.

Clack, Garfield, 'Strikes during the term of collective agreements', in the *Report of the Seventeenth Annual Meeting of the Statistics and Research Committee of the Canadian Association of Administrators of Labour Legislation*, Ottawa, May 1975 (Ottawa: Canada Department of Labour, Economics and Research Branch, forthcoming).

Cliche, Robert (President), Mulroney, Brian and Chevrette, Guy, *Rapport de la commission d'enquête sur l'exercice de la liberté syndicale dans l'industrie de la construction* (Québec: Editeur officiel du Québec, 1975).

——, *Recueil des annexes du rapport de la commission d'enquête sur l'exercice de la liberté syndicale dans l'industrie de la construction* (Québec: Editeur officiel du Québec, 1975).

Cohen, Maxwell, *Report of the Royal Commission on Labour Legislation in Newfoundland and Labrador* (St John's Newfoundland, Newfoundland Department of Labour, 1972).

Comay, Yochanan, 'Migration of professionals, an empirical analysis', *Canadian Journal of Economics*, Vol. V, no. 3 (1972), pp. 419–29.

Cook, Gail C. A. (ed.), *Opportunity for Choice: A Goal for Women in Canada.* (Published by Statistics Canada in association with the C. D. Howe Research Institute, 1975.)

Courchene, Thomas J., 'Interprovincial migration and economic adjustment', *Canadian Journal of Economics*, Vol. III, no. 4 (1970), pp. 550–76.

Cousineau, Jean-Michel and Lacroix, Robert, *Wage Determination in Major Collective Agreements in the Private and Public Sectors* (Ottawa: Economic Council of Canada, 1977).

Craig, Alton, 'The Consequences of Provincial Jurisdiction for the Process of Company-Wide Collective Bargaining: A Study of the Packinghouse Industry', (Ph. D. Dissertation, Cornell University, 1964).

——, 'A model for the analysis of industrial relations systems', in *Canadian Labour and Industrial Relations: Public and Private Sectors*, ed. by H. C. Jain (Toronto: McGraw-Hill Ryerson Limited, 1975), Part I, pp. 2–12.

Cram, John, 'Differential need satisfaction of mine workers in Northern Canada', *Canadian Journal of Behavioural Science*, Vol. 4 (1972), pp. 135–45.

Crispo, John, *International Unionism – A Study in Canadian-American Relations* (Toronto: McGraw-Hill of Canada Ltd., 1967).

——, 'Multinational corporations, international unions, and industrial relations: the Canadian case', *Relations Industrielles*, Vol. 29, no. 4 (1974), pp. 673–83.

——, *The Canadian Industrial Relations System* (Toronto: McGraw-Hill Ryerson, 1978a).

——, *Industrial Democracy in Western Europe* (Toronto: McGraw-Hill Ryerson, 1978b).

Crysler, A. C., *Labour Relations and Precedents in Canada* (Toronto: The Carswell Company Ltd., 1949).

——, *Handbook on Canadian Labour Law* (Toronto: The Carswell Company Ltd., 1957).

——, *Restraint of Trade and Labour* (Toronto: Butterworths, 1967).

Cunningham, W. B., *Compulsory Conciliation and Collective Bargaining: The New Brunswick Experience* (Montreal: Quality Press Limited, 1958. Published jointly by the New Brunswick Department of Labour and Industrial Relations Centre, McGill University).

——, 'Conciliation: the end of compulsory boards', *Relations Industrielles*, Vol. 25, no. 1 (1970), pp. 62–82.

Curtis, C. H., *Labour Arbitration Procedures* (Kingston, Ontario: Industrial Relations Centre, Queen's University, 1957).

——, *The Development of the Enforcement of the Collective Agreement* (Kingston, Ontario: Industrial Relations Centre, Queen's University, 1966). Research Series no. 4.

Cutler, Philip, *Labour Relations and Court Review: A Study in the Supervision and Control of Administrative Tribunals* (Montréal: Tundra Books, 1968).

——, *Code du travail du Québec* (Montréal: Les Livres Toundra, 1970).

D'Aoust, Claude and Rousseau, André, *Le contrat individuel de travail en droit québécois* (Montreal: Les Presses de l'Université de Montréal, 1970).

Davis, N. H. W. and Gupta, M. L., *Labour Force Characteristics in Post-War Immigrants and Native Born Canadians: 1956–67* (Ottawa: Dominion Bureau of Statistics, 1968), Special Labour Force Studies no. 6.

De Bonville, Jean, *Jean-Baptiste Gagnepetit: Les travailleurs Montréalais à la fin du XIXe siecle* (Montréal: Editions de l'Aurore, 1975).

Denton, Frank T., *The Growth of Manpower in Canada*, 1961 Census Monographs Programme (Ottawa: Dominion Bureau of Statistics, 1970).

Denton, Frank T. and Ostry, Sylvia, *Historical Estimates of the Canadian Labour Force*, 1961 Census Monographs Programme (Ottawa: Dominion Bureau of Statistics, 1967).

Department of Manpower and Immigration, Planning and Evaluation Branch, Program Development Service, *The Canadian Adult Training Program*, Paper prepared for OECD (July 1968).

Desrosiers, Richard, and Héroux, Denis, *Le travailleur québécois et le syndicalisme*, 2nd ed. (Montréal: Cahiers de l'Université du Québec, 1973) no. 31.

Dion, Gérard, 'La CTCC et l'unité ouvrière canadienne', *Relations Industrielles*, Vol. 12, nos. 1–2 (1957), pp. 32–54.

——, 'La concurrence syndicale dans le Québec', *Relations Industrielles*, Vol. 22, no. 1 (1967), pp. 74–85.

—— (ed.), *La politisation des relations du travail.* XXVIIe Congrès des relations industrielles de l'Université Laval (Québec: Les Presses de l'Université Laval, 1973).

——, *Vocabulaire français-anglais des relations professionnelles – Glossary of Terms Used in Industrial Relations, English-French* (Revised Edition, Québec: Les Presses de l'Université Laval, 1975).

64   *Industrial Relations in International Perspective*

——, *Dictionnaire canadien des relations du travail* (Québec: Les Presses de l'Université Laval, 1976).

Dodge, David A., *Returns to Investment in University Training – The Case of Canadian Accountants, Engineers and Scientists* (Kingston, Ontario: Industrial Relations Centre, Queen's University, 1972).

Dodge, David A., 'Occupational wage differentials, occupational licensing, and returns to investment in education: an exploratory analysis', in *Canadian Higher Education in the Seventies*, ed. by Sylvia Ostry (Ottawa: Economic Council of Canada, Queen's Printer, 1972), pp. 113–76.

Dofny, J. and Bernard, P., *Le syndicalisme au Québec: structure et mouvement*, Study no. 9, Task Force on Labour Relations (Ottawa: Queen's Printer, 1970).

Doucet, René, 'La résiliation du contrat de travail en droit québécois', *Revue juridique Thémis* (Université de Montréal), Vol. 9, no. 2 (1974) pp. 249–316.

Downie, Bryan M., *Relations Between Canadian-American Wage Settlements, An Empirical Study of Five Industries* (Kingston, Ontario: Industrial Relations Centre, Queen's University, 1970), Research and Current Issues Series, no. 18.

——, 'Centralized collective bargaining: U.S.–Canada experience', *Relations Industrielles*, Vol. 26, no. 1 (1971), pp. 38–63.

Dumas, Evelyn, *Dans le sommeil de nos os* (Ottawa: Editions Leméac, Inc., 1971). Translated by Arnold Bennett, *The Bitter Thirties* (Montreal: Black Rose Publications, 1975).

Dunlop, John, *Industrial Relations Systems* (New York: H. Holt, 1958).

Dunsmore, R. Ross, 'The employer, the employee and the legal strike', *Queen's Law Journal*, Vol. 2 (1973), pp. 3–39.

Dymond, William R., 'The role of benefit/cost analysis in formulating manpower policy', in *Cost-Benefit Analysis of Manpower Policies*, ed. by G. G. Somers and W. D. Wood (Kingston, Ontario: Industrial Relations Centre, Queen's University, 1969), pp. 42–55.

Economic Council of Canada, *Economic Goals for Canada to 1970*, First Annual Review (Ottawa: Queen's Printer, 1964).

Evans, M. G., 'Herzberg's Two Factor Theory: one more test', *Studies in Personnel Psychology*, Vol. 3, no. 1 (1971), pp. 45–9.

——, 'Relations among weighted and non-weighted measures of job satisfaction', *Studies in Personnel Psychology*, Vol. 4, no. 2 (1972), pp. 45–54 ——, 'The moderating effect of internal vs. external control on the relationship between various aspects of job satisfaction', *Studies in Personnel Psychology*, Vol. 5, no. 1 (1973), pp. 37–46.

Finkelman, Jacob, *Employer-*Employee Relations in the Public Service of Canada (Ottawa: Information Canada, 1974).

Flood, Maxwell, *Wildcat Strike in Lake City*, Study no. 15, Task Force on Labour Relations (Ottawa: Queen's Printer, 1968).

Forsey, E., 'The movement towards labour unity in Canada: history and implications', *Canadian Journal of Economics and Political Science*, Vol. 24, no. 1 (1958), pp. 70–83.

——, 'Insights into labour history in Canada', *Relations Industrielles*, Vol. 20, no. 3 (1965), pp. 445–75.

Francoeur, Jean (ed.), *En grève* (Montréal: Editions du Jour, 1963).

Frankel, Saul J., *Staff Relations in the Civil Service* (Montreal: McGill University Press, 1962).

———, *Report of the Royal Commission on Employer-Employee Relations in the Public Services of New Brunswick* (Fredericton, New Brunswick: Queen's Printer, 1967).

Fraser, Donald and Goldenberg, Shirley B., 'Collective bargaining for professional workers: the case of the engineers', *McGill Law Journal*, Vol. 20, no. 3 (1974), pp. 456–79.

Freedman, Mr Justice Samuel, *Report of the Industrial Inquiry Commission on Canadian National Railways 'Run-Throughs'* (Ottawa: Queen's Printer, 1965).

French, Doris, *Faith, Sweat and Politics, The Early Trade Union Years in Canada* (Toronto: McClelland and Stewart Limited, 1962).

Fryer, John, 'The implication of technological change for collective bargaining', *Relations Industrielles*, vol. 22, no. 3 (1967), pp. 411–21.

Gagnon, Robert P., LeBel, Louis, and Verge, Pierre, *Droit du travail en vigueur au Québec* (Québec: Les Presses de l'Université Laval, 1971).

Garant, Patrice, 'Le statut de la fonction publique au Québec', *Les cahiers de droit* (Les Presses de l'Université Laval), Vol. 12, no. 3 (1971), pp. 361–417.

———, 'Le droit disciplinaire dans la fonction publique', *Relations Industrielles*, Vol. 27, no. 3 (1972), pp. 454–96.

Gérin-Lajoie, Jean, 'La fusion et les possibilitiés', *Relations Industrielles*, Vol. 12, nos. 1–2 (1957), pp. 86–95.

Goldenberg, H. Carl, *Report of the Royal Commission on Labour Management Relations in the Construction Industry* (Toronto: Queen's Printer, 1962).

Goldenberg, H. Carl and Crispo, John (eds.), *Construction Labour Relations* (Ottawa, Canadian Construction Association, 1968), English and French.

Goldenberg, Shirley B., *Professional Workers and Collective Bargaining*, Study no. 2, Task Force on Labour Relations (Ottawa: Queen's Printer, 1970).

———, 'Collective bargaining in the provincial public service', *Collective Bargaining in the Public Service* (Toronto: Institute of Public Administration of Canada, 1973a), pp. 11–43.

———, 'Dispute settlement in the public sector: the Canadian scene', *Relations Industrielles*, Vol. 28, no. 2 (1973b), pp. 267–94.

———, *Labour Relations in Quebec: Past and Present* (Kingston, Ontario: Industrial Relations Centre, Queen's University, 1975), Reprint Series no. 28.

Gray, Hon. Herb, *Special Report on Foreign Direct Investment in Canada* (Ottawa: Information Canada, 1972).

Green, Judge N., *Industrial Inquiry Commission Regarding Fisheries in the Ports of Canso, Mulgrave and Petit de Gras* (Halifax: Nova Scotia Department of Labour, 1970).

Gunderson, Morley, 'The case for government supported training programs', *Relations Industrielles*, Vol. 29, no. 4 (1974), pp. 709–24.

——— (ed.), *Collective Bargaining in the Essential and Public Service Sectors* (Toronto: University of Toronto Press, 1975).

Hameed, S. M. A., 'A theory of collective bargaining', *Relations Industrielles*, Vol. 25, no. 3 (1970), pp. 531–52.

—— (ed.), *Canadian Industrial Relations: A Book of Readings* (Toronto: Butterworth and Co. (Canada) Limited, 1975).

Hamelin, Jean; Larocque, Paul and Rouillard, Jacques, *Répertoire des grèves dans la Province de Québec au XIXe siècle* (Montréal: Les Presses de l'Ecole des Hautes Etudes Commerciales, Editions Fides, 1970).

Hann, Russell G.; Kealey, Gregory S.; Kealey, Linda, and Warrian, Peter, *Primary Sources in Canadian Working Class History 1860–1930* (Kitchener, Ontario: Dumont Press, 1973).

Hardin, Einar, 'Benefit-cost analyses of occupational training programs: a comparison of recent studies', in *Cost Benefit Analysis of Manpower Policies*, ed. by G. G. Somers and W. D. Wood (Kingston, Ontario: Industrial Relations Centre, Queen's University, 1969), pp. 97–118.

Hardy, L. S., *Brève historie du syndicalisme ouvrier au Canada* (Montréal: Les Editions de l'Hexagone, 1958).

Hawkins, Freda, *Canada and Immigration – Public Policy and Public Concern* (Montreal: McGill Queen's University Press, 1972).

Heaney, A. D. P. (chairman), *Report of the Preparatory Committee on Collective Bargaining in the Public Service* (Ottawa: Queen's Printer, 1965).

Hébert, Gérard, 'La négociation sectorielle par décision de l'état: le cas de la construction au Québec', *Relations Industrielles*, Vol. 26, no. 1 (1971), pp. 84–123.

——, *Les Relations du travail dans la construction au Québec* (Ottawa: Economic Council of Canada, 1977), French and English.

Herman, E. E., *Determination of the Appropriate Bargaining Unit* (Ottawa: Queen's Printer, 1966).

Hickling, M. A., *Labour Disputes and Unemployment Insurance Benefits in Canada and England* (Toronto: CCH Canadian Limited, 1974).

Higgins, R. D. (chairman); Fryer, J. L.; Fomalty, G. L.; Ruff, N. J., and Richards, N. T., *Making Collective Bargaining Work in British Columbia's Public Service: Report and Recommendations of the Commission of Inquiry into Employer–Employee Relations in the Public Service of B.C.* (Victoria, B.C.: Queen's Printer, (1972).

Hettich, Walter, *Expenditure, Output and Productivity in Canadian University Education*, Economic Council of Canada, Special Study no. 14, 1971.

Hodgetts, J. E. and Dwivedi, O. P., *Provincial Governments as Employers* (Montreal: McGill–Queen's University Press, 1974).

Horowitz, Gad, *Canadian Labour in Politics* (Toronto: University of Toronto Press, 1968).

Hurd, W. B., 'Demographic trends in Canada', *Annals of the American Academy of Political and Social Science*, Vol. 253, (September 1947), pp. 10–15.

Illing, Wolfgang, M., and Zsigmond, Zoltan E., *Enrolment in Schools and Universities 1951–52 to 1975–76*, Economic Council of Canada, Staff Study no. 20, 1967.

Illing, Wolfgang, M., *Population, Household and Labour Force Growth to 1980* (Ottawa: Economic Council of Canada, 1967), Staff Study.

Isaac, J. E., *Compulsory Arbitration in Australia*, Study no. 4, Task Force on Labour Relations (Ottawa: Queen's Printer, 1970).

Isbester, A. F., Coates, D. and Williams, C. B., *Industrial Relations in*

Canada, A Selected Bibliography (Kingston, Ontario: Industrial Relations Centre, Queen's University, 1965) Bibliography Series no. 2.

Jain, Harish (ed.), *Contemporary Issues in Canadian Personnel Administration* (Scarborough, Ontario: Prentice-Hall of Canada, 1971).

Jain, Harish C. and Kanungo, R. N., *Behavioural Issues in Management: The Canadian Context* (Scarborough, Ontario: McGraw-Hill Ryerson, 1977).

Jain, Hem C., *Canadian Cases in Labour Relations and Collective Bargaining* (Don Mills, Ontario: Longman Canada Limited, 1973).

—— (ed.), *Canadian Labour and Industrial Relations, Public and Private Sectors* (Toronto: McGraw-Hill Ryerson Limited, 1975).

Jamieson, Stuart, *Times of Trouble*, Study no. 22, Task Force on Labour Relations (Ottawa: Queen's Printer, 1970).

——, 'Multi-employer bargaining: the case of B.C. coast lumber industry', *Relations Industrielles*, Vol. 26, no. 1 (1971), pp. 146–68.

——, *Industrial Relations in Canada*. Revised edition (Toronto: Macmillan of Canada, 1973).

Jenness, Robert A., 'Manpower mobility programs', in *Cost-Benefit Analysis of Manpower Policies*, ed. by G. G. Somers and W. D. Wood (Kingston, Ontario: Industrial Relations Centre, Queen's University, 1969), pp. 184–220.

Johnston, D. L. (chairman); Alden, R. E.; Turrell, A. S., and McKenna, I. B., *Report of the Hospital Inquiry Commission* (Toronto: Queen's Printer, 1974).

Judy, Richard W., 'Costs: theoretical and methodological issues', in *Cost-Benefit Analysis of Manpower Policies* ed. by G. G. Somers and W. D. Wood (Kingston, Ontario: Industrial Relations Centre, Queen's University, 1969), pp. 16–29.

Kalbach, Warren E., *The Impact of Immigration on Canada's Population*, 1961 Census Monographs Programme (Ottawa: Dominion Bureau of Statistics, 1970).

Kaliski, S. F., 'The relation between unemployment and the rate of change of money wages in Canada', *International Economic Review* (January 1964), pp. 1–33.

——, *The Trade-Off between Inflation and Unemployment: Some Explorations of the Recent Evidence for Canada*, Economic Council of Canada. Special Study no. 22 (Ottawa, 1972).

Kasahara, Y., and Le Nevue, A. H., 'Demographic trends in Canada, 1941–1956, and some of their implications', *Canadian Journal of Economics and Political Science*, Vol. 24, no. 1 (1958), pp. 9–20.

Kealey, Gregory S., *Hogtown: Working Class Toronto at the Turn of the Century* (rev. ed. Toronto: New Hogtown Press, 1974).

Kellock, R. L., (chairman); McLaurin, C. C., and Martineau, Jean, *Report of the Royal Commission on Employment of Fireman and Diesel Locomotives in Freight and Yard Service on the Canadian Pacific Railway* (Ottawa: Queen's Printer, 1958).

Kelly, L. A., *Settlement Methods in Ontario Collective Bargaining 1970–1973* (Kingston, Ontario: Industrial Relations Centre, Queen's University, 1974), Research and Current Issues Series, no. 22.

Kelly, L. A. and Kumar, P., *Inflation and Collective Bargaining* (Kingston,

Ontario: Industrial Relations Centre Queen's University, 1974), Research and Current Issues Series, no. 24.

Keyfitz, Nathan 'The growth of Canadian population', *Population Studies*, Vol. IV, no. 1 (June 1950), pp. 47–63.

Keys, B. A., and Wright, H. H., *Manpower Planning in Industry – A Case Study* (Ottawa: Economic Council of Canada, Queen's Printer, 1966), Staff Study no. 18.

King, William Lyon Mackenzie, *Industry and Humanity* (Toronto: Thomas Allen, 1918. Republished in the Social History of Canada Series, University of Toronto Press, 1973).

Kovacs, Aranka E., 'The philosophy of the Canadian Labour Movement', in *Canadian Labour in Transition*, ed. by Richard U. Miller and Fraser Isbester (Scarborough, Ont: Prentice-Hall of Canada, 1971), Ch. 4, pp. 119–44.

Kruger, Arthur M., *International Unions and Canadian-American Relations* (published for the Canadian Institute of International Affairs, Toronto: Baxter Publishing Co., 1964).

——, 'The right to strike in the public sector: Canadian legislation and experience', *Proceedings of the 1970 Annual Spring Meeting*, Industrial Relations Research Association (Chicago: Commerce Clearing House Inc., 1970) p. 455–63.

——, 'Human adjustment to technological change: an economist's view', *Relations Industrielles*, Vol. 26, no. 2 (1971), pp. 265–307.

——, 'Collective bargaining in the public sector: the Canadian experience', *International Labour Review*, Vol. 109, no. 4 (April 1974), pp. 319–31.

Kumar, Pradeep, *Long-Run Changes in the Labour Share of National Income in Canada, 1926–1966* (Kingston, Ontario: Industrial Relations Centre, Queen's University, 1971).

Kwavnick, David, 'Pressure group demands and the struggle for organizational status: the case of organized labour in Canada', *Canadian Journal of Political Science*, Vol. 3 (1970), pp. 56–72.

——, *Organized Labour and Pressure Politics: The CLC, 1956–1968* (Montreal: McGill-Queen's University Press, 1972).

——, 'Pressure group demands and organizational objectives: the CNTU, the Lapalme affair and national bargaining units', *Canadian Journal of Political Science*, Vol. 6 (1973), pp. 582–601.

Labour Relations Law Casebook Group, *Labour Relations Law: Cases, Materials and Commentary* (Kingston, Ontario: Industrial Relations Centre, Queen's University, 1970; second edition, 1974).

Langdon, Steven, *The Emergence of the Canadian Working Class Movement, 1845–1875* (Toronto: New Hogtown Press, 1975).

Larouche, Viateur and Belzile, Bertrand, 'Motivation au travail des parents de familles à faible revenue: modèle conceptual', *Relations Industrielles*, Vol. 29, no. 4 (1974), pp. 643–84.

Larouche, Viateur and Delorme, François, 'Satisfaction au travail: reformulation théorique', *Relations Industrielles*, Vol. 27, no. 4 (1972), pp. 567–602.

Larouche, Viateur; Lévesque, A. and Delorme, F., 'Satisfaction au travail: problèmes associés à la mesure', *Relations Industrielles*, Vol. 28, no. 1 (1973), pp. 76–109.

Le Blanc, André and Thwaites, James D., *Le monde ouvrier au Québec*, bibliographie rétrospective (Montréal: Les Presses de l'Université du Québec, 1973).

Levitt, Kari, *Population Movements in the Atlantic Provinces* (Frederiction, New Brunswick: Atlantic Provinces Economic Council, 1960).

——, *Silent Surrender* (Toronto: Macmillan of Canada, 1972).

Little, Judge Walter, *Collective Bargaining in the Ontario Government Service* (Toronto: Queen's Printer, 1969).

Logan, H. R., *Trade Unions in Canada* (Toronto: Macmillan of Canada, 1948).

——, *State Intervention and Assistance in Collective Bargaining: The Canadian Experience, 1943–54* (Toronto: University of Toronto Press, 1956).

Loubser, J. J. and Fullan, M., *Industrial Conversion and Workers' Attitudes to Change in Different Industries*, Study no. 12, Task Force on Labour Relations (Ottawa: Queen's Printer, 1970).

Malles, Paul, 'Industrial relations and technological change: Swedish trade union and employers' views and agreements', *Relations Industrielles*, Vol. 23, no. 2 (1968), pp. 265–94.

——, *Trends in Industrial Relations Systems of Continental Europe*, Study no. 7, Task Force on Labour Relations (Ottawa: Queen's Printer, 1969).

——, *The Institutions of Industrial Relations in Continental Europe* (Ottawa: Queen's Printer, 1973).

——, *Employment Insecurity and Industrial Relations in the Canadian Construction Industry* (Ottawa: Economic Council of Canada, Queen's Printer, 1975), English and French.

Manitoba Labour–Management Review Committee, *Report on Public Sector Employee–Employer Relations in Manitoba* (Winnipeg: Department of Labour, 1974).

Marsh, L. C., *Employment Research*, McGill Social Research Series no. 1 (Toronto: Oxford University Press, 1935).

Masters, D. C., *The Winnipeg General Strike* (Toronto: University of Toronto Press, 1950).

McDougall, Duncan M., 'Immigration into Canada, 1851–1920', *Canadian Journal of Economics and Political Science* (May 1961), pp. 162–75.

McKechnie, Graeme H., 'Multi-employer bargaining – Ontario Trucking: a case study', *Relations Industrielles* Vol. 26, no. 1 (1971), pp. 169–83.

McKinnon, Judge Alexander H., *Report of Fact-Finding Body re Labour Legislation* (Halifax, Nova Scotia: Queen's Printer, 1962).

McNaught, Kenneth, *A Prophet in Politics* (Toronto: University of Toronto Press, 1959).

McNaught, Kenneth and Bercuson, David J., *The Winnipeg Strike: 1919* (Don Mills, Ontario: Longman Canada Ltd., 1974).

Meissner, Martin, 'The long arm of the job: a study of work and leisure', *Industrial Relations*, Vol. 10, no. 3 (1971), pp. 239–60. Reprinted in *Canada: A Sociological Profile*, ed. by W. E. Mann (Toronto: Copp-Clark, 1971), pp. 362–77.

Mélanges Beaulieu, *Etudes juridiques en l'honneur de monsieur le professeur Marie-Louis Beaulieu* (Québec: Université Laval, Les cahiers de droit, 1967–68).

Meltz, Noah, *Changes in the Occupational Composition of the Canadian Labour Force 1931–1961* (Ottawa: Queen's Printer, 1965).

——, 'Manpower research: its economic aspects and its application to industrial relations', *International Conference on Trends in Industrial and Labour Relations* (Jerusalem Academic Press, 1974), pp. 304–14.

Melzer, L. Paul and Philbrooke, Thomas V., *Sociological Factors Influencing Labour Mobility: A Pilot Study of Two Sub-Regions of New Brunswick* (Fredericton, N.B.: Department of Labour, 1974).

Mikalachki, A., Forsyth, G. and Wettlaufer, J. J., *Management's Views on Union–Management Relations at the Local Level*, Study no. 17, Task Force on Labour Relations (Ottawa: Queen's Printer, 1970).

Miller, Richard U., 'Organized labour and politics in Canada', in *Canadian Labour in Transition*, ed. by Richard U. Miller and Fraser Isbester (Scarborough, Ontario: Prentice-Hall of Canada, 1971), pp. 204–39.

Montague, J. Tait, *Labour Markets in Canada: Processes and Institutions* (Scarborough, Ontario: Prentice-Hall of Canada, 1970).

Montpetit, Mr Justice André, *Report of the Royal Commission of Inquiry into Working Conditions in the Post Office Department* (Ottawa, Queen's Printer, 1966).

Morin, Fernand, 'L'Accréditation syndicale au Québec: mise en relief des effets de l'accréditation' (avec commentaires par Claude d'Aoust et Raymond Lachapelle), *Relations Industrielles*, Vol. 25, no. 3 (1970), pp. 401–44.

—— (avec la collaboration de Rodrigue Blouin), *L'Arbitrage des griefs au Québec* (Québec: Département des relations industrielles, Les Presses de l'Université Laval, 1975), Collection relations du travail, Etude no. 9.

Morrison, Robert N., *Corporate Adaptability to Bilingualism and Biculturism: A Study of Policies and Practices in Large Canadian Manufacturing Firms* (Ottawa: Queen's Printer, 1970).

Morton, W. L., *Manitoba: A History* (Toronto: University of Toronto Press, 1957).

Muir, J. Douglas, *Collective Bargaining by Canadian Public School Teachers*, Study no. 21, Task Force on Labour Relations (Ottawa: Queen's Printer, 1968).

——, 'Decentralized bargaining: its problems and direction in the public education systems of Ontario and the Western Provinces', *Relations Industrielles*, Vol. 26, no. 1 (1971), pp. 124–45.

Norris, Mr Justice T. G., *Report of the Industrial Inquiry Commission Concerning Matters Relating to the Disruption of Shipping on the Great Lakes, The St. Lawrence River System and Connecting Waters* (Ottawa: Queen's Printer, 1963).

North, George and Griffin, Harold, *A Ripple, A Wave: The Story of Union Organization in the B.C. Fishing Industry* (Vancouver: Fisherman Publishing Society, 1974).

Officer, Laurence H., 'Immigration and emigration', in *Canada's Economic Problems and Policies* (1970). Referred to in *Labour Economics in Canada* by Sylvia Ostry and Mahmood A. Zaidi (Toronto: Macmillan of Canada, 1973), p. 21.

Ostry, Sylvia, *Occupational Composition*, 1961 Census Monograph Programme, (Ottawa: Dominion Bureau of Statistics, 1967).

Ostry, Sylvia and Zaidi, Mahmood A., *Labour Economics in Canada*, second edition (Toronto: Macmillan of Canada, 1972).

Ouellette, Yves, 'Les unités de négociation dans les secteurs hospitaliers et scolaires' (avec commentaires par Jean Réal Cardin), *Relations Industrielles*, Vol. 25, no. 3 (1970), pp. 445–64.

Ozay, Mehmet, 'A critical appraisal of the economic rationale of government–subsidized manpower training', *Relations Industrielles*, Vol. 25, no. 3 (1970), pp. 568–81.

Palmer, Earl E., *Responsible Decision-Making in Democratic Trade Unions*, Study no. 11, Task Force on Labour Relations (Ottawa: Queen's Printer, 1970).

——, *Collective Agreement Arbitration* (Scarborough, Ontario: Butterworths, 1977).

Pankhurst, K. V., 'Migration between Canada and the United States', *The Annals of the American Academy of Political Science*, Vol. 367 (September 1966), pp. 53–62.

Parai, Louis, *Immigration and Emigration of Professional and Skilled Manpower During the Post-War Period* (Ottawa, Economic Council of Canada, Queen's Printer, 1965), Special Study no. 1.

Patterson, J. C., 'Union secondary conduct: a comparative study of the American and Ontario position', *U.B.C. Law Review*, Vol. 8 (1973), pp. 77–103.

Peitchinis, Stephen G., *Labour-Management Relations in the Railway Industry*, Study no. 20, Task Force on Labour Relations (Ottawa: Queen's Printer, 1970).

——, *Canadian Labour Economics* (Toronto: McGraw-Hill of Canada Limited, 1970).

Perlman, Selig, *A Theory of the Labour Movement* (New York: The Macmillan Co., 1928. Reprinted, New York: Augustus M. Kelley, 1949).

Phillips, Paul, *No Power Greater: A Century of Labour in B.C.* (Vancouver: B.C. Federation of Labour, 1967).

——, 'Theoretical problems of public interest sector industrial relations: explorations through a simple bargaining model', Appendix to the *Report of the Manitoba Labour—Management Review Committee on Public Sector Employee—Employer Relations* (Winnipeg, Manitoba: Department of Labour, 1974).

Phillips, W. G., 'Government conciliation of labour disputes: some recent experience in Ontario', *Canadian Journal of Economics and Political Science*, Vol. 22 (November 1956), pp. 523–34.

Picard, Gérard, *Code du travail/Labour Code, Québec* (Montréal: Librairie Beauchemin, 1957).

Picard, L. A., *Report of the Inquiry Commission on the St. Lawrence Ports* (Ottawa: Queen's Printer, 1967).

Pickett, James, 'An evaluation of estimates of immigration into Canada in the late nineteenth century', *Canadian Journal of Economics and Political Science* (November 1965), pp. 499–508.

Porter, Allan, A., *Directory of Canadian Labour Statistics*, Canadian Studies no. 6 (Montreal: National Industrial Conference Board, 1963).

Portigal, Alan H. (ed.), *Measuring the Quality of Working Life* (Ottawa: Canada Department of Labour, Research and Development Program, 1974).

Quinet, Félix, 'Le rôle de la recherche dans la négociation collective centralisée', *Relations Industrielles*, Vol. 26, no 1 (1971), pp. 184–212.

——, 'L'Analyse des coûts des ententes et conventions collectives: quelques aspects techniques et quelques objectifs suggérés', in *Négociations collectives dans le contexte canadien* (Toronto: CCH Canadian Ltd., 1974), pp. 57–74, English and French.

Rand, Ivan C., *Report of the Royal Commission Inquiry into Labour Disputes* (Toronto, Ontario: Queen's Printer, 1968).

Reed, G. W., *White-Collar Bargaining Units Under the Ontario Labour Relations Act* (Kingston, Ontario: Industrial Relations Centre, Queen's University, 1969), Research Series no. 8.

Reuber, G. L., 'The objectives of Canadian monetary policy 1949–61; empirical trade-offs and the reaction of the authorities', *Journal of Political Economy*, Vol. 72 (April 1964), pp. 109–32.

——, *Wage Determination in Canadian Manufacturing Industries*, Study no. 19, Task Force on Labour Relations (Ottawa: Queen's Printer, 1969).

Revell, J. J., *Collective Bargaining in the Public Services of Prince Edward Island* (unpublished report to the Government of Prince Edward Island, 1972).

Roback, Leo, *Formes de politisation du syndicalisme à Québec* (Montréal: Ecole de relations industrielles, Université de Montréal, 1975).

Roberge, Pierre, 'Les conflits intersyndicaux au Québec (1957–1967)', *Relations Industrielles*, Vol. 24, no. 3 (1969), pp. 521–58.

Robin, Martin, *Radical Politics and Canadian Labour, 1880–1930* (Kingston, Ontario: Industrial Relations Centre, Queen's University, 1968), Research Series no. 7.

Robson, Judge J. A., *Royal Commission to Enquire into and Report on the Causes and Effects of the General Strike which Recently Existed in the City of Winnipeg for a Period of Six Weeks, Including the Methods of Calling and Carrying on Such a Strike* (Winnipeg, 1919).

Rose, Joseph B., *A Report on Accreditation and the Construction Industry* (Frederiction, N.B.: New Brunswick Department of Labour, 1972).

——, 'Accreditation and the construction industry: five approaches to countervailing employer power', *Relations Industrielles*, Vol. 28, no. 3 (1973), pp. 565–82.

Ross, David P., 'Reopeners: the Task Force on Labour Relations', *Relations Industrielles*, Vol. 26, no. 1 (1971), pp. 213–22.

Rouillard, Jacques, *Les travailleurs du coton au Québec (1900–1915)* (Montréal: Les Presses de l'Université du Québec, 1974).

Rowley, J. C. R. and Wilton, D. A., 'Empirical foundations of the Canadian Phillips curve', *Canadian Journal of Economics*, Vol. VII, no. 2 (1974), pp. 240–59.

Royal Commission on the Relations of Labour and Capital (Ottawa: Queen's Printer, 1889. Republished Toronto University Press, 1973).

Ryder, Norman B., 'Components of Canadian population growth', *Population Index*, (April 1954) pp. 71–9.

Samlalsingh, Ruby S., *Broadcasting, An Industry Study*, Study no. 1, Task Force on Labour Relations (Ottawa: Queen's Printer, 1970).

Sauvé, Robert, 'La négociation collective sectorielle', *Relations Industrielles*, Vol. 26, no. 1 (1971), pp. 3–37.

Scoville, J. G., *The Job Content of the Canadian Economy, 1941, 1951, and 1961*, Special Labour Force Studies no. 3 (Ottawa: Dominion Bureau of Statistics, 1967).

Selekman, B. M., *Postponing Strikes* (New York: Russell Sage Foundation, 1927).

Sexton, Jean, 'Le placement des travailleurs dans l'industrie de la construction au Québec', *Recueil des annexes du rapport de la commission d'enquête sur l'exercice de la liberté syndicale dans l'industrie de la construction* (Québec: Editeur officiel du Québec, 1975), pp. 705–817.

Smith, Arthur J., *Report of the Industrial Inquiry Commission into Certain Conditions, Conduct and Matters Giving Rise to Labour Unrest at the Ports of Montreal, Trois-Rivières and Quebec* (Ottawa: Queen's Printer, 1970).

Smith, David C., *Incomes Policy: Some Foreign Experiences and their Relevance for Canada* (Ottawa: Economic Council of Canada, 1966), Special Study no. 4.

——, *Incomes and Wage-Price Policies – Some Issues and Approaches* (Kingston, Ontario: Industrial Relations Centre, Queen's University, 1967).

Smith, Douglas A., 'Determinants of strike activity in Canada', *Relations Industrielles*, Vol. 27, no. 4 (1972), pp. 663–78.

Solasse, Bernard, *Syndicalisme, consommation et société de consommation*, Study no. 3, Task Force on Labour Relations (Ottawa, Queen's Printer, 1970).

Somers, Gerald G., 'Federal manpower policies', in *Canadian Labour in Transition*, ed. by Richard U. Miller and Fraser Isbester (Scarborough, Ontario: Prentice-Hall of Canada, Ltd 1971), pp. 56–84.

Somers, G. G. and Wood, W. D. (eds.), *Cost-Benefit Analysis of Manpower Policies* (Kingston, Ontario: Industrial Relations Centre, Queen's University, 1969).

Steinberg, Charles, *The Impact of Municipal Assistance on Labour Force Participation in Nova Scotia*. The Province of Nova Scotia in concert with the Economic Council of Canada and Council of Maritime Premiers (Halifax: Queen's Printer, 1974).

——, 'The economics of bargaining rights in the fisheries of Nova Scotia and Atlantic Canada', *Relations Industrielles*, Vol. 30, no. 2 (1975), pp. 200–17.

Swan, N. and Wilton, D. (eds.), *Inflation and the Canadian Experience*. Sponsored by the Institute for Economic Research (Kingston, Ontario: Queen's University, 1971).

Thompson, Mark, 'Judicial review of labour arbitration in Ontario', *Relations Industrielles*, Vol. 26, no. 2 (1971), pp. 471–89.

Tremblay, Louis-Marie, *Bibliographie des relations du travail au Canada (1940–1967)* (Montréal: Les Presses de l'Université de Montréal, 1969).

——, *Le syndicalisme québécois: idéologies de la CSN et de la FTQ, 1930–1970* (Montréal: Les Presses de l'Université de Montréal, 1972).

Trudeau, P. E. (ed.), *La grève de l'amiante* (Montréal: Cité Libre, 1956) Trans. by James Boake, *The Asbestos Strike* (Toronto: James, Lewis and Samuel, 1974).

Urquhart, M. C. and Buckley, K. A. (eds.), *Historical Statistics of Canada* (Cambridge University Press, 1965).

Vanderkamp, John, 'Wages and price level determination: an empirical model for Canada', *Economica*, Vol. XXXIII (May 1966), pp. 194–218.

——, 'The effect of out-migration on regional employment', *Canadian Journal of Economics*, Vol. III, no. 4 (1970), pp. 541–9.

——, *Mobility Behaviour in the Canadian Labour Force*, Economic Council of Canada, Special Study no. 16, 1973.

Verge, Pierre, *Les critères des conflits créant une situation d'urgence*, Study no. 23, Task Force on Labour Relations (Ottawa: Queen's Printer, 1970).

——, 'De la souveraineté décisionnelle de l'arbitre', *McGill Law Journal*, Vol. 19 (1973), pp. 543–76

Waisberg, Harry (Commissioner), *Report of the Royal Commission on Certain Sectors of the Building Industry* (two volumes), Toronto: Queen's Printer for Ontario, 1974).

Weatherill, J. F. W., 'Labour relations boards and the courts', *Relations Industrielles*, Vol. 21, no. 1 (1966), pp. 58–78.

Weiermair, K., 'Estimating of educational requirements in occupations and occupational groups', *Relations Industrielles*, Vol. 29, no. 1 (1974), pp. 128–57.

Weiler, Paul C., *Labour Arbitration and Industrial Change*, Study no. 6, Task Force on Labour Relations (Ottawa: Queen's Printer, 1969).

——, 'The slippery slope of judicial intervention: the Supreme Court and Canadian labour relations, 1950–1970', *Osgoode Hall Law Journal*, Vol. 9 (1971), pp. 1–79.

——, 'The remedial authority of the labour arbitrator: revised judicial version', *Canadian Bar Review*, Vol. 52 (1974), pp. 29–58.

Weisbrod, Burton A., 'Benefits of manpower programs: theoretical and methodological issues', in *Cost Benefit Analysis of Manpower Policies*, ed. by G. G. Somers and W. D. Wood (Kingston, Ontario: Industrial Relations Centre, Queen's University, 1969), pp. 3–15.

Westley, William A. and Westley, Margaret W., *The Emerging Worker* (Montreal: McGill–Queen's University Press, 1971).

Willes, J. A., *The Craft Bargaining Unit: Ontario and U.S. Labour Board Experience* (Kingston, Ontario: Industrial Relations Centre, Queen's University, 1970), Research Series no. 19.

Williams, C. Brian, *Manpower Management in Canada* (Kingston, Ontario: Industrial Relations Centre, Queen's University, 1968).

——, 'Collective bargaining in the public sector: a re-examination', *Relations Industrielles*, Vol. 28, no. 1 (1973), pp. 17–33.

Williams, Jack, *Unions in Canada* (J. M. Dent and Sons (Canada) Limited, 1975).

Winder, John W. L., 'Structural unemployment,' in *The Canadian Labour Market*, ed., by Kruger and Meltz (Toronto: Centre for Industrial Relations, University of Toronto, 1968), pp. 125–220.

Wood, W. Donald, 'An Analysis of Office Unionism in Canadian Manufacturing Industries', (Ph.D. Dissertaion, Princeton University, 1959).

——, 'White-collar organizing challenges', in *Canadian Labour and Industrial Relations*, ed. by Hem C. Jain (Toronto: McGraw-Hill Ryerson Ltd, 1975), part 5, pp. 273–9.

——, *The Current Industrial Relations Scene in Canada* (Kingston, Ontario: Industrial Relations Centre, Queen's University, annual).

Wood, W. D., and Campbell, H. F., *Cost-Benefit Analysis and the Economics of Investment in Human Resources, An Annotated Bibliography* (Kingston, Ontario: Industrial Relations Centre, Queen's University, 1970), Bibliography Series no. 5.

Wood, W. D., Kelly, L. A., and Kumar, P., *Canadian Graduate Theses: 1919–1967 (An Annotated Bibliography Covering Economics, Business and Industrial Relations)*, (Kingston, Ontario: Industrial Relations Centre, Queen's University, 1970), Bibliography Series no. 4.

Wood, W. D., and Kumar, Pradeep (eds.), *Canadian Perspectives on Wage–Price Guidelines* (Kingston, Ontario: Industrial Relations Centre, Queen's University, 1976). ·

Woods, H. D. (ed.), *Patterns of Industrial Dispute Settlement in Five Canadian Industries* (Montreal: McGill Industrial Relations Centre, 1948).

———, 'Canadian collective bargaining and dispute settlement policy', *Canadian Journal of Economics and Political Science*, Vol. 21 (1955), pp. 447–65.

———, 'Public policy and labour arbitration in Canada', Developments in American and Foreign Arbitration, *Proceedings of the Twenty-First Annual Meeting of the National Academy of Arbitrators*, Bureau of National Affairs, Washington, 1968, Chap. 1, pp. 19–36.

———, *Labour Policy in Canada* (2nd edition), (Toronto: Macmillan of Canada, 1973).

Woods, H. D., *Report of the Commission of Inquiry into Industrial Relations in the Construction Industry* (Halifax: Nova Scotia Department of Labour, 1970).

———, 'A Reply to David P. Ross', *Relations Industrielles*, Vol. 26, no. 1 (1971), pp. 222–8.

———, 'Technological change and the right to strike', *Relations Industrielles*, Vol. 27, no. 4 (1972), pp. 718–35.

Woods, H. D. (chairman); Carrothers, A. W. R.; Crispo, John, and Dion, Gerard, *Canadian Industrial Relations*, Report of the Task Force on Labour Relations (Ottawa: Queen's Printer, 1968).

Woods, H. D., and Ostry, Sylvia, *Labour Policy and Labour Economics in Canada* (Toronto: Macmillan of Canada, 1962).

Young, F. John L., *The Contracting Out of Work: Canadian and U.S.A. Experience* (Kingston, Ontario: Industrial Relations Centre, Queen's University, 1964), Research and Current Issues Series no. 1.

Zaidi, M. A., *A Study of the Effects of the $1·25 Minimum Wage Under the Canadian Labour Code*, Study no. 16, Task Force on Labour Relations (Ottawa: Queen's Printer, 1970).

Zsigmond, Z. E., and Wennas, C. J., *Enrolment of Educational Institutions by Province: 1951–52 to 1980–81*, Staff Study no. 25, Economic Council of Canada, 1970.

Note: The designation 'Queen's Printer' on Federal Government publications was changed to 'Information Canada' in 1971. Publications of Federal Government departments and agencies and reports of federally appointed inquiries are available from Supply and Services Canada (Ottawa). Quebec government publications are available from l'Editeur officiel du Québec. Each of the other provinces has its own Queen's Printer for printing and distributing government reports and documents.

3 Industrial Relations Research in the United States

George Strauss and Peter Feuille

An analysis of the present state of United States academic industrial relations research is complicated by the absence of clear definition of the field. This was less of a problem during the forties and fifties, when industrial relations had a clear identity as an interdisciplinary, institutionally oriented, problem-oriented field centred heavily on developments in collective bargaining. During that period, scholars from a number of basic disciplines – economics, history, law, psychology and sociology – dealt with roughly similar problems and much of the work overlapped a single discipline. Today, however, collective bargaining practice has become somewhat stabilized and union–management relations serve less effectively as a central organizing focus for scholarly effort. As a consequence, the basic fields have grown apart and the number of scholars who identify their work with industrial relations has declined. Further, even among those who call their field industrial relations, many are concerned chiefly with 'manpower' problems relating to poverty and unemployment. Manpower studies have little to do with collective bargaining, and the boundary between manpower and mainstream economics is quite blurred. Thus the focus and boundaries of industrial relations have become increasingly vague. Fortunately, recent developments provide mild hope that new paradigms will develop.

This diminution of a central focus has presented us – as authors – with several dilemmas. Should we view industrial relations broadly or narrowly? Should we organize our material in terms of the various research disciplines or problem by problem? Our solution is a compromise. We begin with a sketchy history of the field as a whole and then look at developments within the basic disciplines – economics, the behavioural sciences, history and law – which may have implications for industrial relations. Finally, we give somewhat more detailed consideration to what we call 'mainstream' research, primarily collective bargaining.

The reader should note carefully: since we are concerned with the state of industrial relations as an academic field, we ignore industrial relations in the real world, except as it impinges on academia.

An Historical Introduction

At the cost of considerable oversimplification, academic industrial relations can be divided into three periods: the Early Days (pre-1933), the Golden Age (1933–59), and the Doldrums (1959 until the present). Perhaps, however, we are entering a fourth period which we venture to call a renaissance.

The Early Days

Academic interest in labour problems in the United States dates back at least to the work of Barnett and Motley at Johns Hopkins, but the first great name in academic industrial relations was John R. Commons. Commons and his colleagues and students at Wisconsin, especially Selig Perlman and Edwin Witte, comprised the Wisconsin school, which together with colleagues with similar interests, such as Harry A. Millis and Robert Hoxie at Chicago, defined the nature of the field and the chief questions that it has considered over the years.

The Wisconsin school was part of a revolt of 'institutionally' oriented economists against what they felt were the sterilities of classical economic theory. Wisconsin, during the early 1900s, was the stronghold of the reform-oriented progressive movement. The Wisconsin school economists were pragmatic reformers in tune with the spirit of the American labour movement, as defined by its leader, Samuel Gompers, and were instrumental in making Wisconsin a laboratory for social legislation. In current terminology, the Wisconsin school was 'involved' with 'socially relevant' approaches to remedying social injustice.

Early labour economics was concerned with two sets of closely related problems. Firstly, it sought to describe, explain and legitimize the struggling trade union movement and to loosen the legal barriers (especially injunctions) inhibiting union growth. Second, it sought to enact social legislation dealing with such subjects as accidents and workman's compensation, employment exchanges, health insurance, minimum wages, and retirement benefits.

The early labour economists were encyclopaedic in their approach, moving easily from economics, to history, to law, and to what might best be called social work. Commons edited an eleven-volume *Documentary History of American Industrial Society* (1919–21) followed by a two-volume *History of Labor in the United States* (1918–35) covering the period to 1890, which was later updated to 1932. Commons and Andrews (1916) contributed a major textbook, *The Principles of Labor Legislation*. A group at Chicago – Douglas, Hitchcock, and Atkins – prepared a widely read book, *The Worker in Modern Economic Society* (1923), which included material ranging from William James through John Dewey, the Webbs, to Karl Marx, F. W. Taylor, and Roscoe Pound. Douglas and Kornhauser (1922), one a labour economist and future US senator and the other a distinguished psychologist, pioneered a personnel text. Millis and Montgomery's (1945) three-volume *Economics of Labor*, though not published until 1945, well indicates the field's domain, as it was seen in the early days. Volume 1 is primarily concerned with the then-current major problems, such as hours of work, child labour, women in industry, and income insecurity. Volume 2 discusses one solution to these problems: social insurance and allied forms of legislation. Volume 3 takes up the second solution: trade unionism; it starts with labour history, moves on to union government, then takes up what we would now call collective bargaining (significantly titled 'Trade-union Policies and Practices'), and ends up with labour relations law.

Early labour economics were generally suspicious of theory. However, Perlman wrote his *Theory of the Labor Movement* in 1928. The works of Tannenbaum (1921), Hoxie (1917) and Commons (1934) contain theories of the labour movement. Commons' theory provided an alternative to the Marxian explanation for the role of trade unions which was probably more realistic and ideologically compatible with the American experience than was the Marxian one. But this theory was quite restricted in its scope, dealing only with the functions of unions and the reasons why workers organized.

The Golden Age

The period from the National Industrial Recovery Act of 1933 to the Landrum–Griffin Act of 1959 might well be called the American academic industrial relation's Golden Age. Industrial relations became the focus of national attention as unions and collective bargaining spread rapidly. During much of the period, it was an open question whether union–management strife could be contained within socially manageable levels.

Many of the Wisconsin school's dreams were realized during the thirties: the principal of collective bargaining was enshrined in law; one by one, after a series of dramatic battles, the great manufacturing firms were unionized; and a relatively comprehensive social security programme (absent health insurance) was established. This was a heroic period for both labour and industrial relations researchers, who breathed a common air of hope and idealism (Allen, 1962). Many professors were called to Washington and the state capitals to draft, lobby for, and administer the growing body of social and labour legislation.

Prior to the Second World War, academics in the field of industrial relations were largely partisan. The war gave industrial relations a claim to neutrality and respectability. Academicians played a major role in the War Labor Board (the major wartime dispute settlement body). Under the leadership of scholars such as George Taylor, this board did much to shape the distinctive characteristics of United States collective bargaining (for example, the almost universal acceptance of arbitration for grievance resolution). Not the least of its contributions was the training of a generation of arbitrators who dominated the field for thirty years.

The postwar wave of strikes made industrial relations the country's number one social problem – or at least many Americans thought so, including a large cohort of returning veterans who entered graduate study. Witte wrote in 1947 that 'there are more members of the American Economic Association who list labor as their major field of interest than any other. . . . No courses are more popular than those in Labor'. The professors who date their Ph.D.s from this zesty era constitute the core of many academic industrial relations groups today.

The motivations of this postwar group were varied and complex. Made reformist by a Depression-ridden childhood, yet conditioned by their wartime experience to be practical, they saw collective bargaining as a realistic means to give the working man a new sense of dignity and to improve society. Combined with sympathy for unions was a desire to understand and help to reduce the causes of industrial unrest. The important point is that industrial relations at that time was both intellectually challenging and socially meaningful and it attracted many of the best students.

Responding to student and public demand, schools and institutes of industrial relations were established in many states, often with strong political support. Offerings at all levels – undergraduate, masters and doctoral – expanded. Faculties were thrown together from a wide variety of fields, contributing to industrial relations' interdisciplinary approach and reducing economics' primacy.

Industrial relations gradually increased its domain beyond the Wisconsin school's original interests in labour law, collective bargaining, social insurance and labour history. Psychologists, sociologists and political scientists were drawn to the fold, contributing particularly to the understanding of the internal life of the union. Perhaps the most notable of many interdisciplinary approaches was the Illini City series (Derber *et al.*, 1953, 1954; see also Kornhauser, Dubin and Ross, 1954). Although few scholars attempted to cover all the sub-fields in the newly enlarged subject (as Millis and Montgomery had done when the subject was more narrowly defined), there was some notable work bridging two fields, e.g. Bakke, psychology and economics; Slichter, economics and law; and Bernstein, history and economics. As jobs in management opened for industrial relations graduates, personnel joined the list of approved courses. A new field, human relations – largely inspired by the Western Electric studies at Hawthorne (Roethlisberger and Dickson, 1939) – dealt with the non-economic, primarily social, needs of workers.

The leading young labour economists of the period – Kerr, Dunlop, and Ross – had served in the War Labor Board, an experience which taught them the limitations of classical economic theory in explaining institutional reality. But, by contrast with their Wisconsin school predecessors, they did not reject theory outright. Instead they sought to develop a combination of theory and practice that led 'to middle-level generalizations that stood between overall principles or ideologies and case-by-case or historical-period-by-historical-period studies' (Kerr, 1978, p. 133). The focus of their concern was the relative importance to be given competitive market forces as opposed to institutional influences in explaining labour mobility and wages as well as the impact of unions on wages, income shares, and inflation. Machlup and Lester debated the value of marginalism in 1946, but particularly after the publication of Ross's *Trade Union Wage Policy* (1948), most industrial relations students concluded (prematurely) that classical economics and marginalism had been soundly defeated. On the other hand, Slichter's great *Union Policies and Industrial Management* (1941) was well ahead of its time in presenting a primarily economic analysis of the impact of the interrelationships between the union and the economy.

These economists were interested in the *results* of collective bargaining. Other scholars were concerned with the process of bargaining and especially with what came to be known as the 'conditions of industrial peace'. There were numerous studies dealing with labour relations at the shop, plant and company levels, as well as with the still-developing fields of mediation and arbitration. Much of this work involved field research and case studies; there was little quantification. Yet another literature, much by non-lawyers, was spawned by the Wagner, Taft–Hartley, and Landrum–Griffin Acts. Finally, a considerable number of industrial relations specialists turned their attention to manpower problems in developing countries (for the results of a twenty-year collaboration, see Dunlop, Harbison, Kerr and Myers, 1975).

The Doldrums

By the late fifties, industrial relations research seemed to lose much of its former excitement. Perhaps the main reason for this was that industrial relations problems had become less urgent and the field's reason for existence less clear. The main focus of academic industrial relations during the thirties and forties was the rapidly developing system of collective bargaining. By the mid-1950s, this system was established and working, and the percentage of the work force unionized began to decline. Strikes had not been eliminated – on the contrary – but the United States system had learned to adjust to them. Indeed during the sixties and seventies the industrial relations system was one of the few stable institutions in American life (perhaps a tribute to those who had contributed to its development). Details remained to be worked out (especially with regard to public employees), but the main principles were generally accepted. The remaining unsolved bargaining problems were not especially attractive to graduate students.

As the sixties unfolded, other issues appeared more pressing and socially 'relevant', particularly to the younger generation. These included unemployment, inflation, discrimination and poverty. Even though most of these 'newer' topics had been treated by the old industrial relations, younger researchers were less likely to identify their work as industrial relations, and they largely ignored the role of collective bargaining.

It was identification with unions that brought many older scholars to the field. The sixties saw a revival of student idealism and radicalism, but the younger generation of students viewed unions as bastions of the establishment rather than engines of social reform. Thus, conventional industrial relations had little interest for radical students (and radical students were often the best and most imaginative ones). Industrial relations became increasingly identified with conservative elements such as unions, personnel managers and public officials. Perhaps significantly the Industrial Relations Research Association was among the few scholarly organizations in the early seventies not to have a radical caucus.

These developments were occurring at a time when the pendulum in most of the social sciences was swinging from interdisciplinary research, raw empiricism and primarily applied work, to theory-making, theory-testing and quantification (the latter in part the result of computers and money to run them). As a consequence, industrial relation's old interdisciplinary amalgam began to fall apart.

For the highly influential 'new labour economists' the relevant theory was that of neoclassical economics. The University of Chicago assumed the leading role once played by Wisconsin. The new labour economists were quantitatively rather than institutionally oriented. They posed their hypotheses in traditional terms (going back as far as Adam Smith) but tested them through use of sophisticated quantitative techniques. They were concerned with questions of income distribution, labour supply and demand, employment and unemployment, and welfare, but had little interest in (or knowledge of) the practical operation of collective bargaining. To the extent that strikes, union growth, or union impacts on wages were studied, it was in purely quantitative, aggregative terms.

Similar disciplinary parochialism occurred in other areas. Except for a few old-timers, labour history today is being written by historians and appears in historical journals. Similarly, the leading articles on labour law are written by lawyers and appear in law journals. Sociology has become more quantitative. There has been much recent interest in strikes, work alienation and the sociology of occupations, and a great many studies concerned with the relationships among technology, environment and structure. However, certainly by comparison with Britain, there has been little collaboration between sociologists and those scholars who call their field industrial relations; further, few sociologists have been concerned with collective bargaining.

'Human relations', once considered by some as part of industrial relations, was included in a new field, 'organizational behaviour'. In some business schools, organizational behaviour and industrial relations were taught jointly. However, the two fields began drawing apart, especially as organizational behaviour joined labour economics in becoming quantitative and more oriented towards classical theory, this time the classical psychological theory of stimulus and reward.

As these associated disciplines went their respective ways, scholars remaining in the industrial relations core began a certain amount of not especially productive soul-searching. The period *circa* 1960 saw a number of articles concerned with defining industrial relations as a field, with some authors believing that industrial relations should have a theoretical base of its own and others concluding that the only appropriate theories were those of the more basic disciplines such as economics (e.g. Chamberlain, 1960; Tripp, 1963). Dunlop contributed his *Industrial Relations Systems* in 1958. Although more a set of questions than a theoretical statement, it did attempt to provide a structure for the field, which emphasized its interrelated nature. The work has had more influence in Britain than in the United States. The broader Kerr, Dunlop, Harbison and Myers formulation (1960) added an element of dynamism to the original Dunlop theory. Although perhaps the closest approach to a purely industrial relations theory to date, this work has served chiefly as a focus for studies of industrializing countries. In 1969, Somers attempted to stimulate further consideration of theoretical issues, but the discussion was desultory. One thing was clear: industrial relations had lost its central focus. Further, many of those who had been leaders in the fifties moved on, either to other scholarly problems (such as economic development) or to academic administration or public service (e.g. as Secretary of Labor or of the Treasury).

For those who were left in industrial relations, there were two research foci. The first was collective bargaining. As labour relations in manufacturing became routine, interest switched to the professional and then public sectors. The early research here was concerned chiefly with differences and similarities between public and private sectors. Later studies, which became increasingly quantitative, examined the impact of bargaining on wages and personnel policies. There were few studies of the bargaining process itself, either public or private, the chief exceptions being important multidisciplinary works by Stevens (1963) and Walton and McKersie (1965). Unfortunately, these studies failed to set the pattern for other research, and there was little apparent interaction between industrial relations scholars and those studying conflict and bargaining behaviour in other contexts.

The other (and better financed) core of industrial relations interest was manpower (with the distinction between this field and labour economics fuzzy). Manpower developed as a result of the interventionist governmental labour-market policies of the sixties and the consequent liberal funding of studies in these areas. Manpower studies were sometimes institutional but perhaps more frequently applications of human capital theory to specific training programmes. In any case, they were heavily focused on the unemployed and the non-union sectors and thus largely ignored collective bargaining.

By the early seventies the industrial relations field showed signs of splitting. On one side was a group of older, institutionally oriented scholars who retained the older interests in union–management relations. On the other were the younger economists and manpower specialists. Certainly the old identity between industrial relations and labour economics had come in doubt. Some argued that there was a danger that industrial relations was becoming a practitioner's rather than a researcher's field. As Rees (1971, p. 2) put it, 'Training in industrial relations is primarily the training of practitioners, while training in labour economics is largely the training of teachers and researchers'. Practitioner-oriented masters' programmes (e.g. at Minnesota) continued to draw students, particularly for late-afternoon and evening classes; enrolment in more research-oriented curricula declined. Considerable semi-verbalized tension developed between practitioners and academicians in the Industrial Relations Research Association. IRRA's largely practitioner-oriented local chapters grew faster than the national body, and even the national meetings allocated increasing time to papers by practitioners as opposed to those by academicians.

The status of American industrial relations was reflected in the introductory textbooks. Arthur Ross (1964, pp. 3–4) wrote that the typical introductory course was 'obsolete', primarily because it was dominated by unionism and manualism and ignored management, international developments and the growing white-collar sector. Despite Ross's argument, most industrial relations texts of 1978 are either little different from those of fourteen years earlier or have changed in what he would have called the wrong direction. Fleisher (1970), Rees (1973) and Mabry (1973) have written texts which concern themselves strictly with labour *economics* and narrowly define this to be wage and employment theory, with relatively little attention given to the impact of unions, and almost none to the institutional workings of collective bargaining. Another version of the newer texts (e.g. Marshall, Cartter and King, 1976; Kreps, Somers and Perlman, 1974) deals with some of the newer economic questions, such as poverty, discrimination, manpower development and human capital, and the old favourites such as wages, unemployment and theories of the labour movement. But collective bargaining details (e.g. seniority, fringe benefits, or grievance procedure) receive relatively little attention from such texts, and personnel questions (e.g. foreman–worker relations, managerial and sales compensation programmes) are almost completely ignored. Even the seventh edition of Reynolds (1978), possibly the most respected book in the field, is far more oriented towards theoretical and neoclassical economics than was its first edition in 1949. Aside from limited-focus collective bargaining texts, only Mills (1978) centred upon union–management relations, although more inter-disciplinary efforts were in the pipeline (Kochan, forthcoming).

A Renaissance?

Interest in industrial relations research probably hit bottom eight years ago, for since then the field has enjoyed a mild revival. One cause of this apparent renaissance has been the emergence of large-scale unionism among government employees. Industrial relations meetings and journals are now devoting a considerable portion of their time and space to public sector papers, from almost nothing 12–15 years ago (Lewin, 1977). Probably the two most analysed subjects are impasse resolution procedures and strikes. Our familiarity with various methods of resolving negotiating disputes is considerably broader today than it was when collective bargaining existed almost solely in the private sector.

A second, but closely related, area of research interest includes bargaining theory, behaviour and outcomes. As will be discussed below, one stream of this research consists of experimental studies conducted mostly by psychologists (Rubin and Brown, 1975; Magenau and Pruitt, 1979; another involves attempts to measure rigorously the many personal and environmental influences on bargaining behaviour and outcomes (Peterson and Tracy, 1977; Kochan and Wheeler, 1975; Gerhart, 1976). Much of this latter work is based on the study of public-sector impasse resolution procedures.

Thirdly, there has been a so-far poorly integrated wave of studies of strike behaviour by psychologists, sociologists, economists, and even a political scientist. Finally, a variety of miscellaneous studies are appearing, most of which focus on specific industries or occupations (Juris and Feuille, 1973; Northrup and Foster, 1975; Rehmus, 1977; Somers, 1980), especially academia (e.g. Garbarino, 1975).

Perhaps the most notable characteristic of this new research is its substantial behavioural foundation. A new generation of scholars is emerging who have been broadly trained in economics, the behavioural sciences, quantitative methods *and* the institutional aspects of industrial relations. The work turned out by these individuals is more heavily grounded in theory than the more descriptive work of the forties and fifties; it makes greater use of quantitative data and more rigorously tests hypotheses; and much of it is interdisciplinary.

A few examples (other than those previously mentioned) may be illustrative. Psychologists have begun to study various forms of union participation, using multivariate analysis. A psychologist joins with two lawyers to examine the validity of behavioural assumptions in the law with regard to the impact of union–management campaign practices. Economists include job satisfaction in their models explaining turnover. Careful evaluations are conducted by psychologists of so-called 'quality of work life' experiments under joint union–management sponsorship.

The new interdisciplinary wave appears to be affecting collective bargaining studies more than manpower. So far, much of this research appears to be concerned with developing methods rather than providing insights or proving broad propositions. As yet little of it is of practical value. Yet change is occurring, and after a long period of inertia it is much to be welcomed.

On this optimistic note, let us look first at the industrial relations contributions of the basic disciplines – labour economics, the behavioural sciences, labour history and labour law – and then at three 'mainstream' areas: collective bargaining, unions and manpower.

Labour Economics

Economics is industrial relations' 'mother discipline', and for many years industrial relations and labour economics were viewed as virtually synonymous. Labour economists were extremely actively studying unionism and collective bargaining during the Golden Age. Labour economics continues as an active field today, but there is less concern with collective bargaining and more with questions relating to poverty, racial discrimination, skill acquisition, unemployment–inflation trade-offs, and the general operation of the labour market. The 'new labour economics' has become quantitative (according to Mitchell (1975), it was perhaps the last major economics field to become so), and it makes use of regression analysis and related multivariate techniques to study topics that might have been studied institutionally in earlier years. Through applying the standards of science to the study of labour markets, it has directed more careful attention to the interface between theory and evidence than we find in earlier literature. This increased research rigour has exacerbated the continuing debate between institutionalists, on one side, and those whose chief orientation is neoclassical theory, on the other, with the second group emphasizing the operation of equilibrium-seeking market forces and the first stressing imperfections in the market. Yet today, even the institutionalists make greater use of formal analysis and quantitative methods than did their predecessors.

The Economic and Political Context of Manpower Concerns

Labour-market research has been heavily affected by the economic and political events of the last twenty years. Continued unemployment and apparent secular stagnation through the early sixties spurred fears as to whether automation would plunge the United States into a permanent depression and stimulated debate as to whether unemployment was traceable to deficient demand or to structural imbalances. Adherents of the former thesis preached monetary and fiscal policy; those of the structural school believed the solution for both inflation and unemployment to be an active manpower policy on the Swedish model, including a massive retraining programme, measures to increase geographical and occupational mobility, and a more adequate labour-market information system. The emphasis here was on the supply side, and human capital theory was quite consistent with this development.

By the end of the sixties, it was clear that increased demand had done much to reduce unemployment; however, training alone was not enough to eliminate what was left. Overall unemployment rates were reduced below the 4 per cent mark, nevertheless black unemployment remained stubbornly twice that of whites, while there was only a slight reduction in interracial income differentials. In this atmosphere, public policy switched towards greater emphasis on 'affirmative action' in employment and dual labour-market theory became popular in economics. The latter emphasized the demand factor and provided an institutional (but theory-related) explanation of differences in employment and income.

The mid-1970s saw another shift, however, with considerable emphasis being placed on lay-offs and short spells of unemployment as explanations of aggregate unemployment (Vickery, 1977).

Labour Supply and Human Capital Theory

Let us begin, as most labour economists do, with the neoclassical theory of the labour market, which consists of a theory of demand based on the profit-maximizing behaviour of employers and a theory of supply based on household utility maximization. The supply side involves two sets of questions, the first involving the quantity of labour, and the second, its quality. Quantity is determined by the aggregate of individual income–leisure choices regarding labour force *participation* and the supply of work-hours. Quality is determined by a variety of decisions by individuals, employers and government agencies as to how much time and money to invest in skill training. An integrating theme in this approach is the treatment of time as the ultimate scarce resource, so that any labour-supply decision can be analysed from the standpoint of the costs and returns for alternative uses of time.

There has been a variety of recent work on participation rates (Parnes, 1970), much of it policy-related. Theoretical articles, particularly by Mincer (e.g. 1962) and Becker (1965), have suggested that the income–leisure choice is not as simple as classicists once thought: (*a*) the choice must be made from at least four alternatives: 'pure' leisure, 'paid' work, housework, and investment in one's own human capital, (*b*) the relevant decision-making unit is the household, not the individual, (*c*) decisions may take into account expectations over an entire life-cycle, and (*d*) the decision to enter or leave the labour market depends in part on the worker's assessment of the probable wages he may earn from various jobs he might find as compared to the cost of looking for them.

A multitude of empirical studies, using both cross-sectional and longitudinal data, have measured the effect on participation of numerous demographic (age, colour, marital status, etc.) and economic factors (wages, spouse's income, stage of the business cycle, etc. – see especially Bowen and Finnegan (1969)). Of special interest to policy-makers has been the impact of a recession on the size of the labour force. As unemployment increases, do additional workers (especially wives) enter the labour market to make up for lost income, or do workers become discouraged in their job search effort and leave the labour force altogether? Research during the sixties concluded that on balance the 'discouraged worker' exceeds the 'additional worker' effect, leading to severe 'hidden unemployment' (but see Mincer, 1966). Later research was concerned with the question of whether increased female participation would raise the 'natural' rate of unemployment (Hall, 1970; Vickery, Bergmann and Swartz, 1978). Recent theoretical and empirical studies have also examined the extent to which transfer payments (such as the 'negative income tax') might lead low-income employees to reduce their labour force participation (Watts and Rees, 1977; Lewis, 1975).

The question of hours of work involves such issues as whether individuals want to work full time or part time, or whether they are willing to accept overtime or to 'moonlight' (i.e. take a second job). There have been numerous empirical and theoretical studies of these issues by both economists and sociologists (e.g. Dankert, Mann and Northrup, 1965; Kerton, 1971; Perlman, 1966; Finnegan, 1962; Wilensky, 1963). A continuing question here (as with participation) is whether, as wages go up, workers will 'buy' more leisure or accept more work.

The 'human capital theory', the most significant recent development in labour economic theory, burst upon the profession at a propitious moment, when there was great interest in government manpower programmes and when the existence of computers made it feasible to process large amounts of data. By adding an elegant new dimension to market analysis, it brought labour economics back into the mainstream of the economics profession.

The theory formalized (mathematically) and elaborated concepts originally stated by Adam Smith. By treating the cost (or length) of training as essentially a proxy for labour quality (productivity), it added a new element of sophistication to explanations of income distribution, wage levels, manpower flows and the demand for labour (especially Schultz, 1971; Becker, 1964; Mincer, 1974). By contrast with postwar studies which related wages to job categories under the assumption that all workers in a given job category were alike, research today can deal with differences in labour quality (skill) and personal characteristics. A number of predictions based on this theory have turned out to be reasonably accurate, for example with regard to turnover rates. The theory has been used frequently in cost–benefit analyses of government training programmes (though the value of these has been debated) (Dunlop, 1977).

Human capital theory is logical, consistent, and stated in a form in which its influence can be measured. Critics argue, however, that 'its simple elegance, powerful implications, and successful predictions make it easy to sweep under the rug answers incongruous with the theory' (Hamermesh, 1973, p. 231; see also Bowles and Gintis, 1975). Too often, problems are redefined to fit the theory, which is more powerful than the often unreliable data used in its analyses.

A controversy has arisen over the alleged *screening* value of education (Berg, 1970; Arrow, 1973). The evidence suggests that a high-school diploma increases one's income. At least some employers view the diploma as an inexpensive device for screening-out the incompetent, but critics argue that higher returns to education demonstrate that employers *think* education is valuable, not that it is.

Labour Markets in Operation

Human capital theory assumes that workers respond to small changes in economic net benefit and that the labour market serves as an efficient allocation mechanism. Mobility studies test both sets of assumptions, while dual labour-market theory seriously challenges the latter.

Labour mobility

Labour mobility has been intensively studied in the United States. Among the forms of mobility subject to research have been movements between firms, between occupations and between geographical regions. Mobility rates have been compared by age, sex, race, occupation, earnings and a variety of other factors, intended to identify the 'pure' independent effect of each factor, and also to isolate the impact of business-cycle changes. Individuals have been followed through their careers (Parnes, Miljus and Spitz, 1969); studies have been made of patterns of job change (sociologists call these careers), and workers' perceptions of job opportunities and willingness to move have been measured.

Several notable studies during the fifties and sixties examined job-search behaviour after plants had shut down and found it haphazard, particularly for blue-collar workers. The studies suggest substantial pay-offs from the development of an improved labour-market information system which can better link job searchers with job vacancies.

High mobility is traditional in the United States, between regions, occupations and employers. The postwar period brought the growth of unionism, seniority and fringe benefits, especially pensions. Have such developments led to a decline in mobility? Or, as Ross (1958) put it, is the United States on the road to a new industrial feudalism? Research suggests that inter-firm mobility is less today than it was before the war but that the rate has remained fairly stable since 1945 (Parker and Burton, 1967). Unionized firms enjoy lower quit rates than non-union firms, but this can be explained by differences in wage rates (Burton and Parker, 1969; but see Parnes, 1970, pp. 51–2). The mobility-inhibiting effects of pension plans are, at the most, weak.

Dual labour-market theories

Mobility studies indicate that there are substantial imperfections in the labour market, and dual labour-market theories attempt to explain the characteristics of some of these. Doeringer and Piore (e.g. 1971; Piore, 1973) postulate the existence of two labour markets: a primary market characterized by stable employment, strong unions, and well-trained, committed, 'socialized' employees; and a second market with low wages, spotty employment, high turnover and absenteeism, demoralization, and employees (many women and members of minority groups) who lack the technical and *social* skills to succeed in the primary market. Within the primary market, jobs are distributed by collective bargaining and bureaucratic rules (especially seniority) and are subject to labour-market constraints only when the labour market is tight.

Dual labour-market theorists can be divided into at least two groups. The more *conservative* wing attempted to explain the existence of dual labour-markets originally in terms of technology (i.e. certain jobs require a stable, committed labour force) and later in terms of such factors as unionism (the secondary labour force is largely non-union); indeed recent writers view union members as exploiters rather than as exploitees. *Radical* economists (e.g. Gordon, 1972; Edwards, Reich and Gordon, 1973) go well beyond either view. They see the dual labour market and its discrimination against women and minority groups as an inevitable concomitant of monopoly capitalism's efforts to divide the labour force and prevent the formation of working-class consciousness and solidarity. Public policy interventions recommended by the conservative dual-market theorists include expanded public employment, wage subsidies and anti-discrimination, as well as extensive macropolitics to insure full employment (Cain, 1975, p. 22; Doeringer *et al.*, 1972). For radical economists this is thin gruel. Their solution is the wholesale re-ordering of the social and economic system.

These theories, which challenged the neo-orthodox labour-market theories that prevailed *circa* 1970, represented a return to earlier institutional traditions that stressed the role of unionism. Clark Kerr (1954b) introduced the concept of 'Balkanized' labour markets, each with its port of entry and internal labour force (see also Dunlop, 1957). Kerr, of course, was interested in explaining labour markets under collective bargaining. His analysis, particularly its distinction between horizontal (craft) and vertical (industrial) mobility, in some ways goes beyond that of Piore and Doeringer. Piore and Doeringer's description of internal labour markets is in the tradition of Slichter (1941) and Slichter, Healy and Livernash (1960). The analysis of the internal primary market is probably less of a contribution than the theory of the secondary market.

Dual theory has caused much controversy. Supporters argue that it provides a reasonably convincing explanation of many of the imperfections in the labour market, especially the concentration of unemployment among minorities, the relative failure of many training programmes, and the insulation of 'protected' primary markets from labour-market pressures. By contrast with neoclassical theory, dual-market theory views taste for work, not as a given, but as endogenous, something caused by the operation of the labour market. The dual-market theory also provides an explanation of poverty and can potentially be linked up with the work of psychologists and sociologists. Critics contend that it is not appropriate to label the dual-market view a theory (Cain, 1975); they argue that it is at most a description of certain behaviour, but provides no testable explanation of why primary or secondary markets exist (or, if they exist at all), that its propositions, for example with regard to turnover (Flanagan, 1974), are not supported by empirical evidence, and that its 'internal market' is not evidence of market imperfection, but merely an example of specific on-the-job training (Wachter, 1974). Nevertheless by bringing institutional realities, especially the role of unions, back into labour economics, dual-market theory performs a notable service.

Economics of Discrimination

Consistent with developments in society generally, labour economists have shown increasing interest in discrimination, first with racial discrimination and more recently with discrimination based on sex (e.g. Bergmann, 1971).

Theoretical models have been developed which explain discrimination in neoclassical terms. Becker's (1971) model postulated a 'taste for discrimination', a preference for which people were willing to pay (see also Alexis, 1974). Arrow's (1974) model also allows for a presumably inaccurate 'perception of reality'. However, as Marshall (1974) and Cain (1975) convincingly argue, these models contain grave flaws. Since these models assume pure competition, they fail to explain the failure of non-discriminatory employers to drive discriminators out of business. They are inconsistent with research findings (Flanagan, 1974), and they incorrectly assume that the main problem consists of equally qualified employees receiving different wages for the same type of work. The real problem, at least until recently, was that for a variety of institutional reasons minorities were either (*a*) unlikely to become qualified in the first place, or (*b*) not allowed to make on-the-job use of any qualifications they did acquire. Finally, among other limitations, these theories treat discrimination as an exogenous 'given'; dual labour-market theories of discrimination have at least the merits of explaining why discrimination exists. Dual theory, for example, suggests that one reason for discrimination is that unions treat it as a means of job control rather than as a simple 'taste' for avoiding blacks.

Though these ideas have generally been only loosely linked to theory, there have been numerous econometric studies that seek to evaluate the impact of 'pure' discrimination on wages and income. The typical study attempts to determine how much of observed differences in wages between blacks and whites, for example, is due to differences in experience, informal training, education, length of service, geographical location, etc. – and how much can be explained only by discrimination. Such studies are useful in a variety of ways: not only do they provide a means of checking progress in reducing discrimination, but they help to pinpoint critical areas where remedial work is most necessary. However, many of the observed differences in education, etc. are themselves caused by discrimination, and there is now a considerable debate as to the relative significance of discrimination occurring in the labour market (e.g. in extent of training), as opposed to discrimination occurring elsewhere in society (e.g. education and in everyday sex role models).

Wages, Prices, Unemployment and Union Impacts

In the research just discussed, unions occupied only secondary roles.

Other research gives top billing to unions and the impact of union policies. At first, the main concern was with possible 'monopolistic' distortions that unions might introduce into the normal economic processes. As interest in this problem decreased, more attention was given to possible interactions among wages, employment and inflation.

As with labour-market research, there were strong differences between neoclassically oriented scholars, who stressed the inevitability of market forces, and institutionalists who emphasized other factors, especially collective bargaining. Slichter was perhaps the most prominent early proponent of the view that unionism could have a significant effect on both the distribution of income and the rate of inflation. Milton Friedman disputed both points, arguing that 'laymen and economists alike tend, in my view, to exaggerate the extent to which labour unions affect the structure and level of wage rates. . . . The strategic position of unions will be stronger in the short than in the long run' (1951, pp. 204, 209). Friedman was answered by Ulman (1955) and others and, to some extent, this debate set the terms of a discussion which has continued to the present, with the opposing sides ever escalating the theoretical and statistical sophistication of their arguments.

Frequent high levels of unemployment, coupled with growing inflation, spurred interest in Phillips-curve studies of wages, prices and employment on a macro level (Eckstein and Wilson, 1962; Perry, 1966; Pierson, 1968). Research attempts to discover a straightforward inflation–unemployment relationship showed it to be heavily affected by other factors (profits, time-lags, expectations, etc.). A variety of statistical techniques was utilized to disentangle these factors, with many of the techniques themselves becoming the focus of sharp debates. By 1970, it was generally agreed that there was some kind of short-run inverse relationship between inflation and unemployment, but with considerable dispute as to whether the relationship was sufficiently stable to be called a 'curve', and concern over the nature of the interactive mechanisms involved, especially the role of unions. By 1978, the relationship had become quite unclear since both inflation and unemployment were high.

A key question was whether unions contributed to inflation. The evidence suggests that during economic peaks wages generally tend to rise more slowly in the union than in the non-union sector (especially since union contracts tend to run for several years); that profit and employment shifts have less of an effect on wages in unionized industries; and that unions introduce a downwards rigidity that gives an upward bias to wage–price relationships generally. Adding to the confusion here is the debate as to whether non-union wages are determined by changes in union wages, or vice versa (Flanagan, 1976).

Numerous studies (Perry, 1967; Mills, 1975; Mitchell, 1975) attempted to evaluate the effectiveness of the government's efforts to influence wage and price changes via the sixties' wage guideposts and the seventies' wage–price controls (both of which were aimed at unionized industries). Again, the lessons from this research are somewhat conflicting. Controls hardly stopped inflation; however, they may have slowed down or at least postponed wage increases.

Our own view is that, while econometric studies have somewhat advanced our understanding of these phenomena, more attention should be given to institutional factors, including the relationship between trade unions and the government.

Unions and Income Differentials

How does unionism affect income differentials, the percentage of national income going to labour, the relationship between union and non-union wages, and differentials between the earnings of blacks and whites? The first two questions received considerable attention during the fifties. Recent research has made use of more detailed data and more sophisticated statistical tools, yet its results have not seriously disturbed earlier findings.

Though measurement is difficult (Schultze and Weiner, 1964), the early evidence suggests that the percentage of national income going to labour (as opposed to profits, rents, etc.) was remaining stable, or perhaps slightly increasing. Once cyclical impacts were ironed out, the measurable impact of unionism here was slight (Hildebrand, 1958; Simler, 1961). Recent evidence suggests that profits are now falling in many countries; the role of unions in this new development needs to be investigated.

The impact of unionism on wages has been difficult to isolate. There is a substantial impact variation among industries and occupational groups. Unionism in a firm or industry seems to cause a one-time increase in relative wages; aside from this, the aggregate union–non-union wage ratio seems relatively constant (again, aside from cyclical variations). There are some disagreements as to the size of this ratio (e.g. Lewis, 1963; Fuchs, 1968), with estimates ranging from '0 to 20 per cent' (Ashenfelter and Johnson, 1972, p. 505) to over 35 per cent, depending on the occupational groups studied and the methodologies used. Part of the differential can be explained by two factors: high-wage firms are more prone to be organized, and they may counteract their enforced wage increases by insisting on further improving the quality of their labour. Thus 'wages, unionism, and labor quality' may be 'jointly determined' (Ashenfelter and Johnson, 1972, p. 505; but see Kahn, 1977). More recently, economists have begun systematic measurement of union impacts on fringes, productivity and profits.

Early labour economists hoped that unionism would reduce income inequality. Recent evidence casts doubt as to whether this is occurring (Lewis, 1963; Rees, 1963). Johnson and Mieszkowski conclude, 'Most, if not all, of the gains of union labour are made at the expense of nonunionized workers, and not at the expense of earning on capital' (1970). On balance, unionism seems to have increased black wages more than white (Ashenfelter and Johnson, 1972); on the other hand, it may have depressed those of women (Johnson, 1975).

Some Evaluations

One of the most persistent themes in labour economics is the tension between classical (largely marginal) and institutional explanations of labour-market behaviour (Cain, 1975). There is a long tradition here, dating back at least to J. S. Mill's criticism of Adam Smith's classical theory as failing adequately to explain why dirty work was paid less than clean work. The Wisconsin school represented an institutional revolt against the then dominant classic theory, and institutionalists were generally supreme during the Golden Age, despite alternative views expressed by such traditionalists as Machlup (1946) and Rottenberg (1956). The pendulum swings, however. The Chicago school of 'new labour economics', *circa* 1965, was classical with a vengeance and even today its influence dominates the field. Dual labour-market theories – both radical and conventional – represented a reversion to institutionalism.

A synthesis between the two schools is badly needed. Classical theory explains continuities and general tendencies; the institutional approach emphasizes the rigidities and imperfections that prevent these tendencies from being realized. In the short run, perhaps, the rigidities are most important; in the long run it is the continuities. Good research should emphasize both. Unfortunately, however, many younger labour economists are weak on the institutional side. This may be as harmful to the new labour economics as lack of theory has been (in our opinion) to traditional industrial relations. Labour economists today deal with important social issues, but individual studies tend to be rather narrow and their findings dull. Much of current research involves imaginative feats of data manipulation, yet too often this requires specifying the problem in a form that fits the available and often unreliable data and ignores many interesting elements. Despite these limitations, the new labour economics centres its attention on important subjects. Hopefully, it will continue to do so, by combining its present breadth of subject-matter with a wider scope of theory and methodology, and with greater cross-fertilization with other disciplines.

The Behavioural Sciences

During industrial relations' Golden Age, considerable numbers of sociologists, psychologists, and even anthropologists, showed interest in the problems of unionism and collective bargaining. For example, as sociologists Lipset *et al.* (1956) and Wilensky (1956) both made significant contributions to the study of union government. Whyte (1951), using essentially anthropological techniques, focused attention on human interaction patterns within unions and collective bargaining relations. Psychologists such as Purcell (1953) and Rosen and Rosen (1955) studied member attitudes towards their unions.

After 1960, most of these behavioural scientists who showed interest in collective bargaining and unionism switched their attention to other areas. On the other hand, a new field – organizational behaviour – arose which includes large numbers of sociologists and psychologists. Until quite recently they have shown but peripheral interest in collective bargaining problems.

Organizational Behaviour

The field of organizational behaviour is now well established in the United States, although the relationship between the field and industrial relations is somewhat uncertain. It does represent a merger between the two earlier fields of management and human relations. In its early days, management was primarily concerned with formal organizational structure and was heavily influenced by bureaucratic theory and the scientific management movement (e.g. Taylor, 1911). Human relations stemmed largely from the Western Electric Hawthorne experiments of the thirties (Roethlisberger and Dickson, 1939). Its focus was on the informal organization, on Social Man as opposed to Economic or Rational Man, and arose in part as a reaction against the excessive impersonality of contemporary organizational practice.

It became obvious by the sixties that the two approaches were complements rather than substitutes. The traditional management approach of 'organizations without people' (Leavitt, 1965) paid little attention to human needs and motivation and was no longer appropriate in an age of unionism. However, the human relations approach almost exclusively emphasizing interpersonal relations left the nature of work organization itself unchanged.

Organizational behaviour, a term which became common in the early sixties, differed from both *traditional* management and human relations in two important ways. In the first place, it was concerned with both organization (the nature of tasks, structure, reporting relations) and people. Secondly, a number of its advocates recognized that people wanted more than financial rewards, job security, humane treatment and a satisfying social life – the forms of motivation stressed by earlier students.

Human resources

Those who placed primary emphasis on this second factor (McGregor, 1960; Likert, 1967), sometimes called the human resources school (Miles, 1964), argued that beyond physical and social needs, man has the desire to gain recognition and fulfilment from doing meaningful work. Managers, therefore, should redesign jobs, decision-processes and control-systems to provide greater opportunities for gaining a sense of accomplishment from work. Although the human resources approach represents a considerable advance over the simplified human relations approach, for many scholars this is inadequate. Early human resources seemed wedded to finding the 'one best method' appropriate to all situations. It also focused primarily on the work team (the manager and his immediate subordinates), it did not directly address itself to the growing concern for coordination across departmental and hierarchical lines. In part, to answer these two objections, there arose two new lines of research, one of which has become known as the *contingency approach* and the other as *macro-organization*.

Contingency theory

Contingency researchers argue that people differ greatly in their desires and capabilities and that not all jobs require the same degree of motivation or permit equal opportunities for worker self-direction. As a consequence, there have been many studies which seek to specify which forms of motivation, supervisory practices, etc. work best with what sorts of people and what sorts of jobs. From this research has emerged a host of complicated, multivariate models of motivation (Porter and Lawler, 1968), job design (Hackman and Lawler, 1971), leadership (Fiedler, 1967), and departmentalization and coordination (Lawrence and Lorsch, 1967).

Macro-organization

Organizational sociologists went beyond the human relations–human resources emphasis on individual and group relations to consider complex organization and the relationship between organizations and their environment. Macro-organization deals with interrelationships among such variables as structure, technology, control, organizational size, organizational politics, and control of scarce resources. Students of organization – environment relations are concerned with the mechanisms by which the organization adjusts to, and seeks to change, its environment. Organizational sociologists are heavily contingency-oriented. Indeed, one of their fundamental hypotheses is that loose, participative organizational structures are best suited for turbulent, uncertain, unpredictable environments. Tight, controlled, 'autocratic' structures are more appropriate when the environment is stable and predictable. Both contingency theory and organizational sociology are heavily influenced by the pioneering research of European scholars such as Crozier, Woodward, Burns and Stalker, Emery and Trist, and Pugh. The better-known American research in the area has been done by Chandler (1962), Thompson (1967), Lawrence and Lorsch (1967), Blau and Schoenherr (1971) and Pfeffer (1978).

Worker alienation and job enrichment

Job alienation has emerged as an issue of special interest to industrial relations. Beginning about 1970, great attention was given in the popular press to allegations of rapidly increasing worker dissatisfaction with their jobs, especially in mass-production industries. This interest was accentuated by a much publicized government-sponsored report, *Work in America* (1973), advocating widespread work-place reforms. Although available attitudinal (Quinn and Staines, 1978) and behavioural data (Flanagan, Strauss and Ulman, 1974) provide mixed support for the hypothesis that dissatisfaction is increasing, there are clearly many psychologically unrewarding jobs in American society. As a consequence there has been considerable interest in the quality of work life, particularly concerning experiments in job enrichment and the development of autonomous work groups (see especially Walton, 1974; Hackman, 1976), some under joint union– management sponsorship (Trist, Susman and Brown, 1977).

Organization development

Organization development (OD) is concerned with organizational change. At one time, OD consultants were closely identified with sensitivity training (T-groups), and their typical approach to every organizational problem was to seek improvements in the 'interpersonal competence' of the people involved. Today, many of these consultants are contingency-oriented and giving increasing consideration to questions of structure, reward systems, etc. Recently there has been interest in applying OD techniques to labour–management relations.

Industrial Psychology

The relationship between psychology and organizational behaviour is as fuzzy as that between economics and industrial relations. Perhaps a distinction can be drawn between *organizational* psychologists who are interested in such subjects as leadership, motivation, communications and small-group behaviour, and *industrial* psychologists who work in older areas such as selection, training, turnover and fatigue. The main current concern of the latter group is developing selection techniques that withstand legal tests as not being racially or sexually discriminatory.

Other important work deals with the psychological impact of wage and fringe benefits (though little of this is integrated with collective bargaining). As will be discussed below, there have been a few recent studies of the psychological correlations to participation in strikes and grievance processing. In addition, laboratory studies of bargaining have advanced sufficiently to have some relevance for industrial relations. Nevertheless, the sum total contribution of psychology to industrial relations is somewhat thin (Strauss, 1979).

Sociology

From 1960 until very recently, American sociologists have had little to say about such subjects as unionism, collective bargaining, or other aspects of traditional industrial relations. Two exceptions have been the continuing work of Robert Dubin, and Selznick's (1969) study of industrial justice. True, sociologists have contributed to the debate regarding alienation and job satisfaction (Blauner, 1964; Sheppard and Herrick, 1972) and also to careers (Van Maanen, 1977). Some of the studies of underprivileged workers (Liebow, 1967) may have significance for dual labour-market theory. But little of this work has been of direct relevance to labour relations. American industrial sociology has been narrow in its focus; it has been generally 'closed system' in its approach; and it has avoided integrating theories (Hirsch, 1975). There are few American counterparts (an exception: Form, 1976) of the rich European studies which look at the plant social system as a whole, relating the worker to his social and technological environments, and tying these to his attitudes towards the company, union and the job.

Outside industrial sociology, things are more promising. There has been an avalanche of recent studies examining strikes as specific manifestations of collective behaviour (among others, Britt and Galle, 1974; Stern, 1976; Snyder, 1977; Lincoln, 1978) and some work on unions as formal organizations (for a summary, see Strauss, 1977).

Labour History

General Developments

The founders of American industrial relations research combined labour history with institutional labour economics in the grand tradition of the Webbs in England. Much valuable research was done during the period 1890–1933 in such schools as Johns Hopkins, Columbia and Wisconsin, with the crowning glory of the period being the previously mentioned work by Commons and his associates. The Wisconsin school tended to be strictly chronological, but those in the Johns Hopkins school wrote economic history (for an analysis, see Galenson, 1957). Interest in labour history declined after the New Deal in the early thirties, although much important research was still done by those steeped in the Wisconsin (e.g. Taft, 1951) and Hopkins traditions (Ulman, 1955).

Some of the most interesting recent writing (e.g. Bernstein, 1960, 1969; Derber, 1970) is anchored in social and intellectual as well as economic history. By and large, however, industrial relations specialists have lost interest in historical subjects, leaving these matters to professional historians. One symptom of this change is that the proportion of *Labour History* contributors identified as historians has more than doubled since the journal's establishment in 1960.

Union history

There have been some recent attempts to survey the entire chronological panorama of the United States labour movement (Dulles, 1960; Pelling, 1960; Taft, 1964); the books highlight main trends but offer relatively little analysis. In addition, there have been some books which treat particular time-periods in some detail (Millis and Brown, 1950; Seidman, 1953; Galenson, 1960). Others look at particular unions or industries: e.g. needle trades (Carpenter, 1972); carpenters (Christie, 1956); longshoring (Jensen, 1974); airline pilots (Hopkins, 1971); and automobiles (Fine, 1963). A common theme, through much of this work, relates to how changes in labour and product markets has led to increased concentration of power not only in the international union but also in the hands of international officers (for a good statement of this theme, see Ulman, 1955).

A related, but somewhat separate line of writing consists of union leader biographies, a genre which seems to be holding up well over time. The autobiographies of Powderly (1940) and Gompers (1943) still make good reading. Other relevant work deals with such leaders as Reuther (Howe and Widick, 1949); Lewis (Alinsky, 1949; Dubofsky and Van Tine, 1977); Hillman (Josephson, 1952) and Bridges (Larrowe, 1972). Some of these studies have provided more insight into union operations than have the more general historical studies. The best of this category is the James and James (1965) insightful investigation of Hoffa's rise to power.

Working-class history

Increasingly, labour history is being written by historians who lack the
strong interest in unions as institutions which characterized the work of
those previously mentioned. This new labour history might better be
known as working-class history; it is part of a broad reaction among
historians against political history or history focused on great men or
great events. Its concern is with the average man, with recapturing the
life-style and values of earlier working-class generations. Historians of
this school seize their data where they can – from church registries,
original census records, military muster rolls, newspaper want ads, and
the like. Unions are not ignored by such studies, but the emphasis is on
their members, not the institution itself. Although economic, intellectual
and technological factors receive considerable attention, this is really
social history (e.g. Gutman, 1976; Van Tine, 1973; Brody, 1979). The
theme of much of this work relates to resistance to underutilization and
loss of skill (e.g., Nelson, 1975; Montgomery, 1976).

There is a radical 'revisionist' wing among American historians, but
despite the appeal of the working class as a topic, there has been
relatively little written by radical labour historians to date (for one
example, see Aronowitz, 1974; for an older Marxian genre, see Foner,
1947, 1965). On the other hand, there has been considerable interest in
explanations as to why American unionism turned to job consciousness
rather than socialism during its formative stage (e.g. Laslett, 1970). An
important book (Cochran, 1977) dispassionately examines the role of
communism in American unions.

Labour Law

Just as labour history has become increasingly the province of
historians, so labour law has become the province of lawyers. The
primary focus is on technical details rather than questions of policy. The
present situation represents a marked change from the not-too-distant
past. During the infancy of industrial relations and in the Golden Age,
both lawyers and non-lawyers (e.g. Commons, Witte, Millis, Slichter)
played a major role in the debate that helped formulate the basic
principles of United States labour law. This debate, which perhaps
reached its zenith with the passage of the Taft–Hartley Act in 1947, is
now largely stilled. This quiescence in what for one hundred years had

been a major national debate reflected the stability of American labour relations. Except for a 1974 law bringing non-profit hospitals under the national regulatory scheme, no legislation aimed at the labour relations *process* has been passed since 1959. (In 1978, an unsuccessful attempt was made to pass a labour reform act which might have made it easier for unions to win NLRB elections. Although of considerable symbolic significance, the proposed law would not have materially affected bargaining procedures once a union was certified.)

Since the main legal structure is firmly established, the focus has shifted to the technical details of statutory administration and interpretation (for a review, see Aaron and Meyer, 1971). Substantively, some of the recent writing deals with NLRB procedures, studying means of coping with the board's exploding work-load and with the adequacy of its remedies. The bulk of the significant work, however, has been concerned with harmonizing conflicting policy *objectives* and reconciling different adjudicatory *systems*. A large share of this research has focused on the provisions of collective bargaining agreements and the requirements of national policies regarding such issues as equal employment and safety. Such issues often involve the relative responsibilities of arbitrators, courts and the NLRB.

There have been few attempts to deal with labour law in broad terms. Gregory (1958) analysed the dilemmas underlying the development of the law, and Cohen (1961) sought to develop a theory that would account for the timing and the nature of changes in national labour policy. Cox (1960) specified the major problems in each principal area of public policy regulation. Wellington (1968) provided a broad overview of how unions and collective bargaining are regulated, and his major theme seemed to be that less legal regulation is desirable. His conclusion reinforced the judgements of an earlier group of well-known industrial relations scholars (Independent Study Group, 1960). Whether or not one agrees with Wellington, his is one of the few works to raise fundamental questions as to how unions and collective bargaining should be regulated. Another is Feller's (1973) attempt to develop a general legal theory of the collective bargaining agreement which will consistently relate the rights and obligations of employers, employees and unions under the labour contract.

A general criticism of labour law writers involves the values and biases they bring to their analyses. Most writers seem to accept the basic outlines of our regulatory system, which means that there are very few assessments of the legal, economic and behavioural premises on which the system is based (see Roomkin and Abrams' (1977) proposal to establish an NLRB behavioural research unit). For instance, do collective bargaining mechanisms work well or poorly in spite of or because of the laws which regulate them? A second criticism is that relatively little labour law writing is interdisciplinary. Exceptions to this tendency include Bok's (1964) use of social psychological findings to examine the probable impact of union organizing tactics, Meltzer's (1965) use of economic data in his analysis of union activity and the antitrust laws, Philip Ross's (1965) empirical examination of NLRB good-faith bargaining requirements, and Getman, Goldberg and Herman's (1976) major new study of worker reactions to union and management campaign practices during NLRB elections.

In contrast to the dominance of lawyers in the settled areas of private-sector labour law, non-lawyers are reasonably active in the two key unsettled public policy areas of the seventies – public-sector labour relations and employment discrimination.

The public sector

Research here reflects issues that have long been studied in the private sector, especially those relating to dispute settlement procedures and the scope of bargaining. The fundamental question is the degree to which governmental labour relations systems should resemble those of the private sector. The jurisdictional diversity (fifty States and countless municipalities) of the existing systems provides a substantial body of data for scholars to mine.

Employment discrimination

The other 'hot' area of labour law research is employment discrimination. The various regulations, especially Executive Order 11246 (affecting government contractors) and Title VII of the 1964 Civil Rights Act, represent the government's strongest intervention yet on the demand side of the labour market. The blanket prohibitions of discriminatory activities and the vigorous enforcement of these prohibitions by government agencies and the courts have resulted in considerable turmoil in many organizations as established hiring, assignment, promotion and pay practices have come under attack. (This turmoil bears considerable resemblance to the late-thirties' turmoil in those companies experiencing first-time union organizing pressures under the aegis of the new national labour policy.)

This turbulence has given scholars a great deal to write about (e.g. Gould, 1977). Psychologists have reported the difficulties of developing non-discriminatory selection tests. Lawyers naturally have focused on the substance of government regulations and court decisions, with a critical dispute over the question of how far the law should require 'compensatory discrimination' to remedy past discriminatory practices (compare Sovern, 1966 and Gould, 1967). Unfortunately there has been almost no cross-fertilization of ideas or dialogue between disciplines (for example, between psychologists and lawyers regarding the development of appropriate criteria for determining whether specific selection techniques are non-discriminatory). With few exceptions, traditional industrial relations scholars have ignored the implications of affirmative action programmes (but see Hausmann *et al.*, eds., 1977).

With this brief discussion of the contributions of the basic disciplines – economics, the behavioural sciences, history and law – to industrial relations, we turn to three 'mainstream' areas: collective bargaining, unions and manpower. With varying emphasis over the years, each area has been the subject of much industrial relations research.

Collective Bargaining

Although collective bargaining receives less attention today than it did during the Golden Age, a substantial amount of research in this area is still being done. This can be classified under four headings: structure, process, issues and the public sector.

Bargaining Structures

Bargaining structure (which might be loosely defined as involving regularized patterns of union–management interaction and influence) has been the subject of much attention, primarily because of the US emphasis on exclusive jurisdiction and bargaining rights. This issue blossomed in the late thirties and forties largely on account of the craft versus industrial contests between the AFL and CIO, the postwar strike wave which dramatically illustrated the huge size of some negotiation units, and the fact that many bargained wage settlements were inter-linked via patterned relationships.

During the fifties, industrial relations scholars examined different structural issues (industry-wide bargaining, centralized bargaining, decision-making, union representational policies), and the realization grew that bargaining structures were complex. These varied con-siderably from industry to industry and encompassed many more dimensions than the NLRB's determination of an 'appropriate unit'. Dunlop's analyses (1958, 1961) suggested that any set of structural arrangements in a particular industry can be fully understood only as a part of the entire industrial relations system in that industry.

Bargaining structure evolved into a formal analytical concept with Weber's analyses (1961, 1967) of the various structural components (election districts, negotiation units, etc.) and determinants (market factors, power considerations, public policy, etc.). Weber's writings reflect the primary interest of most writers in this area: how do structural arrangements vary across industries and what are the determinants of these variations? Clearly, market structure (both of the product and the labour market) plays the major role, but historical accidents (such as which union organized the industry first), political rivalries between unions, technological change, and the vagaries of NLRB policy, all influence the process.

Authors have written about the centralization and decentralization in negotiation of various bargaining issues (Weber, 1967; Chamberlain, 1961), mergers on both the corporate and union sides of the table (Alexander, 1971; Shils, 1971), union attempts to accommodate diver-gent interests within the bargaining unit (Weber, 1963), the fragmented nature of craft bargaining structures (Chandler, 1967), and strikes to change the structure of bargaining (Dunlop, 1967). Recent attention has been given to decentralization of bargaining in the steel and automobile industries and to its centralization in construction. All these issues have significant impact on the parties' relative bargaining powers.

The spread of collective bargaining to the public sector has given rise to a considerable literature dealing with structural questions. Into how many bargaining units should the employees of a given governmental unit be divided? Should supervisors be given the right to bargain? Should they be included in the same unit as their subordinates? Should policemen and firemen be paid the same amount? Should municipalities or school districts in the same geographical area coordinate their bargaining efforts?

Most structural research has been concentrated on the union side, and little has been written about employer organization for bargaining. 'How to do it' manuals for management abound, but the few academic studies of the decision-making process from management's point of view have been concerned chiefly with employers' associations and the relative power of the industrial relations staff as opposed to line management (Myers and Turnbull, 1956; Ritzer and Trice, 1969; Goldner, 1970; Freedman, 1979).

Collective Bargaining Process

The collective bargaining process is perhaps the heart of industrial relations. Unfortunately, the scholarly approach to bargaining is somewhat disorganized, ranging from highly abstract attempts to develop a theory of bargaining to purely descriptive accounts of the latest negotiated settlement. We have bits and pieces of knowledge and insight, but little integration of the separate elements.

Industrial relations climate

During the late forties and fifties, there was an outpouring of literature on the 'character of the union–management relationship'. Some of this material consisted of intensive case-study analyses (sponsored by the National Planning Association) to see why various labour–management relationships were harmonious or conflict-ridden, while others sought to classify different relationships according to degree of conflict (Bakke, 1946; Selekman, 1949). Perhaps the most useful of the latter was Harbison and Coleman's (1951) distinction between what they called armed truce, working harmony and union–management cooperation (the first two being akin to Walton and McKersie's (1965) distinction between distributive and integrative bargaining). There was increasing agreement among the authors that sound industrial relations depended on more than good will; it also required the development of effective bargaining techniques (Garfield and Whyte, 1953) and probably also an appropriate economic and social environment, e.g. industrial strife is more likely to occur in a pattern-leading than in a pattern-following industry (Harbison and Dubin, 1947) or where workers live isolated from the rest of society, as on shipboard or in mines (Kerr and Siegel, 1954). In any case it was clear that industrial relations had to be viewed in systems terms: social and economic conditions, attitudes, behaviour and patterns of human interaction all affect each other (Whyte, 1951; Dunlop, 1958).

Bargaining power

Collective bargaining involves the use of power, and there have been numerous attempts to develop a theory of bargaining power. Chamberlain (1951) advanced the widely used concept that bargaining power involved the ability to manipulate the adversary's costs of agreement and disagreement, but his concept has proved too general to be tested empirically. Kuhn (1964) analysed the forces affecting the favourableness of the parties' negotiating positions and the manoeuvring that occurs during negotiations. Somers (1969) carried this dichotomy further by separating collective bargaining power into an objective notion of a negotiating position determined by environmental factors and a subjective notion of a propensity to withhold labour services.

Union goals

A related line of inquiry has sought to answer the question: what do unions really want? This body of writing dates back to the late forties' debate over whether unions were primarily political (Ross, 1948) or economic (Dunlop, 1944) organizations (Kerr, 1978). In the forties and fifties, there was considerable interest in 'pattern' bargaining, as union wage goals seemed to be determined by bargained settlements elsewhere. Later, Levinson (1966) closely examined the relative importance of economic and political goals in six industries. Ashenfelter and Johnson (1969) developed a formal, three-party model of the bargaining process based on interactions between employers, union leaders and members; Mitchell (1972) tried to reconcile the political and economic interpretations with the concept of employer resistance, and Atherton (1973) proposed a rigorous theory of union bargaining goals. This line of inquiry has yielded some useful concepts, especially the distinction between the goals of the union members and the leaders, and the idea that 'orbits of coercive comparisons' shape member goals and constrain leader behaviour.

Negotiations

Power is exercised and goals are achieved through negotiations. The negotiation process has yet to be adequately studied. Research is difficult because the critical episodes usually occur in private and the presence of an outside observer may well affect the result. A variety of research methods has been utilized: observation (Ann Douglas, 1962), reconstruction from archival data (Comay, Melnik and Subotnik, 1974), questionnaires completed by negotiators (Tracy, 1974), laboratory experiments with labour and/or management negotiators (Balke, Hammond and Meyer, 1973), and experimental manipulations of negotiating behaviour under laboratory conditions (to be discussed). All these methods have their advantages and disadvantages, and all differ in the degree to which they sacrifice institutional reality for methodological controls, or vice versa. Economists and psychologists are both interested in bargaining, but until recently there was little convergence in their approaches.

Economic models

Collective bargaining research originally developed within the province of economics, and most attempts to develop bargaining theories have been made by researchers with backgrounds in economics. There has been a steady stream of efforts by game and decision theorists to develop a rigorous (i.e. mathematical) model of bargaining going back at least to Zeuthen (1930) and continuing through Nash (1950), Harsanyi (1956) and Cross (1965).

Specific models of the collective bargaining process started with the still-classic work of Hicks (1932) and have been developed since then by Pen (1959), Stevens (1963), Walton and McKersie (1965) and Cross (1969). These latter attempts not only were concerned with the economists' utility curves and outcome points, they incorporated such psychological and decision elements as expectations and risk-taking preferences. Schelling (1956), Stevens (1963) and Chamberlain and Kuhn (1965), for example, have been concerned with the path by which agreement is reached, as well as the result of the process. Some attempts have been made to test these models either through laboratory experiments or through comparing predicted results with real-world data, such as strike rates. As a result, the more recent bargaining models seem closer to reality in their awareness of both economic and psychological variables, though the economists' primary orientation seems to be with some quantifiable measure of the bargaining outcome (usually the wage rate) rather than the process itself. Further, many of these models ignore the social, economic and institutional context within which bargaining takes place.

Psychological approaches

Of late, psychologists and organizational behaviour scholars have become increasingly concerned with conflict and conflict resolution (Deutsch, 1973; Rubin and Brown, 1975). Unfortunately, they have made few attempts to apply these theories to industrial relations; nor have industrial relations scholars shown much interest in them.

Understandably, the psychologists' approach differs considerably from that of economists. Economists generally assume that the root cause of conflict is scarcity, the desire to increase income or utility in situations where resources are limited. Psychologists, for their part, emphasize lack of understanding, inadequate information, and emotional barriers. Psychologists seek to reduce or eliminate the *causes* of conflict; industrial relations people are more interested in conflict as a *process* and, specifically in methods of containing and limiting it. Economists are concerned with the 'quantity' of the bargaining solution, especially if it can be expressed in monetary terms; psychologists are more interested in the solution's 'quality', e.g. whether it is accepted by the parties and will strengthen their long-run relationships.

Although economists have shown some interest in *how* a bargaining solution is reached, psychologists have much richer theories as to the processes involved. Their concern is with attitudes and communications. Though much psychological research has dealt with situations considerably less complex than the typical bargaining relationship and has assumed essential harmony between the parties, recently psychologists have shown increasing concern with power, 'real' differences of interest, and institutional as well as interpersonal factors. Recent psychological research can be divided into two streams:

(1) Laboratory experiments (often using undergraduate students as subjects) are directed chiefly towards the development of a general theory of bargaining which might be appropriate in a variety of situations (for summaries see Deutsch, 1973; Rubin and Brown, 1975;

Magenau and Pruitt, 1979). There are numerous problems with research of this sort. External environments are difficult to simulate; the most commonly used laboratory games make it difficult to observe the various phases through which 'real life' bargaining goes; and even at best, the games remotely reproduce reality. Recently, however, greater complexity and reality have been introduced into the experiments. Inter-party trust has been manipulated, suggesting the equivalent of past history. Game conditions have been changed, so that each move is affected by previous moves, thus simulating the need to maintain a long-term relationship. Games have been played before audiences and the parties in various degrees made responsible to 'constituencies'. Third-party mediators have been introduced. Communications channels have been constricted, enlarged or distorted, power differences simulated, time-limits imposed, and small rewards provided. Thus some progress has been made towards reproducing the reality of union–management relations (for example, see Notz and Starke, 1978).

(2) Organization development specialists are greatly concerned with conflict resolution techniques. Their approach stresses the development of personal and group skills for making communications more honest and more open. If organizational development people had their way, dispute settlement would be converted from 'win–lose' to 'problem-solving', a process which would transform 'distributive' bargaining into 'integrative' bargaining. There have been only a limited number of attempts to apply these approaches to labour–management relations (Blake, Sheppard and Mouton, 1964; Lewicki and Alderfer, 1973), and to date they have only limited value for collective bargaining (Strauss, 1977). On the other hand, the research of Walton (1969) and Lawrence and Lorsch (1967), particularly with regard to third-party 'facilitators' (mediators), is extremely relevant, even though their work has so far been confined largely to management.

Walton and McKersie's landmark *Behavioral Theory of Labor Negotiations* (1965) represented an ambitious attempt to formulate a general theory of negotiations, linking together in a single package game theory (from economics), the behavioural theories of conflict and bargaining and institutional collective bargaining. Though the authors' terminology has entered the language, there have been few attempts as yet to test their hypotheses (but see Peterson and Tracy, 1977).

Aside from negotiations, the bargaining process, broadly viewed, also involves strikes, impasse procedures and contract administration.

Strikes and contract rejection

The strike represents partial failure of negotiations (though it may also be viewed as an essential part of the bargaining process). Since strike activity can be measured, there has been a stream of research focusing on the measures and determinants of strike activity, including some recent work by sociologists (as mentioned above), psychologists (Herman, 1977) and a political scientist (Hibbs, 1976). The weight of the evidence (Weintraub, 1966; Skeels, 1971; Walsh, 1975) suggests that strikes in the United States and Canada are more likely to occur during a time of prosperity. Other researchers have investigated possible connections between strike activity and such variables as technology, community character, union structure and plant size (Gifford, 1974; Eisele, 1974; Butler, 1976; Roomkin, 1976; Lincoln, 1978). Another form of negotiation failure occurs when the union members reject a contract negotiated by their leaders. A number of writers have tried to explain this phenomenon (Summers, 1967; Simkin, 1968; Odewahn and Krisov, 1973). Recently there has been considerable interest in the shape of strikes – their frequency, average duration, and breadth (number of workers involved). See, for example, Stern (1978).

Impasse procedures

Given the cost of strikes, there has been considerable attention on alternative methods of reducing their incidence. Lovell (1952), Kerr (1954a) and Stevens (1967) contributed substantially to understanding the skills of the mediator and the conditions under which his interventions might be successful. There have been few recent studies of the mediation process (see Rehmus, 1965). During the mid-1950s, there was urgent concern with 'emergency strikes' which might jeopardize public health and safety. Among mechanisms proposed to deal with these were compulsory arbitration, 'cooling-off' periods, partial strikes and government seizure of affected properties (Chamberlain and Schilling, 1954; Bernstein, Enarson and Fleming (eds.), 1955).

With the growth of public-sector bargaining, unions and management have been experimenting with a variety of forms of innovative mediation, fact-finding and arbitration processes (Gilroy and Sinicropi, 1972; Feuille, 1975; Anderson and Kochan, 1977). For the most part these techniques involve either third-party decision-making or restrictions on the economic weapons available to the parties.

Contract administration

'Contract administration' refers to the handling of disagreements which may arise *during* the life of the contract, especially the processing of grievances. Most of the discussion has emphasized the final and most visible stage, arbitration. Relatively little attention has been given to the earlier stages of the grievance procedure, or to the forms of bargaining and international union politics associated with them (but see Sayles and Strauss, 1953, Kuhn, 1961), yet it is clear that the success of a particular grievance depends on the psychological meaning of the grievance procedure to the participants (Glassman and Belasco, 1975), as well as the social support which it receives (Sayles, 1958; Ronan, 1963).

The voluminous arbitration literature is devoted primarily to analyses of specific contract issues (Slichter, Healy and Livernash, 1960; Cullen and Greenbaum, 1966; Baer, 1972), to descriptions of various functional aspects of the arbitration procedure itself (Prasow and Peters, 1970; Elkouri and Elkouri, 1973), or to the judicial philosophy of specific arbitrators (Yaffe, 1974). Together these elements combine to form the field of 'industrial jurisprudence'. A continuing set of themes throughout this literature relates to the balancing of organisational efficiency with humanity and of stability (and predictability) with flexibility. Recently there has been great concern with the growing conflict between arbitration, as a means of dispute resolution, and the requirements of various laws regulating equal employment and safety (e.g. Feller, 1977).

The literature suggests that grievance and arbitration procedures serve the interests of the parties well, that there are relatively few 'distressed' procedures (Ross, 1963), that the manner in which contracts are administered reaches an equitable balance between the interests of employees in security and the interest of employers in efficiency (Slichter, Healy and Livernash, 1960), and, in short, that arbitration represents one of the outstanding success areas of United States industrial relations. There has been relatively little literature which challenges this conventional wisdom (for an exception, see Hays, 1966). This near-unanimity of opinion is perhaps understandable given the fact that most of the authors involved are arbitrators.

Evaluation

The collective bargaining process and its component parts have been studied from a variety of points of view, from the legal to the psychological. The common concern of the research has been to increase the efficiency of the conflict-resolution process. Though there is general agreement that collective bargaining is a system (and that each part has to be studied in the context of the whole), there are few recent authors who have done this. Walton and McKersie (1965), Dunlop (1958) and Chamberlain (1951) may be exceptions to this statement, but one has to go back to the case studies of 1945–55 to find an attempt to present the picture as a whole. Case studies, however, tend to give substantial weight to idiosyncratic elements. Further, there seems to be a clear gap between labour relations scholars studying collective bargaining and scholars studying bargaining in such arenas as civil rights and international relations (for one exception, see Chalmers and Cormick, 1971). In the bargaining field, above all, the interdisciplinary cross-fertilization, which once characterized industrial relations, is urgently required again. Fortunately, as we mentioned earlier, recent developments – especially the wave of strike studies by scholars from a variety of disciplines, and the experimental, field and theoretical research on bargaining, mediation and arbitration – all give us hope that a renaissance is under way.

Bargaining Issues

Much of the research literature has been issue-oriented rather than process-oriented. The unifying theme running through the research on issues has been the extent to which the unions have been able to exert influence on the terms of employment.

Wages

A substantial amount of wage research has been done in recent years (see Livernash, 1970, for a review). The main question has been the unions' impact on relative wages, wage structures and wage determination processes. Do key union contracts set a pattern which the rest of the economy follows, or are these contracts themselves determined by more fundamental economic forces? Although labour economists have moved from institutional descriptions to theoretical formulations which are tested by various regression equations (Flanagan, 1976), useful insights concerning union effectiveness can still be obtained from historical and institutional studies of specific companies and industries (e.g. James and James, 1965; Ozanne, 1968; and especially Levinson, 1966). Even at the industrial level, quantitative studies are becoming more common (Mills, 1972).

Other research has investigated a union's impact on wage systems *within* the firm (Slichter, Healy and Livernash, 1960), including job evaluation and incentive pay plans. More recently, economists have looked at organizational wage determination and job allocation processes within the analytical construct of the internal labour market (Doeringer and Piore, 1971). Organizational behaviour groups have expressed considerable interest in the psychological aspects of pay systems, and in how payment methods are related to job performance and satisfaction (Lawler, 1971). As with conflict resolution research, there is little cross-fertilization between fields (but see Belcher, 1974). Yet behavioural scientists should have much to say regarding how union members and unions (as political institutions) make and react to 'coercive comparisons' (Patchen, 1961).

Fringe benefits

The fringe-benefit literature is very large, but much of this is technical or descriptive and directed to the practioner (e.g. the journal *Compensation Review*). The major fringe-benefit issue addressed by academic research has been the impact of fringe benefits on labour mobility (Garbarino, 1964). There have also been studies on the unions' role in the growth of fringe benefits (Slichter, Healy and Livernash, 1960) and of union–non-union differentials (Davis and David, 1968). Mabry (1973) presented a 'theory of fringe benefits' which generated numerous testable hypotheses, but its main thrust seems to be that fringe benefits have increased because employers, employees and unions like them.

Management of the work effort

The rapid spread of union contracts during the thirties, forties and fifties produced a large body of literature dealing with the unions' impact on management's ability to manage its human resources in an efficient and equitable manner and, especially, to introduce technological change. In addition to such all-inclusive studies as Slichter, Healy and Livernash's *magnum opus* (1960), empirical studies have dealt with subcontracting (Chandler, 1964), grievance bargaining (Kuhn, 1961), the impact of building trades on productivity (Haber and Levinson, 1956) and the relationship between union bargaining strength and work rules in construction (Strauss, 1958) and manufacturing (Strauss, 1962). Union–management attempts to adjust to technological change were also extensively studied (Somers, Cushman and Weinberg, 1963), with special attention being given to what might be called 'productivity agreements' in Europe (e.g. Healy, 1965), particularly in West-Coast longshoring (Hartman, 1969), in which unions agreed to relax work rules in exchange for substantial economic gains. Though recently there have been a new series of such agreements, notably in railroads and printing, these have received little academic attention. On the other hand, there has been considerable interest in 'ability to manage' in the public sector (Stanley, 1972).

Participation

Outside the United States, 'participation' usually refers to *formal* schemes for worker participation in management, often through representation on works councils or company management boards. In the United States, by contrast, 'participation' is normally considered managerial 'style' (Likert, 1967; McGregor, 1960) and is primarily concerned with relations between subordinates and their direct bosses. (For a left-wing American work which takes a European viewpoint, see Hunnius *et al.*, 1973.)

European-style worker participation is not completely unknown in the United States. Union–management productivity committees existed during the twenties and the Second World War (Slichter, 1941; de Schweintiz, 1949). The Scanlon plan has persisted in a select group of unionized companies for over thirty years. This plan combines a group incentive system with departmental worker committees whose function it is to recommend methods of improving productivity (Lesieur, 1958; Frost, Wakeley and Ruh, 1974). As mentioned earlier there have been a number of recent carefully monitored joint union–management programmes to improve quality of work life (Trist, Susman and Brown 1977).

The Public Sector

Although labour relations research has been in a state of relative decline, a chief exception is the government. Public sector collective bargaining came late in the United States. There was an explosive growth in public unionism during the sixties and seventies, followed by the acceptance of various forms of collective bargaining at different governmental levels, notably in the large cities. Accompanying this growth has been an upsurge in research interest, much of it government- or foundation-funded (for a review, see Jones, 1975).

Much of the writing in this field has been concerned with whether the differences between public and private sectors were so great as to make public collective bargaining inappropriate. Early authors assumed this as a matter of course. In the sixties, numerous others took the opposite position, i.e. that the differences were insignificant. Increasingly there has been a realization that collective bargaining docs exist in the public sector, but that it takes a different character from that in private industry. The main debate then shifted to the question of how great this difference is (or should be). The most provocative work of this genre is Wellington and Winter's highly controversial book (1971), which concludes that public-sector bargaining mechanisms should differ substantially from those in the private sector.

Early research merely reported on the extent of organization, and described formal rules or argued inductively. As bargaining spread, however, researchers increasingly began to turn out union impact studies: on personnel decision-making (Burton, 1972); on wage determination processes (Derber *et al.*, 1973); on union wage impacts (Lipsky and Drotning, 1973; Ehrenberg, 1973, etc.) and the union's role in managing the work force and formulating policy (Stanley with Cooper, 1972; Juris and Feuille, 1973; Perry and Wildman, 1970). Other authors have dealt with the ground rules under which bargaining occurs, and numerous articles have appeared concerning specific issues as they have emerged one by one: recognition, duty to bargain, union security, right to strike, the multilateral nature of the bargaining process (Feuille, 1974; Kochan, 1974), and the environmental variables associated with bargaining outcomes (Kochan and Wheeler, 1975). A high percentage of the research has related to fire-fighters and police.

Public collective bargaining differs most visibly from the private sector by (generally) prohibiting strikes and substituting third-party procedures to resolve negotiating impasses. As a result, most jurisdictions with lengthy bargaining histories have accumulated substantial experience with various forms of mediation, fact-finding and arbitration. In turn, these procedures have attracted a lot of research attention, with the lion's share of this effort focused upon arbitration (for one example, see the 'public-sector impasses' symposium in

Industrial Relations, October 1977). The two primary concerns of these investigations have been the procedures' impacts upon bargaining outcomes (do employees get more with arbitration than without it?) and upon the health of the bargaining process (do these procedures cause the parties to bargain less diligently?). Some of this research has had a direct impact on public-sector labour relations policy (Kochan, 1978) and most of it has shown that collective bargaining can function without the right to strike. As long as public strike prohibitions exist, these impasse procedures will form the most visible segment of governmental labour relations research (and perhaps of labour relations research generally).

Research on Unions

Research on problems related to the growth, organizing, government and political activity of unions has undergone the steepest decline of all the subject matter discussed here, although there are recent signs of an upswing.

Union growth and development

The literature dealing with union growth traces its ancestry back to the early attempts by writers such as Marx, Commons, Tannenbaum and Perlman to develop 'theories of the labour movement' which would explain why workers organized into collectivities, how unions developed, what functions they performed, and how they fit into the larger society.

Modern versions of this literature date to the mid-1950s, when scholars began to argue whether the slow-down in union growth, which occurred about that time, was permanent or not. Numerous authors debated the reasons for previous union expansion and then stagnation and issued prognostications (see Ginsburg, 1970, for a review). An influential school of left-wing intellectuals (e.g. Jacobs, 1963) argued that labour was suffering from premature hardening of the arteries. Most writers failed to foresee the spread of unionism among public employees in the late sixties and seventies. More recently, Ashenfelter and Pencavel (1969) reported good results in explaining union growth by specifying their variables in a regression equation, but their results added little explanatory power to the previous studies. Northrup and

Foster (1975) discuss the growth of non-union work in construction, a process which may also be seen in other industries.

Union government

In the early days, it was difficult to distinguish between studies of collective bargaining, labour history and union government. Although these early studies of unions were primarily descriptive, there was some explicit or implicit analysis, as in Hoxie's classification of unions by central purpose (1917).

Immediately after the Second World War, unions and union government were the subject of much interdisciplinary attention, with a notable group of sociologists and psychologists studying the attitudes and behaviour of union members, officers and work groups at the local level (for a review, see Strauss, 1977). There was a second wave of interest around 1960, this time with an emphasis on structural issues related to trade union democracy, especially in national and large local unions (see particularly Galenson (ed.), 1962). Since that time the subject has been largely ignored except by a few sociologists studying unions as examples of formal organizations (e.g. Edelstein and Warner, 1976). Quite recently, however, there has been a revival of interest by psychologists (Anderson, 1978).

Among the subjects of special interest have been the following: worker attitudes towards collective bargaining in general and their union in particular; the determinants of participation, especially in local meetings; the relationships between local and national unions; and the protection of individual member's rights. Implicitly or explicitly most studies have been concerned with normative and descriptive questions relating to union democracy, and many have sought to discover the conditions under which Michel's '*iron law of oligarchy*' might or might not work. Much of the debate converges on two alternative approaches to democracy, an informal approach, concerned with the existence of an occupational community with which a member can identify and participate (see especially Lipset, Trow and Coleman, 1956), and a structural approach concerned with formal arrangements which facilitate the development of power bases independent of the top leadership (e.g. Edelstein and Warner, 1976).

Obviously unions deserve renewed research interest. Much has happened since the early wave of union studies, making even replications of the old studies worth while. Furthermore, the period since

1960 has seen the development of a host of new methodologies (e.g. multivariate analysis) and new conceptual tools which can be applied to unions (e.g. Freeman and Brittain's (1977) study of union mergers in terms of the new sociological theory of organizational ecology). Representation theory, a political science concept (e.g. Pitkin, 1968), and the theory of boundary relationship management (Thompson, 1967) are both relevant here.

Unions and politics

American unions shed their traditional non-political stance during the New Deal. Today, unions are one of the key private-interest groups affecting political candidates and issues. Union political activities generally have a pragmatic focus (strengthening barriers against competition by non-members, or improving power positions *vis-à-vis* employers) rather than an ideological one (a workers' government). Nevertheless they have been in the forefront of recent campaigns for progressive social legislation; and electorally they are almost continually engaged in campaigns to elect friendly politicians at all levels. Although American unions have no official political ties, there are substantial *de facto* affiliations with the Democrats (Greenstone, 1969).

The relatively small amount of academic attention that union political activities have received has come mainly from political scientists, who tend to view unions as just another pressure group. There are analyses of union involvement in a variety of political affairs (Rehmus and McLaughlin, 1967), of the limitations inherent in such involvement (Greenstone, 1969), of how union members vote (Wolfe, 1969; Kornhauser, Sheppard and Mayer, 1956), of how union political action campaigns are organized (Calkins, 1955), and of how unions have tried to influence labour legislation (McAdams, 1964), with some of this material written as 'muck-rakerism' (Caddy, 1974).

Manpower Research

Manpower is the third area of 'mainstream' research and is in a sense the oldest and the newest of the areas being studied. It is the oldest because it is philosophically akin to the Wisconsin school's interest in social insurance legislation designed to improve workers' labour-market experiences. Further, there were manpower studies during the fifties (e.g. Haber, Harbison, Klein and Palmer (eds.), 1954) and Eli Ginzberg has written extensively about the subject for years. But 'manpower' did not become established as a recognized research field until the advent of the interventionist federal government labour-market policy in the sixties and seventies, starting primarily with the Manpower Development and Training Act of 1962. This policy stemmed originally from anxiety over automation and structural unemployment during the early sixties (Somers, Cushman and Weinberg (eds.), 1963).

As with the term 'industrial relations', manpower research means different things to different people. While formal definitions tend to claim jurisdiction over all studies concerned with the human resource utilization, actual 'manpower' studies consist mainly of descriptions and assessments of specific recent programmes (primarily public) designed to improve labour-market effectiveness and provide better job opportunities for the unemployed and disadvantaged. (For an excellent review, see Mangum, 1971; also Levitan, Mangum and Marshall, 1972.)

The proliferation of manpower research in the sixties was a direct result of a large-scale infusion of federal (and some foundation) funds to assess government manpower policies and programmes. The lion's share of this money has gone to researchers with backgrounds in economics. As a consequence, there has been a continuing stream of cost–benefit analyses which have measured the economic costs and benefits of various programmes, frequently in terms of human capital theory (Hamermesh, 1971; Somers and Woods, 1969; Perry, *et al.*, 1975). Other manpower research has concentrated on the political foundations and administrative systems associated with programme implementation (Mangum, 1969; Davidson, 1972). A modest number of studies have sought to determine which demographic (trainee) and organization (trainer) characteristics are most predictive of success in training the 'hard core', i.e. the most disadvantaged. (For a review, see Goodman, Salipante and Paransky, 1973.)

Among the questions studied have been the following. To what extent do manpower programmes lead to higher levels of long-run employability? Have these programmes in fact been directed chiefly to those easy to train ('creaming') or have the hard core actually benefited? Is it better (by a variety of standards) to provide training in specific skills for specific jobs – or broad education designed to improve reading, writing and arithmetic abilities as well as personal grooming – or work experience on real jobs (regardless of how menial)?

The research efforts to date have done a reasonably good job of evaluating specific manpower programmes, but there has been relatively less attention paid to basic macro-issues. Relatively few generalizations have emerged from this vast outpouring of research which will be of help in designing better manpower programmes, or which significantly advance our knowledge of either the labour market or the skill-acquisition process.

Conclusions

Our conclusions deal with four interrelated issues: the relevance of academic industrial relations in the United States as an applied field; its normative *status quo* orientation; its lack of clear, central focus; and the role of industrial relations theory.

Relevance

A key characteristic of United States industrial relations research has been its unremitting focus upon the institutional realities of the employment relationship. As a consequence, over the years this research has had considerable impact on the development of public policy and private practice. Industrial relations scholars strongly influenced the labour and social legislation during the New Deal. Later, as arbitrators, they helped shape the private industrial jurisprudence which gave meaning to public policy. And as teachers, they trained a high percentage of the management practitioners and, through various labour schools, had some (though not so great) impact on the labour side.

Industrial relations influence continues, especially in the government sector. It is no accident that industrial relations professors have served as chairmen or members of the committees which fashioned the public-sector laws in many States. Once more, industrial relations extension units are busy training practitioners on both sides. And the large sums spent for evaluation of manpower programmes *may* have influenced the nature of labour-market programmes (or at least alerted policy-makers to these programmes' deficiencies).

Nevertheless there are growing complaints that the increasing rigour of research methods makes contemporary industrial relations and labour economics research less and less useful (Dunlop, 1977). Although this perception may not be universally shared (see Dunlop's respondents in the October 1977 *Industrial and Labor Relations Review*), it is certainly true that recent research largely ignores the institutional problems which make the task of policy-makers particularly difficult. Lack of policy relevance may not be entirely a loss, however, for American industrial relations research may have stressed policy too much, seeking immediate application rather than basic understanding. Thus, the need for relevance may have inhibited the development of theory.

A status quo orientation

Industrial relations' founders, over fifty years ago, were reformers, if not radicals: they advocated fundamental changes in the nature of the employee–employer relationship. Today the field is essentially conservative: it is more concerned with training practitioners than questioning practice. Few scholars (particularly arbitrators) question the wisdom of the present arrangement. Criticism from the right is now practically stilled. Criticism from the left, to date, has focused on issues other than collective bargaining. Yet this strong consensus that (almost) all is well in American industrial relations is somewhat disturbing. The field would benefit from the intensive questioning of fundamental verities now occurring in Britain.

There is little *systematic* thinking, for example, about the limits which society should place on the private use of power or the degree to which conflict should be permitted, especially when it hurts third parties. There is much debate about the relative merits of final-offer and conventional arbitration to resolve public-sector impasses; there is less debate about whether any kind of compulsory arbitration is appropriate in a democratic system. The field's pragmatic approach has led to basic questions, as to the nature of pluralistic society, being ignored. One reason for this complacency is that a fair amount of industrial peace has been purchased in America. Probably the price for this has not been excessive, so far, but the framework for analysing these questions does not exist. Indeed the questions have hardly been raised.

Bargaining as a central focus?

Despite (and perhaps because of) its applied orientation, industrial relations suffers from a lack of definition and focus as an academic field. During the Golden Age, it had a clear mission: making collective bargaining work. Today the work done at industrial relations centres has become increasingly divided between manpower and collective bargaining (in part because of liberal financing of the former field). Manpower is concerned chiefly with those not in the labour market, the unemployed, and the low-wage non-union employed; by contrast, collective bargaining involves the better-paid employed in the primary labour market. Aside from an increasingly quantitative methodology (now shared among the social sciences generally), the two fields have little in common. At the practitioners' level the split is even sharper: arbitrators and poverty programme administrators have almost no reason to be interested in each other's work.

This growing split between the fields has serious implications for some industrial relations centres, as the retirement age is being approached by a distinguished older generation of institutionally-oriented labour economists who have spent their lifetime studying collective bargaining. Since the economics departments which employed these men refuse to replace them with either institutionalists or new-wave behaviouralists, the strong institutional ties between economics and the industrial relations centres may become strained. On the other hand, some of the younger generation of industrial relations scholars feel more comfortable in psychology, sociology and organizational behaviour.

Of course, industrial relations institutes often argue that their jurisdiction covers 'all aspects of the employment relationship' (see the masthead of the journal *Industrial Relations*), but this is much too broad because the 'employment relationship' encompasses such diverse fields as occupational selection and testing, collective bargaining, health and safety, equal employment rules, career patterns, government labour-market programmes, and the entire field of organizational behaviour (now probably employing more academicians than does industrial relations). In most universities, it would be politically impossible to pull this conglomeration together under a single head; further, it would be intellectually meaningless.

In practice, the narrow focus on traditional topics has meant that other issues are either ignored or viewed from a limited perspective. Equal employment opportunity (EEO, the elimination of discrimination based on race and sex) may be a far more important practical issue in the United States today than is collective bargaining. Yet to the extent that industrial relations scholars have studied the topic, it has been treated as something peripheral, e.g. in terms of its impact on collective bargaining or labour markets. The impact of EEO on personnel policies and career ladders is almost ignored, as is the EEO compliance bargaining process between employers and government agents. Similarly, in the employment relationship, employers and employees exchange a variety of positive and negative rewards, but little of exchange–rewards systems research from sociology and psychology is reflected in the industrial relations literature.

Thus, despite its broader claims, academic industrial relations today consists chiefly of manpower and collective bargaining. And, for reasons we have explained, we believe the relations between these two fields will become increasingly tenuous (despite some limited research on the impact of collective bargaining on the secondary labour market). Since manpower has a logical home in economics, collective bargaining is likely to be industrial relations' future core – as it was in the United States' Golden Age and as it is in Britain today, which is enjoying a Golden Age of its own.

The role of theory

There have been frequent calls for a distinctive, integrating industrial relations theory, which goes beyond economic theory, and some largely unsuccessful efforts have been made to develop such a theory. Interest in theory is far greater today in Britain than in the United States, in part because in Britain there is greater agreement as to the field's domain. But even in Britain, 'theory' seems to be more an exercise in defining boundaries than in erecting hypotheses.

We see little likelihood of a specifically industrial-relations theory being developed in the United States. Certainly were the field broadly defined it would make little sense to erect a single theory explaining such diverse topics as employment testing, union bargaining demands, and labour force participation. A narrowly defined theory makes more sense; however, one weakness of industrial relations research is that researchers have tended to regard collective bargaining as a unique phenomenon rather than merely as one of a family of interorganizational relationships. To be meaningful, collective bargaining theory should incorporate the process of collective bargaining into behavioural science, as much as labour economists have drawn manpower studies into mainstream economics. Such a theory might indicate the commonalities and differences between collective bargaining and international relations, for example, or family conflicts, or vendor–purchaser relations. Further, it might explain why industrial relations techniques were so difficult to apply during the sixties, in the context of racial negotiations and student–university conflicts.

Toward the future

Recent developments have left us more optimistic than when we began this chapter in 1974. Collective bargaining research was very late in entering the mainstream of the social sciences (later even than labour economics), yet the last few years have seen an outpouring of research that is considerably more quantitative and more specifically designed to test hypotheses than were the more institutional studies of previous periods. Further, behavioural scientists have rediscovered that collective bargaining provides an almost unique laboratory for studying a variety of social phenomena. To take one example, psychologists have begun to examine individual decisions to engage in strikes, sociologists to look upon strikes as examples of collective behaviour, and political scientists to examine how strike activity is related to governmental and political policies. Cross-fertilization among these separate disciplinary approaches may be difficult to accomplish; however, modern multi-variate analysis makes it possible to introduce variables from a variety of disciplines into a single analytic exercise. Depending on researchers' inclinations, the data can be used to test hypotheses from either a single discipline or a variety of disciplines.

The younger generation of industrial relations scholars is more broadly trained than the old, thus facilitating communications among the fields, each of which has its own contribution to make. Economists, for example, may study national aggregatives (e.g. the relationship between unemployment rates and union growth or labour-market supply and wages), while psychologists and organizational behaviour specialists may be more concerned with organizational-level factors (e.g. the attitudinal correlates of the decision to join a union or the forms of organizational adjustments to declining numbers of job applicants).

There is always the danger that the process of each discipline taking snapshots of the industrial relations 'elephant' from its own particular perspective will result in the living dynamics of the 'beast', as a whole, being lost. This loss could be avoided in part by the revival of old-fashioned case studies, provided these are focused on newer questions. There is a danger, too, that the new-wave research will lose the realism and policy relevance of the old. Nevertheless the new approaches permit the systematic analysis of a wide range of factors largely ignored by both institutional and econometric studies in the past (e.g. the psychological and sociological correlates of wildcat strikes in mining). Though much of this new research will lack direct policy relevance, it should provide a theoretical framework that may improve the quality of applied studies.

To summarize, there is an encouraging ferment among industrial relations scholars who specialize in collective bargaining. Equally important, scholars from other disciplines have rediscovered union–management relations. For the moment we are optimistic.

Acknowledgement Some of the main themes in this chapter were developed in camp-fire conversation between the senior author and Professor Robert Flanagan on the shores of Wire Lake, Emigrant Wilderness, California. We wish to pay tribute to Professor Flanagan's skills as a fisherman, cook and economist. Helpful comments were also received from Professors Irving Bernstein, Milton Derber, Peter Doeringer, Howard Foster, Thomas Kochan, Charles Myers, Lloyd Ulman and Clair Vickery. To our knowledge, none of these rivals Professor Flanagan as a fisherman.

REFERENCES

Aaron, Benjamin and Paul Seth Meyer, 'Public policy and labor-management relations', in *A Review of Industrial Relations Research*, Vol. II. (Madison, Wisc.: Industrial Relations Research Association, 1971), pp. 1–60.

Alexander, Kenneth O., 'Conglomerate mergers and collective bargaining', *Industrial and Labor Relations Review*, 24 (April 1971), 354–74.

Alexis, Marcus, 'The political economy of labor market discrimination: synthesis and exploration', in A. Horowitz and G. von Furstenberg (eds.), *Patterns of Discrimination* (Lexington, Mass.: Heath-Lexington, 1974).

Alinsky, Saul, *John L. Lewis: An Unauthorized Biography* (New York: G. P. Putnam's Sons, 1949).

Allen, Russell, 'The professional in unions and his educational preparation', *Industrial and Labor Relations Review*, 16 (October 1962), 16–29.

Anderson, John C., 'A comparative analysis of local union democracy', *Industrial Relations* (October 1978).

Anderson, John and Thomas Kochan, 'Impasse procedures in the Canadian Federal Service', *Industrial and Labor Relations Review*, 30 (April 1977), 283–301.

Aronowitz, Stanley, *False Promises: The Shaping of American Working Class Consciousness* (New York: McGraw-Hill, 1974).

Arrow, Kenneth H., 'Higher education as a filter', *Journal of Political Economy*, 81 (August 1973), 355–74.

Arrow, Kenneth J., 'The theory of discrimination', in Orley Ashenfelter and Albert Rees (eds.), *Discrimination in Labor Markets* (Princeton, N.J.: Princeton University Press, 1974).

Ashenfelter, Orley and George E. Johnson, 'Trade unions, bargaining theory, and industrial strike activity', *American Economic Review*, 59 (1969), 35–49.

Ashenfelter, Orley and George E. Johnson, 'Unionism, relative wages, and labor quality in U.S. manufacturing industries', *International Labor Economics*, 13 (October 1972), 488–508.

Ashenfelter, Orley and John H. Pencavel, 'American trade union growth: 1900–1960', *Quarterly Journal of Economics*, 83 (August 1969), 434–47.

Atherton, Wallace N., *Theory of Union Bargaining Goals* (Princeton, N.J.: Princeton University Press, 1973).

Baer, Walter E., *Practice and Precedent in Labor Relations* (Lexington, Mass.: D. C. Heath, 1972).

Bakke, E. Wight, *Mutual Survival* (New York: Harper, 1946).

Balke, Walter N., Kenneth R. Hammond, and G. Dale Meyer, 'An alternative approach to labor-management relations', *Administrative Science Quarterly*, 18 (September 1973), 311–27.

Becker, Gary, *Human Capital* (New York: National Bureau of Economic Research, 1964).

Becker, Gary, 'A theory of the allocation of time', *Economic Journal*, 75 (September 1965), 493–517.

Becker, Gary, *The Economics of Discrimination*. 2nd ed. (Chicago: University of Chicago Press, 1971).

Belcher, David, *Compensation Administration* (Englewood Cliffs, N.J.: Prentice-Hall, 1974).

Berg, Ivar, *Education and Jobs: The Great Training Robbery* (New York: Praeger, 1970).

Bergmann, Barbara, 'The effects on white incomes of discrimination in employment', *Journal of Political Economy*, 79 (March 1971), 294–313.

Bernstein, Irving, *The Lean Years, A History of the American Worker 1920–1933* (Boston, Mass.: Houghton-Mifflin, 1960).

Bernstein, Irving, *Turbulent Years, A History of the American Worker, 1933–1941* (Boston, Mass.: Houghton-Mifflin, 1969).

Bernstein, Irving, Harold L. Enarson, and R. W. Fleming eds., *Emergency Disputes and National Policy* (New York: Harper & Brothers, 1955).

Blake, Robert R., Herbert Sheppard, and Jane Mouton, *Managing Intergroup Conflict in Industry* (Houston, Texas: Gulf, 1964).

Blau, Peter and R. A. Schoenherr, *The Structure of Organizations* (New York: Basic Books, 1971).

Blauner, Robert, *Alienation and Freedom* (Chicago: University of Chicago Press, 1964).

Bok, Derek C., 'The regulation of campaign tactics in representation elections under the National Labor Relations Act', *Harvard Law Review*, 78 (November 1964), 38–141.

Bok, Derek C. and John T. Dunlop, *Labor and the American Community* (New York: Simon & Schuster, 1970).

Bowen, William G. and T. Aldrich Finnegan, *The Economics of Labor Force Participation* (Princeton, N.J.: Princeton University Press, 1969).

Bowles, Samuel and Herbert Gintis, 'The problem with human capital theory', *American Economic Review*, 65 (May 1975), 74–82.

Britt, David W. and Omar R. Galle, 'Structural antecedent of the shape of strikes: a comparative analysis', *American Sociological Review*, 35 (October 1974), 642–51.

Brody, David, 'The Old Labor History and the New: In Search of an

American Working Class', *Labor History*, 20 (Winter, 1979), 111–26.

Burton Jr., John F., 'Local Government Bargaining and Management Structure', *Industrial Relations*, 11 (May, 1972), 123–140.

Butler, R. J., 'Relative deprivation and power: a switched replication design using time series data of strike rates', *Human Relations*, 29 (July 1976), 623–41.

Caddy, Douglas, *The Hundred Million Dollar Payoff* (New Rochelle, N.Y.: Arlington House, 1974).

Cain, Glen G, 'The challenge of dual and radical theories of the labor market to orthodox theory', *American Economic Review*, 65 (May 1975), 16–22.

Calkins, Fay, *The CIO and the Democratic Party* (Chicago: University of Chicago Press, 1955).

Carpenter, Jesse, *Competition and Collective Bargaining in the Needle Trades, 1910–1967* (Ithaca, N.Y.: New York State School of Industiral and Labor Relations, 1972).

Chalmers, W. Ellison and Gerald W. Cormick, *Racial Conflict and Negotiations: Perspectives and First Case Studies* (Ann Arbor, Mich.: University of Michigan, Institute of Labor and Industrial Relations, 1971).

Chamberlain, Neil W., *Collective Bargaining* (New York: McGraw-Hill, 1951).

Chamberlain, Neil W., 'The problem of strikes', in Emanuel Stein (ed.), *Proceedings* of the New York University Thirteenth Annual Conference on Labor (Albany, N.Y.: Matthew Bender and Company, 1960).

Chamberlain, Neil W., 'Determinants of collective bargaining structures', in Arnold R. Weber (ed.), *The Structure of Collective Bargaining* (New York: The Free Press, 1961).

Chamberlain, Neil W. and James Kuhn,. *Collective Bargaining*. 2nd ed. (New York: McGraw-Hill, 1965).

Chamberlain, Neil W. and J. M. Schilling, *The Impact of Strikes* (New York: Harper & Brothers, 1954).

Chandler, Alfred D., Jr, *Strategy and Structure* (Cambridge, Mass.: MIT Press, 1962).

Chandler, Margaret K., *Management Rights and Union Interests* (New York: McGraw-Hill, 1964).

Chandler, Margaret K., 'Craft bargaining', in John T. Dunlop and Neil W. Chamberlain (eds.), *Frontiers of Collective Bargaining* (New York: Harper and Row, 1967).

Christie, Robert, *Empire in Wood: A History of the Carpenters Union* (Ithaca, N.Y.: New York State School of Industrial and Labor Relations, 1956).

Cochran, Bert, *Labor and Communism* (Princeton, N.J.: Princeton University Press, 1977).

Cohen, Sanford, 'An analytical framework for labor relations law', *Industrial and Labor Relations Review*, 14 (April 1961), 350–62.

Comay, Yochanan, Arie Melnik, and Abraham Subotnik, 'Bargaining, yield curves, and wage settlements: an empirical analysis', *Journal of Political Economy*, 82 (March/April 1974), 303–13.

Commons, John R., *Institutional Economics: Its Place in Political Economy* (New York: Macmillan, 1934).

Commons, John R. and John B. Andrews, *Principles of Labor Legislation* (New York: Harper & Brothers, 1916).

Commons, John R. *et al.* (eds.), *Documentary History of American Industrial Society*. 11 vols. (Cleveland, Ohio: A. H. Clark, 1919–21).

Commons, John R. *et al.*, *History of Labor in the United States*. 4 vols. (New York: Macmillan, 1918–1935).

Cox, Archibald, *Law and the National Labor Policy* (Los Angeles, Calif.: Institude of Industrial Relations, University of California, 1960).

Cross, John G., 'A theory of the bargaining process', *American Economic Review*, 55 (March 1965), 67–94.

Cross, John G., *The Economics of Bargaining* (New York: Basic Books, 1969).

Cullen, Donald E. and Marcia L. Greenbaum, *Management Rights and Collective Bargaining: Can Both Survive?* Bulletin 58 (Ithaca, N.Y.: New York State School of Industrial and Labor Relations, 1966).

Dankert, Clyde, Floyd C. Mann and Herbert R. Northrup (eds.), *Hours of Work* (Madison, Wisc.: Industrial Relations Research Association, 1965).

Davidson, Roger H., *The Politics of Comprehensive Manpower Legislation.* Policy Studies in Employment and Welfare No. 15 (Baltimore, Md.: Johns Hopkins University Press, 1972).

Davis, William and Lily Mary David, 'Pattern of wage and benefit changes in manufacturing', *Monthly Labor Review*, 91 (February 1968), 40–8.

Derber, Milton, *The American Idea of Industrial Democracy: 1865–1965* (Urbana, Ill.: University of Illinois Press, 1970).

Derber, Milton, William E. Chalmers, and Ross Stagner, *Management Relations in Illini City*. Vols. 1, 2 (Urbana, Ill.: Institute of Labor and Industrial Relations, University of Illinois, 1953, 1954).

Derber, Milton, Ken Jennings, Ian McAndrew and Martin Wagner, 'Bargaining and budget making in Illinois public institutions', *Industrial and Labor Relations Review*, 27 (October 1973), 49–62.

de Schweinitz, Dorothy, *Labor and Management in a Common Enterprise* (Cambridge, Mass.: Harvard University Press, 1949).

Deutsch, Morton, *The Resolution of Conflict* (New Haven: Yale University Press, 1973).

Doeringer, Peter B. and Michael J. Piore, *Internal Labor Markets and Manpower Analysis* (Lexington, Mass.: Heath, 1971).

Doeringer, Peter B., Penny H. Feldman, David M. Gordon, Michael J. Piore, and Michael Reich, *Low-Income Labor Markets and Urban Manpower Programs*. Research and Development Findings, No. 12 (Washington, D.C.: U.S. Department of Labor, Manpower Administration, 1972).

Douglas, Ann, *Industrial Peacemaking* (New York: Columbia University Press, 1962).

Douglas, Paul H. and A. W. Kornhauser, *Cases and Problems in Personnel Administration* (Chicago: University of Chicago Press, 1922).

Douglas, Paul H., Curtice N. Hitchcock, and Willard E. Atkins, *The Worker in Modern Economic Society* (Chicago: University of Chicago, Press, 1923).

Dubofsky, Melvyn and Warren Van Tine, *John L. Lewis: A Biography* (New York: Quadrangle, 1977).

Dulles, Foster Rhea, *Labor in America: A History*. 2nd rev. ed. (New York: Thomas Y. Crowell, 1960).

Dunlop, John T., *Wage Determination Under Trade Unions* (New York: Macmillan, 1944).

Dunlop, John T., 'Policy decisions and research in economics and industrial relations', *Industrial and Labor Relations Review*, 30 (April 1977), 275–82.

Dunlop, John T., 'The task of contemporary wage theory', in George W. Taylor and Frank C. Pierson (eds.), *New Concepts in Wage Determination* (New York: McGraw-Hill, 1957).

Dunlop, John T., *Industrial Relations Systems* (New York: Holt, Rinehart, and Winston, 1958).

Dunlop, John T., 'The industrial relations system in construction', in Arnold R. Weber (ed.), *The Structure of Collective Bargaining* (New York: Free Press, 1961).

Dunlop, John T., 'The function of the strike', in John T. Dunlop and Neil W. Chamberlain (eds.), *Frontiers of Collective Bargaining* (New York: Harper & Row, 1967).

Dunlop, John T., Fredrick Harbison, Clark Kerr, and Charles Myers, *Industrialism and Industrial Man Reconsidered* (Princeton: Inter-University Study of Human Resources in National Development, 1975).

Eckstein, Otto and Thomas A. Wilson, 'The determination of money wages in American industry', *Quarterly Journal of Economics*, 76 (August 1962), 379–414.

Edelstein, J. David and Malcolm Warner, *Comparative Union Democracy* (New York: Wiley, 1976).

Edwards, Richard C., Michael Reich and David M. Gordon, 'A theory of labor market segmentation', *American Economic Review*, 63 (May 1973), 359–65.

Ehrenberg, Ronald G. 'Municipal government structure, unionization, and the wages of fire fighters', *Industrial and Labor Relations Review*, 27 (October 1973), 36–48.

Eisele, C. Frederick, 'Organization size, technology, and frequency of strikes', *Industrial and Labor Relations Review*, 27 (July 1974), 560–71.

Elkouri, Frank and Edna A. Elkouri, *How Arbitration Works*. 3rd ed. (Washington, D..C.: Bureau of National Affairs, 1973).

Feller, David E., 'A general theory of the collective bargaining agreement', *California Law Review*, 61 (May 1973), 663–856.

Feller, David E., 'Arbitration: the days of its glory are numbered', *Industrial Relations Law Journal*, 2 (Spring 1977), 97–130.

Feuille, Peter, 'Police labor relations and multilateralism', *Proceedings* of the Twenty-Sixth Annual Winter Meeting of the Industrial Relations Research Association (Madison, Wisc.: 1974).

Feuille, Peter, *Final Offer Arbitration: Concepts, Developments, Techniques*. PERL no. 50 (Chicago: International Personnel Management Association, 1975).

Fiedler, Fred W., *A Theory of Leadership Effectiveness* (New York: McGraw-Hill, 1967).

Fine, Sidney, *The Automobile Under the Blue Eagle: Labor, Management and the Automobile Manufacturing Code* (Ann Arbor, Mich.: University of Michigan Press, 1963).

Finnegan, T. Aldrich, 'Hours of work in the United States', *Journal of Political Economy*, 70 (October 1962), 452–70.

Flanagan, Robert J., 'Labor force experience, job turnover, and racial wage differentials', *Review of Economics and Statistics*, 56 (November 1974).

Flanagan, Robert, 'Wage interdependence in unionized labor markets', *Brookings Papers on Economic Activity*, no. 3 (1976), 635–73.

Flanagan, Robert, George Strauss and Lloyd Ulman, 'Worker discontent and work place behavior', *Industrial Relations*, 13 (May 1974), 1–23.

Fleisher, Belton M., *Labor Economics: Theory and Evidence* (Englewood Cliffs, N.J.: Prentice-Hall, 1970).

Fleming, R. W., *The Labor Arbitration Process* (Urbana, Ill.: University of Illinois Press, 1965).

Foner, Philip Sheldon, *History of the Labor Movement in the United States* (New York: International Publishers, 1947, 1965).

Form, William H., *Blue-Collar Stratification: Auto Workers in Four Countries* (Princeton, N.J.: Princeton University Press, 1976).

Freedman, Audry, *Managing Labor Relations* (New York: The Conference Board, 1979).

Freeman, John and Jack Brittain, 'Union merger process and industrial environment', *Industrial Relations*, 16 (May 1977), 173–86.

Friedman, Milton, 'Some comments on the significance of labor unions for economic policy', in David M. Wright (ed.), *The Impact of the Union* (New York: Harcourt Brace, 1951).

Frost, Carl F., John H. Wakeley, and Robert A. Ruh, *The Scanlon Plan of Organization Development: Identity, Participation, and Equity* (East Lansing, Mich.: Michigan State University Press, 1974).

Fuchs, Victor, *The Service Economy* (New York: National Bureau of Economic Research, 1968).

Galenson, Walter, *The CIO Challenge to the AFL: A History of the American Labor Movement, 1935–1941* (Cambridge, Mass.: Harvard University Press, 1960).

Galenson, Walter, 'Reflections on the writing of labor history', *Industrial and Labor Relations Review*, 11 (October 1957), 85–95.

Galenson, Walter (ed.), *Trade Union Monograph Series.* Center for the Study of Democratic Institutions (New York: Wiley, 1962).

Garbarino, Joseph, *Faculty Bargaining: Change and Conflict* (New York: McGraw-Hill, 1975).

Garbarino, Joseph W., 'Fringe benefits and overtime as barriers to expanding employment', *Industrial and Labor Relations Review*, 17 (April 1964), 426–42.

Garfield, Sidney and William F. Whyte, 'A human relations view of collective bargaining', in George P. Shultz and John R. Coleman (eds.), *Labor Problems and Readings* (New York: McGraw-Hill, 1953).

Garnel, Donald, *The Rise of Teamster Power in the West* (Berkeley, Calif.: University of California Press, 1972).

Gerhart, Paul F., 'Determinants of bargaining outcomes in local government labor negotiations', *Industrial and Labor Relations Review*, 29 (April 1976), 325–41.

Getman, Julius, Stephen Goldberg, and Jeanne Herman, *Union Representation Elections: Law and Reality* (New York: Russell Sage, 1976).

Gifford, Adam, Sr, 'The impact of socialism on work stoppages', *Industrial Relations*, 13 (May 1974), 208–12.

Gilroy, Thomas P. and Anthony V. Sinicropi, 'Impasse resolution in public employment: a current assessment', *Industrial and Labor Relations Review*, 25 (July 1972), 496–511.

Ginsburg, Woodrow, 'Review of literature on union growth, government and structure – 1955–1969', *A Review of Industrial Relations Research*, Vol. 1 (Madison, Wisc.: Industrial Relations Research Association, 1970), pp. 207–60.

Glassman, Alan M. and James A. Belasco, 'The chapter chairman and school grievances', *Industrial Relations*, 14 (May 1975), 233–41.

Goldner, R., 'The Division of Labor: Process and Power', in Meyer Zald (ed.), *Power in Organizations* (Nashville, Tenn.: Vanderbilt University Press, 1970).

Gompers, Samuel, *Seventy Years of Life and Labor, An Autobiography by Samuel Gompers* (New York: E. P. Dutton, 1943).

Goodman, Paul, Paul Salipante, and Harold Paransky, 'Hiring, training and retraining the hard core unemployed: a selected review', *Journal of Applied Psychology*, 58 (1973), 23–32.

Gordon, David M., *Theories of Poverty and Unemployment* (Lexington, Mass.: Heath, 1972).

Gould, William B., *Black Workers in White Unions* (Ithaca, N.Y.: Cornell University Press, 1977).

Gould, William B., 'Employment security, seniority, and race: the role of Title VII of the Civil Rights Act of 1964', *Howard Law Journal*, 13 (Winter 1967), 1–50.

Greenstone, J. David, Labor in American Politics (New York: Alfred A. Knopf, 1969).

Gregory, Charles O., *Labor and the Law* (New York: W. W. Norton, 2nd rev. ed., 1958).

Gutman, Herbert G., *Work, Culture, and Society in Industrialized America* (New York: Knopf, 1976).

Haber, William and Harold M. Levinson, *Labor Relations and Productivity in the Building Trades* (Ann Arbor, Mich.: University of Michigan, Bureau of Industrial Relations, 1956).

Haber, William, Frederick H. Harbison, Lawrence R. Klein, and Palmer Gladys L. (eds.), *Manpower in the U.S.: Problems and Policies* (New York: Harper and Brothers, 1954).

Hackman, J. Richard, 'Work design', in J. Richard Hackman and Lloyd Suttle (eds.), *Improving Life in Organizations* (Los Angeles, Calif.: Goodyear, 1976).

Hackman, J. Richard and Edward E. Lawler, III, 'Employee reactions to job characteristics', *Journal of Applied Psychology*, 55 (June 1971), 259–86.

Hall, Robert, 'Why is the unemployment rate so high at full employment?' *Brookings Papers on Economic Activity*, 3 (1970), 369–96.

Hamermesh, Daniel S., *Economic Aspects of Manpower Training Programs* (Lexington, Mass.: Heath, 1971).

Hamermesh, Daniel S., 'Potential problems in human capital theory'.

Proceedings of the Twenty-Sixth Annual Winter Meeting of the Industrial Relations Research Association (Madison, Wisc.: 1973).

Harbison, Frederick H. and John R. Coleman, *Goals and Strategy in Collective Bargaining* (New York: Harper & Brothers, 1951).

Harbison, Frederick H. and Robert Dubin, *Patterns of Union–Management Relations* (Chicago: University of Chicago Press, 1947).

Harsanyi, John C., 'Approaches to the bargaining problem before and after a theory of games', *Econometrica*, 24 (April 1956), 144–57.

Hartman, Paul T., *Collective Bargaining and Productivity: The Longshore Mechanization Agreement* (Berkeley, Ca.: University of California Press, 1969).

Hausmann, Leonard *et al.* (eds.), *Equal Rights and Industrial Relations* (Madison, Wisc.: Industrial Relations Research Association, 1977).

Hays, Paul R., *Labor Arbitration: A Dissenting View* (New Haven, Conn.: Yale University Press, 1966).

Healy, James J. (ed.), *Creative Collective Bargaining* (Englewood Cliffs, N.J.: Prentice-Hall, 1965).

Herman, Jeanne, 'Conformity and wildcat strikes in the coal mining industry'. Paper presented to the American Psychological Society, August 1977.

Hibbs, Douglas, 'Industrial Conflict in Advanced Industrial Societies', *American Political Science Review*, 70 (1976), 1033–1058.

Hicks, J. R., *The Theory of Wages* (New York: Macmillan, 1932).

Hildebrand, George H., 'The economic effects of unionsim', in Neil W. Chamberlain, Frank C. Pierson, and Theresa Wolfson (eds.), *A Decade of Industrial Relations Research 1946–1956* (New York: Harper & Brothers, 1958a).

Hirsch, Paul, 'Organizational analysis and industrial sociology: an instance of cultural lag', *The American Sociologist*, 10 (February) (1975), 3–12.

Hopkins, George E., *The Airline Pilots: A Study of Elite Unionization* (Cambridge, Mass.: Harvard University Press, 1971).

Howe, Irving and B. J. Widick, *The UAW and Walter Reuther* (New York: Random House, 1949).

Hoxie, Robert, *Trade Unionism in the United States* (New York: Appleton-Century-Crofts, 1917).

Hunnius, Gerry, G. David Garson, and John Case (eds.), *Workers' Control: A Reader on Labor and Social Change* (New York: Vintage Books, 1973).

Independent Study Group. *The Public Interest in National Labor Policy* (New York: Committee for Economic Development, 1960).

Jacobs, Paul, *The State of the Unions* (New York: Atheneum, 1963).

James, Ralph and Estelle James, *Hoffa and the Teamsters: A Study of Union Power* (Princeton, N.J.: D. Van Nostrand, 1965).

Jensen, Vernon H., *Strife on the Waterfront: The Port of New York Authority Since 1945* (Ithaca, N.Y.: Cornell University Press, 1974).

Johnson, George E., 'Economic analysis of trade unionism', *American Economic Review*, 65 (May 1975), 23–8.

Johnson, H. G. and P. Mieszkowski, 'The effects of unionization on the distribution of income: a general equilibrium approach', *Quarterly Journal of Economics*, 84 (November 1970), 539–61.

Jones, Ralph T., *Public Sector Labor Relations: An Evaluation of Policy-Related Research* (Belmont, Mass.: Contract Research Corporation, 1975).

136   *Industrial Relations in International Perspective*

Josephson, Matthew, *Sidney Hillman: Statesman of American Labor* (Garden City, N.Y.: Doubleday, 1952).

Juris, Hervey A. and Peter Feuille *Police Unionism: Power and Impact in Public Sector Bargaining* (Lexington, Mass.: Heath, 1973).

Kahn, Lawrence M., 'Union impact: a reduced form measure', *Review of Economics and Statistics*, 59 (November 1977), 503–7.

Kerr, Clark, 'Industrial conflict and its mediation', *American Journal of Sociology*, 60 (November 1954a), 230–45.

Kerr, Clark, 'The Balkanization of Labor Markets', in E. Wight Bakke, *et al.*, *Labor Mobility and Economic Opportunity* (Cambridge, Mass.: MIT Press, 1954b).

Kerr, Clark and Abraham Siegel, 'The interindustry propensity to strike – an international comparison', in Arthur Kornhauser, Robert Dubin, and Arthur Ross (eds.), *Industrial Conflict* (New York: McGraw-Hill, 1954).

Kerr, Clark, *Labor Markets and Wage Determination* (Berkeley, Ca.: University of California Press, 1978).

Kerr, Clark, John Dunlop, Fredrick Harbison, and Charles Myers, *Industrialism and Industrial Man* (Cambridge, Mass.: Harvard University Press, 1960).

Kerton, Robert R., 'Hours of work: Jevon's theory after 100 years', *Industrial Relations*, 10 (May 1971), 227–30.

Kochan, Thomas A., 'A theory of multilateral collective bargaining in city governments', *Industrial and Labor Relations Review*, 27 (July 1974), 525–42.

Kochan, Thomas A., 'The politics of interest arbitration', *The Arbitration Journal*, 33 (March 1978), 5–9.

Kochan, Thomas A. and Hoyt N. Wheeler, 'Municipal collective bargaining: a model and analysis of bargaining outcomes', *Industrial and Labor*

Kochan, Thomas, *Collective Bargaining and Industrial Relations: From Theory to Policy and Practice* (Homewood, Ill.: Irwin, forthcoming).

Kornhauser, Arthur, Robert Dubin, and Arthur Ross (eds.), *Industrial Conflict* (New York: McGraw-Hill, 1954).

Kornhauser, Arthur, Harold Sheppard, and Albert J. Mayer, *When Labor Votes: A Study of the Autoworkers* (New York: University Books, 1956).

Kreps, Juanita M., Gerald G. Somers, and Richard Perlman, *Contemporary Labor Economics* (Belmont, Ca.: Wadsworth, 1974).

Kuhn, Alfred, 'Bargaining power in transactions: a basic model of interpersonal relationships', *American Journal of Economics and Sociology*, 23 (January 1964), 49–63.

Kuhn, James, *Bargaining in Grievance Settlement* (New York: Columbia University Press, 1961).

Larrowe, Charles P., *Harry Bridges – The Rise and Fall of Radical Labor in the U.S.* (New York: Lawrence Hill, 1972).

Laslett, John M., *Labor and the Left: A Study of Socialist and Radical Influences on the American Labor Movement, 1881–1924* (New York: Basic Books, 1970).

Lawler, Edward E., III, *Pay and Organizational Effectiveness: A Psychological View* (New York: McGraw-Hill, 1971).

Lawrence, Paul R. and Jay W. Lorsch, *Organization and Environment: Managing Differentiation and Integration* (Boston, Mass.: Harvard University, Graduate School of Business Administration, Division of Research, 1967).

Leavitt, Harold, 'Applied organizational change in industry: structural, technological and humanistic approaches', in James March (ed.), *Handbook of Organizations* (Chicago: Rand McNally, 1965).

Lesieur, Frederick G. (ed.), *The Scanlon Plan: A Frontier in Labor–Management Cooperation* (New York: Wiley, 1958).

Lester, Richard A., 'Shortcomings of Marginal Analysis for Wage-Employment Problems', *American Economic Review*, 36 (March, 1946), 63–82.

Levinson, Harold M., *Determining Forces in Collective Wage Bargaining* (New York: Wiley, 1966).

Levitan, Sar A., Garth L. Mangum, and Ray Marshall, *Human Resources and Labor Markets: Labor and Manpower in the American Economy* (New York: Harper & Row, 1972).

Lewin, David, 'Public sector labor relations: a review essay', *Labor History*, 18 (Winter 1977), 133–45.

Lewis, H. Gregg, *Unionism and Relative Wages in the United States: An Empirical Inquiry* (Chicago, Ill.: University of Chicago Press, 1963).

Lewis, H. Gregg, 'The economics of time and labor supply', *American Economic Review*, 65 (May 1975).

Lewicki, Roy J. and Clayton P. Alderfer, 'Tensions between research and intervention in intergroup conflict', *Journal of Applied Behavioral Science*, 9 (1973), 424–49.

Liebow, Elliot, *Tally's Corner: A Study of Negro Streetcorner Men* (Boston, Mass.: Little, Brown, 1967).

Likert, Rensis, *The Human Organization* (New York: McGraw-Hill, 1967).

Lincoln, James R., 'Community structure and industrial conflict', *American Sociological Review*, 43 (April 1978), 199–219.

Lipset, S. M., M. A. Trow, and J. S. Coleman, *Union Democracy: The Internal Politics of the International Typographical Union* (Chicago, Ill.: Free Press, 1956).

Lipsky, David and John Drotning, 'The influence of collective bargaining on teachers' salaries in New York State', *Industrial and Labor Relations Review*, 27 (October 1973), 18–35.

Livernash, E. Robert, 'Wages and benefits', in *A Review of Industrial Relations Research*, Vol. 1 (Madison, Wisc.: Industrial Relations Research Association, 1970).

Lovell, Hugh G., 'The pressure lever in mediation', *Industrial and Labor Relations Review*, 6 (October 1952), 20–30.

Mabry, Bevars D., *Economics of Manpower and the Labor Market* (New York: Intext, 1973).

Machlup, Fritz, 'Marginal analysis and empirical research', *American Economic Review*, 37 (September 1946), 519–54.

Magenau, John M. and Dean G. Pruitt, 'The social psychology of bargaining', in Geoffrey M. Stephenson and Christopher Brotherton (eds.), *Industrial Relations: A Social Psychological Approach*, (London: Wiley, 1979).

138   *Industrial Relations in International Perspective*

Mangum, Garth L., *The Emergence of Manpower Policy* (New York: Holt, Rinehart, and Winston, 1969).

Mangum, Garth L., 'Manpower research and manpower policy', in *A Review of Industrial Relations Research*, Vol. II (Madison, Wisc.: Industrial Relations Research Association, 1971).

Marshall, Ray, 'The economics of racial discrimination: a survey', *Journal of Economic Literature*, 12 (September 1974), 849–71.

Marshall, F. Ray, Allan Cartter, and Allan King, *Labor Economics* (Homewood, Ill.: Irwin, 1976).

McAdams, Alan K., *Power and Politics in Labor Legislation* (New York: Columbia University Press, 1964).

McGregor, Douglas, *The Human Side of Enterprise* (New York: McGraw-Hill, 1960).

Meltzer, Bernard D., 'Labor unions, collective bargaining, and the anti-trust laws', *University of Chicago Law Review*, 32 (Summer 1965).

Miles, Raymond E., 'Conflicting elements in managerial ideologies', *Industrial Relations*, 4 (October 1964), 77–91.

Millis, Harry A. and Emily Clark Brown, *From the Wagner Act to Taft–Hartley* (Chicago, Ill.: University of Chicago Press, 1950).

Millis, Harry A. and Royal A. Montgomery, *The Economics of Labor*; Vol. I, *Labor's Progress and Some Basic Labor Problems* (1938); Vol. II, *Labor's Risks and Social Insurance* (1938); Vol. III, *Organized Labor* (1945) (New York: McGraw-Hill).

Mills, Daniel Q., *Government, Labor and Inflation in the United States* (Chicago, Ill.: University of Chicago Press, 1975).

Mills, D. Quinn, *Industrial Relations and Manpower in Construction* (Cambridge, Mass.: MIT Press, 1972).

Mills, Daniel Q., *Labor–Management Relations* (New York: McGraw-Hill, 1978).

Mincer, Jacob, 'Labor force participation of married women: a study of labor supply', in National Bureau of Economic Research, *Aspects of Labor Economics* (Princeton, N.J.: Princeton University Press, 1962).

Mincer, Jacob, *Schooling, Experience, and Earnings* (New York: National Bureau of Economic Research, 1974).

Mincer, Jacob, 'Labor force participation and unemployment: a review of recent evidence', in Robert A. Gordon and Margaret S. Gordon (eds.), *Prosperity and Unemployment* (New York: Wiley, 1966).

Mitchell, Daniel J. B., 'Union wage policies: the Ross-Dunlop debate reopened', *Industrial Relations*, 11 (February 1972), 46–61.

Mitchell, Daniel J. B., 'Phase II wage controls', *Proceedings* of the Twenty-Seventh Annual Winter Meeting of the Industrial Relations Research Association (Madison, Wisc.: 1975).

Montgomery, D., 'Workers Control of Machine Productivity in the 19th Century', *Labor History*, 17 (1976), 485–509.

Myers, Charles A. and John G. Turnbull, 'Line and staff in industrial relations', *Harvard Business Review*, 34 (July–August 1956), 113–24.

Nash, J. F., 'The bargaining problem', *Econometrica*, 18 (April 1950), 155–62.

Nelson, David, *Managers and Workers* (Madison, Wisc.: University of Wisconsin Press, 1975).

Northrup, Herbert R. and Howard G. Foster, *Open Shop Construction* (Philadelphia, Pa.: University of Pennsylvania, 1975).

Notz, William M. and Frederick A. Starke, 'Final offer versus conventional arbitration as means of conflict management', *Administrative Science Quarterly*, 23 (June 1978), 189–203.

Odewahn, Charles A. and Joseph Krislov, 'Contract rejections: testing the explanatory hypotheses', *Industrial Relations*, 12 (October 1973), 389–96.

Ozanne, Robert, *Wages in Practice and Theory* (Madison, Wisc.: University of Wisconsin Press, 1968).

Parker, John E. and John F. Burton, Jr, 'Voluntary labor mobility in the U.S. manufacturing sector', *Proceedings* of the Twentieth Annual Winter Meeting of the Industrial Relations Research Association (Madison, Wisc.: 1967).

Parnes, Herbert S., 'Labor force participation and labor mobility', in *A Review of Industrial Relations Research*, Vol. 1 (Madison, Wisc.: Industrial Relations Research Association, 1970).

Parnes, Herbert S., Robert C. Miljus, Ruth S. Spitz, and Associates, *Career Thresholds: A Longitudinal Study of the Educational and Labor Market Experience of Male Youth 14–24 Years of Age*, Vol. 1 (Columbus, Ohio: Ohio State University, Center for Human Resource Research, 1969).

Patchen, Martin, *The Choice of Wage Comparisons* (Englewood Cliffs, N.J.: Prentice-Hall, 1961).

Pelling, Henry, *American Labor* (Chicago, Ill.: University of Chicago Press, 1960).

Pen, J., *The Wage Rate Under Collective Bargaining*. Translated by T. S. Preston (Cambridge, Mass.: Harvard University Press, 1959).

Perlman, Richard, 'Observations on overtime and moonlighting', *Southern Economic Journal*, 33 (October 1966), 237–44.

Perlman, Selig, *A Theory of the Labor Movement* (New York: Macmillan, 1928).

Perry, Charles R. and Wesley A. Wildman, *The Impact of Negotiations in Public Education: The Evidence From the Schools* (Worthington, Ohio: Charles A. Jones, 1970).

Perry, Charles, Bernard E. Anderson, Richard L. Rowan, and Herbert R. Northrup, *The Impact of Government Manpower Programs* (Philadelphia, Pa.: University of Pennsylvania, Wharton School, 1975).

Perry, George L., *Unemployment, Money Wage Rates, and Inflation* (Cambridge, Mass.: MIT Press, 1966).

Perry, George L., 'Wages and the guideposts', *American Economic Review*, 57 (September 1967), 897–904.

Peterson, Richard B. and Lane Tracy, 'Testing a behavioral theory model of labor negotiations', *Industrial Relations*, 16 (February 1977), 35–50.

Pfeffer, Jeffrey, *Organizational Design* (Arlington Heights, Ill.: AMH Publishing, 1978).

Pierson, Gail, 'The effect of union strength on the U.S. "Phillips Curve"', *American Economic Review*, 57 (June 1968), 456–67.

Piore, Michael J., 'The importance of human capital theory to labor economics—a dissenting view', *Proceedings* of the Twenty-Fifth Annual Winter Meeting of the Industrial Relations Research Association (Madison, Wisc.: Industrial Relations Research Association, 1973).

Pitkin, Hanna, *The Concept of Representation* (Berkeley, Ca.: University of California Press, 1968).

Porter, Lyman and Edward E. Lawler, III, *Managerial Attitudes and Performance* (Homewood, Ill.: Irwin, 1968).

Powderly, Terence Vincent, *The Path I Trod: The Autobiography of Terence V. Powderly.* Edited by Harry J. Carman, Henry David, and Paul N. Guthrie (New York: Columbia University Press, 1940).

Prasow, Paul and Edward Peters, *Arbitration and Collective Bargaining* (New York: McGraw-Hill, 1970).

Purcell, Theodore V., *The Worker Speaks His Mind on Company and Union* (Cambridge, Mass.: Harvard University Press, 1953).

Quinn, Robert P. and Graham Staines, *1977 Quality of Employment Survey* (Ann Arbor, Mich.: University of Michigan, Institute for Social Research, 1978).

Rees, Albert, 'The current state of labor economics', Reprint no. 16 (Industrial Relations Centre, Queen's University, 1971).

Rees, Albert, *The Economics of Work and Pay* (New York: Harper, 1973).

Rees, Albert, 'The effects of unions on resource allocation', *Journal of Law and Economics*, 6 (October 1963), 69–78.

Rehmus, Charles U., 'The mediation of industrial conflict: a note on the literature', *Journal of Conflict Resolution*, 9 (1965), 118–20.

Rehmus, Charles (ed.), *The Railway Labor Act at Fifty: Collective Bargaining in the Railway and Airline Industry* (Washington: D.C.: GPO, 1977).

Rehmus, Charles M. and Doris B. McLaughlin (eds.), *Labor and American Politics: A Book of Readings* (Ann Arbor, Mich.: University of Michigan Press, 1967).

Reynolds, Lloyd G., *Labor Economics and Labor Relations.* 7th ed. (Englewood Cliffs, N.J.: Prentice-Hall, 1978).

Ritzer, George and Harrison Trice, *An Occupation in Conflict: A Study of the Personnel Manager* (Ithaca, N.Y.: New York State School of Industrial and Labor Relations, 1969).

Roethlisberger, Fritz J. and W. J. Dickson, *Management and the Worker* (Cambridge, Mass.: Harvard University Press, 1939).

Ronan, W. W., 'Work group attributes and grievance activity', *Journal of Applied Psychology*, 47 (1963), 38–41.

Roomkin, Myron, 'Union structure, internal control, and strike activity', *Industrial and Labor Relations Review*, 29 (January 1976), 198–217.

Roomkin, Myron and Roger Abrams, 'Using behavioral evidence in NLRB regulation: a proposal', *Harvard Law Review*, 90 (May 1977), 1441–74.

Rosen, Hjalmar and R. A. H. Rosen, *The Union Member Speaks* (New York: Prentice-Hall, 1955).

Ross, Arthur M., *Trade Union Wage Policy* (Berkeley, Ca.: University of California Press, 1948).

Ross, Arthur M., 'Do we have a new industrial feudalism?' *American Economic Review*, 49 (December 1958), 903–20.

Ross, Arthur M., 'Distressed grievance procedures and their rehabilitation', *Labor Arbitration and Industrial Change*, Proceedings of the Sixteenth Annual Meeting of the National Academy of Arbitrators (Washington, D.C.: BNA Books, 1963).

Ross, Arthur M., 'Labor courses: the need for radical reconstruction', *Industrial Relations*, 4 (October 1964), 1–17.

Ross, Philip, *The Government as a Source of Union Power* (Providence, R.I.: Brown University Press, 1965).

Rottenberg, Simon, 'On choice in labor markets', *Industrial and Labor Relations Review*, 9 (January 1956), 183–99.

Rubin, Jeffrey and Bert Brown, *The Social Psychology of Bargaining and Negotiation* (New York: Academic Press, 1975).

Sayles, Leonard R., *Behavior of Industrial Work Groups* (New York: Wiley, 1958).

Sayles, Leonard R. and George Strauss, *The Local Union* (New York: Harpers, 1953).

Schelling, T. C., 'An Essay on Bargaining', *American Economic Review*, 46 (June 1956), 281–306.

Schultz, Theodore, *Investment in Human Capital* (New York: Free Press, 1971).

Schultze, Charles L. and Louis Weiner (eds.), *The Behavior of Income Shares, Studies in Income and Wealth*. Vol. 27 National Bureau of Economic Research (Princeton, N.J.: Princeton University Press, 1964).

Seidman, Joel, *American Labor from Defense to Reconversion* (Chicago, Ill.: University of Chicago Press, 1953).

Selekman, Benjamin M., 'Varieties of labor relations', *Harvard Business Review*, 27 (March 1949), 175–99.

Selznick, Philip, *Law, Society, and Industrial Justice* (New York: Russell Sage, 1969).

Sheppard, Harold L. and Neal Q. Herrick, *Where Have All the Robots Gone? Worker Dissatisfaction in the 70's* (New York: Free Press, 1972).

Shils, Edward B., 'Union fragmentation: a major cause of transportation crises', *Industrial and Labor Relations Review*, 25 (October 1971), 32–52.

Simkin, William E., 'Refusal to ratify contracts', *Industrial and Labor Relations Review*, 21 (July 1968), 518–40.

Simler, Norman J., *The Impact of Unionism on Wage-Income Ratios in the Economy* (Minneapolis, Minn.: University of Minnesota Press, 1961).

Skeels, Jack W., 'Measures of U.S. strike activity', *Industrial and Labor Relations Review*, 24 (July 1971), 515–25.

Slichter, Sumner H., *Union Policies and Industrial Management* (Washington, D.C.: Brookings Institution, 1941).

Slichter, Sumner H., James J. Healy, and E. Robert Livernash, *The Impact of Collective Bargaining on Management* (Washington, D.C.: Brookings Institution, 1960).

Snyder, David, 'Early North American Strikes: A Reinterpretation', *Industrial and Labor Relations Review*, 30 (April, 1977), pp. 325–341.

Somers, Gerald G., 'Bargaining power and industrial relations theory', in Gerald G. Somers (ed.), *Essays in Industrial Relations Theory* (Ames, Iowa: Iowa State University Press, 1969).

Somers, Gerald G. (ed.), *Collective Bargaining: Contemporary American*

Experience (Madison, Wisc.: Industrial Relations Research Association, 1980).

Somers, Gerald G., Edward L. Cushman, and Nat Weinberg (eds.), *Adjusting to Technological Change* (New York: Harper & Row, 1963).

Somers, Gerald G. and W. D. Woods (eds.), *Cost-Benefit Analysis of Manpower Policies* (Kingston, Ontario: Industrial Relations Centre, Queen's University, 1969).

Sovern, Michael I., *Legal Restraints on Racial Discrimination in Employment* (New York: Twentieth Century Fund, 1966).

Stanley, David T. with Carole L. Cooper, *Managing Local Government under Union Pressure* (Washington, D.C.: Brookings Institution, 1972).

Stern, Robert N., 'Intermetropolitan patterns of strike frequency', *Industrial and Labor Relations Review*, 29 (January 1976), 218–35.

Stern, Robert, 'Methodological Issues in Quantitative Strike Analysis', *Industrial Relations*, 17 (February 1978), 32–42.

Stevens, Carl M., *Strategy and Collective Bargaining Negotiation* (New York: McGraw-Hill, 1963).

Stevens, Carl M., 'Mediation and the role of the neutral', in John T. Dunlop and Neil W. Chamberlain (eds.), *Frontiers of Collective Bargaining* (New York: Harper & Row, 1967).

Strauss, George, *Unions in the Building Trades: A Case Study* (Buffalo, N.Y.: University of Buffalo Series no. 24, 1958).

Strauss, George, 'The shifting power balance in the plant', *Industrial Relations*, 1 (May 1962), 65–96.

Strauss, George, 'Social psychology and industrial relations, perspectives and suggestions', in Geoffry M. Stephenson and Christopher J. Brotherton (eds.), *Industrial Relations: A Social Psychological Point of View* (London: Wiley, 1979).

Strauss, George, 'The study of conflict: hope for a new synthesis between industrial relations and organizational behavior?' *Proceedings* of the Twenty-ninth Annual Meeting, Industrial Relations Research Association (Madison, Wisc.: 1977), pp. 329–37.

Strauss, George, 'Union government in the U.S.: research past and future', *Industrial Relations*, 16 (May 1977), 215–42.

Summers, Clyde W., 'Ratification of agreements', in John T. Dunlop and Neil W. Chamberlain (eds.), *Frontiers of Collective Bargaining* (New York: Harper & Row, 1967).

Taft, Philip, *History of Labour in the United States*. Vol. 4 (New York: Macmillan, 1951).

Taft, Philip, *Organized Labor in American History* (New York: Harper & Row, 1964).

Tannenbaum, Frank, *The Labor Movement* (New York: Putnam, 1921).

Taylor, Frederick W., *The Principles of Scientific Management* (New York: Harper & Brothers, 1911).

Thompson, James D., *Organizations in Action* (New York: McGraw-Hill, 1967).

Tracy, Lane, 'The influence of noneconomic factors on negotiators', *Industrial and Labor Relations Review*, 27 (January 1974), 204–15.

Tripp, L. Reed, 'Collective bargaining theory', in Gerald G. Somers (ed.), *Labor, Management and Social Policy* (Madison, Wisc.: University of Wisconsin, 1963).

Trist, Eric, Gerald Susman, and Grant R. Brown, 'An experiment in autonomous working in an American underground coal mine', *Human Relations*, 30 (1977), 201–36.

Ulman, Lloyd, 'Marshall and Friedman on union strength', *Review of Economics and Statistics*, 37 (November 1955), 384–401.

Ulman, Lloyd, *The Rise of the National Trade Union: The Development and Significance of Its Structure, Governing Institutions, and Economic Policies* (Cambridge, Mass.: Harvard University Press, 1955).

Van Maanen, John (ed.), *Organization Careers* (New York: Wiley, 1977).

Van Tine, Warren R., *The Making of the Labor Bureaucrat: Union Leadership In the United States, 1870–1920* (Amherst, Mass.: University of Massachusetts Press, 1973).

Vickery, Clair, 'The impact of turnover on group unemployment rates', *Review of Economics and Statistics*, 54 (November 1977), 415–26.

Vickery, Clair, Barbara Bergmann, and Katherine Swartz, 'Unemployment rate targets and anti-inflation policy as more women enter the Labor force', *American Economic Review*, 68 (May 1978), 90–4.

Wachter, Michael, 'The primary and secondary labor market mechanism: a critique of the dual literature'. A paper presented to the Brookings Institution Economic Panel Meetings, 5–6 December 1974.

Walsh, William D., 'Economic conditions and strike activity in Canada', *Industrial Relations*, 14 (February 1975), 45–54.

Walton, Richard E., *Interpersonal Peacemaking: Confrontations and Third Party Consultation* (Reading, Mass.: Addison-Wesley, 1969).

Walton, Richard E., 'Innovative restructuring of work', in Jerome W. Rosow (ed.), *The Worker and the Job* (Englewood Cliffs, N.J.: Prentice-Hall, 1974).

Walton, Richard A. and Robert B. McKersie, *A Behavioral Theory of Labor Negotiations* (New York: McGraw-Hill, 1965).

Watts, Harold W. and Albert Rees, *The New Jersey Income–Maintenance Experiment*. Vols. 2 and 3 (New York: Academic Press, 1977).

Weber, Arnold R. (ed.), *The Structure of Collective Bargaining* (New York: Free Press, 1961).

Weber, Arnold R., 'The craft-industrial issue revisited: a study of union government', *Industrial and Labor Relations Review*, 16 (April 1963), 381–404.

Weber, Arnold R., 'Stability and change in the structure of collective bargaining', in The American Assembly, Lloyd Ulman (ed.), *Challenges to Collective Bargaining* (Englewood Cliffs, N.J.: Prentice-Hall, 1967).

Weintraub, Andrew R., 'Prosperity versus strikes: an empirical approach', *Industrial and Labor Relations Review*, 20 (January 1966), 231–38.

Wellington, Harry H., *Labor and the Legal Process* (New Haven, Conn.: Yale University Press, 1968).

Wellington, Harry H. and Ralph K. Winter, Jr. *The Unions and the Cities* (Washington, D.C.: Brookings Institution, 1971).

Whyte, William F., *Patterns of Industrial Peace* (New York: Harpers, 1951).

Wilensky, Harold, *Intellectuals in Labor Unions: Organizational Pressures on Professional Roles* (Glencoe, Ill.: Free Press, 1956).

Wilensky, Harold L., 'The moonlighter: a product of relative deprivation', *Industrial Relations*, 3 (October 1963), 105–24.

Witte, Edwin E., 'The university and labor education', *Industrial and Labor Relations Review*, 1 (October 1947), 3–17.

Wolfe, Arthur C., 'Trends in labor union voting behavior', *Industrial Relations*, 9 (October 1969), 1–10.

Work in America. Report of a Special Task Force to the Secretary of Health, Education, and Welfare (Cambridge, Mass.: MIT Press, 1973).

Yaffe, Byron, *The Saul Wallen Papers: A Neutral's Contribution to Industrial Peace* (Ithaca, N.Y.: Cornell University Press, 1974).

Zeuthen, F., *Problems of Monopoly and Economic Welfare* (London: Routledge, 1930).

4 British Industrial Relations Research in the Sixties and Seventies

Derek Robinson

In the late fifties and early sixties there was a growing movement for legislation to reconstruct British industrial relations, particularly as they involved the activities of union and shop stewards. The Royal Commission on Trade Unions and Employers' Associations (the Donovan Commission) was created in 1965 in response to this movement.

The Donovan Commission provides a useful starting point for a discussion of current labour–management relations. The commission acted as a clearing-house in which various views of collective bargaining were examined. Its report (1968) gave rise to considerable debate in academic circles, management and trade union groups, and political parties. In addition to examining collective bargaining, it gave impetus to study in other areas of government intervention in industrial relations and wage determination.

The Donovan Report

The report of the Donovan Commission identified two systems of industrial relations in Britain: the formal system embodied in the official institutions and the informal system created by the actual behaviour of trade union and employers' associations, of managers, shop stewards and workers. Specifically, it emphasized that 'the keystone of the formal structure is the industry-wide collective agreement' (1968, para. 50), while the 'informal system is founded on reality, recognizing that the organizations on both sides of industry are not strong. Central trade union organization is weak, and employers' associations are weaker' (1968, para. 49). The report summarized the situation in the following manner: 'Other countries also have both formal systems of industrial relations and informal systems created by the behaviour of people and organizations. But in Britain the informal system is often at odds with the formal system' (1968, para. 52).

The report restricted itself to the procedures and processes of collective bargaining, with emphasis on the performance of the existing dual system in this respect. Thus, for example, inflation and its relationship to collective bargaining was not regarded as a crucial element in evaluation, and excessive increases in money wages which could reflect a shift from the formal to the informal system were treated as an outcome of the bargaining system without making normative judgement. This emphasis reflected the view that industrial relations is about the processes of job regulation which naturally stress the importance of institutions and procedures.

The separation of the formal and the informal system leads, in the British context, to a distinction between trade unions and employers' associations bargaining nationally, and shop stewards, work groups and managers bargaining at local levels. It rests on the fact that even though local groups of workers are members of trade unions, their bargaining may be distinct from that of their trade unions. Although this development has been discussed in terms of increasingly local union government, it is not viewed as reflecting adversely on the nature of the official trade unions as representatives of their members. It is seen more as a commentary on the development of procedures and pro cesses which, no matter what their original purpose, now prevent the official union structure from participating in all aspects of collective bargaining.

The official union representatives have been replaced by other agencies either as a result of changing bargaining requirements or of the extension of bargaining to new areas. Thus, while the role and position of shop stewards can be analysed within terms of union government, it is their role as bargainers that underpins the two-systems approach. This has led to increasing attention to the concept that in many areas it is necessary to analyse collective bargaining not as a process involving two constant parties – employers' associations and unions – but as labour and management solving problems as they develop at various levels in the bargaining structure.

The existence of multilevel bargaining was recognized earlier (Clegg, 1972; Robertson, 1960, 1961, 1968). Nancy Seer, however, pointed out that there were many exceptions to this general stereotype, in particular the nationalized industries and, in the private sector, a considerable number of firms who are not members of industry-wide bargaining associations (Roberts (ed.), 1962). To these can be added some 4 million workers covered by Wages Councils or Boards (Bayliss, 1962; Ministry of Labour, 1965).

However, even where a simple single system operated and most bargaining took place between unions and employers' associations, it was recognized that local variations always existed. For example, industry agreements seldom provide for industry-wide piece-rates. Instead, industry agreements would generally include such phrases as 'piece-work rates shall be such as to enable a worker of average ability to earn at least 12 per cent more than a time worker employed during the same period on the same job' (Chemical and Allied Industries, 1974) or more than a certain percentage above his basic rate (Lerner *et al.*, 1969). In some cases, the terminology of the agreements could well be taken to mean that the fixing of piece-work prices was a matter between the individual employer and the individual workman.

The Donovan Report gave greater attention to multilevel bargaining in British industrial relations than had previous research. It also used this concept as the basis of analysis and as the foundation for a framework of recommendations for the reform of the system of industrial relations.

The Donovan analysis has been criticized for overestimating the extent of the two-system phenomenon, for adopting a particular viewpoint, and for generalizing from a limited case (H. A. Turner, 1969a). Similar views have been expressed by Robertson and Hunter (1970), who believed the report concentrated too much on the manufacturing and manual worker sectors, and that this area of interest, while continuing to be important, was not as central as it had been. H. A. Turner also has noted that only a small proportion of workers (4 million out of 23 million) were subject to the two systems, and that 'It is pretty clear, in fact, that it [the Donovan Commission] was persuaded to accept as the typical situation of British industrial relations that of the mass-production operative in a large engineering establishment' (1969). Crossley (1968) feels that the power to determine wages has not shifted from the industry to the work-place level, but has been *added on* to the continuing operation of industry agreements.

In general, the picture that emerges from Donovan and other studies seems to be that while there is something that can be called a system, it refers only in a general and somewhat loose way to the state of industrial relations. There are various and quite different parts of the economy. In some cases, the 'formal' system predominates. In other cases, there is a large amount of supplemental bargaining activity carried out by shop stewards at plant level.

The Oxford school

The Donovan Report is also important in that it represents the views of an informal organization of individuals referred to as the Oxford school (H. A. Turner, 1968; Blain and Gennard, 1970; Goldthorpe, 1974; Eldridge, 1975). In the period 1965–70, this group strongly influenced the development of ideas and attitudes and of government policy.

There is a long tradition of British academics being involved in government and quasi-government activities. The Oxford school's influence probably rested on three factors. Firstly, they shared a common conceptual approach to a wide range of subjects concerning industrial relations; problems were not tackled *ad hoc*. Secondly, they advocated adaptation and change within the existing economic, political and social systems rather than expressing a view of siciety that offered hope only through fundamental changes. Thirdly, they were willing to combine academic work with real-world responsibilities. There was no alternative school or set of individuals acting in a reinforcing manner.

The essential theme of the Oxford School was 'voluntary pluralist' (Fox, 1968, 1971, in Child (ed.). 1973). The group believed that industrial relations reforms should come through voluntary methods rather than statutory intervention. The law might have a role to play in providing a framework of minimum provisions of bargaining institutions and practices to encourage the extension and development of collective bargaining (Flanders, 1966, 1969; in Alexander, (ed.) 1970; Clegg, 1960, 1972; McCarthy and Ellis, 1973). Collective bargaining was seen as a form of democracy or joint regulation of employment conditions, with a view towards extension of democratic control over a much wider area of subjects relevant to people's working lives.

The voluntary–pluralist approach to industrial relations relies on the 'consent' view that management cannot govern without the cooperation of those it seeks to govern, which depends on the extent of joint regulation rather than unilateral management decision-making. This provides the basis for rejecting rigid state or legislative interference with the processes of collective bargaining as well as support for the extension of joint regulation (McCarthy and Ellis, 1973; Daniel and McIntosh, 1972; Weekes *et al.*, 1975).

The basic proposition of the voluntary–pluralist position was reflected in the Donovan proposal for greater formalization of plant and company bargaining. This proposal's goal was an integrated system in which bargaining would take place between employers and unions, perhaps with unions represented by shop stewards, who would operate within a framework created by and subject to the influence of the unions. Great virtue was seen in the clarification of rights and obligations, privileges, and responsibilities, accepted and obtained by joint regulation, which was seen as a process which should be carried out by properly recognized parties acting within an agreed system (CIR Report no. 17, 1971).

In addition, the lack of agreed rights and obligations was seen as leading to wage drift, disorderly pay structures, inefficient utilization of resources, and unofficial or unconstitutional strikes.

This should not be interpreted, however, as meaning that the reason for advocating joint regulation had to do with the distribution of power within the Union hierarchy. Rather the emphasis was on the processes of decision-making. Nor does the Oxford school's criticism of disorder and lack of control imply that there should be a return to unilateral management control. Overall, emphasis here has been on the process of union–management agreement rather than advocacy of certain results. At the same time, the concern over inflation and the support of incomes policy meant that some views were implicit concerning the results of bargaining, and there was an inherent belief that fragmented bargaining was bad for the individuals affected by it and for other workers and society as a whole.

More recent contributions by Fox (Child (ed.), 1973; Fox, 1974b) have criticized at least some interpretations or redefinitions of the pluralist position from the viewpoint that it may lead to a continuation of the *status quo* in terms of power allocation, thus preventing any seriously radical challenge to the power structure extant in society and industry. Attention has been called to the inherent possibility that individuals will somehow be misled into believing that many social arrangements, in this case as they apply particularly to work situations, are less amenable to change than they are or might be (see also Goldthorpe, 1971).

In addition, the view that workers affected by inefficient utilization of resources—excessive overtime, disorderly pay structures and degenerate piece-work schemes – might in fact prefer that disorder to a more formal structure has been advanced by Goldthorpe (1974) and Eldridge (1975) and implicitly by radical left protagonists (see also Topham in Coates, Topham and Barratt Brown, 1969; Collins in Coates, Topham and

Barratt Brown, 1970). However, while the Oxford school's position is open to criticism, its impact on government policy in the current period should not be underestimated.

With this review of some of the main themes of industrial relations in Britain, some more specific areas can be considered: the different levels of bargaining, the role of the parties in bargaining, and then some of the major issues in the past fifteen years.

Levels of Bargaining

Industry level

Most studies of industry-level bargaining have concentrated on wage bargaining, although there are some exceptions (Flanders and Clegg, 1954, ch. 5; Clegg, 1972, ch.6). Analyses of the increases received in different industry agreements have been made, primarily to test the 'wage round' thesis (Knowles and Thorne, 1961; Knowles and Robinson, 1962). If the term is interpreted as including common annual patterns of settlements, there is little evidence that rounds existed in the fifties.

It is nevertheless widely, and probably rightly, believed, that the terms of some individual settlements have effects on others. The apparent existence of longer-term similarities, however, has led some writers to propose the establishment of a national framework, or, say, confederal bargaining, between the TUC and CBI (E. H. Phelps Brown, in evidence to the Donovan Commission, 1968). The two main organizations themselves do not appear to support this, although they may join in tripartite discussions with the government when incomes policies are discussed.

The engineering industry, perhaps because it is the largest industry-wide agreement, is thought of as crucial in affecting the general climate of wage developments. There are data on the industry agreements going back a considerable period of time, and the industry is frequently regarded as the main source of the pressures for wage drift (Knowles and Robertson, 1952, 1954). Marsh (1965) has produced a clear description and a sharp analysis of the negotiation of engineering wage agreements. Subsequent work has continued the investigation of how the industry-wide 'procedure' agreement actually works at plant level (Marsh, Evans and Garcia, 1971; Marsh and Coker, 1963; Marsh and Jones, 1964; Engineering Employers Federation, in Donovan Commission Report,

1968; Hyman, 1972; Marsh and McCarthy, Donovan Research Paper 2, part 2 1968).

A picture emerges of considerable diversity of practice, both with regard to wage developments and adaptations of the outline of the procedure agreement, to meet perceived special needs of each plant. The existence of multi-unionism in plants – a common feature of engineering – adds to the complexity of analysis. Although this has been thought to be a major cause of Britain's industrial relations problems, various studies suggest that, in practice, many individual establishments have devised procedures, both formal and informal, at the plant level to control the situation.

The National Board for Prices and Incomes (NBPI) argued against industry wage settlements if they led to across-the-board general increases (Report no. 49, 1964). In engineering agreements, where such increases are common, there have been attempts since 1964 to consolidate the national rate structure by creating minimum earnings levels. But these have included across-the-board increases even for individuals already receiving rates of pay in excess of the newly established minima (Marsh, 1965).

However, the NBPI, in Report no.49, did support a common framework for hours and holidays, as well as for the reform of plant payment systems. This is a view that can be seen as consistent with the Donovan 'two systems' approach but could also be used to challenge the Donovan interpretation of the function of the system. The formal system assumes that pay is determined by industry-wide agreements (Donovan Report, 1968, para. 146). In engineering, this does not seem to have been assumed by those negotiating the industry agreements (Lowry, 1968). Other industries have been studied:

Docks (HMSO, cmnd. 2934, 1965; Mellish, 1972; ACAS, 1975; Wilson, 1972; Jackson, 1973).

Shipbuilding (CIR, 1971; NBPI, National Incomes Committee Report, 1965; Brown et al., 1972; Nicholson in Coates, Topham and Baratt Brown (eds.), 1969; Daly, 1969; Oldham in Coates, Topham and Baratt Brown (eds.), 1969).

Coal-mining (HMSO, Cmnd. 4903, 1972; Hughes and Moore, 1972; Heath in Coates, Topham and Barratt Brown (eds.), 1969.

Exhibition contracts NBPI Reports no. 2, 1963; no. 117, 1969; Liddle, 1972).

Printing (Child, 1967; HMSO, Cmnd. 3184, 1967; NBPI Report no. 2, 1965; Brown and Sisson, 1975; Sisson, 1975).

Construction (HMSO, Cmnd. 3396, 1967; HMSO, Cmnd. 3714, 3714–1, 1968;HMSO, DEP, 1970; NBPI, Cmnd. 3838, 1968; NBPI, Cmnd. 3982, 1969).

The reports of the NBPI provide information on additional industries, as do the reports of Courts of Inquiry and similar bodies. Some of the reports suggest that improvements in industrial relations will require changes in the structure of the product market or pattern of ownership. Others emphasize the need to improve bargaining arrangements at the plant level by additional procedures.

Although the Courts of Inquiry have usually dealt with specific disputes, in some cases they have examined general problems. The Phelps Brown report on building, for instance, recognized 'the need to strengthen the industrial relations system in building to ensure that earnings and conditions of employment are under the effective joint control of employers and trade unions' (HMSO, Cmnd. 3714, 1968, para. 22). The report put forward proposals for strengthening both trade unions and employers' organizations and illustrated the problems arising from multilevel bargaining.

Plant level

While there has been much interest in plant level bargaining, there has been little academic research in this area until recently. However, the Commission on Industrial Relations (CIR) included detailed surveys and analyses of plant bargaining that have been followed by ACAS, and these documents provide a rich source of information on plant-level activities.

A short general survey of the developing trends in plant and company bargaining is provided by Roberts and Gennard (Robertson and Hunter (eds.), 1970), and the results of comprehensive surveys of workshop relations, with emphasis on the role of the shop steward in this process, were carried out for the Donovan Commission and subsequently updated (Government Social Survey, 1968; McCarthy and Parker, Donovan Research Paper no. 10, 1968; Parker, 1974). These surveys provided evidence on such things as the election and appointment of shop stewards, the items of bargaining, the procedures of bargaining and the evaluations of the practices as reported by the stewards, managers and union officials in the surveys. The later survey indicated that there had been an extension of plant and shop-floor bargaining with shop stewards apparently gaining a more prominent role. There has probably been an increase in the use of written agreements at plant or shop-floor level, but relatively little evidence that the emphasis given by Donovan to the formalization of bargaining practices and procedures has had very much effect. A study by the Department of Employment in 1971 suggested that there might be a little more progress towards bargaining reform but the implementation of simple Donovan proposals might be inappropriate in some cases.

Aspects of plant-level bargaining with particular emphasis on the effects on wage development have been brought out in various studies. Lerner, Cable and Gupta (1969) have illustrated the relative importance of various elements in earnings and considered the levels at which pay decisions are made in engineering, chemicals, baking and the soap industry. Robertson's early work (1960) was based on the engineering and ship building industries, while Brown (1973), as mentioned, has analysed bargaining in engineering. The ship building and ship-repairing report by the Commission on Industrial Relations (CIR, 1971) recommended the establishment of company joint councils with supporting yard councils (equivalent to plant-wide) where necessary. A number of other company analyses were undertaken by the CIR, which included descriptions or analyses of the existing bargaining arrangements. Although these were primarily based on the company, they also included information about the arrangements at plant level.

The motor industry has been the subject of a number of studies which include analyses of plant-level bargaining. The major work by Turner, Clack and Roberts (1967) surveys the industry as a whole as well as discussing activities at shop-floor level. Clack, in an occasional paper for the Cambridge Department of Economics (1967), discussed industrial relations in one plant in more detail and provided insights into the way shop-floor activity expresses itself. His study is based on a piece-working factory, and to that extent some of the problems and attitudes might differ from other car plants. Although Clack found no great dissatisfaction on the part of assembly-line workers, Graham Turner (1964) reported considerable dissatisfaction at Ford, which is a time-based company, and Benyon (1973), writing from a sociological point of view, came to similar conclusions. D.G. Rhys (1974) criticizes both labour and management and in particular draws attention to the deleterious effects of making wage comparisons between plants without there also being effort comparisons.

In general, the studies of bargaining practices have tended to concentrate on two main areas. Some scholars have examined the use made of the formal procedures set by joint industry boards (W. Brown,

1972; A. Flanders, 1969). Other scholarly works have emphasized the importance of informal custom and practice (*Journal of Management Studies*, October 1969, May 1970, October 1971 and 1972; Goldthorpe, 1966).

Worker Attitudes

Sociologists studying work groups and individual motivation and attitudes towards work have provided valuable insights into behaviour at shop-floor level. Goldthorpe *et al.* (1968a) emphasized the importance of external influences on workers' attitudes and priorities and put forward a social group theory of worker behaviour as opposed to the 'human relations' or sociotechnological explanations. Daniel (1970) produced an alternative interpretation of attitudes towards work. Roger Bennett (1974) has written that the Goldthorpe – Daniel debate 'would appear to be concerned with two apparently simple issues; namely, (1) are a worker's priorities "fixed" by forces external to the working situation and (2) do these priorities remain constant over a period of time?

Additional work has been done in this area: Ingham (1970) sought to document the monetary preferences in certain types of work. Wedderburn and Crompton (1972), while emphasizing the role that technology plays in worker attitudes, also stressed the interconnection between experience inside and outside the workplace; Benyon and Blackburn (1972) studied workers' involvement in their employment situation and demonstrated that workers within the same technological system had quite different perceptions of that situation, emphasizing the importance of the orientations a worker brings with him.

Other sociologists have made intensive studies of worker behaviour in specific plant situations. The main contributions came from the Manchester Business School, influenced by Lupton, whose pioneering British work on shop-floor behaviour (Lupton, 1963) generated a microlevel intensive-study approach, to which have been added economic variables.

Gowler (1969) tested a theory of the importance of workers' perceptions of different elements in a pay packet in a situation requiring high but varying amounts of overtime, low basic pay rates and limited job mobility. He found that these factors led to increased absenteeism and labour turnover. Legge (1970) and Legge and Hilling (1974, 1975) applied similar tests to different situations and found that absenteeism and turnover were less marked, or even absent, when bonus earnings formed a large and stable element of the pay. Other studies by Legge and Gowler have demonstrated that work organization, work allocation policies and payments systems can interact to undermine job satisfaction and even generate wage drift (Gowler in Robinson (ed.), 1970; Gowler and Legge in Robinson (ed.), 1970; Gowler and Legge, 1972a and b).

Shop Stewards

One of the distinguishing features of the British system of industrial relations, certainly in the postwar period, is the role of shop stewards. Trade union rule-books and procedure agreements fail to reflect their true roles, as stewards frequently enjoy far wider privileges and 'rights' (Donovan Research Paper no.1, 1968). The growth of work-place bargaining transformed the role of the steward from the guardian of national agreements at the work-place to a more active concern with improving the conditions of employment of his constituents (Goodman and Whittingham, 1969, revised 1973). This has in turn encouraged the further growth of work-place bargaining. These tendencies are perhaps most pronounced in engineering, but similar trends appear elsewhere.

Surveys of shop stewards and their activities, and of how these are perceived by managers, were carried out by the Donovan Commission (Research Paper no. 10, 1968). The general picture that emerges is that the steward in a multi-union establishment spends his time on a variety of issues and believes himself to be a representative of his constituents to management. Many stewards prefer time-rated pay systems to piece-work and, by and large, managers appear quite happy to deal with shop stewards, preferring this to bargaining with full-time trade union officials for many of the issues that arise. Most stewards are not active, class-oriented militants, eager for every opportunity to indulge in pressure bargaining with management. They do, however, present constant challenges to managerial prerogatives.

There is a general agreement that the growth of shop steward power is related to the tight labour market conditions that have existed since the Second World War. It has also been argued that there is a broad relationship between the stewards' ability to influence earnings and their importance in the work-place (Donovan Research Paper no.1, 1968), but this has been challenged on analytical and empirical grounds (Benyon, 1973; Lerner and Bescoby, 1966; HMSO,Cmnd. 131, 1957, Cmnd. 1999, 1963). The main conceptual challenge has been from the

Liverpool steel study (Scott *et al.*, 1956) and the Tavistock study (Trist *et al.*; 1963), which argue that different technologies give rise to different industrial relations problems.

The growth of shop steward committees and combine committees, both of which can be seen as responses to fragmented union organization and as attempts to obtain greater cohesion and uniformity in bargaining practices and results, have been studied, again primarily in the engineering industry.

These committees are often seen as having considerable power, *vis-à-vis* both management and trade unions. This is reflected in the changes in the structure of bargaining in a number of companies. Shop stewards are being incorporated into the formal company-level bargaining machinery. Proposals to formalize the shop stewards' position were also made in the Donovan Report and the CIR has encouraged this in a number of reports.

Donovan Research Paper no. 10 considered the various proposals that were being made relating to changes intended to induce union officials to exert greater influence on their members, to observe agreements entered into by the unions and to make unions responsible in a legal and/or financial sense for the actions of their stewards, particularly when they act unconstitutionally. The paper cast considerable doubt on the ability of unions to exert such pressures, suggesting that measures intended to achieve this sort of result might lead to unions having less rather than more control over their members.

Productivity Bargaining

The emergence of productivity bargaining is probably the most important development in British industrial relations in this period. The term was first used by Flanders (1964), in his account of the bargaining development at the Esso refinery at Fawley, and covered any type of collective bargaining in which an increase in productivity is achieved. He concluded that, 'The principle common to all productivity bargaining is the furnishing of an economic inducement for an acceptance of change. . . . ' The experience of studying Fawley exercised great influence on Flanders. It permeated the rest of the Oxford school and produced policy questions as can be seen in the Donovan Report and in the earlier reports of the NBPI and the CIR.

Flanders advocated productivity bargaining so strongly because he saw this as a way by which collective bargaining could become the means of regulating *all* aspects of the employment situation. The acceptance of voluntarist – pluralist views combined with a belief in the advantages of joint regulation within a formal framework were linked to a process of economic change beneficial not only to the bargaining parties but to the economy as a whole. Improvements covered, for example, efficiency and manpower utilization, the production of formal and controlled wage structures, and the reduction of unnecessary overtime.

McKersie and Hunter (1973) provide a valuable source of information on the development of productivity bargaining and draw a distinction between the agreements that were made in the first wave after Fawley and the second wave which occurred during the Labour Government's 1965–70 incomes policy, when the productivity exception clause was widely used as a means of obtaining pay increases in excess of the norm. It is probably the case that these negotiations would not be regarded as full productivity bargaining by Flanders, and the devaluation of the concept under pressures of incomes policy contributed to its subsequent decline. Clegg (1971) and Towers (Towers *et al.*, 1972) argue that productivity bargaining made little effective contribution to the economic problems during the incomes policy period, while Daniel (1970; Daniel and McIntosh, 1972) and Robinson (1971, 1973) have arrived at somewhat more favourable assessments.

Various studies of productivity agreements and their effects have been made by government agencies. The Donovan Research Paper no. 4 (1968) summarized some of the existing material and commented briefly on how different parties to bargaining perceived productivity bargains. The NBPI produced three general reports on productivity bargaining with special emphasis given to its role in an incomes policy (NBPI Reports no. 23, Cmnd. 3167, 1966; no. 36, Cmnd. 3311, 1967; no. 123, Cmnd. 4136, 1969).

The first two followed a broad Flanders line, with specific advice on how the controls of incomes policy could be applied to test whether there had been an increase in efficiency or productivity and whether this was due to the contribution of the workers concerned. The third general report on the subject in August 1969 considered productivity bargaining under a more relaxed incomes policy and argued that the agreements contributed to the easing of inflation. The NBPI also discussed productivity agreements in its general studies of payment-by-results systems and job evaluation (Report no. 65, Cmnd. 3627/3627–1, 1968; Report no. 83, Cmnd. 3772, 3772–1, 1968). It also discussed this issue in several industries (Report no. 50, Cmnd. 3498, 1967; Report no. 51, Cmnd. 3499, 1968; Report no. 94, Cmnd. 3847, 1968). An excellent case study of productivity was that done by Owen Smith (1971) on the steel industry. This was the main follow-up to Flanders' study of Fawley.

The effect of changes in productivity deals on internal pay structures was discussed by the NBPI and others (North and Buckingham, 1969; McKersie and Hunter, 1973). The NBPI and Addison also addressed the question of whether productivity bargains were inflationary in that they generated pay-level comparisons but not comparison of effort levels (NBPI Report no. 36, Cmnd. 3311, 1967; Addison, 1974; Towers, in Towers, Whittingham, and Gottschalk, 1972). When wage increase agreements are made in a tight labour market with incomes policy restraints, increases in pay may also be the result of collusion between employers and workers, rather than of a straight comparison effect.

Productivity bargaining is now in decline, partly as a result of its perceived abuse under incomes policies and partly because of union resistance in the face of high unemployment.

Wage Drift

The interest shown in wage drift in Britain arose from concern over inflationary effects of increasing wages, and the extension of shop-floor bargaining. Phelps Brown's article in *Economica* (1962) surveyed the problems encountered in measuring drift and discussed some of the causes. His definition of drift, 'that the effective rate of pay per unit of labour input is raised by arrangements that lie outside the control of the recognized procedures for scheduling rates', has been widely accepted.

H. A. Turner (1956) produced a statistical analysis and explanation of drift, and his subsequent debate with S. W. Lerner explored in more detail the statistical difficulties involved in measuring drift and its causes (H. A. Turner, 1960, 1964, 1967; Lerner and Marquand, 1962; Lerner, 1965). The *Department of Employment Gazette*, August 1975, uses data from the New Earnings Survey to test Turner's earlier approach. The Office of Manpower Economics produced a useful review of literature and research on wage drift in 1973.

By and large, discussion centres around two main approaches. The first postulates that in a favourable economic climate managers will increase the pay of their employees in order to keep a good labour force. Thus attempts to demonstrate that wage drift is correlated with the size of an industry settlement may be an argument developed on the premise that the size of the industry settlement is a function of general demand (Gillion, 1968).

The second approach concentrates on the bargaining practices, the role of shop stewards, and the pressures within a company to sustain internal pay relationships (Wilfred Brown, 1973; Robinson, 1968; Robinson (ed.), 1970).

Studies of internal pay relationships in a number of plants in the same industry have shown that very considerable differences exist, although there are common economic pressures (MacKay *et al.*, 1971, Robinson, 1968; Robinson (ed.), 1970, and Robinson's 'Myths of the local labour market', *Personnel*, vol. 1, no. 1, 1967). In some sectors there is little wage drift. Pay is settled by industry negotiations in coal-mining, multiple-plant baking, and large areas of white collar employment in the public sector. If there are pressures, they are more likely to take the form of job grading and effort bargaining, both of which are factors which the usual measures of drift do not, and probably cannot, pick up.

Pay Systems and structures

Discussion of wage drift and the investigations of the NBPI and CIR encouraged consideration of pay systems and led to considerable questioning of the desirability or effectiveness of payment by results. Wilfred Brown (1962) made a strong plea, based on his experience at Glacier Metal, for ending piece-work. The effects of payment by results, particularly in the case of individual or small group piece-work schemes in fragmented bargaining situations, was criticized by the Donovan Commission and NBPI for their adverse impact on pay structures and collective bargaining, and the problems created for incomes policies. However, the NBPI and others have encouraged the creation of wider-based incentive schemes, particularly in the public sector (North and Buckingham, 1969; R. B. McKersie in Royal Commission on Trade unions and Employee Associations Research Paper no. 11, 1968; Gray, 1973; Bentley, 1964).

Changes from payment by results have been attacked from the radical left on the grounds that this would seriously weaken the power of the shop-floor or make stewards responsible for the enforcement of agreements and standards (Cliff, 1970; Allen, 1966). However, surveys of shop stewards, compiled for the Donovan Research Papers suggested that a majority of them preferred not to have piece-work systems.

The discussion of wage drift emphasizes the importance of piece-work earnings but there is as yet relatively little assessment of the longer-term consequences of a movement to a time-based system, particularly one in which pay levels are settled by national bargaining as in parts of the public sector. Thus, for example, little is known of the effects of a single wage structure in coal-mining on the levels of demand for wage increases. Those who used to negotiate pay at pit levels no longer do so, and so may be less constrained in their demands.

Job evaluation was advanced as a solution to the vexing question of pay relationships. The NBPI has favoured it (Report no. 83, Cmnd. 3772, 1968 and Supplement). Lupton and Bowey (1974), and Bowey and Lupton (1973) have surveyed various types of job evaluation systems and suggested ways of comparing pay levels of similar-weighted jobs in different companies. Paterson (1972) has produced proposals for pay determination within companies, and Phelps Brown (1972) has suggested a central consortium in which those with the power to impose decisions about pay – the unions – should exercise the responsibility of making wage decisions.

The Pay Board's report on relativities (Cmnd. 5535, 1974) recognized the importance of comparisons and perceptions of equity of pay relationships. It emphasized the structure of bargaining and decision-making, and its proposals for a Relativities Board to deal with special cases within the statutory incomes policy was intended to permit some overall view of pay relationships on an ad hoc basis. The one report produced by the Pay Board, acting as the Relativities Board, on coal-miners' pay, did not in fact adopt a strict job evaluation approach but took account of both the industry's ability to pay and manpower shortages (Cmnd. 5567, 1974). A Pay Board report on Civil Service scientists recommended some limited relationships with other Civil Service grades while retaining comparability through the pay research method (Cmnd. 5602, 1974).

There was an interesting shift of emphasis between the 1973–74 and the 1965–70 incomes policies. The latter gave little weight to comparability while the former recognized the crucial role that fairness plays in British pay determination. Hyman and Brough (1975) have produced a survey of notions of fairness which also discusses values and ideology in industrial relations.

Studies of pay at plant level have shed some light on the actual pay structures, again mainly in engineering (MacKay *et al.*, 1971; Robinson, 1968, (ed.), 1970; Brown, 1973). Even within the field of engineering itself there seems to be little consistency in internal pay structures among plants, each having developed through time in response to particular pressures. Moreover, there is often a considerable spread of pay for individuals within the same occupation in a single plant, using gross pay as a measure of earnings.

Incomes Policy

In the sixties and seventies, the national government has been concerned with some form of incomes policy.Interest has centred around two issues: its administration and tests of policy measures already introduced. The last area involves econometric analysis more than industrial relations. It is apparent that some of the increase in the Wage Rates Index in the past decade was caused by the type of agreement negotiated – for example, from across-the-board increases in rates to minimum earnings level guarantees, so making this an unsatisfactory statistical source (HMSO, DEP, 1971; Parkin and Sumner, 1972; Laidler and Purdy, 1974; NBPI 3rd General Report, Cmnd. 3715, 1968). (See also list of government White Papers in the bibliography.)

Accounts of the development of such policies during the sixties include Blackaby (ed.), 1972; Clegg, 1971; Fels, 1972; Ulman and Flanagan, 1971; Liddle and McCarthy, 1972; Turner, 1970). Basically, employers do not favour statutory intervention in collective bargaining and the government does not want to be put in a position of implementing unpopular legislation. Nevertheless, there is a consistent growing realization that the inflationary consequences of unhindered collective bargaining are placing too heavy a burden on the economy and inhibiting the government's ability to pursue its social and economic policies.

Advocates of incomes policy include Jones (1973), Clegg (1971), Robinson (1968) and Flanders, whose 1966 paper is the best conceptual approach to the problem of the reconciliation of voluntarism and statutory intervention through incomes policy. Critics from the market position include Parkin and Sumner (1972) Laidler and Purdy (1974), Paish (1971), Jackman and Klappholz (1975), IEA Readings, no. 14 (1974).

The academic debate has centred on the causes of inflation with particular concentration on the Phillips curve (Phillips, 1958). Critics of the Phillips curve have argued that the statistical treatment of the data used to derive the original curve was such that little use can be made of the approach for actual policy-making (Knowles and Winsten, 1959; Robinson, 1968; Jackson, Turner and Wilkinson, 1972; Laidler, 1975; Phelps, 1967; Wood, 1972, 1975). There is now wide agreement, however, on the importance of inducing changes in attitudes and expectations in order to reduce inflation. Agreement now exists as well on the need to introduce policies directed to the structure of the labour market (Topham, in Coates, Topham and Barratt Brown, 1969, and in Coates *et al.*, 1970).

Critics of incomes policy from the left are Cliff (1970, 1975); Cliff and Barker (1966), Allen (1966), and Coates and Topham (1968). Discussions of both sides of the question can be found in Corina (1966) and Robinson (1971). The annual reports of the NBPI (19, 40, 77, 122 1970) contain discussions of the problems encountered by the Labour Government in implementing its incomes policy in 1965–70. This period has been discussed in Jones (1973) and Clegg (1972). The Pay Board issued a report on the 'Experience of Operating a Statutory Incomes Policy' (1974) immediately prior to its demise, which pointed out some of the difficulties of administering it.

Strikes

The starting-point of a discussion of strike activity in Great Britain is Knowles' pioneering work (1952). He analysed the causes of strikes, using available official statistics. Turner (1963) and Hyman (1972) have continued this analysis of strike trends.

During the postwar period, the coal industry had, until recently, suffered a large number of strikes, and the National Coal Board recorded stoppages more systematically and comprehensively than many other employers. The Donovan Commission's Report discussed strike activity in Britain and appeared particularly concerned to make international comparisons of Britain's record. The subsequent debate between Turner and McCarthy on the quality of the data and the conclusions that could be drawn from international comparisons has added to an overall knowledge of strike statistics and has provided desirable guidance on their interpretation (Turner, 1969b; McCarthy, 1970).

It seems that the recent sharp decrease in coal-mining strikes has followed the move from pit bargaining to a uniform day-wage system throughout the industry, with wages being negotiated now only by industry-level or national bargaining. Analyses of more recent data have emphasized the importance of excluding coal-mining from aggregate statistics in order that the very marked reduction of strikes in coal-mining does not distort the general patterns and trends. Silver (1973) challenges one of Turner's themes by arguing that if coal-mining is excluded, strike activity has increased in recent years.

The general consideration of strike activity within a sociological work is well represented by Hyman (1972), Ingham (1974) and Eldridge (1968). These works, in general, provide a wide range of liberal to radical views. Ingham emphasizes the importance of the institutionalization of industrial conflict and the effects of structural variations of unions in the plants. Hyman points out the importance of the political aspects and dimensions of strikes. Eldridge discusses various aspects of strike activity. In general, he emphasizes conflict between normative systems, as well as the impact of belief that others have broken the (written or unwritten) rules of bargaining behaviour.

One of the major early studies of an industry-wide strike was in the engineering industry (Clegg and Adams, 1957). This study examined the roles of the parties and the government in a situation that was perceived first to be inflationary, and later as an intolerable disruption of British industry. The interactions of government and a major employers' association were well developed, as were the consequences for future government – employer relations. This signalled a dramatic change of government policy, probably a sound and perceptive forecast.

Foot (1967) has produced a shorter, more radical study of an industry dispute which brings out the internal union factors. A detailed account of a strike in one company (Lane and Roberts, 1971) illustrates the differences between the overt reasons and the underlying causes of strikes, drawing attention to a long and growing worker dissatisfaction with both management and their own union. Similar in-depth studies have been produced by Barlow (1969), who looks at a strike of white-collar workers, and Arnison (1970). Arnison's work concerns a strike in an American-owned company which became a major issue of trade union recognition and ultimately affected many workers.

There are, in addition, a number of sociological studies of conflict which may fall short of strike action but demonstrate complexity of causation. White (1974) shows how conflict can be generated by the formal provisions of a new work arrangement, which may place intolerable burdens on the participants, particularly if they have been accustomed to informal adaptation to work situations.

Those who are more concerned with reform of the industrial relations system designed to bring joint regulatory activities within the control of the 'proper' parties, are also interested in the distinction between official and unofficial strikes. The latter may be seen as an indication that the formal parties to the bargaining procedures have lost effective control.

This is one motive for some of the legislative proposals to reduce the incidence of unofficial strikes by making trade unions legally responsible for their members' strike participation.

Other interesting studies of strikes in particular areas or sectors shed light on both statistical incidence and causes. Brown *et al.* (1972), after studying the ship building industry, conclude that a class explanation of strikes is inappropriate. Workers have strong group identity on an occupational basis, and it is accepted that groups can, within certain limits, pursue their own claims independently. As the success of some individual groups is perceived by others as adversely affecting their own position, the pattern of disputes is self-perpetuating. This conclusion is also reached in the CIR study of the ship building and ship-repairing industry (1971). Strikes in the north-east's ship building industry are also discussed by Cameron (1964).

The effect of payment of social security benefits to strikers or their families has been raised as both a research issue and a political debate (Conservative Political Centre, 1968; HMSO, Cmnd. 3888, 1969; Society of Conservative Lawyers, 1974; Lasko, 1975). Gennard and Lasko (1974, 1975) have produced factual analyses of the results of state financial support to strikers and have discussed the various proposals for change without coming to any firm policy recommendations. Duncan and McCarthy (1974), after examining data for the past fifteen years, conclude that the argument that the increase in strikes is a result of the payment of benefits to strikers is not proven.

Legislation and Government Intervention

The Donovan Commission's hearings provided an opportunity for both sides of the industrial relations system to state their views on legal intervention, with the result that both sides advocated minimum intervention. This advocacy, however, was moderated by each side's desire to have legal intervention work in favour of attaining their objectives (1968), presumably while restraining the opposition.

The Commission was, of course, part of a major debate over legislative reform of industrial relations. Its report emphasized a *voluntary* system, but recommended a number of legal and procedural changes to help achieve reform. Firstly, the Commission recommended the establishment of factory- or company-wide agreements, placing heavy responsibility on company directors for achieving industrial relations improvements.

Secondly, the commission proposed an Industrial Relations Act to bolster voluntary strategies. This Act would require employers to register their (new) agreements with the Department of Employment, and would create a Commission on Industrial Relations (CIR) to examine cases referred to it and obtain desired reforms. The CIR would also examine recognition and inter-union disputes. Legal enforcement was left an open question, pending the results of voluntary reform.

There were additional proposals for legislative change of such things as the legal status of unions and union rules. A majority of the commission wanted to persuade unions to register, by extending protection against legal action for inducing breaches of contract only to registered unions, while a minority (7 to 5) wanted registration to be mandatory. Contracts stipulating that an employee could not be a union member were to be void, and an employer's refusal to recognize a union or bargain effectively was to be referred to compulsory unilateral arbitration.

The general reaction to the Donovan Report was that it did not go far enough and, in particular, that it did not offer any quick or even perhaps reasonable hopes of solving the problems of unconstitutional and unofficial strikes and the general issue of trade union control over their members.

The Labour Government reacted by producing its White Paper, 'In Place of Strife', in January 1969. The CIR was to be established, and the government could enforce its rulings on inter-union disputes. Reserve powers were established to provide a 28-day 'conciliation pause' in disputes that might seriously affect the economy. In official strikes, there was a provision for a government-called strike ballot of the members, if the national interest were deemed threatened. In April 1969, the government announced that it would give preliminary priority to the 'legal sanctions' clauses, and leave much of the rest to be introduced later. The first announcement of this was made by the Chancellor of the Exchequer, emphasizing that the reforms were considered a contribution to anti-inflation policy (Robinson, 1968).

The proposal created immense dissension inside the Labour Party and between the government and trade unions, and it appeared for a time that the government would fall (Peter Jenkins, 1970). In the end, the TUC agreed to new procedures to deal with unconstitutional strikes (TUC Report, 1969). Fay (1970) has written a highly readable commentary on this situation.

The Conservative Government of 1970 was committed to reform involving much more legal intervention and enacted the Industrial

Relations Act of 1971. Provisions were made for procedure agreements proposed by the CIR to be made legally enforceable.

The CIR was also made responsible for investigating recognition cases both in the voluntary stages and under the more formal procedures of Industrial Relations Act. Its basic approach was to seek a solution on the bargaining unit that was acceptable to all parties, although this was not always possible. In considering the most appropriate bargaining unit, the commission examined such things as the payment system, grading structure, promotion and recruitment policy of the company (CIR Study no. 5, 1974). The decision to recommend a bargaining agent and the choice of that agent was determined by a combination of union membership and potential membership. Considering that the Commission's task was to encourage collective bargaining, it is not surprising that, on occasion, they recommended recognition even when the members of the bargaining unit were in a minority in the plant.

Under the 1971 Act, strikes and irregular industrial action could be penalized under certain conditions. The legal protection against inducing breaches of contract in furtherance of a trade dispute was confined to registered trade unions, and the great majority of unions decided not to register. The concept of unfair industrial practices was then introduced and provision made for individuals to refuse to belong to a trade union (Clegg, 1972; Simpson and Wood, 1973; Paterson, 1971).

The Act set up the National Industrial Relations Court to hear cases arising from the reform. The court received much adverse comment from trade unions, and on occasion from scholars, who believed not merely that the law it was applying was ill conceived, but that the court's methods were ill suited to the problems it confronted, and that some of the court's decisions and statements may have worsened the situation (National Industrial Relations Court, 1973; Donaldson, 1973). At the same time, it should be recognized that trade union hostility to the Industrial Relations Act and the NIRC was such that strong criticism was inevitable.

Weekes *et al.* (1975) examined the implementation of the 1971 Act and concluded that this sort of legislation is unlikely to be effective, not the least because of reluctance of most of the participants to utilize its legal sanctions.

Although Donovan's recommendations served to focus debate on industrial relations, the Commission was not the only author of research in this field. Several other major research lines need to be mentioned.

There have been significant analyses of various issues that have been the subject of legislation, Weekes *et al.* (1975) being the most sustained and important. Rideout has looked at trade union rules on discipline and on admission to membership (1964, 1966). Foster (1973) and O'Higgins (1973) have considered the legal effects of a strike notice. Kidner (1973) has examined the law as it affects the right to stand for union office. Hepple (1972) has discussed the relationship between a trade union and its shop stewards, with emphasis on the question of liability for action taken. Lewis (1974) has discussed the Con–Mech case which appeared before the National Industrial Relations Court and proved to be of great political significance. Probably the most important case was Heaton, discussed by Otto Kahn-Freund (1972).

An excellent outline of current legislative provisions is to be found in Hepple and O'Higgins, *Encyclopedia of Labour Relations Law*, which is periodically updated to take account of current developments. Accounts of labour law can also be found in Wedderburn (1971), Kahn-Freund (1972) and Clegg (1972).

In general, academic work *has* had some influence on attitudes towards government intervention. For example, both before and after the Industrial Relations Act, the CIR's approach relied heavily on the Oxford school viewpoint.

Unions in Britain are prepared (apparently increasingly so) to accept legislative intervention to provide floors from which their rights can be established and increased. They are, however, totally unprepared to accept restraints on their bargaining positions except in incomes policy situations, and then only with extreme reluctance. In addition, they are unwilling to have outside intervention in such things as union de-marcations or enforceability of contracts, especially where this has a connotation that union organization has to accept legal responsibility for the actions of its members. There is a very powerful attachment to the belief that voluntarism and persuasion by trade unions at the plant level is the most appropriate way of sustaining agreements.

Trade Union Growth

The Donovan Commission examined union growth in Research Paper no. 6, in which Bain (1966) concluded that further expansion of trade union membership, a condition for the extension of collective bargain-ing, would require government intervention to encourage trade union recognition.

This was particularly true of the white-collar field, where, he had argued earlier, the density of union membership was rising and the increase in the number of members reflected the growth in white-collar employment. Bain's 1970 study of the growth of white-collar unionism and Bain *et al.* (1973) found no relationship between growth of aggregate white-collar union membership and sociodemographic characteristics of white-collar workers, their earnings, or other terms and conditions of employment (including job security, promotion and other aspects of the work situation, as well as such things as the union's image and recruitment policies). Instead, growth was related to employment concentration, union recognition and government action. Studies of individual sectors of white-collar unionism have included more specific variables to explain the particular cases (Blackburn, 1967).

Attention has also focused on the growth of professional associations with union-type activities, and suggestions have been made that an increase in bargaining activities and militancy should be expected (Prandy, 1965; Blain, 1972; Coates, 1972; Roberts, Loveridge and Gennard, 1972).

On the question of total union membership, the Donovan Report concluded that the most important factor determining the level of trade union membership is the level of the economy. However, there are considerable problems involved in measuring trade union membership; the figures are of varying reliability, and no really satisfactory way has yet been found of ascertaining membership in different sectors of industry.

H. A. Turner's 1962 study of cotton unions provided an important point for further work on union growth, and his classification of unions into 'open' and 'closed' offered an alternative to the usual 'craft, industrial and general' classification.

Trade Union Structure and Government

Donovan Research Paper no. 5 examines union structure and development, membership participation and union government. It also discusses the process of amalgamation, which has increased in recent years as part of a growing interest in merging competing unions at the workplace.

The major contribution to trade union government and administration was made by Roberts (1956). Part 2 of Research Paper no. 5 of the Donovan Report returned to the subject and started from the premise that membership participation was of central importance in the functioning of unions. The paper attempted to classify unions with different membership participation characteristics. This question is also discussed in much of the literature on shop stewards. Hughes writes briefly of the activities of the Communist Party in unions (Research Paper no. 5, part 2) within the context of the possibility of having 'opposition' within trade unions. The argument for this was earlier advanced by Jenkins and Mortimer (1965), two trade union officials.

Related Issues

Worker participation

The increase in research activity in this field has preceded recent political interest. Clegg (1960) provided a critical examination of workers' participation in management. The traditional attitude of British unions was that industrial democracy and worker participation could be best achieved by an extension of collective bargaining through more representation at the individual plant level (Labour Party, 1967; J. Jones in Coates, Topham and Barratt Brown (eds.) 1969).

Some shift in emphasis occurred in 1974. In part, this was a response to anticipated membership in the EEC. It also reflected a change in the attitudes of some trade union leaders, who had come to believe that participation in some form of supervisory board could prevent undesirable decisions such as lay-offs and plant shut-downs (TUC, 1974). The question of participation and collective bargaining is discussed from a non-trade union point of view by Clarke *et al.* (1972), who conclude that direct participation of workers in management will not increase rapidly, although legislation might stimulate it.

Commentators from the left have advocated workers' control as an advanced form of participation. These views are sometimes related to the broad stream of ideas developed from the early syndicalist writers (Coates and Topham (eds.), 1968). The leading advocates, from the Institute for Workers' Control, combine proposals for workers' control with criticism of what is seen as the excessively bureaucratic structure of trade unions and the undemocratic powers of management (Coates and Topham, 1972).

Studies of various forms of participation or control in individual companies or organizations have been made. Flanders *et al.* (1968) examined a retail store with a special form of participation and assessed the extent of effective diffusion of decision-making. The Fairfields (later Upper Clyde Shipbuilders) experiment in finance and union participation on the board of a company which would otherwise have closed down has provoked some interesting studies (Alexander and Jenkins, 1970; Paulden and Hawkins, 1969; Buchan, 1972).

Suggested legislation for worker directors, provisions allowing trade union representatives to sit on bodies such as safety committees, and proposals to require management to disclose information to trade unionists (CIR Report no. 31), show promise of changing present bargaining practices and realigning the balance of power. At the same time, there is a growing interest in questions of work organization, job content and the quality of working life. In these areas, further research will undoubtedly follow (Goldthorpe, 1974, Fox, 1974b).

Lay-offs, or redundancy

Loss of jobs, particularly when associated with the closure of plants, has been a cause of concern on both political and industrial fronts. The legislative provisions of the Redundancy Payments Act and the unfair dismissals clauses of the Industrial Relations Act, improved and amended in the current Employment Protection (Consolidation) Act, 1978, illustrate the attention given to this issue by successive governments. Wedderburn (1964, 1965) has studied the effects of lay-offs on white-collar workers following cancellation of a defence contract. He has also studied railway employees. Thomas (1969), too, has examined lay-offs following a defence contract cancellation. Martin and Fryer (1973) studied a severe cutback in employment by a firm and commented critically on the Redundancy Payments Act. Fryer's appendix contains a stimulating discussion of lay-offs at the Upper Clyde Shipbuilders, and raises questions concerning the effectiveness of government provisions for dealing with the question of job search and re-employment in such a situation. Daniel (1972) studied this aspect in a situation involving lay-offs following a merger of two electrical companies. He concluded that a higher proportion of people in his study were placed in jobs through government services than had been publicized in a national survey (Parker *et al.*, 1971).

Discussion of the effectiveness of lay-off provisions has become intertwined with assessments of labour markets and of the government's manpower policies. For example, interesting light is being shed on new jobs taken by laid-off workers and the extent to which they stay in similar occupations in different industries rather than change occupations (Martin and Fryer, 1973).

Low pay

Although wages councils have been introduced to set pay in low-wage industries (Bayliss, 1962), the question has continued to interest researchers, trade unions and government. Marquand has discussed the incidence of low pay using the former official statistics series (1967). The NBPI produced a general report (no. 169, 1971) on the subject just before closing down in 1971. This was a broad survey which adopted the concept of 'lower paid' as the 'lowest decile', for the board had throughout its life refused to define low pay at a money level. Specific reports made by the NBPI included agricultural workers and workers in the retail drapery, outfitting and footwear trades. The reports were made in February and March 1967, during the period of severe restraint (Report no. 25, Cmnd. 3199, 1967; Report no. 27, Cmnd. 3224, 1967). The board also issued a report on the clothing industry (no. 110, Cmnd. 4002, 4002–1, 1969), in which it concluded that the wage council machinery was ill-suited to deal with the problems of low pay. Additional reports covered ancillary workers in National Health Service hospitals (no. 166, Cmnd. 4644, 1971), workers in the laundry and dry cleaning industry (no. 167, Cmnd. 4647, 1971), and workers in the contract cleaning trade (no. 168, Cmnd. 4637, 1971) (See also CIR Reports 23, 37, 46, 47, 48, 49, 50, 51, 77 and 83).

Incomes policy has tended to be regarded as providing an opportunity for special treatment of low-paid workers, but the results, so far as they can be inferred from the available statistics, do not seem to have been particularly encouraging (Field (ed.), 1973; Fisher and Dix, 1974). It is unclear whether this is because the machinery of incomes policy was inadequate in that it merely permitted relatively larger increases for some low-paid workers, rather than insisting that preferential treatment be given to them (which would have involved further intervention in bargaining), or because such preferential treatment, once obtained, would be offset by the action of others seeking to restore previous pay relationships. The use of aggregate data is less than fully satisfactory, and it is clear that further work needs to take place in this area, perhaps on a disaggregated basis if and when improved statistical data are available. A government report in 1969 discussed the possibility of a national minimum wage as a way of dealing with the problem, but did not come out in favour of such a solution (HMSO, *A National Minimum Wage*, 1969). The TUC has turned its attention to low pay, but there is a conflict inside trade unions as to the extent to which additional improvements should be sought through collective bargaining (TUC, *Low Pay*, 1970; TUC *Economic Review*, 1968 onwards).

An Overview

The current state of theory might be summarized as one in which various attacks are being made on the general position associated with the Oxford school. The pluralist approach has been criticized for its perceived implication of endorsement of the existing balance of power (Fox, 1974b; Goldthorpe, 1974; for a reply see Clegg, 1975). Productivity bargaining is being criticized on theoretical as well as practical grounds, and the basic voluntarist position appears to be suffering setbacks as an increasing amount of legislation is introduced by the current Labour Government. Such laws have had the effect of providing trade unions with rights and opportunities in collective bargaining, although stopping short of making agreements enforceable at law. What appeared to be the strongest coherent approach to industrial relations theory and practice is thus being attacked on a number of fronts.

At the same time, there is a growing body of Marxist writing which has hitherto contained little beyond partial criticism of more orthodox approaches. Thus pluralism was challenged as a distorting ideology which concealed the fundamental dichotomy mediated by the inequality of class power. The definition of industrial relations in terms of job control or regulation is seen as suggesting a greater degree of stability and order than really exists. There has, however, been little systematic approach seeking to relate these and similar arguments to a Marxist theory of industrial relations. It is likely that such treatment, will be forthcoming as writers seek to place recent developments in industrial relations in a broader social, economic and political context. This would see the system of industrial relations, if there is a system, as one beset by internal contradictions, and conclude that the traditional approach will be unable to explain the 'disorder' with which it so concerns itself because of the deficiencies of its own methods of analysis. (Hyman and Brough, 1975).

The radical critics of the Oxford school (Fox, Goldthorpe and Eldridge) have not as yet produced a general framework of analysis within which the processes of industrial relations can be examined and explained. However, the Oxford school's emphasis on the role of the *traditional* parties to collective bargaining is seen as excessively conservative, ignoring growing shop-floor demand for greater direct involvement in determination of terms and conditions of employment. At the same time, the problems generated by governments' attempts to establish an incomes policy have not yet been fully incorporated into a systematic analysis of industrial relations.

The creation of bodies such as the National Board for Prices and Incomes, the Commission on Industrial Relations, and the Advisory Conciliation and Arbitration Service has had a beneficial effect on industrial relations research. These bodies have undertaken many studies, both broad and specific, of industrial relations and wage problems. Research methodology has been improved by these bodies. In addition, they have had a direct effect in spreading research experience. The NBPI and the CIR have made widespread use of academics to reproduce their studies. Thus, although it was not one of their original objectives, the NBPI and the CIR have been of significant benefit to the training of research workers and the production of research material.

The industrial relations scene itself is subject to considerable and rapid change. The trends towards greater decentralisation of power and the rejection of both managerial and union authority by shop-floor workers, coinciding with the greater involvement of national trade unions in the government's formulation of social and economic policy, are creating a new context of industrial relations. While the British trade union movement has always been political, it is now much more involved in the processes of political decision-making than in any other peacetime period. Trade unionists' perception of their power to prevent undesirable legislation has to some extent undermined the government's confidence in its ability to deal with industrial and related economic issues. Whether this confidence will be restored if adverse economic conditions reduce the real or perceived power of trade unions is unknown. It is, however, a question that both major parties are considering.

In practical terms, a major issue is the attention which can and should be given to considerations of the public interest in the results of collective bargaining. There is a substantial body of opinion that recent experiences have demonstrated that the government cannot compel trade unions to pay regard to the 'public interests', in either incomes policy or industrial relations reform. To this extent, the voluntarists seem to be gaining ground. However, should voluntarist methods prove insufficient, there will be no doubt be a revival of the interventionist strategy of safeguarding the public interest (however defined) by legislation and acts of government.

LIST OF ABBREVIATIONS USED IN REFERENCES

ACAS	– Advisory Conciliation and Arbitration Service
BJIR	– *British Journal of Industrial Relations*
BOUIES	– *Bulletin of Oxford University Institute of Economics and Statistics*
CIR	– Commission On Industrial Relations
DAE	– Department of Applied Economics
DEP	– Department of Employment and Productivity (now Department of Employment)
ILJ	– *Industrial Law Journal*
IEA	– International Economics Association
IPM	– Institute of Personnel Management
IRJ	– *Industrial Relations Journal*
JMS	– *Journal of Management Studies*
NBPI	– National Board for Prices and Incomes
NHS	– National Health Service
NIESR	– National Institute For Economic and Social Research
NIRC	– National Industrial Relations Court
PEP	– Political and Economic Planning
SSRC	– Social Science Research Council

REFERENCES

ACAS, 'Difficulties affecting London Docks', Report no. 2 (1975).

Addison, J. T., 'Productivity bargaining: the externalities question', *Scottish Journal of Political Economy* (June 1974).

Alexander, K. J. W. and C. L. Jenkins, *Fairfields: A Study of Industrial Change* (London: Allen Lane, 1970).

Allen, V. L., *Militant Trade Unionism* (London: Merlin Press, 1966).

Arnison, Jim, *The Million Pound Strike* (London: Lawrence & Wishart, 1970).

Bain, George Sayers, 'The growth of white-collar trade unionism in Great Britain', *BJIR*, Vol. IV, no. 3 (November 1966).

——, *The Growth of White-Collar Unionism* (Oxford: OUP, 1970).

——, Coates, David and Ellis, Valerie, *Social Stratification and Trade Unionism* (London: Heinemann Educational, 1973).

Barlow, Graham, 'Some latent influences in a pay claim: an examination of a white-collar dispute', *BJIR*, Vol. VII, no. 2 (July 1969).

Bayliss, F. J., *British Wages Councils* (Oxford: Blackwell, 1962).

Beck, Tony, *The Fine Tubes Strike* (London: Stage 1, 1974).

Bennett, Roger, 'Orientation to work and some implications for management', *Journal of Management Studies*, Vol. 11, no. 2 (May 1974).

Bentley, F. R., *People, Productivity and Progress* (London: Business Publications, Ltd, 1964).

Benyon, H. and R. M. Blackburn, *Perceptions of Work: Variations within a Factory* (Cambridge: CUP, 1972).

——, *Working for Ford* (Harmondsworth: Allen Lane Penguin, 1973).

Blackaby, F. (ed.), *An Incomes Policy for Britain (London: NIESR & SSRC, 1972)*.

Blackburn, R. M., *Union Character and Social Class* (London: Batsford, 1967).

Blain, A. N. J., *Pilots and Management* (London: George Allen & Unwin, 1972).

Blain, A. N. J. and John Gennard, 'Industrial relations theory: a critical review', *BJIR*, Vol. VIII, no. 3 (November 1970).

Boraston, Ian, Hugh Clegg and Malcolm Rimmer, *Workplace and Union* (London: Heinemann Educational, 1975).

Bowey, Angela and Tom Lupton, *Job and Pay Comparisons* (London: Gower Press, 1973).

Brown, R. K., P. Brannen, J. M. Cousins and M. L. Samphier, 'The contours of solidarity: social stratification and industrial relations in shipbuilding', *BJIR*, Vol. X, no. 1 (March 1972).

Brown, Wilfred, *Piecework Abandoned* (London: Heinemann Educational, 1962).

——, *The Earnings Conflict* (London: Penguin, 1973).

Brown William, 'A Consideration of Custom and Practice', *BJIR*, Vol. X, no. 1 (March 1972).

——, *Piecework Bargaining* (London: Heinemann Educational, 1973).

——, and Keith Sisson, 'The use of comparisons in workplace wage determinations', *BJIR*, Vol. XIII, no. 1 (March 1975).

Buchan, Alasdair, *The Right to Work: The Story of the Upper Clyde Confrontation* (London: Calder & Boyars, 1972).

Cameron, G. C., 'Post-war strikes in the north-east shipbuilding and shiprepairing industry', *BJIR*, Vol. II, no. 1 (March 1964).

Chemical and Allied industries Joint Industrial Council, *Constitution and Schedule of Wage Rates and Working Conditions*, Clause 9 (September 1974).

Child, John, *Industrial Relations in the British Printing Industry* (London: George Allen & Unwin, 1967).

——(ed.), *Man and Organisation* (London: George Allen & Unwin, 1973).

CIR, 'Facilities afforded to Shop Stewards', Report No. 17 (London: HMSO, 1971).

——, 'Shipbuilding and Shiprepairing', Report No. 22 (London: HMSO, 1971).

——, Study No. 5, *Trade Union Recognition: CIR Experience*, 1974.

——, Reports: 23, 31, 37, 46, 47, 48, 49, 50, 51, 77, 83.

Clack, G., *Industrial Relations in a British Car Factory*, Cambridge Department of Applied Economics, Occasional Paper No. 9 (1967).

Clarke, R. O., D. J. Fatchett and B. C. Roberts, *Workers' Participation in Management in Britain* (London: Heinemann Educational, 1972).

Clegg, H. A., *A New Approach to Industrial Democracy* (Oxford: Blackwell, 1960).

——, *How to Run an Incomes Policy and Why We Made Such a Mess of the Last One* (London: Heinemann, 1971).

——, *The System of Industrial Relations in Great Britain* (Oxford: Blackwell, 1972).

——, 'Pluralism in industrial relations', *BJIR*, Vol. XIII, no. 3 (1975).

Clegg, H. A. and Rex Adams, *The Employers' Challenge* (Oxford: Blackwell, 1957).

Cliff, Tony, *The Employers' Offensive: Productivity Deals and How to Fight Them* (London: Pluto Press, 1970).

——, *The Crisis: Social Contract or Socialism* (London: Pluto Press, 1975).

Cliff, T. and Barker, C., *Incomes Policy, Legislation and Shop Stewards* (London: Industrial Shop Stewards Defence Committee, 1966).

Coates, Ken and Anthony Topham (eds.), *Industrial Democracy in Great Britain: a book of readings and witnesses for workers control* (London: MacGibbon & Kee, 1968).

——, *The New Unionism: The Case for Workers' Control* (London: Peter Owen, 1972).

Coates, Ken, Tony Topham and Michael Barratt Brown (eds), *Trade Union Register* (London: Merlin Press, 1969; and also 1970).

Coates, R. D., *Teachers' Unions and Interest Group Politics* (Cambridge: CUP, 1972).

Conservative Political Centre, *Fair Deal at Work* (London, 1968).

Corina, J., The Development of Incomes Policy', (London: *IPM*, 1966).

Crossley, J. R., 'The Donovan Report: a case study in the poverty of Historicism', *BJIR*, Vol. VI, no. 3 (1968).

Daly, L., 'A Future for the Miners' in Coates, Topham, and Barrat Brown (eds) (1969).

Daniel, W. W., *Beyond the Wage-work Bargain,* (London: PEP Broadsheet, 519, July 1970).

——, *Whatever happened to the workers in Woolwich?* (London: PEP, Broadsheet 537, July 1972).

——, and Neil McIntosh, *The Right to Manage* (London: MacDonald, PEP, 1972).

Department of Employment Gazette (August 1975). Donaldson, Sir John, President of the NIRC, speech of 18 October 1973, reported in *Industrial Review Review and Report* (IR-RR), no. 67 (1973).

Duncan, J.W. and W. E. J. McCarthy, 'The state subsidy theory of strikes: an examination of statistical data for the period 1956–1970', *BJIR*, Vol. XII, no. 1 (March 1974).

Eldridge, J. E. T., *Industrial Disputes: Essays in the Sociology of Industrial Relations* (London: Routledge and Kegan Paul, 1968).

——, 'Panaceas and pragmatism in industrial relations', *IRJ*, Vol. 6, no. 1 (Spring 1975).

Employment Protection Act (1975).

Fay, Stephen, *Measure for Measure: Reforming the Trade Unions* (London: Chatto & Windus, Charles Knight, 1970).

Fels, Allan, *The British Prices and Incomes Board* (Cambridge: CUP, 1972).

Field, Frank (ed.), *Low Pay* (London: Arrow Books, 1973).

Fisher, Alan and Bernard Dix, *Low Pay and How to End It* (London: Pitman, 1974).

Fisher, Malcolm R., *The Economic Analysis of Labour* (London: Weidenfeld & Nicolson, 1971).

Flanders, Allan, *The Fawley Productivity Agreements* (London: Faber & Faber, 1964).

——, 'The future of voluntarism', *Personnel Management*, Vol. XLVII, no. 378 (1966).

——, 'Productivity bargaining as a rule-changing exercise', in D. C. Alexander (ed.), *A Productivity Bargaining Symposium* (London: Engineering Employers' Federation, 1969).

——, *Management and Unions* (London: Faber & Faber, 1970).

——, and H. A. Clegg, *The System of Industrial Relations in Great Britain* (Oxford: Blackwell, 1954).

——, R. Pomeranz and J. Woodward, *Experiment in Industrial Democracy: a Study of the John Lewis Partnership* (London: Faber & Faber, 1968).

Foot, P., 'The seamen's struggle', in R. Blackburn and C. Cockburn (eds.), *The Incompatibles: Trade Union Militancy and the Consensus* (London: Penguin, 1967).

Foster, Ken, 'Strike Notice: Section 147', *Industrial Law Journal*, Vol. 2, no. 1 (1973).

Fox, Alan, *Industrial Sociology and Industrial Relations*, Donovan Research Paper No. 8 (1968).

——, *A Sociology of Work in Industry* (London: Collier–Macmillan, 1971).

——, *Man Mismanagement* (London: Hutchinson, 1974a).

——, *Beyond Contract: Work, Power and Trust Relations* (London: Faber & Faber, 1974b).

Gennard, John and Roger Lasko, 'Supplementary benefits and strikers', *BJIR*, Vol. XII, no. I (March 1974).

Gennard, John and Roger Lasko, 'The individual and the strike', *BJIR*, Vol. XIII, no. 3 (November 1975).

Gillion, C., 'Wage rates, earnings and wage drift', *NIESR* (1968).

Goldthorpe, J. H., 'Attitudes and behaviour of car assembly workers: a deviant case and a theoretical critique', *British Journal of Sociology*, Vol. 17, no. 3 (September 1966).

——, 'Theories of Industrial society reflections on the recrudescence of Historicism and the future of futurology', *Archives Europeenes de sociologie*, Vol. XII (1971).

——, 'Industrial relations in Great Britain: a critique of reformism', *Politics and Society* (1974).

Goldthorpe, John H., David Lockwood, Frank Bechhofer, Jennifer Platt, *The Affluent Worker: Industrial Attitudes and Behaviour* (Cambridge: CUP, 1968a).

——, *The Affluent Worker: Political Attitudes and Behaviour* (Cambridge: CUP, 1968b).

——, *The Affluent Worker in the Class Structure* (Cambridge: CUP, 1969).

Goodman, J. F. B. and T. G. Whittingham, *Shop Stewards* (London: Pan Management Series, 1973).

——, *Strikes* (London: Fontana/Collins, 1972).

Government Social Survey, *Workplace Industrial Relations* (1968).

Government White Papers, Incomes Policy, Cmnd. 1844 (1962); Cmnd. 2577 (1965); Cmnd. 2639 (1965); Cmnd. 2808 (1965); Cmnd. 3073 (1966); Cmnd. 3150 (1966); Cmnd. 3235 (1967); Cmnd. 3590 (1968); Cmnd. 4237 (1969); Cmnd. 5205 (1973); Cmnd. 5247 (1973); Cmnd. 5779 (1974).

Gowler, Dan, ' Determinants of the supply of labour to the firm', *Journal of Management Studies*, Vol. 6, no. 1 (February 1969).

Gowler, Dan and Karen Legge, 'Occupational role development: Part 1', *Personnel Review*, Vol. 1, no. 2 (Spring 1972a); 'Part II' (Summer 1972b).

Gray, R. B., 'The Scanlon Plan-A case study', *BJIR*, Vol. IX, no. 3 (November 1973).

Hepple, Bob, 'Union responsibility for shop stewards', *ILJ*, Vol. 1, no. 4 (1972).

Hepple, B. A. and P. O'Higgins, *Encyclopedia of Labour Relations Law* London: Sweet and Maxwell and Edinburgh: W. Green & Son (periodically updated).

Herron, Frank, *Labour Markets in Crisis: Redundancy at Upper Clyde Shipbuilders* (London: Macmillan, 1975).

HMSO, 'Interim Report on Joint Standing Industrial Councils', Cmnd. 8606 (1917).

——, 'Supplementary Report on Works Committees', Cmnd. 9001 (1918).

——, Committee on Trade and Industry (Balfour Committee), 'Survey of Industrial Relations' (1926).

——, Courts of Inquiry Reports of Briggs Motor Bodies and Fords, Cmnd. 131 (1957); Cmnd. 1999 (1963).

——, 'Final Report of the Committee of Inquiry under the Rt. Hon. Lord Devlin into certain matters concerning the Post Transport Industry', Cmnd. 2934 (1965).

——, 'Report of a Court of Inquiry into the problems caused by the introduction of Webb-offset machines in the printing industry, and the problems arising from the introduction of other modern printing techniques and the arrangments which should be adopted within the industry for dealing with them', Cmnd. 3184 (1967).

——, 'Report of a Court of Inquiry into trade disputes at the Barbican and Horseferry Road Construction sites in London', Cmnd. 3396 (1967).

——, 'Report of the Committee of Inquiry under Professor E. H. Phelps Brown into Certain Matters concerning the Labour in Building and Civil Engineering', Cmnd. 3714 (1968); Research Supplement, Cmnd. 3714–1 (1968).

——, *In Place of Strife: A Policy for Industrial Relations*, Cmnd. 3888 (1969).

——, *A National Minimum Wage*, Report of an Inter-Departmental Working Party (1969).

——, Department of Employment (DEP), 'Menon Site: Ten Case Studies in Building Management' (1970).

——, 'The Reform of Collective Bargaining at Plant and Company Level', Manpower Papers, No. 5 (1971).

———, 'Report of a Court of Inquiry into a dispute between the National Coal Board and the National Union of Mineworkers under the Chairmanship of the Rt. Hon. Lord Wilberforce, C.M.G., O.B.E., Cmnd. 4903 (1972).

———, DEP, *New Earnings Survey 1973* (1974) (issues are available for 1968, 1970, 1971, 1972).

Hughes, John and R. Moore, *A Case for Special Treatment* (Harmondsworth: Penguin, 1972).

Hyman, Richard, *Disputes Procedure in Action* (London: Heinemann Educational, 1972).

Hyman, R. and I. Brough, *Social Values and Industrial Relations: A Study of Fairness and Equality* (Oxford: Blackwell, 1975).

IEA Readings, *Inflation: Causes, Consequences and Cures*, no. 14 (1974).

Ingham, Geoffrey K., *Size of Industrial Organisation and Worker Behaviour* (Cambridge: CUP, 1970).

———, *Strikes and Industrial Conflict: Britain and Scandinavia* (London: Macmillan, 1974).

Jackman, Richard and Kurt Klappholz, *Taming the Tiger*, Hobart Paper 63 (1975).

Jackson, Dudley, H. A. Turner and Frank Wilkinson, *Do Trade Unions Cause Inflation?* University of Cambridge Department of Applied Economics Occasional Paper 36 (1972).

Jackson, M., *Labour Relations in the Docks* (London: Saxon House, 1973).

Jenkins, Clive and J. E. Mortimer, *British Trade Unions Today* (Oxford: Pergamon, 1965).

Jenkins, Peter, *The Battle of Downing Street* (London: Charles Knight, 1970).

Jones, Aubrey, *The New Inflation: The Politics of Prices and Incomes* (London: André Deutsch and Penguin, 1973).

Journal of Management Studies (October 1969; May 1970; October 1971; October 1972).

Kahn-Freund, Otto, *Labour and the Law* (London: Stevens, 1972).

Kidner, Richard, 'The right to be a candidate for union office', *ILJ*, Vol. 2, no. 2 (1973).

Knowles, K. J. C. C., 'Strikes: A Study in Industrial Conflict' (Oxford: Blackwell, 1952).

Knowles, K. G. J. C. and D. J. Robertson, 'Earnings in engineering, 1926–1948', *BOUIES*, Vol. 13, no. 6 (June 1952).

———, 'Structure of engineering earnings', *Bulletin*, Vol. 16, nos. 9 and 10 (1954).

——— and E. M. Thorne, 'Wage rounds, 1948–1959', *BOUIES* (February 1961).

——— and D. Robinson, 'Wage rounds and wage policy', *BOUIES* (May 1962).

Knowles, K. G. J. C. and C. B. Winsten, 'Can the level of unemployment explain changes in wages?' *BOUIES*, Vol. 21, no. 2 (May 1959).

Labour Party, 'Industrial Democracy: Working Party Report' (London, 1967).

Laidler, David E. W., *Unemployment versus Inflation*, IEA Occasional Paper 44 (1975).

180   *Industrial Relations in International Perspective*

Laidler, D and D. E. Purdy (eds.), *Inflation and Labour Markets* (Manchester: Manchester UP, 1974).

Lane, T. and K. Roberts, *Strike at Pilkingtons* (London: Pan Books, 1971).

Lasko, Roger, 'The payment of supplement benefits to strikers' dependants – misconceptions and misrepresentation', *Modern Law Review* (January 1975).

Legge, K., 'The operation of the "Regressive Spiral" in the labour market', *Journal of Management Studies*, Vol. 1, no. 1 (February 1970).

Legge, K. and S. Hilling, 'Overtime, absence and the structure of the pay packet: some methodological points – Part I', *Journal of Management Studies*, Vol. 11, no. 3 (October 1974), and 'Part II', *JMS*, Vol. 12, no. 1 (January 1975).

Lerner, Shirley W. and John Bescoby, 'Shop steward committees in the British engineering industry', *BJIR*, Vol. IV, no. 2 (July 1966).

Lerner, S. and J. Marquand, 'Workshop bargaining, wage drift and productivity in the British engineering industry', *Manchester School* (January 1962).

Lerner, Shirley W., John R. Cable and S. Gupta, *Workshop Wage Determination* (Oxford: Pergamon Press, 1969).

Lewis, Norman, 'Con-Mech: Showdown for the NIRC', *ILJ*, Vol. 3, no. 4 (December 1974).

Liddle, R. J., 'Third party intervention in the exhibition contracting industry: a case study of bargaining reform', *IRJ*, Vol. 3, no. 4 (Winter 1972).

Liddle, R. and W. E. J. McCarthy, 'The Impact of the Prices and Incomes Board on the Reform of Collective Bargaining', *BJIR*, Vol. X, no. 3 (November 1972).

Lowry, J. P., 'The future of national wage bargaining', EEF (1968).

Lupton, T., *On the Shop Floor* (Oxford: Pergamon, 1963).

Lupton, Tom and Dan Gowler, *Selecting a Wage Payment System*, Engineering Employers' Federation, Research Paper III (London, 1969).

Lupton, T. and A. M. Bowey, *Wages and Salaries* (Harmondsworth: Penguin, 1974).

MacKay, D. I., D. Boddy, J. Brack, J. Diack and N. Jones, *Labour Markets Under Different Employment Conditions* (London: George Allen & Unwin, 1971).

Marquand, J., 'Which are the lowest paid workers?' *BJIR*, Vol. 5, no. 3, 1967.

Marsh, A., *Industrial Relations in Engineering* (Oxford: Pergamon Press, 1965).

Marsh, A. I., E. O. Evans and P. Garcia, 'Workplace relations in engineering', EEF Research Paper no. 4 (London, 1971).

—— and W. E. J. McCarthy, Donovan Research Paper 2, Part 2 (1968).

Marsh, A. I. and R. S. Jones, 'Engineering Procedures and Central Conference at York in 1959: a Factual Analysis', *BJIR*, Vol. 2, no. 2 (1964).

Marsh, A. I. and E. Coker, 'Shop steward organisation in the engineering industry', *BJIR*, Vol. 1, no. 2 (1963).

Martin, Roderick and R. H. Fryer, *Redundancy and Paternalist Capitalism* (London: George Allen & Unwin, 1973).

Mathews, John, *Ford Strike: The Worker's Story* (London: Panther, 1972).

McCarthy, W. E. J., 'The nature of Britain's strike problem', *BJIR*, Vol. VIII, no. 2 (1970).

McCarthy, W. E. J. and N. D. Ellis, *Management by Agreement* (London: Hutchinson, 1973).

McKersie, R. B. and L. C. Hunter, *Pay, Productivity and Collective Bargaining* (London: Macmillan, 1973).

Mellish, M., *The Docks after Devlin* (London: Heinemann, 1972).

Ministry of Labour, 'Written Evidence to Donovan', Fifth Memorandum (1965).

Mukherjee, Sanrosh, *Changing Manpower Needs: A Study of Industrial Training Boards*, PFP Broadsheet 523 (November 1970).

——, *Through No Fault of their Own* (London: MacDonald-PEP, 1973).

'National Industrial Relations Court . . .', in M. Barratt Brown and K. Coates (eds.), *Trade Union Registers* (Bristol: 1973).

NBPI, 'Report on the Agreement of February–March 1963 in Electrical Contracting in Heating Ventilating and Domestic Engineering, and in Exhibition Contracting', Report no. 2, Cmnd. 2098 (1963).

——, Report no. 49 (1964).

——, Report on Shipbuilding by National Incomes Committee (1965).

——, 'Wages, Costs and Prices in the Printing Industry', Report no. 2, Cmnd. 2750 (1965).

——, *Pay of Workers in Agriculture in England and Wales*, Report no. 25, Cmnd. 3199 (1967).

——, *Pay of Workers in the Retail Draper Outfitting and Footwear Trades*, Report no. 27, Cmnd. 3224 (1967).

——, Reports, no. 65, Cmnd. 3627 and 3627–1 (1968); Cmnd. 3772, 3772–1 (1968); no. 50, Cmnd. 3498 (1967); no. 51, Cmnd. 3499 (1968); no. 94, Cmnd. 3847 (1968).

——, 'Job Evaluation', Report no. 83, Cmnd. 3772 (1968).

——, 3rd General Report, Cmnd. 3715 (1968).

——, Reports, no. 23, Cmnd. 3167 (1966); no. 36, Cmnd. 3311 (1967); no. 123, Cmnd. 4136, 1969.

——, 'Pay and Conditions in the Building Industry, the Civil Engineering Industry and the Construction Industry other than Building and Civil Engineering', (Statistical Supplement), Cmnd. 3982 (1969).

——, *Pay and Conditions in the Clothing Manufacturing Industries*, Report no. 110 and Supplement, Cmnd. 4002 and 4002–1 (1969).

——, 'Pay and Conditions of Workers in the Exhibition Industry', Report no. 117, Cmnd. 4088 (1969).

——, Annual Reports: Cmnd. 3087 (1966); no. 40, Cmnd. 3394 (1967); no. 77, Cmnd. 3715 (1968); no. 122, Cmnd. 4130 (1969).

——, *The Pay and Conditions of Service of Ancillary Workers in NHS Hospitals*, Report no. 166, Cmnd. 4644 (1971).

——, *Pay and Conditions of Service Workers in the Laundry and Dry Cleaning Industry*, Report no. 167, Cmnd. 4647 (1971).

——, *Pay and Conditions in the Contract Cleaning Trade*, Report no. 168, Cmnd. 4637 (1971).

——, General Report, no. 169 (1971).

North, D. T. B. and G. J. Buckingham, *Productivity Agreements and Wage Systems* (London: Gower Press, 1969).

O'Higgins, Paul, 'Strike notices: another approach', *ILJ*, Vol. 2, no. 3 (1973).

Owen Smith, E., *Productivity Bargaining: A Case Study in the Steel Industry* (London: Pan Piper, 1971).

Paish, F. W., *Rise and Fall of Incomes Policy*, Hobart Paper 47, 2nd edition (1971).

Parker, S. R., *Workplace Industrial Relations, 1972* (London: HMSO, 1974).

——, C. G. Thomas, N. D. Ellis and W. E. J. McCarthy, *Effects of the Redundancy Payments Act* (London: HMSO, 1971).

Parkin, M. and M. T. Sumner, *Incomes Policy and Inflation* (Manchester: Manchester University Press, 1972).

Paterson, Peter, *An Employer's Guide to the Industrial Relations Act* (London: Kogan Page (Associates), 1971).

Paterson, T. T., *Job Evaluation, Volumes 1 and 2* (London: Business Books, 1972).

Paulden, Sydney and Bill Hawkins, *Whatever Happened at Fairfields?* (London: Gower, 1969).

Pay Board, *Report on Civil Service* Cmnd. Science Group; Cmnd. 5602 (1974).

——, Report, 'The Experience of Operating a Statutory Incomes Policy' (1974).

——, *Report on Anomolies*, Cmnd. 5249 (1973).

——, *Report on Relativities*, Cmnd. 5535 (1974).

——, Special Report, 'Relative Pay of Mineworkers', Cmnd. 5567 (London: HMSO, 1974).

Paynter, W., *British Trade Unions and the Problems of Change* (London: George Allen & Unwin, 1970).

Phelps, E. S., 'Phillips Curves, expectations of inflation, and optimal unemployment over time', *Economica* (August 1967).

Phelps Brown, E. H., 'Wage Drift,' *Economica*, November 1962.

Phelps Brown, E. H., 'Inter-industrial job evaluation and collective bargaining', in a symposium, *Some Approaches to National Job Evaluation* (London: Foundation for Business Responsibilities, November 1972).

Phillips, A. W., 'The relation between unemployment and the rate of change of money wage rates in the United Kingdom, 1951–1957', *Economica* (November 1958).

Prandy, Kenneth, *Professional Employees* (London: Faber, 1965).

Rhys, D. G., 'Employment, efficiency and labour relations in the British motor industry', *IRJ*, Vol. 5, no. 2 (Summer 1974).

Rideout, Roger W., 'The content of trade union disciplinary rules', *BJIR*, Vol. II, no. 2 (1964) and 'The content of trade union rules regulating admission', *BJIR*, Vol. IV, no. 1 (1966).

Roberts, B. C., *Trade Union Government* (London: London School of Economics and Political Science and G. Bell & Sons Ltd., 1956). (London: Methuen, 1962).

——, Ray Loveridge and John Gennard, *Reluctant Militants* (London: Heinemann Educational, 1972).

Robertson, D. J., *Factory Wage Structures and National Agreements*, (Cambridge: CUP, 1960).

——, *The Economics of Wages and the Distribution of Income* (London: Macmillan, 1961).

Robertson, D. J., 'The implications of the proposed new look in industrial relations', *BJIR*, Vol. VI, no. 3 (November 1968).

—— and L. C. Hunter (eds.), *Labour Market Issues of the 1970s* (Edinburgh: Oliver & Boyd, 1970).

Robinson, Derek, 'Myths of the local labour market', *Personnel*, Vol. 1, no. 1 (1967).

——, *Wage Drift, Fringe Benefits and Manpower Distribution* (Paris: OECD, 1968).

—— (ed.), *Local Labour Markets and Wage Structures* (London: Gower Press, 1970).

——, *Incomes Policy*, Ditchley Paper, no. 38 (Ditchley Park, 1971).

——, 'Labour market policies', in Wilfred Beckermann (ed.), '*The Labour Government's Economic Record: 1964–1970*' (London: Duckworth, 1972).

——, *Incomes Policy and Capital Sharing in Europe* (London: Croom Helm, 1973).

Royal Commission on Trade Unions and Employers' Associations, *Report* (London: HMSO, 1968).

——, Research Papers, 1–11 (London: HMSO, 1966–1968).

Scott, W. H., A. H. Halsey, J. A. Banks and T. Lupton, *Technical Change and Industrial Relations* (Liverpool: Liverpool U.P., 1956).

Silver, Michael, 'Recent British Strike Trends: A Factual Analysis', *BJIR*, Vol. XI, no. 1 (March 1973).

Simpson, R. C. and John Wood, *Industrial Relations* (London: Pitman, 1973).

Sisson, Keith, *Industrial Relations in Fleet Street* (Oxford: Blackwell, 1975).

Smith, David C., *Incomes Policies: Some Foreign Experiences and Their Relevance for Canada* (Ottawa: Queen's Printer, 1966).

Society of Conservative Lawyers, *Financing Strikes* (Conservative Political Centre, 1974).

Thomas, R. R., *An Exercise in Redeployment* (Oxford: Pergamon, 1969).

Towers, B., T. G. Whittingham and A. W. Gottschalk (eds.), *Bargaining for Change* (London: George Allen & Unwin, 1972).

Trist, E. L., J. W. Higgin, H. Murray, and A. B. Pollack, *Organizational Choice* (London: Tavistock, 1963).

TUC, *Incomes Policy*, Report of a Conference of Executive Committees of Affiliated Organizations (London: 1965).

——, Reports of Annual Congresses (1968–1975).

——, *Economic Review* (1968 onwards).

——, *Low Pay*, General Council Discussion Document (1970).

——, 'National Industrial Relations Court: An Object Lesson in Missed Opportunities', in M. Barratt Brown and K. Coates (ed.), *Trade Union Register 3* (Bristol: 1973).

——, *Industrial Democracy*, Supplementary Report B (1974).

184   *Industrial Relations in International Perspective*

Turner, Graham, *The Car Makers* (Harmondsworth: Penguin, 1964).

Turner, H. A., 'Wages: industry rates, workplace rates and wage drift', *Manchester School* (1956).

——, *Trade Union Growth, Structure and Policy: A Comparative Study of the Cotton Unions* (London: George Allen & Unwin, 1962).

——, *The Trend of Strikes* (Leeds: Leeds University Press, 1963).

——, 'The disappearing drift (or, in defence of Turner)', *Manchester School* (May 1964).

——, 'That damned drift; a note on the Turner–Lerner controversy', *Manchester School* (1967).

——, 'The Royal Commission Research Papers', *BJIR*, Vol. VI, no. 3 (November 1968).

——, 'The Donovan Report', *Economic Journal*, Vol. LXXIX, no. 5 (1969a).

——, *Is Britain really strike-prone?* (Cambridge: CUP, 1969b).

——, 'Wages, productivity and the level of unemployment: more on wage drift', *Manchester School* (January 1970).

——, 'Collective bargaining and the eclipse of incomes policy: retrospect, prospect and possibilities', *BJIR*, Vol. VIII, no. 2 (July 1970).

——, Garfield Clack and Geoffrey Roberts, *Labour Relations in the Motor Industry* (London: George Allen & Unwin, 1967).

Ulman, Lloyd and Robert J. Flanagan, *Wage Restraint: A Study of Incomes Policies in Western Europe* (University of California Press, 1971).

Wedderburn, D., *White Collar Redundancy: A Case Study* (University of Cambridge, DAE Occasional Paper 1 (Cambridge: CUP, 1964).

——, *Redundancy and the Railwaymen*, University of Cambridge, DAE Occasional Paper 4 (Cambridge: CUP, 1965).

—— and R. Crompton, *Workers' Attitudes and Technology* (Cambridge: CUP, 1972).

Wedderburn, K. W., *The Worker and the Law*, 2nd ed. (Harmondsworth: Penguin, 1971).

——, and P.L. Davies, *Employment Grievances and Disputes Procedures in Britain* (University of California Press, 1969).

Weekes, Brian, Michael Mellish, Linda Dickens and John Lloyd, *Industrial Relations and the Limits of Law* (Oxford: Blackwell, 1975).

White, Phillip, 'The gasworkers' strike, 1972/3: analysis of causes', *IRJ*, Vol. 5, no. 1 (Spring, 1974).

Wilson, David F., *Dockers: the Impact of Industrial Change* (London: Fontana, 1972).

Wood, J. B., *How Much Unemployment?* IEA Research Monograph 28 (1972).

——, *How Little Unemployment?* IEA Hobart Paper 65 (1975).

5 Sweden: Conflict, Power and Politics in Industrial Relations

Walter Korpi

Research on Industrial Relations

The standard picture of industrial relations in Sweden as seen from abroad appears to have three distinctive characteristics: the near absence of industrial disputes; the strength and centralization of unions and employers' organizations; and the regulation of industrial relationships without the intervention of the state. For some observers, Sweden would thus appear to be approaching the ideal of industrial relations in advanced societies, where industrial conflict has been resolved, where social justice is being achieved, and where the institutions for decision-making in the economic field function independently from those in the political area. The stability of these characteristics would also appear to be taken more or less for granted.

Although superficial and simplified, this picture has some basis in reality. Its tenuous nature is, however, often overlooked. Up to the early thirties, state intervention in industrial relations was common, and Sweden actually ranked as the country most prone to industrial conflict among Western industrial nations. After the coming to power of the Social Democratic Government in 1932, industrial conflict in Sweden rapidly decreased and in the postwar period Sweden had one of the lowest rates among Western nations. The principle of non-intervention of the state in industrial relations became recognized. The foundations of a Welfare State were created in the early postwar period.

Since the late sixties, however, significant changes have taken place in Swedish industrial relations. The level of industrial disputes, although still low, is increasing. Problems concerning quality of work, work safety and work environment have entered the political forum. The issues of industrial and economic democracy have been revived. The idea that the state should not intervene in labour–management relations is no longer taken for granted. Concern with inequalities has emerged again.

The basic questions to be posed in research on industrial relations in Sweden are, then, how are we to account for the changes from one extreme to another in the level of industrial conflict over the years; how has the industrial relations system functioned in the postwar period, and why is it presently undergoing changes? Available research can give only partial answers to these questions. This has to do both with the organization of research on industrial relations as well as with positions on basic issues taken in mainstream industrial relations research.

Organization of research

Industrial relations is not an independent discipline at Swedish universities, nor is it an area of specialization in any of the established disciplines. In fact, no Swedish term exists corresponding to 'industrial relations'. Research on different aspects of industrial relations in Sweden can be found in studies originating in different academic disciplines, but there has been no attempt to integrate this information into an industrial relations framework.[1]

Economists have discussed stabilization policies and described the distribution of income, and political scientists have analysed political aspects of labour–management relations. Sociologists and psychologists have done research in industrial sociology and personnel administration. Historians have studied the development of the labour movement and of social conditions.[2] Some relevent research has also been done in the area of labour law. The Swedish Institute for Social Research, established in 1972, has industrial relations research in its programme.[3] Significant research has also been done in connection with different official commissions of enquiry. A large government fund for applied research on work environment and work safety has also been established. In 1977, the relatively large Centre for Research into Working Life was established. It is directed at social science research, especially concerning industrial democracy. Industrial relations in Sweden have also attracted some interest among scholars abroad (e.g. Johnston, 1962; Barbash, 1972; Martin, 1973; Scase, 1977, Fulcher, 1973; Ingham, 1974).

Various employers' associations have sponsored institutes, where research of relevance to industrial relations has been carried out. The Swedish Employers' Confederation (SAF) has sponsored an institute for research, consultation and information in personnel administration, which has conducted a considerable amount of research in its area.[4] The Federation of Swedish Industries has a research institute,[5] where work has been done, e.g. on income distribution and labour market problems. An association of leading persons in industry has sponsored research in industrial sociology and economics.[6]

Until recently, the unions have been less inclined to engage in research. However, some empirical studies have been carried out in connection with historical accounts of specific unions and by staff members of the Confederation of Swedish Trade Unions (LO) (Lindblad, 1960; Björklund, 1965; Meidner, 1954; LO, 1973). In recent years the research activities of the unions have increased, and sample surveys among union members have been initiated.

In the seventies research on industrial relations has become more openly controversial. There has been criticism that too much research has focused on adapting the individual worker to the existing industrial organization, without questioning the alternatives (Flord, *et al.*, 1969; Gardell, 1969). On the other hand, employers have accused researchers of bias in their work. Research contracts have been cancelled and researchers have been denied access to factories and employer controlled statistical sources such as wages (Hammarström, 1975).

Basic issues in industrial relations research

Research on industrial relations concerns the relationship between labour and capital, by many regarded as the main sources of conflict in Western societies. It is only natural that values and beliefs of an ideological nature, implicitly or explicitly, enter into research in this area (Fox, 1974, ch. 6). The fragmented and non-institutionalized character of research on industrial relations in Sweden has allowed for a relatively high degree of pluralism in approaches to the subject. Yet, Swedish research also shares the characteristics of mainstream industrial relations research, in that it limits its potential to explain the evolution and present changes in industrial relations in Sweden.

If the capacity of industrial relations research to explain change is to be improved, we must locate the theoretical areas of importance in this context. The options chosen, explicitly or implicitly, on the following three issues affect the ability of theories in this area to account for changes in industrial relations.

Harmony versus a conflict of interests

Although conflict is recognized in mainstream industrial relations research, the assumption of a basic harmony of interests between the parties on the labour market tends to dominate. An alternative perspective would view conflicts of interests between the parties on the labour market as derived from enduring features of societies, the economic organization of which is based on the private ownership of the means of production and search for factors which affect the extent and forms in which these conflicts become manifest.

Institutions versus power

Mainstream industrial relations research tends to assume that institutions for the resolution of industrial conflict will emerge with the development of industrial society and the institutions are often regarded as independent factors affecting industrial conflict. An alternative approach would, instead, take the web of rules and the institutions on the labour market as intervening variables, dependent in turn on the structure of power in society.

Separation versus unity of conflict

Mainstream industrial relations research tends to share the assumption expressed, for example, by Dahrendorf (1959) that in 'post-capitalistic' societies industrial and political conflict will be structurally and institutionally separated. An alternative approach would view conflicts in the industrial and in the political area as related expressions of conflicts of interests derived from the differing positions of social collectivities in the system of production.

An industrial relations frame of reference

The fragmentation of research on industrial relations makes it necessary here to assemble information from diverse sources to form a picture of the development and functioning of the Swedish industrial relations system. In order to give meaning to these data, a frame of reference must be developed in terms of which the data can be interpreted. To facilitate the understanding of the central issues concerning the evolution and current changes in industrial relations in Sweden, such a frame of reference should differ from the approaches suggested above.

An industrial relations system here is conceived broadly as embracing all the institutions and practices related to the organization of production and the distribution of the results of production. The central components of the industrial relations system are the arrangements for ownership of the means of production, unions, employers' organizations and the institutions on the labour market, including the legal structures as well as agreements between the parties and the informal practices that have developed to arrive at decisions concerning production and the distribution of its results.

The position of individuals in the production organizations and their relations to the means of production are the main factors forming the stratification system and class structure in society. The industrial relations system thus becomes closely related to the system of stratification and class. A central variable in the analysis of the relationships between these systems is the distribution of power resources among social groups. Ownership of the means of production, on the one hand, and political and union organization, on the other, are the central power resources, the relationship of which is a primary determinant of the structure of power in society.

While the division of labour introduces a multitude of potential conflicts in capitalist societies, the disparity of interests between sellers and buyers of manpower tends to relate and to superimpose a series of important differences deriving from the class system in society. The latent conflicts of interest between sellers and buyers of manpower concern the distribution of rewards and results of production, and also control in the production organization and in the economy. The extent and forms in which latent conflicts of interest become manifest depends largely on the shape and changes in the distribution of power resources between the main social groups. Changes in the distribution of power resources may affect the degree of overlap between conflicts in the political and in the industrial arena (Korpi, 1974a, 1978).

The state – i.e. the institutions for making and implementing political decisions – has an important role *vis-à-vis* the industrial relations system, since the actions of the state can also be assumed to reflect the differences in power resources between the main social groups and interest factions in society. Where unions and political parties based on working-class parties are weak, state action can be expected to be biased against the interests of the sellers of manpower. When a working-class-based political party becomes the dominant government party, the actions of the state may be modified. This can also affect the relationship between industrial and political conflict, by providing the sellers of manpower with a political alternative to industrial action.

Power in the industrial relations system

Of basic importance for understanding the functioning of the industrial relations system is the distribution of power resources between sellers and buyers of manpower and the changes in this distribution. The power resources that concern us here are, on the one hand, the pattern of ownership of capital and of organization among employers, and, on the other hand, union organization and political power.

Ownership and employers' organizations

Contrary to apparently widespread beliefs abroad, the Swedish economy is to a large extent based on private ownership. Employees in the state-owned corporations thus constitute only about 3 per cent of the number of employees in firms in the SAF. The main source of data on the distribution of ownership and power in the private sector of the economy is the report of a parliamentary commission (SOU, 1968: 7); also Hermansson (1959) and Meidner *et al* (1977). This report shows that in the postwar period the concentration of ownership in the large companies has increased. The two hundred largest private companies, employed 25 per cent of all employees in the private sector in 1942, but 32 per cent in 1964. At that time the two hundred largest manufacturing companies accounted for 49 per cent of total employment in manufacturing and 52 per cent of the value of production. Although by international standards the largest Swedish companies are of relatively modest size, the concentration of ownership of the largest firms appears to be higher in Sweden than in Britain or the United States.

In the mid-1960s, seventeen different groups of owners had control over firms accounting for 36 per cent of the total value of production in manufacturing. Fourteen of these groups were families. Among these, one single family clearly dominated and controlled firms producing 15 per cent of the product value in manufacturing. During the last decade, the degree of concentration of ownership in the private sector has increased considerably, due to the rapid amalgamation of companies since the fifties (Rydén, 1971).

Only small changes in the pattern of ownership of private property appear to have taken place since the thirties (SOU, 1968, p. 7; Spånt, 1975a). (For a study of changes in the pattern of ownership of property among primary-school teachers, bricklayers and textile workers in the period 1925–59, see Kuuse, 1970.) Of significance in this context, however, are the funds created in connection with the introduction of the supplementary pensions scheme in the sixties, which have become a very important source of capital under state control. By the end of 1969, the value of these funds was equal to the value of the total stock of private companies listed on the stock exchange (Spånt, 1975a, pp. 45 and 52).

Swedish employers are highly organized in centralized employers' organizations, as well as in other organizations. The formation of the Swedish Employers' Association in 1902 appears to have been a response to the increasing strength of working-class-based organizations (Lohse, 1963). Its very high level of organization facilitates the mobilization of the employers' power, makes the lock-out a very effective weapon against the unions (von Otter, 1975a), and makes it difficult for the unions to take advantage of splits between employers.

The power resources of unions

Industrialization came late to Sweden, with a breakthrough around the turn of the century, but the industrialization process was relatively rapid (Jörberg, 1970). The first trade unions were formed in the 1880s, primarily by skilled workers and largely as a protection against encroachment from unskilled labour migrating to the cities (Carlsson, 1969; Karlbom, 1969; Casparsson, 1966; Bäckström, 1971; Forsebäck, 1976). It is, however, of considerable importance in the development of the Swedish labour movement that the craft unions were soon replaced by industrial unions. The union movement therefore became more united and radical.

By the end of the nineteenth century, unions were dominated by socialists in the Social Democratic Party, which was formed in 1889. On the initiative of the Social Democratic Party a national 'top organization' for the manual unions – the Confederation of Swedish Trade Unions, the LO – was formed in 1898. The first statutes of the LO required the union branches to become collective members of the Social Democratic Party (Blake, 1960). The unions increased their membership rapidly around the turn of the century and reached a relatively high level of organization at an early stage (e.g. in the metal-working industry roughly 45 per cent of all workers appear to have been organized around 1906). Defeat in the general strike of 1909 almost halved the membership of the LO and it took a decade to recover the losses. Since then its membership has been steadily increasing, except for the stagnation of the Depression years after the First World War and in the early thirties.

Of significance to the relative power position of the LO is the high level of organization among workers, the relative absence of inter-union rivalry and the general goodwill towards the unions among the public. The level of union membership is very high. A survey among a random sample of the Swedish population in 1968 indicates that, among workers employed in manufacturing, 85 per cent reported union membership. All persons working more than one hour in the preceding week were included in this statistic, but the figure for full-time employees would be considerably higher. The level of unionization is somewhat lower in the service sector, especially in the 'secondary labour market' characterized by part-time work and low wages (von Otter, 1975a).

In the manual sector, 'splinter unionism' has on the whole been absent. An aftermath of the general strike was the formation of a syndicalist union organization in 1910. The size of its membership was for some years about 10 per cent that of the LO, but is now only 2 per cent.

Organizational efforts among white-collar workers began in the thirties (Croner, 1962, 1963; Nilstein, 1966; Tobisson, 1973; Adams, 1975; Wheeler, 1972): The present top organization for unions of lower white-collar employees, the TCO, was formed in 1944, and for employees with academic training, the SACO, in 1947. The level of organization is also high in the white-collar sector and has increased rapidly in the last decade, although it is still less marked than in the LO.

Of great significance to the industrial relations system in Sweden is the pattern of social stratification that is evident in the organizations among employees. The core of SACO members are thus from the higher professions, while the bulk of the TCO's membership is drawn from the lower middle-class occupations. The LO members are manual workers with a minority in the lower middle-class occupations. Although the LO thus has been able to contain most of the internal splits and conflicts in the working class, differences among wage-earners in general have thus become more or less institutionalized. In the seventies, however, the LO and the TCO have been co-operating relatively closely.

Political power

In contrast with many other countries, the labour movement in Sweden has a relatively strong power position, indicated by its control of the government in the period from 1932 to 1976. The Social Democrats formed a government in 1932 on a programme for combating unemployment (Öhman, 1966; Steiger, 1973; Lewin, 1967). This programme laid the basis for Social Democratic strength in the coming years. In the 1938 elections they received over 50 per cent of the vote. The entrenchment of the Social Democrats as a government party in the thirties separated political power from economic power and thus significantly changed the power structure of society. In the following decades their vote has fluctuated around 45 per cent, which, together with the support of the small Communist Party, gave them a generally narrow majority in the Riksdag up to 1976, when a bourgeois coalition government was formed.

About 75 per cent of the working class have regularly voted for the left-wing parties, which have also received about 30 per cent of the middle-class vote. This contrasts with the situation in Britain for instance, where middle class support for labour is less and the labour vote comes primarily from the working class. In comparison with workers in Britain, Swedish workers would appear to be more aware of inequalities in the distribution of rewards in society and tend more often to see these differences as results of the economic system (Scase, 1977).

Social stratification is reflected in the party preferences of the members of different organizations of employees. In the 1973 elections, 77 per cent of the LO members thus voted for the left-wing parties as against 38 per cent of the TCO members and 25 per cent of the SACO members (Petersson and Särlvik, 1974). Although the TCO and the SACO maintain political neutrality, the LO has close ties with the Social Democratic Party. Since the twenties, roughly 30 per cent of LO members have belonged to branches with collective membership in the party, and account for about 70 per cent of the membership of the party. Both the TCO and the SACO/SR take stands on political issues of importance to the welfare of their members.

The political influence of the organizations on the labour market is not only exerted through pressure-group activities and through their spokesmen in the Riksdag. Since the forties the government has appointed lay members to the executive boards of major government administrative bodies. Representatives from the main labour-market organizations (LO, TCO, SACO and SAF) thus serve on the executive boards and advisory committees, ranging from the Labour Market Board to the chancellery of the universities. In this way the organizations have good opportunities to affect not only legislation, but also its implementation (see Elvander, 1969, 1974, for an analysis of the political influence of the organizations). These developments have also been viewed as indications of the growth of a corporative society and of the development of a state–interventionistic capitalism (Dencik, 1974a and b).

Despite the strength of labour, the influence that employers have over investments and the level of employment has generally tended to place them in a very strong bargaining position *vis-à-vis* the Social Democratic Government, since the maintenance of a high level of employment has been a political necessity for the government. (For a discussion of the relationship between the Social Democrats and industry, see Svenning, 1972.) To stimulate economic growth the government has introduced tax credits and concessions favouring firms that expand (Bergström, 1971; Södersten, 1971). It can be noted, for instance, that in 1974 Sweden's largest and quite profitable firm, Volvo, paid no taxes to the state.

Changing power structure

Changes in the power structure of Swedish society that result from the entrenchment of the Social Democrats as the governing party in the latter part of the thirties had important consequences for industrial relations. There was an end to the pattern of state intervention in industrial relations in favour of the employers (Eklund, 1973, 1974; Hultén, 1971), and the idea of non-intervention by the state in industrial relations became established. The changes in power structure are also important in understanding the changes in the level of industrial conflict.

The pattern of industrial conflict in Sweden reflects a long-standing struggle between well-organized workers and employers. Increasing organizational power of the unions around the turn of the century led to an increasing incidence of disputes, which tended to be of long duration. During the first decades of this century, employers used large-scale lock-outs with relative success. The general strike in 1909 was a response to the threat of a mass lock-out (Schiller, 1967). In face of the threat of a lock-out, the LO accepted an agreement with SAF in 1906, by which the employers recognized the right of workers to belong to unions and the LO accepted the 'managerial prerogatives' of the employers concerning the right to hire and fire and to direct work. This agreement, known as the 'December Compromise', was of considerable importance in shaping subsequent developments.

Up to the late thirties, however, employers claimed the right to hire strike-breakers. In 1931 the use of strike-breakers led to large-scale demonstrations in Ådalen, with military intervention and the shooting of five persons. Strikes and lock-outs were very common in the twenties and continued with a large number of disputes and lost man-days up to 1933–5. After this period, industrial disputes by and large died down. A clear turning-point in the level of industrial conflict thus came a couple of years after the Social Democratic Government took office.

Little research has been done on the drastic decline in industrial conflict in Sweden in the mid-1930s. Often the low level of conflict is seen as a result of the elaborate structures of the Swedish labour market. Ingham (1974) has suggested that the differing levels of industrial conflict between Britain and Sweden reflect differences in the industrial infrastructure of the two countries, which has led to differences between them in the institutional structure of industrial relations. The changes in the institutional structure on the labour market, however, were not timed in a way that makes it reasonable to see them as major causal factors affecting the level of industrial conflict. Some of the most important institutions thus developed before or during the twenties without decreasing the level of conflict. Other institutions came into being after the decrease in the level of conflict. The existence of labour-market institutions has been unable to prevent an increase in conflict since the late sixties.

The decline of industrial conflict in Sweden in the mid-1930s may instead be accounted for by the change in power structure resulting from the entrenchment of the Social Democrats after 1932. The policies this government initiated, and the effect of these policies, strongly increased support for the labour movement. The improved and apparently stable political base of the Social Democrats significantly affected the distribution of power in society, and provided the basis for a new relationship between labour and capital founded on the common interest in increasing economic growth and efficiency of production.

The clearest sign of the new relationship between employers and unions was the central negotiations between the LO and the SAF, which started in 1936 and led to the conclusion of the Main Agreement in 1938. This agreement included rules for handling grievances and negotiations between the parties, as well as a procedural framework for industrial conflict. Its main significance, however, was as a symbol of the new relationship between the parties on the labour market. Another sign of the new conditions was the LO's acceptance of the laws concerning collective agreements and of the Labour Court, which it had opposed a few years earlier. (For a discussion of these developments, see Korpi, 1978.)

The interrelation of economic, labour market and wage policies

The main problem confronting most Western governments in the postwar period has been to maintain simultaneously a high level of employment and a low level of inflation. (For descriptions and discussions of recent economic postwar policies in Sweden see Lindbeck, 1975; Martin, 1973.) This dilemma has been especially pronounced in Sweden since expectations with regard to the employment level have been set very high by the members of the LO and the voters for the Social Democratic Party.

A policy model for the solution of the full employment–economic stability dilemma was developed in the late forties by economists attached to the LO, with the primary inspiration of Gösta Rehn and Rudolf Meidner. Its main distinguishing feature is the key role of an active labour-market policy for the stabilization of the economy (Turvey, 1952; LO, 1951; Rehn and Lundberg, 1963; Andersson and Meidner, 1973).

The starting-point for this model is the assumption that full employment and stable prices cannot be achieved simultaneously through policies that affect general demand. Since there is considerable variation between different sectors of the economy, such policies inevitably lead to excess demand and inflationary tendencies in some sectors of the economy. Instead, a moderate level of demand in the economy should be maintained and be combined with selective measures designed to affect the labour market in areas where the increase in demand is most needed. Such measures would include the creation of employment through public works, sheltered employment and support to firms in depressed areas, as well as the stimulation of geographical mobility of workers through improved Labour Exchange services, occupational training and inducements to migration (see Öhman, 1970, 1973). The general principle behind this model were accepted by the LO.

Parallel with this economic policy, the LO gradually developed a policy for wages known as the 'solidaristic wage policy' (Meidner, 1973; Meidner and Öhman, 1972; Öhman, 1970, Holmberg, 1963; Ullenhag, 1971). This term was introduced in the late thirties, and has deep roots in the union movement, where the need to help the worst-paid workers has been stressed since its early days. At the same time, there have been internal tensions within the union movement between skilled and unskilled workers, and between industrial and craft unions. The issue of the solidaristic wage policy has been interwoven with the question of the degree of centralization of decision-making within the unions and from the unions to the LO.

In its early versions, the solidaristic wage policy highlighted a reduction in the wage differentials between skilled and unskilled workers. Towards the end of the thirties, it stressed that the profitability of the firms should not affect wages and that there should be equal pay for equal work. To achieve an equalization of wages between different branches, it was argued that the LO must be given greater power in wage negotiations. Changes in the constitutions of the LO unions making this possible were introduced in 1941. Towards the end of the forties, the arguments for coordinated wage negotiations under LO leadership were phrased primarily in terms of the necessity to maintain economic stability and full employment (Meidner, 1973, pp. 15–16).

In the mid-1950s, coordinated wage rounds between the LO and SAF were finally introduced. More recently towards the end of the sixties, the equalization of wages was again brought into the foreground and various modifications were gradually undertaken to make the solidaristic wage policy more effective in this respect. The LO began to stress that the coordination of wage negotiations should concern the unions outside the LO as well. Here the LO ran into conflict with the salaried staff unions, especially the SACO. These unions had been using the percentage wage increases for industrial workers as the basis for their wage claims to maintain wage differentials (for a theoretical discussion, see Andersson, 1973). Aided by the institutional arrangements in the wage rounds, where the LO – SAF negotiations generally were concluded first, these organizations were relatively successful in maintaining wage differentials between manual workers and salaried employees.

In the first half of the seventies, the combination of rapid inflation and a system of progressive taxation made it necessary also for the LO to demand very high gross increases in wages in order to increase the net wages of their members. This led to settlements between the government and the unions over adjustments of the tax structure, preceding the wage negotiations between unions and employers in which the LO and the salaried employees have begun to cooperate.

Distribution of rewards

The rewards distributed through the industrial relations system are not limited to wages and income. Rewards related to the quality of work and work environment are also of crucial importance and may have consequences for physical and mental health. Moreover, in the Swedish context, the consequences of the labour-market policies are of relevance.

Wages and income

In the three-tiered bargaining system now obtaining in Sweden, wages can be affected at all three levels. Considerable attention has been focused on wage drift (i.e. the gap between centrally negotiated wage increases and actual changes in earnings). Wage drift can result from structural changes in the work force, rationalization, increased productivity and negotiation of piece-rates. The high proportion of piece-rates in combination with minimum rather than normal wages in the contracts have contributed to wage drift.

In the sixties, wage drift accounted for about half the total wage increases in the LO–SAF area and has been viewed as a major nuisance by both the LO and the SAF. The LO has regarded it as an obstacle to a solidaristic wage policy since it has tended to restore wage differentials (Meidner, 1973). Jacobsson and Lindbeck (1969), analysing factors related to wage increases resulting from industry-wide contracts, as well as from wage drift in the period 1955–67, found that variations in the level of unemployment accounted for both types of wage increase (see also Edgren *et al.*, 1970)

A model for the relation between wage formation and economic stability has been developed by economists in the SAF, the TCO and the LO (Edgren *et al.*, 1969, 1970). In this model the economy is seen as divided into a competitive sector, subject to competition in the international export market and from imports, and a protected sector, not subject to international competition. The competitive sector includes primarily manufacturing and has had a more rapid productivity increase than the protected sector, which includes public service and administration, construction and agriculture. International price increases and productivity increases in the competitive sector define the 'room' for wage increases when the wage–profit distribution is assumed to be stable. In the fifties and sixties, increases in wages and salaries in the competitive sector were by and large contained within this 'room'. These wage increases have, however, been passed on to the protected sector, where productivity increases have been considerably smaller and have thus contributed to inflation.

Wage-determining processes at the level of the work-place have by and large remained *terra incognita* for the social scientists. A pioneering attempt to shed light on these processes was made by two sociologists, in case studies at four different manufacturing firms (Hart and von Otter, 1973). Their observations point to the wide discrepancies between the formally set wages and the actual earnings of the workers, due to differences in number of hours worked and the amount of overtime. Another factor is the ability of management in local negotiations to define the occupational structure of the local plant. In a wage-policy programme accepted in 1973, the Swedish Metal Workers' Union indicated that staffing patterns should also be subject to negotiations.

Cross-sectional studies of the relationship between wages and age among workers have generally shown that wages tend to be lowest among the youngest and among the oldest, with a maximum level in the middle age-bracket (Holmberg, 1963). This has often been interpreted to mean that as workers grow older they tend to experience a decline in real wages. A longitudinal study of the changes of wages from 1951–66, carried out by the Low Income Commission[7] on a random sample of the adult Swedish population, indicates that such assumptions are not necessarily warranted (I Eriksson, 1970). The findings indicate that wages generally tend to increase with age, but less rapidly. (For studies on wage structures in selected sectors of the labour market, see Klevmarken, 1972 and Gustafsson, 1976.)

The studies by the Low Income Commission indicate that the question of low income is not only a matter of low wages but also, to a considerable extent, a question of employment opportunities. Large groups in the population, especially among women, may for various reasons not work as much as they would have liked to (SOU, 1970: 34).

A special study of the 15 per cent of wage-earners with the lowest hourly wages indicates that, in terms of their standard of living, these low-wage groups are clearly disadvantaged. To a large extent these low-wage employees were not union members, or worked in branches where the level of organization was low (Sundbom, 1970).

Ullenhag (1971), reviewing changes in the differences between average wages in the LO area from 1923 to 1965, came to the conclusion that the solidaristic wage policy has, by and large, been a failure (see also Olsson, 1970). Later studies, however, indicate that the policy has been effective since the late sixties. Meidner (1973) shows that an index of wage differentials set at 100 in 1951 remained relatively stable up to 1961, but decreased to 49 in 1972. Allowing for structural changes in the size of various branches, Dencik (1974b) finds that the variation in wages between men in different sectors of manufacturing has clearly decreased. Wages for low-paid groups like farm workers and women have increased especially rapidly. In manufacturing, the wages for women were 69 per cent of wages for men in 1960 but 82 per cent in 1971. Wage statistics based on individual workers confirm the decrease in differentials during the sixties in engineering, and during the seventies in the major part of the LO–SAF area (Meidner, 1973; Olsson, 1975). Studies on the distribution of income indicate that in the period 1930–50, there was some decrease in the dispersion of income (Bentzel, 1951; Lydall, 1968). Since 1950, however, the distribution of pre-tax income among men has remained relatively stable (Spånt and Selander, 1971; Spånt, 1975b; Kuuse, 1970).

The relationship between changes in wages and in productivity has been insufficiently analysed. Meidner (1973) found that, since the fifties, increases in the nominal wage for adult men in manufacturing have been somewhat higher than increases in productivity measured in real prices. Dencik (1974b), however, argues that for this category, increases in real wages have generally lagged behind increases in productivity measured in nominal prices. He suggests that by limiting the wage demands of labour to increases in productivity the solidaristic wage policy has in practice functioned as an income policy.

In 1973/74 when profits, especially in the export sector, were extraordinarily high, attention was drawn to the inability of the solidaristic wage policy to channel high profits from one sector of industry to other sectors where wages were low. The wage restraint implied by this policy for workers in the most profitable sectors means increased profits for the owners. This has important effects on the distribution of income between capital and labour. One of the architects of the solidaristic wage policy of the LO, Rudolf Meidner (1973), stated that this issue is 'one of the most central problems of the solidaristic wage policy – perhaps its crucial question'. (For a study of the functional distribution of income in Sweden, 1870–1950, see Jungenfeldt, 1966.)

The quality of work and the work environment

In the seventies, the issues of the quality of work and work environment have come into the foreground of public debate in Sweden (Lidman and Uhrbom 1968; Palm, 1972, 1974). A decade earlier the union movement had focused attention on these problems. The LO presented a report on technological change to its congress in 1966 (LO, 1966). While this report underlined union acceptance of increased efficiency at work as a necessary requirement for the increase in material standards of the members, it also stressed the possibility and the need to combine an effective production organization with a technology which would give the workers increased potential for deriving intrinsic job satisfaction. In this connection the LO invited a group of sociologists to prepare a report on the relationship of technological structure and change to work adjustment and mobility of the labour market (Dahlström *et al.*, 1966). A comprehensive empirical study on the relationship between the technological requirements imposed on work and the possibility of workers achieving job satisfaction has been done by Gardell (1971 see also Gardell, 1976).

A crucial aspect of the quality of work is the health hazards to which individuals are exposed. Sample surveys carried out by the LO have indicated the surprisingly great extent to which manual workers are exposed to health hazards at their places of work (Bolinder *et al.*, 1970; Ohlström, 1970). The government Low Income Commission has provided empirical data on the distribution of various negative aspects of work and work environment in the Swedish population (Sundbom, 1971). The survey included indicators for measuring physical requirements and exhaustion at work, as well as the experiences of strain in the form of hectic or monotonous work and of mental exhaustion. Work environment was described in terms of level and type of noise, climate, and air pollution. The frequency of these negative aspects of work is clearly and negatively related to the socio-economic status of the occupation and the wage level.

The different negative aspects of work environment were clearly correlated. The survey also documents a positive correlation between various symptoms of ill health and the presence of negative aspects in the work environment. Work experiences have also been found to be related to the activities of workers outside the job (Karasek, 1976; Westlander, 1976). Nelander (1971) has shown that in spite of decreases in the number of working hours down to a 40-hours week in the seventies, the total time spent in travel to and from work, as well as the time at work, is still surprisingly high.

The issue of the type of wage has come up as a central question in the debate on quality of work and work environment. Traditionally a very high proportion of manual work in manufacturing (during the sixties about 65 per cent) has been done on a piece-rate basis. For a long time, unions and workers have viewed piece-rates favourably, since they have provided an opportunity to increase wages, partly by increases in effort. Management has also favoured the piece-rate system, but has wanted to change the system in the direction of a basic wage combined with a relatively small variable based on effort. As more advanced methods for setting piece-rates have been introduced (based on time and motion study), as the pace of work has increased, and the possibility of increasing wages through piece-rates has decreased, the workers have come to view this system of payment much more negatively. The piece-rate system has also been seen as detrimental to the solidaristic wage policy by providing opportunities for wage drift.

The data from the Low Income Commission indicate among male workers in manufacturing a correlation between reports of physical exhaustion after work and the type of wage. Physical exhaustion is lowest among workers on time-rates and highest among workers on individual piece-rates based on time studies. Sundbom (1971), Gardell (1971) and Korpi (1978) noted indications of a relationship between mental strain and the type of wage system. A positive correlation between piece-rates and mental stress as well as between shift work and stress has also been documented by Bolinder and Ohlström (1971).

A change from piece-rates to fixed wages also appears to decrease the accident rate (Kronlund, 1974). The unions have, with a few exceptions, come to oppose the piece-rate system, and the proportion of work done on piece-rates has been decreasing since the early seventies.

Labour-market policies

Of particular relevance here are studies of the effects of active labour-market policies. Some studies indicate that in cases of plant closure, labour-market policies have been relatively ineffective in providing new jobs for the workers concerned. A relatively high proportion of the workers remain unemployed or leave the labour force (Pettersson, 1971; Gonäs, 1974).

Analyses of the social and economic consequences of workers relocated from depressed areas with the aid of the labour-market authorities show that the benefits from mobility (indicated by cost–benefit analyses) were considerably greater for the national economy than for the migrants. The job opportunities of the migrants were considerably improved, but difficulties were found in forming new social relationships and in other aspects of adjustment (SOU, 1974, 29; Åberg, 1974; Rundblad, 1964, 1971). Cost–benefit analyses of programmes of occupational training to avoid unemployment indicate that the net outcome of these programmes is more favourable for the individual than for the national economy (SOU, 1974:29; Dahlberg, 1972).

The Labour Court and the legal system

A dense web of rules covers the relationships between the parties on the Swedish labour market (descriptive summaries are found in Forsebäck, 1976 and Fredriksson, 1973). The Labour Court has played an important, but often misunderstood, role in this system of rules. When collective agreements became legally binding in 1928, the Labour Court was established to adjudicate violations of or disputes concerning the interpretation of the collective agreements.

The LO strongly protested when the court was established by a conservative government. A major objection was that the court would come to rule in favour of the employers on issues of managerial prerogatives concerning the right to hire and fire and to manage work. The LO regarded these issues as an unsettled area in the conflict of interests between labour and management. Relatively soon, however, the LO came to accept the court. This was in spite of the fact that the court in 1932 ruled that these managerial prerogatives were derived from general principles inherent in the legal foundations of the nation. Even in cases where the contracts did not make it explicit, the managerial prerogatives thus rested with the employers. By thus vastly enlarging the area considered to be settled by the collective agreement, this ruling strongly increased the scope of the ban on strikes during the term of the contract, on issues covered by the collective agreement.

The court also ruled that the prerogative of interpretation in cases of disputes concerning the content of the contract belonged to management. This made it unnecessary for employers to sue at the court in a wide area of issues, but made it the only avenue open for employees. Since only a small proportion of all disputes could be taken to the court, the employers were thereby given important opportunities to use the contracts to their advantage.

A circumstance contributing to the acceptance of the court by the LO was the fact that the unions were able to force smaller firms not belonging to employers' organizations to follow stipulations in contracts and in social legislation. The unions thus came to sue at court much more often than the employers. The court soon gained the LO's unreserved acceptance (Johnston, 1962).

In the seventies the evaluation of the court has again changed drastically. It has been pointed out that the proportion of cases taken to the court by various parties is not a decisive indicator of the court's role. Attention has again been drawn to the important judicial role of the court in establishing the legal framework of the labour market. The court has adhered strictly to the precedents set in the thirties without regard to changes that have taken place since then in the general conceptions concerning the proper relationship between employers and employees (Edlund, 1967, 1973; Korpi, 1970).

The role of law in shaping the relationships between the parties in the labour market has not received much attention by researchers. In his dissertation on the functioning of the Labour Court, Lennart Geijer, later Minister of Justice in the Social Democratic Government, argued that the rules of the law were not always expressions of values common to all groups in society but rather that the rules reflect 'the values among the groups in society which were in power at the time the rule was accepted' (Geijer and Schmidt, 1958, p. 338). That this is true to a considerable degree in the case of laws concerning the relations between the parties on the labour market has been argued by Eklund (1973), who analyses the role of the law in its attempts to repress the growth of the labour movement up to the beginning of this century. (For international comparisons of the legal system concerning industrial disputes see Schmidt, 1962, 1972.) Cottino (1973) has analysed the effects of law on enforcing minimum standards in the relations between employers and employees in the 'grey' labour market. Rules and conflict on the labour market are also discussed in Brantgärde *et al* (1974).

Conflict and change

Since the late sixties, the industrial relations system in Sweden has been undergoing rather drastic changes (von Otter, 1975a). These changes are related to an increase in the level of industrial conflict. They have brought industrial relations into the centre of the political debate.

Increasing industrial conflict

In 1969 the calm on the Swedish labour market was shaken by a wave of unofficial strikes. The largest of them occurred in the nationalized iron-ore mines in northern Sweden and ended in a relative victory for the workers (Thunberg, 1970; Korpi, 1970; Dahlström *et al.*, 1971). The wage negotiations in the winter of 1969/70 were accompanied by a series of unofficial strikes. Although such strikes were not unknown in Sweden (Abrahamsson, 1968; Korpi, 1968), and although they remained few by international standards, the change was large enough to seem a dramatic increase. A new wave of strikes came in 1974/75.

In about half of the unofficial stoppages in the years before 1969 the reasons for the strikes referred to wage issues, while the other half related to work environment and issues concerning controls at the place of work. In the strike waves since then, wage issues have predominated. In some of the largest strikes (accounting for the major part of striker-days) issues of the work environment, focusing on the demand for a change from piece-rates to monthly wages, has played a central role (Korpi, 1978).

An important part of the background to the new developments is found in cumulative processes and changes that have affected the level of living of the working class in Sweden during recent years. Of particular importance is the increased economic pressure on the workers in connection with stagflation, with its high levels of unemployment and rapid inflation. This pressure is reflected in the increase in the use of means-tested social assistance, which almost doubled from 1965 to 1972, when it reached its highest level of the postwar period (Korpi, 1975). The two strike waves in 1969/70 and 1974/75 came in periods when the rate of price increases was exceptionally high. Another and more long-term development is the increased efficiency in the utilization of work time, which may have led to increased stress and new types of health hazards at work. The decrease in labour force participation among men, especially among elderly men, would appear to be a result of this development (Berglind and Lindqvist, 1972).

Tensions have also been generated by the relationship among different union federations. This has primarily concerned wage issues. The wage negotiations of 1970/71 dramatically illustrated the conflicting wage policies of the SACO and the LO (Nycander, 1972). As a part of the policy of 'increased equality', the Social Democratic Government took the initiative for extraordinarily high wage increases for the lowest-paid employees in the public sector. The LO also demanded that the policy of equalization of wages should be extended to the whole labour market, including senior government officials. This met with strong resistance from SACO and its ally, the smaller SR, which represented the commissioned officers in the armed forces and minor groups such as train dispatchers on the state-owned railways.

When SACO and SR failed to reach comparable wage increases for their members, some minor membership groups in the SR, among them the train dispatchers, embarked on a strike that soon paralysed the railways. The bargaining organization of the government responded by issuing a lock-out warning to the SR, including military officers. Before the lock-out went into effect, however, the government took the initiative to pass a law which fixed salaries at the level of the latest offer by the board of conciliation. This intervention of the government was viewed negatively by some of the LO unions, but it forced the SACO to reconsider its basic policies (Nycander, 1974).

The wave of unofficial strikes has also led to some discussion of the internal government of the unions. The process of centralization of decision-making in unions accelerated in the late thirties. The formal structure of the unions has also changed drastically in recent years as a result of amalgamation of unions and of branches. In the LO unions about two-thirds of the branches disappeared as independent units during the sixties (K. Eriksson, 1973; Johannesson, 1975). Although goodwill towards the unions remains relatively high among the general public, survey data also indicate a rather widespread feeling of distance among the rank and file members in relation to the union leaders (Korpi, 1970, Lewin, 1977).

The unions have tried to counteract the negative aspects of these developments by increasing their communication efforts with the members, and by devising new channels for the upward flow of information within the union structure. Thus several unions and the LO have submitted policy questions for discussion in members' 'study circles', with written replies to be sent to the union headquarters.

The politics of industrial relations.

The increasing level of industrial conflict has occurred during a period when the political situation has become more unstable (Elvander, 1974; Högström, 1973). In the elections during the 1968 recession, the Social Democrats won one of their greatest victories. They received over 50 per cent of the vote, apparently as a result of their old image as the 'party of full employment' and of a new industrial policy that promised better employment opportunities. The party also appeared as more radical in this period by making 'increased equality' a central political issue (Menningen, 1971).

In the early seventies, the political fortunes of the party declined, and the electorate appeared more volatile than before. The response by the Social Democratic government and the LO in this situation was to maintain the political intiative by acting positively to satisfy the demands of wage-earners. This has had crucial consequences for industrial relations. Following the show of dissatisfaction among its members the LO has changed its long-standing policy of preferring negotiations to legislation on the labour market. It has demanded legislation to increase the influence of the workers at their place of work.

In the early seventies, the Social Democratic Government thus took the initiative to introduce legislation giving the elected safety officers at the factory level increased authority; making it more difficult for management to fire workers; and improving the possibilities for the elected union representatives at plant level to carry out their tasks. The government also proposed a law concerning minority representation by employees on company boards. All these changes were gradually accepted by the employers and by the opposition parties.

The LO and the Social Democratic Party, however, have continued to press industrial democracy as a political issue. (See Schiller, 1973, for an analysis of this shift in LO policy. For different theoretical approaches to industrial democracy, see Dahlström, 1969; Karlsson, 1969; Rehnman, 1964.) Experiments on increasing the participation by employees in decision-making in nationalized companies and public administration have been initiated with mixed success (Kronlund, 1974; Karlsson and Söderlund, 1973; Karlsson, 1969; von Otter, 1975b). Employers have shown relatively more interest in job enlargement and in the introduction of semi-independent work groups (Hansson *et al.*, 1973).

In 1975 the discussion on industrial democracy took a new turn. One impetus came from a parliamentary commission appointed to put forward proposals for limiting the traditional managerial prerogatives. The commission delivered its report at the beginning of 1975 (SOU, 1975: 1). The two Social Democrats on the commission joined the representatives from the bourgeois parties and the SAF in recommending that the increasing influence of labour should be implemented along the lines of the German codetermination system. A minority on the commission, consisting of the representatives of the LO and the TCO, rejected this approach, demanding instead that the increased influence of the workers should be channelled through the union organization. They thought that the power of the local unions should be increased by measures giving the unions a temporary veto over the introduction of changes and by prerogatives in interpreting collective agreements. They also thought that the right to strike on issues other than wages should be extended during the term of the contract, that all issues should be negotiable, and that there should be increased access to information on company affairs, by the union. In some areas concerning health hazards, the LO and TCO thought that the unions should have the decisive voice. The SAF has strongly opposed these suggestions. Legislation incorporating important parts of the LO–TCO proposal was enacted in 1976 (Edlund and Gustafsson, 1976).

In 1975 the Social Democratic Party revised its party programme. The new programme stressed economic democracy as the third stage of its political strategy following the achievement of political and social democracy. One of the proposals to the programme committee for achieving economic democracy was to establish tripartite membership of company boards, with equal representation from shareholders, employers, and the local government in the area where the firm is located (Johansson, 1974; Bergström, 1973).

A very important proposal concerning economic democracy was set forth by an expert committee in the LO (Meidner, Hedborg and Fond, 1975). This committee was appointed to tackle the problem of 'excess' profits in the most profitable firms, which had become recognized as a strain on the solidaristic wage policy. The committee, headed by the most prominent member of the LO staff, Rudolf Meidner, set out a proposal aimed at curbing the growing concentration of power in the economy.

The proposal aims at establishing funds controlled by wage-earners. To these 'wage-earner funds', firms over a certain size would contribute shares, without compensation, equivalent to a certain proportion of their real profits. Depending on the size of the profits to be given to the funds, the funds would after some years have a dominating control over the shares of the more profitable private companies.

The LO congress in 1976 accepted the basic principles of collective wage-earner funds (LO, 1976). Within the TCO a proposal has been set out concerning 'wage-earner capital', involving the creation of collective funds through the issuing of shares from the most profitable firms (TCO, 1976). This proposal has basic similarities with the LO proposal. The employers have countered these proposals with profit-sharing programmes directed at the individual employee, which do not alter the power structure in the economy (SAF, 1976).

Conclusions

Three areas have been indicated where industrial relations theory faces significant choices that will affect not only the approaches to the subject but also the results of research. These choices concern: (*a*) the relative emphasis to be placed on harmony versus enduring conflicts of interest between the parties on the labour market, (*b*) the relative importance of social norms and institutions versus the structure of power in affecting the actions of social groups, and (*c*) the independence versus the interdependence of conflict in industrial and political areas. The evolution and recent changes of the industrial relations system in Sweden are difficult to understand unless an enduring conflict of interests is assumed between the parties in the labour market and unless the system of industrial relations is placed firmly in the context of the political economy, the class system and the power structure of society.

It can be argued that Sweden differs from other nations with capitalistic economic systems primarily by having a stronger labour movement, something reflected in the record tenure of the Social Democratic Party in government. In nations where the imbalance in power between the parties in the labour market is greater, the power structure will have different but nevertheless crucial effects in shaping the nature and functioning of industrial relations. Industrial relations research can profit from broadening its theoretical frame of reference by focusing on the structure of economic and political power in society, on the interplay between industrial relations and the class structure of society, and on the conditions under which the latent conflicts of labour and management become manifest in political and industrial conflict.

210   *Industrial Relations in International Perspective*

NOTES

1. The following bibliographies include research of relevance for industrial relations: Svensk arbetsmarknad 1950—1968. Bibliografi över debatt och forskning; Grahm, *Svensk arbetsmarknadsforskning ur sociologisk belysning*; Niklassqn *et al.*, *Svensk arbetsmarknadsforskning ur samhällsekonomisk belysning*; Boethius, *Svensk företagssociologisk bibliografi* and Suikkila, *Arbetsforskning inom samhällsvetenskaplig fakultet.*
2. Recently a journal for studies in labour history was established, *Arkiv för studier i arbetarrörelsens historia* (Archives for the study of the history of the labour movement).
3. For a review of on-going research at the Swedish Institute for Social Research, see the sections on 'Research in Progress' in *Industrial and Labour Relations Review.*
4. Personaladministrativa rådet (PA-Council).
5. Industrins utredningsinstitut (Industrial Institute for Economic and Social Research).
6. This association, *Studieförbundet Näringsliv och Samhälle*, sponsored two of the three pioneering studies in industrial sociology done in Sweden in the fifties. One was a study of work and leisure in two industrial communities of different types (Segerstedt and Lundquist, 1952 and 1955) while the other analysed the position of salaried employees in manufacturing (Dahlström, 1954). The third study (Boalt, 1954), which concerned work groups in the electro-technical industry and replicated as well as criticized the Hawthorne studies, was sponsored by the Social Science Research Council. Boalt also co-authored the first Swedish book on the sociology of work (Boalt and Westerlund, 1954, see also Boalt, Lantz and Westerlund, 1967). The PA-Council sponsored by the SAF has been influential in initiating work-related research, e.g. concerning the role of foremen (Lennerlöf, 1966) and personnel turnover (Hedberg, 1967).
7. The Low Income Commission was established in 1966 and published about 20 reports before it was dissolved prior to having completed its work. For a presentation and discussion of its work see review symposium in *Acta Sociologica*, Vol. 16 (1973) (3), pp. 211–39.
8. Only a very small fraction of all unofficial strikes are prosecuted at the Labour Court by the employers. In the period 1949–68 only 3 per cent of all stoppages in the metal-working sector reported by the employers to the union were thus taken to the court (Korpi, forthcoming).

REFERENCES

Åberg, Rune, 'Strukturarbetslösheten' (Structural unemployment). *Sociologisk Forskning*, Vol. 11, no. 4, pp. 35–55 (1974).
Abrahamsson, Bengt, *Konfliktkontroll och konfliktlösning: en studie av vilda strejker inom Svenska Metallindustriarbetareförbundet* (Conflict control and conflict resolution. A study of wildcat strikes in the Swedish Metal Workers' Union) (Stockholm, 1968) (Mimeo).
Anderson, Bo, 'Några   reflexioner om rättvisa och jämlikhet' (Some

reflexions on justice and equality), pp. 49–68 in von Otter (ed.), *Arbetslivet i kris och förvandling* (Stockholm: Rabén & Sjögren, 1971).

Andersson, Rolf and Rudolf Meidner, *Arbetsmarknadspolitik och stabilisering* (Labour market policy and stabilization). Report no. 4 from the Swedish Institute for Social Research (Stockholm: Prisma, 1973).

Barbash, Jack, *Trade Unions and National Economic Policy* (Baltimore: Johns Hopkins Press, 1972).

Bentzel, Ragnar, *Inkomsfördelningen i Sverige* (Income Distribution in Sweden) (Uppsala: 1951).

Berglind, Hans and Anna-Lena Lindqvist, *Utslagningen på arbetsmarknaden* (The stamping-out process at the labour market) (Lund: Studentforlaget, 1972).

Bergström, Villy, 'Industriell utveckling, industrins kapitalbildning och finanspolitiken' (Industrial development, capital formation in industry and financial policies), pp. 282–321 in Erik Lundberg, *et al.*, *Svensk finanspolitik i teori och praktik* (Stockholm: Aldus, 1971).

Bergström, Villy, *Kapitalbildning och industriell demokrati* (Capital formation and industrial democracy) (Stockholm: Tiden, 1973).

Björklund, Bertil, *Svenska Typografförbundet* (The Swedish Typographers' Union) (Stockholm: Tiden, 1965).

Blake, Donald J., 'Swedish trade unions and the Social Democratic Party', *The Scandinavian Economic History Review*, Vol. VIII, no. 1, pp. 19–44 (1960).

Bolinder, Erik, Egon Magnusson, and Lars Nyrén, *Risker i jobbet: LO-enkäten* (Health hazards at work: The LO inquiry) (Stockholm: Prisma, 1970).

Bolinder, Erik and Bo Ohlström, *Stress på svenska arbetsplaster* (Stress at work-places in Sweden) (Stockholm: Prisma, 1971).

Bäckström, Knut, *Arbetarrörelsen i Sverige* (The labour movement in Sweden), two volumes (Stockholm: Rabén & Sjögren, 1971).

Carlsson, Bo, *Trade Unions in Sweden* (Stockholm: Tiden 1969).

Casparsson, Ragnar, *LO: Bakgrund, utveckling och verksamhet* (The LO – Background, development and activities) (Stockholm: Tiden, 1966).

Cottino, Amedeo. *Slavmarknad – eller om lagens effektivitet* (The slave market – or on the efficiency of law (Umeå: Department of Sociology, 1973).

Croner, Fritz, *Soziologie der Angestellten* (Cologne: Kiepenheuer & Witsch, 1962). Revised edition in Swedish: *Tjänstemännen* (Salaried employees) (Stockholm: Rabén & Sjögren, 1963).

Dahlberg, Åke. *Arbetsmarknadsutbildning – verkningar för den enskilde och samhället* (Labour market training – consequences for the individual and society). Reports from the department of economics, University of Umeå (1972).

Dahlström, Edmund, *Fördjupad företagsdemokrati* (Industrial democracy extended) (Stockholm: Prisma, 1969).

Dahlström, Edmund, Bertil, Gardell, Bengt G., Rundblad, Bo Wingårdh, and Jan Hallin, *Teknisk förändring och arbetsanpassning* (Technological change and work adjustment) (Stockholm: Prisma, 1966).

Dahlström, Edmund, Kjell Eriksson, Bertil Gardell, Olle Hammarström and Ruth Hammarström, *LKAB och demokratin* (The LKAB and democracy) (Stockholm: Wahlström & Widstrand, 1971).

Dahrendorf, Ralf, *Class and Class Conflict in Industrial Society* (Stanford, Calif.: Stanford University Press, 1959).

Dencik, Peter, 'Statsinterventionismen' (State interventionism), pp. 9–22 in Peter Dencik and Bengt-Åke Lundvall (eds.), *Arbete, kapital och stat* (Work, capital and state) (Stockholm: Zenit–Rabén & Sjögren, 1974a).

Dencik, Peter, 'Solidarisk lönepolitik som inkomst-politik' (Solidaristic wage policy as incomes policy), pp. 191–216 in Peter Dencik and Bengt-Åke Lundvall (eds.), *Arbete, kapital och stat* (Work, capital and state) (Stockholm, Zenit–Rabén & Sjögren, 1974b).

Edgren, Gösta, Karl-Olof Faxén, and Odhner, Claes-Erik. 'Wages, Growth, and the Distribution of Income', *Swedish Journal of Economics*, Vol. LXXI (3) (1969), pp. 133–60.

Edgren, Gösta, Karl-Olof Faxén and Clas-Erik Odhner, *Lönebildning och samhällsekonomi* (Wage formation and the economy) (Stockholm: Rabén & Sjögren, 1970).

Edlund, Stren, *Tvisteförhandlingar på arbetsmarknaden. En rättslig studie av två riksavtal i tillämpning* (Negotiation procedures on the labor market. A legal study of the functioning of two national collective agreements (Stockholm: Norstedt, 1967).

Edlund, Sten, 'Perspektiv på arbetsdomstolen' (Perspectives on the Labour Court), pp. 455–84 in LO: *Tvärsnitt* (Prisma: Stockholm, 1973).

Edlund, Sten and Stig Gustafsson, *Medbestämmanderätten* (The right of codetermination) (Stockholm: Tiden, 1976).

Eklund, Per, 'Rätten i klasskampen – en studie i rättens funktioner' (The law in class conflict – a study in the functions of law), pp. 399–454 in LO, *Tvärsnitt* (Stockholm: Prisma, 1973).

Eklund, Per, *Rätten i klasskampen* (The law in the class struggle) (Stockholm: Tiden, 1974).

Elvander, Nils, *Intresseorganisationerna i dagens Sverige* (The interest organizations in Sweden today) (Lund: Gleerup, 1969).

Elvander, Nils, 'In search of new relationships: parties, unions, and salaried employees' associations in Sweden', *Industrial and Labour Relations Review*, Vol. 28, pp. 60–74 (October 1974).

Elvander, Nils, 'Staten och organisationerna på arbetsmarknaden i de nordiska länderna' (The state and the organizations on the labour market in the Nordic countries), in L. Brantgärde, N. Elvander, F. Schmidt, and A. Victorin, *Konfliktlösning på arbetsmarknaden* (Lund: Gleerup. 1974).

Eriksson, Ingalill, *Ålder och inkomst* (Age and income) (Stockholm: Allmänna Förlaget, 1970).

Eriksson, Kjell, *Facklig demokrati* (Union democracy). Report no. 6. Department of Sociology, University of Göteborg (1973).

Flord, Christina *et al.*, *Konsten att dressera människor* (The art of taming people) (Stockholm: Prisma, 1969).

Forsebäck, Lennart, *Industrial Relations and Employment in Sweden* (Stockholm: Swedish Institute, 1976).

Fox, Alan, *Beyond Contract: Work, Power and Trust Relations* (Faber and Faber, London, 1974).

Fredriksson, Bert, *Arbetsmarknadens lagar och avtal* (The laws and agreements on the labour market) (Stockholm: Prisma, 1973).

Sweden: Conflict, Power and Politics in Industrial Relations 213

Fulcher, James, 'Class conflict in Sweden', *Sociology*, Vol. VII (1973).

Gardell, Bertil, 'Vrångbild av svensk arbetsvetenskap' (Distorted picture of Swedish research on work), *Sociologisk forskning*, Vol. 6 (4), pp. 305–17 (1969).

Gardell, Bertil, *Produktionsteknik och arbetsglädje* (Production technology and joy in one's work) (Stockholm: PA-radel, 1971).

Gardell, Bertil, *Arbetsinnehåll och livskvalitet* (Content of work and quality of life) (Stockholm: Prisma, 1976).

Geijer, Lennart and Folke Schmidt, *Arbetsgivare och fackföreningsledare i domarsäte* (Employers and union leaders in the judge's seat) (Lund: 1958).

Gonäs, Lena, *Företagsnedläggning och arbetsmarknadspolitik* (Plant shutdown and labour market policy). Reports from the Department of Cultural Geography, no. 10 (Uppsala: University of Uppsala, 1974).

Gustafsson, Siv, *Lönebildning och lönestruktur inom den statliga sektorn* (Wage formation and wage structure in the state sector) (Stockholm: Industriens Utredningsinstitut, 1976).

Hammarström, Olle, 'Vad har den företagsdemokratiska forskningen givit? (What have been the results of research on industrial democracy?) *Psykolognytt*, Vol. 21, no. 16 (appendix), pp. 11–13 (1975).

Hansson, Reine, Lars Björk and P. Hellberg, *Ökat inflytande i jobbet* (Increased influence at work) (Stockholm: PA-rådet & Utvecklingsrådet, 1973).

Hart, Horst and Casten von Otter, *Lönebildning på arbetsplatsen* (Wage formation at the place of work). Report no. 3 from the Swedish Institute for Social Research (Stockholm: Prisma, 1973).

Holmberg, Per, *Arbete och löner i Sverige* (Work and wages in Sweden) (Stockholm: Almänna förlaget, 1963).

Hultén, Gösta, *Arbetsrätt och klassherravälde* (Labour law and class supremacy) (Stockholm: Rabén & Sjögren, 1971).

Högström, Gunnar, 'Recent trends in collective bargaining in Sweden', *International Labour Review*, Vol. CVII (March 1973).

Ingham, Geoffrey K., *Strikes and Industrial Conflict*: Britain and Scandinavia (London: Macmillan, 1974).

Jacobsson, Lars and Assar Lindbeck, 'Labour market conditions, wages and inflation – Swedish experiences 1955–67', *Swedish Journal of Economics*, Vol. LXXXI, pp. 64–103 (1969).

Johannesson, Conny, *De centrala avtalsförhandlingarna och den fackliga demokratin* (Centralized collective bargaining and union democracy). Lund political studies no. 18 (Lund: Department of political science, University of Lund, 1975).

Johansson, Sten, *När är tiden mogen?* (When is the time ripe?) (Stockholm: Tiden, 1974).

Johnston, T. L., *Collective Bargaining in Sweden* (London: Allen & Unwin, 1962).

Jungenfeldt, Karl G., *Löneandelen och den ekonomiska utvecklingen* (The share of wages and the economic development (Stockholm, IUI, 1966).

Jörberg, Lennart, *The Industrial Revolution in Scandinavia* (London: Fontana, 1970).

Karasek, Robert Allen, *The Impact of Work Environment on Life Outside the Job.* (Ph.D. dissertation, Massachusetts Institute of Technology). Mimeo (Stockholm: Swedish Institute for Social Research, 1976).

Karlbom, Torvald, *Arbetarnas facköreningar* (The unions of the workers) (Stockholm: Bok & Bild, 1969).

Karlsson, Lars Erik, *Demokratipå arbetsplatsen* (Democracy at the place of work) (Stockholm: Prisma, 1969).

Karlsson, Lars Erik and Jens, Söderlund, *Lägesrapport Från Arvikaprojektet* (Interim report from the Arvika study) (Stockholm: Företagsdemokratidelegationen, 1973).

Klevmarken, Anders, *Statistical Methods for the Analysis of Earnings Data* (Stockholm: Almqvist & Wiksell, 1972).

Korpi, Walter, *Vilda strejker inom metall – och verkstadsindustrin. En rapport till Svenska Metallindustriarbetareförbundet* (Wildcat strikes in the metal working industry). A report to the Swedish Metal Workers Union (Stockholm: 1968) (Mimeo).

Korpi, Walter, *Varför strejkar arbetarna? En betraktelse över konflikter, makt och rätt pa* arbetsmarknaden?* (Why do workers strike? An essay on conflicts, power and justice on the labour market) (Stockholm: Tiden, 1970).

Korpi, Walter, 'Gruvarbetarnas syn på strejken vid LKAB' (The mineworkers' view on the LKAB strike), *Fackföreningsrörelsen*, Vol. 50, no. 26, pp. 390–4 (1970).

Korpi, Walter, 'Conflict and the balance of power', *Acta Sociologica.* Vol. 17 (2) pp. 99–114 (1974a).

Korpi, Walter, 'Conflict, power and relative deprivation', *The American Political Science Review.* Vol. LXVIII· pp. 1569–78 (December 1974b).

Korpi, Walter, 'Social policy and poverty in post-war Sweden', *Acta Sociologica*, Vol. 18, no. 2–3 pp. 120–41 (1975).

Korpi, Walter, *The Working Class in Welfare Capitalism. Work, Unions and Politics in Sweden* (London: Routledge & Kegan Paul, 1978).

Kronlund, Jan *Demokrati utan inflytande* (Stockholm: Prisma, 1974).

Kuuse, Jan, *Inkomstutveckling och förmögenhetsfördelning* Changes in income and distribution of property). Report no. 23 from the department of economic history Göteborg: (University of Göteborg, 1970).

Lewin, Leif, *Planhushållningsdebatten* (The debate on the planned economy) (Stockholm: Almqvist & Wiksell, 1967).

Lewin, Leif, *Hur styrs facket? Om demokratin inom fackföreningsrörelsen* (How are the Unions Governed? On democracy in the Union Movement) (Stockholm: Rabén & Sjogren, 1977).

Lidman, Sara and Odd Uhrbom, *Gruva* (The mine). (Stockholm: Bonnier, 1968).

Lindbeck, Assar, *Swedish Economic Policy* (Stockholm: Aldus, 1975).

Lindblad, Ingemar, *Svenska Kommunalarbetareförbundet 1910–1960* (The Swedish Municipal Workers' Union, 1910–1960) (Stockholm: Tiden, 1960).

LO, *Fackföreningsrörelsen och den fulla sysselsättningen* (Trade unions and full employment) (Stockholm 1951. A modified version translated into English see Turvey (1952).

LO, *Fackföreningsrörelsen och den tekniska utvecklingen* (Stockholm: Prisma, 1966). Translated into English: *Trade Unions and Technological Change* S. D. Anderman (ed.) (London: Allen & Unwin, 1967).

Sweden: *Conflict, Power and Politics in Industrial Relations* 215

LO, *Tvärsnitt. 7 forskningsrapporter utgivna till LO:s 75-års-jubileum* (Cross-section. Seven research reports to the 75th anniversary of the LO) (Stockholm: Prisma, 1973).

LO, *Kollektiv kapitalbildning genom löntagarfonder* (Collective capital formation through wage earners' funds). Report to the Congress of the LO (Stockholm: Prisma, 1976).

Lydall, H., *The Structure of Earnings* (London: Oxford University Press, 1968).

Martin, Andrew, *The politics of Economic Policy in the United States: A Tentative View from a Comparative Perspective* (Beverly Hills: Sage Publications, 1973).

Meidner, Rudolf *Svensk arbetsmarknad under full sysselsättning* (The Swedish labour market under full employment) (stockholm: Norstedt, 1954).

Meidner, Rudolf, 'Samordning och solidarisk löne politik under tre decennier', pp. 7–73 (Coordination and solidaristic wage policy during three decades), in LO: *Tvärsnitt* (Stockholm: Prisma, 1973).

Meidner, Rudolf and Berndt Öhman, *Solidarisk lönepolitik* (Stockholm: Tiden, 1972). Published in English by LO: *Fifteen Years of Wage Policy* Stockholm: 1972).

Meidner, Rudolf, Anna Hedborg and Gunnar Fond, *Löntagarfonder* (Stockholm: Tiden, 1975). Revised edition in English, *'Employee Investment Funds. An Approach to Capital Formation* (London: Allen & Unwin, 1977).

Menningen, Walter (ed.), *Ungleichheit im Wohlfahrtsstaat. Der Alva-Myrdal-Report der schwedischen Sozialdemokraten* (Hamburg, Rowohlt, 1971).

Nelander, Sven, *Löntagarnas faktiska arbetstider* (The actual working hours of the wage earners) (Stockholm: Allmänna Förlaget, 1971).

Nilstein, Arne, 'White collar unions in Sweden', in Adolf Strumthal (ed.), *White Collar Trade Unions* (Urbana, Ill.: University of Illinois Press, 1966).

Nycander, Svante, *Kurs på Kollision* (Collision course) (Stockholm: Askild & Kärnekull, 1972).

Nycander, Svante, 'Genombrott för en ny lönepolitik' (Break-through for a new wage policy), *Skandinaviska Enskilda Bankens kvartalstidskrift*, no. 3 (1974).

Ohlsson, Ingvar, 'Den solidariska lönepolitiken – resultat och problem' (Solidaristic wage policy – results and problems), *Tiden*, no. 1 pp. 16–24 (1975).

Ohlström, Bo, *Kockumsrapporten* (Kockum's report) (Stockholm: Prisma, 1970).

Öhman, Bernt, *Svensk arbetsmarknadspolitik 1900 – 1947* (Swedish labour market policy 1900–1947) (Stockholm: Prisma, 1970).

——, 'LO och arbetsmarknadspolitiken efter andra världskriget' (LO and labour market policy since the Second World War), pp. 73–150 in LO: *Tvärsnitt* (Stockholm: Prisma, 1973).

Olsson, Ulf, *Lönepolitik och lönestruktur* (Wages policy and wage structure). Report no. 19, from the department of economic history (University of Göteborg, Göteborg, 1970).

von Otter, Casten, 'Arbetarnas fackliga organisationsgrad' (The level of unionization among workers), *Arkiv för studier i arbetarrörelsens historia*, no. 4, pp. 21–38 (1973).

von Otter, Casten, 'Lockouten i kampen mellan arbete och kapital' (The lockout in the struggle between labour and capital), pp. 237–54 in Peter Dencik and Bengt-Åke Lundvall (eds.). *Arbete, Kapital & Stat* (Stockholm: Zenit–Rabén & Sjögren, 1974).

von Otter, Casten, 'Sweden: labour reformism reshapes the system', pp. 194–234 in S. Barkin (ed.), *Worker Militancy and its Consequences, 1965–75* (New York: Praeger, 1975a).

von Otter, Casten, *Försök med förvaltningsdemokrati – en utvärdering* (Experiments with democracy in public administration – an evaluation) (Stockholm: Delegationen för förvaltningsdemokrati, 1975b).

Palm, Göran, *Ett å på LM* (A year at the LM) (Stockholm: Författar förlaget, 1972).

Palm, Göran, *Bokslut från LM* (Balance account from the LM) (Stockholm: Författarlaget, 1974).

Petersson, O. and B. Särlvik, *Valet 1973* (The 1973 Election) (Stockholm: The Central Bureau of Statistics, 1974) (mimeo).

Pettersson, William, 'Vad kostar en företagsnedläggning den drabbade arbetskraften' (What does a plant closure cost the affected labour force), pp. 127–58 in Casten von Otter (ed.), *Arbetslivet i kris och förvandling* (Stockholm: Rabén & Sjögren, 1971).

Rehn, Gösta and Erik Lundberg, 'Employment and welfare: some Swedish issues', *Industrial Relations*, Vol. 2, no. 2 (February 1963).

Rehnman, Erik, *Företagsdemokrati och företagsorganisation* (Industrial democracy and enterprise organisation) (Stockholm: Norstedt, 1964).

Rundblad, Bengt G., *Arbetskraftens rörlighet* (Labour force mobility) (Stockholm: Almqvist & Wiksell, 1964).

Rundblad, Bengt G., 'Inflyttad arbetskrafts anpassning i en expanderande arbetsmarknad' (The adjustment of migrating labour into an expanding labour market), pp. 159–78, in Casten von Otter (ed.). *Arbetslivet i kris och förvandling* (Stockholm: Rabén & Sjögren, 1971).

Rydén, Bengt, *Fusioner i svensk industri* (Fusions in Swedish industry) (Stockholm: IUI, 1971).

SAF. *Företagsvinster, kapitalförsörjning, löntagarfonder* (Company profits, capital supply, wage-earners' funds) (Stockholm: Svensak Arbetsgivareföreningen och Sveriges Industriförbund, 1976).

Scase, Richard, *Social Democracy in Capitalist Society: Working Class Politics in Britain and Sweden* (London: Croom Helm, 1977).

Schiller, Bernt, *Storstrejken 1909* (The general strike of 1909) (Göteborg, Akademiförlaget, 1967).

Schiller, Bernt, 'LO, paragraf 32 och företagsdemokratin' (LO, paragraph 32 and industrial democracy), pp. 283–398 in LO, *Tvärsnitt* (Stockholm: Prisma, 1973).

Schmidt, Folke, *The Law of Labour Relations in Sweden* (Stockholm: TCO 1962).

Schmidt, Folke, in Aaron, Benjamin and K. W. Wedderburn (eds.), *Industrial Conflict: A Comparative Legal Survey* (London: Longmans, 1972).

SOU 1968:7. *Ägande och inflytande i det privata näringslivet* (Ownership and influence in the private industry) (Stockholm: 1968).

SOU 1970:34. *Svenska folkets inkomster* (Incomes of the Swedish people) (Stockholm: 1970).

SOU 1974:29. *Att utvärdera arbetsmarknadspolitik* (To evaluate labour market politics) (Stockholm: 1974).

SOU 1975:1. *Demokrati på arbetsplatsen* (Democracy at the work-place) (Stockholm: 1975).

Spånt, Roland, *Förmögenhetsfördelningen i Sverige* (The distribution of property in Sweden). Report no. 5 from the Swedish Institute for Social Research (Stockholm: Prisma, 1975a).

Spånt, Roland, *Den svenska inkomstfördelningens utveckling* (The development of the distribution of income in Sweden). Report from Department of Economics, University of Uppsala (Uppsala: 1975b) (mimeo).

Spånt, Roland and Pebbe Selander, 'Distribution of income', pp. 173–89, in SOU 1970:71. *The Swedish Economy 1971–1975. The 1970 Long-term Survey* (Stockholm: 1970).

Steiger, Otto, 'Bakgrunden till 30-talets social-demokratiska krispolitik' (The background to the crises policy of the Social Democrats in the 1930's). *Arkiv för studier i arbetarrörelsens historia*, Vol. 1, pp. 4–28 (1973).

Sundbom, Lars, *De extremt lågavlönade* (Persons with extremely low wages) (Stockholm: Allmänna Förlaget, 1970).

Sundbom, Lars, *De förvärvsarbetandes arbetsplats-förhållanden* (Workplace conditions of the gainfully employed) (Stockholm: Allmänna Förlaget, 1971).

Svenning, Olle, *Socialdemokratin och näringslivet* (Social Democracy and Industry) (Stockholm: Tiden, 1972).

Svensk Arbetsmarknad 1950–1968. Bibliografi över forskning och debatt (The Swedish labour market 1950–1968. Bibliography on research and debate) (Stockholm: Institutet för arbetsmarknadsfrågor, 1969).

Svensson, Jörn, *Det korporativa samhället* (The corporativistic society) (Stockholm: Arbetarkultur, 1969).

Södersten, Jan, 'Företagsbeskattning och resursfördelning' (Company taxation and the distribution of resources), pp. 322–59, in Erik Lundberg *et al.*, *Svensk finanspolitik i teori och praktik* (Stockholm: Aldus, 1971).

TCO, *Löntagarkapital* (Wage-earners' capital). Report to the Congress of the TCO (Stockholm: 1976).

Thunberg, Anders (ed.), *Strejken* (The strike) (Stockholm: Rabén & Sjögren, 1970).

Tobisson, Lars, *Framväxten av statstjänstemännens förhandlingsrätt* (The development of the bargaining rights of state employees) (Stockholm: Jucist- och samhällsvetareförbundets förlag, 1973).

Turvey, R. (ed.), *Wages Policy under Full Employment* (London: , 1952).

Ullenhag, Jörgen, *Den solidariska lönepolitiken i Sverige* (Solidaristic wage policy in Sweden) (Stockholm: Läromedekförlagen, 1971).

Westlander, Gunnela, *Arbetets villkor och fritidens innehåll* (Conditions of work and content of leisure) (Stockholm: Pa-Council, 1976).

Wheeler, Christopher W., *Interest Groups in Swedish Politics: The Case of the Central Organisation of Salaried Employees*. Ph.D. dissertation (Faculty of Political Science, Columbia University, 1972).

6 Industrial Relations in West Germany

Heinz Hartmann and Wolfgang Conrad

The present industrial relations system of West Germany has obvious historical precedents. Works councils, for example, became strong under the Weimar Republic following the First World War and anticipated postwar proposals for employee participation in management, or codetermination (Schneider and Kuda, 1969; Vetter, 1975). This long tradition can be explained, in part, by the government's interest in industrial relations, particularly concerning the issue of industrial peace. As early as 1869 there was legislation regulating problem-solving in industrial relations. Such legislation led to the formal recognition of organized labour in 1916 and to government supervision of labour–management relations. Since the Second World War, the government has tended to intervene less often and to give greater scope for 'autonomous' interaction between organized labour and employer associations.

The development of research in this area shows a pattern similar to its history. There seems to have been no evolution in the narrow sense, but rather, continuing research on recurring themes. In the early twenties, for example, work-place allowances for 'the nature of production' were instituted (Böhle and Sauer, 1975).

Legal protection against dismissal exists but is limited in its effectiveness because employees have to prove that they were dismissed because their employer 'misused his superior position of power in the company'. In fact, employers can counter such an argument by reference to 'overriding exigencies in production' (Hartwich, 1970).

When Braun (1972) studied the system and functions of social security measures in the Federal Republic, he found that in financial terms, old-age insurance represents the largest component of the social security system. This insurance system is divided along traditional lines, with

218

separate systems for blue-collar workers, white-collar workers, and miners. In spite of recent efforts towards a standardization of different systems, the almost feudal structure of institutional differentiation has persisted. Similarly, disability and redundancy compensation provide only limited payments scaled to the personal details of the recipients, so that social security measures only incompletely replace lost earnings (Böhle and Altmann, 1972).

Another sector of state social policy relates to skill-training. West Germany has a labour promotion law, which was designed to help workers adjust to changing occupational requirements. The primary objective of the law – to reduce unemployment and to utilize the potential of the work force – is, of course, difficult to achieve. Lutz and Sengenberger (1974) as well as Böhle and Sauer (1975) explicitly attest to such limitations. The law is least effective for those groups in the labour force that suffer most from the risk of unemployment. Its benefits are available to those who have graduated from a complete programme of occupational training. By and large, the unskilled and semi-skilled are not covered. In addition, the law is geared to general capabilities or occupational skills and not to job-centred qualifications.

Welfare State versus Capitalism

Research on the role of the state is primarily concerned with inputs (Mayntz, 1974). Outputs, such as actions of political bodies, are neglected. This was obvious in the beginnings of research on democracy, which marked the transition from the Nazi tradition. Even the emergence of criticism of the established system did not change the focus, only the tone of the assessment: critical statements centred on the deficiencies of democratic decision-making and participation rather than on the problem of administrative inefficiency. A similar trend can easily be demonstrated in studies on the political activities of labour and management organizations. The powerful position of such organizations since the middle of the sixties drew attention to their role in decision-making. At the end of that decade, the discussion changed again towards the evaluation of these organizations as instruments of class interest in a capitalist framework (Narr and Naschold, 1971).

Because of this change in orientation, theorists are no longer confined to a discussion of the evolutionary laws of capital, but question the relationship of economic conflicts to the stabilizing and management functions of the political system. As Offe (1973) puts it, theorists are now in a position to investigate the 'crises of crisis management'.

Critics of capitalism all agree that the solution to the problems of the established system cannot be found in change by gradual reform. The system lacks opportunities for such change because of the strong incentives for private capital accumulation. In theories of advanced capitalism, the antagonism between private decisions and social effects is not considered a primary cause of crisis in the system. Instead, interest is centred on an analysis of mechanisms, such as collective bargaining, which help to balance the antagonism (Offe, 1972). The limited effectiveness of these mechanisms, however, leads to increasing discrepancies between social problems and the ability to deal with them.

The Public Sector

Almost half the employees active in the public sector are civil servants and therefore barred from collective bargaining. But these civil servants do belong to professional associations concerned with Civil Service regulations and their application (Hartwich, 1970). There is very little research available on industrial relations in the public sector. However, in view of the higher incidence of public-sector labour conflicts at the end of the sixties, mostly in the form of 'working to rule', there was more discussion of the 'right to strike' for employees in the public sector generally, and specifically for civil servants (Däubler, 1970; Hoffacher, 1973). So far, however, there have only been two studies of any importance: one of these (Lutz *et al.*, 1970) concentrates on changes in technology and organization and their effects on the public sector. The second study (Billerbeck *et al.*, 1975) rejects the assumption that the special status of employees in the public sector, and especially of civil servants, leads to orientations different from those in private industry.

The Contemporary Role of Trade Unions

After the collapse of national socialism, trade union policy was faced with a choice: either to strive towards social innovation in the sense of a socialist-planned economy, or to participate in a social recovery oriented to the tradition of the First German Republic. Because of the influence of the occupation powers, organized labour decided in favour of the second option: a concentration of all social resources on material recovery. Since then, German trade unions have avoided any serious break with the established social order (Széplabi, 1973; Schmidt, 1971; Conert, 1970). This is mainly because trade unions have been accepted by their political and economic counterparts. As a result, labour–management relations have shown flexibility during crisis. Codetermination is an indication of this flexibility and reflects an attitude towards society and the management of conflict inherent in German industrial relations policy.

It is only in recent years that empirical studies have been undertaken on the relationship of social and economic development, on the one hand, and of the structure and activities of organized labour on the other (Bergmann *et al.*, 1975). The special merit of this study is its emphasis on the importance of the motivation of union members. Trade union policy in this view is considered the natural representative of the interests of union members rather than something independent of the rank and file. The German Trade Union Federation, as well as its 16 constituent industrial unions, depends on the support of a strong membership that accepts the goals of the organization and is willing to support these goals by striking if necessary.

The degree of participation among workers in the various West German trade unions averages about 35 per cent. The low levels of membership must be attributed to the 'free rider' effect, which allows employees to avoid the comparatively high membership fees. Another factor seems to be that, in the interpretation of the rank and file, the *raison d'être* of trade unions is to be found in the initiatives which they take to promote favourable legislation in social policy (Wallraff, 1970). When this activity is preempted by initiatives of the government, workers see less need for active membership. Thus the more success that union objectives have politically, the less there is to bargain about (Briefs, 1965; Nickel, 1974; van de Vall, 1966). (The van de Vall analysis is concerned with the situation in the Netherlands, but it has contributed significantly to discussions in the Federal Republic.)

Functions and functional change

In evaluating trade unions in West Germany, three general questions emerge:
(1) What are the contributions of trade unions to the satisfaction of member interests?

(2) What is the contribution of organized labour to the increased emancipation of workers from doctrinaire work rules?

(3) What is the union contribution to the stability of the socio-economic system?

The major problem in a discussion of trade union functions is the basic incompatibility of these three roles and the identification of the effects of the predominance of one of the three (Mayer, 1973; Bergmann *et al.*, 1975). The basic concept of necessity must be adapted to changing economic and social situations (Pizzorno, 1972). This process of adaptation to new situations has recently been described as 'functional change' in trade unions. In this context, there is special emphasis on two trends of trade union development: their recognition by employers and the state (Hirsch, 1966) and their social integration, or acceptance of conditions of economic and political stability.

There is emphasis on the fact that trade union activities today are no longer quasi-autonomous, or at least are significantly reduced in function when compared to the situation sixty years ago (Mayer, 1973). This stems from the social integration of organized labour and can only be compensated for by obtaining new areas of influence. There has been reference to the fact that an increase in public functions strengthens trade unions as independent institutions rather than making them an adjunct of the economic process (Briefs, 1965; van de Vall, 1966).

Consequences of functional change

As a rule, discussions centre on the relationship of newly organized local trade unions to employers and to the state, rather than on the wider repercussions of changes in the relationships between trade unions and their members or in their organizational structure. Apart from theorizing, as in Michels (1911) well-worn work, but confirmed, on oligarchy, little attention has been devoted to the consequences of the transition to a consolidated or 'co-operative' trade union movement (Bergmann *et al.*, 1975).

The problem of functional effects on the organizational structure of trade unions so far has been discussed only in theories of advanced capitalism or in the context of the crisis of motivation in advanced capitalist systems. Some references to the current situation, however, are to be found in Weitbrecht (1969). He argues that under current economic and political conditions, the area of independent decision-making by the bargaining parties has been reduced by the application of objective standards. This places a great deal of stress on the conventional commitment of union members to traditional union policies, particularly in the area of quasi-participation, mentioned earlier. More insights into this problem are presented in a study by Streeck (1976).

Trade unions and political parties

German trade unions have remained neutral in their relationship to political parties. But there is a traditional, symbolic relationship with the Social Democratic Party, which has its origins in the simultaneous establishment of trade unions and working-class parties in Germany many decades ago. Such a relationship does not mean, however, that trade unions are formal members of the party at either the local or national level. At most, the relationship reflects the joint representation of trade unions and political parties in institutions of the state and a certain tendency on the part of the governing Social Democrats to take trade union objectives into account.

Statements on this subject must remain vague since as yet, no empirical research has emerged. However, a study is now being conducted at Frankfurt (Herding *et al.*) which is devoted precisely to this problem. Otherwise, the only systematic contributions have been made by Eliassen (1974), who developed a typology of political participation and party commitment by the trade unions to West Germany. Finally, Hirsch-Weber (1969) pointed out the efforts of political parties to exercise control over trade unions and to avoid trade union pressure on politics by forming partisan political groups inside the unions.

Problems and Developments in Collective Bargaining

Bargaining autonomy and its legal framework

The system of collective bargaining in West Germany has been unusually stable. There have been few interventions by the state, and these have been most discreet. The absence of government intervention attests to extensive autonomy of bargaining in the Federal Republic: trade unions and employers' associations exercise their power in wage bargaining based upon a mutual recognition of the bargaining system, and reach a compromise decision (Himmelmann, 1971). However, the general legal provisions affecting the actual autonomy of the parties to bargaining should not be under-estimated. Weitbrecht, who is the author of the most widely known German study on the collective bargaining system (1969), maintains that autonomy is dependent on such regulations because they imply a political guarantee of such autonomy (see also Streeck, 1976; Himmelmann, 1971).

Weitbrecht also points to the role of the state which would otherwise have to be recognized as a third party in the system of interaction between organized labour and employers' associations. In this relationship, interaction between the bargaining parties may be interpreted as the internal aspect of bargaining autonomy, while the relationship between these two parties and the state might be considered its external aspect.

The opportunities and limits of joint decision-making by the bargaining parties are defined by the boundary of the autonomous area and its interactions with the state (Hartwich, 1970). Industrial unionism in West Germany is not company centred. Agreements emphasize regional differentials in growth, since the predominant pattern of bargaining over wages and salaries is regional (Schacht and Unterseher, 1971, 1972).

Schacht and Unterseher have also pointed out that the two issues of hierarchical control in the firm and grievance procedures are matters of concern not only for the parties to bargaining but for the institutions created by the Works Constitution Act and the Co-determination Law. The regulation, by means of the Works Constitution Act, of conflicts that are experienced daily and directly by the employee greatly relieves the agenda of the collective bargaining system. Another issue that conceivably might be made the subject of collective bargaining is deciding on the interpretation of collectively agreed work norms, and this will be discussed in more detail later. Finally, detailed regulations on safety and other working conditions serve to lessen the functional load carried by collective bargaining in West Germany.

The legal standardization of bargaining procedures in part emerges from labour law. The law determines the pattern of conflict (prohibition of wildcat strikes, recognition of the fairness rule or of the "*ultima ratio*" – demand) and it sets the procedure for collective bargaining. Labour courts, for instance, almost always fully commit both parties to peaceful conduct during the course of their deliberations. While contracts are in force, strikes cannot be called to modify them or to impose new contracts. Furthermore, trade unions cannot strike without a general vote of at least 75 per cent of all members.

Mediation

The system of mediation which occurs in bargaining impasses is geared so that the settlements take into account both the interests of the parties involved and the public policy favouring income redistribution (Unterseher, 1972). According to Luhmann (1969), mediation can be interpreted as the vital factor in a learning process enabling participants to come to terms with possible disappointments. Weitbrecht (1969) also sums up the process of collective bargaining as a procedure for committing participants to disappointing compromise. Compromise, and of course the effectiveness of a bargaining system, depends upon the relationship of the delegates to the members of the organization.

Another aspect of mediation procedures is 'concerted action', an institution established by the government in which representatives of the government, of employers, and of organized labour discuss the guidelines of the government incomes policy. There are doubts, however, concerning the effectiveness of concerted action. Unterseher (1972a), in fact, suspects that the wildcat strikes in 1969 and the attempts at bargaining in the metal industries in 1970 may be interpreted as rebellions against long-range planning.

Mention should be made also of a study by Külp (1972) on the results of different styles of mediation. The results of the survey show that mediation as it is variously practised is accepted by most of the participants.

Labour courts

Unterseher (1975) concludes that the function of the labour courts depends on the frequency and degree of intervention, by the state. The more immediate the intervention, the less is the importance of the labour courts. In a system featuring fairly autonomous bargaining and a state limiting itself to control of the context of bargaining, as in West Germany, the main role of the labour courts is the maintenance and consolidation of the established patterns of bargaining. According to Schacht and Unterseher (1972), there are four aspects to such limitation:
(1) The commitment to peaceful conduct;
(2) The development by the federal Labour Court, of the concept of 'social adequacy', which permits labour courts to accept as legitimate only strikes that satisfy certain criteria established by the court themselves.

(3) The concept of 'parity in conflict' which establishes the formal balance between strikes and lock-outs. Strikes are a suspension of work relationships while this is true for lock-outs only under specified conditions which, in turn, are subject to interpretation by the courts.

(4) The illegality of wildcat strikes, as well as of political strikes.

Collective Conflicts

Official strikes organized by trade unions

There has been little research on strikes, except for wildcat actions which have attracted increasing attention since the wave of metalworkers' strikes in 1969. Data on 'official' strikes organized by the trade unions are collected by the Federal Labour Exchange. Information is included on establishments affected, workers involved in strikes and lock-outs, and work-days lost. The reporting methods, however, do not give a clear statistical picture of industrial conflict. For instance, length of strike and number of people involved are usually under-estimated; individual actions (e.g. absenteeism) are not covered and collective forms of conflict which are restricted to one firm, like short-term spontaneous work stoppages are not reported in official statistics.

Studies of official strikes include a history of strikes and lock-outs over two decades: 1948–68 (Kalbitz, 1973); comparative case studies of the strikes of employees in the chemical industries in 1972 (Dzielak *et al.*, 1974); and analyses of strikes in the Federal Republic in the late sixties and early seventies (Steinhaus, 1975).

Scholars of 'labour studies' have undertaken occasional examinations of strikes and strike threats (Wiedemann, 1971), while economists (Külp, 1969) have studied the question of whether a lack of recognition of trade union officers by the rank and file may stimulate strikes.

As is demonstrated by the study of strikes and lock-outs 1948–68 (Kalbitz, 1973), official strikes have led to a subsequent improvement in the economic situation of employees. Exceptions have been in mining where there is a significantly larger incidence of 'political strikes', in the metal industries where wildcat strikes are dominant (strikes not necessarily for economic purposes), and in the public services where the prohibition on strikes for civil servants has created a situation in which 'political strikes' have become the predominant type of conflict. For a more recent period, Kern (1974) has concluded that there is a change in the collective interests and types of conduct shown in conflict situations. His thesis is that there is increasing interest in the control and improvement of working conditions and growing resistance to the hierarchical organization of work.

Case studies of strikes in the chemical industries (Dzielak *et al.*, 1974) do not allow for similar generalizations. They do, however, show the contribution made by the show of strength in individual firms to the overall development of trade union power in industrial conflict.

Wildcat strikes

The literature on wildcat strikes is far more extensive than the investigations of strikes organized by trade unions. Researchers are obviously more attracted by illegal conflicts than by strikes which follow normal patterns.

The increase in the number of studies on wildcat strikes since September 1969 may also be due to the fact that the limits of economic growth first became visible towards the end of the sixties.

The upward trend in wildcat strikes, for example in the metal and building industries, has been accelerating steadily. Kalbitz (1973) sees wildcat strikes as a permanent feature of industrial relations which becomes widespread when the pressures on workers are increased.

After 1969 some observers noted the revival of class feeling and solidarity. This is denied by Kalbitz (1973) for whom wildcat strikes are a more or less regular, normal aspect of industrial conflict. Schumann *et al* (1971) also refute, at least in part, the thesis of working-class revival. Instead Schumann emphasizes the fact that wage demands, which until then had been conventional claims for an increase in wages and salaries, in 1969 for the first time involved arguments aiming at adequate participation in economic growth. As Bergmann (1972) has shown, the unusual configuration of circumstances in that year (government coalition between the two most important political parties, cooperation of the trade unions in 'concerted action', public discussions on economic policy and a general election) contributed to a growing awareness among employees of the discrepancy between a growing national product and rising profits on the one hand and lags in income on the other. These comments are confirmed by data from an opinion survey among officials of three industrial trade unions, carried out in 1970 by the Institute for Social Research in Frankfurt (Bergmann *et al.*, 1975).

There is one aspect of investigation on wildcat strikes in the Federal Republic which should not be neglected here – the question of whether the increasing incidence of spontaneous striking is indicative of a crisis of trade union policy. This argument was first raised in a study by the Institute for Marxist Social Research (IMSF, 1969), which concluded that workers were willing to fight for their immediate economic interests, so that it would be possible to mobilize large numbers of workers in favour of strikes, but that trade unions lack the militance required for such mobilization. Similar conclusions have been reached by another research team (Express, 1974) which investigated the background and the chronology of strikes in 1973. They also speak of a crisis in the 'social partnership' orientation of trade union policy. In consequence the team recommends trade union activities which are able to absorb and activate the conflict potential of the rank and file, and endorses political education.

Furthermore, the investigations by this research team on strikes in individual companies tend to show that strikes in 1973 did not represent a united movement but were started and concluded in relative isolation. There was often a lack of coordination even when strike activities extended to several units of one large industrial company. Unlike 1969, however, strikes were not confined to iron and steel and mining, sectors with relatively stable trade union organizations and characterized by a certain amount of strike experience. Instead, strikes focused on the automobile industry and related industries as well as on the electrical industry.

Changes in Economic Structure and Their Implications

Long-term changes in occupational structure have occurred. Agriculture constituted 25 per cent of employment in 1950 and 7 per cent in 1973. In contrast, employment in manufacturing rose from 43 per cent in 1950 to 47 per cent in 1973. Employment in the service sector also changed significantly, rising from 33 per cent in 1950 to 46 per cent in 1973. In 1973, 45 per cent of the working population were classified as blue-collar workers, 32 per cent as white-collar workers, 8 per cent as Civil Service officials (*Beamten*), 9 per cent as self-employed, and 6 per cent as miscellaneous (Institut der Deutschen Wirtschaft, 1975).

These shifts have been variously attributed to technological change, industrial reorganization, shifts in demands for goods and services, and changes in labour supply. On balance, there has been a modest upgrading of skills required. The skill level of blue-collar workers is said to have remained fairly stable whereas white-collar and Civil Service sectors are apparently becoming more skilled.

Empirical data tend to support the early theses by Kern and Schumann (1970) suggesting occupational polarization(Oppelt, Schrick and Bremmer, 1972; Gerstenberger *et al.*, 1974; Mickler, 1975) which show that within most industries there is an increase in the demand for both highly skilled and less-skilled manpower, while the demand for employees with average qualifications is decreasing. Clearly, developments in this area are of serious importance to the future of industrial relations in the Federal Republic. Will employers be dealing with a labour force better equipped with skills and know-how than before? Or will they be facing employees holding comparatively low qualifications. Or will labour be divided into experts and assistants, with a widening gap between the two groups?

Determinants of change

During the sixties, public as well as academic assessments of occupational change focused on technological change which was thought to have a *Sachzwang*, that is to say, an exogenous force, independent of social policy. The most thorough investigation of the impact of technology on qualifications was undertaken by Kern and Schumann, who studied innovation in nine firms in different industries (1970). Their description offers many conclusive results; however, it stops short of policy recommendations – unlike others who call for the development of managerial strategies to adjust technology to the demands of different kinds of markets (Altmann and Kammerer, 1970). There is evidence that management has considerable discretion in reacting to technological problems (Schultz-Wild and Weltz, 1973).

It was not until the mid-70s that this bias was questioned by industrial sociologists (Fricke, 1975), although earlier research had shown that technology has social implications and plays an important role in changing occupational structure. Else and Werner Fricke (1973, 1974) emphasize, from their studies in mining, that organization, not technology, is a determining factor in change of qualification. Gerstenberger *et al.*(1974) argue forceably that technology itself is a product of other determinants, notably profitability, and this is also supported by Mickler (1975) who traces technological change to management control and to the returns on capital investment. Hesse (1972) discusses employer and employee associations; Gerstenberger (1974) trade unions; Kern and Schumann (1970) educational institutions an market factors.

All these studies, however, agree that management decisions control change in job content, and that long-term management interests are an important consideration in determining whether a job will be upgraded or downgraded.

Controversies on Training

There is an on-going controversy over vocational training. A primary issue is the apparent 'functionalism' of conventional training and its tendency to be dominated by managerial interests, particularly in the area of apprenticeship training and continuing education for adults (Sass, Sengenberger and Weltz, 1974; Axmacher, 1974).

Following the early lead of Dahrendorf (1956), social scientists became aware that training does not pertain just to technical skills, but also involves building traits such as loyalty, dependability, and the like, which promote social stability at the work-place. Weltz (1974) and Lempert (1971) have shown that the utilization of skilled workers is in part explained by managerial preference for the attitudes that they possess.

Reform of apprenticeship training

Apprenticeship first ran into massive criticism in the wake of university reform when several authors denounced the conservative, exploitative character of industrial training programmes (Baethge, 1970; Crusius, Lempert and Wilke, 1974). The government is pressing for a new law that would replace the employer-dominated system with a federal agency to supervise programmes supported by a general payroll levy.

Research shows that employers are using a number of strategies to subvert the government's reform proposals (Binkelmann and Schneller, 1975). In addition, Marxist writers have charged the government with collusion with capitalists (Becker and Jungblut, 1972), and reformers have pressed for more substantial changes in the system (Binkelmann, Böhle and Schneller, 1975; Crusius, Lempert and Wilke, 1974; Offe, 1975).

Wages, Working Conditions and 'Humanization' of Work

There has been growing criticism of the structure of industrial work in West Germany, as it has become more subject to the influence of employees, organized labour and empirical researchers. These developments make a brief look at working conditions imperative.

Wages and working conditions

An inventory on earnings of industrial workers compiled by the Centre of Sociological Research at Göttingen describes their situation as 'rather favourable' (Osterland *et al.*, 1973). Yet, there are still wide differences in the earnings of blue- and white-collar workers (Eckart *et al.*, 1974). Wages have been eroded by inflation (Blechschmidt, 1974), and the distribution of private property markedly favours a minority of the well-to-do (Bosch, 1973).

Wages and salaries are determined by base-rates and by incentive pay. Two decades ago, incentive systems were given little chance of survival because increasing mechanization was said to destroy the basis for evaluation of individual performance. Nevertheless, there has been a slight increase in the proportion of employees subject to the incentive system (Mergner, Osterland and Pelte, 1974).

The application of incentives is accompanied by a growing emphasis on job evaluation. In consequence, performance on industrial jobs is becoming more and more standardized. Blue-collar workers, especially, are said to be the focus of increased efforts on the part of management to measure and control their work.

Studies of working conditions have included the effects of work on man – involving engineering, physiology, psychology, sociology and medicine. Most of the case studies to date have been published in specialized periodicals such as *Zentralblatt für Arbeitswissenschaft*. Summaries of work in this field so far are rare, but see Mergner, Osterland and Pelte (1974).

One of the main targets which organized labour has pursued in the improvement of working conditions has been job security. Today, half the employees covered by current bargaining contracts are protected in some degree against the effects of 'rationalization measures'. Typically, agreements provide for compensation in case of transfer, lay-off, or retraining, or for actual job guarantees (Böhle and Lutz, 1974). Nevertheless, unusually high unemployment rates still cause considerable concern among employees in some industries.

Research on other forms of risk and stress at work and their consequences for social policy, has barely scratched the surface of these questions (Böhle and Altmann, 1972; Thomas, 1964).

Supervision and hierarchy

There has been no systematic research on issues of hierarchical control – the communication of orders, the recognition of managerial prerogative, and the application of discipline. Curiously enough, many observers in the sixties believed that formal hierarchies would be dismantled in industrial firms. They thought that increasing mechanization would allow more worker autonomy (Fürstenberg, 1969). For a while, managerial indecision on optimal strategies for dealing with employees (*Führungsstile*) encouraged the belief that management would be less authoritarian. Actual developments have failed to bear this out. There is instead growing talk of Taylorism, of 'restrictive work', and of more efficient utilization of labour (Böhle and Sauer, 1975).

Comparisons are often drawn with the rationalization strategies of the twenties and thirties. One exception is Mickler (1975), who shows that problems in technological change may lead temporarily to the suspension of profit orientation, to more leeway for specialists and to cutbacks in close supervision. Also, case studies of mechanization did produce data on the emergence of new jobs with some measure of autonomy (Kern and Schumann, 1970; Oppelt, Schrick and Bremmer, 1972).

If there is evidence at all on a sustained relaxation of control, however, it is within management. A survey of executives in 412 companies showed a growing preference for frequent consultation, team-like co-operation, and the demonstration of initiative by their subordinates. In particular, this pattern emerged in large firms, firms with a high proportion of university graduates and firms with high degrees of mechanization in administration and programmes of advanced training (Lukatis, 1972b).

The humanization of work

Organized labour as well as the government apparently are unwilling to count on employee-centred management policies for the improvement of working conditions. The government has designed an elaborate programme of labour–management research, soliciting studies from scholars in the field, and the German Federation of Trade Unions launched a Congress on Humanization in 1974 which heard contributions from a number of research specialists (Vetter (ed.), 1974).

At the heart of humanization efforts is the Works Constitution Act revised in 1972. In particular, the Act provides for 'introduction of employee-centred working conditions' when employees are adversely affected by changes in jobs, the sequence of work activities, or the context of work. Works councils are to be informed and consulted in all stages of planning, but the Act does not grant full worker-determination on this issue.

Neither the government nor organized labour, however, are likely to confine their humanization efforts to technological change. In particular, the trade unions have evolved a complex catalogue of demands: safety and hygiene, job content, technology and organization, wages and salaries, working hours, and research (Helfert, 1975). German unions have begun to incorporate such demands in collective bargaining and employers have begun to be willing to consider humanization as an issue. Progress is slow at present as economic recession and unemployment are crowding out problems secondary to income and job security.

One other source of resistance will also impede progress: a sizeable group of trade unionists together with labour ideologists object to the humanization of work as a 'defensive strategy of capital' or, at best, a 'strategy for the containment of conflict' (Mendner, 1975). They feel that as long as incentive systems and efficiency-oriented job evaluation persist in the enterprise, no amount of change in other conditions of work can compensate for the inhumanity of such inducements to stress and breakdown.

Worker Participation: Codetermination

Codetermination (*Mitbestimmung*), West Germany's contribution to participatory democracy in industry, is a complex and sturdy scheme. Enacted into law in the early fifties, codetermination has become entrenched as a social institution (for a historical account, see Vetter, 1975). This particular design for worker participation in management has attracted a great deal of international attention. Surprisingly, next to no research has been undertaken in the seventies on the effects of this system. Elaborate accounts of codetermination are available, including some in English (Fürstenberg, 1969; Roberts, 1973; Szakats, 1974; this account follows Hartmann, 1970).

The idea of industrial democracy, of course, had well-established roots in the history of the German labour movement. Steps towards a legal consolidation of informal gains and towards formal prescriptions beyond such advances led to the Codetermination Law of 1951. The law applied to the coal, iron and steel industries. It stipulated that half the seats on the supervisory board (roughly corresponding to the board of directors) should be allocated to employee representatives, and that executive committees should include a 'labour director'. The supervisory boards were to be chaired by a 'neutral'. In addition, the law gave more powers to works councils, including the right to participate in some major management decisions.

The labour director, certainly one of the most advanced features of codetermination, is appointed by the supervisory board on a trade union ticket, usually following joint deliberations between representatives of the employees of the individual company and representatives of the national trade unions (which in Germany are not officially organized at company level even though more or less formally represented by *Vertrauensleute*, i.e. shop stewards). The labour director is a full-fledged member of the executive board, i.e. his responsibility and privileges are not limited to personnel administration and social services, but extend to general management.

In 1952, one year after the passage of the Codetermination Law, the West German Parliament passed an Act pertaining to industries other than coal, iron and steel. Although this law, the Works Constitution Act, was intended by the trade unions to extend codetermination beyond its early confines, the attempt failed. The Act provided for increased powers of the works council and, among other things, required supervisory boards to reserve one third of their seats for employee representatives. This seemed to represent a gain for organized labour. But, although the Works Constitution Act produced codetermination outside the coal and steel industries, it was a greatly diluted version of employee control, and the trade unions soon became dissatisfied with this weak form of worker participation.

In the following years labour made tenacious efforts to improve on its legislative success of 1951. In 1955, parliament passed a personnel representation law which introduced some worker participation into decision-making in public administration. One year later, a new law subjected holding companies in the coal and steel industries to codetermination. But provisions here were less advantageous to organized labour than in operating companies. Then, many mergers in the coal and steel industries between 1952 and 1968 reduced the number of companies subject to codetermination by more than one-third. The unions therefore fought for, and managed to conclude, an agreement with respective employers' associations which allowed all supervisory boards and labour directors to continue to function in a minor form in spite of mergers.

The evaluation of results

A government commission headed by Kurt Biedenkopf published a summary evaluation of codetermination in the past two decades (Deutscher Bundestag, 1970). The report covers three major subjects: the general effectiveness of codetermination, the relative value of specific institutions within the system, probable lines of reform.

There had been considerable speculation that codetermination would be so costly and cumbersome that it would seriously impede industrial efficiency. The commission was unable to find more than incidental evidence of conflict between codetermination and managerial efforts at efficiency. And the system was shown to be accepted not only by labour but by management as well. Not all of the specific institutional arrangements proved beyond criticism. The commission discounted the value of having a neutral chairman for the supervisory board, for it revealed significant evidence of cooperation between top management and the works council at the expense of the supervisory board. It also discounted the merits of the economic committee which was supposed to be a clearing-house for information. In addition, the commission touched on the role of minority groups inside firms and on the influence of organized labour.

The commission endorsed some general trends such as an increase in the power of management, i.e. the executive board, and it favoured keeping codetermination subject to the protection of the right to maintain private property and to earn profits. In a sense, the conservative tenor of its recommendations stands in marked contrast to the favourable evaluation of the recent record of codetermination.

There are also research results on decision-making processes in the supervisory board (Brinkmann-Herz, 1972). This study deserves special attention since it seeks to assess the capacity of the board to serve as an instrument of codetermination. The study concludes with policy recommendations, a rare feature in German industrial relations research.

Mention should also be made of an analysis of the most complex problem in this field: the effects of codetermination on managerial decision-making, company policies, production, markets and social policy (Tegtmeier, 1973). In a sense, this is a sequel to the Biedenkopf Report.

Tegtmeier confirms that supervisory boards were pre-empted by 'collusion' between top management and the works councils. He also presents more specific evidence on decision-making at the apex of this two-tier structure; for example, he supplies data on the policy objectives of workers and on the structure of voting. Worker members of the supervisory board are most concerned with workers' problems in the narrowest sense, followed by problems of capital investment, the general organization of the firm and the staffing of the executive board.

In spite of such apparent worker concern with matters of management, cases of outright show-downs in voting are extremely rare: in the coal and steel industries, no more than 20 such incidents were registered over a period of four years. These analyses by Tegtmeier reveal tell-tale differences in the style of participation by members of the executive board and of the works council. Worker representatives are much more prone to emphasize workers' initiatives in the supervisory board and to rate them highly than are members of top management.

Finally, questions are raised here concerning the implications of data for codetermination as a generalized pattern of worker participation. Tegtmeier, for example, tends to refute the idea that the even allocation of votes to employee and employer representatives in the supervisory board ('parity') in the coal and steel industries is likely to lead to stalemate in decision-making. He does agree that, in its manifest objective, this pattern is not designed with an eye to effective decision-making. But his findings are that parity is practiced 'preventively', that is, the parties involved are anxious jointly to prevent situations of deadlock. In fact, then, the parity arrangement produces 'pressure towards cooperation'. This certainly is one result that was difficult to anticipate by logic or theory; only empirical investigation can demonstrate in cases like this how well social innovations measure up to their purpose.

Late in 1975, the government decided to present parliament with a Bill on codetermination to introduce the 'parity' arrangement, then confined to the coal and steel industries, into most of the large German firms. This is a somewhat stronger version of the Works Constitution Act of 1952, since it provides for an even allocation of votes to employee and employer representatives in the supervisory boards of such firms. However, the employee group will include one or more representatives of middle and upper management (*Leitende Angestellte*); in rank, they extend from immediately below the executive board to the level of bureau chief or staff specialist. Since managerial personnel of this kind cannot be expected to share the interests and ideologies of employees at lower levels of the hierarchy (Hartmann, Bock-Rosenthal and Helmer, 1973), the objectives of the Bill are questionable. As a result, the Bill has been contested by the trade unions, employers' federations and the organizations of managerial executives (Hartmann, 1975).

The Bill does provide for labour directors to be regular members of executive board. But worker representatives would no longer be granted the privilege of nomination, nor would they have the power of veto if a candidate did not have their full approval. While codetermination, then, will be extended within German industry, it will not be at the advanced levels it has reached in coal and steel.

Codetermination on the job was introduced to some extent by provisions in the newly revised Works Constitution Act. This allows for some employee influence in the areas of quality of work, safety and protection of minority groups (Kittner, 1975). There is a general consensus, however, that these concessions are difficult to make use of because they are closely hedged, and fairly limited to begin with. Organized labour has been loath, though, to demand an entirely new type of codetermination legislation. Rather, it has been pressing for improvements in the Works Constitution Act, and continuing to champion a general adoption of the 'parity model'. The trade unions are apparently unwilling to risk acquiring an infinite proliferation of power through codetermination against a promise to use any newly increased influence in the interest not only of general concerns but also of specific advantages on individual jobs.

Finally, codetermination has proved attractive to observers outside Germany. (Roeder-Sorge and Nagels, 1977). In particular, the European Commission has looked towards codetermination as a model in its effort at reorganizing industrial relations in member states. To date, the Commission has made two proposals relating to participation: the draft Fifth Directive (1972) aimed at the harmonization of company law and the draft proposal for a 'European Company' (1970). Both provided for the establishment of a two-tier system in the enterprise and both suggested the same pattern of worker participation in the supervisory board that had been introduced by the Works Constitution Act, i.e. one-third worker representation.

The Research Outlook

There is no doubt that industrial relations problems in West Germany have received considerable attention from research workers. Empirical case studies, historical accounts and legal commentaries add up to a remarkable volume. Many disciplines are involved in this endeavour; while it is true that sociologists are particularly active in industrial relations research, there are many significant contributions from other fields, notably *Arbeitswissenschaft*. By and large, research methods and results show analysts to be non-partisan students of industrial relations. This is largely due to the fact that the major parties involved do not share in this research effort: the investigation of industrial relations is almost exclusively in the hands of academic specialists. This may explain in part why contacts between research workers and the actual participants in industrial relations have remained few and unproductive; there is little feedback of research findings into the world of work. This in turn is a handicap to the systematic exploration of the industrial relations scene. The choice of new topics is largely at the mercy of academics and, therefore, may appear haphazard.

Our material in fact shows that there are curious gaps in research with regard to some of the major problems of industrial relations in West Germany. There is surprisingly little information on the structure and functions of codetermination, even though *Mitbestimmung* has been one of the most-vaunted innovations of the German scene. The management side generally has been given little research attention. Very few data are available, for instance, on managerial behaviour in the industrial relations context. No investigations have been undertaken on employers' associations. Not even the trade unions have been studied thoroughly. Recently, a study on trade union structure was funded by a German foundation precisely because it was considered a topic deplorably neglected. As one would expect, there is even less information on specialized subjects like the Europeanization of industrial relations, even though this would be a problem of considerable topical interest.

Industrial relations research in West Germany will soon receive a new impetus from the many innovations which are now being worked out with regard to research methods. Rightly or wrongly, the comparative inefficiency of research has been aggravated by the inefficiency of conventional methods. By way of remedy, members of several research centres have designed innovations in the area of surveys ('camera research', worker correspondence, narrative analysis), in-depth research (sociobiography, longitudinal studies, 'animation') and application ('crisis seminars', process innovation). Some of these new techniques represent a genuine break with methodological conventions in this field of research and there is hope that the use of these novel methods will lead to an increase in research findings.

POSTSCRIPT

The manuscript of this book was delivered to the general editor, Peter Doeringer, in January 1976. While most of our account pertains to the current situation without qualification, regrettably it was impossible to include references to studies and comments which were published since 1976.

REFERENCES

Achinger, Hans, *Sozialpolitik als Gesellschaftspolitik* (Hamburg: Rowohlt, 1958).

Altmann, Norbert and Guido Kammerer, *Wandel der Berufsstruktur* (Frankfurt: RKW, 1970).

Altmann, Norbert and Guido Bechtle, *Betriebliche Herrschaftsstrukturen und industrielle Gesellschaft* (München: Hanser, 1971).

Apel, Günter and Roland Issen, *Miteigentum: Probleme und Lösungen* (München: Nymphenburger, 1970).

Axmacher, Dirk, *Erwachsenenbildung im Kapitalismus* (Frankfurt: Fischer, 1974).

Baethge, Martin, *Ausbildung und Herrschaft* (Frankfurt: Europäische Verlagsanstalt, 1970).

Baethge, Martin, et al., *Produktion und Qualifikation* (Hannover: Jänecke, 1974).

Becker, Egon and Gerd Jungblut, *Strategien der Bildungsproduktion*, (Frankfurt: Suhrkamp, 1972).

Bergmann, Joachim, 'Neues Lohnbewußtsein und Septemberstreiks', in Otto Jacobi, Walther Müller-Jentsch and Eberhard Schmidt, (eds.), *Gewerkschaften und Klassenkampf 1972* (Frankfurt: Fischer, 1972).

Bergmann, Joachim, et al.: *Gewerkschaften in der Bundesrepublik* (Frankfurt/Köln: EVA, 1975).

Bergmann, Joachim, and Walter Müller-Jentsch, 'The Federal Republic of Germany: Cooperative Unionism and Dual Bargaining System Challenged' in *Worker Militancy and Its Consequences*, ed. Solomon Barkin (New York: Praeger, 1975), pp. 235–276.

Benno Biermann, 'Zur Zielstruktur der wirtschaftlichen Führungsausbildung', *Zeitschrift für die Gesamte Staatswissenschaft*, CXXVIII (1972), pp. 498–518, especially p. 518.

Billerbeck, Isenberg und Körber, *Gesellschaftliche Widersprüche und*

240   *Industrial Relations in International Perspective*

öffentliche Verwaltung: Reaktionen auf Struktur- und Funktionswandel der öffentlichen Verwaltung im Bewußtsein ausgewählten Gruppen von Verwaltungsangehörigen, unpublished manuscript (Frankfurt: Institut für Sozialforschung, 1975).

Binkelmann, Peter and Irmtraut Schneller, *Reaktionen auf Reformen des Berufsausbildungsrechts* (Köln: Europäische Verlagsanstalt, 1975).

Binkelmann, Peter, Fritz Böhle and Irmtraut Schneller, *Industrielle Ausbildung und Berufsbildungsrecht* (Köln: Europäische Verlagsanstalt, 1975).

Blechschmidt, Aike, *Löhne, Preise und Gewinne (1967–1973)* (Lampertheim: Kübler, 1974).

Böhle, Fritz and Norbert Altmann, *Industrielle Arbeit und Soziale Sicherheit: Eine Studie über Risiken im Arbeitsprozeß und auf dem Arbeitsmarkt* (Frankfurt: Athenäum, 1972).

Böhle, Fritz and Dieter Sauer, *Betriebliche Arbeitskräfteeinsatz und öffentliche Interventionen – Zum Verhältnis von Staat und Produktionsprozeß* (München: Institut für Sozialwissenschaftliche Forschung, 1974), unpublished manuscript.

Böhle, Fritz and Dieter Sauer, 'Intensivierung der Arbeit und staatliche Sozialpolitik', *Leviathan*, 3 (1975), pp. 49–78.

Böhle, Fritz and Burkart Lutz, *Rationalisierungsschutzabkommen – Wirksamkeit und Probleme* (Göttingen: Schwartz & Co, 1974).

Bosch, Heinz-Dieter, *Zur Vermögenssituation der privaten Haushalte in der Bundesrepublik Deutschland*, Vol. I (Berlin: Duncker & Humblot, 1973).

Braun, Hans, *Soziale Sicherung: System und Funktion* (Stuttgart, Berlin, Köln, Mainz: Kohlhammer, 1972).

Braun, Siegfried and Jochen Fuhrmann, *Angestelltenmentalität* (Neuwied: Luchterhand, 1970).

Briefs, Götz, 'Gewerkschaften: Theorie', in v. Beckerath *er al.* (eds.), *Handwörterbuch der Sozialwissenschaften*, Vol 4 (Stuttgart: 1965), pp. 545–61.

Brinkmann-Herz, Dorothea, *Entscheidungsprozesse in den Aufsichtsräten der Montanindustrie* (Berlin: Duncker & Humblot, 1972).

Conert, Hansgeorg, *Gewerkschaften heute – Ordnungsfaktor oder Gegenmacht?* series 'Arbeit und Leben' (DGB: 1970).

Crusius, Reinhard, Wolfgang Lempert, and Manfred Wilke, *Berufsausbildung – Reformpolitik in der Sackgasse?* (Reinbek: Rowohlt, 1974).

Däubler, Wolfgang, *Das Grundrecht auf Mitbestimmung* (Frankfurt: EVA, 1973).

Däubler, Wolfgang, *Der Streik im öffentlichen Dienst* (Tübingen: Mohr, 1970).

Dahrendorf, Ralf, 'Industrielle Fertigkeiten und soziale Schichtung', *Kölner Zeitschrift für Soziologie und Sozialpsychologie*, 8 (1956), pp. 540–68.

Deutscher Bundestag, *Bundestagsdrucksache VI/334* (Bad Godesberg: Heger, 1970).

Dzielak, Willi *et al.*, *Offene und verdeckte Konflikte im Betrieb*, unpublished manuscript (Dortmund: Sozialforschungsstelle, 1974).

Eckart, Christel *et al.*, *Soziale Ungleichheit und materielle Ansprüche*, unpublished manuscript (Frankfurt: Institut für Sozialforschung, 1974).

Eliassen, Kjell A. 'Politische Beteiligung und Parteipolitische Bindung der

Gewerkschaften in Westeuropa: Ein Überblick', *Soziale Welt*, 25 (1974), pp. 71–90.

Redaktionskollektiv 'express', *Spontane Streiks 1973: Krise der Gewerkschaftspolitik* (Offenbach: Verlag 2000, 1974).

Fricke, Else and Werner Fricke, 'Auf dem Wege zu einer dynamisierten Theorie der Qualifikation', *Soziale Welt*, 25 (1974), pp. 415–31.

Fricke, Else, Werner Fricke and Manfred Schönwälder, 'Qualifikation und betriebliche Organisation', *Soziale Welt*, 24 (1973), pp. 219–41.

Fricke, Werner, *Arbeitsorganisation und Qualifikation* (Bonn–Bad Godesberg: Verlag Neue Gesellschaft, 1975).

Fürstenberg, Friedrich, 'Workers' participation in management in the Federal Republic of Germany', *Bulletin of the International Institute for Labour Studies* (June 1969), pp. 94–148.

Fürstenberg, Friedrich, *Die Soziallage der Chemiearbeiter* (Neuwied: Luchterhand, 1969).

Gerstenberger, Friedrich *et al.*, *Produktion und Qualifikation* (Göttingen: SOFI, 1974).

Grünewald, Uwe and Gunter Kohlheyer, *Zur Anhebung der Qualität der Berufsausbildung* (Bielefeld: Bertelsmann, 1974).

Hartmann, Heinz, 'Codetermination in West Germany', *Industrial Relations*, 9 (1970), pp. 137–47.

Hartmann, Heinz, 'Structure and process in industrial relations, unpublished statement contributed to 3rd World Congress, Sect. I/5, International Relations Association (London, 1973).

Hartmann, Heinz, 'Managerial employees – new participants in industrial relations', *British Journal of Industrial Relations*, 12·(1974), pp. 268–81. This account is based on Heinz Hartmann, Erika Bock-Rosenthal, and Elvira Helmer, *Leitende Angestellte: Selbstverständnis und kollektive Forderungen* (Neuwied: Luchterhand, 1973).

Hartmann, Heinz, 'Codetermination today and tomorrow', *British Journal of Industrial Relations*, 13 (1975), pp. 54–64.

Hartwich, Hans-Hermann, *Sozialstaatspostulat und gesellschaftlicher status quo* (Köln and Opladen: Westdeutscher Verlag, 1970).

Helfert, Mario, 'Ziele und Durchsetzung der Humanisierung der Arbeit', *WSI-Mitteilungen*, 28 (1975), pp. 245–56.

Hesse, Hans A., *Berufe im Wandel*, 2 ed. (Stuttgart: Enke, 1972).

Himmelmann, Gerhard, *Lohnbildung durch Kollektivverhandlungen: Eine politologische Analyse unter besonderer Berücksichtigung der Strategie und Taktik der Gewerkschaften* (Berlin: Duncker & Humblot, 1971).

Hirsch, Joachim, *Die öffentlichen Funktionen der Gewerkschaften: Eine Untersuchung zur Autonomie sozialer Verbände in der modernen Verfassungsordnung* (Stuttgart: Klett, 1966).

Hirsch-Weber, Wolfgang, *Gewerkschaften in der Politik: Von der Massenstreikdebatte zum Kampf um das Mitbestimmungsrecht* (Opladen: Westdeutscher Verlag, 1969).

W. Hoffacher, 'Der Streik der Beamten', *Leviathan*, 1 (1973), pp. 254–67.

Hondrich, Karl Otto, *Demokratisierung und Leistungsgesellschaft* (Stuttgart: Kohlhammer, 1972).

Institut für Angewandte Sozialwissenschaft (INFAS), *Umfragen zu*

Problemen der Arbeitszufriedenheit (Bad Godesberg, 1973) (unpublished).

Institut für Marxistische Studien und Forschung (IMSF), *Die September-streiks 1969: Darstellung, Analyse, Dokumente* (Frankfurt: IMSF, 1969).

Institut der Deutschen Wirtschaft (ed.), *Zahlen zur wirtschaftlichen Entwicklung der Bundesrepublik Deutschland* (Köln: Deutscher Instituts-Verlag, 1975).

Kalbitz, Rainer, 'Die Entwicklung von Streiks und Aussperrungen in der BRD', in Otto Jacobi, Walther Müller-Jentsch and Eberhard Schmidt (eds.), *Gewerkschaften und Klassenkampf 1973* (Frankfurt: Fischer 1973), pp. 163–76.

Keller, Berndt, 'Allgemeine Kritik der collective bargaining-Theorien', *Soziale Welt*, 24 (1973), pp. 242–56.

Kern, Horst, 'Die Bedeutung der Arbeitsbedingungen in den Streiks 1973', in Otto Jacobi, Walther Müller-Jentsch und Eberhard Schmidt (eds.), *Gewerkschaften und Klassenkampf 1974* (Frankfurt: Fischer, 1974), pp. 25–43.

Kern, Horst *et al.*, *Materialien zur 'Humanisierung' der Arbeit*, SOFI–Forschungsbericht (1975).

Kern, Horst and Michael Schumann, *Industriearbeit und Arbeiter-bewußtsein*, Vol. I, (Frankfurt: 1970).

Kerr, Clark, 'Industrial conflict and its mediation', *American Journal of Sociology*, 60 (1954/55), pp. 230–45.

Kittner, Michael 'Mitbestimmung der Arbeitnehmer über die Arbeits-organisation und über die Ausgestaltung und Umgebung des Arbeitsplatzes', *WSI-Mitteilungen*, 28 (1975), pp. 256–69.

Kliemt, Gundolf, *Die Praxis des Betriebsverfassungsgesetzes im Dienst-leistungsbereich* (Tübingen: Mohr, 1971).

Külp, Bernhard, *Streik und Streikdrohung: Ihre Rolle in der Volkswirtschaft und im Sozialprozeß* (Berlin-West: Berlin Verlag, 1969).

Külp, Bernhard, *Der Einfluß von Schlichtungsformen auf Verlauf und Ergebnis von Tarif- und Schlichtungsverhandlungen* (Berlin: Duncker & Humblot, 1972).

Külp, Bernhard and Wilfried Schreiber (eds.), *Arbeitsökonomik* (Köln: Kiepenheuer & Witsch, 1972).

Laske, Stephan, 'Emanzipatorische Arbeitswissenschaft: Zur Begründung einer Konzeption der Arbeitswissenschaft als Sozialwissenschaft, *AFA-Informationen* (1974) pp. 179–88.

Leminsky, Gerhard, 'The Central Trade Union Organization and the individual union in Federal Germany', unpublished statement contributed to 3rd World Congress, Sect. III/e, International Industrial Relations Association (London, September 1973), 26 pages.

Lempert, Wolfgang, *Leistungsprinzip und Emanzipation* (Frankfurt: Suhrkamp, 1971).

Lenhardt, Gero, *Berufliche Weiterbildung und Arbeitsteilung in der Industrieproduktion* (Frankfurt: Suhrkamp, 1974).

Luhmann, Niklas, *Legitimation durch Verfahren* (Neuwied, Berlin: Luchterhand, 1969).

schinenschlosser im industriellen Produktionsprozess (Berlin: Max Planck-Institut für Bildungsforschung, 1972).

Lukatis, Ingrid, *Organisationsstrukturen und Führungsstile im Wirt-*

schaftsunternehmen (Frankfurt: Akademische Verlagsgesellschaft, 1972a).

Lukatis, Wolfgang, *Akademiker in Wirtschaftsunternehmen* (Frankfurt: Akademische Verlagsanstalt, 1972b).

Lutz, Burkart, *Krise des Lohnanreizes* (Frankfurt: EVA, 1975).

Lutz, Burkart *et al.*, *Rationalisierung und Mechanisierung im öffentlichen Dienst: Ein Gutachten für die Gewerkschaft ÖTV* (München: Hanser, 1970).

Lutz, Burkart and Werner Sengenberger, *Arbeitsmarktstrukturen und öffentliche Arbeitsmarktpolitik: Eine kritische Analyse von Zielen und Instrumenten* (Göttingen: Schwartz & Co., 1974).

Mackenroth, Gerhard, *Die Reform der Sozialpolitik für einen deutschen Sozialplan,* Schriften des Vereins für Sozialpolitik (Berlin: 1952).

Mandel, Ernest, 'Systemkonforme Gewerkschaften', *Gewerkschaftstheorie heute,* ed. DGB (Bad Kreuznach: 1970), pp. 63–73.

Mayer, Evelies, *Theorien zum Funktionswandel der Gewerkschaften* (Frankfurt: EVA, 1973).

Mayntz, Renate, *Trend Report: Staat und politische Organisation,* paper, presented at the '17. Deutscher Soziologentag' (Kassel 1974).

Mendner, Jürgen H., *Technologische Entwicklung und Arbeitsprozess* (Frankfurt: Fischer, 1975).

Mergner, Ulrich, Martin Osterland, and Klaus Pelte, *Die Entwicklung ausgewählter Arbeitsbedingungen in der BRD* (Göttingen: SOFI, 1974).

Michels, Robert, *Zur Soziologie des Parteiwesens in der modernen Demokratie* (Leipzig: Klinkhardt, 1911); *Political Parties – A Sociological Study of the Oligarchical Tendencies in Modern Democracy* (London: Jarrold & Sons, 1961).

Mickler, Otfried, *Technik, Arbeitsorganisation und Arbeit* (Göttingen: SOFI, 1975).

Müller, J. Heinz, 'Wirtschaftliche Fragen der Bildung breitgestreuten Eigentums', in Bernhard Külp and Wilfried Schreiber (eds.), *Soziale Sicherheit* (Köln, Berlin: Kiepenheuer & Witsch, 1971), pp. 385–401.

Müller-Jentsch, Walther, 'Entwicklung und Widersprüche in der westdeutschen Gewerkschaftsbewegung', in Otto Jacobi, Walther Müller-Jentsch and Eberhard Schmidt (eds.), *Gewerkschaften und Klassenkampf 1973* (Frankfurt: Fischer, 1973), pp. 150–62.

Narr, Wolf-Dieter and Frieder Naschold, *Theorie der Demokratie: Einführung in die moderne politische Theorie,* Vol. 3 (Stuttgart: 1971).

Nickel, Walter, *Zum Verhältnis von Arbeiterschaft und Gewerkschaft* (Köln: Bund-Verlag, 1974).

Offe, Claus, *Strukturprobleme des kapitalistischen Staates* (Frankfurt: Suhrkamp, 1972).

Offe, Claus, 'Krisen des Krisenmanagement: Elemente einer politischen Krisentheorie' in M. Jänicke (ed.), *Herrschaft und Krise* (Opladen: Westdeutscher Verlag, 1973), pp. 197–223.

Offe, Claus, *Leistungsprinzip und industrielle Arbeit* (Frankfurt: Europäische Verlagsanstalt, 1970).

Offe, Claus, *Berufsbildungsreform: Eine Fallstudie über Reformpolitik* (Frankfurt: Suhrkamp, 1975).

Offe, Claus, *Industry and Inequality: The Achievement Principle in Work and Social Status* (London: Arnold, 1976).

Oppelt, Claus, Gerd Schrick, and Armin Bremmer, *Gelernte Maschinenschlosser im imdustriellen Produktionsprozess* (Berlin: Max Planck-Institutfür Bildungsforschung, 1972).

Osterland, Martin *et al.*, *Materialien der Lebens- und Arbeitssituation der Industriearbeiter in der BRD* (Frankfurt: EVA, 1973).

Pizzorno, Alessandro, 'Zukunftaussichten der Gewerkschaft in der Gesellschaft des organisierten Kapitalismus', in *Aufgabe Zukunft: Qualität des Lebens*, Col. 9, ed. Industriegewerkschaft Metall (Frankfurt: EVA, 1972), pp. 45–73.

Ramm, Thilo, 'Labour Relations in the Public Sector in the Federal Republic of Germany', unpublished statement contributed to 3rd World Congress, Sect. V/6, International Industrial Relations Association (London, September 1973), 24 pages.

Roberts, Ivor L., 'The Works Constitution Acts and industrial relations in West Germany: implications for the United Kingdom', *British Journal of Industrial Relations*, 11 (1973), pp. 338–67.

Roeder-Sorge Arndt, and Karl Heinz Nagels, *Industrielle Demokratie in Europa* (Frankfurt: Campus, 1977).

Sass, Jürgen, Werner Sengenberger, and Friedrich Weltz, *Weiterbildung und betriebliche Arbeitskräftepolitik* (Köln: Europäische Verlagsanstalt, 1974).

Schacht, Konrad and Lutz Unterseher, 'Streiks und gewerkschaftliche Strategie in der Bundesrepublik', in Dieter Schneider (ed.) *Zur Theorie und Praxis des Streiks* (Frankfurt: Suhrkamp, 1971), pp. 289–324.

Schacht, Konrad and Lutz Unterseher, 'Das Tarifverhandlungssystem der Bundesrepublik', in Werner Meißner and Lutz Unterseher (eds.), *Verteilungskampf und Stabilitätspolitik* (Stuttgart, Berlin, Köln, Mainz: Kohlhammer 1972), pp. 79–118.

Scharpf, Fritz W. *Planung als politischer Prozeß: Aufsätze zur Theorie der planenden Demokratie* (Frankfurt: Suhrkamp, 1973).

Schmidt, Eberhard, *Ordnungsfaktor oder Gegenmacht: Die politische Rolle der Gewerkschaften* (Frankfurt: Suhrkamp, 1971).

Schneider, Dieter and Rudolf Kuda, *Mitbestimmung* (München: Deutscher Taschenbuchverlag, 1969).

Schultz-Wild, Rainer and Friedrich Weltz, *Technischer Wandel und Industriebetrieb* (Frankfurt: Athenäum, 1973).

Schumann, Michael, Frank Gerlach, Albert Gschlössl and Petra Milhoffer, *Am Beispiel der Septemberstreiks – Anfang der Rekonstruktionsperiode der Arbeiterklasse?* (Frankfurt: EVA, 1971).

Steinhaus, Kurt, *Streiks in der Bundesrepublik 1966–1974: Eine Untersuchung des Instituts für marxistische Studien und Forschungen (IMSF)* (Frankfurt: Marxistische Blätter, 1975).

Streeck, Wolfgang, 'Das Dilemma der Organisation: Tarifverbände zwischen Interessenvertretung und Stabilitätspolitik', in Werner Meißner and Lutz Unterseher *Verteilungskampf und Stabilitätspolitik* (eds.) (Stuttgart, Berlin, Köln, Mainz: Kohlhammer, 1972).

Szakats, A., 'Workers' participation in management: the German experience', *Journal of Industrial Relations*, 16 (1974), pp. 28–44.

Széplabi, Michael, *Das Gesellschaftsbild der Gewerkschaften: Eine wissenssoziologische Analyse gesellschafstheoretischer Programm-Aussagen des DGB* (Stuttgart: Enke, 1973).

Tegtmeier, Werner, *Wirkungen der Mitbestimmung der Arbeitnehmer* (Göttingen: Vanderhoeck & Ruprecht, 1973).

Thomas, Konrad, *Die betriebliche Situation der Arbeiter* (Stuttgart: Enke, 1964).

Unterseher, Lutz, *Arbeitsvertrag und innerbetriebliche Herrschaft: Eine historische Untersuchung* (Frankfurt: EVA, 1969).

Unterseher, Lutz, 'Arbeitsrecht – eine deutsche Spezialität', in Otto Jacobi, Walther Müller-Jentsch und Eberhard Schmidt (eds.), *Gewerkschaften und Klassenkampf 1972* (Frankfurt: Fischer, 1972a), pp. 190–201.

Unterseher, Lutz, 'Tarifliche Schlichtung: ein ökonomisches Gerichtsverfahren?' in Werner Meißner und Lutz Unterseher (eds.), *Verteilungskampf und Stabilitätspolitik*, (Stuttgart, Berlin, Köln, Mainz: Kohlhammer 1972b), pp. 119–29.

Unterseher, Lutz, *Kollektives Arbeitsrecht und Tarifsystem* (Diss. Frankfurt, 1975).

van de Vall, Mark, *Die Gewerkschaften im Wohlfahrtsstaat* (Opladen: Westdeutscher Verlag, 1966).

Vetter, Heinz-Oskar (ed.), *Humanisierung der Arbeit als gesellschaftspolitische und gewerkschaftliche Aufgabe* (Frankfurt: EVA, 1974).

Vetter, Heinz-Oskar (ed.), *Vom Sozialistengesetz zur Mitbestimmung* (Köln: Bund-Verlag, 1975).

Vilmar, Fritz, *Mitbestimmung am Arbeitsplatz* (Neuwied: Luchterhand, 1971).

Vilmar, Fritz (ed.), *Menschenwürde im Betrieb* (Reinbek: Rowohlt, 1973a).

Vilmar, Fritz, *Strategien der Demokratisierung*, Vol. I, II, (Neuwied: Luchterhand, 1973b).

Vogel, Bernhard (ed.), *Neue Bildungspolitik* (Herford: Nicolaische Verlagsbuchhandlung, 1975).

Volpert, Walter, *Die 'Humanisierung' der Arbeit und die Arbeitswissenschaft* (Köln: Pahl-Rugenstein, 1974).

Wallraff, Herman-Josef, 'Funktionswandel der Gewerkschaften', *Gewerkschaftstheorie heute*, ed. DGB (Bad Kreuznach: 1970), pp. 51–61.

Weinstock, S. A., 'Role elements: a link between acculturation and occupational status', *British Journal of Sociology*, 14 (1963), pp. 144–9.

Weitbrecht, Hansjörg, *Effektivität und Legitimität der Tarifautonomie: Eine soziologische Untersuchung am Beispiel der deutschen Metallindustrie* (Berlin: Duncker & Humblot, 1969).

Weitbrecht, Hansjörg, 'Das Machtproblem in Tarifverhandlungen', *Soziale Welt*, 25 (1974), pp. 224–34.

Weltz, Friedrich, Gert Schmidt, and Jürgen Sass, *Facharbeiter im Industriebetrieb* (Frankfurt: Athenäum, 1974).

Wiedemann, Klaus, *Streik und Streikdrohung: Darstellung und Kritik der theoretischen Beiträge zur Streikproblematik* (Herford: Maximilian, 1971).

Wils, Wilber *et al.*, *Changing Industrial Relations*, unpublished manuscript (Amsterdam: European Cultural Foundation, 1975), 58 pages.

Winterhager, Wolfgang Dietrich, *Anforderungen an ein Beruf-bildungssystem* (Göttingen: Schwartz & Co., 1973).

Winterhager, Wolfgang Dietrich, *Humanisierung der Arbeitswelt* (Berlin: de Gruyter, 1975).

7 Industrial Relations Research in France 1960–75: A Review

Jean-Daniel Reynaud

This presentation of a review of industrial relations research in France necessarily expresses a personal point of view. The selection of texts and important themes, along with the argument developed in the discussion itself, brief as it is, represents a highly subjective process. For better or for worse, it would be wise to consider this essay as the author's own reflections on the past fifteen years.

Although our purpose is not to discuss the French situation itself, but to define the general direction taken by research, it is useful to recall three important characteristics of the present situation.

(1) As in most industrial countries, there is a marked contrast between the early sixties, the expansion of production and trade, and the more recent social and economic crises related to inflation. But this contrast is more marked in France than elsewhere because belief in the benefits of growth had been stronger and represented a sharp break with the past and the breach took the form of the profound crisis of May 1968. This same contrast is noticeable in the research, for many of the works have aged prematurely.

(2) It has been brought out that the relative weakness of labour unions in France, the fluctuating mobilization of the rank and file, and a lack of bargaining commitment often led to alternating periods of dormancy and explosion. But it must not be forgotten that these same characteristics – those of militant trade unionism – also make the unions particularly sensitive to emerging needs and problems. Bureaucratic opacity is weak, but the capacity for responsiveness is strong. The updating of themes and priorities is therefore considerable.

(3) French society is made up of sharp contrasts, often expressed in

doctrinal terms. Ideology is a constant and vital feature. But for the past ten years conflicts and their resolution have been characterized by a surprising pragmatism, often bypassing established legal principles and precedents. The distance between fairly rigid legal doctrines and flexible strategies and tactics makes analysis even more difficult. We can only conclude that research in this area is still weak and poorly developed.

For convenience of presentation, the material is divided according to certain issues. The problem of this method is that it emphasizes public debates of a doctrinal nature. Yet it has the advantage of presenting the research in better relation to the social problems that are at the heart of the debates.

The main controversies have centred around four topics: (*a*) the 'new working class' of the sixties, (*b*) the prominent debate of the seventies regarding 'working conditions and plant organization', (*c*) a new style of strikes and conflicts that have emerged and studies devoted to exploring their consequences, and (*d*) a parallel development of new trends in collective bargaining. Special attention will be given to the problems of employment and training, and how the changing context and crises of the period has had deep implications for the structure of trade unions and employers' associations. In conclusion, topics for further study will be suggested.

The New Working Class

Owing to the crises of the Labour Party, the 'new working class' in Britain was typified by the *embourgeoisement* of the traditional working class. In France, on the contrary, the 'new working class' has been a modernist concept of the left, which has tried to reconcile economic progress with the possibility for revolution.

Today we can better distinguish the different components of the theory. Technological change has (*a*) had serious consequences for industrial organization, skill requirements and the orientation of the workers' consciousness (Touraine, 1955, 1966), (*b*) transformed methods of production and consumption and modified the economic perspectives, needs and demands of labour and management (Touraine *et al.*, 1965; Dofny *et al.*, 1966; Belleville, 1963), and (*c*) affected union behaviour through the development of plant-level action and organization, and altered political behaviour as well. It is this set of ideas that Serge Mallet (1963) took up in a neo-Marxist perspective, portraying automation as a technical, economic and social force uniting workers, technicians and in certain cases management (*cadres*) of high-technology industries into a new avant-garde, the 'new working class', strongly attached to the firm and anxious above all to control its management. Certain aspects of the May 1968 strikes seemed to confirm this interpretation (Mallet, 1969, 1971).

However, from the start (*Arguments*, 1959), the weakness of this thesis and the very different interpretations it received were apparent. Touraine's analysis is very different; for him, it was not a matter of new actors taking up the same class struggle, but a transformation of class structure itself (Hamon, 1962). Then for the most part, he abandons the theme of the new working class in order to identify a new class struggle between the highest-level policy-making managers and lower-level managers and technicians who must carry out the policies; this new struggle would be the central conflict of post-industrial society (Touraine, 1969). He interprets the May 1968 conflicts in this light (Touraine, 1968).

More generally, the economic and technological bases of the analysis were very superficial and ignored the growing amount of data gathered by statisticians and historians, either on the historical development of firms, markets and technology (Gille, 1959; Friedenson, 1972), or on the characteristics of the production system (INSEE, 1974). The philosophy of history (broadly Marxist but in a narrow technological way) that underlines Mallet's thesis has been the major factor in its popularity and influence. But it has also been the root of its weaknesses: automation is too broad a category; the direct link between the effects of technological transformation and those of growth and prosperity has not been proven. An underlying evolutionism is hardly defendable (Reynaud, 1972). Studies on the transformation of jobs and skills point in other directions (Naville, 1961, 1963). A 1969 study of the attitudes of union militants, members, and sympathisers, has shown that technicians and managers are still poorly organized even though the extreme left has found a sizeable following among them. The idea of self-management was better received by skilled workers than by technicians. Thus, in spite of a few changes and some novelties, the image of the workers that emerged was much closer to the traditional one (Adam *et al.*, 1971; Adam, 1968c, 1972). Likewise, the study of specific conflicts by Barrier (1975) denied the aspiration for self-management and showed the complexities of group strategy.

Interest thus shifted to the technicians and managers, two rapidly growing categories whose roles within the firm were ill-defined. Their part in the 1968 strikes and especially their participation in the debates within the occupied factories seemed to confirm that at least in scientific research and in laboratories, typically modern activities, the most qualified employees seemed to initiate the contestation. But further research has contradicted this thesis. Firstly, the participation of these groups in the 1968 strikes was limited to a few specific cases, but above all the position of the managers has been ambiguous. Were they the envoys of employers for maintaining contact with the strikers, were they strikers themselves or were they a third force? Were the reforms which they elaborated modernization according to the employers' gospel or democratization of a rigidly stratified society? Or was it even conquest of new power for themselves? The results of the elections to the works committees are revealing; immediately after the 'events', the Union of Technicians and Supervisory Employees (CGC) saw its influence grow at the expense of the other union organizations (Jean Dubois *et al*, 1971; Willener *et al.*, 1969; Reynaud *et al.*, 1971; Maurice *et al.*, 1972).

In place of the loose theme of 'class struggle', the interests and strategies of the various categories of employees appeared. In the place of broad economic analyses a new type of organizational analysis emerged (Crozier, 1960; Sainsaulieu, 1972).

The supervisory employees thus emerged with their own cultural values which above all emphasize individual capability and free competition and consequently leave only a minor role for collective action (Benoit and Maurice, 1960; Benoit, 1962; Maurice, 1967, 1968). This unease undoubtedly came from the profound transformation of the large firms. What was their place in these new structures? On what criteria were they judged? What determined their career and employment security? The transition from a paternalistic model, defined by reciprocal loyalty, to a model where efficiency is the foremost criterion and mobility is encouraged, has often been traumatic. This is especially true when this social change is coupled with the feeling that the highest echelons of power belong to another caste, the traditional élite of money or prestigious schools (Bachy, 1971; J. Dubois, 1971; Confremca, 1971; Leboucq, 1972).

For the technicians, the difficulties are more limited and more acute. Their dissatisfaction is rather that of a group whose mobility runs into a very rigid barrier, that of the 'movement into management' (*passage cadres*). Often well educated, with a schooling that whets the appetite for promotion and makes the discrepancy between diplomas and re-muneration cruelly felt, the technicians take the supervisory employees, not the manual workers, as a reference group (Douard *et al.*, 1973;

Durand and Durand, 1971; Guillon and Pigelet, 1974; Bonis, 1969; Legoux, 1962, 1972).

These changes have found little echo in the structure and goals of the unions. The federation of technicians and supervisory employees has remained stable (Malterre, 1969, 1971). Agitation has none the less resulted in minor internal disputes and in increased activity by the unions. The particular demands of each category of employees have been reinforced even in the blue-collar unions (Meunier, 1970; Doublet and Passelecq, 1973).

Thus interest tends to shift towards analysis of organizations. Recently large firms have increased the number of studies of their own supervisory employees. The period of direct importation of new management techniques has been succeeded by a period of reflection and policy elaboration. The centre of interest has shifted to the firm (Sudreau, 1975).

While the highest skilled workers might have appeared the most militant in the early sixties, it is the emergence of conflicts among semi-skilled workers that has characterized the early seventies (Mallet, 1971). The reversal has been complete. The economically and tech-nologically backward sectors are asserting themselves. The initiative now lies with those left behind by expansion and no longer with its champions. The skilled workers, who had been the solid, stable nucleus of unionism, have lost power not to those from above, but to those from below. One of the principal problems with economic growth, in the eyes of public opinion, is the fate of those who are excluded from it (Belorgey and Dupeyroux, 1974).

There remains today little of the thesis as originally stated. It has at least had the consequence of awakening interest in the orientations and reactions of new groups of salaried workers. Paradoxically, in relation to its point of departure, it has led to recognition of their originality, or at least, their specific characteristics. It has certainly contributed to enlarging the horizons of union leaders and politicians.

But perhaps its most important contribution is the least obvious at first glance; it has favoured the renaissance of a very old workers' theme – the autonomy of production – by adorning it with the colours of modernity. The interest of the 'new working class' in management practices and in the firm itself was an elaboration of a shop-floor association of producers. Historical studies have been very active in analysing this old national tradition, in fact a mixture of anarchist ideas, as incorporated by Pelloutier (Maîtron, 1951; Julliard, 1971), and trade union practices. Revolutionary syndicalism as it developed in the first fourteen years of this century may still have something to say, if one disregards the ideological rhetoric and notices how much it has been able to adapt to different economic contexts (Julliard, 1965, 1968). It has taken a new form in the French union movement today with the self-management demands of the CFDT (Chauvey, 1970; Detraz *et al.*, 1973; Maire, 1971; Maire and Julliard, 1975).

Autogestion, or self-management, is admittedly vague as a strategy for transforming work and society. However, it does revive very old aspirations of manual workers and combines them with the recent trends of revolt against 'bureaucratic' or 'authoritarian' hierarchies. It has been used by the CFDT in bargaining for more rank and file autonomy (not without sharp disagreements with the CGT) and also to dismiss the co-determination schemes popular in a large part of Europe. It has inspired a new style of socialism clearly opposed to the Communist Party's 'democratic centralism'. Although referring more to a sensitivity and a cluster of attitudes than to a specific solution, it has real appeal for union militants and may serve to orient their action.

Working Conditions and Plant Organization

The term 'working conditions' has taken on a particular meaning in France since the early seventies. Before then, it meant the mere terms of employment (salary, working hours, job requirements, etc.); it has now come to mean more strictly the non-monetary conditions of work: health and safety, work-load and fatigue, comfort, interest, the opportunity to learn and progress, the chances for promotion and even more flexible working hours and forms of pay. The unifying themes of this broad concept are unclear: whether it is new demands which have become more urgent, or areas formerly untouched by negotiation or, finally, whether it concerns everything that determines workshop organization.

The common characteristic of these themes is that they open new areas for conflict and bargaining. It is, in fact, conflict that has brought them to public attention. After an initial period in which they were themes used by the far left movements, the Renault–Le Mans (1971) conflict demonstrated their more general appeal. The national organizations took up positions, the employers for once preceding the labour unions (CNPF, 1971; CGT, 1972; CFDT, 1972b), and a report was made to the minister of labour (Delamotte, 1972).

Some studies were already available: of ergonomists (Wisner *et al.*, 1972; Wisner, 1974), of organizers (Prestat, 1972; Montmollin, 1974), and of sociologists (Douard and Reynaud, 1973) in which opposing points of view and arguments were presented. From the beginning, the problem has been considered not a problem of management but a problem of industrial relations.

Job enrichment or the creation of autonomous work groups clearly touches on the managerial prerogatives of coordination and control and on the status of supervisors and even of upper management. Likewise, for those most concerned with occupational health and safety, the involvement of specialists, especially outside experts, is far less satisfactory than plant-level negotiations over these issues. Is it not better to let the actors define their own approaches and open the way to self-organization?

The division of responsibility for such matters has some technical basis. But it is more a matter of organizational methods than of technology, of guiding principles than of machines. And it is thus closely tied to the problems of power. When manpower is easy to replace, personnel administration is easier, but also the discretionary power of management is greater. If all information is sent up the hierarchical ladder to those who have the right to judge and act on their judgement, as in Taylorist systems, management can lead without opposition. This also encourages the centralization of grievance procedures and bargaining. A high rate of conflict, or at any rate, of opposition, also promotes centralization (Douard and Reynaud, 1975; Gorz, 1973).

Counteracting these pressures for decentralization is the extreme centralization of management control in France. The social basis of hierarchy is best illustrated by international comparisons. With the same technology and in similar economic conditions, German and French firms have neither the same number of levels, nor the same number of people in these levels, nor the same wage differentials between levels. The description and explanation of these differences, with the above hypotheses in mind, are the object of a study in progress (Sellier *et al.*, 1973).

The tension between the levels of an organization is, in fact, an opposition of social groups. The logic (or culture) of the workers is not that of management, not because of a logic of feelings versus a logic of efficiency, but rather that of differences in class or group interests (Bernoux *et al.*, 1973; Bernoux, 1972). We would find analogous problems with other categories of workers, notably in the difficult adaptation of young wage-earners to industry.

In view of these conclusions the limits of a psychological analysis of authority relations are evident. Human relations are not only a function of organizational structure, but they also result from collective strategies. On the other hand, good studies do exist in the field of group psychology, but rarely have these investigations been scientific. Laboratory psychologists have not applied their skill and insight very frequently to industrial relations situations. This lack of scientific interest in the psychology of human relations should not be summarily ascribed merely to an old intellectual tradition stressing 'structural' explanations, but also to the rather widely accepted view that human relations result from the accommodation of contradictory collective interests.

Giving more equal status to manual and non-manual workers, such as *mensualization* tried to achieve, has met with the same sort of difficulties. Besides the fact that the distinctions between supervisory employees and the other employees persist and are even somewhat reinforced, it does not seem that superficially equalizing the pay of different occupational groups significantly alters the hierarchical structure (Bunel, 1973; Moller, 1971). This has led some researchers to re-examine the qualifications and skills of supervisory personnel and to show the extent to which they were the result of social distinctions inside and outside the firm, rather than the reason for the hierarchical difference (Gajdos, 1972; Benguigui and Monjardet, 1973).

Any attempt at self-management challenges the entire hierarchy and leads to either serious difficulties or profound changes, or both. At the same time, it touches on the traditional state of relations between management and labour representatives (Borzeix and Chave, 1975), since the latter do not want to be left aside nor be responsible for reorganization. These relationships and the chances for their evolution are a rich area for further study.

Negotiations on working conditions kept the Confederation of Employers and the union federations busy for nearly two years (1973–75). The difficulties they encountered before reaching an agreement (17 March 1975) which the two principal unions, the CGT and the CFDT, did not sign, would merit further examination, but probably more for the dynamics of the negotiation process than for its final outcome. On the other hand, the expected extensions (the agreement calls for negotiations by industry and firm) should give industrial relations experts a better understanding of the difficulties and the stakes involved.

Conflicts

Under French law and even more in practice, conflict is never limited by collective bargaining agreements. It is not forbidden for the duration of the agreement. The right to strike even exists in cases where the right to bargain does not. It is thus legitimate and necessary to treat conflict independently, both as a form of expression and as an indication of larger social changes.

The crisis of 1968 generated an immense, often purely ideological or exhortatory literature. Objective factual descriptions are not numerous. The *Cahiers Libres* collection of the Maspero publishing house contained numerous specific and detailed monographs (*Notre Arme, C'est la Grève*, 1968; Talbo 1968, etc.). The union organizations also drew up their own accounts (CGT, 1968, 1972; CFDT, 1972).

A comprehensive view is still difficult, but the real scale of the phenomenon can be estimated (Adam, 1970). On the basis of some fifty monographs and some thematic studies, Reynaud *et al.*, (1971), sought to draw up a synthetic picture. The strike mechanism was not unusual, but it was reinforced by a longer than usual period of latency; the university crisis and the social crisis were connected only by the fact that the former was the detonator of the latter. On the other hand, the political crisis was a direct extension of the social crisis. The concurrence of the two explains the amplitude of the reaction to long-standing defects in the system of industrial relations and without creating new themes stimulates negotiations. Dubois *et al.* (1971) undertook a broad inquiry into principal aspects of the strike. Touraine (1972) sees the 1968 movements as a mixture of the traditional labour conflicts in the older industrial sectors and of the new class conflict of post-industrial society, present in utopian form among the students and in a more realistic but still imprecise form in some offices and research centres. Some of the case studies merit special attention for the quality of their analysis as well as for the peculiarities of the strikes studied (Kergoat, 1973; Naville *et al.*, 1971).

In the following years, the number of conflicts has been moderate (more or less equivalent to the average for the preceding years). On the other hand, certain characteristics of these conflicts have been new enough to attract special attention (Mallet, 1969; Durand and Dubois, 1975; Lorant *et al.*, 1972; Maire and Piaget, 1973; Barrier, 1975).

The most obvious are the new types of action. Most strikes are increasing violations of certain basic legal restrictions. The practice of sit-down strikes is becoming frequent and is increasingly felt to be legitimate in the eyes of the strikers. Their expulsion often serves to cement the unity of the workers. The besieging of management has profoundly shocked public opinion, especially that of supervisory personnel (P. Dubois, 1973), as did a refusal, in one sit-down strike, to maintain machinery in running order. The occupation of bankrupt enterprises by workers, to block lay-offs and apply pressure for reopening, has been illustrated by the Lip case (Maire and Piaget, 1973), and has been frequent since 1973. There are also several cases of 'wildcat' production and sales. Finally, there is the appeal to public opinion, and its support – especially financial – has often been effective. All these forms of conflict have little to do with the traditional image of the strike as a form of purely economic pressure. As a means of social action, a strike is far more complicated than that.

Jurisprudence seems to be changing profoundly, not only on the problem of the sit-down strike, on which the courts are becoming more flexible, but also on the very conception of its role. For Javillier (1973), this means the gradual disappearance of a doctrine in which the judge must and can arbitrate on a conflict, in favour of a practice in which he is a mediator, promoting agreement between the parties. The importance of such an evolution in French law can be appreciated from the resistance it has generated (Latournerie, 1972).

Sociologists have noted the shift in the level where conflict is initiated. Not only are strikes more often triggered by the rank and file, but they are more frequently led by the local union, often supported by a strike committee and/or assembly of wage-earners. The role of the national unions is sometimes very limited, and the role of local decisions is intensified. Even if this 'spontaneity' is that of the militants rather than of the non-unionized, it often changes the way conflict develops and even its conclusion.

Furthermore, new actors are appearing. There has not been any drastic change in the laws granting workers, professionals, and civil servants a wide right to organize and bargain. But groups which were weakly organized or were subservient to larger movements are coming to the foreground and presenting their own specific demands. These new groups include white-collar workers such as bank and store clerks, semi-skilled workers, women, immigrant workers and very young wage-earners. Even if the relative weight of these 'new' groups is exaggerated, the fact that they have become organized is significant.

The new groups in the movement have also changed the stakes of conflict. They are often much more localized, and the demands proceed more directly from the groups involved, who refuse to call off a strike until their demands are met.

How should these changes be interpreted? First, the phenomena are not confined to France, but *mutatis mutandis*, are found in most countries of Europe (Spitaels, 1971), to the point where it is possible to speak of a crisis of industrial relations. The interpretation which Phelps Brown gives of the phenomena seems to be the most convincing and the most comprehensive. Is it not a shift of power to the shop-floor, for which the reasons are complex, both economic and social (Reynaud, 1973)?

If the overall assessment is correct, one sees how difficult it is to make firm predictions or analyses for the future (Scardigli, 1973a and b). These shop-floor conflicts are evidence of an upheaval, if not a crisis, in social relations themselves, more than an indication of a well-defined trend. In any case, they no doubt limit the chances for any development of a commitment to bargaining in France.

It may be significant that, while the existing legal procedures for mediation, conciliation and arbitration are hardly used any longer, very little effort has been made to devise effective new ones. In fact, the direct settlement of conflict by the parties, more or less tempered by *ad hoc* intervention at different levels by public authorities, seems for the time being the only practical procedure (Sudreau, 1975).

The development of conflicts at plant level and the attention that has been given them has enabled researchers to document the negotiation sessions. Previously, the secrecy of the bargaining committees had made this impossible in France. It thus favours strategy analyses. The existing studies are still weak, especially compared to those in the United States, but the potential exists and interest is awakening. They could bring out more clearly the striking difference between the very strict limits of American negotiations and the very open (and very unforeseeable) character of French conflicts in recent years.

Another consequence is the strengthening of the importance of personnel functions in the firm and the importance of forecasting and knowledge of the social context in these functions. Much more so than before, the large firms have the feeling of being alone in their social responsibilities and of being responsible for their own policy (in contrast to a tradition in which the advice of employers' associations weighed heavily). They are thus making considerable efforts to study the area of personnel relations (Bosquet, 1975).

Historians have provided us with a very complete picture of the development of past conflicts through (*a*) monographs describing the various conflicts (Kriegel, 1964), (*b*) the study of a whole period combining statistical analysis and case studies (Perrot, 1974), or (*c*) by-products of the longitudinal study of an industrial group (Trempé, 1971). This allows a better appreciation of the continuities and discontinuities in strike patterns.

Trends in Negotiation

Theorists of the French cultural model of behaviour hypothesized the existence of a fear of face-to-face relations and an absence of negotiation; this doctrinal intransigence rejects, along with compromise, all change in the field of industrial relations. If this model were true, major changes have taken place in the past ten years: the development of the practice of negotiation, its frequency, the extent of commitments made and the new areas covered demonstrate a departure from the 'stalemate society' (Crozier, 1970). The will of employers (and, after 1969, of the government as an employer) has given new life to bargaining in the traditional areas: wages, with much hesitation but with little renewal if we refer to Meyers' analysis (1965), and the length of the work day. There are also new areas: employment (for both unemployment insurance and lay-off regulation); vocational training; and working conditions.

Particularly remarkable are the 'policy agreements' which elaborate a joint policy between the employers' group and the unions at inter-industry level. Despite their traditional form, their ambition and their newness have attracted research attention (Reynaud, 1969; Delamotte, 1969b). Often ignored is the fact that they considerably extended the areas covered by negotiation. This was not done by reinforcing existing agreements; rather it was accomplished by making agreements more flexible and by providing on-going opportunities for mutual consultation instead of dictating how the final resolution of a disagreement would be arbitrated.

At the enterprise level, this flexibility is even stronger. Opportunities for meeting are numerous. Works committees, instituted for consultation and participation (Montuclard, 1963), traditionally played a more limited role (Spyropoulos, 1961) and sometimes have been a farce. However, these works committees have assumed a wider function to deal with employment, working conditions, profit-sharing and so forth, to the point where unions sometimes fear that the employer will turn to these committees rather than to them for negotiation (Baron *et al.*,

1974). Could they become a substitute for the union? In addition, shop stewards continue to figure in labour representation in the work-place (Pierre Dubois, 1971), as do the union delegates recognized by law in 1968. In spite of the multiple interlocutors and even more varied forms of discussion, there has been no commitment to any particular system except to avoid any over-rigid framework of formal collective agreements in the plant (Adam *et al.*, 1972; Bachy *et al.*, 1974).

Other authors dismiss the importance of these developments, arguing that they mask what are really class relations. They depict discussion and agreement as a system of oppression and compulsion that no faithful description of the work relationship could disguise (Dassa *et al.*, 1973).

Public-sector Bargaining

Bargaining in the public sector merits separate treatment. More specifically, wage negotiations had been a recurrent problem in the fifties: tight government control, with extreme centralization of decisions, kept bargaining within very narrow limits and unions felt quite powerless. On the other hand, wage drift frustrated any central control, causing confusion and mutual distrust (Toutée, 1964). A proposal to correct these weaknesses was rejected by the unions and eventually dropped in 1968. The constraint it imposed (bargaining on the total payroll of the company, not on wage rates), was deemed too severe; but it did serve to highlight the situation. More specifically, it made clear the relevance of internal personnel administration for wage negotiations and that decisions based on total payroll do not settle the question of differentials (Rochecorbon, 1968; Lavorel, 1968).

The efforts towards a 'contractual policy' after 1969 fostered managerial autonomy and changed the tone of industrial relations (Bunel and Meunier, 1972; Delors, 1975). Although the appraisals are contradictory (P. Dubois, 1974), decentralization of decisions has clearly occurred.

How is this trend to be interpreted? There is little doubt that this policy sought to develop a contractual basis for industrial relations by offering important concessions (as evidenced by the conciliation clause of the 1968 agreement of the national electricity company) and by establishing as firmly as possible the rules of the game. Despite its timidity and obscurities, the agreement eventually recognized the union as a partner; for the first time, it created a limited commitment to labour peace and it permitted joint administration of the contract.

The history of agreements, however, evolved in a different direction: they have eliminated conciliation procedures as well as provisions linking wages to the prosperity of individual firms; their duration has been in most cases reduced to one year and most agreements now contain some form of escalator clause.

Any basic assessment of public-sector labour–management relations should perhaps emphasize the variety of channels of communication (as in the large private-sector firms) and the numerous possibilities for grievance settlement and ameliorating agreements that it offers. The extreme pragmatism of these developments is striking; the development of contractual policy in public enterprises has been established not only without a legal basis, but in contradiction to official provisions for the approval of wage increases by the minister of finance (Voisset, 1970).

Collective Bargaining and the State

Where collective bargaining cannot supplant legal provisions, it has encouraged their modification. For instance, the new law on collective bargaining of 1971 was prepared after thorough consultation with both labour and management and was passed unanimously by parliament. Other cases are still more striking: the 1966 law on training and education found its implementing provisions not in a ministerial decree but in a collective agreement – the 1970 inter-industry agreement on training. Maternity-leave compensation for manual workers was incorporated into social security by a law which in fact just reproduced the inter-industry agreement. We are thus witnessing a change in the role of the state, to an enlarged delegation of authority to interest groups and to a change in the sources of the law (Delamotte, 1971; Verdier and Langlois, 1972; see also Hayward, 1966, 1967; Darricau and Flandin, 1963; Le Brun, 1965; Lavau, 1965).

The unions, and more especially the CFDT, have come to prefer direct contact with the political authorities, contrary to certain predictions (Oppenheim, 1973; Reynaud, 1967). The independent socialist federation, FO, has been the major partner of government and private employers in the development of the 'contractual policy' and claims as its own some of the main innovations of this policy (e.g. training). The ex-Christian CFDT has espoused the cause of 'marginal' workers (semi-skilled workers, working women, etc.) and supported unusual means of exerting pressure.

Employment and Training

The recent preparation of the Sixth Economic Plan (1971–5) has led to an examination of the data, practices and ideas concerning employment, training and unemployment compensation (Mouriaux, 1972). An important survey of employment issues is contained in the plan itself (Commissariat Général du Plan, 1971a and b); an attempt has been made to define more clearly employment and unemployment, as well as marginal employment; manpower policy and new labour-market statistics have been studied (Courtheoux, 1971). The determinants of labour-market success have been analysed from a purely sociological perspective by Ledrut (1966).

More interesting, because it is perhaps more original, is the development of joint committees on employment matters (Reynaud, 1969; Delamotte, 1969a and b). Starting with the 1958 agreements on supplementary unemployment benefits, collective bargaining has linked employment policies to the firm's economic activity. The goal has not only been to compensate unemployment, but still more to encourage productivity increases and industrial expansion by making them socially acceptable. Delamotte, in a comparative study (1971), has shown how the differences in provisions and approaches in Britain, Germany, Sweden and France reflected the differences in the respective systems of industrial relations (Delamotte, 1969a).

Somewhat different considerations apply in the case of firms in financial difficulty. Isolated cases like Lip in 1973, and more and more frequent ones in 1974 and 1975, have attracted public support for strike action in these conflicts, but insufficient recognition has been given to the responsibilities taken on by the unions (Maire and Piaget, 1973). Investment plans have been jointly modified (at Rateau, 1974). Elsewhere, agreements have been signed on the creation of new firms (at Romans, 1974; at Neogravure, 1974/75; at Titan–Coder, 1975). A general study has yet to be done, but the new practices have already attracted the attention of specialists. The lasting social consequences of group lay-offs have been studied by Combe *et al.* (1974).

Immigrant workers have been the subject of numerous works (Grandjeat, 1966; Commissariat Général du Plan, 1971a; Mottez, 1972). Although knowledge of their situation has progressed considerably as a result of statistical data, studies of nationalities, and case studies by firm, at present few comprehensive analyses have appeared.

Temporary or contract labour firms in France have been on the increase. This raises the question of whether the improvement in employment security and increased protection against lay-offs has contributed to this increase (Lyon-Caen and Bonnetête, 1973). Do these developments portend a 'dualism' in employment as described by Doeringer and Piore? The answer is still uncertain (Caire, 1973; Guilbert *et al.*, 1970).

There has been a long series of studies on the social and individual consequences of labour mobility. Case studies have stressed the impact on the local community and on the individual (Girard and Meutey, 1965; Barbichon and Moscovici, 1962; Vidal, 1967). Some have described the emergence of a new work culture and community (Moscovici, 1961; Loux, 1974). Recently, traditional economic analysis has been challenged. Does it make practical sense to classify under the same heading the quite different social processes of plant shut-downs, limited dismissals, and individuals actively looking for a better job (Delors, 1970a)? The direct effects of technological change attracted much attention at the beginning of the wave of 'automation'; but the centre of interest soon shifted, as has already been noted, from general economic or social analysis to the consideration of the way these changes are handled and bargained over.

Like employment, vocational training (initial as well as continued training) has been regulated by collective agreement and by law (1972), but always with close collaboration between the unions, the employers and the state. There is an increasing number of studies on the role of training for the firm – that is, its impact on the organization and the changes it introduces – enlarging an already old tradition (Vatier, 1960; Reynaud, 1963; Caspar, 1970), and also on the meaning of training to the interest groups concerned, or the social strata within the firm (Durand and Durand, 1971; Fritsch, 1971; Guillon and Pigelet, 1974). The questions of how these group strategies are articulated by institutions (such as, for example, the works committee) or express themselves in union action, have been studied by Belorgey and Dupeyroux (1973).

Labour Organizations

Comprehensive studies on the labour movement include Lefranc (1969, 1973), Bruhat and Piolet (1966), Bouvier-Ajam (1969).

The important role played by union leaders in the debates on ideas, using the different platforms offered them, is one of the characteristics of the French political scene. Particular attention has been paid to the

CFDT–CFTC because it is the organization which has changed the most in its social basis as well as in its orientation (Adam, 1964b). Its change of name reflects the transformation of the union itself as well as that of the political role played by Catholics and the Church in France (Adam, 1965b; Marchal, 1965; Maurice, 1965a; Reynaud, 1965).

The union leaders themselves have written extensively: bringing together principal doctrinal texts for the CFDT (Bonety *et al.*, 1971); a stock-taking of major events for the CGT (1968; Seguy, 1972), or developing discussions of ideas and positions (Krasucki, 1969, 1972; Bergeron, 1975; Maire, 1971; Maire and Julliard, 1975).

Measuring political shifts in unions is difficult. Membership can only be estimated, but election results are known with precision (Adam, 1964a, 1968a and b; Perrot and Commaille, 1966), and results of elections to the works committees – a good measure of the respective weight of the unions – are published every year. The history of trade unions gives some flesh to these statistics. It shows, for example, the very high stability of affiliation: the 1921 split in the CGT, when closely examined, reveals enduring loyalties (Kriegel, 1966). The growth of the CGT in the years 1934–6, when examined by industry, shows the strengths and weaknesses of the federation (Prost, 1962).

Much of what has been discussed concerning the most recent labour–management relations has underplayed the often dominant role of the national industrial unions. This is obvious in cases where traditions of craft unionism remain very strong, such as in the printing industry (P. Chauvet, 1971; Sales, 1967) or again where there is a strong sense of community as among the dockers (Delamotte, 1973). Drawing from studies of workers in the glass industries and of maritime workers, Segrestin illustrated the craft dimension of union action, particularly in the CGT. In an approach related to Commons and the Wisconsin school, he shows how the workers' craft community serves as a basis for resistance to the economic logic of employers. Though the unions employ the language of traditional Marxism, it may conceal more pragmatic strategies (Segrestin, 1974, 1975).

The French unions, poor in membership and money, remain unions of militants, in which the essential element of the organization is the initiative and devotion of men motivated by conviction and the need for action (Berthon, 1962; Maurice, 1965b; Schifres, 1972; Andrieux and Lignon, 1973; Capdevielle and Mouriaux, 1968; Mothé, 1965, 1973). The accounts some of these militants have given of their activity, therefore, is often invaluable (Descamps, 1971; Declercq, 1974; Seguy, 1975).

In spite of the scant number of studies on problems of internal structure and organization, some trends may be noted in the research. Some recent studies have tried to stress the relationship between objectives (as defined by platform or by ideological tenets) and structure. This approach may have broader relevance for a system where ideology is strong and active. It is also more natural when much seems to rest on voluntary action and conviction-inspired projects, made easier by the possibility of comparing different objectives (and different ideologies) in the same context (Adam, 1966; Erbes-Seguin, 1968, 1971; Reynaud *et al.*, 1966a and b). Interesting comparisons can be made with Kriegel's approach to the Communist Party (Kriegel, 1968).

Following the theories of Touraine (1955, 1960, 1966), a research team led an important survey of union militants. The results only partially confirm the hypothesis made at the outset (*l'Action Syndicale*, 1968; Durand, 1972). On the other hand, the 'spin-off' of this study is important since the rich materials assembled have nourished a whole series of publications, of fairly diverse inspiration (Erbès-Seguin, 1971).

Employers' Organizations

The employers' organizations remain extremely discreet on their internal functioning. Nearly twenty years after its first publication, Ehrmann's book (1959) is still the best account. Their leaders, it is true, have often presented the major outlines of the employers' associations (Villiers, 1960), or its possible and desirable evolution (Huvelin, 1963), with a great deal of clarity and mastery; but the reform of the CNPF (1969), has not been studied. Efforts have been made to throw light on the action of voluntary groups, such as the young employers' group. They show a light-weight organization, capable of seizing the opportunities of the moment to affirm its leadership and initiative, assembling small entrepreneurs (Bernoux, 1974). Last and most important, there have been some analyses of the economic and structural conditions (size of the firms, market situation, etc.) which permit and favour an active employers' organization, or else reduce it to a decorative role (Jacob-Ory, 1969); and more generally, the conditions under which an industry policy is developed (Lautman, 1966; Szokoloczy-Syllaga, 1965). Studies are in progress for connecting industry and firm policies, particularly in the area of conflict (Bernoux *et al.*, 1973).

Labour, Employers and Politics

The relationship between the unions and political parties has changed much in the past fifteen years. The most stable case, that of the CGT and the Communist Party, has passed from a period in which the avant-garde demanded very strict obedience, to a period of a more balanced relationship (Ranger, 1969; Adam, 1968b). A masterly study of the beginnings of the Communist Party shows how it used opportunism to graft itself on to the workers' movement in France (Kriegel, 1964). Another study by the same author sees the Communist Party as a counter-society with the stable characteristics of a Leninist organization and the enduring traits of its relations with mass organizations like trade unions (Kriegel, 1968). The fluctuations for the CFDT have been greater. It has changed allies, passing from the MRP (Christian Democrats) in 1945 to the Socialist Party in 1975, but it has also changed its type of affiliation from the religious association to the labour movement. Studies of labour's vote (Dogan, 1960, 1965; Hamon, 1962; Bon and Michelat, 1970) and those, more rare, of the tie between vote and union membership (Adam *et al.*, 1971) show both the grouping of the labour vote in the left-wing parties (and also the impossibility of reducing the Communist votes to those of the working class alone), and the diversity of the unions. The CGT and FO find themselves close when faced with the united left; the CFDT goes further to the left but also further to the right. The alliance, that is, the unity of action, between the CGT and the CFDT (Adam, 1968b), does not seem, from this point of view, to have brought them any closer together. One could make the hypothesis, to enable a prediction, that the relationships between parties and unions in France follow different models in each of the three cases (Reynaud, 1975).

Very little is known on the relations between employers and political parties, except in a few cases where their financial support has been investigated (Brizay, 1975) or where some orientations in government social policy can be traced to support from employer groups (Bunel, 1973).

Conclusions

Several attempts have been made to convey a comprehensive image of industrial relations in France, whether based on the union movement or on negotiations (Sellier and Tiano, 1962; Caire, 1971, 1973b; Rioux,

1960, 1972; Weiss, 1973, 1974; Reynaud, 1975). The approach that seems the most fruitful is the one used by Sellier (Sellier, 1961; see also Sellier, 1970), in speaking of strategies of social struggle, especially as it showed how legal formulas which are formally opposed can lead to the same result depending on the context. Technically speaking, there was freedom of wage negotiation, but in fact, it meant arbitration, a situation similar to the wage controls of the 1945–50 period. The studies also show how economic analysis furnishes only a part of the explanation of behaviour, especially in conflicts, because economic power is only one type of power among many others. They show the necessity for treating political resources and mobilization capabilities in the same way. This mode of analysis, clarifed and reinforced by contributions from games theory and the study of international military strategy, shows promise of refinement and development.

Because the French situation has often been considered, especially by outside observers, as quite unique, too little attention has been paid to comparative research. Today, the opportunities seem better than ever. The political shift of the Catholic Church and its organizations should be studied comparatively in Quebec, Italy and France. The new patterns and the new results of conflict deserve a general review, but special comparison should be made between Italy and France. The emphasis on procedural instead of substantive content in the agreements should induce French scholars to scrutinize the British experience closely. For the role played by 'working conditions' as an issue in industrial relations, attention should be given to Norway and Sweden. This comparative orientation will, we think, be the most useful one for the years to come.

Many gaps could be underscored in the existing literature. Little is known of the industries where bargaining does not take place or is only a formality (it *is* known that they employ a high proportion of wage-earners). Public service bargaining has been only cursorily examined; balanced judgement of its successes and inefficiencies would be a very useful contribution. More generally, labour economics is still very weak in France, with the important exception of the Aix laboratory already mentioned.

New developments are taking place at the plant level. Particularly striking are the negotiations on 'working conditions'. In fact, the admittedly vague phrase of 'working conditions' encompasses larger and larger problems. Plant-level concerns of hierarchy and control are coming to the fore and furthering local bargaining. Regulation of health and safety by law and by joint commissions, a hot issue today, and the specific duties of worker representatives and management specialists, are probably changing – this deserves attention. To some degree, the same would apply to the questioning of disciplinary rules in the plant.

The effects of the new training provisions need evaluation. They may be far-reaching, not only for the work of employees, but also for hierarchical relationships in the companies and their personnel policies.

The rising tide of unemployment at the end of 1974 and during 1975 and the rather pessimistic forecasts for the duration of the Seventh Plan (1976–80) stimulate new reflections on the labour market. At the same time, the new decisions (by law and by collectively bargained agreement) granting almost full pay to employees laid off for economic reasons or restricted dismissals may begin to look less like a temporary expedient and more like an important step towards a change in the employment relationship. This trend should be scrutinized and the consequences assessed; some unexpected ones might show up.

The evolution of ideas over fifteen years could perhaps be characterized as the progress of realism in political debates – and there is no reason to confuse this realism with conformity and the acceptance of the established order. The depth of economic changes and of certain social changes has had the effect of concentrating discussion on short- and middle-term measures, rather than on long-term perspectives. Although the word 'change' is fashionable, on the right as well as on the left, it is referring to precise programmes and limited objectives (Delors, 1975).

This tendency, connected with the closer and closer concentration of the expression of problems, that is, the conflicts and compromises to which they lead in the firm (Reynaud, 1968), explains the political importance of the Sudreau Report, but also the form it took (Sudreau, 1975), in contrast to one of the best studies of the previous decade (Bloch-Laine, 1963). It was to make proposals for a reform in the enterprise, understood as leading not to plans for a general reshaping based on a global theory or on a doctrine, but as a list of suggestions, addressed in large part to the unions and to management, asking the government to play the role of permitting and participating more often than of imposing. The reception given the proposed measures, as well as the echo of the debate, obviously are geared to the political context, in the narrow sense of the term, that is, the fluctuations of public opinion and of governmental positions. But the general climate, indicated by this report is an indication, perhaps, of a more general significance.

GLOSSARY

Cadres: Cadres are managerial or professional salary earners, as opposed to manual workers, or lower white-collar workers (top supervisors are not *cadres* in collective agreements). The law allows them to organize. A specific national union (Confédération générale des cadres) groups *cadres*, supervisors and other groups. Manual workers' unions accept cadres in their ranks and the main federations have interindustry *unions* to cater for their special interests.

CGT: *Confédération générale du travail*. The most important union federation in France, communist controlled.

CGT-FO: (*Force ouvrière*). Split from the CGT in 1947 and has assumed a strong non-partisan trend. It is socialist orientated.

CFDT: *Confédération française démocratique du travail*. The old Catholic federation (CFTC, *Confédération française de travailleurs chrétiens*) changed its name in 1964 for the present one.

Mensualisation: On the President's initiative in 1970 a drive was launched to equalize and when possible identify the benefits and privileges of manual workers and lower white-collars (*cadres* not included). Accompanied by a change to monthly salary, this was called *mensualisation*.

Shop stewards: We have called the French *délégués du personnel* shop stewards. They are elected by all wage- and salary-earners in a plant; unions have the right to nominate them for elections (if the turnout is under 50 per cent, anybody can be a candidate). They should be distinguished from union delegates, elected in the union according to its own internal procedures, and accredited to the management of the company (1968 law).

Works committees: The *comité d'entreprise* groups around the director of the company delegates elected by all wage- and salary-earners. They must be consulted about the economic and technical problems of the company and about special problems (safety, through a special commission, training plans, profit-sharing plans, etc.).

REFERENCES

'Données et problèmes de la lutte ouvrière', *Les temps modernes* (sept.–oct. 1962) pp. 385–736.

L'action syndicale, Sociologie du Travail, n° special (1968), n° 2, pp. 113–232.

L'activité syndicale au niveau de l'entreprise, Paris, Sirey, Faculté de Droit et des Sciences économiques de l'Université de Lille (1966).

La grève généralisée en France (mai–juin 1968), Supplément à Informations-correspondance ouvrière, Paris (juin–juillet 1968).

Le mouvement ouvrier en mai 1968, n° spécial de Sociologie du Travail (1970), n° 3.

Lutter dans un grand magasin des travailleurs de la Samaritaine et la CFDT (Paris: Gît le Coeur, 1973).

Notre arme, c'est la grève (la grève chez Renault-Cléon) (Paris: Maspéro, 1968).

Ouvriers face aux appareils. Une experience de militantisme chez Hispano-Suiza, Cahiers libres 183–4, (Paris: Maspéro, 1970).

Positions et action de la CFDT au cours des événements de mai–juin 1968, *Syndicalisme Hebdo*, n° 1266A (novembre 1969).

'Qu'est-ce que la classe ouvrière?', *Arguments*, n° 12–13 (janvier–mars 1959).

'Structure des salaries et des emplois dans les entreprises françaises et allemandes Documents du Centre d'étude des revenus et des coûts', *Documentation Française* n° 23.

Abboud, Nicole de Maupeou, *Les blousons bleus, étude sociologique des jeunes ouvriers de la région parisienne* (Paris: A. Colin, Coll. Sciences Sociales de travail, 1968).

Abboud, Nicole, 'Les grèves et les changements de rapports sociaux', *Sociologie du Travail*, n° 4/73, n° Spécial 'Les grèves' (1973).

Abboud, Nicole, 'Grèves et rapports sociaux du travail: modèles classiques ou schémas nouveaux? *Sociologie du Travail*, n° 3/74, n° Spécial 'Mouvements sociaux d'aujourd'hui' (1974).

Adam, Gérard, *Atlas des élections professionnelles en France*, Cahiers de la Fondation nationale des sciences politiques (Paris: A. Colin, 1964a).

Adam, Gérard, *La C.F.D.T., 1940–1958, Histoire politique et d'idéologique* (Paris: Fondation nationale des sciences politiques, 1964b).

Adam, Gérard, *La C.F.T.C.* (Etudes syndicales) (Paris: Fondation nationale des sciences politiques, 1964c).

Adam, Gérard, *La C.G.T.-F.O.* (Etudes syndicales) (Paris: Fondation nationale des sciences politiques, 1965a).

Adam, Gérard, *Le syndicalisme ouvrier*, fasc 2 (Paris: IEP, 1969–1970).

Adam, Gérard, 'De la C.F.T.C. à la C.F.D.T.', *Revue Française de Science Politique 15 (1)* (février 1965b), pp. 87–103.

Adam, Gérard, 'Stratégies syndicales et types d'organisation', *Revue Française de Science Politique 5* (1966).

Adam, Gérard, 'L'unité d'action C.F.D.T. – C.G.T.', *Revue Française de Science Politique 17 (3)* (juin 1967) pp. 576–90.

Adam, Gérard, 'La représentativité des organisations syndicales', *Revue Française de Science Politique* (avril 1968a), pp. 278–314.

Adam, Gérard, 'Eléments d'analyse sur les liens entre le PCF, et la CGT', *Revue Française de Science Politique* (juin 1968b), pp. 530–1.

Adam, Gérard, 'Ou èn est le débat sur la "nouvelle classe ouvrière"?' Etat des Travaux, *Revue Française de Science Politique* (octôbre 1968c), pp. 1004–23.

Adam, Gérard, 'L'unité d'action C.G.T. – C.F.D.T. (bilan et perspectives janvier 1966–septembre 1968)', *Droit Social* (novembre 1968a), p. 567.

Adam, Gérard, 'Etude statistique des grèves en mai-juin 1968', *Revue Française de Science Politique*, (fevrier 1970), pp. 105–19.

Adam, Gérard, 'Introduction à un débat sur la nouvelle classe ouvrière', *Revue Française de Science Politique*, 1972, pp. 509–28.

Adam, Gérard, Bon F., Capdevielle J., Mourlaux R., *L'ouvrier français en 1970, Enquête nationale auprès de 1116 ouvriers d'industrie* (Paris: A. Colin, 1971).

Adam, Gérard, Reynaud, Jean-Daniel, Verdier, Jean-Maurice, *La négociation collective en France* (Paris: Éd. ouvrières, 1972).

Aglietta, Michel, 'L'évolution des salaires en France au cours des vingt dernières années', *Revue Economique* (janvier 1971), pp. 69–117.

AGREF, *Bas salaires et disparités dans la croissance économique* (Paris: nov. 73).

AGREF, *Le processus inflationniste* (Paris: 1974a).

AGREF, *Les effects de l'inflation* (Paris: 1974b).

Alasseur, Remy, *Le revenu disponible des salariés en France de 1920 à 1969. Elements de détermination* (Paris: Ecole pratique des Hautes Etudes 1974).

Andrieux, André, Lignon, Jean, *L'ouvrier d'aujourd'hui* (Paris: Ed. ouvrières, 1961).

Andrieux, André, Lignon, Jean, *Le militant syndicaliste d'aujourd'hui* (Paris: Denoël, 1973).

Arliaud, Michel, *Contribution à l'analyse du comportement de l'emploi*, 1 ère partie (CERS-LEST, 1974).

Arliaud, Michel, 'La problématique économique de la mobilité de l'emploi', *Sociologie du Travail*, 2/74.

Arliaud, Michel, Maurice, M., Picon, B., Quatrepages, G., *Mobilité des entreprises et mobilité de la main-d'oeuvre, approche sociologique* (LEST, 1969).

Audibert, Jacques, 'La mobilité de la main-d'oeuvre', *Droit Social*, n° 11 (novembre 1973).

Audinet, J., 'Une année du Conseil de Prud 'hommes: Marseille 1966', *Droit Social* (janvier 1970).

Bachy, Jean-Paul, *Les cadres en France* (Paris: A. Colin, Dossiers U2, 1971).

Bachy, Jean-Paul, Dupu, Francois, Martin, Dominique, *Représentation et négociation dans l'entreprise* (sous la direction de G. Adam) (Paris: CRESST, 1974).

Balmes, Grassi, Mouton, Peperstraete, Tessier, *Les principales clauses salariales contenues dan les conventions collectives et les accords d'entreprise. Essaide systématisation*, Travaux de groupe de relations professionelles. Centre de formation des inspecteurs du travail et de la main-d'oeuvre, Session 74, multigr.

Baraquin, Y., Mercier, P. A., *Pratiques contractuelles et conflits de travail. Etude de cas des hypermarchés* (Paris: Credoc, 1973).

Barbichon, Guy, Moscovici, Serge, 'Modernisation des mines, conversion des mineurs', *Revue française de travail* (juillet–septembre 1962).

Barjonet, André, *La C.G.T.* (Paris: Seuil, coll. Politique, 1968a).

Barjonet, André, 'CGT 1968, le subjectivisme au service de l'ordre établi', *Les Temps modernes* (juillet 1968b).

Baron, Chicotte, Hazenbergue, Lefevre, Markey, *L'évolution des fonctions des comités d'entreprise*, Travaux de groupe de relations professionnelles, Centre de formation des inspecteurs du travail et de la main-d'oeuvre, Session 1974 multigr.

Barrier, Christiane, 'Techniciens et grèves à l'électricité de France', *Sociologie du Travail* (Janvier-mars 1968), pp. 50–71.

Barrier, Christiane, *Le combat ouvrier dans une entreprise de pointe* (Paris: Ed. ouvrières, coll. relations sociales, 1975).

Baumfelder, E., Cazes, S., Dassa, S., Durand, Claude, Kergoat, Danièle,

Mallet, Serge, Vidal, Daniel, 'Le mouvement ouvrier en mai 68', *Sociologie du Travail*, n° Spécial, 3/1970.

Bazex, M., *L'administration et les syndicats* (Paris Ed. Berger-Levrault, coll. d'administration nouvelle, 1973).

Beauchesne, M. N., *Recherche d'indicateurs sociaux concernant les conditions de travail*, 2ème partie: la législation et les organismes, analyse et bilan critique (LEST: 1973).

Beauchesne, M. N., Guelaud, F., Romagnan, B., *Recherche d'indicateurs sociaux concernant les conditions de travail* (LEST: 1972).

Belleville, Pierre, *Une nouvelle classe ouvrière* (Paris: Julliard, 1963).

Belorgey, Jean-Michel, Dupeyroux, Jean-Jacques, 'La formation professionnelle continue', *Droit Social*, n° Spécial (septembre–octobre 1973).

Belorgey, Jean-Michel, Dupeyroux, Jean-Jacques, 'L'exclusion sociale', *Droit Social*, n° Spécial (novembre 1974).

Benton, Philippe, Touchard, Jean, Les interprétations de la crise de mai-juin 1968, *Revue française de science politique*, Vol. 20, n° 3 (juin 1970), pp. 503–43.

Benguigui, G., Gajdos, C., Gaulon, J., Guillon, R., Lagneau, G., Lautman, J., Maurice, M., Monjardet, D., Monteil-Tartanjon, C., Sales, A., Walbert, D., Williner, A., 'Les cadres dans l'entreprise et dans le mouvement syndical', *Sociologie du Travail*, n° spécial, 3/68.

Benguigui, G., Monjardet, D., La mesure de la qualification du travail des cadres *Sociologie du Travail*, n° 2/73.

Benoit, Odile, 'Statut dans l'entreprise et attitude syndicale des ouvriers', *Sociologie du travail*, n° 3 (1962), pp. 230–42.

Benoit, Odile, Maurice, Marc, 'Groupes professionnels et relations collectives de travail dans l'entreprise', *Sociologie du Travail*, n° 2, (1960) pp. 151–69.

Bergeron, André, *Lottre ouverte à un syndiqué* (Paris: Albin Michel, 1975).

Bernoux, Philippe, Motte, Dominique, 'L'accord et le conflit Berliet de 1970', *Droit Social*, n° 7–8 (juillet-août 1971).

Bernoux, Philippe, *Les nouveaux patrons* (Paris: Ed. ouvrières, 1974).

Bernoux, Philippe, 'Les O.S. face à l'organisation industrielle', *Sociologie du Travail* (Paris: Editions Seuil, n° 4/72).

Bernoux, Philippe, Motte, Dominique, Saglio, Jean, *Trois ateliers d'O.S.* (Paris: Ed. ouvrières, 1973).

Bernoux, Philippe, Saglio, Jean, Bunel, Jean, *Les nouvelles politiques sociales patronales. Participation et institutionalisation des conflits* (Lyon: CORDES, Economie et Humanisme, 1973).

Bernoux, Philippe, Ruffier, Jean, *Les groupes semi-autonomes de production*, Caluire, Economie et Humanisme (novembre 1974).

Berthon, Jean, 'Les militants de la CFTC', *Sociologie du Travail* n° 2, (1962) pp. 174–85.

Bloch-Laine, François, *Pour une réforme de l'entreprise* (Paris: Ed. du Seuil, 1963).

Bodiguel, Jean-Luc, *La réduction du temps de travail* (Paris: Ed. ouvrières, 1969).

Bois, P., 'Les comités d'entreprises. Un espoir longtemps déçu peut-il renaître?' *Dròit Social*, n° 2 (Février 1969).

Bon, Frédéric, Brunier, Michel-Antoine, *Les nouveaux intellectuels* (Paris: Cujas, 1966).

Bon, Frédéric, Burnier, Michel-Antoine, *Classe ouvrière et révolution* (Paris: Seuil, 1971).

Bon, Frédéric, Michelat, Guy, *Attitudes et comportements politiques à Boulogne-Billancourt*, (Paris: A. Colin, travaux de recherches de science politique, 1970).

Bon, Frédéric, Capdevielle, Jacques, Mouriaux, René, *L'ouvrier conservateur* (Paris: Foundation nationale des sciences politiques. août 1973).

Bonety, Gilbert, Bouladoux, Maurice, Declercq, Gilbert, *et al.*, *La C.F.D.T.* (Paris: Seuil, coll. politique, 1971).

Bonis, Jean, 'Les cadres, ''enterprise et l'environement', *Sociologie du Travail*, n° 3 (1969) 241–58.

Bonnaud, Jean-Jacques, 'La participation des organisations professionnelles à la planification économique et sociale en France', *Revue internationale du travail* (avril 1966), pp. 378–403.

Borkel, Alain, *La participation des syndicats ouvriers aux fonctions économiques et sociales de l'état*, (Paris: Librairie générale de droit et de jurisprudence 1965).

Borzeix, Anni, Chave, Daniel, *Réorganisation du travail et dynamique des conflits*, Laboratoire de sociologie du travail du Conservatoire des Arts et Métiers, mimeographed report, (Paris, 1975).

Bosquet, Robert (sous la direction de), *L'évolution du context social 1974–1985* (Paris: Entreprise et Personnel, 1975).

Bourdet, Yvon, *La déliverance de Prométhée. Pour une théorie politique de l'autogestion* (Paris: Anthropos, 1970).

Bourdet, Yvon, *Pour l'autogestion* (Paris: Anthropos, 1974).

Bourdieu, Pierre, Darbel, Alain, Rivet, Jean-Paul, Seibel, Claude, *Travail et travailleurs en Algérie* (Paris – The Hague: Mouton, 1963).

Bouvier-Ajam, Maurice, *Histoire du travail en France depuis la Révolution* (Paris: Libr. Générale de Droit et de Jurisprudence, 1969).

Brault, Carpentier, Chelle, Guaroliolle, Roland, *Le rôle de l'inspecteur du travail dans le reglement des conflits collectifs du travail*, Centre de formation des inspecteurs du travail et de la main-d'oeuvre, Session 1974.

Brecy, Robert, *Le mouvement syndical en France, 1871–1921, Essai bibliographique* (Paris: Mouton, 1963).

Brethe de la Gressaye, J., 'La présence du syndicat dans l'entreprise', *Droit Social* no 3 (mars 1969).

Brizay, Bernard, *Le patronat, histoire, structure, stratégie du CNPF* (Paris: Seuil, 1975).

Bruhat, Jean, Piolet, Marc, *Esquisse d'une histoire de la C.G.T., (1895–1965)* (Paris: C.G.T. Centre confédéral d'education ouvière, 1966).

Brun, Jean, *Histoire du mouvement ouvrier français*, Tome 3, 1950–1972 (Paris: Ed. ouvrières, 1973).

Bunel, Jean, *La mensualisation, une réforme tranquille?* (Paris: Ed. ouvrières, 1973).

Bunel, Jean, Meunier, Paul, *Chaban-Delmas . . .* (Paris: Stock, 1972).

Butler, M., Gaudemar, J. P. de, Pitoeff, L., Torreau, R., 'Formations et carrières professionnelles', *Sociologie du Travail*, 1/74, pp. 65–85.

Caire, Guy, *Les Syndicats et l'automation* (Aix-on-Provence: La pensée universitaire, 1960).

Caire, Guy, *Les syndicats ouvriers* (Paris: PUF, 1971).

Caire, Guy, *Les nouveaus marchands d'hommes? Etude du travail intérimaire*, (Paris: Ed. ouvrières, 1973a).

Caire, Guy, *Les relations industrielles* (Paris: Dalloz, 1973b).

Camerlynck, G. H., *Contrat de Travail*, Tome 1 de Camerlynch, G. H., *Traité de Droit du Travail* (Paris Dalloz, 1968).

Capdevielle, J., Mouriaux, R., *Les militants de la CGT et de la CFDT* (Paris: Fondation nationale des sciences politiques, 1968).

Capdevielle, J., Mouriaux, R., 'Le militantisme syndical en France', *Revue Française de Science Politique*, Paris, *22*, 3 (1972), pp. 566–81.

Capitaine, Eyssette, Barret, Paoli, Seguela, *L'inflation et la négociation*, Travaux de groupe de relations professionnelles. Centre de formation des Inspecteurs du travail et de la main-d'oeuvre, Session 1974.

Caspar, Pierre, *Formation des adultes ou transformation des structures de l'entreprise* (Ed. d'organisation, 1970).

Centi, C., *Responsabilité, pouvoir et formation du salaire: essai d'un modèle théorique*, (Aix-on-Provence: L.E.S.T., Laboratoire d'Economie et de Sociologie du Travail).

Centre national des dirigeants d'entreprise, *La participation dans l'enterprise* (Paris: Seuil, 1969).

CFDT, 'Les conditions de travail des ouvriers spécialisés et des travailleurs postés', *Bulletin du Militant*, supplt. au n° 359 (juillet Fédération générale de la métallurgie C.F.D.T. 1972).

CFDT, *Situation des travailleuses* (Paris: Etudes économiques, Dec. 1972b).

CGT, 'La grève générale de mai 1968', *Le Peuple n° 799/800/801* (15 au 30 juin 68).

CGT, *Pour des conditions de travail plus humaines en rapport avec notre temps*, Document adopté par la Commission exécutive de la C.G.T. dans sa réunion du 2 février 1972, *Le Peuple, n° 887* (17 au 29 février 1972).

Chauvet, Paul, *Les ouvriers du livre et du journal* (Paris: Ed. ouvrières, 1971).

Chauvey, Daniel, *Autogestion* (Paris: Ed. du seuil, 1970).

Chenevier, Jean, *L'éducation permanente* (Paris: CRC, Cahier n° 13, 1969).

Cheverny, Julien, *Les cadres, essai sur les nouveaux prolétaires* (Paris: Julliard, 1967).

Chombart de lauwe, Paul H., 'Y a-t-il encore une classe ouvrière?', *Revue de l'action populaire 135* (février 1960), pp. 125–203.

Clerc, Jean-Marc, ed., *Expériences en vue d'une organisation plus humaine du travail industriel*, Compte rendu d'un colloque international, établi par Jean-Marc CLERC, 1973, Collection sciences sociales du travail.

Club, Jean Moulin, *L'Etat et le citoyen* (Paris: Seuil, 1961).

CNPF, *Le problème des O.S., Rapport au groupe d'études du C.N.P.F.* (Paris: octobre 1971).

Combe, Maurice, *L'alibi. Vingt ans d'un comité central d'entreprise* (Paris: Gallimard, 1969).

Combe, M., Ziegler, H., Ziegler, M. P., *Les effets traumatisants d'un licenciement collectif*, Centre d'ethnologie sociale et de psychosociologie, rapport CORDES (Paris: 1974).

Comité d'étude et de liaison du travail féminin, 'Problèmes du travail féminin', *Revue Française des Affaires Sociales* (juillet–septembre 1969).

Commissariat général du Plan, *Rapport general de la Commission de la main-d'oeuvre de 5ème plan* (Paris: CGP, mars 1966).

Commissariat Général du Plan, *Rapport de la commission emploi* du 6ème plan, Paris, Documentation Française (1971a), 2 vols.

Commissariat Général du Plan, *Rapport de l'intergroupe formation qualification* professionable du 6ème plan (Paris: Documentation Française 1971b).

Confremca, *Etude psychosociologique sur les attitudes des cadres français* (août 1971).

Cornu, R., 'Marché du travail et mobilite deś travailleurs. Note critique', *Année sociologigue* (1972), pp. 465–84.

Cornu, R., Duplex, J., Picon, B., *Analyse contextuelle de la mobilité. lère partie les industries portuaires à Marseille* (Aix-en-Provence: LEST).

Cornu, R., Maurice, M., 'Revendications, orientations syndicales et participation des cadres àla grève', *Sociologie du travail*, n° 3, (1970), pp. 328–38.

Courbis, Raymond, 'Productivité globale des facteurs, prévision des prix et politique des revenus', *Revue économique* (juillet 1968), pp. 563–606.

Courtheoux, Jean-Paul, *La politique des revenus* (Paris: PUF, Coll. Que sais-je?, 1966).

Courtheoux, Jean-Paul, 'La nation d'activité selon la coutume statistique', *Revue Française de Sociologie*, *12*, 1 (1971), pp. 40–56.

Courtheoux, J.P., Lacombe, Y., 'Les fonctions complémentaires des salaires minima', *Droit Social*, n° 9 (septembre–octobre 1972), pp. 449–53.

Crozier, Michel, 'Classes sans conscience ou préfiguration de la société sans classes', *Archives Européennes de Sociologie*, n° 2 (1960), pp. 233–47.

Crozier, Michel, 'Sociologie du syndicalisme', in Friedmann George, Naville, Pierre, *Traité de Sociologie du travail* (Paris: Armand Colin, 1962), tome 2, pp. 170–91.

Crozier, Michel, *Le Phénomène bureaucratique* (Paris: Seuil, 1963).

Crozier, Michel, *La société bloquée* (Paris: Ed., Seuil, 1970).

Danaho, Raoul, 'La conception moderne de l'administration de d'emploi', *Droit Social*, n° 12 (décembre 1969), pp. 556–70.

Darricau, André, Flandin, William, 'La participation syndicale au Plan', *Revue de l'action populaire* 174 (janvier 1963), pp. 59–67.

Dassa, Sami, Fournier, Jean-Yves, Mercier, Nicole, *Les relations professionnelles dans l'entreprise* (Paris: 1973), multigr. 377 p.

Dassa, Sami, 'L'analyse contextuelle appliquée aux orientations et aux comportements syndicaux', *Sociologie du Travail*, n° 4 (1968), pp. 407–15.

Daubigney, J. P., 'Actualité du Système Parodi dans les comportements salariaux des entreprises', *Revue Économique*, Vol. XX, n° 3 (mai 1969), pp. 497–514.

Daubigney, J. P., 'Croissance des salaires et évolution de la hiérarchie ouvrière. Analyses des comportements d'entreprise', *Economie et société*. Cahiers de l' ISEA, Tome III (12) (décembre 1969), pp. 2115–40.

Daubigney, J. P., *Hiérarchie des salaires et conventions collectives* (LEST, 1970).

Daubigney, J. P., 'Les différences de salaires entre enterprises. Etude micro-économique, *Revue Économique*, Vol. XXII, n° 2 (mars 1971), pp. 214–46.

Daubigney, J. P., 'Les disparités de salaires internes à la firme', *Revue Économique* Vol. XXII, n° 3 (mai 1971).

Daubigney, J. P., Silvestre, J. J., 'La signification de la corrélation éducation–salaire, commentaire', *Revue Économique*, Vol. XXIV, n° 3 (mai 1973), pp. 370–3.

David, Marcel, *Les travailleurs et le sens de leur histoire* (Paris: Cujas, coll. 'Temps de l'histoire', 1967).

Dayron, Barnet, Combes, Gullaumin, Tissier, *L'inspecteur du travail et les conditions de travail*, C.F.I.T.M.O., Session 1974.

Dechartre, Philippe, 'Bilan et perspectives de l'ordonnance de 1967 sur la participation des salariés aux fruits de l'expansion des entreprises'. Communication de M. Philippe Dechartre, Secrétaire d'Etat auprès du Ministre du Travail, de l'emploi et de la Population au Conseil économique et Social 4.2.7. janvier 1971, *Droit social*, n° 6 (juin 1971).

Declercq, Gilbert, *Syndicaliste en liberté* (Paris: Seuil, 1974).

Declercq, Gilbert, 'Démocratie nouvelle et syndicalisme moderne', *Nouvelle revue française 18 (6)* (avril–juin 1961), pp. 91–105.

Delamotte, Yves, 'Le recours ouvrier, réflexion sur la signification psycho-logique des règles juridiques', *Sociologie du Travail*, n° 2 (1961), pp. 113–23.

Delamotte, Yves, 'Relations collectives et règles juridiques du travail et de la sécurité social', in Friedmann, G., Naville, P., *Traité de sociologie du travail*, Vol. 2 (Paris: A. Colin, 1962), pp. 203–31.

Delamotte, Yves, 'L'incidence des systèms de relations industrielles sur la contribution des conventions collectives à la recherche de solutions aux problèmes d'emploi', *Droit Social* (avril 1969a), pp. 227–32.

Delamotte, Yves, 'L'accord interprofessionnel sur la sécurité de l'emploi du 10 février 1969', *Droit Social*, n° 9–10 (septembre-octobre 1969b), pp. 498–508.

Delamotte, Yves, 'Les tendances récentes de la négociation collective en France', *Revue internationale du travail* (avril 1971).

Delamotte, Yves, *Les partenaires sociaux face aux problèmes de productivité et d'emploi*, (Paris: OECD, 1971).

Delamotte, Yves, *Recherches en vue d'une organisation plus humaine du travail industriel* (Paris: Documentation française, 1972).

Delamotte, Yves, 'Changements dans les règles et pratiques de travail des dockers', in *Une nouvelle civilisation? Hommage à Georges Friedmann* (Paris: Gallimard, 1973), pp. 153–96.

Delamotte, Y., Walker, K. F., *L'humanisation du travail et la qualité de la vie de travail. Tendances et problèmes*, Institut International d'Etudes Sociales, Genève, Bulletin n° 11 (janvier 1974).

Delon, Pierre, *Les employés* (Paris: Editions sociales, 1969).

Delors, Jacques (ed.), *Mobilité et coûts de l'adaptation*, Plan et prospectives, Commissariat général du Plan (Paris: A. Colin, 1970a), pp. 89–132.

Delors, Jacques, 'La nouvelle sociéte', *Preuves* (2ème trimestre 1970b), pp. 95–108.

Delors, Jacques, *Changer* (Paris: Stock, 1975).

Demains, Bruno, 'Les cadres en question', *Revué Française des Affaires Sociales* (janvier–mars 1970).

Denojean, Demory, Lecoutour, Lemaire, Mulmann, *La représentativité des organisations syndicales*, Travaux de groupe de relations professionnelles. Centre de formation des inspecteurs du travail et de la main-d' oeuvre, Session 1974.

Derouin, Philippe, 'Une expérience de participation du personnel à l'entreprise', *Droit Social*, n° 1 (janvier 1969), pp. 27–32.

Descamps, Eugène, *Militer, une vie pour un engagement collectif* (Paris: Fayard, 1971).

Despax, Michel, *Conventions collectives*, tome 7 de Camerlynck, G. H., *Traite de Droit du Travail* (Paris: Dalloz, 1966).

Despax, Michel, 'Les accordes de participation', *Droit Social*, n° 6 (juin 1969), pp. 378–87.

Despax, Michel, 'La réforme du droit des conventions collectives de travail par la loi 71.561 du 13 juillet 1971', *Droit Social*, n° 9–10 (septembre–octobre 1971), pp. 530–43.

Desseigne, Gérard, *L'évolution des structures de l'emploi dans l'industrie aerospatiale française* (Paris: Cujas, 1966).

Detraz, A., Krumnow, F., Maire, E., *La CFDT et l'autogestion* (Paris: Cerf, 1973).

Dofny, Jacques, Durand, Claude, Reynaud, Jean-Daniel, Touraine, Alain, *Les ouvriers et le progrès technique* (Paris: A. Colin, coll. Sciences sociales du travail, 1966).

Dofny, Jacques, Maurice, Marc, Willener, Alfred, *Travail, salaire et production*, tome 2, *Pouvoir et rémunération* (Paris: Mouton, 1972).

Dogan, Mattéi, 'Le vote ouvrier en Europe occidentale', *Revue Francaise de Sociologie 1 (1)* (1960), pp. 25–44.

Dogan, Mattéi, 'Le vote ouvrier en France. Analyse écologique des élections de 1962', *Revue Française de Sociologie* (octobre–décembre 1965), pp. 435–71.

Douard, H., Reynaud, J. D., Chave, D., Saglio, J., *Evolution de l'autorité dans l'entreprise industrielle* (Entreprise et personnel, multigr., 1973).

Douard, H., Reynaud, J. D., 'The quality of working life, a central issue in industrial relations', in L. Davis (ed.) *Quality of Working Life: Problems, Prospects and State of the Art*, vol. 1 (Free Press, 1975).

Doublet, Jacques, Passelecq, Oliver, *Les Cadres* (Paris: PUF, coll. Que sais-je? 1973).

Dubois, Jean *et al.*, *Les cadres, enjeu politique* (Paris: Seuil, 1971).

Dubois, Pierre, *Recours ouvrier, évolution technique, conjoncture sociale* (Collection Sciences Sociales du Travail), (Paris: A. Colin, 1971).

Dubois, Pierre, *Mort de l'Etat-patron* (Paris: Editions ouvrières, 1974).

Dubois, Pierre, 'Le traitement de la réclamation dans l'industrie textile', *Sociologie du Travail*, n° 4 (octobre–décembre 1968), pp. 393–406.

Dubois, Pierre, 'Implantation syndicale et recours ouvrier', *Projet*, n° 41 (janvier 1970), pp. 79–87.

Dubois, Pierre, 'Les types de revendications dans l'industrie textile', *Revue Française des Affaires Sociales* (janvier–mars 1970).

Dubois, Pierre, 'La négociation d'entreprise en période de crise sociale',

Revue Française des Affaires Sociales (avril–juin 1970).

Dubois, Pierre, 'Etude d'une pratique revendicative: l'action directe', *Revue Française des Affaires Sociales* (octobre–décembre 1970).

Dubois, Pierre, 'L'information des ouvriers pendant le temps du travail, *Revue Française des Affaires Sociales* (1971).

Dubois, Pierre, 'La séquestration', *Socilogie du Travail*, n° Spécial 'Les grèves' (1973), pp. 410–27.

Dubois, Pierre, 'Les grèves et la droit à l'emploi', *Revue Française des Affaires Sociales* (janvier–mars 1974).

Dubois, Pierre, Dulong, Renaud, Durand, Claude, Erbes-Seguin, Sabine, Vidal, Daniel, *Grèves revendicatives ou grèves politiques?* (Paris: Editions Anthropos, 1971).

Dunajweski, H., *Décisions d'amélioration des conditions de travail sans influence sur la productivité: étude d'un cas particular aux garages en France* (LEST 1973).

Dupeyroux, Jean-Jacques (ed.), 'La Securité de l'emploi et du salaire', special issues of *Droit Social*, n° 6 (juin 1976), n° 9–10 (septembre–octobre 1975).

Duraffourg, J., Laville, A., Raquillet, M. Teiger, C., Wisner, A., *Charge de travail et vieillissement*, C.N.A.M., rapport CORDES (1973).

Durand, Claude, 'Signification politique de l'action syndicale', *Revue Française de Sociologie, 9, 3* (juillet–septembre 1968), pp. 320–37.

Durand, Claude, *Conscience ouvrière et action syndicale* (Paris-The Hague: Mouton, 1972).

Durand, Claude, 'Revendications explicites et revendications latentes', *Sociologie du Travail*, n° 4, n° Spécial 'Les grèves' (1973), pp. 394–409.

Durand, Claude, Dubois, Pierre, *La grève* (Paris: A. Colin, Fondation nationale des Sciences politiques, 1975).

Durand, Claude, Durand, Michelle, *De l'O.S. a l'ingénieur. Carrière en classe sociale* (Paris: Éditions ouvrières, 1971).

Durand, Claude, Prestat, Claude, Willener, Alfred, *Travail, salaire, production*, Tome 1, *Le controle des cadences* (Paris, The Hague: Mouton, 1973).

Durand, Claude, Maurice, Marc, Dofny, Jacques, Willener, Alfred, *Travail, salaire, production*, Tome 2, *Pouvoir et rémunération* (Paris, The Hague: Mouton, 1973).

Durand, Michelle, 'Initiative économique, politique d'emploi et conflict social', *Sociologie du Travail*, n° 1 (1971), pp. 53–72.

Durand, Michelle, Guillon, Roland, Hagege, Claude, *L'entreprise et les politiques d'emploi. Etude des politiques patronales et syndicales* (Paris: ISST, 1972).

Ehrmann, Henri W., *La politique du patronat français (1936–1955)* (Paris: A. Colin, 1959).

Erbes-Seguin, Sabine, 'Des buts de l'action aux structures syndicales', *Sociologie du Travail*, n° 2 (1968), pp. 168–89.

Erbes-Seguin, Sabine, 'Relations entre travailleurs dans l'entreprise en grève', *Revue Française de Sociologie*, Editions du C.N.R.S., n° Xl-3 (juillet-septembre 1970).

Erbes-Seguin, Sabine, *Démocratie dans les syndicats* (Paris: Moutin, 1971).

Fremontier, Jacques, *La fortaresse ouvrière: Renault* (Paris: Fayard. 1971).

Friedenson, Patrick, *Histoire des usines Renault – I – Naissance de la grande entreprise, 1898–1939* (Paris: Seuil, 1972).

Fritsch, Philippe, *L'éducation des adultes* (Paris, The Hague: Mouton, 1971).

Froidevaux, Gravejat, *La participation des travailleurs aux décisions dans l'entreprise*, Rapport DGRST, IRAS (Lyon, 1972).

Gajdos, Catherine, 'Culture et impasse de la technique, les cadres del'industrie', *Revue Française de Sociologie*, XIII, supplément (1972), pp. 666–90.

Gille, Bertrand, *Recherche sur la formation de la grande entreprise capitaliste 1815–1848* (Paris: S.E.V.P.E.N., coll. Affaires et gens d'affaires, 1959).

Girard, Alain, Meutey, Pierre, *Développment économique et mobilité des travailleurs. L'individu, la profession, la région* (Paris: INED, 1956).

Goetz-Girey, Robert, *La mouvement des grèves en France 1919–1962* (Paris: Sirey, Collection l'économique, 1965).

Gorz, Andre, *Neócapitalisme et stratégie ouvrière* (Paris: Seuil, 1964).

Gorz, André, *Le socialisme difficile* (Paris: Seuil, 1967).

Gorz, André, 'Technique, techniciens et lutte des classes', *Temps modernes* (août-septembere 1971), n° 301–2.

Gorz, André (sous la direction de), *Critique de la division du travail* (Paris: Seuil, Collection Politique, 1973).

Grandjeat, Pierre, *Les migrations de travailleurs en Europe* (Paris: Librairie sociale et économique, Cahiers de l'Institut international d'études sociales, *1*, 1, Octobre-Décembre 1966).

Grossin, William, *Le travail et le temps* (Paris: Anthropos, 1969).

Grumbach, Tiennot, 'En partant del'expérience de Flins "base ouvrière", Renault-Fline 1971', *Les Temps Modernes* n° 301–2 (août-septembre 1971).

Guelaud-Leridon, Françoise, *Le travail des femmes en France* (Paris: PUF, 1964).

Guelaud, Françoise, 'Modifier et améliorer les conditions de travail', *Dirigeant* (avril 1972), pp. 21–5.

Guelaud, Françoise, Beauchesne, Marie-Noël, Gautrat, Jacques, Roustang, Guy, *Pour un analyse des conditions du travail ouvrier dans l'entreprise* (Aix-en-Provence: LEST, 1974).

Guilbert, Madeleine, *Les fonctions des femmes dans l'industrie* (Paris: Mouton, 1966).

Guilbert, Madeleine, Lowit, Nicole, Creusen, J., *Le travail temporaire*, Société des amis du Centre d'études sociologiques, travaux et documents, n° 2 (1970).

Guillon, Roland, Pigelet, Jean-Luc, *Cadres, techniciens et agents de maîtrise devant la qualification et l'emploi. Leurs pratiques de négociation collective* (Paris: CRESST, 1974).

Guin, Yannick, *La commune de Nantes* (Paris: Maspéro, 1969).

Hamon, Léo (sous la direction de), *Les nouveaux comportements de la classe ouvrière* (entretiens de Dijon, sous la direction de Léo Hamon) (Paris: PUF, 1962).

Hasson, Guy, *La formation dans l'entreprise et ses problèmes* (Paris: Editions de l'entreprise moderne, 1975).

Hatzfeld, Henry, Freyssinet, Jacques, *L'emploi en France* (Paris: Editions ouvrières, 1964).

Hayward, J. E. S., *Private interests and public policy. The experiences of the French Economic and Social Council* (London: Longmans, 1966).

Hayward, J. E. S., 'Le fonctionnement des commissions et la préparation du Ve Plan. L'exemple de la commission de la main-d'oeuvre', *Revue Française de Sociologie 8*, 4 (1967), pp. 447–67.

Humblet, Jean, *Les cadres d'entreprises, France, Belgique, Royaume-Uni* (Paris: Editions universitaires, 1966).

Huvelin, Paul, 'L'avenir de l'organisation professionelle', *Cahiers du C.R.C.*, n° 10 (1963), pp. 5–46.

Idiart, Pierre, *Les jeunes travailleurs de 15 à 25 ans dans la France d'aujourd'hui*, (Paris: Editions, ouvrieres, 1964).

INSEE, *Presque historique du système productif*, Collections de l'Institut National de la Statistique et des Etudes économiques, Série E, n° 27 (octobre 1974).

Iribarne, Alan D', 'Les besoins d'emploi des entreprises', *Revue économique* (juillet 1969), pp. 601–57.

Isambert, F. A., *Christianisme et classe ouvrière, jalons pour une étude de sociologie historique* (Paris: Castenman, 1961).

Jacob-Ory, A. M., 'Formes d'organisation patronale et limitations de la concurrence', *Revue Française de Sociologie*, 10, 5 (1969), pp. 631–43.

Jacob-Ory, A. M., *Les syndicats patronaux dans le système économique*, thèse de doctorat, spécialité 3 ème cycle (1972).

Javillier, Jean-Claude, 'La partie "obligatoire" de la convention collective', *Droit Social* (Avril 1971), pp. 258–76.

Javillier, Jean-Claude, *Recherche sur les conflits du travail*, Thèse pour le doctorat en droit (Paris, 1973).

Jobert, Annette, *Pratiques contractuelles et conflits sociaux, Etude de cas: la société nationale des chemins de fer français* (Paris: Credoc, 1973).

Jobert, Annette, *Pratiques contractuelles et conflits sociaux – Syndicats et patronat face à la politique contractuelle* (Paris: Credoc, 1973).

Jobert, Annette, Mercier, P. A., *Pratiques contractuelles et conflits sociaux. L'opinion face aux conflits de travail* (Paris: Credoc, 1973).

Julliard, Jacques, *Clémenceau briseur de grèves. L'affaire de Draveil. Villeneuve St.-Georges (1908)* (Paris: Julliard, coll. Archives, 1965).

Julliard, Jacques, 'La grève', *Formation 19 (69)* (septembre–octobre 1966).

Julliard, Jacques, 'Théorie syndicaliste révolutionnaire et pratique gréviste', *Le Mouvement Social*, n° 65 (octobre–décembre 1968), pp. 55–70.

Julliard, Jacques, *Fernand Pelloutier et les origines du syndicalisme d'action directe* (Paris: Seuil, 1971).

Kergoat, Danièle, *Bulledor ou l'histoire d'une mobilisation ouvrière* (Paris: Seuil, 1973).

Krasucki, Henri, *Syndicats et lutte de classes* (Paris: Editions sociales, 1969).

Krasucki, Henri, *Syndicats et socialisme* (Paris: Editions sociales, 1972).

Kriegel, Annie, *Aux origines du communisme française, 1914–1920. Contribution à l'histoire du mouvement ouvrier français* (Paris – The Hague: Mouton, 1964), 2 vols.

Kriegel, Annie, *La croissance de la CGT, 1918–1921*. Essai statistique (Paris – The Hague: Mouton, 1966).

Kriegel, Annie, *Les communistes français* (Paris: Seuil, coll. Politique, 1968).

Labi, Maurice, *La societé en révolution* (Paris: Editions syndicalistes, 1968).

Lagandre, Francois, *Rapport au Conseil économique et social sur la concentration France* (Paris: Conseil économique et social, 1966).

Lambert, Jean, *Le patron* (Paris: Bloud et Gay, 1969).

Lannier, *Le sous-emploi féminin dans quelques zones industrielles et portuaires*, Rapport CORDES, AFPA (1972).

Laroque, Pierre, 'Droits de l'homme, travail social et politique sociale, *Droit Social*, n° 12 (Décembre 1968).

Latournerie, Roger, *Le droit français de la grève* (Paris: Sirey, 1972).

Laubier, Patrick de, 'Esquisse d'une théorie du syndicalisme', *Sociologie du travail*, n° 4 (1968), pp. 362–92.

Lautman, Jacques, Jacob, Annie, 'Rôle du syndicalisme patronal et évolution économique' in Reynaud, Jean-Daniel (ed.), *Tendances et volontés de la société française* (Paris: Sédéis, 1966), pp. 268–84.

Lavau, Georges (ed.), *La planification comme processus de décision*, Cahiers de la fondation nationale des sciences politiques (Paris: A. Colin, 1965).

Lavorel, Lucien, 'Procédure Toutée et disparités sociales', *Droit Social* (novembre 1968) pp. 592–605.

Lavorel, Lucien, Mounier, A. 'Influence de la formation sur les types d'action de syndicats', *Projet 11*, (mai 1967), pp. 48–65.

Lebon, André, 'Les principaux accords salariaux signés en 1970 et 1971 dans les secteurs publics et nationalisés', *Droit social* (juillet 1971).

Leboucq, Philippe, *Les cadres* (Paris: C.R.C., Cahier 20, 1972).

Le Brun, Pierre, *Questions actuelles du syndicalisme* (Paris: Seuil, 1956).

Lecaillon, J., *Croissance et politique des revenus* (Paris: Cujas, 1964).

Lecaillon, J., *La politique des revenus* (Paris: Cujas, 1965).

Ledrut, Raymond, *Sociologie du chômage* (Paris: PUF, 1966).

Leenhardt, Jacques, 'La nouvelle classe ouvrière en grève', *Sociologie du Travail* n° 4 (1968), pp. 441–9.

Lefranc, Georges, *Le mouvement syndical. De la libération aux évènéments de mai–juin 68* (Paris: Editions Payot, 1969).

Lefranc, Georges, *Le syndicalisme en France* (Paris: PUF, Que sais-je, 1973).

Legoux, Yves, 'Le choix professionnel des techniciens de la chimie', *Sociologie du travail* n° 4 (1960), pp. 300–13.

Legoux, Yves, 'Formation et aspirations chez les techniciens de chimie et de l'électronique', *Cahiers de l'automation*, n° 4 (1962).

Legoux, Yves, *Du compagnon au technicien. L'école Diderot et l'évolution des qualifications 1873–1972* (Paris: Technique et vulgarisation, 1972).

Lesire-Ogrel, Hubert, *Le syndicat dans l'entreprise* (Paris: Seuil, 1967).

Lorant, Guy, Mandray, Noël, Anseime, Daniel, *Quatre grèves significatives* (Paris: Epi, 1972).

Loux, Françoise, *Le passé dans l'avenir, conduites économiques ouvrières en milieu rural* (Paris: Maisonneuve, Mémoires d'anthropologie française, 1974).

Lyon-Caen, Gerard, *Les salaires*, Tome 2 de Camerlynck, G. H., *Traité de Droit du Travail* (Paris: Dalloz, 1967).

Lyon-Caen, Gérard, 'La convention sociale de l'E.G.F. et le système français de relations professionnelles', *Droit Social* (avril 1970).

Lyon-Caen, Gérard (ed.), *La juridiction du travail en France*, *Droit Social*, n° Spécial (février 1974).

Lyon-Caen, Gérard, and Bonnetête, M. C., 'La réforme du licenciement a travers la loi du 3.7.73', *Droit Social* (novembre 1973), pp. 493–507.

Macpherson, W., 'Les conseils de prud'hommes. Une analyse et leur fonctionnement', *Droit Social* (1962).

Magniadas, Jean, Mouriaux, René, Piolot, Marc, *Les militants de la C.G.T. en formation syndicale* (Paris: Confédération Générale du Travail, 1972).

Maire, Edmond, *CFDT* (Paris: Epi, 1971).

Maire, Edmond, Julliard, Jacques, *La C.F.D.T. d'aujourd'hui* (Paris: Seuil, 1975).

Maire, Edmond, Piaget, Charles, *Lip 73. Combats* (Paris: Seuil, 1973).

Maitron, Jean, *Histoire du mouvement anarchiste en France, 1880–1914* (Paris: 2ème Éd. 1955; 1ère Éd.: 1951).

Mallet, Serge, *La nouvelle classe ouvrière* (Paris: Seuil, 2ème édition, 1969; 1ère édition, 1963).

Mallet, Serge, *Le pouvoir ouvrier* (Paris: Editions anthropos, 1971).

Malterre, André, *Les cadres et la réforme des entreprises* (Paris: Editions France-Empire 1969).

Malterre, André, *Positions et propositions de la C.G.C.* (Paris: CGC, octobre 1971).

Marchal, Jean, 'Un tournant pour le syndicalisme francais. La C.F.T.C. devient la C.F.D.T.', *Revue internationale du socialisme 2 (J)* (janvier–février 1965), pp. 94–112.

Massé, Pierre, *Rapport sur la politique des revenus établi à la suite de la conférence des revenus* (Paris: Documentation française, Rapports et monographies, 1964).

Maurice, Marc, 'L'évolution de la C.F.D.C.', *Sociologie du Travail 7 (1)* (janvier–mars 1965a), pp. 83–95.

Maurice, Marc, 'Déterminants du militantisme et projet syndical', *Sociologie du Travail*, n° 3 (1965b), pp. 254–72.

Maurice, Marc, *Les cadres et l'entreprise.* (Etude sociologique des rapports entre profession et organisation parmi les cadres, les ingénieurs et les techniciens de l'aéronautique) (Paris: ISST, 1967).

Maurice, Marc, 'Professionalisme et syndicalisme', *Sociologie du Travail*, n° 3 (1968), pp. 243–56.

Maurice, Marc, 'Les cadres et les relations professionnelles', *Droit Social* (avril 1969), pp. 241–5.

Maurice, Marc, *Le travail par equines–avantages économiques et coûts sociaux* (Genèva: BIT, 1971).

Maurice, Marc, 'Propos sur la sociologie des professions', *Sociologie du Travail* (1972), pp. 213–25.

Maurice, Marc, Arliaud, M., 'Une critique de la thèse de l'embourgeoisement de la nouvelle class ouvrière: the affluent worker', *Sociologie du Travail* (1970), pp. 74–86.

Maurice, Marc, Cornu, R., Garnier, J-C., *Les cadres en mai–juin 1968 dans la region d'Aix-Marseille* (Aix-en-Provence: LEST, Rapport CORDES, 1972).

Meignant, Alain, 'La formation dans les entreprises après la loi du 16 juillet 1971', *Sociologie du Travail* 1 (1973), pp. 45–53.

Melucci, Alberto, *Idéologies et pratiques patronales pendant l'industrialisation capitaliste: le cas de la France* (Paris: Ecole pratique des Hautes Etudes, 1974) (thèse de doctorat de 3ème cycle).

Meunier, Paul, 'Le syndicalisme des cadres en France', *Droit Social* (nov. 1970), pp. 506–15.

Meyers, Frédéric, 'Deux aspects du rôle des negotiations collectives en France', *Sociologie du Travail*, n° 1 (1965), pp. 1–33, n° 2, pp. 113–50.

Milhau, Jules, 'Indexation des salaires sur le coût de la vie', *Droit Social*, n° 7–8 (juillet–août 1969); n° 9–10 (septembre–octobre 1969).

Moller, Louis-Antoine, 'La mensualisation: bilan des accords professionnels signés à la fin de 1970', *Droit Social* (mars 1971).

Montmollin, Maurice de, 'Taylorisme et antiTaylorisme', *Sociologie du Travail*, n° 4 (1974), pp. 374–82.

Montuclard, Maurice, *La dynamique des comités d'entreprise* (Paris: CNRS, 1963).

Moscovici, Serge, *Reconversion industrielle et changements sociaux* (Paris: Armand Colin, Cahiers de la Fondation nationale des Sciences politiques, 1961).

Mothé, Daniel, *Militant chez Renault* (Paris: Seuil, 1965).

Mothé, Daniel, *Les O.S.* (Paris: Cerf, 1972).

Mothé, Daniel, *Le métiér de militant* (Paris: Seuil, 1973).

Mottez, Bernard (ed.), *Les travailleurs immigrés, Sociologie du Travail*, n° Spécial 3, (1972), pp. 257–368.

Mouriaux, Marie-Françoise, L'Emploi en France depuis 1945 (Paris: Armand Colin, Coll. U2, (1972).

Mouriaux, René, 'Transformations de la classe ouvrière et idéologies du changement', *Etudes* (mars 1973), pp. 337–46.

Naude, François, 'Réflexions à propos du projet de loi modifiant le droit de licenciement', *Droit Social* (mars 1973).

Naville, Pierre, *L'automation et le travail humain* (Paris: CNRS, 1961).

Naville, Pierre, *Vers l'automatisme social? Problèmes du travail et de l'automation* (Paris: Gallimard, 1963).

Naville, Pierre, Bardou Jean-Pierre, Brachet, Phillippe, Levy, Catherine, *L'Etat entrepreneur. Le cas de la Régie Renault* (Paris: Anthropos, 1971).

Oppenheim, Jean-Pierre, *La CFDT et la planification* (Paris: Téma-Action, 1973).

Parodi, Maurice, *Croissance économique et nivellement hiérarchique des salaires ouvriers* (Paris: Éd. Rivière, 1962).

Perrot, Michèle, *Les ouvriers en grève. France, 1871–1890* (Paris–The Hague, Mouton, 1974), 2 vols.

Perrot, Michèle, Commaille, Jacques, 'Elections professionnelles', *Le Mouvement Social*, n° 55 (avril–juin 1966), pp. 93–107.

Pesquet, Jacques, *Des Soviets à Saclay* (Paris: Maspéro, Cahiers Libres, 1968).

Prestat, Claude, *A case of autonomous groups* (Paris: Avril 1972).

Prost, Antonie, *La CGT à l'époque du Front Populaire. Essai de description numérique* (Paris: A. Colin, Cahiers de la Fondation Nationale de Sciences Politiques, 1962).

Ranger, Jean, Adam, Gérard, 'Les liens entre le PCF et la CGT, éléments d'un débat', *Revue Française de Sciences Politiques* (février 1969), pp. 182–7.

Reynaud, Jean-Daniel (ed.), *Formation et promotion dans l'entreprise, Sociologie du Travail*, n° Spécial (1963), 4, pp. 313–432.

Reynaud, Jean-Daniel, 'De la CFTC a la CFDT', *Droit Social* (mars 1965), pp. 199–201.

Reynaud, Jean-Daniel, 'The role of Trade Unions in national political economic, developed countries of Europe', in Barkin, Solomon, Dymond, William Kassalow, Everett M., Meyers, Frederic, Myers, Charles A., *International Labor* (New York: Harper, Industrial Relations Research Association, 1967), pp. 33–61

Reynaud, Jean-Daniel, L'avenir des relations professionnelles en Europe occidentale: perspectives et hypotheses', *Bulletin de l'Institut International d'Etudes sociales*, 4 (fev. 1968), pp. 76–106.

Reynaud, Jean-Daniel, 'La convention sociale de la Siderurgie lorraine', *Droit Social* (avril 1969).

Reynaud, Jean-Daniel, 'La nouvelle classe ouvrière, la technologie et l'histoire', *Revue Française de Sciences politiques, 22*, 3 (juin 1972), pp. 529–42.

Reynaud, Jean-Daniel, 'Les relations professionnelles et la négociation du changement', *Bulletin de l'Institut International d'Etudes sociales*, n° 9 (1972), pp. 318.

Reynaud, Jean-Daniel, 'Tout le pouvoir au peuple, ou de la polyarchie à la pléistocratie', in *Une nouvelle civilisation? Homage à Georges Friedmann* (Paris, Gallimard, 1973), pp. 76–92.

Reynaud, Jean-Daniel, 'Trade Unions and political parties in France. Some recent trends', *Industrial and Labor Relations Review, 28*, (jan. 1975), pp. 208–22.

Reynaud, Jean-Daniel, *Les syndicats en France* (Paris: Seuil, nouv. ed. 1975, 2 vols.

Reynaud, Jean-Daniel, Bernoux, Philippe, Lavorel, Lucien, 'Les syndicats ouvriers et leurs politiques des salaires', *Revue Française du Travail* (1966a), 3, pp. 3–28.

Reynaud, Jean-Daniel, Bernoux, Philippe, Lavorel, Lucien, 'Organisation syndicale, idéologie et politique des salaires', *Sociologie du Travail* (1966b), 4, pp. 368–88.

Reynaud, Jean-Daniel, Bernoux, Philippe, Lavorel, Lucien, *Les syndicats ouvriers et leurs politiques des salaires* (Paris: ISST, 1966c).

Reynaud, Jean-Daniel, Sassa, Sami, Dassa, Josette, Maclouf, Pierre, *Mai–Juin 1968 et le système français des relations professionnelles* (Paris: CORDES-CNAM, 1972).

Reynaud, Jean-Daniel, Dassa, Sami, Dassa, Josette, Maclouf, Pierre, 'Les événéments de mai-juin 1968 et le systeme français des relations profession-nelles', *Sociologie du Travail*, n° 1 (1971), pp. 73–97; n° 2, pp. 191–209.

Reynaud, Roger, 'Les nouvelles stratégies syndicales' in *Le travail et les travailleurs dans la société contemporaine* (Lyon: Chronique sociale de France, (1965), 51ème semaine sociale, 1964, Lyon), 422 p., pp. 335–350.

Ribettes-Tilhet, Jeanne, 'La mensualisation', *Droit Social* (juin 1970).

Rioux, Lucien, *Où en est le syndicalisme?* (Paris: Buchet-Chastel, 1960).

Rioux, Lucien, *Clefs pour le syndicalisme* (Paris: Seghers, 1972).

Rivero, Jean, 'Historique des relations entre les syndicats et l'Etat', *Droit Social* (mars 1965), pp. 166–73.

Rochecorbon, G., 'Feu la procédure Toutée?' *Droit Social* (nov. 1968), pp. 578–91.

Rolle, Pierre, 'Qualités de travail et hiérarchie des qualifications', *Sociologie du Travail* (1973), 2 pp. 157–75.

Roustang, G., 'Proportion des cadres supérieurs dans le total des salariés et économie d'échelle', *Revue Économique*, XX (sept. 1969), pp. 888–93.

Roustang, Guy, 'La formation des salaires des cadres', *Revue Économique*, 22, 2 (mars 1971), pp. 247–70.

Roustang, Guy, 'Prospective du travail', *Prospective et société*, La Documentation Française (1972), pp. 87–94.

Roustang, Guy, 'Travail et Société', *Economie et Humanisme* (sept.–oct. 1973), pp. 15–26.

Roustang, Guy, 'Conditions de travail et changement social', *Connexions* (1974).

Roustang, G., 'Méthode d'analyse des conditions de travail', ouvr. collectif sur *La charge de travail de l'opérateur vieillissant* (Paris: Éd. Naturalia et Biologia, 1974).

Saglio, Jean, 'La matiére et les signes: les ouvriers face au savoir', *Sociologie du Travail* (1972), 4, pp. 437–54.

Sainsaulieu, Renaud, 'Pouvoirs et stratégies de groupes ouvriers dans l'atelier', *Sociologie du Travail* (1965), 2, pp. 162–74.

Sainsaulieu, Renaud, *Les relations de travail à l'usine* (Paris: Ed. d'Organisation, coll. Sociologie des organisations, 1972).

Sales, Hubert, *Les relations industrielles dans l'imprimerie française* (Paris: Cujas, 1967).

Savatier, Jean, 'La Révolution" de mai et le droit du travail', *Droit Social* juillet–août 1968).

Scardigli, Victor, *Pratiques contractuelles et conflits du travail. Société française et conflits sociaux* (Paris: CREDOC, 1973a).

Scardigli, Victor, *Pratiques contractuelles et conflits du travail. Synthèse: le système francais de relations professionnelles. Bilan et perspectives* (Paris: CREDOC, 1973b).

Schifres, Michel, *La CFDT des militants* (Paris: Stock, 1972).

Segrestin, Denis, *La CGT et les métiers. La dimension professionnelle de l'action syndicale vue à travers le cas des marins et des verriers* (Paris: Fondation nationale des Sciences Politiques, 1974).

Segrestin, Denis, 'Du syndicalisme de metier au syndicalisme de classe: pour une sociologie de la CGT', *Sociologie du Travail*, 2 (1975), pp. 152–73.

Seguy, Georges, *Le mai de la CGT* (Paris: Julliard, 1972).

Seguy, Georges, *Lutter* (Paris: Stock, 1975).

Sellier, François, *Stratégie de la lutte sociale en France* (Paris: Editions ouvrières, 1961).

Sellier, François, *Dynamique des besoins sociaux* (Paris: Editions ouvrières, 1970).

Sellier, François, 'L'évolution des négociations collectives dans la sidérurgie et la métallurgie en France (1950–1969), *Droit Social* (sept.–oct. 1970).

Sellier, François, Tiano, André, *Economie du travail* (Paris: PUF, Coll. Thémis, 1962).

Sellier, François *et al.*, *La hiérarchie d'encadrement dans l'entreprise: recherche d'un effet societal* (Aix-en-Provence: CORDES, 1973).

Silvestre, Jean-Jacques, 'Le marché du travail', *Encyclopedia universalis*, tome 1, pp. 483–8.

Silvestre, Jean-Jacques, 'Présentation théorique sur les disparités de salaires', *Revue Économique, 22*, 2 (mars 1971), pp. 193–213.

Silvestre, Jean-Jacques, 'La dynamique des salaires nominaux en France', *Revue Économique, 22*, 3 (mai 1971), pp. 431–49.

Silvestre, J.-J., *Les salaires dans l'industrie française* Paris: Bordas, coll. Etudes économiques, 1973).

Silvestre, J.-J., Benhayoun, R., 'Relations salaires–chômage; recherche d'un effet régional', *Economie appliquée* (1974).

Sinay, Hélène, *La Grève*, tome 6 de Camerlynck, G. H., *Traité de Droit du Travail* (Paris: Dalloz, 1966).

Sinay, Hélène, *Exercise des libertés syndicales dans les entreprises* (Strasbourg: CORDES, Institut du Travail,   ).

Spitaels, Guy (ed.), *Les conflits sociaux en Europe* (Verviers: Marabout, 1971).

Spyropoulos, G., *L'administration des oeuvres sociales par les comités d'entreprise* (Paris: Librairie générale de Droit et de jurisprudence, 1961).

Stockel-Fizaine, F., 'Deux analyses du marché du travail urbain en France et aux Etats-Unis. Méthodes et interprétations théoriques', *Revue Économique, 25*, 1 (janvier 1974), pp. 98–104.

Sudreau, Pierre, *La réforme de l'entreprise. Rapport du comité présidé par Pierre Sudreau* (Paris: Union générale d'Editions, 1975).

Szokoloczy-Syllaga, Janos, *Les organisations professionnelles françaises et le Marché commun* (Paris: Armand Colin, Cahiers de la Fondation nationale des Sciences politiques, n° 133, 1965).

Talbo, J.-PH. (ed.), *La grève à Flins* (Paris: Maspéro, 1968).

Tchobanian, R., *Réflexions sur l'analyse économique des conditions de travail* (Lest, 1972).

Testaniere, J., *Mobilité sociale et niveau d'éducation. La réconversion du bassin Minier Nord–Pas de Calais*, DGRST (Paris: CSE, 1972).

Tiano, André, *L'action syndicale ouvrière et la théorie économique du salaire* (Paris: Génin, 1957).

Tiano, André, 'L'action des syndicats ouvriers. Etat des travaux', *Revue Française de Sciences Politiques*, 10, 4 (decembre 1960), pp. 912–30.

Touraine, Alain, *L'evolution du travail ouvrier aux usines Renault* (Paris: CNRS, 1955).

Touraine, Alain, 'Contribution à la sociologie du mouvement ouvrier: le syndicalisme de contrôle', *Cahiers internationaux de sociologie 28* (janvier–juin 1960), pp. 57–88.

Touraine, Alain, *La conscience ouvrière* (Paris: Seuil, 1966).

Touraine, Alain, *Le mouvement de mai ou le communisme utopique* (Paris:

Seuil, 1968) (2ème édition réduite, et enrichie d'une postface: *Le communisme utopique. Le mouvement de mai 1968*, Paris, Seuil, coll. Politique, 1972).

Touraine, Alain, *La société post-industrielle. Naissance d'une société* (Paris: Denoël, Médiations, 1969).

Touraine, Alain, 'Les nouveaux conflits sociaux', *Sociologie du Travail*, n° 1 (1975), pp. 1–17.

Touraine, Alain, Ragazzi, O., *Ouvriers d'origine agricole* (Paris: Seuil, (1961).

Touraine, Alain, Durand, Claude, Pecaut, Daniel, Willener, Alfred, *Les travailleurs et les changements techniques* (Paris: OECD, 1965).

Toutée, 'Mission sur l'amélioration des procédures de discussion des salaires dans le secteur public, Paris', *La Documentation Française* (1964).

Trempé, Rolande, *Les Mineurs de Carmaux* (Paris: Éd. ouvrières, 1971), 2 vols.

Trentin, Bruno, 'Tendances actuelles de la lutte de classes et problèmes du mouvement syndical face aux développements récents du capitalisme européen', *Les Temps Modernes* (février 1967) pp. 1389–430.

Tripier, Maryse, 'La revendication des "Conseils d'unité" au Commissariat à l'Energie Atomique, en mai–juin 1968. Essai d'interprétation', *Revue Française de Sociologie* (juillet–septembre 1970), pp. 351–67.

Van Bockstaele, Maria, Schein P., 'Limites des négociations et négociation des limites', *Sociologie du Travail* (1971) 1, pp. 1–24.

Vatier, Raymond, *Développement de l'entreprise. Promotion des hommes* (Paris: Éd. de l'Entreprise moderne, 1960).

Verdier, Jean-Maurice, *Syndicats*, tome 5 de Camerlynck G. H., *Traité de Droit du Travail* (Paris: Dalloz, 1966).

Verdier, Jean-Maurice, Langlois Philippe, 'Aux confins de la théorie des sources du droit, une relation nouvelle entre la loi et l'accord collectif', *Dalloz Sirey*, 39ème cahier (1972), pp. 253–260.

Vidal, Daniel, *Changements industriels et productivité. Crise et décentralisation à Reims* (Paris–The Hague: Mouton, 1967).

Vidal, Daniel, *Essai sur l'idéologie; le cas particulier des idéologies syndicales* (Paris: Anthropos, 1971).

Vignaux, Paul, 'La CFDT: Du syndicalisme chrétien au "gauchissement"', *Contrepoint*, n° 9 (1973).

Villiers, Georges, 'Forces patronales' *Encyclopédie Française*, tome 9, *L'Univers économique et social* (Paris: Societé nouvelle de l'Encyclopédie Française, 1960), pp. 9.62.2–9.62.3.

Vincens, Jean, *La prévision de l'emploi* (Paris: PUF, coll. sup., 1970).

Vincens, Jean, 'Les prévisions par profession', *Revue économique, 20*, 4 (juillet 1969), pp. 531–600.

Voisset, Michele, 'Concertation et contractualisation dans la fonction publique', *Droit Social* (sept.–oct. 1970).

Vuillod-Mounier, Anne, *La formation des militants dans les syndicats ouvriers: son rôle et son influence dans l'activité syndicale* (Paris: Ecole pratique des Hautes Etudes, 1969).

Weiss, Dimitri, *Relations Industrielles* (Paris: Sirey, 1973).

Weiss, Dimitri, *Les relations du travail. Employeurs, personnel, syndicats, Etat* (Dunce: Dunod-Entreprise, 1974).

Werner, Pascale, 'Lip: les femmes dans la lutte des classes', *Les Temps Modernes* (juillet 1974).

Willener Alfred, *Autonomie et intégration des cadres dans l'entreprise* (Paris: DGRST, 1972).

Willener A., Benguigui G., Cajdos C., *Les cadres en mouvement* (Fondation Royaumont, Éd. de l'Epi, 1969).

Wisner, Alain *et al.*, *Conséquences du travail répétitif sous cadence sur la santé des travailleurs et les accidents*, rapport n° 29 (mars 1972).

Wisner, Alain, 'Contenu des tâches et charge de travail', *Sociologie du Travail* (1974), 4, pp. 339–57.

8 The Japanese System of Industrial Relations

Mikio Sumiya

Theory and Methodology in Industrial Relations Research

When Japan was less developed, research in labour economics was one of the many disciplines heavily influenced by ideas from the advanced nations. However, Japan reacted to these ideas in a particular way.

The German school of social policy science was introduced into Japan at the end of the nineteenth century when the country first faced the need to analyse and solve its labour problems. At that time, Japanese scholars, following the German example, organized the Society for the Study of Social Policy. Since then, in Japanese universities, labour problems have been researched and taught within the discipline of social policy.

The history of the Society for the Study of Social Policy is at the same time a history of research in labour problems in Japan. The society was extremely active prior to 1920. In the twenties, however, it suddenly lost its impetus and ceased to function. The society was reorganized in 1950, and it now operates as an academic society for labour studies.

The dissolution of the society in the twenties took place because young scholars after the First World War came under the influence of socialism, which created a fundamental gap in philosophy between them and the older generation. The society's reorganization after the Second World War was a result of the vigorous debate among Marxists over the meaning of social policy. A Marxist reformation of 'social policy' had begun during the thirties and the necessary tools and theories were developed to analyse labour problems. Though there had been very severe political repression, after the end of the war, pressure against research in the social sciences was removed.

In the past thirty years, research on social policy in Japan has

287

undergone the following two changes. Firstly, because of the great influence of Marxist economics, it has been very difficult to debate social policy without involving the pros and cons of Marxism. Secondly, up until the twenties, social policy included problems such as the protection of the small farmer, or the problems of the small businessman. However, these problems were picked up by agricultural and industrial economics and the discipline of social policy focused solely on research involving employed labour. Even today in Japanese universities, research in labour problems goes by the name of social policy.

The leading influence on research in labour problems in Japan was Kazuo Ohkochi. Ohkochi argued that capitalism contains an incentive to reduce labour costs and, therefore, working conditions. If this incentive becomes excessive it will not be possible for the economy to maintain its momentum because of the shortage of a healthy labour force. Accordingly, social policy involves preservation and cultivation of the labour force and is the responsibility of 'total capital' (the economy as a whole) (Ohkochi, 1940). The theory was influential during the wartime period in protecting the economic livelihood of workers; i.e. it was concluded that if workers were overworked and their livelihood reduced greatly, their physical strength would suffer, their productivity would decline, and as a result the country's defences would be endangered.

Because of Ohkochi's theory, the field of social policy was able to maintain scientific objectivity even during the period of militarism in Japan. After the war, this influence remained important. However, as Ohkochi explained the need for social policy from the viewpoint of the reproduction of capital, when workers began to demand the improvement of labour conditions (at the start of the labour movement) as a principle in itself, the centre of debate turned to how to theoretically evaluate this movement in relation to social policy. Until about 1955, the question of the essential meaning of social policy absorbed most of the researchers in lively debate (Kishimoto, 1953). Gradually this discussion isolated itself from labour problems and drifted in an abstract direction (JFEA, 1975).

The movement toward using the theories of labour economics after 1955 was occasioned by criticism of this state of affairs. The call for a change in the state of the discipline tended to direct research specifically to labour problems themselves, not to policy problems, though recognizing the significance of research in social policy (Sumiya, 1954).

Behind this change in theory and methodology lay two new trends.

One was the development of the field survey. In prewar days, research was suppressed, so that field surveys were difficult to carry out unless one was in an institution associated with the government. After the war these restrictions were lifted, but surveys were prohibitively expensive. Fortunately, this problem was overcome to some extent by the Institute for the Study of Social Sciences at Tokyo University, where Kazuo Ohkochi was organizing research. With the cooperation of scholars outside Tokyo University, the Institute carried out surveys and published the results, starting in 1947 with a labour market study.[1]

All of the surveys up until 1955 contained the common hypothesis that there was an extremely traditional relationship between labour and management in Japan. The surveys gave evidence of this traditional relationship and attempted to examine the possibility of a change to a modernized labour–management relationship. The theme of the first survey on labour unions concerned the democratization of the unions (Tokyo Daigaku Skk, 1950).

An article which analysed the social character of Japanese workers divided the labour force into three social groups—(1) migrant workers from agriculture, (2) workers dividing their time between farm and industry, and (3) craftsmen, considering the first two to link the traditional farm village with the reproduction of labour, and the last to be at the root of a traditional social status-oriented labour–management relationship. In this sense it concluded that the labour force still had not lost its feudal characteristics (Sumiya, 1951). This point became the basis for further debate.

The way in which Japan's labour force was categorized was heavily influenced by Ohkochi's theory about migrant workers. Since the prewar days, there have been two views concerning how best to characterize capitalism in Japan. One group considered it to be part feudal, while the other group claimed it to be fundamentally modernized. Ohkochi, who supported the former dominant view stressed that one should consider Japanese workers as migrant workers who were yet to be completely separated from the traditional farm village, and that such a social characteristic of these workers corresponded to semi-feudal capitalism (Ohkochi, 1950). The field surveys of labour unions and the labour market up until 1955 were all based on this theoretical hypothesis to varying degrees. Also, as I will mention later, the concepts of the enterprise union and the *nenkō* system were borne out and developed in relation to this context.

Research on labour unions never suffered from a lack of analytic tools. From before the war the works of Sidney and Beatrice Webb and

G. D. H. Cole had been introduced into Japan, and the Marxist theories on labour unions had been translated into Japanese. The situation was different, however, for research on the labour market. Understanding among the researchers seemed to be rather ambiguous, even in 1952 and 1953 when labour market surveys were being taken.

The term 'labour market' first came into use as the fundamental concept in labour research after labour economics was introduced from the United States following the Second World War. It was difficult to incorporate labour economics into any academic discipline since in Japan research in labour problems always had taken the form of social policy. However, labour economics found acceptance among the bureaucracy of the Ministry of Labour, the reason being that it was incorporated into Japan's labour administration by the United States occupation forces. In 1949, the Ministry of Labour began to publish the yearly 'Labour White Paper' under the title of 'An Analysis of the Labour Economy'.[2] In this publication the heading 'labour market' appears, but 'labour market' was used to mean the market for employed labour and, therefore, activities of the Job Stabilization Board were analysed.

The second new trend in the field of industrial relations has been the introduction of labour studies. Sumiya approached the theories of labour economics by borrowing and utilizing them from the viewpoint of the reproduction of the wage labour force (Sumiya, 1954). The surveys mentioned above, as well as the writings of Ujihara (1953, 1954a, b), were powerful sources of support for what was called 'the release of labour research from social policy'. This met with strong reaction from the supporters of social policy because the new approach criticized the traditional methods and tools of analysis, and the labour economics which it introduced was considered as a vulgar Americanization of social science (Kishimoto, 1955).

It is rather questionable to wnat extent the disciplines of labour economics and industrial relations have become recognized in Japan since that time. But the analytical tools exist, and this chapter presents the results of research in Japan on the labour market, wages, industrial relations, and labour history, in that order, since 1955.[3]

One continuing serious barrier for foreigners who would like to study the Japanese industrial relations system is that almost all detailed studies are in Japanese. Several excellent overviews by American and European scholars exist, however, and a recent survey by Japanese scholars (written in English) analyses the basic characteristics of Japanese industrial relations, covering the whole field from historical development, legal framework, labour market, wages, and labour unions to social security systems (Ohkochi, Karsh, and Levine (eds.), 1973).

Labour Market Analysis

Development of Labour Market Theory

Since industrial relations has been approached through the discipline of social policy, factory legislation and social insurance have been the centre of research. Even though unemployment and concealed unemployment were serious problems for Japanese society, study of the labour market was delayed. There was no clear understanding among scholars as to what the question of 'labour market' meant. Even in the White Paper on Labour published after 1949 by the Ministry of Labour, the only topic covered under the heading of 'labour market' was, for several years, the number of job applications and job vacancies as reported by the government.

In the early 1950s research on the labour market began as a search to find the historical roots of enterprise unionism. However, the emphasis was placed on exposing the feudal character of Japan's labour market (Shakaieisaku Gakkai, 1955).

Subsequently, as the features of Japan's labour market were brought out into the open, the need to crystalize the theoretical framework of the labour market became evident. This need was answered by the essays of Shojiro Ujihara and Eiichi Eguchi (Ujihara, 1957a; Eguchi, 1957). Ujihara's essay criticized the fact that the research up until that time, both on wage labour, and on labour unions, was discussed without any relation to the labour market. He defined the labour market from a macro point of view as a mechanism for the transactions involving the distribution of the labour force. Eguchi's essay described the micro-labour market through the development of a rather simple model, and defined the fundamental relations in the labour market.

Problems of Overpopulation

Research on the labour market evolved ahead of the development of new theoretical tools and centred around identifying the Japanese characteristics of workers and the labour market. During the 1950s the 'dekasegi' (workers temporarily away from home) theory of Ohkochi had a decisive influence on this research. According to Ohkochi, Japanese agriculture is feudalistic and the agrarian population is still tied to rural villages: the labour force is made up of sons and daughters of farm families who leave the village in search of work and come back when they are needed at home (Ohkochi, 1950, 1952a).

In opposition to the 'dekasegi' theory is the idea that Japan's labour force is best understood by studying the circumstances of workers dividing their time between farm and industry, a phenomenon that has accompanied the development of capitalism (Takagi, 1953). In both cases, however, the labour market is examined from the point of view of labour supply.

This tendency was also seen consistently in the studies on latent overpopulation, which has been the greatest problem in the labour market since the Second World War. Research was conducted on the existence of excess population in farm villages and the flow of this population to the cities. Conceptions of overpopulation were based upon such theories as the optimum theory of population (Nōson Jinkō-Mondai Kenkyukai, 1952), or were adaptations of Joan Robinson's theory of disguised unemployment (Tobata, 1956), but the most popular ideas were those based upon the Marxist relative overpopulation theory (Ohuchi, 1947; Takagi, 1959). All of these ideas, however, have in common the notion that rural villages were pools of excess population, and the out flow corresponded to the increase and decrease in employment.

Criticism of this viewpoint developed from two directions. First the impact of technological innovation led to the view that demand must be taken into consideration in research on the labour market. Studies connecting the approach from the agricultural viewpoint and that from labour demand analyses appeared. The work which reviewed the research in this field attempted to resolve this problem logically from a Marxist position, and at the same time demonstrate this point historically (Kobayashi, 1961).

The other criticism denied the hypothesis that rural villages had become pools for excess population. This view, based on past data, claimed that there was very little change in the population of rural villages, asserting that the excess population flowed out to the cities regularly (Namiki, 1956, 1957).

On the other hand, when it was realized that the excess population was settling in the cities, research began on urban poverty. These studies, while keeping in mind the research of sociologists on social stratification, analysed the class structure of the poor based on original field surveys (Ujihara *et al.*, 1956, 1959). However, the focus here was on poverty rather than on labour markets.

The conflict between the 'dekasegi' theory and Namiki's conception was mediated when, from a labour market viewpoint, the poverty class of the cities was described as a stratum of workers doing minor, miscellaneous jobs. It was made clear that this stratum, rather than the farm families, was the pool of excess labour, which increased and decreased with fluctuations in business activity (Sumiya, 1964).

Lifetime Employment

The point of view that lifetime employment ('*nenkō*') is Japan's fundamental employment custom was developed by J. C. Abegglen. Abegglen believes that it is possible to explain lifetime employment in terms of Japan's traditional social relationship of loyalty toward one's employer (Abegglen, 1958).

Among Japanese scholars as well, when the *nenkō* system became apparent, it was recognized that Japanese employees worked in the same work-place generally for long periods of time. Shōjiro Ujihara showed that key workers with long tenure were the mainstay in maintaining discipline in the work-place, and he also formalized the notion that the labour market of big industry was closed within each firm (Ujihara, 1953, 1954a). In big business, where enterprise labour markets are closed, lifetime employment was theoretically inevitable.

Nevertheless, Ujihara did not go so far as to say that lifetime employment was an essential part of Japan's labour market. Surely, this was because he was not able to shake off completely the influence of the theory concerning the dekasegi labourers.

However, research on lifetime employment was mainly developed by managerial scientists and sociologists who, through the discussion based upon the loyalty of workers toward their employers, coupled lifetime employment with 'Kazoku-Shugi' of management or the management principle of 'firm as family' (Mori, 1961; Matsushima, 1962). In particular, the influence that Japan's family system exerted upon labour management was precisely stipulated from a sociological viewpoint. This influence was analysed persuasively through actual examination of the process of the development of lifetime employment (Hazama, 1964). However, recently a new hypothesis has appeared that life-time employment was a result of 'position improvement' behaviour rather than simply loyalty (Mannari and Marsh, 1973).

There has also been criticism from economists concerning the coupling of lifetime employment with the traditional relationship of loyalty. However, there is general agreement that the *nenkō* system has not existed traditionally in Japan, but developed in the process of industrialization. The generally accepted theory on this issue states that it was firmly established in the 1920s (Sumiya, 1959; Ohkochi, 1963; Hazama, 1964). There is also a minority opinion that lifetime employment developed during the Second World War as a result of labour legislation (Magota, 1965).

Finally, Marxist economics tries to explain lifetime employment by placing the focus on large monopolistic industry, and its desire to control the labour supply by dividing the labour market into enterprise segments (Kishimoto, 1964).

The Dual Structure of the Labour Market

The pattern of lifetime employment first established among big business is less prevalent in small and medium businesses, where the market is more open. In addition, there are large differences in wages and labour conditions between large firms and smaller firms. For these reasons, these two labour pools and two exclusive labour markets exist, leading to dualism of the labour market. The first person to draw up a model of this dualism was Shojiro Ujihara. This theory was first accepted among labour economists (Ohkochi and Sumiya (eds.), 1955) and it became widely held after 1957, when the Economic White Paper (1957) endorsed a dualist view of the Japanese economy.

Research on the quite different labour market of small- and medium-sized industry lagged behind the progress made in studies of lifetime employment. At first, the labour force of small and medium business was analysed in relation to the feudal aspects of wage labour (Matsumoto, 1955). In general research centred on demonstrating the validity of the hypothesis which claimed that low wages and poor living conditions were an inevitable outgrowth of the huge supply of labour from the excess agrarian population (Ohara Shakai Mondai Kenkyujo, 1960). The supply and demand for labourers in small and medium business was examined by Takanashi in relation to the findings on the labour market mentioned above (Takanashi, 1967b).

The dual structure of the labour market is far more visible in the contrast between permanent workers and temporary workers than between the workers of big and small industry. As the length of service of workers in the big firm became longer in the 1920s, employment became unresponsive to changes in business conditions. Thus temporary workers were employed as a means of regulating the level of employment (Sumiya, 1964). Temporary workers disappeared during the wartime economy, and reappeared during the Korean War and thereafter. The problem of temporary workers first caught the attention of labour law scholars over the question of whether labour contracts could also be applied to this kind of worker (Minemura, 1952). Subsequently, the Hokkaido-ritsu Institute of Labour Science associated the temporary workers with the controversy over Japan's labour feudalism, saying that the postwar temporary workers were a result of the dissolution of the work gangs (which had been previously preserved by the feudal labour supply mechanism) and the rehiring of workers directly by industry. Poor wages and working conditions were emphasized as more important than employment instability (Hokkaido-ritsu Rodo-kagaku Kenkyujo, 1956).

The economic growth and technological change occurring after 1955 had a major effect on the temporary workers. One view stated that since economic growth permitted continuous rehiring and the promotion of at least a part of the temporary workers, the role of providing a buffer to changes in economic conditions became less important. Rather, it had become a system, made possible through technological change, where unskilled and semi-skilled labour could be employed at low wages (Sumiya, 1963b, 1964). The other view stresses the importance of the regulation of employment through temporary workers, the prior dominant view. Proponents of this view, by dividing the temporary workers into groups according to their function within the firm, discovered that a large majority of temporary workers were in lower level jobs. Here the existence of competition and selection, and of adjustments in supply and demand, were emphasized (Kobayashi, 1966; Koike, 1966; Yamamoto, 1967).

Tokyo University's Institute for the Study of Social Sciences published an excellent analysis, based on a field survey, of temporary workers and two other groups similar to them: Shagaiko, the skilled workers supplied by subcontractors and the day labourers who obtain work mainly through the Employment Stabilization Office (Tokyo Daigaku Shakai-kagaku Kenkyujo, 1960–69; Ujihara *et al.*, 1962).

In addition, there was substantial research in prewar Japan, when textiles was the main industry, concerning the employment of young female workers. While the role of female workers has become less important in the postwar era, it is unreasonable to say that 'the development of the economics of female labour is just beginning' (Sekiya, 1966). This brings to mind the fact that in large industry female workers are placed outside the framework of lifetime employment and the *nenko* system, and that there are large wage differentials between male and female workers. The debate over equal work, equal pay is rather vigorous.

Recently following the influence of United States research into female labour force participation, econometric research on the Japanese female labour force has begun (Sano, 1972).

Technological Change and the Labour Market

Thus far only research from the viewpoint of the labour supply has been considered. The technological changes that began around 1955 gave stimulus to the idea that consideration of labour *demand* was also necessary. Masumi Tsuda, using a field survey, analysed the influence of technological change in the labour market. Building on Ujihara's achievements, he placed his focus on the changes in the *nenko* system (Tsuda, 1959). Criticizing Tsuda for his emphasis on labour management, a field survey published by another group gave its main concern to the regulations of labour unions on job status and promotion (Meijidaigaku Shakaikagaku Kenkyujo, 1961).

A field survey by the Jinbun Kagakukai on the automobile and chemical industries further expanded research to include analysis of the influence that process standardization had on the internal and external labour markets (Jinbun Kagakukai, 1963). The study also examined the increased use of temporary workers, their promotion to permanent positions, and new methods of accumulating work experience in the internal labour market, as well as the reformation of the *nenko* system.

A field survey of construction workers concluded that as a result of technological change (1) occupations and labour administration were changing; (2) separate labour markets were developing among the divisions of skilled labour; and (3) in the unskilled labour market, the role of the Employment Stabilization Office was extremely important (Jinbun Kagakukai, 1958).

In Europe and the United States, unemployment and the need caused by technological change to retrain older, skilled workers created social tension. In Japan, it was not a serious problem because of the tradition of lifetime employment. Employees were retrained by their own firms and assigned to new jobs rather than being discharged (Arima, 1961).

Rapid Economic Growth and the Labour Market

Japan has been burdened with large disguised unemployment in the rural villages and in the cities. Thus, there has always existed an over-supply of labour, and the low wages resulting from this over-supply are an important problem.

Since 1955, especially when 'rationalization' and technological change were major issues, scholars were theoretically concerned over displacement as a source of unemployment. Labour unions, fearing dismissals and a worsening of wages and labour conditions, resolutely opposed rationalization.

New investment which stimulated 'rationalization', however, more than compensated for the diminishing of employment by technological change, and from 1955, the employed labour force increased by almost one million every year.

The new labour force was filled mainly by the outflow of labour from the rural villages, including the eldest sons who were to be successors on the farms. Later, the farmers themselves left, leaving the farm work to the machinery and farm wives. Econometric inquiry focused mainly on analysing shifts in labour supply. The conclusions were that the transfer of labour power from the rural villages to the cities was promoted by improved wages and labour conditions, and that this had a positive effect on the incomes of self-employed businesses (Umemura, 1961, 1971).

After 1960, the shortage of labour became more apparent, and in small and medium enterprises, where wages and labour conditions were poor, the shortage became particularly severe. Small- and medium-size businesses thus had to improve wages and working conditions in order to be able to compete with large business in the labour market.

In spite of these wage increases, the flow of labour from small- and medium-sized business to large business increased, which had been more or less unheard of before that time. The gradual disappearance of the dual structure in the labour market was described in the Labour White Paper.

In contrast to these optimistic viewpoints, others have pointed out that there were many cases, as in coal and other industries, where industry was declining under technological change and that the number of poverty-stricken workers had increased (Kyushu Keizai-chosa Kyokai, 1964). However, a refutation which gained strong support appeared. It stated that as a result of the *nenkō* system, it was the low-wage, young workers who were in short supply, while the middle- and upper-aged workers were, as before, in surplus (Sumiya, 1964).

In contrast to these institutional studies, an econometric study attempted to demonstrate (using the Lewis model) that the shortage of labour was a shift from the unlimited supply of labour to the limited (Minami, 1970).

Wages

Wage Level

From before the war, the dominant view among Japanese scholars was that the huge surplus labour force pushed wages down, and also that this labour force was forced from the small, high-rent, tenant farms to the industrial labour market to supplement the family budget.[4]

After the war, Ohkochi's 'dekasegi' theory restated this theme in concrete terms. Ohkochi considered the low Japanese wage level to be a result of wages that were based on the actual cost of living for single workers (Ohkochi, 1952b). Later, a critic of this theory modified it to say that it was the abundance of half-farm, half-industrial labourers, that depressed the wage level (Takagi, 1953).

Ujihara refined this theory and had a great influence on later research. He argued that the market for young inexperienced workers determined the wage floor. In equilibrium, rural and industrial wage differences reflected costs of relocation from rural to urban areas. Ujihara then argued that farm work provided additional non-cash income; non-farm workers could not survive on earned wages alone. Dormitories and other welfare facilities of industry were subsidizing the wage-earners, he concluded (Ujihara, 1954b). Later on, there was additional and more concrete research on the price of labour from the farm family. Umemura, using the theory of marginal productivity, maintained that wages were determined by the equilibrium between the marginal productivities of industrial and farm labour. He assumed that the marginal productivity of farm labour could be represented by the farm day-labour wage. Comparing this wage to the industrial wage, he noted that the difference stood for the 'lubricating oil' used for the movement of labour from farming to industry. He also examined the long-range change in the wage level, and produced a wage-level index (Umemura, 1961). Kenichi Kobayashi traced historically the relationship between farmers and workers and changes in wages, and formalized his analysis with empirical evidence (Kobayashi, 1961).

Sumiya criticized the view that wage level was determined in relation to the supply price of labour from farm families, and argued that the supply of labour has become increasingly greater from the urban districts than from farms since around 1930 and that the structure of the labour supply mechanisms should be studied. He analysed the structure of urban labour markets (Sumiya, 1964).

Other research has elaborated on the supply price of urban labour in relation to private, individual business owners (Ozaki, 1960), and with day labourers (Kagoyama, 1959). Also noteworthy is the survey on day labourers which stressed that their wage level determines the quantity and the quality of labour supply from self-employed businesses (Ujihara, Eguchi, and Yamazaki, 1962, 1963).

There was also a widespread movement to explain Japan's low wage level by Marx's law of impoverishment. This interpretation was debated considerably around 1955. With further economic development, the debate was cut off, leaving the discussion incomplete (Kishimoto, 1955; Shimoyama, 1966).

The Internal Wage Structure and the Nenkō Wage System

The *nenkō* wage system existed in Japan prior to the Second World War. However, the recognition that the *nenkō* system pertains to workers in large enterprises is rather new, having been suggested by Ujihara after the war. Ujihara discovered through a survey of the workers in large businesses that their length of service in the same firm was long and that the experience they had accumulated resulted in higher job status, as well as wages. He named this system '*nenkō*' (seniority) (Ujihara, 1948, 1953), and contrasted this situation with his earlier study of unmarried workers from the farm villages.

Later, the *nenkō* wage system was associated with lifetime employment, and came to be regarded as the fundamental characteristic of Japan's labour relations. It has gained the support not only of academia but of management and the labour unions. However, there is a division of opinion among scholars over the conditions which brought the establishment of *nenkō* wages. Those who emphasize its relationship with industrial relations generally give major importance to the traditional family system (Hazama, 1964; Fujita, 1961; Tsuda, 1968). On the other hand, those scholars who emphasize the supply price of labour cite low starting salaries, determined by the competitive labour market for youth, and the fact that *nenkō* wages match the increasing

cost of living in a closed, internal labour market (Funahashi, 1966).
of living in a closed, internal labour market (Funahashi, 1966).

Opinion is divided as to whether or not *nenkō* wages will slowly disappear. Scholars who stress the disappearance of *nenkō* wages emphasize the influence of technological change (Tsuda, 1959) and the evidence of rising starting wages and a reduction in wage differentials between age groups in an expanding economy (Funahashi, 1966). Another view is that while the benevolent aspect of the *nenkō* system has been modified by pressure from the labour union movement, the *nenkō* system still exists in all other aspects (Koshiro, 1958). Kazutoshi Koshiro developed this discussion even further, saying that when monopoly capitalism begins to take hold, even in the United States and Great Britain, craft skills are replaced by a hierarchical division of labour within the enterprise in which increment of wages and staffing patterns are adopted. He also added that there is a difference between the Japanese *nenkō* system and the Western wage increment systems which emerge under other social traditions (Koshiro, 1961).

Koike further theorized that when a large business introduces a mass production system, the tasks of the process are divided and reorganized. On-the-job training takes place, and an internal wage structure is formed (Koike, 1962). However, because the labour market is closed, the need to match wages precisely with particular jobs becomes unnecessary. Therefore, it becomes possible to match wages with length of service. Koike later continued his work on internal wage structures using research conducted in the United States. However, a lack of wage data according to age or number of years of service has been a large obstacle to that research (Koike, 1966, 1973).

Wage System

When the *nenkō* wage system, which had become the fundamental wage system of Japanese big business, began to lose ground as a result of technological change, management proposed a 'shokumukyu' system (wage based on job) as a replacement for *nenkō* wages. Shokumkyu was defined as a system where wages were determined by job evaluation in each enterprise, and it was understood in Japan as being the basis for most wage agreements in Western countries. There were two factors at the time which led to the development of the viewpoint that wages should be based on a job evaluation. The first factor was the belief that the *nenkō* wage system had to be eliminated in order to modernize Japanese industrial relations. The other factor was the belief that the *nenkō* wage system had to be replaced by a different wage structure because employment was becoming too rigid (due to the demands of the labour unions) and because the increasing average age of employees was pushing up the average wage.

As a result, labour unions (Nihon Rōdō Kyokai, 1961; Rodo-kamiai Sōhyogikai, 1960), management (Nikkeiren, 1955, 1960), and scholars all turned their attention to the 'shokumukyu'. Even those who had criticized the *nenkō* system and had supported equal pay for equal work or a national wage scale, joined the debate over 'shokumukyu' (Kishimoto, 1962).

Scholars who were interested in technological changes presented the view that the development of a wage scale based on type of job should be introduced to replace the *nenkō* system (Tsuda, 1959). Others, however, claimed that the 'shokumukyu' system was nothing more than a modified *nenkō* system, altered by the process of technological change (Koshiro, 1958). The Nikkeiren (the Japan Federation of Employers' Associations) also gave their views on 'shokumukyu'. They said that its full implementation would require a considerable increase in funds for wages, and that for the time being, wage scales according to length of service must remain to some degree (Nikkeiren, 1961).

Among those who discussed the 'shokumukyu', there were those who believed it to be equivalent to 'occupational' wage structures in Europe and the United States. It was pointed out, however, that there was no term in those countries that corresponded to 'shokumukyu'. Shokumukyu has been called 'The New Deal of the *nenkō* wage system' (Soeda, 1965) since it formalizes wage agreements.

The Sōhyo (General Council of Trade Unions of Japan) is of the opinion that the 'shokumukyu' idea was inaugurated as a means of wage administration in industry, and while it appears similar to the 'equal pay for equal work', or the national wage scales (by occupation) supported by the labour unions, it is fundamentally different. A similar debate has also been carried out energetically by Eitaro Kishimoto and his group. Originally Kishimoto was in favour of 'shokumukyu', but later became critical of it. His recent view is that on the stage of monopolization, old trades are lost to mechanization. Since this simplifies and standardizes the production process, lateral mobility is possible among enterprises, thus creating an occupational wage scale. The labour unions encourage this. However, management, in order to restrict job changing, organizes jobs in each company separately and attempts to divide up the labour market. This, he concludes, is a wage scale determined by management, 'shokumukyu' (Kishimoto, 1962).

Wage structure

The dual structure of the labour market between large and small companies showed that there was a large wage differential between the two labour markets. The relatively low wages of workers in small- and medium-sized businesses, the temporary workers, and the day labourers were analysed and interpreted as resulting from the pressure of surplus population. Frequently, this whole second labour market was characterized as containing disguised employment (Ohara Shakai-Mondai Kenkyujo, 1960). It came to be recognized that low wages were the basis for the existence of small- and medium-sized businesses.

Sumiya criticized this view, saying that, while there was a large differential in the average wage, this differential was small among the younger workers. In 1960 and after, the wages of workers under 20 years of age in small- and medium-sized enterprises were higher than those in big enterprises. The differential was only large for the middle and upper ages. Small- and medium-sized business employed many young workers and many old workers, whose wages are relatively low. Thus the average wage was low as compared to the large businesses. The differential is based on the fact that the wages of the middle- and upper-aged workers do not rise in the small- and medium-sized businesses as they would in large businesses under the *nenkō* system does not prevail in the small and medium businesses (Sumiya, 1964).

This view differed from the generally held theory, so naturally it came under much criticism. However, it can be said that the fundamental point was recognized. Further examination of this question was carried out by studying different occupations (Takanashi, 1965), and by regression analysis which explained the diminishing wage differentials among the various scales of business (Ono, 1973).

Another analysis on the question of wages differentials among the different sized companies from a completely different angle has maintained that the product market of small- and medium-sized businesses was different from that in big businesses. Thus what appeared as a wage differential among the various sizes of business was actually a difference in types of industry (Imura and Kitahara, 1961). Another interesting explanation of wage differentials is that they are the result of larger capital concentrations in big business and the consequent differences in productivity between big and small business (Shinohara, 1961).

Because the dual structure of the labour market has received such an excessive amount of attention, research on the differentials between industries in different regions has lagged. This type of study was fostered by research in the United States, and began under its theoretical influence. The first study from this point of view examined the geographical movements of textile workers (Nishikawa, 1966). The research started under the hypothesis that geographic wage differentials and farm family income would be the important factors, but the results obtained showed that social-psychological factors of distance were more important.

Recent research has measured econometrically the impact of change in the structure of the labour market, as well as that of unions on the Japanese wage structure. The detailed analysis included workers' age, size of work-place, etc., in the postwar period and particularly during the time that the labour force was switching from surplus to shortage (Ono, 1973). No particularly new viewpoint appeared in this study concerning the wage structure. However, the hard data used in the analysis represent a step forward.

The most recent research has also used this technique to analyse wage differentials between industries, geographical areas, and different sized businesses, as well as the changes in these differentials. The results of this study were all previously known, but the study has merit in that it brought out that any unemployment under 3 per cent had no effect on the wage structure, and that the work force reacts more sensitively to employment opportunity than to wage differentials (Mizuno, 1973).

Industrial Relations

The Enterprise Union

When the war ended and political pressure was lifted, the labour union movement developed rapidly. One year after the war, in June 1946, there were 3.7 million union members; by June 1948, there were 6.7 million. A study was carried out in 1947 by the Tokyo University Institute for the Study of Social Sciences to examine labour unions by means of questionnaires and interviews. The study found that postwar labour unions were composed of all employees of the firms including both white- and blue-collar workers and that unions were enterprise-based, made up only of the employees of one company (Tokyo Daigaku Shakai-kagaku Kenkyujo, 1950). At that time the labour law scholar Suehiro also wrote that the single enterprise organization was the most important characteristic of the Japanese postwar labour union (Suehiro, 1950). Ohkochi went a step further to explain the establishment of the enterprise union on the basis of the previously mentioned dekasegi-type workers (Ohkochi, 1951).

Ohkochi's theory received both wide support and criticism. The most important criticism of the theory was that what was called the enterprise union was actually only a workers' council, and that it was to become the lower branch of a future industrial union (Ohtomo, 1952). Another criticism further maintained that the enterprise union was a re-organization by management of the workers' council (which had been independently developed by the workers themselves) into a cooperative work-place organization (Takahashi 1955). These critics held the opinion that the enterprise union was actually a company union.

When the labour union movement ran into difficulties in the early 1950s, Ohkochi maintained that it was because of the weakness of the enterprise union. The labour union leaders agreed with this view, and suggested a break from enterprise unionism (Ohkochi, 1953; Hamakawa and Tanahashi, 1959). However, because of the difficulty of reformulating the labour union organization, attention was turned to the possibility of improving the function of the enterprise unions. First, Fujita criticized Ohkochi for explaining the formation of the enterprise union only from the viewpoint of labour supply. Fujita associated this labour supply, which was accustomed to the family relations of the rural village, to the *nenkō*-type discipline of the work-place, and suggested that it was this relationship that fostered the enterprise union (Fujita, 1956). This won the approval of the scholars of the *nenkō* system theory. Ohkochi, converted from the dekasegi theory to the *nenko* system (Ohkochi, 1959a), and the group at the Institute for the Study of Social Sciences began empirical research on the work-place organization emphasizing it as the base of strength of the labour union (Ohkochi, Ujihara, and Fujita, 1959b). The study focused on plant-level surveys in steel, electrical appliance, coal, and other industries, and discovered that the *nenkō* system was being reformed as a result of technological change and that some labour unions were operating rather effectively.

Another theoretical hypothesis concerning the work-place organization was Ujihara's theory about the labour movement in the mass production industries (Ujihara, 1957b). The theory stated that difficulties in wage negotiations force unions to adopt policies that regulate the supply and wages of the workers inside the firm, and for this reason the activities of the shop steward become more critical. This theory was effectively used to investigate the work-place organization and collective bargaining in the steel industry and helped to examine the peculiarities of the Japanese situation (Takanashi, 1967a). These studies of work-place organizations and collective bargaining were developed as part of a set of international comparisons of labour unions (Kurita, 1963; Kumazawa, 1970; Koshiro, 1966; Tsuda, 1967).

After recognizing that the labour unions were heavily influenced by the external changes just mentioned, Ujihara and others analysed the leadership qualities of labour union leaders (Ohkochi, Ujihara, Takahashi, and Takanashi, 1965). Also Shirai examined the relationship of labour union finances to their organization and activities (Shirai, 1964).

In analysing the function of the enterprise union, Japanese scholars have used the labour union theories of Sidney and Beatrice Webb and Marx and Engels as a frame of reference. However, there was a movement to break this frame of reference and develop a new theory of the labour union (Katsuyoshi Takahashi, 1968; Banto, 1973). However, attention was concentrated on enterprise union theories, and few new theories were developed. Recently, Sumiya theorized that as promotions took place in the internal labour market and as the length of service became longer within the large business organization, career consciousness was replacing job consciousness, which was the key concept in Selig Perlman's theory. This consciousness had an effect on labour union organization, and collective bargaining has begun to take place at the enterprise or factory level. The enterprise union has become the Japanese variant of career-conscious unions (Sumiya, 1975).

In contrast to the lively research on labour unions, there have been only a few studies on employers' organizations (Sumiya, 1965; Kitagawa, 1968). It is difficult to get enough information to analyse their behaviour and function. Business administrators in Japan have little interest in analysing their relationship to labour, although there are several noteworthy studies on the character of Japanese management.

Industrial Relations in the Nenkō System

In Western nations, the term 'labor relations' usually implies the labour union and its relations with management. In Japan, as a result of the strong influence of Marxism, labour relations first was discussed in terms of the relationship between the working class and the capitalist class. In the postwar period, the discipline of industrial relations was introduced from the United States, and the two types of labour relations have existed together – the labour union versus management and employee versus employer. This duality was recognized as basic for studying industrial relations (Fujibayashi, 1963). Sumiya made clear the distinction that industrial relations dealt with a functional relationship, while the Marxist worker–capitalist relation deals with the primary substantive theory, and he emphasized the significance of functional analysis (Sumiya, 1967a). Even now among Japanese scholars there are many supporters of the view that emphasizes worker–capitalist relations.

Scholars have, however, focused more attention on the peculiar characteristics of labour relations in Japan. The dekasegi theory of Ohkochi, mentioned previously, described the paternalistic and un-stable aspects of the traditional relations between labour and management. Following this, the 'Kazoku-shugi' (family-ism) concept appeared, which was thought to be a basis for the *nenkō* system. Here the attempt was made to explain Japanese labour relations in terms of sociological concepts. Sociologists are eager to examine the management-family concept theoretically and historically as the central theme in Japanese labour relations (Hazama, 1964).

In contrast to this approach, Fujita, Ujihara and others consider that the *nenkō* system has been the foundation of Japan's labour relations. In a survey on the work-place by the Institute for the Study of Social Sciences, Fujita framed the hypothesis that the structuring of the labour force according to the *nenkō* principle and its breaking up, were the keys to understanding the labour union movement (Ohkochi, Ujihara, Fujita, 1959b). Fujita identified the following three elements: (1) the composition of employees by social position, i.e. blue or white collar; (2) lifetime employment, the rising income provided by *nenkō* wages, and subsidies through welfare facilities; and (3) the relationship between promotions (which are based on loyalty to the firm), and estrangement. Fujita said this was the nucleus of Japan's labour relations (Fujita, 1961). He then described the conflicts which would most divide the labour unions: the blue- versus white-collar worker; the ambitious and loyal versus the indifferent; and the middle and upper aged, with long service, versus young workers.

Tsuda also critically examined the various *nenkō*-system theories, and expanded upon them (Tsuda, 1968). Tsuda differed from Fujita in maintaining that *nenkō*-type labour relations, which were based on the relationship of social status and loyalty, would dissolve under changing technology. He perceived that management would come to stress 'ability', while from the labour unions side, a more Westernized movement would appear.

Koshiro was critical of the view that *nenkō*-type labour relations would dissolve. Koshiro had earlier espoused the view that in the process of monopolization, industry generally creates job clusters with fixed grades of jobs. As internal promotion becomes common, the labour market becomes closed, and a *nenkō* system develops. However, the similarity of this process with Japan's *nenkō* system is superficial. Staffing practices and the wage structures in Japanese enterprise do not coincide entirely with the model (Koshiro, 1958, 1961).

Kazuo Koike, however, recognized no special characteristics of Japan's case and tried to explain the *nenkō* system by the closed nature of the labour market during the process of monopolization and by internal promotions. Koike re-evaluated Japanese labour relations from an international perspective, and pointed out that because Japan lacked training systems such as apprenticeship, internal promotions fulfilled a training function and readily became a part of labour relations (Koike, 1966, 1973).

Sumiya examined these theories and, using United States research on internal labour markets as a reference, concluded that *nenkō* system developed quickly in Japan because there was no resistance from labour unions. Also, Sumiya analysed those elements of the Japanese *nenkō*-type labour relations that would dissolve, and those that would not, and brought out the fact that in Korea there existed an even more rigid *nenkō* system. The particular characteristic of Japan's *nenkō* system of labour relations is the fact that there are both old and new concepts of labour-relations existing together (Sumiya, 1975).

Collective Bargaining and Shunto

Despite the facts that labour unions are organized widely throughout Japan and that wages are commonly determined by collective bargaining, due to the strong influence of Marxism and the Marxist wage theories, there had been no worthwhile research done on wage determination through collective bargaining. Koike opened the door to this field of research. By analysing wage bargaining on the industrial level (Koike, 1962), he has hypothesized that wages at the industrial level are determined by the specific characteristics and scope of competition among industries.

Research was also carried out by the Ohkochi group. They studied various industries, although the analytical methods and tools used varied among them. Some of the research approached the problem from the industrial level, or the company level, as did Koike, while other research was based on an analysis of the labour market. The quality of the methods used has not been carefully examined (Ohkochi, 1965a). Since 1955, the determination of wages through negotiation with the labour unions has occurred during the spring months, and is called the *Shuntō* (spring offensive). Under the enterprise union system, labour union members maintain a sense of loyalty to the union as well as to the firm. Since these two loyalties coincide to a certain degree, under severe competition there is a limit to the force of any wage conflict. In order to avoid this weakness, union leaders maintain that unions in the same industry must join together by uniting their demands and strikes and thereby attempt to gain greater bargaining power. This theory holds that the more frequently labour unions carry out simultaneous strikes, the more bargaining power the unions will have.

Sumiya explained the *Shuntō* in conjunction with oligopolistic competition in the Japanese economy. The year that the *Shuntō* first began, 1955, was when big businesses began to compete fiercely within the same industries. Thus it was impossible for a labour union of one firm individually to win any large pay increase. It is easier to have demands met when the unions join together to negotiate with competing firms. This is the basis for the large unified battles in each industry (Sumiya, 1964; Ohkochi, 1965b).

Sano has used econometric methods to analyse the criteria governing wage determination in the *Shuntō* as well as the effect this determination has on other wages. Sano and her group, looking at these criteria, surveyed labour unions, the labour market, and the characteristics of the firm. She found that in big business the influence of collective bargaining was the greatest. The smaller the size of the firm, however, the less pressure from collective bargaining and the more from the labour market (Sano, Koike, and Ishida, 1969). Sano also examined forestry workers, who had no labour organization, and railroad workers, who had a long-established union. She discovered that the differences in the wage criteria between these two industries was due to the variations in the type of work and the flow of information (Sano, 1970). The analysis was expanded to the manufacturing industries, and it was made clear that the direction and strength of wage comparisons among different-sized firms were dependent upon the type of workers, the severity of competition, the extent of labour organization, and the national federation to which they belong (Shimada, 1968). Another group obtained the same type of conclusion through an analysis of wage movements in the two sectors, big business and medium or small business (Furuya, Nakamura, and Suzuki, 1969).

The Sano group carried out a similar survey on medium and small businesses. They discovered that wage determination in medium and small businesses was heavily influenced by labour market forces and that the 'going rate' at the time was also an important standard for wage determination in those businesses (Sano, Ishida, and Inoue, 1971). In addition, this same problem was studied from an institutional point of view, and the theory put forward that the comparatively strong unions among the small and medium businesses set the pattern and paved the way for bargaining (Takanashi, 1965).

Specialists on labour law are also very much interested in labour disputes, as they present various fascinating legal problems. Recently labour disputes were analysed from the viewpoint of legal sociology in connection with Japanese industrial relations (Hanami, 1973).

The unions of the public corporations (national railways, postal service, telecommunications, and others), despite the fact that they have not been granted the right to strike, have played an important role in Japanese industrial relations because of their size, and strategic importance in Japan's labour union movement, especially in the *Shuntō*. Nevertheless, except for a survey carried out after the war on the labour unions of the national railways and postal service (Ohkochi, 1954), there has been little research until recently on these unions. One recent study examined the non-market institutional elements of wage determination and attention was given to the influence of arbitration (Koshiro, 1973).

Labour History

Methodology

In Japan, studies of labour problems were developed at first under the influence of the German school of social policy (also called the historical school), and afterward the influence of Marxism, which attaches great importance to historical processes. Before the Second World War, there was no really worthwhile study of labour history other than the analysis made of the history of social policy in Japan by Kazahaya (1937). Around 1955, some important results of research on labour unions and on the characteristics of the labour market began, for the first time, to be published. One can say that the real study of labour history started at that time. Almost the only exception to this was the study of the labour union movement by Suehiro, who was a pioneer of the study of labour in Japan (Suehiro, 1950, 1954). He analysed the organization and functions of labour unions and took the lead in pointing out that post-war unions were organized by enterprise.

Labour unions in Japan were closely connected with the socialist movement both·before and after the Second World War. Especially in the prewar period, labour unions were often organized by socialists. It was common for unions to split according to different types of socialist ideologies and their programmes for the labour movement. Therefore, the labour union movement has been seen as a link in the chain of social movements. All the works on the history of the labour movement published since the Second World War were written from the viewpoint of the social movement, except Suehiro's. Among them, a study on the labour movement early in the twentieth century by Ohkochi examined documents extensively and rigorously and raised important theoretical problems (Ohkochi, 1959. Ohkochi defined the basic type of Japanese worker as 'Dekasegi'. He argued that, due to the immaturity of workers' consciousness as a working class, they found it difficult to organize themselves by craft or by industry. Under these circumstances, the labour movement tended to choose street demonstrations as their main strategy. The unions had to organize within the enterprise since the labour market between enterprises did not exist.

This viewpoint exerted a major influence on the study of labour history as well as on that of industrial relations. At the same time, there was criticism of this viewpoint. One criticism was that to define the character of the labour movement only from the social condition of labour supply was one-sided, and changes in the conditions of demand for labour, such as that of the production structure, technology, or management policy, should be taken into consideration (Nimura, 1959). As this criticism became accepted, Ohkochi began to attach importance to 'long-term employment customs' and to explain the enterprise union in relation to the formation of the *nenko* system (Ohkochi, 1959, 1963).

On the other hand, views critical of the traditional description of social movement history maintained that the social movement should be divided into three parts: (1) the labour union movement; (2) the socialist movement; and (3) the proletarian political party movement. Thus the substance of each movement and its interrelations should be made clear. Then the study of the labour movement could be reorganized around the union movement as its centre (Watanabe, 1960). Shirai criticized the traditional view of the labour movement, which had observed and described it from a left-wing point of view and tended to neglect non-revolutionary efforts. He maintained that collective bargaining should be given a more adequate place in labour history (Shirai, 1961).

The importance of such criticism was recognized and accepted generally, but even now there is a difference of opinion among scholars as to how to rebuild the interrelationship among these three movements.

Documents and Analysis

The labour union movement in Japan started at the end of the nineteenth century under the influence of the American labour movement. Although the movement was not radical, it was suppressed by the government. As the repressive attitude of the government and of management did not change, the mainstream of the labour movement in Japan tended to be anarchist and suffered more severe oppression. Accordingly, labour leaders were frequently arrested and unions were forced to disband. As a consequence, the basic documents and materials for the study of labour history became scattered and were lost. This is one of the most serious difficulties in the study of the history of the Japanese labour movement.

The first work to be done after the war, therefore, was to collect documents and publish them. In order to accomplish this task, the Committee for the Documentary History of the Labour Movement was organized in 1954, and after 1959, documentary histories were published.[5] The first trade union organ, *The Labour World* (*Rōdōsekai*), which was published from 1897 to 1900, was also reprinted as a by-product of the Committee. Later on, *Yuai Shimpō* (later *Rōdō*), which was the organ of the union organized in 1912, and other basic documents were reprinted.

As the materials became available, studies which made use of these basic documents were published. There was a study which analysed the organization and activities of the National Council of Trade Unions, the documents of which were scattered when the union was forced to disband (Watanabe, 1954).

Another study described the strike at Kobe Shipyards, the largest strike before the war, and its connection with the condition of the labour market, production process, and personnel management (Ohamae and Ikeda, 1966). There has also been a study published which pursued the mechanic's movement down to the shop floor level (Ikeda, 1970); and a study which examined the formation of the enterprise union in the prewar period (Komatsu, 1971). At the same time, comprehensive histories of labour unions began to be published which made use of the materials collected after the war and brought the results of the studies on the labour market and industrial relations into consideration (Sumiya, 1966).

The postwar labour union movement has had a history of rapid growth, repeated splits, and rigorous struggles. However, a characteristic of the studies of the development of the postwar labour movement was that most of them were written by participants in the union movement (rather than by scholars), based on their experiences and materials collected through their activities, and reflecting attitudes of the labour movement at the time. For example, one of the former left-wing leaders focused his analysis on the leadership's ideology of the labour movement and maintained that the mistaken strategy of the Communist Party broke down the postwar labour movement (Saito, 1956).

In the postwar labour movement, there were many interesting labour disputes, and several studies of them. One, in particular, focused on representative disputes and analysed their character (Fujita and Shioda, 1963). The study of the history of labour disputes has gradually become more important (Ikeda, 1970). But due to the immaturity of the methods used in analysis and to the underdevelopment of any theory of labour disputes, no fully developed work on this history has yet been achieved.

Working-Class History

One of the characteristics of the study of labour history in Japan is a series of studies on the history of the working class, which covers a wider field of research than the study of labour unions as such. This has occurred partly because of the restricted influence of the Institutional School, but mainly because of the impact of Marxism and its influence on the study of economic history.

Research has been carried out in particular on the labour market and the creation of an industrial labour force in the late nineteenth century, criticizing the popular view which argued that this labour force was abundant and cheap in the process of industrialization in Japan (Watanabe, 1953). A major study in this field was that of Sumiya (1955).

He analysed the process by which the working class was formed, covering the dissolution of the feudal warrior class, the reorganization of the artisan class, the changes which took place in the farming class, and the appearance of an urban lower class. He maintained that the migration of farm families was the most important element in the whole process. These farm families supplied the labour force for cotton-spinning or textile factories, which was emerging as part of the urban poor. Local labour markets appeared around the silk industry districts which were located in rural regions. Owing to the limited supply of labour in each local labour market, girl workers had to be recruited from remote villages and a dormitory system was created. After examining these developments, Sumiya analysed the industrial relations which developed from these labour market conditions, and also the labour movement which grew under these situations (Sumiya, 1955).

Since then, studies in this field have advanced through research on the change in the farming class, and on the changing stages of development of home industries. There are new studies which examine the historical relationship between farmers and the urban working class (Kobayashi, 1961); which analyse the process by which artisans have changed from feudal to modern relationships without an effective resistance to these changes (Nakanishi, 1968), and which have studied in detail the conditions of the urban lower classes at the beginning of the twentieth century (Tsuda, 1972). At the same time, a comprehensive labour history which covers the period from the Meiji Restoration (1868) to the present has been published (Sumiya, Kobayashi, and Hyodo, 1967b).

A point of dispute in the study of the history of the working class has been the extent to which feudal elements have remained in the Japanese working class or in industrial relations. Ohkochi (1950, 1952a), Sumiya (1951, 1955), and Tsuda (1968), though different in detail, have maintained that those elements played an important part at least up to a certain stage of industrialization, but Kobayashi (1961) and Hyodo (1971) have opposed such a view. This issue was discussed in connection with the gang system (Oyakata system) in mining labour, where feudal labour relations were thought to remain most strongly. One viewpoint has been that the feudal Oyakata (labour boss) system began to dissolve from the beginning of the twentieth century (Sumiya, 1960), and the other viewpoint insists it remained even up to the 1930s (Ohyama, 1964). A second issue which involved the shift from feudal to modern society was how apprenticeship changed and in what way job training was performed. Studies on this subject developed in the 1970s, corresponding to the new tendency to examine the quality of the labour force and industrial education. The role of the government at the beginning of industrialization, and that of the big enterprises after a certain stage of development, has been emphasized (Sumiya, 1970, 1971; Nihon Sangyo-Kunren Kyokai, 1971).

Another focus of studies in labour history has been on the stage at which labour relations based on the *nenko* system and lifetime employment were established. One view found the origin of the *nenko* system in the family relations of the warrior class and in the bureaucracy of the Meiji government (Fujita, 1961). Another argued that control over labour during the Second World War was the real basis for the system (Magota, 1965). The view that the *nenko* system appeared during the early growth of big business after the Russo-Japanese War (1904–5) and became established in the 1920s is now widely accepted (Ohkochi, 1959a; Sumiya, 1959, 1966; Hazama, 1964).

Hyodo analysed the changing phases of labour problems from 1890 to 1930 based on the studies mentioned, but he reorganized them from a Marxian view of labour–capital relations and substantiated them with new data. Hyodo's work represents the present stage of study on the history of the working class (Hyodo, 1971).

Conclusion

One might wonder why American (and to some extent British) influence on labour study has become so strong in Japan, where German *Sozialpolitik* had been influential and where Marxism has built up a strong foundation, even in academic society. First, it is because German social policy was poor in theory. Social policy analysis was provided with theoretical tools by Marxian economics from the 1930s, and Marxian economists subsequently confined their studies on labour problems within the framework of social policy.

Japanese scholars were not provided with adequate tools and theories for analysing labour unions and labour markets, even after the Second World War. American labour economics and industrial relations research seemed to fill the vacuum. Since they were helpful in explaining labour problems, they were accepted gradually, although not without resistance – mainly from Marxists. At present, three types of approach to labour problems can be distinguished: Marxian, American, and a mixed viewpoint. The last is dominant, although it covers a broad range, from pro-Marxian theory to pro-American industrial relations.

Another issue which might be misunderstood is the dual structure of

Japanese labour markets. It is different from the dualism of developing countries and even from the dual labour market of the United States. Japan is a mono-racial society, and the dual structure has had little relationship with ethnic problems. Even small factories are usually provided with reasonably modern equipment and both large and small businesses have to compete in the same labour markets for younger workers. This means that the difference between the two sectors is quantitative rather than qualitative. It is not, of course, correct to say that Japan has no ethnic problems. But any such problems have apparently not yet permeated the awareness of serious labour issues, and research has lagged in this area.

An interesting problem is that although the labour movement in Japan has been very political, even after the Second World War, there has been little research on this. At present, Sohyo, the largest national union (4.5 million members), supports the Socialist Party; Domei, the next largest national union (2.3 million members), supports the Democratic Socialist Party. There have been serious disputes about their affiliations. In national conventions of unions, political issues are given the most serious consideration, and political slogans feature in the *Shunto*. Nevertheless, Japanese social scientists have shown little interest in the political behaviour of the unions. There are three reasons for this lack of interest. Labour economists think that the essence of Japanese labour unionism is economic and that the political side of unions is secondary. For example, notwithstanding its political appeals, the *Shunto* comes to an end when wage bargaining is settled. Secondly, political scientists have shown little interest in trade unions (one exception being Ishida, 1966) because of their tradition of concentrating on the analysis of state political authority rather than management relations. Thirdly, although Marxian influence is strong, Japanese academic Marxism is not so much politically minded, but rather tends to hold objective and scientific attitudes. It seems to restrain most Marxian social scientists from interesting themselves in political issues.

As for the nature of research, two suggestions for the future can be made on the basis of the above remarks. One is that while research on industrial relations has advanced rapidly, it has been concentrated on the nature of Japan's unique characteristics, leaving international comparisons incomplete. For the *nenko* system or for the lifetime employment system, a re-examination is necessary to discover its universal aspects, and those that are peculiar to Japan. This should be done through a comparison of Japan with the United States and Europe on the one hand, and with the developing (Asian) countries on the other.

The second point is that, recently, the use of econometric methods has

316   *Industrial Relations in International Perspective*

become more common and is producing many results, stimulating further research of this sort. It must be remembered, however, that there is a limit to the application of econometric research in the study of Japan's particular situation.

NOTES

1. For the working hypotheses, the objects, the scale, and the results of the field surveys taken in postwar Japan, including those surveys conducted outside the Institute for Research on the Social Sciences, see the Study Group for Labour Field Surveys, *Labour Field Surveys in Japan in the Postwar Period (Sengo Nihon no Rōdōchōsa)* (Tokyo: Tokyo Univ. Press, 1970).
2. Ministry of Labour, *Rōdōkeizai no Bunseki* (An Analysis of Labour Economics), annually from 1949. For a description of the extent of the understanding at the time of the bureaucracy, see Yoneji Masuda, *An Analysis of Labour Economics (Rōdōkeizai no Bunseki)* (Tokyo: 1949).
3. The changing attitude of Japanese scholars on labour problems is analysed in detail by Nakanishi (1971).
4. The work which defined the relationship between conditions of the tenant farmer and the worker, and has had the largest influence on research on wages in postwar Japan is by Noritaro Yamada, *An Analysis of Japanese Capitalism (Nihon Shihonshugi Bunseki)* (Tokyo: Iwanami Shoten, 1934).
5. The Committee has planned to publish 10 volumes of the *Documentary History of the Labour Movement in Japan* which would be equal to Commons and Associates, *Documentary History*. Vols. 1 and 2 (1860–1907), Vol. 3 (1908–1918), Vols. 7, 8, and 9 (1931–1945), and Vol. 10 (statistics) have already been published.

REFERENCES

Abbreviations:

NRKZ = Nihon Rodo Kyokai Zasshi (Japan Institute of Labour)
KGR = Keizai-gaku Ronshu (Tokyo Univ., Economics Faculty)

Abegglen, J. C., *The Japanese Factory*, (Cambridge: MIT Press, 1958).
Arima, Motoharu, *Job Training and the Labour Market* (Shokugyō Kunren to Rōdōshijō), *NRKZ* (April 1961).
Banto, Satoshi, Reconstruction of Labour Union Theory (Rōdōkumiairon no Sai-Kōchiku), *Rōdō Chōsa Jihō*, no. 627 (April 1973).
Eguchi, Eiichi, *Some Problems of the Labour Market* (Rōdōshijō no Mondai), in *Kōza-Shakaigaku*, Vol. VI (Tokyo: Daiamondo, 1963).
Fujibayashi, Keizo *Industrial Relations and the Industrial Consultation System* (Roshi-kankei to Roshi-kyogisei) (1963).
Fujita, Wakao, 'The Enterprise Union and its Critics' (Kigyōbetsu kumiai to sono Hihan), in Shakai Seisaku Gakkai (ed.), *The Labour Unions in Post-War Japan* (Tokyo: Yuhikaku, 1956).

——, *On the Collective Agreement in Japan* (Nihon Rōdōkyōyakuron) (Tokyo: Tokyo Univ. Press, 1961).

—— and Shioda, Shōbei (eds.), *Labour Disputes in Postwar Japan* (Sengo Nihon no Rōdō-Sōgi) (Tokyo: Ochanomizu Shobo, 1963).

Funahashi, Naomichi, *The Labour Market and the Wage System* (Rōdōshijō to Chingin-Keitai) (Tokyo: Hosei Univ. Press, 1966).

Furuya, Kenichi, Nakamura, Atsushi and Suzuki, Takao, *A Study of the Factors of Wage Change* (Chingin Hendo Yoin no Kenkyu) (Tokyo: Econ. Planning Board, 1969).

Hamakawa, Hiroshi and Tanahashi, Taisuke, 'The Way of Overcoming the Enterprise Union' (Kigyōbetsu Kumiai Kokufuku no Hōkō), in Tanahashi (ed.), *Sengo Rōdōkumiai Undō Shi*, part 2 (Ohtsuki-Syoten, 1959).

Hanami, Tadashi, *The Labour Dispute* (Rōdo-Sōgi) (Tokyo: Nihon Keizai Shinbun-sha, 1973).

Hazama, Hiroshi, *A Study of the History of Personnel Management* (Nihon Rōmu-kanri-shi Kenkyū) (Tokyo: Daiamondo, 1964).

Hokkaido-ritsu Rodo-kagaku Kenkyujo (Hokkaido Institute of Labor Science), *The Temporary Workers* (Rinjiko), I, II (1956).

Hyōdo, Tsutomu, *Development of Labour-Capital Relations in Japan* (Nihon ni okeru Rōshi-kankei no Tenkai) (Tokyo: Tokyo Univ. Press, 1971).

Ikeda, Makoto, *On the Formation of Engineers' Unions in Japan* (Nihon Kikaikō Kumiai Seiritsu-shi Ron) (Tokyo: Nihon-hyoron Sha, 1970).

Imura, Kiyoko and Katahara, Isamu [1961], 'Structural characteristics of Japanese industry and so-called wage differentials among enterprises of different sizes' (Wagakuni Kogyō no Kōzōteki Tokushitsu to iwayuru 'Kigyōkibo-betsu Chingin Kakusa), in Shakaiseisaku Gakkai (ed.), *Rōdōshijō to Chingin* (Tokyo: Yuhikaku, 1961).

Ishida, Takeshi, *On Modern Organization* (Gendai Soshiki-ron) (Tokyo: Iwanami-Shoten, 1966).

Japan Federation of Economic Associations (JFEA), *Trends in Economics* (Keizaigaku no Dōkō), Vol. II (Tokyo: Toyo-keizai Shimposha, 1975).

Jinbun Kagakukai, *Social Impact of Technological Changes* (Gijutsu Kakushin no Shakaiteki Eikyō) (Tokyo: Tokyo Univ. Press, 1963).

—— 'The Sakuma Dam' (Sakuma Damu), (Tokyo: Tokyo Univ. Press, 1958).

Kagoyama, Takashi, *Day Labourers and their Minimum Wage* (Hiyatoi to sono Rōchin no Saiteigen), *NRKZ* (Nov. 1959).

Kazahaya, Yasoji, *History of Social Policy in Japan* (Nihon Shakai-Seisaku Shi) (Tokyo: Nihon-Hyoron-sha, 1937).

Keigai-Kikaku-Cho (Economic Planning Board) Economic White Paper (Keizai Hakusho) (July, 1957).

Kishimoto, Eitaro, *The Fundamental Problems of Social Policy* (Shakai-seisakuron no Konpon-Mondai) (Tokyo: Nihon-Hyoron-sha, 1950. Rev. ed. 1953).

——, *The Law of Impoverishment and Social Policy* (Kyuboka Hosoku to Shakai Seisaku), *NRKZ* (Nov. 1955).

——, *History of Wage Problems in Japan* (Nihon Chinginron-shi) (Kyoto: Mineruva Shobo, 1962).

———, *Wage Theory in the Labour Movement* (Undö no naka no Chinginron) (Tokyo: Aoki Shoten, 1964).

Kitagawa, Ryukichi, *The Nikkeiren* (Nikkeiren) (Tokyo: Rôdô Jumpo-sha, 1968).

Kobayashi, Kenichi, *The Employment Structure and Rural Over-Population* (Shûgyo-kôzô to Nôson Kajô-Jinkô) (Tokyo: Ochanomizu Shobo, 1961).

———, *The Employment Structure of Present-day Japan* (Gendai Nihon no Koyô-kôzô) (Tokyo: Iwanami Shoten, 1966).

Koike, Kazuo, *Wage Bargaining in Japan* (Nihon no Chingin Kôshô) (Tokyo: Tokyo Univ. Press, 1962).

———, *Wages – Theory and Analysis* (Chingin – Sono Riron to Genjô-bunseki) (Tokyo: Daiamondo, 1966).

———, 'Internal promotion and industrial relations' (Naibu-shôshinsci to Rôshikankei), *Keizai-kagaku*, Vol. XX, no. 2 (1973).

Komatsu, Ryuji, *Formation of the Enterprise Unions* (Kigyô-betsu Kumiai no Seisei) (Tokyo: Ochanomizu Shobo, 1971).

Koshiro, Kazutoshi, 'Labour problems under monopoly and social theory' (Dokusen no Rôdômondai to Shakai Riron), in Koshimura, Shinzaburo (eds.), *Saikin no Dokusen Kenkyû* (Tokyo: Toyokeizai Shimpo-sha, 1958).

———, 'Labour Market Structure and the nenko-system under monopolization' (Dokusendankai no Rôdô-shijô-kozo to nenkosei) *NRKZ*, (March & April, 1961).

———, *A Study of American Industrial Democracy* (Amerika Sangyô Minshu-sei no Kenkyû) (Tokyo: Tokyo Univ. Press, 1966).

———, *Mechanism of Japanese Wage Determination* (Nihon no Chingin Kettei Kikô) (Tokyo: Nihon-hyoron-sha, 1973).

Kumazawa, Makoto, *The Functions of the Trade Union in Industrial History* (Sangyô-shi ni okeru Rôdôkumiai Kinô) (Kyoto: Mineruva Shobo, 1970)

Kurita, Ken, *A History of British Trade Unions* (Igirisu Rôdôkumiai-shi Ron) (Tokyo: Miraisha, 1963).

Kyushu Keizai-chosa Kyokai (ed.), *Report of the Research on the Labour Market in Kyushu* (Kyûshû Rôdô-shijô Chôsa Hôkoku) (Fukuoka, 1964).

Magota, Ryohei, 'Some questions on wartime labour' (Senji Rôdôron no Gimon), *NRKZ* (July 1965).

Mannari, Hiroshi and Marsh, Robert M., 'Japanese industrial workers and life-time employment' (Nihon no Sangyô-rôdôsha to Shûshinkoyô), in Mannari (ed.), *Atarashii Rodosha no Kenkyu* (Studies on New Workers) (Tokyo: Hakuto Shobo, 1973).

Matsumoto, Tatsuro, 'Workers of medium and small industries' (Chûshô-Kigyô no Rôdôsha), in Ohkochi and Sumiya (eds.), *Nihon no Rôdôsha Kaikayû* (Tokyo: Toyokeizai Shimpo-sha, 1955).

Matsushima, Shizuo, *The Characteristics and Changes of Japanese Personnel Management* (Rômu-kanri no Nihonteki Tokushitsu to Hensen) Tokyo: Daiamondo, 1962).

Meijidaigaku Shakaikagaku Kenyujo (ed.), *Rationalization and Labour of the Iron and Steel Industry* (Tekkôgyô no Gôrika to Rôdô) (Tokyo: Hakuto-Shobo, 1961).

Minami, Ryoshin, *Turning Point of Japanese Economy – From Surplus to Shortage of Labour* (Nihon Keizai no Tenkan-ten) (Tokyo: Sobunsha, 1970).

Minemura, Mitsuro, *The Temporary Workers – Their Conditions and Legal Problems* (Rinjikō–Sono Jittai to Hōritsu-mondai) (Tokyo: Kaname Shobo, 1952).

Mizuno, Asao, *Changes in the Wage Structure* (Chingin-kōzō Hendrō-ron) (Tokyo: Shin-hyoron, 1973).

Mori, Goro, *Labour Management in Post-War Japan* (Sengo Nihon no Rōmukanri) (Tokyo: Daiamondo, 1961).

Nankanishi, Yo, 'Formation of a heavy industry management in Japan' (Nihon ni okeru Jukogyo Keiei no Seisei Katei) *KGR*, Vol. 35, nos. 1–3 1968).

——, 'Present Situation of the Study on the "Social Policy" and the "Labor Problems" in Japan' (Nihon ni okeru 'Shakai Seisaku' to 'Rodo-mondai' Kenkyu no Genchiten) *KGR* (1971).

Namiki, Shoichi, 'Ways of population outflow from farm families (Nōka, no Jinkō Id ō in Showa) Dojinkai (ed.), *Wagakuni Kanzenkoyō no Igi to Taisaku* (Tokyo: Showa Dojinkai, 1957).

Nihon Keieisha Dantai Renmei (Nikkeiren), *A Study on Shokumukyū* (Shokumukyū no Kenkyū) (Tokyo: Nikkeiren, 1955).

——, *Modernization of Wage System and Job Analysis* (Chingintaikei no Kindaika to Shokumu-bunseki) (Tokyo: Nikkeiren, 1960).

——, *Task for the Stabilization of the Japanese Economy and Wage Problems* (Nihonkeizai no Anteika e no Kadai to Chingin-mondai) (Tokyo: Nikkeiren, 1961).

Nihon Rōdō Kyokai (ed.), *Labour Union and Wages* Rōdō-kumiai to Chingin) (Tokyo: Nihon Rodo Kyokai, 1961).

Nihon Sangyo-kunren Kyokai (ed.), *A Hundred Years' History of Industrial Training* (Sangyō-Kunren Hyakunen-shi) (Tokyo: Sangyo-kunren Kyokai, 1971).

Nimura, Kazuo, 'Basic process of the Ashio riot' (Ashio Bōdō no Kōsō-katei), *Hogaku-Shirin* (Hosei Univ.), Vol. 57, no. 1 (1959).

Nishikawa, Shunsaku, *Inter-Regional Labour Mobility and Labour Market* (Chiikikan Rōdō-idō to Rōdō-shijō) (Tokyo: Yuhikaku, 1966).

Nosōn Jinkō-Mondai Kenkyukai, *Studies on Rural Population Problems* (Nōson Jinkō-Mondai Kenkyū), Vol. 1–2 (Tokyo: Norin Tokei Kyokai, 1952).

Ohara Shakai Mondai Kenkyujo, *On Medium and Small Business Workers* (Chūshōkigyō Rōdōsha-ron) (Tokyo: Toyo-keizai Shimpo-sha, 1960).

Ohkochi, Kazuo, *Basic Problems in Social Policy* (Shakaiseisaku no Kihon-mondai) (Tokyo: Nihon-hyoron-sha, 1940).

——, 'The feudalistic character of wage labour, (Chinrōdō ni okeru Hōkenteki narumono), *KGR*, Vol. XIX, no. 2 (1950).

——, 'On Japanese-type labour unions' Rōdōkumiai ni okeru Nihon-gata ni tsuite), *Keizai Kenkyu*, Vol. 11, no. 4 (Oct. 1951).

——, *The Dawn of the Japanese Labour Movement* (Reimeiki no Nihon Rōdōundō) (Tokyo: Iwanami Shoten, 1952a).

——, *Economic Theory of Social Policy* (Shakaiseisaku no Keizairiron) (Tokyo: Nihon-hyoron-sha, 1952b).

——, *On the Labour Union in Japan* (Nihon Rōdōkumiai-ron) (Tokyo: Keiyu-sha, 1953).

——(ed.), *The Japanese Labour Unions* (Nihon Rōdōkumiai-ron), (Tokyo: Yuhikaku, 1954).

320   *Industrial Relations in International Perspective*

—— and Sumiya, Mikio (eds.), *The Working Classes of Japan* (Nihon no Rōdō-kaikyū) (Tokyo: Toyo-keizai Shimpo-sha, 1955).

——, 'A historical examination of the enterprise union' (Kigyōbetsu Kumiai no Rekishi-teki Kentō), *Rōdō Undōshi Kenkyū*, no. 15 (Tokyo: Otsuki Shoten, 1959a).

—— and Ujihara, Fujita (eds.), *The Structure and the Functions of the Labour Union – Analysis of Shop Organization* Rōdōkumiai no Kōzō to Kinō – Shokuba Soshiki no Jittai Bunseki) (Tokyo: Tokyo Univ. Press, 1959b).

——, 'Japanese industrial relations and their tradition' (Nihon teki Roshi Kankei to sono Dentō), *KGR*, Vol. 29, no. 1 (1963).

—— (ed.), *Mechanism of Industrial Wage Determination* (Sangyōbetsu Chingin Kettei no Kikō) (Tokyo: Nihon-Rōdō-kyōkai, 1965a).

——, Ujihara, Takahashi, Takanashi, *Labour Union Leaders in Japan* (Nihon no Yunion Liida) (Tokyo: Toyokeizai Shimpo-sha, 1965b).

——, Karsh, Levine (eds.), *Workers and Employers in Japan* (Tokyo: Tokyo Univ. Press, 1973).

Ohamae, Sakuro and Ikeda, Makoto, *On the Labour Movement in Japan* (Nihon Rōdō-undō-shi Ron) (Tokyo: Nihon-hyoron-sha, 1966).

Ohtomo, Fukuo, 'Organization' (Soshiki), in Endo, Shokichi *et al.*, *Tōitsuteki Rōdōundō no Tenbō* (Tokyo: Rodo-horitsu Jumpo-sha, 1952).

Ohuchi, Tsutomu, *Agricultural Problems of Japanese Capitalism* (Nihon Shihon-shugi no Nōgyō-mondai) (Tokyo: Nihon-hyoron-sha, 1947).

Ohyama, Shikitaro, *Mining Labour and the Gangmaster System* (Kōgyōrōdō to Oyakata-seido) (Tokyo: Yuhikaku, 1964).

Ono, Akira, *Wage Determination in Post-War Japan* (Sengo Nihon no Chingin Kettei) (Tokyo: Toyo-keizai Shimpo-sha, 1973).

Ozaki, Iwao, 'Wage changes and employment structure' (Chingin Hendō to Shūgyō-Kōzō), *Mita-gakkai Zasshi* (Jan. 1960).

Rōdō-kumiai Sohyogikai (Sōhyō), *Present Labour Problems* (Tōmen no Rōdō-mondai) (Tokyo: Rōdō-kumiai Sōhyōgikai, 1960).

Saito, Ichiro, *Post-War History of the Labour Movement in Japan* (Sengo Nihon Rōdō-undō-shi), 2 vols. (Tokyo: Sanichi Shobo, 1956).

Sano, Yoko, Koike, Kazuo, Ishida, Hideo, *Behavioural Science of Wage Bargaining* (Chingin Kōshō no Kōdōkagaku) (Tokyo: Toyo-keizai Shimpo-sha, 1969).

Sano, Yoko, *Econometric Analysis of Wage Determination* (Chingin Kettei no Keiryō-bunseki) (Tokyo: Toyo-keizai Shimpo-sha, 1970).

——, Ishida, Hideo, Inoue, Shozo, *Wage Determination of Medium and Small Business* (Chūshō Kigyō no Chingin Kettei) (Tokyo: Toyo-keizai Shimpo-sha, 1971).

—— (ed.), *Economics of Female Labour* (Joshirōdō no Keizaigaku) (Tokyo: Nihon-Rodo Kyokai, 1972).

Sekiya, Ranko, 'Labour problems of women' (Fujin Rodomondai), in Bunken Kenkyu, *Nihon no Rōdōmondai* (Labour Problems of Japan – Surveys of Literature) (Tokyo: Sogo-rodo Kenkyujo, 1966).

Shakaiseisaku Gakkai (ed.), *Feudalism in Wage Labour* (Chinrōdō ni okeru Hōkensei) (Tokyo: Yuhikaku, 1955).

Shimada, Haruo, 'Behaviour of wage comparisons and the structure of wage spillover' (Chingin 'Hikaku-kōdō to Chingin Hakyū no Kōzō) (1) (2), *Mita-*

Gakkai Zasshi, Vol. 61, nos. 6–7 (1968).

Shimoyama, Fusao, *History of Wage Theories in Japan* (Nihon Chingin Gakusetsu-shi) (Tokyo: Nihon-hyoron-sha, 1966).

Shinohara, Miyohei, 'Capital concentration and wage structure' (Shihon Shūchū to Chingin Kōzō), in Funahashi and Shinohara (eds.), *Nihon-gata Chingin Kōzō no Kenkyū* (Tokyo: Rodo Hogaku Kenkyujo, 1961).

Shirai, Taishiro, 'On the evaluation of pre-war trade unionism – a reconsideration on the methodology of the history of the labour movement' (Senzen ni okeru Rodo-Kumiai Shugi no Hyoka ni tsuite – Rōdō-Undō-Shi Hōhōron e no Hansei), *NRKZ*, no. 23 (1961).

——, *Finance of the Labour Unions* (Rodokumiai no Zaisei) (Tokyo: Nihon-hyoron-sha, 1964).

Soeda, Mitsuteru, 'Shokumukyu in Japan' (Nihon no Shokumukyū), *Kyūdai Keizaigaku Kenkyū* (Feb. 1965).

Suehiro, Itsutaro, *History of Trade Unionism in Japan* (Nihon Rōdōkumiai Undō-shi) (Tokyo: Nihon Rōdōkumiai Undō-shi Kankōkai, 1950; rpt. Tokyo: Chuokoron-sha, 1954).

Sumiya, Mikio, 'Capital and labour – the feudal character of labour relations' (Shihon to Rōdō – Chinrōdō Kankei no Hōkensei), in Jimbum Kagakukai, Hōken Isei, (*The Remnants of Feudalism* (Tokyo: Yuhikaku, 1951).

——, 'The theory of wage-labour – a conception of labour economics' (Chinrōdōno Riron – Rōdōkeizairon no Kōsō), *KGR*, Vol. XXII, no. 1 (1954).

——, *On the History of Wage Labour in Japan* (Nihon Chin-rōdōshi Ron) (Tokyo: Tokyo Univ. Press, 1955).

——, 'Industrialization and the labour unions' (Sangyō Hatten to Rōdō Kumiai), in Sumiya (ed.), *Sangyo to Rodo Kumiai* (Tokyo: Daiamondo, 1959).

——, 'Formation and collapse of the gang system' (Naya-seido no Seiritsu to Hōkai), *Shisō (Iwanami Shoten)* (Sept. 1960).

——, *Social Impact of Industrialization in Japan* (in English) (Tokyo: UNESCO, 1963a).

——, 'Problems of temporary labourers at the present stage' (Gendankai ni okeru Rinjikō Mondai), *NRKZ* (March 1963b).

——, *Labour Problems of Japan* (Nihon no Rōdō-Mondai) (Tokyo: Tokyo Univ. Press, 1964).

——, *Economics of Labour* (Rōdō Keizai-ron) (Tokyo: Nihon-Hyoronsha, 1965).

——, *History of the Labour Union Movement in Japan* (Nihon Rōdōundō-shi) (Tokyo: Yuhikaku, 1966).

——, 'Industrial Relations' (Rōshi-kankei Ron), in Sumiya (ed.), *Nihon no Rōshi-kankei* (Tokyo: Nihon-hyoron-sha, 1967a).

——, Kobayashi and Hyōdō, *Japanese Capitalism and Its Labour Problems* (Nihon Shihonshugi to Rōdō Mondai) (Tokyo: Tokyo Univ. Press, 1967).

—— (ed.), 'Development of job training in Japan' (Nihon Shokugyō Kunren Hatten-shi) (Tokyo: Nihon Rodo Kyokai, Vol. I, 1970, Vol. II, 1971).

——, 'Reconsideration of Japanese industrial relations' (Nihonteki Rōshi-kankei no Sai-kentō), *NRKZ* (Aug. and Oct. 1964).

——, 'Modern capitalism and the labour union' (Gendai Shihon-shugi to Rōdōkumiai), *Toyokeizai Shimpo*, no. 3868 (April 1975).

Takagi, Takuo, 'On the half-farm, half-industrial type worker' (Hannō-

Hanrō-Gata ni tsuite), in Shakaiseisaku-Gakkai (ed.), *Chingin, Seikeihi, Seikatsu Hoshō* (Tokyo: Yuhikaku, 1953).

——, 'An observation on disguised unemployment' (Senzai Shitsugyō ni kansuru Ichikōsatsu), in Shakai Seisaku Gakkai (ed.), *Nihon no Shitsugyō* (Tokyo: Yuhikaku, 1959).

Takahashi, Katsuyoshi, 'Economic theories of British trade unionism' (Igirisu Rōdōkumiai-shugi no Keizai Riron), in Yamanaka Tokutarō, *Hakase Taikan Kinen Ronbun-shu: yuhikaku* (1968).

Takahashi, Ko, 'On the so-called "Enterprise Union"' (Iwayuru 'Kigyō-betsu Kumiai' ni tsuite), in Shakai Seisaku Gakkai (ed.), *Chinrōdō ni okeru Hōkensei* (Tokyo: Yuhikaku, 1955).

Takanashi, Akira, *Labour Problems of Present-day Japan* (Gendai Nihon no Rōdō Mondai) (Tokyo: Toyo-keizai Shimpo-sha, 1965).

——, *Industrial Relations of the Steel Industry in Japan* (Nihon Tekkōgyō no Rōshi-kankei) (Tokyo: Tokyo Univ. Press, 1967a).

——, 'Workers of small and medium business and the petty business' (Chūshōkigyō Rōdōsha Reisaikeiei), in Ujihara (ed.), *Nihon no Rōdōshijō* (Tokyo: Nihon-hyoron-sha, 1967b).

Tobata, Seiichi (ed.), *Disguised Unemployment in Agriculture* (Nōgyō ni okeru Senzai Shitsugyō) (Tokyo: Noson Jinko-mondai Kenkyu Kyokai, 1956).

Tokyo Daigaku Shakai-kagaku Kenkyujo (ed.), *The Facts of Post-War Labour Unions* (Sengo Rōdōkumiai no Jittai) (Tokyo: Nihon-hyoron-sha, 1950).

——, (ed.) *Report of Field Research (on the Shipbuilding Industry)*, no. 2 (1960), 3 (1963), 4 (1964) and 5 (1969) (Tokyo: Tokyo Daigaku Shakai-kagaku Kenkyujo).

Tsuda, Masumi, *Labour Problems and Labour Management* (Rōdōmondai to Rōmukanri) (Kyoto: Minerva Shobo, 1959).

——, *The Structure of American Labour Unions* (Amerika Rōdōkumiai no Kōzō) (Tokyo: Nihon-hyoron-sha, 1967).

——, *Industrial Relations of the Nenkō System* (Nenkoteki Roshikankei Ron) (Kyoto: Minerva Shobo, 1968).

——, *The Urban Lower Classes in Japan* (Nihon no Toshi Kasō-shakai) (Kyoto: Minerva Shobo, 1972).

Ujihara, Shojiro, 'What is the real problem of wages in Japan?' (Wagakuni ni okeru Chingin Mondai no Shozai), *Hyoron* (Aug. 1948).

——, 'The character of the big business employee' (Daikigyō-Rōdōsha no Seikaku), in Nihon Jinbun Kagakukai (ed.), *Shakaiteki Kinchō no Kenkyū* (Studies on Social Tension) (Tokyo: Yuhikaku, 1953).

——, 'A model of the labour market' (Rōdō-Shijō no Mokei), in Kanagawa-ken (ed.), *Keihin Kōgyō-chitai Chōsa Hōkōkusho – Sangyō Rōdō-hen Kakuron* (Yokohama: Kanagawa-ken, 1954a).

——, 'The Japanese farm village and labour market' (Nihon Nōson to Rōdōshijō), in *Noson-mondai Kōza*, Vol. 3 (Tokyo: Kawade Shobo, 1954b).

——, *A Reconsideration on the Labor Market* Rōdōshijōron no Hansei) (Keizai-Hyoron, Nov. 1957a).

——, 'Economic Theory of the Union Shop' (Yunion Shoppu no Keizai Riron), *Koza Rodomondai to Rodoho*, Vol. IV (Tokyo: Kobundo, 1957b).

Ujihara, Eguchi, Takanashi, and Sekiya, 'Distribution and composition of the poor in urban districts' (Toshi ni okeru Hinkonsō no Bunpu to Keisei ni kansuru Ichi-shiryō), *Shakaikagaku Kenkyu*, Vol. VIII no. 1 (1956) and Vol. XI, no. 2 (1959).

Ujihara, Eguchi, Yamazaki, 'Wages of the day labourer and the minimum cost of living' (Hiyatoi Rōdōsha no Chingin to Saitei Seikatsuhi), *Shakaikagaku Kenkyu* (Feb. 1962 and March 1963).

Umemura, Mataji, *Wages, Employment and Agriculture* (Chingin, Koyō, Nōgyō) (Tokyo: Taimeido, 1961).

——, *Structure of the Labour Force and Employment Problems* (Rōdō-ryoku no Kōzō to Koyō-mondai) (Tokyo: Iwanami Shoten, 1971).

Watanabe, Toru, 'On the formation of labour markets in the first half of the Meiji Era' (Meiji Zenki no Rōdōshijō Keisei o megutte), *Jinbun Gakuho*, no. 4 (1953).

——, *A History of the Trade Union Movement in Japan* (Nihon Rōdōkumiai Undō-shi) (Tokyo: Aoki Shoten, 1954).

——, 'Methodology of analysis on the history of the labour movement in Japan' (Nihon Rōdō-undō-shi Bunseki no Hōhōron), *Shakai-Rodo Kenkyu*, no. 12 (1960).

Yamamoto Kiyoshi, *The Structure of the Labour Market in Japan* (Nihon Rōdōshijō no Kōzō) (Tokyo: Tokyo Univ. Press, 1967).

9 The Italian System of Industrial Relations

Gino Giugni

The Italian Industrial Relations System. An outline

The principal components.

We shall be separately considering the role of the trade unions, management and the government.

The Trade Unions

These are generally set up as industrial unions, under a single confederation. A unique aspect of the Italian trade union movement is, and always has been, its close ties with the various political parties. This has in general brought about the creation of as many confederations as there are political persuasions. The three most important confederations are: the CGIL (Confederazione Generale Italiana del Lavoro), with 3 800 000 members, mainly communists and socialists; the CISL (Confederazione Italiana Sindacati Lavoratori) with 2 200 000 members, at first almost exclusively Catholic, (i.e. Christian Democrat) but today showing a greater shift towards the Socialist Party – particularly in industry; the UIL (Union Italiana Lavoratori) with 800 000 members, the majority socialists but also representing the centre non-religious parties (republicans and social democrats).

As can be seen, the Socialist Party is represented in all the confederations. The possibility of unification has thus become more and more relevant since 1966. An agreement, reached in 1972, was eventually revoked, however, due to strong opposition that suddenly sprang up within the UIL and within several sectors of the CISL (mainly from agricultural workers and civil servants). During this period the CGIL–

CISL–UIL Federation was set up, which was intended as a transitional step towards total organic unification. According to this unusual formula, the three confederations were to collaborate – with equal rights – through a joint executive and a general secretariat.

The Federation embraces all the various category organizations, of which the most important is the metalworkers' union. In fact three separate federations go to make up the FLM (Federazione Lavoratori Metal meccanici), uniting the union's policy-making and service organs. The FLM is the largest organization both in terms of members and political strength and has played a leading role in events over the last few years.

The trade union organization at plant level has undergone some radical changes since 1968. Prior to this date the unions did not have, at plant level, a specific autonomous organization and those which did exist were not particularly efficient. This was principally due to the fact that the elected internal committees (Commissioni Interne) which represented the workers – and almost always dependent on the trade union organization itself – could not be considered structurally part of the latter.

After 1968 a new organizational structure was set up spontaneously by the workers: a so-called system of delegates, very similar to that of the shop stewards in Britain.

This system was characterized by the election of a representative (the delegate) for each homogeneous group of workers (on average 30–40 workers). These representatives together formed the works council.

Only at a later date did the trade unions recognize and accept this new structure as part of their own shop-floor structure. It must however be underlined that these works council were and are, unlike the trade union confederations, totally unified.

A further important aspect to stress is the spread of *check-off* systems which have given added economic stability to the trade unions, and led them to a greater self-sufficiency, compared with the period immediately after the liberation when they depended totally on international financing from the two 'cold war' blocs.

Management

Management in Italy, at times deals directly with the unions (it should not be forgotten that Italy has a high percentage of small- to medium-sized firms) but generally it operates through the employers' association.

The most important are, the Confindustria (the Confederation of Industry) and the Intersind, which accounts for a large proportion of the state-controlled companies, often ranking among the leading sectors of the economy. In the 1960s the latter played an important role in trade union policies by taking a more progressive political line compared to the Confindustria.

There are also specialized employers' associations operating in other sectors of the economy.

The Government

The government's role in industrial disputes is regulated by an Act which empowers the local offices of the Ministry of Labour to mediate in local disputes. No provision is made for national disputes but in practice the Ministry of Labour's role has been rapidly increasing.

National disputes are in fact often solved via ministerial intervention in the form of autonomous proposals. This is often seen as an informal system of arbitration.

The bargaining system

It is worthwhile mentioning, at this point, that the predominant view held by the trade union movement is that its role is far more widespread than merely bargaining for wages and work conditions. The political implications of collective bargaining are quite obvious, as the direct agreements reached between the government and the unions on social reform (housing, national health, transportation, etc.) clearly indicate.

An examination of the bargaining structure of wages and work conditions shows distinct differences in contractual levels:

(a) Interconfederal or overall agreements: these were more frequent in the past, but have recently regained greater importance. The 'interconfederal' agreements in industry deal with the following aspects: wage differentials between jobs and geographical areas (the latter eliminated since 1969); automatic wage–cost indexation; internal commissions; collective and individual dismissals (now completely dealt with by law); redundancy pay (guaranteed wages); equality of pay for men and women, etc.

(b) National category contracts. These are in fact the most important types of contract and regulate all work conditions. They are generally renewed every three years (flexibility is guaranteed by supplementary plant agreements stipulated during this three-year period). The principle category agreement is that stipulated with the metal workers' union which usually sets the trend for the whole bargaining system.

(c) Supplementary plant agreements. This has been the most important achievement within the trade unions since 1960. The metal workers contract renewal in 1962 included an agreement (known as the 'Intersind–ASAP' agreement) that provided the possibility of integrating the national collective contract (for certain matters) with individual plant agreements.

Since 1969 supplementary plant agreements have touched all aspects of bargaining and have often been the forerunners of the national contracts which tend to generalize, to all categories, the innovations introduced.

For large enterprises these supplementary agreements are usually 'group agreements', applicable to all industries owned by the enterprise which produce the same product. It is unusual for industries with differing production lines to reach a 'group agreement'.

Labour Conflicts

The trade unions' bargaining and political power lies principally in their right to strike action, which represents their basic form of self-defence.

According to recent statistics, Italy has the highest number of working hours lost through industrial action. Even though these statistics are imperfect, strike action in Italy is, nevertheless, very frequent. Let us examine the main characteristics of this form of action:

(a) the duration of strikes is generally relatively short;

(b) during the bargaining round strikes are usually limited to a series of short stoppages, rather than an unlimited period;

(c) strikes do not always involve deserting the work-place. In fact strikes are often organized as work-to-rule, go-slow or intermittent stoppages, etc. In the more serious cases, for example collective dismissals, the unions resort to sit-in strikes. Picketing in these cases is very stringent and at times leads to acts of violence.

The legality of such stoppages is highly debated, even though their use is now far less frequent. Unlike recourse to strike action, the employer does not have the right to take lock-out action except in retaliation to an illegal strike.

The legal framework

The fundamental legal principles on which the present day system of industrial relations is based, are the following:

(a) The principle of union freedom, guaranteed by Art. 39 of the Constitution and enforced by law in 1970 – the Workers' Statute. This Act (and in particular Art. 28) states, among other things, that the local national trade union associations can – if faced with unfair practice on behalf of the employer aimed at limiting or obstructing union activity and/or freedom – apply to a lower court for a ruling against the employer. This right, deriving from the Statute, is of fundamental importance to trade union activity.

(b) Collective agreements are legally enforceable only for those employers affiliated to the employers' association that stipulated the contracts. Their acceptance, however, is in practice more widespread due to the so-called 'imitation process'. The trade unions, though, are only held in part to these agreements. The legality of the unions' obligation to maintain a peaceful situation is in fact much debated, as was the no-strike clause laid down in the agreements drawn up between 1960 and 1970. Such clauses, however, have now been abolished and the prevailing opinion is that the contract cannot forbid unions from taking direct action to change it prior to its natural expiry date (in this way it is possible to improve the national collective agreement via individual company agreements).

(c) Whilst the Constitution does not acknowledge the 'lock-out', the legality of strike action is universally accepted, even for political aims (as recently ruled by the Constitutional Court). Sit-ins, on the other hand, are not considered legal even though the courts seldom condemn them. Finally it must be remembered that the Workers' Statute provides the unions with certain rights, namely: the right to assemble, during working hours, on the shop floor (up to ten hours per year paid by the employer); paid leave for company union representatives to perform trade union duties (for a limited number of hours); the unions' right to collect workers' membership fees directly from the pay packet.

The Research on Industrial Relations

The first problem that must be faced concerns, naturally, the identification of the area covered by industrial relations; this subject (only recently recognized as worthy of specialized examination) is characterized by a sort of mobile frontier.

It must be pointed out that the term 'industrial relations' is in itself a rather recent introduction into the Italian language; it was first introduced by managers – generally those with Anglo-Saxon training – and only later accepted among the trade unions. In trade union literature of the 1950s the identification of 'human relations' with 'industrial relations' was manifest, both terms being considered as unfortunate expressions of the ruling American sociology and considered by Marxists as an ideological expression of capitalism.

The use of the term is now widespread, expressing a field of social phenomena such as the capital–labour relationship, rather than implying a critical methodology.

The linguistic choice in itself is meaningful, since it can be seen as an attempt to isolate a field of research that (for reasons we shall subsequently explain) had either been confused with political analysis or else studied only from an ideological point of view.

Two approaches can be followed: the first consists in the attempt to create an autonomous methodological research programme, mainly on the lines described by John T. Dunlop in his book *Industrial Relations Systems*, which had a remarkable impact in Italy.[1] The most consistent attempt at utilizing Dunlop's system of analysis was carried out by Piero Merli Brandini.[2] The second approach, outlined in the introduction, written by Gino Giugni, to a survey carried out in 1972,[3] saw industrial relations as a field that studies the interrelations between two conflicting parties; the employers and the workers, and between both of these and the state organs. Industrial relations can thus be pictured as an interdisciplinary subject which touches all the relevant sociological, political, legal, historical and psychological aspects.

An attempt to analyse this matter in greater depth with regards to the Italian experience was undertaken by Giovanni Sartori in 'Il potere del lavoro nella società post pacificata: un futuribile sindacale'.[4] The author accused American industrial relations theory of 'ethnocentrism' and criticized the concept of trade unionism as a pressure group. On the contrary he affirmed that industrial relations were to be regarded as a subsystem of the general political system.[5] Enzo Bartocci reached similar conclusions. While attempting to develop a critical view of the theory of industrial relations[6] (as postulated by American and English experts) on the basis of Marxist theory, he concluded that a system of industrial relations could not exist in a country where there was no basic social consensus (Italy, France).

This criticism of the theory of industrial relations (seen as distinct from the political system) was probably more of a confirmation of the peculiar historical aspects of industrial relations in Italy than proof of any general theoretical value. In Italy, as in other European countries, industrial relations are closely related to the evolution of the political system; this implies that they may be the object of a specific analysis, but that they cannot be considered as distinct from such a system.

The Restraints to the Development of Research

Taking for granted or even in proof of what we have previously stated, it must be pointed out that up to the first half of the 1950s industrial relations were substantially neglected. This was shown in 1952 in a paper by Gino Giugni and Federico Mancini[7] which also pinpointed the defects of existing surveys on this subject, with reference to the various disciplines involved, and attempted to analyse the reasons for such defects. Moreover the two authors upheld that, beyond the strict relationship trade unions–politics, there was a whole area of industrial relations not covered by the social sciences.

A more up-to-date analysis might help to clarify this situation. This might point out:

(a) An institutional limit, due mainly to the organizational structure of university research. In fact the only aspect of labour covered by Italian universities has been labour law. This, however, has been simply the result of historical events. Fascism created the corporative system and, to emphasize its principles, instituted chairs in corporative law in all Law and Economics faculties. After the liberation such chairs were simply transformed into chairs of labour law. During this initial period labour law lacked the backing of any empirical knowledge of the subject. The whole problem was seen from the point of view of civil law.

Some innovations have since been introduced, via the institution of chairs in industrial relations in several universities (Bari, Bologna, Trento, where there were already chairs in industrial sociology); the formation of several labour law and industrial relations institutes; the creation of private research centres (ISRIL, CENSIS) and of research centres within the labour organizations.

(b) Furthermore, an ideological restraint is coupled to this institutional one. The Marxist culture, despite Gramsci's great influence (his greatest achievement was to have been the first scholar who, by means of Marxist theory, carried out an analysis of Italy's social and political history), is principally orientated towards the elaboration of ideological thought. In its historical analysis Marxist culture tends to undervalue the autonomous role of the trade unions, identifying it with the political experience of the workers' movement. This is the real ideological constraint, because the few historians interested in studying the rise of the trade unions in the pre-Fascist period, admit that this period had an enormous institutionalizing effect, in the sense that it had given rise to remarkable contractual and cooperative structures.[8]

(c) Benedetto Croce may be regarded as the principal and most influential Italian philosopher of the twentieth century. His condemnation of positivistic sociology (as upheld by Comte and Spencer, etc.) obstructed, for a long time, the development of any sociology based on empirical research. In fact the first chairs of sociology in Italy were created only after the 1950s.

On the other hand, the tendency that predominated among the various academic disciplines was constructed on marginalistic economics, and on law imbued with normative concepts and pure methodology, totally devoid of economic or sociological facts. A 'living' science did not exist.

(d) The non-Marxist radicals traditionally viewed the trade unions with suspicion, seeing them as an institution aimed at safeguarding their sectoral interests and incapable of proposing any sort of reform. The Italian radicals (Gaetano Salvemini, De Viti De Marco, Ernesto Rossi, etc.) had, prior to the advent of Fascism, pointed out the rapid strengthening of the system based on customs protectionism, which allowed the enterprises in the North to achieve high profits, and the workers of the area to receive pay rises. This underlined the general opinion that the trade union's role in society was, if not altogether negative, at least very minor. This belief was strengthened by the rise of the Communist Party, after Fascism, which had a strong hold over the labour movement. This Communist Party–trade union relationship was in fact seen as a 'transmission belt'. Thus the Marxist view of the secondary role of the trade union was further confirmed.

And so we have a paradoxical situation. On the one hand, after the Liberation, the trade unions assumed a significant role in collective bargaining, with collective bargaining itself becoming increasingly important, whilst on the other, applied research seemed to ignore this change. In fact it was only after many years that the trade unions' role became a matter of serious study.

The trade union was thus seen as one wing of the political parties, or – and this was the opinion generally held within Catholic circles – as an institution to be allocated within the framework of a constitutional system based, at least partially, on the representation of the professional classes.

The beginnings: Legal Studies

Even though the years 1968–9 are seen as the turning-point in research, the 1950s saw a growing interest in labour relations, with a consequent increase in scientific research. The first breakthrough came with legal studies, undoubtedly favoured by the existence of chairs in labour law.

In 1960 a legal theory known as the '*ordinamento intersindacale*' was developed. This theory presupposed the existence of a set of rules, over and above those laid down by the state, which took their force from union–management relationships. These rules defined collective agreements, work conditions, trade practices, administrative procedures and so forth. The aim of this theory was to coordinate these rules into one single system, the '*ordinamento intersindacale*'. This was quite a significant achievement because statutory rules concerning labour relations were at that time relatively scarce. After the fall of the corporative state, two important articles were introduced into the Constitution. One, Art. 39, provided for the legal recognition of trade unions and employers' associations, and consequently gave the power to draw up universally valid collective agreements. This Article, however, required a special statement in order to be implemented and the advantages and disadvantages of this law were heavily debated. The three union confederations were for a long time in disagreement on this point, but eventually a contrary opinion prevailed which was gradually accepted by all the confederations.

In the earlier years, legal studies, following a positive line of thinking, concentrated solely on the Constitution's planning regulations or simply on criticizing or complaining about their non-implementation.

During the same period (we are talking about a period of approximately fifteen years) a new set of rules, independent of the statutory regulations, had developed.

The new trend of research that originated from this course of events can be outlined as follows:

(a) Research into the legal interpretation, not of statutory laws, but of collective agreements. Among the provisions studied, particular (and perhaps excessive) attention was paid to those concerning the relationship between various bargaining levels (the so-called '*clausole di rinvio*') and those – mainly studied by Giorgio Ghezzi – concerning the obligation to maintain industrial peace.[9] Meanwhile the use of historical and socio-economic methods of survey, as a preliminary phase of the legal analysis, continued to grow.[10]

(b) Studies of the evolution of collective bargaining within various sectors of industry such as steel and mining[11] and agricultural[12] sectors.

(c) General studies on the trend of collective bargaining.[13]

(d) Case studies on particular industrial experiences.[14]

(e) Surveys on trade union organization at company level. Among the latter the work by Tiziano Treu on the models and experiences of the FLM–CISL organization between 1954 and 1970[15] pointed out that, before the establishing of shop stewards and works councils, the trade union organization at company level was still just wishful thinking, even though the trade unions had been proclaiming the need for these structures in their programmes for at least ten years.

Another empirical research was carried out by Bruno Veneziani on the role of the government in collective bargaining.[16] He outlined the significant importance of ministerial mediation, *vis-à-vis* the absolute absence of rules regulating the state's power in this matter.

A study was also produced by Gaetano Veneto who analysed industrial behaviour in depth, emphasizing the remarkable contradictions existing between statutory rules concerning employment and the actual practice followed by large enterprises.[17] These empirical studies had their origin in the 'School of Bari', which, being pragmatic in outlook, based its analysis on a large collection of facts and documents.

(f) Another approach was to examine the political aspects of the law. This received its main encouragement from the publication of an important work by Giovanni Tarello,[18] which analysed the political motivations, conscious or unconscious, of Italian jurists in the field of trade union law.

This contribution described how the old school, seeing itself as an interpreter and not creator of rules, had in practice expressed its interpretations in the light of a moderate and perhaps conservative policy. It had, for instance, devised the concept of the right to strike on the grounds of 'professional interest' which, being neither included in statutory rules nor in the Constitution, was in practice a political concept expressed under the guise of impartiality.

Moreover, Tarello examined in greater depth the next stage of legal studies, that developed around the '*ordinamento intersindacale*' theory, which he considered to be of a reformist nature. In fact, he maintained that several aspects of this doctrine implied the integration of the workers' movement into the capitalist system. In a later revised edition, the author was equally critical of the more recent radical theories,[19] attacking the doctrine of the *'ordinamento intersindacale'* by affirming that after the events of 1968, there was no longer a system of industrial relations but a state of self-determination of the working class by the working class itself.[20]

Tarello's critical framework provided a new direction in research, characterized by the profound influence that political and ideological criticism could have over the legal interpretation of affairs. The School of Bologna is also important in this field. Particularly noteworthy is Giorgio Ghezzi's essay *'Diritto di sciopero e attività creatrice dei suoi interpreti'*,[21] that vigorously attacked the decision of the courts in general and of the 'Supreme Court' (*Corte di Cassazione*) in particular, to limit the right to strike on the ground of technicalities.

This view was further strengthened after the introduction of the Workers' Statute in 1970, which gave a significant and fruitful boost to legal studies. The importance of this Act was that it extended the area of judicial intervention in matters of labour law. Furthermore as most decisions were left to the young magistrates (politically more reformist or radical), these were becoming generally more politically determined.

Some outstanding examples of the above-mentioned political interpretation of the law are the following:

(1) The 'Comment to the Workers' Statute' by the School of Bologna[22] and Federico Mancini's report, 'The Workers' Statute following the Labour Conflicts of 1969', written for the Italian Association of Labour Law National Congress, that gave rise to much debate on the methodology used.

(2) The research into the legality of strike action by Edoardo Ghera.[23]

(3) The study by Franco Carinci into the legality of labour conflicts in the constitutional courts.[24]

Historical Research

Research into the historical developments of the Trade Unions is hindered yet further by ideological restraints. Even though the study of history has produced successful results in Italy, the history of the labour movement has not been sufficiently examined, due to reluctance to carry out research that tends to isolate specific aspects of industrial relations, such as the trade unions, collective bargaining, strikes and so on.

A debate was held in 1971 to examine the reasons why the study of the historical developments of the trade union was so limited.[25] Only recently has this field of research moved in a positive direction. Historical research has almost exclusively been approached from the political point of view.[26] A book dealing with the industrial development of the economy rather than the social aspects has also recently been published.[27]

No synthetic appraisal of trade union history has been produced and the university courses in 'History of the trade union movement' and 'history of the labour movement' (both of which are becoming more popular in universities in Italy), use most frequently the Italian translation of Daniel Horowitz's book.[28] However, a documentary history of the pre-Fascist period is to be published shortly, edited by a group of scholars, which will certainly fill a gap.[29]

Dora Marucco's book, *Arturo Labriola e il sindacalismo rivoluzionario in Italia* was an important contribution to the study of the ideological origin of the trade unions.[30] Equally important is Alceo Riosa's survey (1976) on the influence of the revolutionary union movement. This movement, though confined to certain areas, was nonetheless highly significant, particularly among the peasant farmers.[31]

Furthermore a book has just been published that can be considered as the first history of a trade union federation; the railwaymen's union, over the period 1862–1900[32]. This study, above all, emphasized the spontaneous development from job consciousness to class consciousness.

The most important works recently published confirm the sharp difference in the development of the Italian labour movements from that of other countries. This was determined by the fact that the origin of the trade union movement was strongly influenced by the peculiar aspects of the peasant workers' movements: generalized protests, a high degree of political consciousness and, in apparent contradiction, a remarkable capacity for creating autonomous organizations aimed at promoting bargaining and assisting the cooperative movement.[33]

Idomeneo Barbadoro's book, *The history of the Italian Trade Union Movement; from Birth to Fascism* is fundamental, particularly the first volume containing the history of the Federterra (the peasant workers' federation).[34] Barbadoro, a socialist and former CGIL organizer, also drew up a thorough analysis of the workers' movement, and particularly examined in depth the institutional framework within which it operated.

The birth of the workers' movement within industry has been the subject of two works: the first written in 1962 by Giuliano Procacci[35] had a great influence on the second, by Stefano Merli.[36] The latter carried out a detailed analysis of the origin of the labour movement in the textile industry, and reached two important conclusions: (a) that contrary to popular belief, the large-sized firm had already made its appearance in Italy during the last two decades of the nineteenth century; (b) that the development of the local groups of industrial proletariat was contemporary with that of the large firms, which thus prepared the way for the rise of an active labour movement. It is in fact well known that the first strikes and the first collective agreements occurred in the textile industry long before the end of the nineteenth century.

Equally important were the conclusions reached by G. Procacci in his work, concerning the large increase in craft unions during initial industrialization. He recalled how Samuel Compers, during a trip to Europe, was surprised by this phenomenon. The main reason for this was the high degree of artisan work and the low level of technology. In fact at the turn of the century, the labour force was totally made up of unskilled workers (women, children and peasants) or former artisans. However, with the entry into the labour force of semi-skilled manual workers, the process of grouping into federations was very rapid. An important role in this was played by the employment bureaux which succeeded in coupling the interests of the workers with the various crafts and occupations. This aspect was also stressed in the first volume of Barbadoro's work, where the author tried to prove that having overcome the initial period of local craft organization, the trade union movement was motivated by general social and economic objectives.

Thus, according to those two authors, the Italian trade union movement was unique; its ideology was not drawn from one specific party (as in Germany) nor did it give rise to the creation of a certain party (as in Great Britain).

The Italian labour movement therefore followed two different paths: that of an industrial proletariat already bent on collective bargaining and that of a large peasant workers' movement, likewise committed to collective bargaining and to cooperative undertakings as well. Both these aspects were fully examined by Rinaldo Rigola – leader of the Italian labour movement before the Fascist period – in 1949, when he wrote a (largely autobiographical) historical synthesis of the labour movement. This book is still considered important, despite its limitation, for it clearly outlined the two characteristics of the Italian labour movement.[37]

In 1906 the 'Confederazione Generale del Lavoro' (CGIL) was constituted. Historical comment on this event is still being formalized, but an important work has already been published on this matter by Adolfo Pepe, *Storia della Confederazione Generale del Lavoro*.[38] This book – extremely rich in documentation – emphasizes more the organization, the strikes and the political strategies and relations than the unions' bargaining activities.

The Italian history of the trade union movement of that period in fact foregoes this highly significant aspect. A fair amount of material was, however, published at that time by the Labour Office – a government body dependent on the Ministry of Industry – to which the school of jurists (the School of Bologna[39] and the School of Bari[40]) – devoted particular attention.

The emerging industrial proletariat in the crucial area of Turin has been the subject of a work by Paolo Spriano – a communist writer. He tried to stress the historical tie existing between the early forms of organization in the up and coming automobile industry and the great ideological movement led by Antonio Gramsci in 1919. However dubious such a relationship might appear, it must be acknowledged that the author clearly outlined the sort of ambivalence existing between revolutionary inclination and institutional tendencies (shown by the increase in collective agreements), which was present throughout this period and which was of significant importance for a better comprehension and analysis of the following periods.[41] A detailed analysis, that partially covered the same period, but more from the entrepreneurs' point of view, was Mario Abrate's work *La lotta sindacale nell'industrializzazione in Italia (1906–1926)*.[42]

Institutional elements still prevailed in the repressive Fascist period, during which workers were registered with state-controlled trade unions. In fact the collective agreement was seen as the supporting structure of the regime's social policy, even though its contents, rather than being autonomously determined, resulted from government intervention. It should however be underlined that it was not until after 1960 – when the trade unions had gained greater bargaining power[43] – that all influence of the past regime was completely obliterated from bargaining.

The starting-point for any research – either direct or indirect – concerning industrial relations during the Fascist regime, is Louis Rosestock Frank's work. This writer, although French, wrote his dissertation in Italy during the early 1930s.[44] His works, however, covered mainly the period prior to 1934, whilst for the following, historically more important, period no original historical research exists.

The historical events following the fall of Fascism are equally significant, but are more difficult to analyse in depth. Some general background work has however been published.[45]

The wave of criticism generated by the events of 1968–9 has given historians a greater insight into the origins of post-Fascist unionism. Liliana Lanzardo[46] upheld the theory that the growing consciousness of the working classes in the big factories of the north could have led to greater achievements if the Communist Party had not joined the other parties in the capitalistic reconstruction of the country. In her essay on reconstruction, Bianca Beccalli asserted that early post war Italian trade unionism developed as a part of a revolutionary process, channelled, however, by the CGIL within the frame work of the industrial relations of a capitalistic economy.[47]

A short but detailed examination of trade union events up to 1968 was carried out by Vittorio, Foa, an intellectual 'leased' to the trade unions (CGIL). In one of his papers he considered as positive the experience of the reformist socialists during the pre-Fascist era, who were able to build up, step by step, a solid political framework.[48]

Industrial Relations Research in the 1960s

1968–9 has generally come to be considered as the turning-point in the history of the labour movement and in industrial relations in general. It is, however, very unusual for any historical event not to be preceded by a period of preparation, and this case is no exception.

It can in fact be noted that as early as the first half of the 1950s, interest in trade unionism was on the increase. Among the most important articles, the Italian translation of S. Perlman's *A Theory of the Labour Movement* deserves mention. This translation, contained an introduction by Gino Giugni which illustrated and compared 'home-grown' trade unionism and assessed its possible political aspects. Perlman's theory was used as a means of singling out the existence, within the Italian labour movement, of internal pressures aimed at breaking the strict dependence on the political parties – a feature that was also present in the pre-Fascist period. This book had a strong influence on the new young leadership of the CISL, and contributed to the elimination of the view held by the traditional Catholics on cooperation between the social classes.

This 'home-grown' theory can, furthermore, be considered as the basis of a new trade union theory, capable of reconciling both traditional ideologies; the Catholic one and the classist one (typical of the CGIL). According to the new intellectuals within the CISL the past history of trade-unionism was based on a pre-industrial phase of the country, when true history had yet to be converted into facts.

The main contributions to this doctrine are due to Mario Romani's works and teaching, through which English and American sources also circulated.[49]

An important step was the circulation of Anglo-Saxon theories on the 'industrial conflict'. R. Dahrendorf's work was translated in 1962 and published with a rather critical introduction by Alessandro Pizzorno.[50]

Equally important was the impact of the theories contained in *Industrialism and Industrial Man*.[51] These were re-echoed by Franco Ferrarotti in his work on workers' protest.[52] Furthermore Guido Baglioni carried out a useful systematic survey of the topic.[53]

Neither did the Marxists ignore the new doctrine from overseas or the development of French industrial sociology (Touraine, Friedmann, Crozier, etc.). During the mid-1950s there was an increasing tendency simply to analyse the problems of the working class; this placed greater emphasis on an accurate analysis of the meaning and implications of new management policies.[54]

The turning-point of the significant cultural change among pro-union intellectuals of all creeds was a study conference organized in 1960. Ideological disputes were put aside and replaced by a careful analysis of the relations between trade union policies and technological change. A great deal of the ideological restraints were at last overcome, giving rise to a completely new era.[55] Two papers presented at the congress by Vittorio Foa and Bruno Trentin – two CGIL leaders of high intellectual standing – were of particular importance.[56]

Equally important was the paper presented by Franco Momigliano, a Marxist intellectual, in reply to the question raised by George Friedmann in his opening speech. Momigliano answered that the Italian unions *were* capable of reacting effectively to technological change.[57] It is quite obvious that since the beginning of the 1960s the trade union movement had been gaining a new cultural foundation, supported furthermore by increasing intellectual activity.

As for the sociological research, we must once again point to Guido

Baglioni's work which by analysing the different foreign trade union theories, attempted to assert that the trade union was the natural instrument needed to maintain equilibrium in industrial relations. This period, however, still saw a lot of work being devoted to problems of internal migration and to particular aspects of working-class conditions. An exception to this was the research on union leaders in Southern Italy. This study showed how the CISL recruited its officials from the middle classes, whereas the CGIL was more strictly bound to the working class.[58]

A revival in labour economics – previously not studied as a separate subject – occurred during this period. This was mainly because the institutional aspects arising from the changed conditions on the labour market and the increased bargaining strength of the trade unions captured the attention of academic economists.[59]

A further valuable contribution came from the Catholic University of Milan, whose economists had tended to move towards institutional economics.

At the beginning of the 1960s Giancarlo Mazzocchi – considered one of the best economists in recent years – carried out an economic analysis of sectoral and plant bargaining. He arrived at the conclusion that, in an economy where manpower was abundant, plant bargaining was the only means of ensuring the equal distribution of income between wages and profits.[60] During this same period several studies on wage drift confirmed the extent of this phenomenon.[61] In the meantime, after the initial attempts at economic planning, the literature on the subject became increasingly more prolific. The idea of economic planning was shared by the economists of the Marxist school and was the great dream of the reformist intellectuals of the 1960s. Its political expression was reflected in the Christian Democrat and Socialist coalition governments.[62] The analysis of the dualism of the Italian economy prepared the ground for similar work on the dualistic structure of the labour market, which was to develop in the 1970s. However, at that time, the trend was still towards general 'models' which had no empirical backing. An important point in this respect was raised by Vera Lutz in her essay on the labour market. She assumed that wage bargaining affected only large enterprises, with a resulting drop in employment due to higher labour costs. Thus the total effect was a slow-down in the backward sectors which were characterized by excess labour-intensity and discouraged from adopting modern technologies.[63]

On the other hand, studies on bargaining (except from the legal point of view) are very scarce. The survey carried out by Giuseppe Bianchi, a supporter of the CISL and founder of the Institute of Industrial Relations (ISRIL), based on a sample of plant agreements signed in 1968, outlined the differences between the formal structure and ·the autonomous forms of plant bargaining effectively existing.[64] Giuseppe Ammassari tried a more theoretical approach. He tried to create a model capable of explaining the economic effects of collective bargaining and demonstrating that between 1956 and 1966 the wage–price ratio was mainly influenced by the flow of credit from the banking system.[65]

The Autumn of 1969 and Its Repercussions on Industrial Research

1968 saw an end to a historical era that many people thought was tending towards increasing social tranquillity. The students' revolt, occurring simultaneously in France, Germany and in almost all the European countries (not to mention the United States), sparked off industrial conflicts once again. In Italy industrial conflicts had declined after the recovery of 1960–2. The outbreak of unrest in 1968 was thus totally spontaneous. A peculiar aspect of these new conflicts was that they were gradually being placed under union control, and the conflicts of autumn 1969 were just a confirmation of this trend. The years 1968–9 were of fundamental importance, for they were destined to strengthen the position and increase the power of the unions, both politically and within the firm, to a point never previously reached in Italy.

The repercussions of these important events were relevant also in the field of research. They gave rise to lively intellectual, empirical and ideological activity, which resulted in a significant boost to industrial relations research, to varying degrees however among the different sectors of research.

A great part of the studies on the trade union movement carried out during these years was distinguished by a high degree of enthusiasm and improvisation – typical of periods of lively intellectual revival. The most positive aspect of all this was that research spontaneously directed itself towards everyday matters that had an immediate political impact. The day of the 'academics' was over.

For this reason this paper will proceed by topic rather than by subject matter.

The Motivations Behind the 1968–9 Labour Conflicts: The Radical Interpretation

The first aspect to be examined relates to the interpretation of the reasons for the period of violent conflict and for the revival of the power of the trade unions. To do this it is first necessary to examine the significant amount of literature that developed during the 1960s. This principally consisted of politically orientated articles and surveys, seldom of any analytical nature, but that were nonetheless important as they formulated several theories that in the following years were to become the focal point of heated ideological debate. Furthermore, they anticipated the changes that were to occur in shop-floor relations several years later and which were one of the main reasons for the events of the late 1960s.

This approach developed mainly through articles published in journals, with a restricted circulation, but that are today regarded as important material for research. One of the most important journals of this period was *Quaderni Rossi*, published from September 1961 to April 1965.[66] Also worthy of mention is the paper on workers' control by Raniero Panzieri, a socialist intellectual and forerunner of the extra-parliamentarian groups.[67]

An examination of the new structures in work organization (such as incentive schemes, job evaluation, work loads, etc.) can be found in Victor Rieser's essays.[68] There was also Alberto Asor Rosa's work on the composition of the new working class,[69] and Mario Tronti's series of basic articles – again on the composition of the working classes – published in various journals of the extra-parliamentarian groups, as well as those published in *Classe Operaira* attacking the trade union and trade union bureaucracy and upholding the position of rivalry between the working classes and the trade unions.[70]

Vittorio Foa's contribution to radical theory is also worthy of note.[71] Foa, a former CGIL leader and supporter of trade union policies, criticized in particular the elitist approach of the extra-parliamentarians (comprised of small groups of students and workers). Even though his criticism was to the point, it was heavily influenced by the above-mentioned groups.[72]

All these writers had strong ideological viewpoints, were highly critical of the trade unions (in particular the CGIL) and were bent on analysing industrial practices such as piece-work, job assignment and the composition of the working classes.[73]

Finally we must not forget the work carried out by the present leader of the metalworkers' union, Bruno Trentin. In fact his unorthodox views and stimulating contributions have earned him the reputation of being one of the major representatives of the group of intellectual trade union leaders. However unorthodox his views, they have been accepted both by the union's hierarchy and by the Communist Party to which he belongs.[74]

The Sociological Interpretation

A scientific approach, based on a survey covering eleven companies, was carried out by Alessandro Pizzorno.[75] On information obtained from this survey he also wrote a paper concerning the function and historical aspects of the trade unions within the Italian political system.[76]

The most salient correlations discovered appeared under a joint sociological/historical analysis and showed that:

(1) At the end of the 1960s, working class initiatives were a strong force but they did not correspond to a powerful trade union movement.

(2) There was an interesting relationship between the new structure of the working class and its commitment to social conflicts; the events of the autumn of 1969 had shown that the younger the working class the stronger the initiative.

(3) A further correlation was detected between the workers' propensity to enter into conflict and the increase in semi-skilled workers (mainly young people and immigrants). Pizzorno's analysis led to the conclusion that the conflicts which occurred at the end of the 1960s had been generated by a new type of working class; objectively through its modified structure and subjectively through its weak commitment to the labour political organization. Furthermore the author was of the belief that industrial conflicts were historically cyclical.

(4) The most significant correlation revealed concerned the ideological function. Pizzorno upheld that the weaker the union the more probable was its use of ideology as a unifying instrument. This had been true of the Italian trade union throughout its history. Recently the ideology of the trade union movement had identified itself with the Italian Communist Party which, during the 1950s, operated primarily through the parliamentary machine. The events of 1968–9 did nothing to deter the political–ideological commitment of the working class which, however, went beyond the position of the Communist Party itself.

This ideological commitment did, however, help bring a large number of intellectuals into the trade unions, giving the unions a greater elasticity in their outlook, with the result that the unions put forward 'quality' claims rather than simple claims concerning wages and work conditions. These were soon followed by commitments covering the social problems of the country.

On the other hand, this highly significant study (criticized for being too closely centred on the CGIL and not analysing the history of the other trade unions)[77] confirmed on the whole some of the general trends in Italian trade union history. As we have already seen, trade unionism developed largely with the introduction of the semi-skilled worker into the ranks of the artisans and the manual labourers, where ideology was still used as the fundamental aggregating factor. Recent events can still be interpreted along these lines.

Economic Interpretations

Undoubtedly some of the reasons for the social upheavals of the late 1960s can be found in the changes that occurred in the labour market. Of particular significance were the interpretations given of the structural changes in the demand and supply of labour.

Marcello De Cecco's labour demand analysis developed an interesting application of the Ricardian model of land income, using age as a method of ranking workers. On this basis he asserted that the demand for labour during the 1960s was centred on workers belonging to the intermediate age group (25–45), for their suitability to adapt to mechanization, for their stability of character and consequently for their willingness to maintain social peace.[78] As a result, women, old and young people were pushed to the back of the queue in the labour market. This employment policy was, on the other hand, the necessary outcome of the fact that, during those years, Italian industry was rapidly developing thanks to higher productivity – which was not, however, matched by a similar increase in the rate of investment.

An important research into the supply of labour was carried out by Massimo Paci.[79] This work underlined the increasing influence of higher levels of education on the growing refusal to do manual jobs. This well-known phenomenon explained in part the rise in workers' protests. Paci furthermore noted that as a consequence of the above-mentioned phenomenon labour supply became less elastic which, despite a situation of non-full employment, determined an excess supply of labour for the 'better' jobs (civil service, clerical, etc.) and a fall in that for the less skilled ones. Furthermore, the latter are in general characterized by a high level of absenteeism, increasing the demand for labour and thus the existence of under-employment of the productive forces.

This analysis appeared to be quite consistent with the labour demand model elaborated by Marcello De Cecco. From it Paci drew the important conclusion that the unions, even in the presence of a situation of non-full employment, had acquired a strength comparable to that existing in countries characterized by full employment. This newly gained power had also been obtained by trade unions during the recessionary periods (this does not consider the effects of the present cycle as no judgement is yet possible), by taking advantage of the ever-increasing dualistic nature of the labour market.

The economic analysis conducted by Michele Salvati concluded, on the other hand, that the strengthened position of the unions could only be fully explained by political aspects.[80] According to Salvati conflicts began after a period of continued dissatisfaction of the workers concerning increased work-loads introduced by the management to counteract the fall in investment.

The rapid fall in living standards was due to the fast pace of urbanization and to the chronic but ever-increasing lack of social services. There is no doubt – a view also upheld by management – that this political factor played an important role.

One could easily conclude, therefore, that the reasons for the workers' protests were a combination of economic, political and social aspects, all of which are still open to study.

Changes in the Structure of the Trade Unions

After 1968, conflicts increased considerably, bringing about profound changes in the labour organization. Many studies and surveys have been carried out on just this aspect of the trade unions. Here we will deal with the structure of the trade unions and subsequently their doctrines and political behaviour.

The most remarkable change, with regard to the structure, was the introduction of shop stewards. As we have already seen, up to 1968 the local trade union organization was centred in provincial units. The attempts to create a local structure at shop-floor level had not achieved any significant result. In 1968, however, under the pressure of strike action, a new form of representation gradually emerged – the so-called shop-floor delegates. Via a very rapid process of evolution, they were absorbed into the three major confederations and their affiliated federations, and recognized as the basic element of the trade unions within the factory. Research work into this aspect is plentiful.[81]

Among these the one by Guido Romagnoli is of particular interest for his analysis of the shop delegates and works council. The most interesting points revealed by this study concern the delegates' political orientations. Up to 1972 they were, in general, not members of any particular party.[82] An examination of the role played by these delegates in company collective bargaining was carried out by Gaetano Veneto in his research into bargaining and industrial practices at company level.[83]

The case study conducted by Alessandro Pizzorno pointed out a variety of models of existing relationships between the representatives and their electoral base within the enterprise. In particular, this enquiry gave a greater insight into the varying degrees of autonomy of the various sectors or departments within each plant; into the unifying role of the works council (which, if not unifying in itself, could often draw the greatest advantage from party intervention, particularly that of the Communist Party), and into the role of the workers' general assembly.

However – apart from considerations on the structure and role of the works council and delegates – we must stress that the works councils in Italy have greatly contributed to stimulating interest in the problems of worker control. Publications with differing ideological backgrounds are numerous in this field, particularly concerning the relationship between the works councils and Antonio Gramsci's theory of workers' control.[84] Perhaps at the beginning the radical groups and intellectuals in particular had hoped that the new forms of workers' representation could have been the stepping-stone towards self-determination; but none of this has occurred in reality.[85]

Now, after a lapse of some years, it is generally accepted that the system of shop-floor delegates in Italy is simply a variation of the trade union organization and not a new form of worker participation (a view held by the unions themselves). This opinion is further backed by case studies similar to Pizzorno's or to the less exhaustive, but equally valid one by Fabrizio D'Agostini.[86]

The *Quaderni di Rassegna Sindacale* have, furthermore, provided a wide documentation of the federal, confederal, provincial and local trade union structures.[87] Among the articles published, of particular interest was the special issue devoted to the problem of trade union financing[88] (up to now perhaps deliberately avoided). It should be noted that the only attempt made at documenting union finances had been in fact carried out by an American writer, Maurice Neufeld.[89]

The importance of research on labour movement philosophies must also be adequately stressed. The most interesting stream of research is that relating to the CISL, the labour union that underwent the most radical changes — passing from a concept of union–management cooperation, to one of class unity, now accepted by all the industrial federations belonging to the CISL. This issue has been widely discussed, and will probably be further developed. One of the more recent developments was Guido Baglioni's survey on the relationship between the CISL, the Catholics and politics. Together with this there appeared a survey by Guido Romagnoli (member of the sociology department of the Catholic University of Milan; this department is considered the intellectual 'soul' of the CISL left-wing) on the evolution of the sociopolitical tendencies of the leaders and members of the CISL.[90] We should also bear in mind the works of Giamprimo Cella, Bruno Manghi and Paola Piva – three intellectuals of the CISL totally committed to their union – on the FLM–CISL (the metalworkers' union).[91]

Literature on the trends within the CGIL is less abundant; however an important contribution has been made by Aris Accornero, a working-class intellectual who deals with the cultural and educational structures within the CGIL. In his paper on industrial factories in the 1950s he underlined the distinguishing features of this confederation and the concept of class representation. During this period the official CISL doctrine, on the contrary, upheld the view of 'association' between workers with converging interests in the labour market.

One of the principal studies on the CGIL was carried out by the above-mentioned CISL group.[92] This work outlined the characteristics of a union that, despite its Marxist origins, had followed a relatively pragmatic policy. In fact, ideologically the CGIL had in no way scorned the opportunities offered by the capitalist system, seeing that the three confederations had always been willing to negotiate with it. On the other hand, the CGIL was far from being a profession-orientated union.[93]

The Trade Unions, the Political System and Policies

The examination of the institutional mechanisms through which the unions operate gives us the opportunity to develop and study a further stream of research: that carried out by jurists and politicians.

One of the initial problems studied by them was that concerning the relations between the trade unions and the political system, which was also the central theme developed in the two works by Alessandro Pizzorno and Giovanni Sartori, mentioned above.[94]

An essay by Gino Giugni on 'trade union substitution' described the growing importance achieved by the confederation since 1968. He stressed that due to inefficiency on the part of parliament to enforce the required reforms, the trade unions had, so to speak, substituted the political parties. In fact the trade union organizations had set up direct bargaining relationships with the government in order to obtain concessions on social reforms and economic policy.[95]

The political power achieved by the trade unions was, by some authors, defined as 'pan-unionism' and questioned on the grounds of its Marxist orthodoxy.[96]

Leaving aside the institutional aspects, and before passing on to analyse the juridical ideologies, let us not forget that 1970 saw the introduction of the Workers' Statute. This Act was and still is of fundamental importance to any study of the legal aspects. The juridical ideologies inspiring the confederations and the internal changes that have occurred over the years, have been successfully illustrated in two essays written by Tiziano Treu and Mario Ricciardi.[97]

For more than twenty years, the CISL's and the CGIL's attitude towards legislation had been in conflict. The CISL upheld the view of the absolute priority of bargaining, of conciliation and of full trade union jurisdiction on labour grievances. The CGIL, on the contrary, was favourable to legislation and court intervention, principally to safeguard the social rights as laid down by the Constitution (for instance equal pay for men and women, fair wages, etc.).

The Workers' Statute, issued in 1970, and followed in 1973 by an Act on individual labour disputes, modified several aspects that had always been taken for granted. Court proceedings became easier, shorter and less expensive. Art. 28 of the Statute, moreover, introduced a highly significant innovation: it gave the unions the right to apply to the lower courts to proceed against any employer behaving in an anti-union fashion. Soon after 1970, in fact, hundreds of labour disputes were taken before the courts by the unions, thanks to this procedure. However, the working world itself began to criticize the use of this instrument, often taken to extremes, which ironically became known as the 'judicial way to socialism'; what it had done was to create a new relationship between the unions and the law.

The Workers' Statute conciliated the once contrasting positions of the two major confederations on legal philosophy. The relation between judicial action, bargaining and administration of the contract was the subject of three reports that tried to analyse the relative costs and benefits of these forms of action. They each concluded that one does not exclude the other, but rather the choice of which to use should be strictly controlled by the trade union.[98] The Workers' Statute has thus significantly contributed to a greater 'entente' among the unions on legislation and legal action.

The social unrest that broke out in 1968 had a significant impact on the structure of collective bargaining. One of the first researches into the new system of bargaining that resulted was conducted by Edoardo Ghera,[99] who illustrated the profound importance of decentralization on company and shop bargaining. The permanent bargaining model was based on the suppression of the 'peace obligation' from collective bargaining agreements, which prohibited the unions from presenting new wage claims before their natural expiry dates.[100]

These characteristics of collective bargaining have led Umberto Romagnoli – an active legal writer – to conclude that the collective contract can, in truth, no longer be considered a contract.[101]

The Development of Sociological Research

In this field the greatest amount of interest has been directed to the problems of work organization, leaving research into trade union sociology well behind (with the exception of Pizzorno's work, mentioned above). However, we must not forget that the conclusions of this case study were meant to be a historical interpretation of trade unionism.

Other essays worthy of mention are Filippo Battaglia's analysis of trade union officials;[102] the survey on shop stewards by Guido Romagnoli;[103] and an analysis of strikes in Milan between 1950 and 1970 by Bianca Beccalli, which examined the major role played by the unions in every conflict irrespective of the structure of the labour market.[104]

In a wider context of sociological research, the introduction by Marino Regini and Emilio Reyneri in the Italian version of S. Lipset, Coleman and Trow's *Union Democracy*, is of great interest.[105] The foreword dealt with the sociology of organization and stressed the need to specify the union's role within the class conflict structure. These two researchers drew a sharp distinction between the terms 'class' or 'movement' and the term 'organization' with reference to the trade unions and argued in favour of the pre-eminent role of the former.

Finally, an essay by Paolo Zannoni represented the first attempt to construct an explanatory model of the functions and structure of the unions.[106]

The contributions of sociologists on problems concerning workers' conditions and organization are, however, of more importance with respect to their contribution to this science. An investigation was carried out on a sample of 7000 workers to find out how workers felt about their condition after the unrest of 1968.[107] Among the large amount of data obtained, some of which is already widely known, there seemed to emerge the fact that some of the workers' expectations were often very different from the objectives desired by the unions; a clear example of this was the workers' attitude towards the so-called 'career'. The worker sees this as a climb to a different and privileged class for which he needs a high school degree in order to be admitted. The theoretical background of this survey was described in detail in the introduction. It represented, more or less, a synthesis of the theories of some American sociologists (mainly Kornhauser) and of European Marxism.

Work Organization

The results obtained in the research on work organization as seen from the workers' point of view, are more fruitful. On this subject the articles mentioned above by Raniero Panzieri[108] which supported the attack on the capitalistic form of labour organization, are of particular interest; however the greatest number of articles on this topic were written later on, during the period between 1970 and 1973. In fact this argument became the central theme of union action (whilst after 1973 the unions once again had to face more pressing problems, such as un-employment).

The surveys carried out in this field are of remarkable value. Marino Regini and Emilio Reyneri,[109] after extensive field research, came up with a strategy of continuous challenge to the system of capitalistic work organization, without, however, giving in to any form of bargaining. The greatest criticism presented by this work is on incentives and job classification; piece-work and other incentive schemes were neither accepted nor rejected and the authors' conclusions on job classification were to be of great help to the 1971–3 union claims for a unique manual–white-collar worker classification.

On this precise point the survey looks into the different attitudes held by the CISL and the CGIL, on category unification; the CGIL, on the one hand, was inclined to stick to the old professional values, particularly seeing that its members were older and more highly skilled workers. The CISL and FLM–CISL, on the other hand, had younger semi-skilled members and aimed at a greater equality of pay and at reducing as far as possible the numbers of categories in order to eventually reach a situation with one single category of workers.

The period which saw the unions bent on analysing capitalistic labour organization, which led to the introduction of systems of job rotation, enrichment and enlargement, was followed by one of closer and more detailed research.

Trade union writers on this subject were less conditioned by ideological and utopian schemes. On the other hand, Luciano Gallino, an eminent sociologist, sceptically affirmed that there was no alternative system capable of replacing the much criticized Taylorism and that a great deal of time was needed to elaborate others, seeing that the existing models were the product of more than a century of 'intellectual and economic investment'.[110]

Research promoted by ARPES (a consultant group), examining the development of new managerial techniques, concluded that their evolution was not necessarily an antithesis of Taylorism. The report then suggested a change in the quality of labour towards forms of shop floor democracy as experienced in the Scandinavian countries.[111]

Federico Butera stressed in his essay that it was necessary to restructure labour organization on the basis of a new organic relationship between the 'expert' and the working class. Butera's conclusion seemed to fit in well with Antonio Gramsci's theory, according to which the working class should acquire a 'producers' consciousness' and thus control organization.[112]

The attack on capitalist labour organization prepared the way for the most important claims of recent years. What the unions wanted was a total revision of the system of job classification. The '*inquadramento unico*' (single category classification) was seen as the greatest achievement of collective bargaining. It was pursued not only for egalitarian reasons but also in consideration of its potential impact on the division of labour.

This new classification system was accompanied by a series of clauses on vertical labour mobility with a view to improving career opportunities through the various professional skills. It would have thus been possible for even manual workers to have greater career prospects through the recomposition of sectorized jobs.

While the '*inquadramento unico*' has already been fully achieved, the modification of the division of labour within the industrial system is still only at project level. It must be pointed out, however, that the unions' proposals concerning the upgrading of professional skills have led to a great deal of valuable research into the division of labour, particularly that carried out by Giamprimo Cella between 1969 and 1971.[113]

There are very few important studies on industrial democracy. The reason for this is perhaps due to the Italian unions' unwillingness to cooperate and their inclination to think that collective bargaining, which now covers aspects of investment and industrial allocation policies, is able to sustain, within the bargaining round itself, matters that in other countries are dealt with through codetermination or other forms of worker-participation.

Even though debate in this field is now quite extensive, little research work has actually been produced.[114]

The impact of the Economic Recession. The Fall in Employment

The new structure in collective bargaining; the change (thanks to the Workers' Statute) in the balance of power between labour and management; the impact of labour conflicts on power-sharing in the factory; and the theory on the methods of attacking the capitalistic organization of labour, can all be considered as the results of wider experience into the problems of the working class. As we have already seen, both scholars and trade union leaders alike have realized that conflicts cannot be kept within the four walls of the factory but must be solved through political action. The years of social conflict can thus be seen as a confirmation and strengthening of the essential historical characteristics of the Italian trade union movement. It will be up to future studies and research to decide whether the movement has undergone any radical change or whether, as is my opinion, there is no break between the past and recent events, which have tended to confirm the unions' strength and political importance. A further factor that has emphasized action outside the factory has been the rise in inflation and recession over the last few years. In fact, during this period, economic policy has replaced industrial sociology, to the extent that issues such as employment, the labour market and voluntary wage controls (social contracts) have become of utmost importance.

Recently there has also been a significant recovery in labour economics and above all in research on the labour market. Research was focused mainly on the sizeable fall in employment, whilst visible unemployment seemed, however, to remain constant. Different interpretations have been given for this phenomenon, which were clearly outlined in a work by Salvatore Vinci.[115] An optimistic view advanced by Giuseppe De Meo saw the reduction in employment as the product of an increase in economic welfare; this however, was superseded by rather more pessimistic outlooks.[116] An essay by Giorgio La Malfa and Salvatore Vinci described the 'disenchanted worker' who, faced with situation of decreasing demand for labour – mainly among the young, the old and women – decided not to register as unemployed with the local employment offices.[117]

Marcello De Cecco's analysis on the structure of the demand for labour has already been fully described. However another model outlined by Franco Modigliani and Ezio Tarantelli is also of great interest. According to this model, the long-term trend of a developing economy implies an increase in employment, which with an increase in labour productivity – locomotive effect – would have no inflationary effects. This model is valid for the first half of the 1960s, following which the trend was reversed and a drop in demand began to be registered.

Within the framework of this model there was an attempt at reconstructing the Phillip's curve on the basis of a wider disaggregation of the various sub-markets. This sort of analysis has become quite popular among labour economists.[118]

A survey conducted by Luigi Frey on the labour market in Lombardy provided an empirical test of the De Cecco model. According to Frey, a part of the labour supply, determined by sex and age, was marginalized also through a greater use of 'home' work.[119]

Massimo Paci's study of the structure of the labour supply has led to the identification of three divisions within the labour market:

(a) The marginal labour market (women, young people, old people);
(b) The workers' labour market;
(c) The intellectual labour market.

The workers' labour market, was characterized by a high degree of rigidity due to the increased level of education and to the increased costs of urbanization. Both these elements discouraged entry into this sector.

An analysis by Piero Ferri which pointed out the correlation between these subsectors of the market and their geographical distribution between north and south also deserves mention. This essay provided an interpretation of the phenomenon of increasing productivity, in the presence of modest increases in the level of overall investment, as was the case in the years immediately preceding 1968. The author believes that the rise in productivity was due to an increase in employment – rather than to an increase in work loads – in the large industrial concerns, which monopolized investment and thus saw their productivity improve. In short this implied that the 1960s had widened the gap between the advanced and backward sectors of industry.[120]

On the whole, the economists' analysis provided a solid foundation for the theory formulated by the sociologist Luciano Gallino, who stated that the Italian population could be divided into two well-defined blocs: the 'guaranteed' bloc, that comprises dependent workers plus some professional groups, which either by law or through collective bargaining, have reached a higher standard of living; and the 'emarginated' bloc.[121] The increasing dualism in the labour market and in income distribution was seen by Michele Salvati as an effect of the distortion of the capitalist system of accumulation.[122]

The 'Wage Jungle' and the Extent of Parasitism within the Economy

The fragmentation of the labour market, together with the impact of various institutional factors, have led to the creation of the so-called 'wage jungle' – an expression coined by Ermanno Gorrieri.[123]

This situation has led the labour organizations to work out a new policy aimed at limiting inter-industry and inter-sector wage differentials. Dramatic wage differentials in fact exist between the productive and the non-productive sectors (in particular the public sector) in favour of the latter. Thus the inequalities in the distribution of income have become a crucial issue and have stimulated the attention of many scholars.

A very important essay by the economist Paolo Sylos Labini threw light on the relationship between income and social groups. The impact of this short but brilliant essay, together with that of Ermanno Gorrieri on union policies and their leaders, was very strong. Sylos Labini produced evidence that the non-productive sectors employed the largest portion of the population and that the Italian social structure was characterized by parasitism.[124]

An interesting essay by Ezio Tarantelli which examined the first draft of Sylos Labini's work confirmed two important points:

(1) The long-run invariability in the distribution of income, despite wage increases equal to the rise in prices over the last twenty years.

(2) The increase in differentials between dependent and professional

workers, and between civil servants and manual workers, etc.[125] This conclusion will probably stimulate further research into the institutional structures which are the main lifeline of the parasitic sector. Public administration, together with employment in the public sector, have become one of the favourite areas of research.

From a legal point of view this aspect has already been dealt with by Edoardo Ghera.[126]

The Ambiguity Arising from the Legislation on Redundancy Payments

During periods of increasing employment, greater attention is given to the institutional instruments devised for restricting the consequences of unemployment.

One of the most interesting is the existence of a system of social insurance, financed by the government and by the employers, which provides laid-off workers with a temporary subsidy. This subsidy is paid until they are readmitted to work. This system has recently been restructured. It now provides that workers, in certain cases, can be guaranteed up to 80 per cent of their wages for periods of up to one year and more.

The interesting aspect of this instrument is twofold. Firstly, unemployment is kept down since laid-off workers do not register as unemployed, which in fact they are not. Secondly, and this gives rise to the ambiguity, recourse to temporary lay-offs has often been used by the employers to abate the more violent reactions to collective dismissals. Taking this point of view, some extreme left-wing intellectuals consider this system of redundancy payments as an instrument that provides social peace to the advantage of capitalism.[127]

The whole matter is tied to the existence of the legal framework on collective dismissals, which is in itself full of technicalities, thus giving rise to conflicting political opinions.[120] The unions hold that such a mechanism can only be valid if the terms are previously stipulated with the unions themselves. Legislation is now evolving along these lines.

Institutional Relations

Throughout our survey we have alluded to the relationship between research and the agencies or institutions which carry it out. In general we might conclude that the pattern is for a spontaneous increase in research, particularly within the academic field, especially after the events of 1968–9.

After the years of unrest, researchers became increasingly influenced by political motivations, which, by and large, stemmed either from a radical or pro-labour movement attitude. So even though research continued to be confined to the academic structures, it became less and less academic. At times it also tried to provide an answer to questions from outside agents (as we shall see later), principally from the trade unions, but in most cases it was an autonomous process. However, the results were made available to the unions. A few of the mentioned works – those by Marcello De Cecco, Edoardo Ghera and Alessandro Pizzorno – were coordinated by an ISPE committee (Institute for National Planning).[129] The same may be said for several of the studies on the labour market. The influence of the employers' associations had dwindled over the years, as was openly stated by a report, issued in 1971, on the policies of the Confindustria.[130]

All this has determined the trade unions' role as the centre of cultural debate. In the past this was reflected in their publication, *Politica Sindacale*, a bi-monthly journal published by the CISL and circulated both to union members and non-members. This journal helped put over the principles of the new form of trade unionism which the CISL was trying to build up. Many translations of well-known essays published abroad were reproduced in it. This avant-garde position held by the CISL was superseded by the CGIL with their publication of the *Quaderni di Rassegna Sindacale*, again a bi-monthly journal.

Each issue was devoted to a specific topic and now after ten years of continuous publication they have covered most of the basic arguments concerning industrial relations. The journal, which is undoubtedly the most important publication concerning industrial relations, is edited by Aris Accornero, whose works we have already mentioned. Until the end of the 1960s the CISL, together with the Catholic University of Milan, organized annual conventions on economics. These conventions were similar to those promoted by the employers' confederation (Confindustria) and despite their academic approach threw light on some of the hotter issues of industrial relations and economic development.

Having shown the leading role played by academic research we must also underline that its contact with the agents of industrial relations is primarily of an indirect nature. It is very rare for an academic to present a paper at a trade union convention – one exception to this was at the 1972 FLM (metalworkers' union) conference on trade-union power and the law.[131] Furthermore, much of the work carried out in collaboration with the Catholic University of Milan on economic, sociological and legal aspects is closely tied to the local trade unions, because many of the scholars work both for the university and for the CISL.

As is the case with political parties or the institutions directly connected to them, interest in the various aspects of industrial relations is relatively limited. However, the most significant steps forward in the development of a new approach among communist intellectuals have been achieved thanks to the Gramsci Institute.

NOTES

1. John T. Dunlop, *Industrial Relations Systems* (New York: Holt 1958).
2. Pietro Merli Brandini, *Le Relazioni Industriali* (Milan: F. Angeli, 1969).
3. Gloria Pirzo Ammassari, *Gli Studi di Relazioni Industriali in Italia* (Milan: Edizioni Comunità, 1972).
4. Giovanni Sartori, 'Il potere del lavoro nella società post pacificata: un futuribile sindacale', *Rivista Italiana di Scienza Politica*, No 1 (1973).
5. For an analysis of this theory see Dimitri Weiss, 'Relations Industrielles et Science Politique', *Relations Industrielles*. 30, no. 1 (Quebec: Presse de l'Université Laval, 1975).
6. Enzo Bartocci, 'Appunti critici sulla Teoria delle Relazioni Industriali', in *Sindacato, classe e società* (Padua: Cedam, 1975).
7. Gino Giugni and Federico Mancini, 'Per una cultura sindacale in Italia', *Il Mulino*, no. 27 (January 1954) p. 28–45.
8. Angelo Tasca, *Nascita e Avvento del Fascismo. L'Italia dal 1918 al 1922* (Florence: La Nuova Italia, 1950).
9. Giorgio Ghezzi, *La responsabilità contrattuale delle associazioni sindacali. La parte obbligatoria del contratto collettivo* (Milan: Giuffrè, 1963).
10. A clear example can be seen in Umberto Romagnoli, *Le Associazioni Sindacali nel Processo* (Milan: Giuffrè, 1969).
11. Gino Giugni, *L'evoluzione della contrattazione collettiva nelle industrie siderurgica e mineraria (1955–1963)* (Milan: Giuffrè, 1964). Giuffrè, 1964).
12. Bruno Veneziani, 'L'evoluzione della contrattazione collettiva in agricoltura dal periodo corporativo ai nostri giorni', *Rivista di Diritto del Lavoro* (1968), pp. 64–163.
13. Edoardo Ghera, 'Linee di tendenza della contrattazione sindacale 1968–1971', *Quaderni di Rassegna Sindacale*, no. 35 (March–April 1971).
14. Umberto Romagnoli, *Contrattazione e partecipazione. studio di relazioni industriali in un' azienda italiana* (Bologna: Il Mulino, 1968).
15 Tiziano Treu, *Sindacato e Rappresentanze Aziendali: Modelli ed Esperienze di un sindacato industriale, FLM-CISL 1954–1970* (Bologna: Il Mulino, 1971).

16. Bruno Veneziani, *La mediazione dei pubblici poteri nei conflitti collettivi di lavoro* (Bolonga: Il Mulino, 1972).

17. Gaetano Veneto, *Contrattazione e prassi nei rapporti di lavoro* (Bologna: Il Mulino, 1974).

18. Giovanni Tarello, *Teorie ed ideologie del diritto sindacale*, 2nd ed. (1967) (Milan: Edizioni Comunità, 1972).

19. Giorgio Ghezzi, 'Osservazioni sul metodo dell'indagine giuridica nel diritto sindacale', *Rivista Trimestrale di Diritto e Procedura Civile* (June 1970).

20. This practice of self-determination was explicitly criticized by a leading left-wing trade union official, Vittorio Foa.

21. Giorgio Ghezzi, 'Diritto di sciopero e attività creatrice dei suoi interpreti', *Rivista Trimestrale di Diritto e Procedura Civile* (1968).

22. Giorgio Ghezzi, Federico Mancini, Luigi Montuschi and Umberto Romagnoli, *Commentario allo Statuto dei Diritti dei Lavoratori* (Bologna: Zanichelli, Il foro italiano, 1972).

23. Edoardo Ghera, 'Considerazioni sulla giurisprudenza in tema di sciopero', in *Indagine sul sindacato*, ISLE (Milan: Giuffrè, 1970).

24. Franco Carinci, *Il conflitto collettivo nella giurisprudenza constituzionale* (Milan: Giuffrè, 1971).

25. Gloria Pirzo Ammassari, *op. cit.*, pp. 147–84.

26. Gastone Manacorda, *Il movimento operaio italiano attraverso i suoi congressi. Dalle origini alla formazione del Partito Socialista (1853–1892)* 2nd ed. (1953) (Rome: Editori Riuniti, 1963). This author underlines how in countries with political labour organizations trade union history is an abstraction (p. 7).

27. Valerio Castronovo, 'Dall'unità ad oggi', vol. IV in *Storia d'Italia* (Turin: Einaudi, 1975).

28. Daniel Horowitz, *Storia del Movimento sindacale in Italia* (Bologna: Il Mulino, 1960). See also M. F. Neufeld, *Italy: School for Awakening Countries* (Ithaca, New York: 1961).

29. *La condizione e l'impiegazione operaia in Italia dall'unità al 1926*, Istituto di studi storico-politici della Facoltà di Scienze Politiche dell'università di Roma (ed.) (Bari: De Donato).

30. Dora Marucco, *Arturo Labriola e il sindacalismo rivoluzionario in Italia* (Turin: Einaudi, 1970).

31. Alceo Riosa, 'Il sindacalismo rivoluzionario in Italia' (Bari: De Donato).

32. Enrico Finzi, *Alle origini del movimento sindacale: i ferrovieri* (Bologna: Il Mulino, 1975).

33. Renato Zangheri, *Lotte agrarie in Italia* (Milan: Feltrinelli, 1960).

34. Idomeneo Barbadoro, *La storia del sindacalismo italiano: dalla nascita al fascismo.* 2nd ed. (1973) (Florence: La Nuova Italia, 1974).

35. Giuliano Procacci, 'La classe operaia italiana agli inizi del secolo XX' in *Studi Storici*, now in *La classe operaia italiana agli inizi del secolo XX* (Rome: Editori Riuniti, 1970).

36. Stefano Merli, *Proletariato di fabbrica e capitalismo industriale* (Florence: La Nuova Italia, 1972).

37. Rinaldo Rigola, *Storia del movimento operaio italiano* (Milan: Domus, 1949).

38. Adolfo Pepe, *Storia della CGIL* (Bari: Laterza, 1972).

39. Umberto Romagnoli, *Il sindacato tra ill vecchio e il nuovo diritto* (Bologna: Il Mulino, 1974).
40. Bruno Veneziani, 'L'evoluzione della contrattazione collettiva in agricoltura dal periodo corporativo ai nostri giorni' *op. cit.* Gaetano Veneto, *Contrattazione e prassi nei rapporti di lavoro*, in particular chapter II, 'La classificazione dei lavoratori. La mobilità e la carriera', pp. 67–101, and chapter III, 'La retribuzione ad incentivo: il cottimo' pp. 107–38.
41. Paolo Spriano, *Socialismo e classe operaia a Torino dal 1892 al 1913* (Turin: Einaudi, 1958).
42. Mario Abrate, *La lotta sindacale nell'industrializzazione in Italia (1906–1926)* (Milan: F. Angeli, 1967).
43. Gino Giugni, 'Le esperienze corporative e post-corporative' *Il Mulino* no. 51–52; and by the same author, in English, 'Bargaining units and Labour Organization in Italy', *Industrial Labour Relations Review*, (1957). See also, Franco Archibugi, 'Tendenze di Fondo della contrattazione collettiva', *Politica Sindacale* (ed. CISL, 1959) pp. 13–37.
44. Louis Rosestock Frank, *L'économie corporative fasciste en doctrine et en fait: ses origines historiques et son évolution* (Paris: Librarie universitaire J. Gamber, 1934). A later book deals in particular with the general economic policy of the regime, *Les Etapes de l'économie fasciste italienne: du corporativisme à l'économie de guerre* (Paris: La Librairie sociale et economique, 1939).
45. Sergio Turone, *Storia del sindacato in Italia (1943–1969)* (Bari: Laterza, 1973), a highly commendable piece of journalistic work. See also Corrado Perna, 'L'evoluzione storica del movimento sindacale in Italia' in *Il sindacato in Italia* ISLE (Milan: Giuffrè, 1970), and Detlav Albers, 'Il movimento sindacale italiano dal 1944 al 1973', *Quaderni di Rassegna Sindacale*, no. 49 (July–August 1974), pp. 5–43.
46. Liliana Lanzardo, *Classe operaia e partito comunista alla FIAT: la strategia della collaborazione* (Turin: Einaudi, 1971).
47. Bianca Beccalli, 'La ricostruzione del sindacalismo italiano, 1943–1950', in *Italia 1943–1950: la ricostruzione*, Stuart J. Wolf (ed.) (Bari: Laterza, 1974) pp. 319–88.
48. Vittorio Foa, 'Sindacato e lotte sociali', in Vol. V. *Storia d'Itqlia* (Turin: Einaudi, 1975), pp. 1781–1828.
49. See Mario Romani, 'I rapporti sociali nell'azienda', in ACLI, 'Il fattore umano nell'azienda' (proceedings of the 1st national research conference, June 1951) (Rome, 1952). See also *Appunti sull' evoluzione del sindacato*, ISA (Milan, 1951).
50. Alessandro Pizzorno, Foreword to R. Dahrendorf, *Classi e conflitti di classi nella società industriale* (Bari: Laterza, 1962).
51. C. Kerr, J. T. Dunlop, F. H. Harbison and C. A. Myers (translation) *L'industrialismo e l'uomo dell'industria* (Milan: F. Angeli, 1970).
52. Franco Ferrarotti, *La protesta operaia* (Milan: Comunità, 1955).
53. Guido Baglioni, (in collaboration with Bruno Manghi), *Il problema del lavoro operaio. Teorie del conflitto industriale e dell'esperienza sindacale* (Milan: F. Angeli, 1967).
54. The turning-point was perhaps the national convention on 'Workers and technical progress' organized by the Gramsci Institute. See the reports of

this meeting, *I lavoratori e il progresso tecnico* (Ed. Riuniti, 1956). See in particular B. Trentin's report.

55. *Lavoratori e sindacati di fronte alle trasformazioni del processo produttivo*, Franco Momigliano. Acts of the International Study Congress on Technological Progress and Italian Society. 28 June–3 July 1960, Milan, Centro Nazionale di Prevenzione e Difesa sociale, Milan, 28 June–3 July 1960 (Milan: Feltrinelli, 1962), II.

56. *Lavoratori e sindacati di fronte alle trasformazioni del processo produttivo*, pp. 161–86.

57. Franco Momigliano, 'I sindacati di fronte al progresso tecnico ed alle trasformazioni del processo produttivo', now in *Sindacato, progresso tecnico, programmazione economica* (Turin: Einaudi, 1966), pp. 5–87.

58. Luciano Visentini, 'I dirigenti sindacali nel processo di sviluppo del Mezzogiorno' and 'Azione e leadership sindacale nel Mezzogiorno', *Tempi Moderni*, no. 23, pp. 21–49.

59. Gloria Pirzio Ammassari, *op. cit.*, pp. 82.

60. Giancarlo Mazzocchi, *Variazioni di produttività e politica salariale* (Milan: Giuffrè, 1961).

61. Giuseppe Ammassari, *Salari di fatto in Italia* (Milan: Giuffrè, 1963).

62. Giorgio Ruffolo, *Rapporto sulla programmazione* (Bari: Laterza, 1973).

63. Vera Lutz, Il processo di sviluppo in un sistema dualistico', in Salvatore Vinci (ed.) *Il mercato del lavoro in Italia* (Milan: F. Angeli, 1974), pp. 159–78. See the criticism by Luigi Spaventa, 'Dualism in Economic Growth', *Banca Nazionale del Lavoro Quarterly Review* (December 1959) and Augusto Graziani, 'Lo sviluppo di un'economia aperta, Un modello a due settori', in *Il mercato del lavoro in Italia*, pp. 179–88. In fact the view that unions had strong bargaining power in the advanced sectors was not proved.

64. Giuseppe Bianchi, *Sindacati e impresa* (Milano: F. Angeli, 1969).

65. Giuseppe Ammassari, 'Gli effetti economici dell'azione sindacale', in *Indagine sul sindacato* (Milano: Giuffrè, 1969).

66. *Quaderni Rossi*, Raniero Panzieri (ed.), Milano, Instituto Rodolfo Morandi.

67. Raniero Panzieri, 'Sull'uso capitalistico delle macchine nel neocapitalismo', *Quaderni Rossi*, no. 1 (1961), pp. 53–72, but the debate had already begun several years previously in the Socialist Party's review; see: 'Capitalismo contemporaneo e controllo operaio', *Mondo operaio*, no. 12 (1957).

68. See Victor Rieser, 'Salario e sviluppo nella politica della CGIL', *Quaderni Rossi*, no. 3 (1963), pp. 210–36.

69. Alberto Asor Rosa, *Intellettual e classe operaia* (Florence: La Nuova Italia, 1973).

70. Mario Tronti, *Operai e capitale* (Turin: Einaudi, 1971).

71. See Vittorio Foa, 'Lotte operaie nello sviluppo capitalistico', *Quaderni Rossi*, no. 1 (September 1961), pp. 1–17.

72. Vittorio Foa, 'Note sui gruppi estremisti e le lotte sindacali', *Problemi del socialismo*, no. 41 (1969), pp. 658–69. .

73. An up-to-date summary of the positions of the radical groups can be found in Augusto Illuminati's work *Lavoro e rivoluzione: produttivismo e lotte operaie dal 1945 al 1973* (Milan: Mazzotta, 1974).

74. Of special interest is Bruno Trentin's, 'Politica dei redditi e programmazione', *Critica Marxista* (Jan.–Feb. 1964), pp. 11 ff., and by the same author, 'Le dottrine neocapitalistiche e l'ideologia delle forze dominanti nella politica economica italiana', from his report presented at the Convention organized by the Istituto Gramsci (1962) on the 'Tendenze nel capitalismo'. See in *Politica e teoria nel marxismo italiano, 1959–1969,* Giuseppe Vacca (ed.) (Bari: De Donato, 1972), pp. 150–65.

75. See Alessandro Pizzorno (ed.), *Lotte operaie e sindacato in Italia, 1968–1973* Vols. I–IV (Milan: Il Mulino, 1974).

76. Alessandro Pizzorno, 'I sindacati nel sistema politico italiano: aspetti storici', *Rivista Trimestrale di Diritto Pubblico*, no. 4 (Oct.–Dec. 1971), pp. 1510–59. An examination of the behavioural rather than motivational characteristics of the autumn of 1969 can be found in Gino Giugni's essay 'L'autunno caldo sindacale', *Il Mulino*, no. 270 (1970), pp. 24–43, now in *Il sindacato tra contratti e riforme. 1969–1973* (Bari: De Donato, 1973), pp. 9–34.

77. Bianca Beccalli, 'La ricostruzione del sindacalismo italiano. 1943–1950', in Stuart J. Wolf (ed.), *Italia 1943–1950: la ricostruzione* (Bari: Laterza, 1965), pp. 319–88.

78. See Marcello De Cecco, 'Caratteri dello sviluppo economico nella sua fase più recente e sue implicazioni sul mercato del lavoro', in ISPE (ed.), *Gli anni della conflittualità permanente* (Milan: F. Angeli, 1975); and, by the same author, 'Un'interpretazione ricardana della dinamica della forza lavoro in Italia nel decennio 1959–1969', *Note economiche*, no. 1 (1972), pp. 76–118.

79. Massimo Paci, *Mercato del lavoro e classi sociali in Italia: ricerche sulla composizione del proletariato* (Bologna: Il Mulino, 1973).

80. Michele Salvati, *La congiuntura più lunga* (Bologna: Il Mulino, 1974).

81. Tiziano Treu, *Sindacato e rappresentanze aziendali: modelli ed esperienze di un sindacato industriale, FIM-CISL 1954–1970* (Bologna: Il Mulino, 1971); Aris Accornero, 'Le strutture di base negli anni '50', in *Quaderni di Rassegna Sindacale*, no. 49 (1974), pp. 84–121; Roberto Aglieta, Giuseppe Bianchi and Pietro Merli Brandini, *I delegati operai: ricerca su nuove forme di rappresentanza operaia* (Rome: Coines, 1970); L. Albanese, F. Viuzzi and A. Perrella, *I consigli di fabbrica* (Rome: Editori Riuniti, 1973); Fabrizio D'Agostini, *La condizione operaia e i consigli di fabbrica* (Rome: editori Riuniti,1974); Gianni Salvarani and Alberto Bonifazi, *Le nuove strutture del sindacato: origini, esperienze e prospettive del movimento dei delegati in Italia* (Milan: F. Angeli, 1973), G. Censi, N. de Pamphilis, A. Fasola, G. Fassio, A. La Porta, G. Mantovani, M. Polverari, M. Ricceri, S. Scaiola, *Delegati e consigli di fabbrica in Italia* (Milan: F. Angeli, 1973); 'Il sindacato e le sue strutture', no. 49 of *Quaderni di Rassegna Sindacale* (1974).

82. Guido Romagnoli, 'Democrazia di base ed organizzazione di classe nell'esperienza dei consigli', *Prospettiva Sindacale* (April 1973), pp. 49 ff.

83. Gaetano Veneto, *Contrattazione e prassi nei rapporti di lavoro*, already mentioned. An interesting investigation promoted by the employers' association pointed out, on the other hand, that in 1973, in almost half the Italian enterprises, the workers' representation structure had begun to change, but that the old 'commissioni interne' (internal committees), still

362   *Industrial Relations in International Perspective*

existed. See: *Le rappresentanze dei lavoratori in fabbrica* (Confindustria, 1973).

84. Antonio Gramsci, *L'Ordine Nuovo. 1919–1920* (Turin: Einaudi, 1954). See also: AAVV, *I consigli operai* (Rome: Samonà and Savelli), 1972, and the review *Mondo Operaio*, no. 3 (1974), pp. 69–76, and no. 4 (1974), pp. 73–8, which contains a debate on industrial democracy with the participation of trade union leaders, intellectuals and politicians belonging mainly to the Socialist Party.

85. It is useful to remember the authors of the extra-parliamentary left already cited and in particular the *Quaderni Rossi* group and the innumerable articles reproduced in the many journals of the various groups.

86. Fabrizio D'Agostini, *La condizione operaia e i consigli di fabbrica* (Rome: Editori Riuniti, 1974).

87. 'Il sindacato c le sue strutture', no. 49, *Quaderni di Rassegna Sindacale*.

88. 'Il finanziamento del sindacato', no. 50 of *Quaderni di Rassegna Sindacale* (Sept. – Oct. 1974).

89. M. F. Neufeld, Italy: School for Awakening Countries, op. cit.

90. Guido Baglioni, 'La CISL, il mondo politico e il mondo cattolico', *Prospettiva Sindacale*, no. 15 (Dec. 1974), pp. 9–31; Guido Romagnoli, 'L'evoluzione nella composizione sociopolitica dei dirigenti e militanti CISL', *Prospettiva Sindacale*, no. 15 (Dec. 1974), pp. 33–51.

91. Giamprimo Cella, Bruno Manghi and Paola Piva, *Un sindacato italiano negli anni Sessanta, La FIM-CISL dall'associazione alla classe* (Bari: De Donato, 1972).

92. Giamprimo Cella, Bruno Manghi, Renzo Paldini, *La concezione sindacale della CGIL: un sindacato per la classe* (Rome: Edizioni ACLI, 1969).

93. bis Aris Accornero, *Gli anni '50 in fabbrica* (Bari: De Donato, 1973).

94. Giovanni Sartori, 'Il potere del lavoro nella società post-pacificata: un futuribile sindacale', op. cit.

95. Gino Giugni, 'Stato sindacale, pansindacalismo, supplenza sindacale', *Politica del diritto*, no. 1 (1970), pp. 49 ff.

96. Giorgio Gasparotti, 'Prassi sindacale e avventura pansindacalista', *La Rivista Trimestrale*, no. 35–36 (Dec. 1972), pp. 289 ff.

97. Tiziano Treu, 'La CISL degli anni cinquanta e le ideologie giuridiche dominanti', pp. 267–396, and Mario Ricciardi, 'Appunti per una ricerca sulla politica della CGIL: gli anni 50', pp. 161–262, both in Giovanni Tarello (ed.), *Dottrine giuridiche e ideologie sindacali*, (Bologna: Il Mulino, 1973).

98. Gino Giugni, 'Azione sindacale e politica giudiziaria', *Quaderni di Rassegna Sindacale*, no. 46 (Jan.–Feb. 1974), pp. 57–74; Maria Vittoria Ballestrero, 'Nuove prospettive del diritto del lavoro', *Democrazia e Diritto*, no. 1 (1975), pp. 105–21; Carlo Smuraglia, 'Giuslavoristi e movimento operaio', *Democrazia e Diritto*, no. 1 (1975), pp. 121–33.

99. Edoardo Ghera, 'Linee di tendenza della contrattazione sindacale 1968–1971' op. cit.

100. See the relation to the congress organized by the FLM (Federazione Lavoratori Metalmeccanici) written by Gino Giugni and Federico Mancini, 'Movimento sindacale e contrattazione collettiva', in *Potere sindacale*

e *ordinamento giuridico*, proceedings of the national Conference of FLM (Bologna, 10–11 July 1972) (Bari: De Donato, 1973).

101. Umberto Romagnoli, 'Il contratto collettivo difficile', *Politica del diritto*, no. 1 (Feb. 1971), pp. 1–84 (report at the 2nd National Conference of AISRI, Italian Industrial Relations Research Association).

102. Filippo Battaglia, 'I dirigenti sindacali italiani: alcuni dati', *Rassegna Italiana di Sociologia*, no. 2 (1971), pp. 335–60.

103. Guido Romagnoli, 'Democrazia di base ed organizzazione di classe nell'esperienza dei consigli', op. cit.

104. Bianca Beccalli, 'Scioperi e organizzazione sindacale. Milano, 1950–1970', *Rassegna Italiana di Sociologia*, no. 1 (1971), pp. 80, 300.

105. Seymour M. Lipset, Coleman and Trow, *Union Democracy* (trans.), *La Democrazia sindacale* (Milan: Etas Compass, 1972).

106. Paolo Zannoni, 'Strutture e funzioni dei sindacati', *Rivista Italiana di Scienze Politiche*, no. 1 (1973), pp. 73–127.

107. Domenico De Masi and Giuseppe Fevola (eds.), *I lavoratori nell'industria italiana*, (Milan: F. Angeli, 1974).

108. Raniero Panzieri, 'Sull'uso capitalistico delle macchine nel neo-capitalismo', op. cit., and 'Plusvalore e pianificazione, punti di lettura del "Capitale"', *Quaderni Rossi*, no. 4 (1963), pp. 257–88.

109. Marino Regini and Emilio Reyneri, *Lotte operaie e organizzazione del lavoro* (Padua: Marsilio, 1971).

110. Luciano Gallino, 'La crisi dell'organizzazione del lavoro', *Economia e Lavoro*, no. 3 (1972), pp. 250 ff.

111. ARPES, 'La organizzazione del lavoro operaio in fabbrica', *Quaderni di formazione ISFOL*, no. 9 (Nov. 1974).

112. Federico Butera, 'Mutamento dell'organizzazione del lavoro ed egemonia', *Economia e Lavoro*, no. 1 (January–February 1974), pp. 39–80.

113. Giamprimo Cella, *Divisione del lavoro ed iniziativa operaia* (Bari: De Donato, 1972).

114. 'La via italiana alla democrazia industriale', *Mondo operaio*, no. 2 (1974), pp. 49–52; no. 3 (1974), pp. 69–76; and no. 4 (1974), pp. 73–8.

115. Salvatore Vinci, 'Il funzionamento del mercato del lavoro in Italia. Un'analisi comparata delle varie interpretazioni', in *Il mercato del lavoro in Italia*, pp. 19–78.

116. Giuseppe De Meo, 'Evoluzione storica e recenti tendenze delle forze di lavoro in Italia', in *Il mercato del lavoro in Italia*, pp. 225–36.

117. Giorgio La Malfa and Salvatore Vinci, 'Il saggio di partecipazione della forza lavoro in Italia', *L'industria*, no. 4 (1970).

118. Franco Modigliani and Ezio Tarantelli, 'Una generalizzazione della curva di Phillips per un paese in via di sviluppo', in *Il mercato del lavoro in Italia*, pp. 200–240.

119. See Luigi Frey (ed.), *Lavoro a domicilio e decentramento dell'attività produttiva nei settori tessile e dell'abbigliamento in Italia* (Milan: F. Angeli, 1975).

120. Piero Ferri, 'Il mercato del lavoro in un contesto dualistico', in *Il mercato del lavoro in Italia*, pp. 83–111.

121. Luciano Gallino, 'Politica dell'occupazione e seconda occupazione', *Economia e Lavoro*, no. 1 (1975), pp. 81–95.
122. Michele Salvati, *La congiuntura piu lunga*, op. cit.
123. Ermanno Gorrieri, *La giungla retributiva* (Bologna: Il Mulino, 1973).
124. Paolo Sylos Labini, *Le classi sociali in Italia* (Bari: Laterza, 1974).
125. Ezio Tarantelli, 'Reddito e rinnovi contrattuali', *Rivista Internazionale di Scienze Sociali*, no. 4–5, (July–Oct. 1973), pp. 345–72.
126. Edoardo Ghera, 'Pubblico impiego e relazioni sindacali', *Economia e Lavoro*, no. 5–6 (1974), pp. 513–673; see, too, Carlo Marchese, 'Le strategie rivendicative nel pubblico impiego', *Quaderni di Rassegna Sindacale*, no. 47–8 (March–June 1974), pp. 44–82, and, in the same review, Renzo Razzano and Domenico Cini, 'L'organizzazione sindacale nel pubblico impiego', pp. 83–108.
127. 'Ristrutturazioni aziendali, cassa integrazione, e licenziamenti collettivi.' Proceedings of the Conference on 'Dismissals as a mean for reducing personnel and redundancies' (Bologna, 28–29 April 1973) (Milan: CELUC, 1974).
128. Luigi Mariucci, 'I licenziamenti collettivi tra prassi sindacale e opinioni degli interpeti', *Rivista trimestrale di diritto e procedura civile*, no. 2 (1975); pp. 698–732.
129. The report of this committee was published as: *Gli anni della conflittualità permanente* (Milan: F. Angeli, 1975).
130. 'Rapporto Pirelli', *Mondo Economico* (28 February 1970). As far as state participation companies are concerned, the study 'Dieci anni di attività contrattuale' (Associazione Italiana Intersind 1968) was an important attempt to define the cultural background of the labour–management relations within these companies. The oil and chemical public sectors have significantly contributed with their review 'Notiziario ASAP'. The strong influence that the state-owned companies had on the new legal ideologies had appeared as early as the 1960s and was confirmed by G. Tarello in the above-mentioned work. See also Ada Collida, Lucio De Carlini, Gianfranco Rosetto and Renzo Stefanelli, *La politica del padronato italiano: dalla ricostruzione all'autunno caldo* (Bari: De Donato, 1972).
131. *Potere sindacale e ordinamento giuridico*, op. cit.

10 Multinational Enterprise and Labour

B. C. Roberts

Introduction

This paper examines research into the impact of the development of multinational enterprise on industrial relations (Gunter, 1972, 1974). Although multinational enterprise is not a new phenomenon, the realization that it might have a special significance for organized labour has emerged largely over the past decade.

One of the earliest studies of industrial relations problems of multinational enterprises was made by Fayerweather in 1959. Based upon an examination of experience in Mexico, Fayerweather analysed the problems encountered by United States executives called upon to manage operations in an altogether different cultural environment. The role of United States management in the employment of high-level manpower in overseas subsidiaries in Mexico and Brazil was also examined by Shearer (1960). He expressed the view that United States corporations followed policies in developing countries that were determined by American economic, technological, and cultural factors. The main concern of Shearer (1967) and others such as Myers (1962) was whether the establishment of trade unions and the collective bargaining process based on a Western capitalist society was an appropriate model for developing countries. It was argued that the American model was bound to have only limited success, since it did not grow out of local circumstances, but was the product of America's historical development and its particular economic and social environment. Parts of the American system of industrial relations might be exportable, but the system as a whole was not. Those aspects which might be relevant to the experience of other countries would lie somewhat more in the management area than in that of trade unions and government relations, 'largely because managerial problems around the world appear to be more similar than trade union responses and government policies' (Myers, 1962).

The evolution of research from these studies in the early 1960s followed the emergence of a growing awareness and concern at the remarkable expansion of multinational enterprise during the postwar decades. Within the next few years, there was an upsurge of academic interest in the effect of the growth of multinational business on the world economy. Raymond Vernon (1967), Kindleberger (1969), Rolfe (1969), Polk (1968), Berhman (1969), and others in the United States, began major inquiries into the development and role of multinational business that were to produce important studies before the end of the 1960s.

There were also the first signs of interest by industrial relations scholars in Europe. Houssiaux (1964) analysed the organizational characteristics of large-scale multinational enterprises using the International Telephone and Telegraph Corporation, rather questionably, as a *typical* example. In 1967, Casserini, later to become a senior official of the International Metalworkers' Federation, published a significant article, *L'internationalisation de la production et les syndicats*, which described the centralization of decisions on the use of international resources by multinational enterprises and discussed the implications of this development for trade unions. In 1969 Demonts analysed the institutional characteristics of multinational enterprise in *'La recherche dans la firme plurinationale et la propagation des techniques'*.

Widespread public concern at the growth of American corporate investment in Europe was first aroused by a vigorous and influential attack published in 1967 by the French radical politician and journalist, Jean-Jacques Servan-Schreiber. *Le Défi Américain* (*The American Challenge*) caught the resurgent mood of France and its partners in the European Economic Community. It revealed a threat to Europe's economic independence and cultural values that appeared implicit in the great expansion of American corporate investment during the postwar period. Above all, it gave a focus to the incipient fears of Europe's intellectuals, trade unionists, and politicians that the big corporations controlled and directed from the United States were inexorably achieving total domination of the key sectors of European countries.

Impact of the Growth of Multinational Enterprises

The remarkable growth of the multinational enterprise during the past quarter of a century, whatever its economic, social, and political implications may be, constitutes a major change in the structure of the world economy. As Rolfe (1969), Wilkins (1970), and others have pointed out, this is not the first time that public concern has been aroused by the direct investment of companies overseas. By the end of the nineteenth century, both American and British companies had substantial investments in other countries (Wilkins, 1970). This growth of international business activity gave rise to public anxiety on both sides of the Atlantic. British business saw the influx of 'Yankee capital' as an American invasion of the home market which threatened the destruction of British firms (McKenzie, 1901). These fears were based upon a recognition that American companies had developed superior production technologies.

The concerns of Americans rose not from the fear of competition from British enterprises, but from their belief that international business firms were associated with the creation of international trusts and cartels to circumvent the Sherman Anti-Trust Act. Organized labour on both sides of the Atlantic showed a common fear of trusts and cartels as developments of capitalism which threatened their interests. They were also afraid that the device of multinational firms might be used to curb their own local collective bargaining activities (Pelling, 1954).

The great upsurge of foreign investment came after the Second World War. It has been estimated by Vaupel and Curham (1969) that between 1950 and 1967 the number of overseas manufacturing subsidiaries controlled by 187 United States-based multinational enterprises rose from 988 to 3646. The US Senate Tariff Commission surveyed 3400 US based multinationals and 23,000 majority-owned affiliates in 1966. In a report prepared in 1972 by the United Nations Secretariat, based on 15 selected countries which were the homes of multinationals, the figure arrived at for multinationals with headquarters in their countries was 7276. This total was by no means complete, since the 15 selected countries did not include Australia, Canada, and Japan, nor any of the less developed countries which provide a base for multinational enterprises (Clapham, 1974). Clapham cites the US Treasury Department as giving a figure of 8000 American-based firms with direct investments abroad. No comparable figure is available from public sources for other countries, but the estimate made by Clapham of the world total of multinational parent companies 'as being in the area of 12000 to 15000' is probably not far off.

If all the companies which are directly owned in whole or part, or are linked with multinationals, are added to the parent companies, the total is vastly greater. Unfortunately, it is even more difficult to make an accurate estimate of this total. It is probably, as Clapham suggests, in excess of 100 000 separate companies and it may be as large as 200 000.

The full significance of this astonishing growth of international business firms is not yet apparent, but what is of special significance is the emergence of a belief that the multinational corporation presents a threat to the interests of employees that is different from that of purely national enterprises. The unions, therefore, perceive it to be necessary to extend the institutions and processes of industrial relations from the national to the international level.

An article which had immense influence in spreading the perception of a world dominated by multinational enterprises was published in the *Wharton Quarterly* (winter 1968) by Perlmutter, who advanced the theory that the world was rapidly moving into an era of super-giant firms. By 1985, Perlmutter suggested the world economy would be dominated by two to three hundred huge multinational companies that would be responsible for the major part of world production and trade. Perlmutter's prediction was challenged by Rolfe (1969), who pointed out that 'the relative division of output between small and large companies in the U.S., where the integration process has gone on longest, has not really changed radically since the 1930s. Moreover, if one of the major motives for international investment stems from a company's holding some form of technical advantage, history indicates that standardized production, inviting numerous competitors, in time replaces even great technological leads.' However, Perlmutter's thesis has received considerable support and it has had a profound influence on political and labour leaders (Levinson, 1972; Lea, 1971). Dunning (1971) calculated that 'the foreign output of multinational production enterprises is currently expanding at the rate of 10 per cent per annum, twice the rate of growth of world gross national product and 40 per cent faster than world exports'.

A later statement of the super-giant thesis was made by the Group of Eminent Persons appointed by the United Nations to examine the role of multinational enterprises (1974b). The group stated that 'The typical multinational corporation is a large size, predominantly oligopolistic firm with sales running into hundreds of millions of dollars and affiliates spread over several countries'. It went on to say that 'those with less than $100 million can be safely ignored'. These statements have been severely criticized by Clapham (1974) as grossly misleading. The uneven geographical spread of multinational enterprise has also given rise to concern in countries where the degree of domination has been great. In 1967, of the hundred largest companies in Canada, 75 per cent were foreign-owned; in Australia 40 per cent of her mining and manufacturing was controlled by United States firms, and the subsidiaries of foreign-owned multinationals accounted for 25 per cent of the manufacturing exports of the United Kingdom and Europe (Dunning, 1971).

The implications for national sovereignty which have been raised by the growth of multinational enterprises have been explored by Vernon (1971), Kindleberger (1969), and others in terms of the global benefits of modern welfare capitalism. In the view of these and other authors, the multinational enterprise, by exporting capital, technology, and modern managerial skills, tends to bring about a modernization of less developed nations and a redistribution of wealth and income that benefits these nations and promotes world welfare (Roberts, 1964). Fayerweather (1960) has seen a fundamental conflict between the inherent demands of nationalism and the international character of a multinational enterprise. He has called for a political internationalism which would recognize the needs of the multinational enterprise and the political entity, the nation state, within which a multinational must operate. This notion has received support from both companies and unions in the discussions of the role of the multinational enterprise in the international agencies (United Nations, 1974a).

Marxist analysts have seen the tensions between multinational corporations and nation states and labour movements as an inevitable and predictable consequence of global economic imperialism (Sweezy and Macdoff, 1970; Palloix, 1973). Since the conflict can only be resolved by the eradication of private multinational enterprise by state socialism, no welfare optimum and stable political equilibrium is attainable according to this analysis.

Perlmutter (1965) has conceptualized the evolution of the multi-national enterprise in terms that are related to phases of their development as ethnocentric, polycentric, and geocentric. In its early stages of development a multinational enterprise is likely to be ethnocentric: the pattern of the management of its subsidiaries would mainly reflect the cultural characteristics of the parent corporation. In the polycentric stage of development, the subsidiary units would be managed by nationals of the host country. The dominant elements in the pattern of management would then reflect the culture of the countries in which the subsidiaries were located. The ultimate state of development, the geocentric, would come when a multinational enterprise had grown beyond the ethnocentric and the polycentric. A geocentric corporation would be essentially a corporation which developed its own ethos, a corporate culture which was not tied to any ethnic or national entity. It would recruit its managers on a global basis regardless of nationality and they would be expected to give their loyalty to the enterprise regardless of national considerations (Belford, 1964). At the date of Perlmutter's article there were few, if any, multinational enterprises which had reached the geocentric stage of development, but there were some, such as IBM, Shell, Unilever, and Nestlé, which were perhaps not too far distant from this concept of corporate organization.

The practical and political problems arising for the subsidiaries of multinationals have been analysed in terms of cultural differences in a series of studies (Gennard, 1972; Cleveland and Mangore, 1957; Roberts, 1972). The imperatives of host countries are generally accepted, and it would appear from the vast growth of multinational enterprise that, by and large, corporate and national needs are met (Shearer, 1967; Rocour, 1966; Model, 1967; Fayerweather, 1966; Lee, 1966).

However, in the transfer of technology and the managerial techniques which enable the transfer to take place successfully, an element of cultural shock is inevitable. Some research has suggested that when this shock is too great, the technological transfer either fails or is only sustained by a process of cultural imperialism which brutally changes the character of the host society.

As indicated earlier, it has been argued that both American-based corporations and trade unions which have sought to transfer their own concepts of organization to less developed countries have largely failed to make them effective (Shearer, 1967; Myers, 1962; Howe, 1964). However, there is also evidence, in both developed and developing countries, that multinationals have successfully transferred managerial methods which have been grafted on to host country industrial relations systems without causing a violent disturbance or provoking a hostile response (Steuer and Gennard, 1971).

The problem of comparisons between multinationals and national firms in terms of their employment conditions has received relatively little systematic research attention. Such information as there is suggests these points: in some important respects multinational companies have been innovators, through their role as transferers of technology and managerial skills; they also tend to adopt employment policies which keep them in line with the best of prevailing local practice, but not necessarily ahead of it (Warner, 1973).

By proving that they are following a policy of being good employers in host country terms, foreign-owned firms hope to avoid conflict with their employees and to avoid criticism from national employers as disturbers of the local labour market. This policy does not, however, always protect the multinational enterprise from international criticism, as recent attacks on the employment policies of foreign-owned firms in South Africa, Latin America, and Sri Lanka have shown. While there is also evidence that most foreign-owned firms endeavour to conform to local patterns of industrial relations (Walker, 1972), there have been conspicuous examples of some United States-based multinational enterprises vigorously pursuing policies which have been determined in the cultural environment of the corporate headquarters. The policies of these companies have been much quoted as examples of the alien influences of multinational enterprises.

Trade Union Perceptions and Responses

The contemporary concern displayed by unions toward the growth of multinational enterprise begins with the perception by American trade unions that establishment by American corporations of subsidiaries in Canada, the Caribbean, Latin America, Asia, and Europe as 'runaway' companies has resulted in an economic loss to American workers.

It was almost certainly the rise in unemployment in the late 1950s which led the unions in America to show a rising concern at the outflow of American capital. Unemployment was seen primarily at this time as a structural problem arising from the advent of automation and the export of capital overseas which enabled the American companies to escape the attentions of the unions. Goods were produced more cheaply and profitably overseas, thus competing with exports from the United States. The American worker faced losing his job, owing to the competition of cheap imports produced by the subsidiaries of American companies who were able to undercut the conditions of employment established by the American unions (Kujawa, 1975).

The migration of capital to the south in the 1940s and 1950s left many bitter memories of 'runaway' companies in the trade union movement. The organization of the south provided at least a partial solution, but this response to the 'runaway' company was more difficult to achieve when the capital export was across a national boundary. However, in the case of Canada, which raised the most immediate issues, the situation was not totally different from that of a shift across the boundaries of States within the union.

Although the first influence on trade union development in Canada was British, unions with their headquarters in the United States have been a dominant force in Canada since the mid-nineteenth century. The spead of United States-based unions across the border was due to the wish of Canadian workers to belong to unions which offered them a passport to jobs when they went south in search of employment. There were many other reasons, which have been listed by John Crispo in *International Unionism: A Study in Canadian-American Relations* (1967). Some United States unions were concerned with protecting their members from low-wage competition. Many simply felt the urge to grow, and Canada was sufficiently alike and close enough to be an obvious and inviting area in which to expand. In some cases, United States unions were invited to move in to compete with a left-wing union or to protect a jurisdiction threatened by another union moving into Canada.

Crispo does not mention the existence of the multinational enterprise, as such, as a significant factor in the concern of United States-based unions to organize Canadian workers. Although there was worry about job loss earlier, it was not until the late 1960s that the unions began to press for parity of wages and conditions of employment in the plants of companies that straddled the Canadian–United States border. Although the headquarters of the United Automobile, Aerospace, and Agricultural Implement Workers of America is situated on the river facing Canada, the first agreement covering both countries was only negotiated in 1967 (Blake, 1972). Blake has examined the factors that brought this agreement about and has emphasized that despite the fears on both sides, there is a 'high degree of integration in the automobile industry and the friendly environment in terms of the general social, cultural, economic, historical, and political interactions between the two countries'. He believes that this set of circumstances provided a favourable atmosphere for international collective bargaining.

Compared to their close ties to Canada, unions in the United States have much less in common with unions in the Caribbean, Latin America, Asia, and Africa. Nevertheless, the AFL–CIO and its affiliates have shown a strong desire to assist in the development of effective unions in these areas. They have actively supported the International Confederation of Free Trade Unions (ICFTU) and its regional bodies.

One of the first specific actions taken by a union in the United States to assist another union organizing in the same industry occurred in 1952 when the United Steel Workers of America (USW), which had amalgamated with the Aluminum Workers of America (AWA), sent an international representative to Jamaica to help striking bauxite workers. During the next few years, the USW contributed considerable sums of money to this organizing drive. This assistance was by no means entirely altruistic. It was motivated by a concern to ensure that the Jamaican union was strong enough to raise the pay of its members, to prevent the union from being taken over by left-wing communist-oriented leaders and thus threaten the supply of bauxite ore to the United States. At the same time, an increase in labour costs would raise the price of aluminium which was beginning to replace steel in many uses and therefore posed a threat to the jobs of steel-workers (Knowles, 1959). Jeffrey Harrod (1972) has discussed the motives of the United Steel Workers and concluded that the unions, the Canadian and American corporations, and the United States Government (he does not mention the Canadian Government) in the Cold War period, had a common interest in ensuring the shipment of aluminium to North American plants.

The common interest in the development of orderly industrial relations based upon the pattern of the home country was most clearly demonstrated in the active collaboration between British trade unions and British-based multinational enterprises making direct investments in British colonial territories (Roberts, 1964). However when goods produced in the colonies, or former colonial territories, were imported into Britain and undercut domestic prices, there was an outcry for protection and some criticism of low wages and other costs of production. Generally, however, unions in the home countries did not perceive that the companies they negotiated with at home had direct control over their subsidiaries. In any case, they did not link cheap imports with particular British companies.

At the end of the 1960s and the beginning of the 1970s, unions in European countries began to become concerned at a possible loss of jobs due to capital migration to developing countries and the subsequent import of lower-priced products. That American unions were quicker to perceive a threat from the export of capital by multinational companies can probably be explained by the higher levels of unemployment in the United States in the post war period and by the previous experience with companies migrating from the high-wage, industrial States in the north to the lower-wage States in the south.

The rising concern of the AFL–CIO at the domestic effects believed to result from the export of capital by United States-based multinationals was strongly expressed to Congress (Goldfinger, 1970; AFL–CIO Industrial Union Department, 1971; Jennings and Biemiller, 1970).

The upshot of this campaign was a Bill introduced by Senator Vance Hartke in September 1971, 'to amend the tariff and trade laws of the United States to promote full employment and restore a diversified production base; to amend the Internal Revenue Code of 1954 to stem the outflow of U.S. capital, jobs, technology and production and for other purposes'. A similar Bill was introduced into the House of Representatives by Representative James A. Burke.

As a result of the growing pressure from the AFL–CIO a number of massive inquiries were made by the US Department of Commerce (1972), in a report to the US Senate Finance Committee (1973), and by Stobaugh (1971). The methodological problems of determining the loss of employment caused by multinational firms are considerable (Hawkin, 1972). The outcome of the studies so far suggests that there is not much substance in the general charges made by the AFL–CIO regarding large-scale job losses. After considerable research effort, it is not possible to be absolutely certain, but the evidence seems to indicate that the effects of United States foreign investment have probably been of net benefit to employment in the United States (Stobaugh, Telesio and de la Torre, 1973).

The main effect on employment would seem to be on the change in its pattern in both home and host countries (Stobaugh *et al.*, 1973). British unions have been particularly concerned at the extent to which the research function has been deemed by foreign-owned companies to be a matter for the parent company, thus denying British scientists an opportunity for employment and the development of a body of indigenous technical knowledge.

Although Britain recognized early the threat that an invasion of American capital might pose, most countries, including Britain, have been extremely ready to welcome foreign investment (TUC [Trades Union Congress] Report on International Companies, 1970). In a paper prepared for the Conference on Industrial Relations and Multinational Corporations held in Chicago in 1973, Gunter Kopke, Secretary of the European Metalworkers' Federation, stated: 'Generally speaking, our criticism of the multinational corporations is not primarily directed at their size as to capital and turnover, but to their powerful position in society, the economy, towards consumers, working people and national governments. The European trade union movement does not oppose the existence of multinational corporations, but it objects to the attitudes and practices of the capitalists and their responsible managers in a number of multinational companies' (Kopke, 1973).

Anxiety on the part of British trade unions over the impact of multinational companies led to a report to a special congress in October 1970. This report indicated that there had been problems of adaptation to British industrial relations practice, including the finding that a 'substantial number of foreign owned firms had refused unions recognition' (TUC, 1970). However, since the report was made, a number of companies have decided to recognize unions and to enter into collective bargaining arrangements. Indeed, Moss Evans, a leading British trade union official, speaking at a conference at Michigan State University in November 1974, said they had given more complete cooperation with the unions than many British firms (Evans, 1974). Moreover there is evidence that foreign-owned companies have been innovators in advanced industrial relations policies (Gennard, 1972; Gennard and Steuer, 1971; Forsyth, 1973). There is also evidence that they have tended to adopt wage policies which have placed them near the top of the pay scales (Kujawa, 1971; Gennard, 1972; Dunning, 1976; Dunning, 1980).

The 1970 TUC Report concluded that 'the difficulties so far encountered by British trade unions in their dealings with foreign-owned subsidiaries have on the whole been relatively minor'. Nevertheless, the TUC saw a long-term threat in the growth of multinational enterprises, related in particular to aspects of their bargaining power arising from their ability over the course of time to switch their investments. A later TUC Report (1972) found that 'the direct problem of runaway companies to low-cost areas is relatively small'.

Unions in Europe have shown increasing concern with job redundancy and have sought to secure laws which would ensure compensation for any worker dismissed for economic reasons. Although steps have been taken in the direction of making redundancy highly expensive, unions have been particularly concerned with both threats and actual decisions of multinational companies to close down plants.

The threat by Henry Ford that the Ford Motor Company might be compelled to reconsider its investment programme if British unions failed to honour their agreements, and similar threats by other foreign-owned companies operating in Britain, evoked a strong response from the unions (Matthews, 1972). The TUC has made clear that it does not believe that any company with a massive investment would suddenly decide to establish its business elsewhere. The cases of AKZO in the Netherlands, Roberts Arundel in England, and General Electric in Ireland show that multinational enterprises are not proof against militant bargaining tactics if these are provoked by an unacceptable decision to close down plants or impose anti-union policies (Northrup and Rowan, 1974a). Nevertheless, the threat to switch investment to another country is one that unions find hard to counter if it is carried out gradually.

The vulnerability of the company depends upon a variety of circumstances. If a company is making massive losses and can satisfy its supply needs from other sources that cannot be stopped by the unions, it will be able to close down a plant, as Litton Industries' decision to close down its Imperial Typewriter plants in Britain has shown. If, on the other hand, a union can strike at the plant or prevent a market from being supplied from other plants, it is in a strong bargaining position, especially if, as in the AKZO case, it can secure the support of public opinion, government assistance, and international union aid (Northrup and Rowan, 1974).

The aspect of multinational enterprise which incites the most acute dislike on the part of unions is the fact that final decisions relating to investment, transfers of production, introduction of new methods, plant closures, and other issues of crucial importance to union members' interests may be made thousands of miles away at corporate headquarters, beyond the reach of the unions in the host country affected. Union leaders have declared their intense frustration at their apparent helplessness to influence such decisions or to know about them in sufficient time to take effective action (Woodcock, 1974). It is this situation which had led them to look to international trade union action as a means of exercising a greater degree of influence on the decision-making processes of multinational enterprises.

In seeking to bring pressure to bear upon a multinational enterprise at the international level, unions are confronted by a variety of difficult problems. Although there may be a transnational union interest in bargaining with a multinational enterprise, the strength of this interest may vary considerably between the national unions involved. Indeed, in some cases the conflict which they have in common with the multinational enterprise may turn out to be a conflict among themselves nationally. A victory leading to the raising of wages in a less developed country may well bring a greater benefit in terms of pay and jobs in a more advanced country.

Unions display a certain degree of altruism in the pursuit of their goals, but there are limits to the sacrifice that union members in one country are prepared to provide in fraternal support of union members in another country. In many countries, there will be legal obstacles to overcome; these may not be unsurmountable, but they could present serious difficulties (Wedderburn, 1972). The difficulties of 'coalition bargaining' have been pertinently discussed by Chernish (1969) in the United States. They are inevitably considerably greater when the coalition and coordination has to be achieved across national boundaries. If the problems of communication, confidence, and effective decision-making are great within the United States, they are clearly infinitely greater on an international scale.

International Role of Unions

In the mid-1960s, the international trade union organizations began to take an active interest in the development of multinational enterprises. Their response was inevitably affected by the fact that the international trade union movement had long been racked by ideological dissension. At the end of the 1960s there were three world organizations: the International Confederation of Free Trade Unions (ICFTU), which represented unions in non-communist countries; the World Federation of Trade Unions (WFTU), which represented trade unions in communist countries or in other countries which had unions with a communist ideology; and the successor of the International Federation of Christian Trade Unions (IFCTU), the World Confederation of Labour (WCL) (formed in 1968 to extend the organization to third-world groups).

International Trade Secretariats (ITS) were established before the First World War to act as centres of information and coordination for the unions concerned with particular industries (Lorwin, 1929). There has been considerable research interest in the response of the secretariats to multinational enterprises. The International Metalworkers' Federation (IMF), the International Union of Food and Allied Workers' Association (IUF), and the International Chemical and General Workers' Federation (ICF) appear to have been the first to recognize a need to develop a policy aimed at achieving some degree of common understanding of the threat posed by multinational enterprises. The world-wide development and rapid growth of the international automobile industry induced the IMF to develop a new policy (Kassalow, 1974). Unions responsible for organizing workers in the automobile industry, under the leadership of the United Automobile Workers' Union of America (UAW) (Reuther, 1964) held their first conference on the specific problems common to employees of General Motors and Ford in 1966 (Kassalow, 1974). This conference led to a decision to establish world automobile industry councils which would meet at regular intervals to exchange information and discuss bargaining tactics and strategies (IMF, 1968).

In 1964, the subject of multinational corporations was discussed at a world conference of the IUF. Following this conference the Secretariat of the IUF began to carry out research into one of the largest of the international food companies, Nestlé (Northrup and Rowan, 1974b). In the same year, Charles Levinson, an official of the IMF, left that organization to become General Secretary of the virtually moribund ICF. Levinson, knowing that the world chemical industry was dominated by a relatively small number of capital intensive giant multinational corporations, quickly recognized the opportunity to make the ICF into a powerful international organization. In 1967, at a world conference, Levinson persuaded the federation to adopt 'coordinated international collective bargaining' as a 'top priority policy objective'. Since that time Levinson has made frantic efforts to achieve this goal and with minimum resources but with an amazing public relations ability he was, perhaps more than anyone else, responsible for making the multinational corporation into a world-wide political issue for the unions (Northrup and Rowan, 1974a and b; Roberts, 1973).

Levinson has suggested that in the creation of an 'international global counterforce the first stage is a country-wide support of a single union in one country engaged in a dispute in a foreign subsidiary'. The second stage involves 'a jump to the level of multiple negotiations with a company in several countries at the same time'. The third stage is 'one of integrated negotiations around common demands' involving the parent and some or all of the subsidiaries (Levinson, 1972).

The establishment of a data bank of information relating to the terms and conditions of employment established in automobile plants owned by General Motors, Ford, Chrysler, Fiat, Toyota, Volkswagen, British Leyland, and Renault was an important step taken by the IMF, and was made possible by the resources of the UAW and IG-Metall, which enabled affiliated unions to obtain information they could use in the conduct of their own negotiations (IMF Report, 1968).

The International Food and Allied Process Workers' Federation (IUF) followed a somewhat different information strategy. Starting with the Nestlé Company, profiles of the main multinationals, with whom their affiliates had to deal, were carefully compiled by IUF research staff. These profiles were then made available to affiliated organizations to use as they thought fit in their own negotiations with the multinationals concerned (Northrup and Rowan, 1974b).

The ICF, as well as the IMF, has sought to establish world councils based on multinationals as a means of bringing together on a regular basis representatives of unions negotiating with particular enterprises and of coordinating their bargaining tactics. This organizational innovation has not yet been as effectively developed by the IMF in the automobile industry, but the federation believes emphatically that it is moving toward a more effective coordination of collective bargaining with major automobile manufacturers.

One of the main objectives of the federation is to try to bring about a common date for the termination of agreements between the unions and the major automobile manufacturers in the advanced industrial countries. This proposal was first made by Reuther (1964). Some progress has been made toward the achievement of this goal, more by accident than design, in the negotiations with the Ford Motor Company in Europe, but no serious attempt has been made to coordinate union demands and bargaining tactics. Although union leaders are prepared to support the idea of common contract termination dates, they have reservations based upon private worries of possible embarrassment caused by pressures to provide mutual support.

One of the first, and subsequently much quoted examples, of the coordination of international union action organized by an ITS was the case of the international glass manufacturing company, St Gobain. In 1969, Charles Levinson, General Secretary of the International Chemical and General Workers' Federation, convened a meeting of union representatives from seven countries in which the St Gobain company had plants, to coordinate bargaining strategy. The representatives agreed that no negotiations should be concluded in any country without their approval, and in the event of a strike in one country, all the unions would provide financial assistance if needed. They also agreed that if the strike was prolonged, overtime would be boycotted at other St Gobain plants, and any attempt to transfer production to another country during the strike would be opposed.

After the successful settlement of claims made by the unions in the German and Italian plants, a deadlock occurred in the United States when the company refused to concede a pay increase on the grounds that no profits had been made for the previous three years. A strike followed and was eventually settled more or less on the union's terms. In France, the communist unions were not a party to the coordination policy of the ICF, and accepted a far more modest settlement than had been gained by the United States unions. The ICF was able to claim the settlement in the United States as a tremendous victory for the coordination plan (Litvak and Maule, 1972).

In publicity terms Levinson brilliantly exploited the 'victory' over St Gobain (Northrup and Rowan, 1974a). In fact, it was an extremely limited victory since it resulted in a prolongation of the losses that the American company had sustained for a long period of time. The settlement finally convinced the parent company to sell the ailing subsidiary.

In 1973, the ICF seized the opportunity to promote its aim of coordinating collective bargaining in an industrial conflict which arose when AKZO, the Netherlands-based chemical and textile fibres company, sought to close down five plants in Switzerland, the Netherlands, Germany, and Belgium. An account of the events which led to the union occupation of the AKZO plant at Breda has been published as the *Enka Dossier Handboek Voor Bezetters* (1973) (Northrup and Rowan, 1974a; Piehl, 1973).

It is generally agreed by international union leaders that the possibility of negotiating a world-wide collective agreement with any multinational enterprise is extremely difficult, but some believe that the negotiation of more limited European-wide agreements may not be too distant.

In 1967 Philips Gloeilampenfabrieken of Eindhoven, one of the world's largest multinational enterprises, with a labour force of 390 000 in 70 countries, of whom 270 000 were employed in the European Economic Community, was requested to enter into discussions with representatives of European unions in the metal and electrical engineering industries. The company responded favourably to this approach, since it believed 'that economic integration in Europe would logically lead to a certain degree of social integration' (Dronkers, 1973). This meeting was mainly concerned with Philips' production policy in Europe and the levels of decision-making in the company.

Further meetings were held in later years, but the company flatly refused to go beyond a consultative meeting and enter into European-wide agreements on specific matters. Such agreements, the company felt, would infringe the autonomy of its separate national companies and would conflict with national agreements between employer organizations and unions to which Philips was a party. European agreements might also be in conflict with 'national legislation and government policy, with existing agreements and rules on related subjects, and with the legal roles of enterprise councils in some EEC countries' (Dronkers,

1973). However, Dr Dronkers, its director of personnel, 'emphasized the importance of a regular dialogue between partners leading to a better understanding of continuously changing problems experienced on both sides'. Moreover, the company was ready to enter into realistic and concrete projects to improve the quality of working life if a problem-solving approach could be agreed upon with the unions (Dronkers, 1973).

The conditions which must be satisfied to bring about an extension of the collective bargaining process have been generally analysed by Ulman (1975), and by Roberts (1973) and David Blake (1972a) in studies more specifically related to Europe.

The International Confederation of Free Trade Unions (ICFTU) has published in its journal, the *Free Labour World*, a large number of articles on multinational corporations based on its own research and evidence obtained from its affiliates. In its statement, *The Multinational Challenge*, in the Report of the Tenth World Congress held in London in July 1972, the ICFTU supported the efforts of the ITS 'in working toward coordinated collective bargaining with these multinational companies' (ICFTU, 1973) but most of its efforts have been devoted to promoting conferences and giving evidence to international agencies about the need to develop an international system of controls that would regulate the activities of multinational enterprises.

The ICFTU has indicated that it does not oppose the existence of multinational enterprises as such (Maier, 1970). The communist-controlled World Federation of Trade Unions, however, is fundamentally antagonistic to multinational enterprises since they are the product of monopoly capital and by definition are seen as antithetical to the interests of workers. The WFTU has urged the nationalization of multinational corporations in order to protect workers' interests, and to defend each country's right to decide how it should use its economic resources. The international codes of conduct prepared by the ICFTU are attacked as a deception. 'Some trade union leaders in the reformist tradition . . . are expressing views supporting the multinational companies and . . . are trying to bring the trade unions to seek international norms and institutions which would compel the multinational companies to make their social policy more progressive. To hope that the multinational companies will allow themselves to be liberalized by the monopolistic state, or by a supra-national bridge set up by the monopolies is an illusion about changing the nature of capitalism' (Kassalow, 1974b).

The World Confederation of Labour has denounced multinational corporations in the same Marxist terms as the WFTU and it has emphasized the need to create a true international solidarity and to achieve a new society, 'the basic characteristics of which must be oriented towards the socialization of the means of production, democratic planning of the economy and self-government of the economy and society by the workers' (WCL, World Congress Report, 1973).

These ideological divisions make the task of developing an effective coordination of union action at the international level extremely difficult, and of creating unified organizations that would bargain as a single international unit virtually impossible. The most that has been achieved has been a degree of unity for specific and limited purposes, as has been achieved between communist, socialist, and Christian unions in Belgium, Holland, France and Italy. In the national context this level of unity, though confined to particular collective bargaining situations, has been quite effective in these countries but there has been little evidence that such cooperation is possible at the international level.

A much more difficult problem for the unions is the conflict of national economic interests, since this can and does occur between unions of like-minded ideological views. Although the ITS have achieved a degree of success in securing transnational support in a number of disputes, none of them so far has been able to reach the stage where they could make a common claim and be confident that they could conduct negotiations knowing that they could rely on the unswerving support of every union that might be involved. As Lloyd Ulman has pointed out, an international agreement is only likely when both sides are fully convinced by the hard facts of the situation that it would be in their economic interests to make such a concord, *and* when this position has the support of the nation states involved (Ulman, 1975).

Attitudes of Multinational Enterprises to the Challenge of Unions

The general attitude of multinational enterprise managers toward union demands for multinational bargaining procedures has been either to deny that they were multinational enterprises, or to argue that even if they were, they pursued a policy of national devolution which made any notion of company-wide industrial relations policy impossible. At the Third World Congress, International Industrial Relations Association, London, 1973, Douglas H. Soutar, Vice President, American Smelting and Refining Company, declared: 'Many if not most of us in management deny the existence of such an entity, for it exists neither in law nor in fact' (Soutar, 1973).

The problem of defining a multinational has been widely discussed (Dunning, 1971; Lea and Webley, 1973). It is quite clear that the range of organizations that might be covered by this term is extremely wide. Multinational enterprises vary greatly in all respects. They differ in size, technology, type of product or service produced, pattern of organization, and philosophy of the parent company. At one extreme is the company which wholly owns all its subsidiaries, has a clearly defined philosophy, an integrated structure, and a highly centralized pattern of management. At the other extreme is the company whose subsidiaries are national companies linked to a multinational enterprise through participating shareholdings; the multinational company makes no attempt to impose its own views on its subsidiaries and allows them to follow their own policies as long as they are able to pay a reasonable rate of return on the capital they employ.

All these factors will have an influence on the behaviour of management and the response of the parent company and subsidiaries to the industrial relations problems they encounter (Roberts, 1972).

Well aware of conflicts with national interests that might arise, the management of subsidiaries of multinationals tend to seek maximum identification with the country in which they are located. They fear that national unions would be neither satisfied with agreements negotiated internationally nor *able* to honour such agreements. (IOE [International Organization of Employers], 1974). It is firmly the view of management that industrial relations are a product of national cultures and therefore company organization must be administered within the framework of a national culture (IOE, 1974; Denise, 1973). This view is emphatically asserted even by multinational corporations which have a strongly projected corporate industrial relations philosophy.

For their part trade union leaders tend to speak even more disingenuously of multinational enterprises as if they were all exactly alike, and they seem to believe that the most important decisions affecting employees are made at corporate headquarters situated thousands of miles away in another country (Benedict, 1974). However, the evidence suggests that neither management nor views of uniformity of policy or behaviour are correct (Kujawa, 1971; Brooks and Remmers, 1974).

As one example of cultural differences, American and English companies vary in their treatment of headquarters' involvement in industrial relations. American headquarters tend to become actively involved in a few areas such as collective bargaining, while their British counterparts tend to be more removed.

These differences between American and English companies may arise partly from their broader corporate philosophies (Heise, 1973). It is probably more common for American companies operating abroad to do so through wholly owned subsidiaries to avoid situations such as joint ventures and local capital participation, in which local influence is bound to be greater. Greater emphasis is placed by United States corporations on central financial control, operated through rigorously applied accounting procedures, profit planning, budgetary controls, and other methods of assuring that financial goals are met (Brooks and Remmers, 1970). These policies inevitably have an impact on industrial relations and personnel policies which must be adjusted to permit the achievement of financial goals. British companies have a noticeably less highly developed company philosophy and are more ready to adjust to local circumstances.

Both British and American companies have thought it necessary to employ expatriate managers, but in the advanced industrial countries British companies have emphasized the desirability of employing as many indigenous managers as possible. American companies have tended to show less confidence in a totally foreign management, especially in the early stages, and have generally introduced and often maintained a number of senior American managers. However, in recent years they have become more polycentric, as Rosow (1974) insists has been the trend in Exxon.

Although management of multinational enterprises is extremely hostile to the notion of international collective bargaining, some managers now tend to see its development as highly likely, if not inevitable. When asked when they thought they might have to face this prospect, United States managers thought it would arrive quicker than did their British counterparts. Both British and American managers were convinced that international union pressures would be damaging to their business, but a much higher proportion of United States-based companies were prepared to say that they would resist the organizing and bargaining efforts of the unions. British managers were more ready to seek a compromise. This difference probably reflects the fact that American business firms are more successful in holding unions at bay than British firms (Roberts and May, 1974).

Robert Copp (1974), international liaison manager of the Ford Motor Company, has argued that industrial relations questions 'generally concern remunerations and conditions of employment, including employee benefit plans; recruitment and training of employees; recognition of trade unions or other employee representatives; establishment of collective bargaining and grievance resolutions procedures; and resolution of disputes that might arise concerning these matters. Management decisions about new or redeployed production facilities are not, as such, industrial relations questions. However, the effects of these decisions on employees are the concern of industrial relations executives in management and, in most firms, these effects are an appropriate subject for consultation and bargaining with recognised representatives of designated groups of employees.' It is, in fact, precisely the decisions relating to the location of plants and long-term investment policies that have given rise to some of the strongest union criticism of multinational corporations.

The Role of International Employers' Organizations

The extension of collective bargaining from a local to a national scale required not only the growth of national unions, but also the growth of national employers' organizations.

Parallel developments at the international level might be necessary, if bargaining were based on multinationals. Employers have in the past supported the International Organization of Employers primarily to ensure that their interests were effectively represented to the governing body, conferences and committees of the International Labour Organization. In matters affecting their commercial interests, the International Chamber of Commerce has played a leading role.

Since the establishment of the European Economic Community, the employers of Western Europe have formed a number of organizations to promote their interests. The principal employers' organization is the *Union des Industries de la Communauté Européenne* (UNICE) with which central employers' organizations of each country are affiliated. A number of industry organizations have also been established covering such industries as engineering, chemicals, plastics, textiles, and electronics.

The main concern of UNICE has been with EEC proposals affecting industry. In this respect it has had virtually daily contacts with the representatives of the European Commission. UNICE's role, like that of the European Trades Union Congress (ETUC), is entirely political, though it is conceivable that at some stage it might participate in some form of European-wide agreement with the ETUC. Both, however, would have to achieve a far greater degree of integration and coordination than at present. At this stage UNICE reflects the view of the employers that multinational enterprises do not experience different industrial relations problem from those of their domestic counterparts.

Trade Union and Political Demands for Regulation of Multinational Enterprises

Trade unions have never been simply bargaining agencies; they have always been ready to turn to governments for help and assistance when it would be to their advantage. There have been, however, considerable differences in the emphasis which unions have placed on the collective bargaining and political methods of achieving their goals in different countries and in the same country at different times. The demand by unions for the legal regulation of foreign investments by multinationals and the limiting of taxation privileges, as envisaged in legislative proposals in the United States, for example, arose from a recognition by the AFL–CIO that their objectives could not be achieved by the collective bargaining process alone.

The aims of the unions in the Burke–Hartke Bill were consistent with their demands for tariffs and other forms of protective controls on imports of foreign manufacturers. In both cases, the unions were convinced that these measures would benefit the employment and wages of their members (Ruttenberg *et al.*, 1971).

The demand by unions in the host countries for the legal regulation of foreign-owned companies is motivated by the same objectives as the unions in the home countries, and it is subject to perhaps even greater contradictions. In many host countries, foreign capital is attracted by special tax privileges such as tax holidays, investment grants, training grants, and other incentives. Unions have generally been strong supporters of these investment incentive schemes since they have perceived them as an effective way of creating more employment, introducing new technology, and raising wages and salaries. However, once the capital has been invested, the attitude of the host country unions becomes the same as the unions in the home country. They wish to retain that capital and desire the foreign-owned firm to reinvest its profits, issue local stock, and in effect become a national enterprise. The policy of 'nationalising' foreign capital may well, however, be in conflict with the policy of seeking to attract such capital.

The conflict of interest between home and host unions is illustrated by the code, adopted by the Swedish government at the request of the unions, regulating the export of capital under the government aid programme to developing countries. Swedish firms which seek government underwriting for their investments in developing countries, where they have been urged to expand for aid reasons, are required to satisfy specified social conditions. The Swedish guidelines were more specific and covered a wider range of issues than for a time were called for by the ICFTU in its demands for an international regulatory code for multinationals. In addition to requiring the company concerned 'as far as practicable [to] try to break existing discrimination patterns which counteract economic and social development', they should also (1) recognize trade unions; (2) not restrict union officials in the exercise of their functions; (3) disclose wage statistics before negotiation; (4) enter into collective agreements; (5) give notice of lay-offs and assist readjustment of workers laid off; (6) cooperate with unions in finding a peaceful solution to disputes (Blake, 1973). In terms of social welfare, companies should make provision to increase the skill of their employees through training, substitute local for foreign personnel as quickly as possible, help employees find suitable housing, take adequate steps to ensure those who work for the company or live close to it are maintained in good health, make it possible for employees to enjoy a good standard of nutrition and provide libraries, meeting places, and training and entertainment so as to facilitate workers' adjustment to a new environment (Blake, 1973).

One of the most frequent criticisms of multinational enterprises made by unions is that they are able to adjust their location of profit to suit national tax requirements through transfer price policies (Tugendhat, 1971). The financial administration of multinational enterprise is a highly complex matter and the transfer of funds is inevitably affected by exchange rates, tax policies, and trading regulations (Brooks and Remmers, 1970; Chown, 1974). Undoubtedly in the past, multinationals were able to benefit by lax tax administration. This problem is, however, much less significant, Clapham argues, than most trade unionists think. 'The scale of inter-firm transfers is much smaller than generally supposed, and the freedom to fix transfer prices and royalties is closely circumscribed, so that the multinational's freedom to minimize tax, compete unfairly or dodge exchange controls is relatively small' (Clapham, 1974). Similarly, multinational corporations have been accused of endangering exchange rates and world economic stability by moving funds across national frontiers in an insatiable search for profits and capital growth (Levinson, 1972). The size of the liquid funds controlled by multinational enterprises and speculative movements of money, however, appears to be small relative to monetary flows in connection with world trade, capital flows, and intergovernmental transactions (*OECD Report on Short-term Capital Movements* 1974, Paris); US Senate, *Implications of Multinational Firms for World Trade and Investment and for US Trade and Labor*, 1973).

Nevertheless, the total effect of multinational enterprises on all aspects of the world economy is considerable, and though any single element of their activity may be marginal, it may be sufficient to make a serious impact on economic stability. Although no government may wish to discourage multinational enterprises from commercial activities which would bring economic benefit, most governments have become sufficiently concerned at the possible implications of the growth of multinational enterprise to be willing to respond to trade union pressures to encourage the international agencies to examine the situation and to make proposals for their regulation (Clarke, 1973).

The Role of the International Agencies in Union–Multinational Relations

The international labour organization (ILO)

The first international agency to become concerned with the problems of workers in multinationals was the International Labour Organisation. After two years of discussions, during which the representatives of the employers' organizations opposed the idea that the ILO should investigate multinationals, it was finally agreed that a report should be prepared and then be considered by a special conference convened by the governing body (Jenks, 1972). In the 1973 report prepared for the special conference, the ILO examined (1) the nature and significance of multinational enterprises; (2) the impact of multinational enterprises on manpower; (3) conditions of work and life in multinational enterprises; (4) industrial relations in a multinational framework; and (5) the relevance of international labour standards to multinational enterprises (ILO, 1973).

The opportunity for the ILO to investigate the significance of the multinational enterprise offered the possibility of the ILO developing and applying international labour standards as a solution to the problems of controlling multinational enterprises in the social interest.

This possible development of the international labour code seemed of particular concern to the then Director-General who saw in it a fulfilment of a primary function of the ILO against those who had argued that this type of regulatory activity had lost its former significance (N.M., 1971).

The ILO report and conference produced many suggestions from government, employer, and trade union representatives. The following recommendations were made to the governing body:

That the International Labour Office be requested to undertake intensive and extensive studies concerning issues in the social policy field to provide the comprehensive information needed to identify and determine the problems that may be specific to multinational enterprises as opposed to national firms. . . . In order that such studies can be properly carried out:

(a) governments should be invited to improve their statistics in relation to these studies in consultation with workers and employers. To facilitate such studies in countries where such statistics may not be adequate the International Labour Office, upon request, should assist them in developing statistics and data collecting machinery;

(b) employees and workers and their respective organizations should be invited and encouraged to provide the data necessary for such statistics and studies;

(c) the studies should be based upon appropriate methodology and research techniques to be developed by the International Labour Office in terms of their objectives and in consultation with other relevant institutions. (ILO, 1973)

The Director-General was also instructed to undertake a study of the usefulness of international principles and guidelines in the field of social policy relating to the activities of multinational enterprises. If the study proved that such principles and guidelines were to be useful and feasible, the governing body would initiate action to make them effective.

Following five years study and extensive consultation between all involved parties a *Tripartite Declaration of Principals concerning Multinational Enterprises and Social Policy* was adopted by the Governing Body of the I.L.O. in 1977 (I.L.O. govern 1977).

United Nations

In July 1972, the Economic and Social Council of the United Nations adopted unanimously a resolution calling upon the Secretary-General to appoint 'a group of eminent persons' to study the role of the multinational corporations and their impact on the process of development, especially that of developing countries (United Nations, 1972) Such a group of eminent persons was established to study the Role of MNCs on Development and International Relations. The Department of Economic and Social Affairs of the United Nations Secretariat prepared a factual study for the group which analysed the problems, and discussed various proposals for action (United Nations, 1973). The Group took evidence from 'fifty leading personalities from Government, business, trade unions, special public interest groups and universities' (United Nations, 1974b). The group recommended 'that home countries should not hamper the process of transfer by multinational corporations of the production of labour-intensive and low-skill products to developing countries; and that they should protect the domestic work force displaced by this transfer, through adjustment assistance measures such as re-training and re-employment in more productive and higher paying jobs, and not through restrictions on imports'. It also recommended a detailed set of guidelines which would strengthen the role of unions and the protection of workers involved with multinationals, and a permanent research body to monitor the activities of multinationals.

OECD – Studies of multinational enterprises

As with the other international agencies, the OECD began to show concern at the growth of multinational enterprises in the early 1970s. Its Industry Committee established a working party to conduct investigations into multinational enterprises which produced an interim report in 1972 (not published until 1974). Although meetings of trade union and employer experts had been held earlier, it was only in 1973 that the organization began to be seriously concerned about the industrial relations aspects of the role of multinational enterprises and to discuss with member states and the advisory committees of employers and trade unions actions that might be taken. By the spring of 1974 a programme of study had been agreed upon which would 'permit a comprehensive assessment of the question of whether to cope with possible conflict between the operation of the firms and government policies' (Clarke, 1973). In the field of industrial relations, employment, and wages studies were made of:

(a) the effects of multinational corporation activity on the labour market, in 'host' and 'home' countries, and on wage levels in host countries;

(b) the influence of multinational corporations in promoting advanced management techniques relevant to industrial relations and employment;

(c) the extent of the employment by multinational corporations of foreign nationals in operations in host countries and the specific industrial relations problems connected with such employment (OECD, 1974).

By 1976 agreement was needed between the member governments of the OECD on the adoption of guidelines which were acceptable to the employers and the unions and governments (Roberts and Liebhaberg, 1977). The basic principles on which the guidelines were based were that member countries should treat foreign controlled enterprises no less favourably than they accorded domestic enterprises in like situations. The guidelines were not legally enforceable, but member states undertook to give support to their application.

The most significant use of the guidelines occurred when an American owned electronics company closed down in Brussels without observance of the principles laid down. In the event the Belgium government, with the apparent support of the OECD, succeeded in obtaining exgratia payments for those who lost their jobs (Blanpain, 1979).

In 1979, the guidelines were reviewed by the Ministers of the OECD member countries. They concluded that 'they provide a sound and realistic framework for cooperation not only among governments, but also between governments, enterprises and labour'. Minor alterations were approved and it was agreed that member governments should report every two years on experience and development at national level (International Investment and Multinational Enterprises, Review of the 1976 Declaration and Decisions, OECD, Paris 1979).

The European Economic Community and multinational enterprises

Article 118 of the Treaty of Rome (1957) states that 'the Commission shall have the task of promoting close cooperation between Member States in the social field, particularly in matters relating to employment; labour law and working conditions; basic and advanced vocational training; social security; prevention of occupational accidents and diseases; occupational hygiene; the right of association, and collective bargaining between employers and workers.' The signatories of the Treaty clearly believed that the development of an integrated system of industrial relations would be an important element in the establishment of a viable European Economic Community.

Although, as Georges Spyropoulos (1966) has pointed out, the basic concepts of industrial relations and trends of development in the member states are similar, relatively little progress has been made toward the achievement of a more unified system. This slow progress has been analysed by Michael Despax (in Gunter (ed.), 1972). The obstacles to be overcome, listed by Despax, include (1) differences in national laws governing collective bargaining; (2) uncertainty as to the ways and means whereby transnational industrial relations could be developed; (3) the ideological divisions and structural differences in the national trade union organizations; and (4) the problem of creating machinery which would relate collective agreements made at the European level to national legal systems and to local district and plant circumstances.

The growing influence of multinational enterprises on the economic and political life of the countries in which they operate has given rise recently to deep anxieties in the areas of employment, competition, tax avoidance capital movements, and the economic independence of developing countries (EEC *Bulletin*, 1973). In the same *Bulletin* the Commission declared that the measures to be taken 'should not impede the development of a phenomenon with recognized economic and social advantages but they should merely aim at guarding the community against its harmful effects with the help of a suitable legal framework' (EEC *Bulletin*, 1973). It considered that the growth of European collective agreements would help to solve the problems which multinational corporations have created, and held the view that a multinational enterprise should give straightforward information on the following items: (1) funds invested, reinvested, and transferred to country of origin; (2) the origin and composition of the capital; (3) the number of jobs created and abolished; (4) declared profits and taxes paid, as percentages of turnover; and (5) expenditure on research and income from licences.

Strong pressure has been placed on the EEC by the European Trades Union Confederation (ETUC) to persuade it to adopt measures which would secure the democratic control of multinational enterprises. The ETUC was established in April 1969 to represent and promote in common the social, economic, and cultural interests of European workers, with particular regard to all European institutions, including those of the European Communities and the European Free Trade Area

(Blanpain, 1972). The ETUC was founded by affiliates of the ICFTU, but it is an independent body, and has extended its membership to include the affiliates of the WCL and the communist-led trade union federation of Italy and the CISL.

The Commission proposals already go a good way toward meeting the demands of the ETUC, but apart from specific measures that the Community may take to regulate the activities of multinational enterprises, the successful achievement of the Community's basic economic goals of common product markets, capital markets, and labour markets will inevitably bring about conditions that are likely to promote more uniform levels of pay and conditions of employment. Such a development should foster the growth of agreements that are company-wide and cut across the boundaries of the member states.

If in addition the Community moves toward a common social policy and toward a common legal framework, this set of factors will further encourage and assist the development of European patterns of collective bargaining. The resolution of company law and the growth of consultative processes on a European level, if achieved, would be a significant step in the direction of developing a European system of industrial relations. Within the boundaries of the EEC, unions and employers are likely to become increasingly aware of advances in employment conditions in member countries. It is unlikely, however, that Eurobargaining will supersede national and local plant bargaining, but it may eventually add a significant dimension to the bargaining process in the EEC (Van Dierendonck, 1972; Gunter, 1972).

Conclusions

Research can ascertain facts, reveal trends, and clarify issues, but it cannot settle conflicts of interest or differences of value judgement. The research surveyed here indicates that there is a world-wide concern about the growth of multinational enterprise, but there are sharp divisions of opinion as to the significance of this development among employers, unions and governments.

It appears that a new dimension in industrial relations is emerging at the international level. It is not yet clear, however, whether this will lead to the development of an international level of collective bargaining which will be effectively incorporated into the process of collective bargaining at the national level. There is a strong probability, however, that over the next decade the international trade union organizations will be increasingly called upon by their constituent national affiliates, when engaged in negotiations with multinational companies, to secure assistance from unions in other countries. There is thus likely to be a growth of mutual help and support. Nevertheless, it is likely that national interests will continue to be a predominant influence on the decisions of employers, unions, and governments for many years to come.

Although the systems of industrial relations in each of the nine countries which make up the European Economic Community are different, there is the possibility that the mutuality of interest of the unions and employers will eventually mature to the point where limited agreements might be reached. This will depend, however, on management recognizing the evolution of international agreements as being to their advantage. The possibility of this happening will be made more likely if the EEC consolidates the development of common product, capital, and labour markets and develops a supportive Community-wide social policy and legal framework. It is unlikely, however, at an intercontinental level that mutuality of union action will extend beyond *ad hoc* supportive gestures; in situations where the multinational enterprise involved is vulnerable to such pressures, they may bring the unions concerned positive results without leading to a permanent system of collective bargaining.

At the international level, it is possible that effective pressure on multinational enterprises, compelling them to conform to agreed-upon international standards, may come from the international agencies. The effect of an international code in terms of welfare criteria is difficult to assess. The adoption of a world-wide code might be possible, but how far it would significantly advance the interests of those in a weak bargaining position cannot be predicted with certainty.

In the study of multinational enterprise and labour, it is clear that there are large gaps in factual knowledge and major problems of research methodology to overcome. The monitoring and analysis of the multinational developments following from those covered in this survey will call for a continuous, innovative research effort in the years ahead (Bomers, 1976).

REFERENCES

AFL–CIO, Industrial Union Department, *Needed, a Constructive Foreign Trade Policy* (Washington, D.C.: May 1971).

Belford, John A., 'Centralised Policy Direction of the Industrial Relations Function in an International Company', *I.I.R.A. Proceedings of Seventeenth Annual Meeting* (Chicago: 1964).

Berhman, Jack, *Some Patterns in the Rise of Multinational Enterprise* (Chapel Hill: University of North Carolina Research Paper, 1969).

Benedict, Dan, *Multinational Companies: Their Relations with Their Workers* (Geneva: IMF, 1974).

Blake, David H., 'Multinational corporation, international union and international collective bargaining: a case study of the political, social and economic implications of the 1967 U.A.W.–Chrysler Agreement', in Hans Gunter (ed.), *Transnational Industrial Relations*, (London: Macmillan, 1972).

——, 'International labour and the regulation of multinational corporations: proposals and prospects', *San Diego Law Review*, (November 1973), Vol. II, no. 1.

——, 'The internalisation of industrial relations', *Journal of International Business Studies* (Fall 1972b).

Blanpain, Roger, 'Efforts to bring about community-level collective bargaining in the Coal and Steel Community and the EEC', in Gunter (ed.), *Transnational Industrial Relations* (London: Macmillan, 1972).

Bomers, G. J. B., *Multinational Corporations and Industrial Relations* (Amsterdam: Van Gorcum, 1976).

Bowers, G. B. H., *Multinational Corporations and Industrial Relations* (Netherlands: Van Goram & Co., 1976).

Brooks, Michael I. and Remmers, H. Lee (eds.), *The Multinational Company in Europe: Some Key Problems* (Ann Arbor: University of Michigan Press, 1974).

Brooks, Michael I. and Remmers, H. Lee, *The Strategy of Multinational Enterprise* (London: Longman, 1970).

Casserini, K., 'L'internationalisation de la production et les syndicats', *Revue économique et sociale* (July 1967).

Chernish, William N., *Coalition Bargaining: A Study of Union Tactics and Public Policy* (Philadelphia: University of Pennsylvania Press, 1969).

Chown, John F., *Taxation and Multinational Enterprise* (London: Longman, 1974).

Clapham, Sir Michael, Josiah Stamp Memorial Lecture, University of London (London: November, 1974).

Clarke, R. O., *The Multinational Company: The State and International Organisations*, a paper given at the 3rd World Congress of the IIRA, London (September 1973).

Cleveland, Harian, and Mangore, Gerrard J., *The Art of Overseamanship* (Syracuse University Press: 1957).

Copp, R. 'Levels of Management Decisions', Conference on Industrial Relations Problems Raised by Multinational in Advanced Industrial Societies, Michigan State University (November 1974).

Crispo, John, *International Unionism: A Study in Canadian–American Relations* (Toronto: McGraw Hill, 1967).

Demonts, Roger, 'La recherche dans la firme plurinationale et la propagation des techniques', in François Perroux (ed.), *Recherche et activité économique* (Paris: A. Colin, 1969).

Denise, Malcolm L., 'Industrial Relations and the Multinational Corporation, Inferences from Ford Experience', Graduate School of Business (Chicago: May 1973).

Despax, Michael, 'European Regional Integration and Collective Bargaining' in H. Gunter (ed.), *Transnational Industrial Relations* (London: Macmillan, 1972).

Dronkers, P. L., 'A Multinational Organisation and Industrial Relations: The Philips' Case', a paper presented at the 3rd World Congress of the International Industrial Relations Association (London: September 1973).

Dunning, J. H., *The Multinational Enterprise* (London: George Allen and Unwin, 1971).

European Economic Community, *Bulletin*, (1973).

Evans, Moss, Paper given at the Michigan State University Conference on Industrial Relations Problems Raised by Multinationals in Advanced Industrial Societies (November 1974)

Fayerweather, John, *The Executive Overseas: Administrative Attitudes and Relationships to a Foreign Culture* (New York: Syracuse University Press, 1959).

——, 'Long-range planning for international operation', *Californian Management Review*, (Fall 1960).

——, '19th Century ideology and 20th century reality', *Columbia Journal of World Business*, 1 (1) (Winter 1966), pp. 77–84.

'The Foreign Trade and Investment Act of 1972', S. 2592, 92d Cong., 1st sess., 28 September 1971, Congressional Record 97, no. 142; S15135–42.

Forsyth, David J. C., 'Foreign-owned firms and labour relations: a regional perspective', *British Journal of Industrial Relations* (March 1973).

Gennard, J., *Multinational Corporations and British Labour: a Review of Attitudes and Responses* (London: British North America Committee, 1972).

Gennard, J. and Steuer, M. D.,'The industrial relations of foreign-owned subsidiaries in the U.K.', *British Journal of Industrial Relations* (July 1971).

Goldfinger, Nathaniel, Speech to a conference of the Industrial Union Department of the AFL–CIO (19 March 1970).

Gunter, Hans, 'International Collective Bargaining and regional economic integration: some reflections on experience in the E.E.C.', in Gunter (ed.), *Transnational Industrial Relations*, (1972).

——, 'An overview of some recent research on multinatinational corporations and labour', *IILS Bulletin*, No. 12 (Geneva, 1974).

——, United States Industry in Britain (Wilton House Publications: London, 1976).

——, 'Employee Compensation in US Multinationals and Indigenous Firms; An Exploratory Micro-Macro Analysis', *British Journal of Industrial Relations* (July 1980).

Harrod, J., 'Multinational corporations, trade unions and industrial relations: a case study of Jamaica', in Hans Gunter (ed.), *Transnational Industrial Relations* 1972.

Hawkin, Robert G., *Job Displacement and the Multinational Firm: a methodological review* (Washington: Centre for Multinational Studies, Occasional Paper no. 3, 1972).

Heise, Paul A., 'The multinational corporation and industrial relations: the

American approach compared with the European', *Industrial Relations* (January 1973).

Houssiaux, J., 'La grande entreprise plurinationale', *Economie appliquée* (April–September 1964).

Howe, Martin, *International Business: Principles and Problems* (New York: Free Press, 1964).

ICFTU (International Confederation of Trade Unions), statement on *The Multinational Challenge*, Report of the Tenth World Congress (London, July 1972), (Brussels, 1973).

ILO (International Labour Organization), Report (1973).

ILO, *Multinational Enterprises and Social Policy* (Geneva: 1973).

IMF (International Metalworkers' Federation), Papers and Report of World Auto Conference (Turin: 1968).

IMF, 'World Company Councils, Auto Workers' Answer to World Company Powers', (Geneva: 1967).

IOE, *Multinational Enterprises*, A Report by the International Organisation of Employers (Geneva: 1974).

Jenks, Wilfred, *International Labour Conference* (Geneva: 1972).

Jennings, Paul and Biemiller, A., to the Boggs Sub-Committee of the House Ways and Means Committee on Tariff and Trade Proposals, 19 May 1970 (Washington, D. C.: U.S. Government Printing Office, May 1970).

Kassalow, Everett M., *The International Metalworkers' Federation and the world automotive industry; the early years*, Paper given at the 3rd World Congress, International Industrial Relations Association (September 1973).

———, *The International Metalworkers' Federation and the Multinational automobile companies: A Study of Transnational Unionism*, draft manuscript, Wisconsin: University of Madison, March 1974a.)

———, paper on *Trade Union Policies and Ideologies: their influence on international Bargaining with Multinational Companies* (Michigan State University, November 1974b.)

Kindleberger, C. P., *The International Corporation* (Cambridge: MIT Press, 1969).

Knowles, W., *Trade Union Development and Industrial Relations in the British West Indies* (Berkeley: University of California Press, 1959).

Kopke, Gunter, *Multinational Corporations and International Unions: The Viewpoints and Responses of Continental European Unions*, Conference on Industrial Relations and Multinational Corporations (Chicago: 1973).

Kujawa, Duane, *International Labour Management Relations Management in the Automobile Industry: a Comparative Study of Chrysler, Ford and General Motors* (New York: Praeger, 1971).

———, *International Labor and the Multinational Enterprise* (New York: Praeger, 1975).

Lea, David, 'Multinational companies and trade union interests', in J. H. Dunning (ed.), *The Multinational Enterprise*, (London: George Allen and Unwin, 1971).

Lea, Sperry and Webley, Simon, *Multinational Corporations in Developed Countries: A Review of Recent Research and Policy Thinking* (British North American Committee, 1973).

Lee, James A., 'Cultural analysis in overseas operations', *Harvard Business Review* (March–April 1966).

Levinson, Charles, *International Trade Unionism* (London: George Allen & Unwin, 1972).

Litvak, I. A. and Maule, B. J., 'Unions and international corporations', *Industrial Relations*, Vol. IX (February 1972).

Lorwin, Lewis L., *Labour and Internationalism* (New York: Macmillan, 1929).

Maier, Heribert, Director, Economic, Social and Political Department, ICFTU, in A Foreign Economic Policy for the 1970s, Hearings before the Subcommittee on Foreign Economic Policy of the Joint Economic Committee, Congress of the United States, 91st Congress, 2nd Session, Part 4: 'The MNC and international investment' (Washington, D.C.: US Government Printing Office, 1970), pp. 824–5.

Matthews, John, *Ford Strike: The Workers' Story* (London: Panther, 1972).

McKenzie, Fred A., *The American Invaders: Their Plans, Tactics and Progress* (London: 1901).

Model, Leo, 'The politics of private foreign investment', *Foreign Affairs* (July 1967).

Myers, C., *The American System of Industrial Relations: Is it Exportable?* Presidential Address, IIRA Proceedings of Fifteenth Annual Meeting, Pittsburg (December 1962).

N.M., 'International Labour in Crisis', *Foreign Affairs*, Vol. 49, no. 3 (April 1971).

Northrup, Herbert R., and Rowan, Richard L., 'Multinational collective bargaining activity: the factual record in chemicals, glass and rubber tires', Part 1, *Columbia Journal of World Business* (Spring 1974a).

——, 'Multinational bargaining in food and allied industries: approaches and prospects', *Wharton Quarterly* (Spring 1974b).

——, 'Multinational bargaining in metals and electrical industries: approaches and prospects', *Journal of Industrial Relations*, Vol. 17, no. 1 (1975).

——, 'Multinational union activities and plant closings: the case of AKZO', *Industrial Relations Journal* (Spring 1978).

OECD, Interim Report on the Industry Committee on International Enterprises (March 1974).

——, *Observer* (April 1974).

——, *Short term Capital Movements*, A Report by the High Level Standing Group on Capital Markets (Paris: 1974).

Palloix, C., *Firmes multinationales et l'économie mondiale capitaliste* (Paris: Mespero, 1975).

Pelling, H., *The Origins of the Labour Party 1880–1900* (London: Macmillan, 1954).

Perlmutter, Howard V., 'Super-giant firms in the Future', *Wharton Quarterly* (Winter 1968).

——, 'L'Entreprise Internationale: trois conceptions', *Revue Economique et Sociale* (May 1965).

Piehl, E., 'Internationale Gewerkschaftssolidarität gegen Multinationale Kapitalstrategie am Beispiel des Akzo-Konzeruns', *Das Mitbestimmungespräch* 5 (1973) and 6 (1973).

Polk, Judd, 'The new world economy', *Columbia Journal of World Business* (January/February 1968).

Reuther, Walter P., 'Worldwide labour solidarity – essential for developing international co-operation', *I.M.F. Bulletin 21* (November 1964).

Roberts, B. C., *Labour in the Tropical Territories of the Commonwealth* (London: Bell, 1964).

——, 'Factors influencing the organisation and the style of management and their effect on the pattern of industrial relations in multinational corporations', in H. Gunter (ed.), *Transnational Industrial Relations* (London: Macmillan, 1972).

——, 'Multinational bargaining: a European prospect?' *British Journal of Industrial Relations*, Vol. XI, no. 2 (November 1973).

Roberts, B. C. and Liebhaberg, Bruno, 'The European Trades Union Confederation: influence of regionalism, détente and multinationals', *British Journal of Industrial Relations*, Vol. XIV, no. 3 (November 1976).

——, 'International regulation of multinational enterprises: trade union and management concerns', *British Journal of Industrial Relations*, Vol. XV, no. 3 (Spring 1977).

Roberts, B. C. and May, Jonathan, 'The response of multinational enterprises to international trade union pressures', *British Journal of Industrial Relations*, Vol. XII, no. 3 (November 1974).

Rocour, Jean-Luc, 'Management of European subsidiaries in the United States', *Management International* (1) (1966).

Rolfe, S., *The International Corporation*, International Chamber of Commerce (Paris: 1969).

Rosow, J. M., 'Industrial Relations and the Multinational Corporation – Management Approach', (New York: Exxon Corporation, 1974).

Ruttenberg, Stanley H. and Associates, 'Needed: A Constructive Foreign Trade Policy', a special study commissioned and published by the Industrial Union Department, AFL–CIO, Washington, D.C. (October 1971).

Servan-Schreiber, 'Jean-Jacques, *Le Défi Américain* (Paris: Denoel, 1967).

Shearer, John C., *High Level Manpower in Overseas Subsidiaries* (Princeton University: 1960).

——, 'Industrial relations of American corporations abroad', in Barkin, Dymond, Kassalow, Meyers and Myers (eds.), *International Labour* (New York: Harper & Row, 1967).

Soutar, Douglas H., Vice President, American Smelting and Refining Company, in a paper, 'Forecast and Theoretical Consideration of Multinational Corporation Strategies in Relation to Union Strategies', 3rd World Congress, International Industrial Relations Association (London: 1973).

Spyropoulos, Georges, (Le rôle de la négociation collective dans l'harmonisation des systèmes sociaux européens', *Revue Internationale de Droit Comparé* (1966).

Steuer, M. and Gennard, J., 'Industrial relations, labour disputes and labour utilisation in foreign owned firms in the United Kingdom', in Dunning (ed.), *The Multinational Enterprise* (1971).

Stobaugh, Robert B., in Duane Kujawa (ed.) *American Labour and the Multinational Corporation* (New York: Praeger, 1971).

Stobaugh, Robert B., Telesio, Piers, and de la Torre, José, *The effects of*

U.S. foreign direct investment in manufacturing on the U.S. balance of payments, U.S. employment and changes in skill composition of employment, Center for Multinational Studies, Occasional Paper no. 4 (Washington: 1973).

Sweezy, P. M. and Macdoff, H., 'Anmerkungen zur multinationalen Korporationen', *Sozialistisches Jahrbuch* 2 (Berlin: 1970).

TUC (Trade Union Conference), *Economic Review* (1972).

——, *Report on International Companies* (1970).

Tugendhat, C., *The Multinationals* (London: Eyre & Spottiswood, 1971).

Ulman, Lloyd, 'Multinational unionism: incentives, barriers and alternatives', *Industrial Relations* (February 1975).

United Nations, *The Impact of Multinational Corporations on Development and International Relations* (New York: 1974a).

UN Economic and Social Council, *The Impact of MNCs on the development process and on international relations*, Report of the Group of Eminent Persons to Study the Role of MNCs on Development and on International Relations, 57th Session, Agenda item 8/E5500 (May 1974b).

——, Resolution 1721 (L111), New York (2 July 1972).

UN, *Multinational Corporations in World Development* (New York: 1972).

US Dept. of Commerce, *Survey of American Business Investments in Foreign Countries* 1972).

——, *US Multinational Enterprises and the US Economy* (Washington: 1972).

US Senate, *Implications of Multinational Firms for World Trade and Investment and for U.S. Trade and Labor*, Report to the Committee on Finance of the U.S. Senate and its sub-committee on international trade (Washington: 1973).

Van Dierendonck, J. E., 'Regional economic integration as the creation of an environment favourable to transnational industrial relations', in H. Gunter (ed.), *Transnational Industrial Relations* (London: Macmillan, 1972).

Vaupel, James W. and Curham, Joan P., *The Making of Multinational Enterprise* (Harvard: Harvard Business School, 1969).

Vernon, Raymond, *Sovereignty at Bay: The Multinational Spread of U.S. Enterprises* (London: Longman, 1971).

——, 'Multinational Enterprise and National Sovereignties', *Harvard Business Review* (March–April 1967), pp. 156–72.

Walker, K. F., *Labour Problems in Multinational Firms*: a report on a meeting of management experts (Paris: OECD, June 1972).

Warner, M., *et al.*, in K. P. Tudyka (ed.) *Multinational Corporations and Labour Unions*, Papers presented to a symposium at Nijmegen University (1973).

Wedderburn, K. W., 'Multinational enterprise and national labour law', *Industrial Law Journal*, Vol. 1, no. 1 (March 1972).

Wilkins, Myra, *The Emergence of Multinational Enterprise* (Cambridge, Mass.: Harvard University Press, 1970).

Woodcock, Leonard, 'Labour and Multinationals', a speech to the Conference on Industrial Relations Problems Raised by Multinationals in Advanced Industrial Societies, Michigan State University (November 1974).

World Confederation of Labour, *Solidarity and Liberation*, Report to WCL (1973).

11 Industrial Relations and Politics: Some Reflections

Peter Gourevitch, Peter Lange and Andrew Martin

None of the social science disciplines has played a smaller role in the study of industrial relations than political science. While the essays in this volume show the importance of sociology, social psychology and other fields, there is a noticeable absence of studies concerned with the interaction between politics and industrial relations. The 'behavioural revolution' in political science (especially opinion surveys analysed through sophisticated statistical techniques) has given us a great deal of knowledge about worker attitudes toward many subjects. We still know very little, though, about such matters as the impact of labour market conditions upon political behaviour, the way in which workers' individual priorities are processed by labour organizations and the operation of labour organizations in the political system. It is striking how little attention political scientists have devoted to the role of labour unions in the domestic policy process despite the widespread belief that unions are (too?) powerful.

If political scientists have neglected the impact of labour on politics, the students of industrial relations have neglected the impact of politics on their field of interest as well. Though they may acknowledge at a theoretical level the interdependence of industrial relations with other elements of the social system, American, and to a lesser extent European researchers have tended to treat industrial relations as autonomous. Much of the research reported in this volume seeks to explain labour relations outcomes with variables, usually quantifiable, drawn from the labour market arena itself. Politics has usually remained in the background: part of the stage set but rarely part of the action.

Because the three authors of this essay are political scientists strongly interested in labour, we are particularly aware of these lacunae. Looking at the research examined here, there appear to be frequent instances in which a consideration of the causal role of political factors would have been appropriate, if not necessary. Some of the most striking phenomena of the past two decades (from the French May 1968 and the Italian 'hot autumn' of 1969 to incomes policy and inflation) are only poorly captured by prevailing structures of analysis, or ignored altogether.

It is never very hard to identify gaps in the literature on a given subject; more difficult is filling them. In the time since the essays for this volume were drafted, we have seen the beginnings of more systematic explorations of the interaction between politics and industrial relations. It would undoubtedly be extremely useful if we could provide a theoretical statement which would thoroughly integrate the findings of these recent studies, but we have hardly reached the stage where we can do so. We intend, instead, in this brief essay to do two things. Firstly, we analyse three perspectives which have influenced much of the research reported in this volume. Secondly, we draw on some of the recent research to suggest an additional perspective which might allow a more systematic understanding of the relationship between politics and industrial relations.

Current Perspectives

What are the relationships between workers' roles as producers and as citizens? How do the ways in which these roles are institutionalized in the labour market and the political arena affect each other? How much does the distribution of power within each of these institutional contexts influence the distribution of power in the other? How does the character and intensity of conflict in one impinge on the features of conflict in the other? What impact do the terms of settlements made in one of these contexts have on settlements made in the other? What determines the variations in these relationships among different countries? Under what circumstances do changes in these relationships occur?

American and European researchers have always differed in their treatment of these questions. Still, at the beginning of this project we expected somehow that these differences, having been with us for so long, were in the process of being eroded, and that some new, wider synthesis was being formulated. This is not the case. The research reported by our authors shows that the older differences in perspective remain quite powerful. American and Canadian (and to a lesser extent, British) research still tends to be 'narrower' than its Continental counterpart: it is generally narrower in the questions it asks ('bread and butter issues', rather than 'life chances');[1] and it is narrower in the types of explanations it gives (market forces, not culture, politics, history).

The Liberal Perspective

Interpretations of industrial relations systems are intimately linked to views of society as a whole. In the fifties and sixties, American social science theory was dominated by liberal, pluralist optimism expressed, or perhaps caricatured, in the phrase, 'end of ideology'. This body of thought argued that the traditional political struggles of the West (those among classes and those among confessional groupings) are being replaced by a new politics of interest-group mediation within the institutions of the modern liberal democratic welfare state. Party systems are being transformed as the links between parties and trade unions forged in an era of 'harder' class lines progressively weaken. Unions concentrate increasingly on interest group functions, administering their established collective bargaining rights in the interests of their members. Political parties increasingly bid for support across a broad and fragmented set of interests, committing themselves to administer the state in the interests of the entire community. The separation of workers' roles into producer and citizen becomes institutionalized as a fundamental feature of advanced industrial society.[2]

This same insight was inherent in the theory of industrial relations which is best represented in Kerr *et al.*'s *Industrialism and Industrial Man* and its more narrow predecessor, Dunlop's *Industrial Relations Systems*.[3] The central assumption of this theory of pluralist industrialism was that the basic tensions inherent in the process of industrial transformation have been overcome in the modern industrial countries. As a consequence, the social conflicts and ideologies accompanying the birth-pangs of industrial society are subsiding. The logic of industrialism does allow some variance in institutional forms (communist and non-communist systems) but also compels some convergence. In the West, one can expect to find a growing consensus around liberal democratic institutions and the modern mixed economy. Relations between 'managers and the managed' are increasingly embedded in a web of rules agreed to by both parties. This web is sufficiently bounded, self-adjusting and autonomous to merit being treated as a subsystem which controls and limits both the intensity and the scope of industrial conflict. Issues which arise within the subsystem will tend to be insulated from each other, and from issues and arrangements arising in other subsystems.

At the most abstract level, the pluralist industrial perspective acknowledged that industrial relations was one of a number of subsystems (politics being another) of the larger social system. These subsystems could become ever more institutionally differentiated, but never wholly separable.[4] Nonetheless, as a guide for research, the approach encouraged the treatment of each subsystem as autonomous. By and large, labour markets and politics have been treated as largely independent of one another.

A number of criticisms of the theory of pluralist industrialism are raised by the essays in this volume. Others are evident when one compares expectations derived from the theory with contemporary developments in industrial relations of the countries. Rather than catalogue these criticisms, we will focus on one which seems to us particularly important – the insulation of labour relations from politics (broadly understood as the struggle for office, the content of public policy and the role of the state).

In stressing institutionalization and role differentiation, the view exemplified by Kerr *et al.* encouraged an analysis of industrial relations largely confined to the close examination of the industrial arrangements which directly linked the producing groups: the collective bargaining process and the market conditions which determined the relative power of the parties to the process. Thus, they neglected in practice the analytical importance of the notion that social actors have a multiplicity of goals and types of resources for pursuing them, that the labour market is only one of the arenas in which those goals are pursued and resources deployed, and that politics is another, quite important, one. In doing so, the liberal school obscured the possibility that power relations and policy outcomes in one sphere might have a strong and continuing effect on relationships and outcomes in the other.

Whether this concept of an insulated industrial relations system was correct when it was first formulated is doubtful. Certainly there is little question (as the essays in this volume show) that this model did not, as its proponents expected, spread from the United States to the other advanced industrial countries. Recent developments, on the contrary, have made clear the enormous role politics and governmental policy have in determining the successes and failures of those who meet around a bargaining table. Two examples suffice to demonstrate this point: incomes policy and welfare policies.

So long as it lasted, stable economic growth contributed among other things to optimism, social peace, and the kind of role fragmentation central to the liberal school's analyses. By increasing resources, growth made it easier for labour and management in some countries to achieve relative satisfaction of their goals in both politics and in collective bargaining. Both parties were able therefore to accept a separation of the agenda of politics from that of industrial relations, and had little reason to push demands from one arena to the other.

Economic difficulties burst this bubble. Inflation, stagnation and other economic ills make it harder to satisfy industrial relations demands and intensify political conflicts. Incomes policy, wage–price controls, and tripartite or neo-corporatist arrangements clearly link politics and the industrial relations systems in a way not encompassed by the liberal theory.

Similarly, the expansion of the welfare state has also had marked effects on the character of bargaining. One need not accept the neo-Marxist view of the functions performed by the state in modern capitalism to recognize that welfare state politics have probably influenced the nature and intensity of the demands both employers and employees bring to the bargaining table.[5] By providing services through the government which workers would otherwise have to acquire directly, these policies encourage bargaining peace. Effective national health insurance policies, for instance, may alter the structure of demands for fringe benefits at the labour–management bargaining table. At the same time, welfare state policies may exacerbate industrial conflict. Unemployment compensation may reduce the effectiveness of market 'discipline' on worker demands.

Given the importance of government policy, then, it would seem that political power must join market power as a central explanatory factor in accounting for collective bargaining outcomes in different countries. Welfare policies and the content of incomes policy differ from one system to another, in part because of variations in the relative strength of employers and workers. Where one of these groups is particularly weak in the political arena, it may well seek to achieve its demands in the economic one, and vice versa.[6] The liberal perspective, in insulating the functioning of labour markets from politics and state action, discourages examination of the connection between the two.

The Marxist Perspective

After pluralist industrialism, the most coherent, systematic and far-reaching theory exercising major influence on the study of industrial relations is Marxism. The essays in this volume show clearly that Marxist categories and concepts continue to play a central role in the analyses not only of Continental researchers but of British ones as well. And while the tradition never became as important a strand in the intellectual environment of industrial relations research in the United States, from the days of Commons and Perlman to the present it has been seen as the principal theoretical alternative and ideological target to which liberals directed their attacks.[7] Given the concern of Marxists to root economic conflict in the broader context of the political relations of class, one could reasonably expect to find a useful formulation of the politics–industrial relations linkage within that tradition.

An examination of the theoretical and research literature, however, proves disappointing in this regard. The Marxist tradition does not really provide an alternative model or framework for analysing the varieties of interaction between labour market and political processes. Marxist theorizing on industrial relations and politics has tended to remain on a high level of abstraction. It has been primarily concerned with insisting that class conflict remains inherent in the fundamental structure of capitalism. With few exceptions, Marxist analysis has not specified the ways in which class conflict underlies empirically observable institutional arrangements in the labour market and political arena, nor explained the conditions under which conflict within these spheres becomes latent or manifest. One consequence is that the Marxist view of industrial relations has largely to be inferred from the more general Marxist interpretation of capitalism.

The more serious consequence is that writers in the Marxist tradition have failed to meet the need for a theoretical alternative to pluralist analysis. To be sure, the emphasis on the permanence of class conflict in capitalism, precluding any permanent 'solutions', would seem to put the Marxist approach in a better position to explain the eruption of conflict in the labour market than the pluralistic industrialism approach. Hence, the surge of labour militancy beginning in the late 1960s should have come as no surprise to writers with a Marxist orientation. Yet those phenomena did catch them largely by surprise. As a result, they resorted to essentially *ad hoc*, theoretically unintegrated explanations. The Marxist approach to class conflict cannot provide anything more as long as the 'predictions' or 'explanations' of conflict that flow from it remain so general as to be either trivial or tautological. If the 'hot autumn' and similar phenomena were wholly inconsistent with the expectations flowing from pluralistic industrialism, that view at least offered hypotheses that could be shown wrong by the evidence.

Marxist research is often very sensitive to the importance of politics on labour. At the same time, Marxist writing about politics and theorizing about the state remains, even in its most recent and sophisticated forms, highly reductionist. It has not gone far beyond the classical Marxist conception of the state as a direct expression of capitalist interests, 'the executive committee of the bourgeoisie'.

To the extent it has gone beyond that, it has done so most effectively in terms of a kind of functionalist analysis.[8] In this view, the state is seen as performing functions essential to the legitimacy as well as economic operation of capitalist political economies apart from and even in conflict with the perceived interests of individual capitalists. These functions themselves are seen as potentially in conflict with each other, with the possibilities of reconciling them limited by the extent of working-class power in both the labour market and the political arena.

In the furthest development of this theory, politics is seen not simply as a mechanism for protecting generalized capitalist class interest but as a context in which class conflict occurs. Yet, the potentialities implicit in this approach have so far not been exploited. The issues and outcomes of politics are still seen as determined by the imperatives of capitalist development, leaving intact the reductionist presuppositions of the theory. It has therefore apparently seemed unnecessary to seek explanations for variations in the role of the state by examining the specific characteristics of the political process in different countries. Thus, little significance is attached to the scope, structures, and strategies of employer and employee organizations in the labour market, how the political process screens and channels the impact of the resources that workers and employers deploy in the political arena, and how this impact in turn conditions their relationships in the work-place.

In effect, the Marxists deny the autonomy of political processes from the underlying structure of class relationships to much the same extent as the liberal pluralists affirm the autonomy of industrial relations from politics. Both consequently beg the fundamental question of why relationships between industrial relations and politics take varying forms with varying consequences for the operation of different political economies.

The Contemporary European Perspective

Much of the literature on industrial relations in European countries reflects the inability of either the liberal or Marxist theories to capture the contemporary reality of labour management relations. Analyses of labour in Italy, France, Sweden and, to a lesser extent, Germany and Great Britain, continually overflowed the boundaries of these two perspectives even when nourished by their waters. Drawing heavily on Weberianism, though influenced by Marxist concerns, discussions of the labour movements in those countries were much more likely to try to integrate the examination of the industrial relations subsystem in a broader societal context: to show how the labour market 'piece' of the social system expresses the logic of the whole. Wages, hours, working conditions were more likely to be treated in these discussions as ways of getting at larger issues (the type of social system) and as symptoms of larger forces, not autonomously determined. There is, of course, something about the conditions in these countries which cries out for such an analysis – especially in France, Italy and Sweden, where the politically organized role of labour is so conspicuous. Nevertheless, the issues and connections cannot be assumed to be absent elsewhere. They may be less obvious, further from the surface and more poorly institutionalized, but their latency makes it all the more interesting and necessary to seek to lay them bare.

Despite its openness to broader questions and mechanisms of explanation, however, the European perspective (to call it by a suitably imprecise term) suffers, in comparison with the liberal and Marxist perspective, from a lack of rigour. Aside from stating that it is broader, indeed it is difficult to identify with precision what this third perspective is. Its advantages of descriptive accuracy and sensitivity to factors of particular national importance have not been complemented by the kind of systematization which would make it useful for comparative analysis. Politics is recognized to be of great import (it would be impossible to ignore it in some of the countries) but this insight has remained country-bound. Furthermore, it has not been integrated into a more abstract and systematic approach to the more general study of industrial relations. Thus we find ourselves caught in the unfortunate but thought-provoking dilemma of being sympathetic to the approach which the Europeans appear to be employing but unable to identify clearly what the approach actually represents. Descriptively we are more satisfied, but at the level of theory we feel the need to try to stimulate efforts to make what the Europeans have done more analytically utilizable. Clearly this cannot be done in one essay, but we would feel remiss if we did not make an initial effort to address some aspects of the problem.

Labour and Politics

As our discussions of different models of industrial relations show, we are deeply interested in the interaction of labour and politics. Each model has its own way of viewing this relationship. The liberal view tends towards the separation of labour market and political arenas. The Marxist tradition, while emphasizing the importance of politics to labour market relations, becomes quite reductionist and abstract in its treatment of the connection between them. The European approach sees the relationship as much closer, more intimate, less autonomous than does the liberal interpretation, and more reciprocally interactive than does the Marxist. But the Continental authors have lost in rigour and systematization what they have gained by bringing together some of the best analytical insights drawn from the other two traditions.

We will not pretend to do here what we have said so many others have not done. The space is insufficient, and, far more tellingly, we do not have a systematic theory. Nonetheless, we believe the papers in this volume, as well as more recent research, suggest some relationships between politics and labour which deserve to be drawn out, made explicit, and collated as a way of encouraging further exploration of the problem. In doing so, we ask the reader to bear in mind the speculative character of our enterprise.

In all the Western countries, several cleavage lines cut through the polity: religion, national identity, urban versus rural, agriculture versus industry, industry type versus industry type, rich versus poor, capital versus labour, etc., etc. On some issues workers and employers are in coalition; on others, they are on opposite sides. The relative importance of the different types of cleavage is, of course, a matter of considerable variation from country to country, and the source of considerable theoretical (and ideological) dispute.[9]

We wish here to explore issues over which capital and labour are in conflict. Politics and the labour market may be conceptualized as two arenas in which labour and management pursue their interests. At the most general level, the stakes in the two arenas are the same: the distributions of income and control. What may change is the arena in which each party seeks to maintain or improve its position. Thus an effort to increase the income share of workers may take the form of a struggle for higher pay through collective bargaining or for a reduction in the level of taxation on wage income through legislation. Similarly, unions may seek greater control through increased power at the work-place or by state ownership or investment planning. The specific agenda of issues over which this conflict occurs and why certain issues are pursued in one or the other arena in any particular country are empirical questions which seem to us of great importance.

An initial insight into the ways labour action in the two arenas may be related is suggested by Korpi's analysis of the Swedish case in this volume.[10] As he points out, an extended period of rule by a labour-based party, beginning in 1932, was accompanied by a dramatic decline in strike activity, from one of the highest to one of the lowest in the industrial world. His analysis suggests the causal mechanism involved. A party enjoying the support of most workers won control of the government and carried out policies meeting what those workers understood to be their interests. Given the realization of some of their goals, workers were willing to heed governmental pleas for moderation in the use of their power in the labour market. The increased power of labour in the political arena in turn reduced employer resistance in the collective bargaining process. Together these changes facilitated industrial peace. As long as policy continued to meet workers' interests, low tension in the labour market persisted. By the end of the 1960s, however, the extent of policy satisfaction declined – partly because some expectations from the past had never been fulfilled, partly because new definitions of worker interests had emerged. As a result, strike activity in Sweden during 1969–74 went up.

A similar association of shifts in the level of strike activity with apparent changes in the responsiveness of government policy to worker interests is discernible in the British case. There, as long as labour's expectations concerning such things as full employment and freedom from state intervention in collective bargaining were met, by Conservative as well as Labour governments, tension in the labour market remained low. When Labour or Conservative policies resulted in increased unemployment and greater intervention, tension increased – as in 1957, the late 1960s, and especially the early 1970s.[11]

The Swedish and British cases both suggest that labour's power in the political arena and tension in the labour market are inversely related. When labour's political power is high, strike activity is low, and vice versa. A change in the level of labour's political power will result in a change in the level of labour market tension in the opposite direction. Is this proposition generally valid? A negative answer would sustain those approaches which treat politics and labour markets as largely autonomous subsystems. An affirmative answer would justify the effort to build alternative approaches that systematically integrate the two.

Some evidence pertinent to the validity of the proposition has begun to accumulate. In a study of strike activity in ten advanced industrial capitalist societies between 1950 and 1969, Douglas A. Hibbs, Jr. concludes that over the short run labour-market tension does not fall or rise depending on whether a labour-based party is in power. However, in a study of trends in strike activity over a longer time-span (1900–72), Hibbs finds that it is clearly lower when labour-based parties are in power for extended periods and higher when centrist or conservative parties enjoy sustained control of governments. This conclusion is based on a comparison of changes in average strike volume, measured as man-days lost per thousand non-agricultural civilian employees, and changes in average participation in cabinets by labour-based parties between the interwar and postwar periods in eleven countries.[12]

Hibbs suggests that such 'long-run changes in the volume of industrial conflict arc largely explained by changes in the locus of the struggle over distribution'. The argument is not that occupancy of office by labour-based parties by itself results in lower strike activity, but that the longer they are in office the more the welfare state is expanded, shifting more of the distribution of disposable income 'from the private sector, where property and capital interests enjoy a comparative advantage, to the public sector, where the political resources of the organized working class are more telling'.[13] He provides some evidence for this by showing that there is a strong positive correlation (+ .803) between growth in the share of non-defence government expenditure in GDP and increases in labour-based party cabinet representation, and a strong negative correlation (− .789) between such public sector distribution and long-run trends in strike volume.[14] Thus, long-run labour party governmental presence is seen as altering both the relative importance of the labour market and political arenas for capital–labour distributional conflict and correspondingly, the balance of power between capital and labour.

The existence of a clear linkage between the political power of labour-based parties and governmental policy is confirmed in several other studies. David Cameron too has found growth of the public sector to be related to such power.[15] Christopher Hewitt has shown it to be associated with more egalitarian methods of financing the public sector.[16] And Hibbs, in another study, has shown that labour-based parties place a distinctly higher priority on full employment than price stability, whereas the priorities of conservative, business-based parties are reversed. His comparison of the experience in twelve advanced industrial capitalist countries suggests that actual economic policies have effectively reflected these priorities. The percentage of years between 1945 and 1969 in which labour-based parties participated in the executive has a strong negative correlation (− .68) with mean percentage unemployment from 1960 to 1969, and an even stronger positive correlation (+ .74) with mean inflation rates.[17]

Using somewhat different measures and applying them to a larger number of countries, Korpi and Shalev find broadly similar relationships between strike activity, on the one hand, and labour political power and policy outcomes, on the other.[18] However, what emerges particularly clearly from their study is the considerable variation around the central tendency for labour to use labour market and political action as alternative means for advancing its interests. The clearest and hence most interesting deviant case is that of West Germany. Strike activity in that country is as low as in Sweden over the postwar period as a whole. Yet, over the same period, the labour-based party's participation in the executive has been much shorter. Nevertheless, policy outcomes in West Germany have not been correspondingly less favourable than those in Sweden; German unemployment rates, in fact, have been lower than Swedish ones. And although the German non-defence public sector share of GDP has not been as high as in Sweden, the share of transfer payments to households has been higher. The redistributive effect of the tax and transfer systems is almost as great in Germany as in Sweden according to one estimate, although the tax system alone is less redistributive according to another.[19] How are we to understand the German case?

If policy outcomes are as favourable to labour in Germany as in Sweden, it may mean that German labour has more power in the political arena than is implied when it is measured by cabinet participation of labour-based parties. A more subtle measure would accordingly be required. It might be, for instance, that labour's political power should be measured not just by its governmental presence but by its institutionalized strength in a broad range of social and political institutions (e.g. boards of insurance institutions, governmental commissions) including, but ranging well beyond, traditional work-place trade union structures. Use of such a measure would presumably reveal the German case to be more consistent with the proposition we have suggested.

The coexistence of low strike activity, relatively favourable policy outcomes, and relatively low labour political power – as measured in the reported research – might be explained, however, by an alternative line of reasoning that focuses on a different aspect of politics: political integration. Present literature characterizes the German labour movement as highly integrated into the German polity.[20] It accepts the legitimacy not only of the constitution, but more broadly, of the German political economy, and it has a high level of confidence in government, regardless of which party is in control or specific policy outputs.

This suggests the following causal mechanism. High integration is accompanied by low dissatisfaction, strong confidence about the future and hence an accommodative posture toward technological innovation and work reorganization coupled with low strike activity. The economy is therefore strong, and able to reward the labour force for its industry and peacefulness. High real wages and generous transfer payments are thus the reward for compliance and discipline, rather than militancy.

If this interpretation of the German case is valid, it suggests an alternative to the proposition suggested by Korpi's interpretation of the Swedish case, providing a different explanation of the Swedish and other cases as well. The alternative proposition is that the more integrated the labour movement, the more peaceful are labour relations. High legitimacy means low strike activity, and vice versa. In fact, this is the proposition often implied by discussion of differences between Anglo-American labour behaviour and that in countries (especially France and Italy) having strong communist parties and communist affiliated unions.[21]

Following this reasoning one would expect Italy and the United States to be at opposite poles. Few labour movements in the West appear less integrated than the Italian; few are more integrated than the American. They should therefore have very differing strike volumes: high in Italy, low in the United States. Yet this is clearly not the case. The United States (and Canada) have a remarkably high strike volume, higher than France and close to Italian levels.[22] The integration argument cannot deal with this similarity in strike volume between the United States and Italy.

It would appear, indeed, that if one wishes to develop a general and parsimonious explanation, the proposition linking labour power (as distinct from integration) and strike volume better explains the United States–Italian similarity. Despite dramatic differences in their degrees of integration, labour political power in both countries is relatively low. The political weakness of the Italian labour movement until the last decade is well known. The political weakness of the United States' labour movement, while perhaps more contested, would appear to be supported by indicators like the size of the public sector and level of public social welfare support.[23]

This does not mean that integration of the labour movement is unimportant, only that it contributes little to the explanation of strike volume. Integration does in fact appear important in explaining *the consequences* of high strike volume (and low power). In the United States it is high legitimacy and integration which makes possible the relative autonomy of the labour market and political arenas which the Kerr school took as a pattern for the West as a whole. Labour can be very prone to strike without this having great significance for the legitimacy of the political regime. In such European countries as France and Italy, poor political integration leads to the politicization of all questions in society from religion to culture to labour markets. Strikes, therefore, always have a political dimension there, which they lack in the United States.

Although, as already suggested, it may simply be that our indications of political power are insufficiently developed, Germany may still be a deviant case calling for a special explanation. Korpi and Shalev hold that it is and supply such an explanation, emphasizing particular historical factors that are said to account for the kind of behaviour that has been interpreted as evidence of integration. But more comparative research is needed to explore the ways in which integration may affect the relationships between labour action in the labour market and political arena. For example, we need to understand how the forces making for different degrees of integration affect labour's choice of strategies. How much weight should be assigned to the dimension of political culture, for example, as opposed to institutional ones like political parties? We tend to emphasize the latter (though, of course political culture is not irrelevant to an understanding of the evolution of party systems). Catch-all parties surely link industrial relations and politics quite differently than do mass parties. Thus an interpretation of industrial relations based upon the American situation could plausibly speak of the autonomy of spheres. But the extension of this model to Europe presupposes the transformation of labour movement parties into catch-all ones.[24] To the extent this has not happened, the pluralistic industrialism model does not apply.

While the studies we have cited obviously leave these and many other questions open, they all confirm the interconnectedness of industrial relations and politics. While it is too soon to speak of the emergence of a new school of interpretation, there is some reason to expect at least renewed debate. The work of Hibbs, Korpi and others fits in best with what we have called the European perspective and hopefully will promote the development of systematic theory in that camp. It may also incite the liberal and Marxian schools to reformulate their positions.

Perhaps it will become axiomatic that, to paraphrase Clausewitz, 'for labour, politics is the pursuit of labour market goals by other means'. We will then be able to argue about different models of the interpenetration of industrial relations and politics, not whether the two are connected.

NOTES

1. The most marked exception to this generalization is the burgeoning interest, evident in this volume, in the impact of dual or segmented labour markets on life chances.
2. Otto Kirchheimer, 'The Transformation of Western European Party Systems', in Joseph La Palombara and Myron Weiner (eds.), *Political Parties and Political Development* (Princeton: Princeton University Press, 1966), ch. 6. In the same vein, see Raymond Aron, 'Fin de l'âge idéologique?' in Theodore W. Adorno and Walter Dirks, (eds.), *Sociologica* (Frankfurt: Europäische Verlagsanstalt, 1955), pp. 219–33; Herbert Tingsten, 'Stability and vitality in Swedish democracy', *Political Quarterly*, 26 (1955), pp. 140–51; S. M. Lipset, 'The changing class structure and contemporary European politics', in Stephen R. Graubard, *A New Europe?* (Boston: Beacon Press, 1964), pp. 337–69; Daniel Bell, *The End of Ideology* (Glencoe: Free Press, 1960), esp. pp. 369–75; Ralf Dahrendorf, *Class Conflict in Industrial Society* (Stanford: Stanford University Press, 1959), esp. pp. 214–318; and Chaim Waxman (ed.), *The End of Ideology Debate* (New York: Funk and Wagnalls, 1968).
3. Clark Kerr, John T. Dunlop, Frederick Harbison and Charles A. Meyers, *Industrialism and Industrial Man* (Cambridge: Harvard University Press, 1960) and John T. Dunlop, *Industrial Relations Systems* (New York: Henry Holt and Company, Inc., 1958).
4. The influence of Talcott Parsons on the development of this conceptualization is evident. See, among others, his *The Social System* (Glencoe: The Free Press, 1951). Dunlop in particular was aware that subsystems are not wholly autonomous. Nonetheless, by treating the character and operations of other subsystems with a *ceteris paribus* assumption, he encouraged neglect of the interactions between subsystems.
5. For a systematic presentation of this view, see James O'Connor, *The Fiscal Crisis of the State* (New York: St Martin's Press, 1973).
6. Korpi's essay makes this point skilfully for the Swedish case and there is no reason to think that its theoretical implications do not equally apply to other countries.
7. See the essay by George Strauss and Peter Feuille in this volume, p.
8. See O'Connor, *op. cit.* See also, Jürgen Habermas, *Legitimation Crisis* (Boston: Beacon Press, 1975) and Claus Offe, 'The theory of the capitalist state and the problem of policy formation', in Leon Lindberg *et al.* (eds.), *Stress and Contraction in Modern Capitalism* (Lexington: Lexington Books, 1975), ch. 5.
9. S. M. Lipset and Stein Rokkan, *Party Systems and Voter Alignments: Cross-National Perspectives* (New York: The Free Press, 1967).

10. See Korpi's essay, p. 184 and also his *The Working Class in Welfare Capitalism* (London: Routledge & Kegan Paul, 1978).
11. Data on strike activity in Britain from Douglas A. Hibbs, Jr., 'Trade Union Power, Labor Militancy and Wage Inflation: A Comparative Analysis', Centre for International Studies, Massachusetts Institute of Technology (1977).
12. Douglas A. Hibbs, Jr, 'On the political economy of long-run trends in strike activity', *British Journal of Political Science*, 8, 2 (AprIl 1978) pp. 153–75.
13. Ibid., p. 167.
14. Ibid., p. 168.
15. David R. Cameron, 'The expansion of the public economy', *American Political Science Review* 72, 4 (December, 1978) pp. 1243–1261.
16. Christopher Hewitt, 'The effect of political democracy and social democracy on equality in industrial societies: a cross-national comparison', *American Sociological Review*, 42, 3 (June 1977), pp. 450–64.
17. Douglas A. Hibbs, Jr, 'Political parties and macroeconomic policy', *American Political Science Review*, LXXI, 4 (December 1977), pp. 1467–87.
18. Walter Korpi and Michael Shalev, 'Strikes, power and politics in the Western nations, 1900–1976', *Political Power and Social Theory* (forthcoming).
19. Sources of data on West Germany as follows: on unemployment, Hibbs, 'Political Parties and Macroeconomic Policy', p. 1472; on public sector and transfer payments shares of GDP, 'Expenditure trends in OECD countries', *OECD Economic Outlook, Occasional Studies* (July 1976).
20. In addition to the essay on West Germany in this volume, see Alfred Diamant, 'Democratizing the workplace: the myth and reality of Mitbestimmung in the Federal Republic of Germany', in G. David Garson (ed.), *Worker Self-Management in Industry: The West European Experience* (New York: Praeger, 1977), pp. 25–48; and Joachim Bergman and Walter Muller-Jentsch, 'The Federal Republic of Germany: cooperative unionism and dual bargaining system challenged', in Solomon Barkin (ed.), *Worker Militancy and Its Consequences, 1965–75* (New York: Praeger, 1975), pp. 235–76.
21. See Everett M. Kassalow, *Trade Unions and Industrial Relations: An International Comparison* (New York: Random House, 1969), Part One.
22. Comparative strike data in Hibbs, 'On the Political Economy of Long-Run Trends', and Korpi and Shalev, 'Strikes, Power and Politics'.
23. On Italy, see Ida Regalia, Marino Regini and Emilio Regneri, 'Labour conflicts and industrial relations in Italy', in Cohn Grouch and Alessandro Pizzorno (eds.), *The Resurgence of Class Conflict in Europe since 1968* (London: Macmillan, 1978). On American labour's political efforts, see J. David Greenstone, *Labor in American Politics* (New York: Vintage, 1969); and for a discussion of some results of those efforts, see Andrew Martin, 'The politics of economic policy in the United States: a tentative view from a comparative perspective', *Sage Professional Papers in Comparative Politics* 01–040 (1973).
24. This is Kirchheimer's term for parties that bid for support across a broad range of interests instead of along class or confessional lines.

Index